MARKET
SHARE
REPORTER

ISSN 1052-9578

MARKET SHARE REPORTER

AN ANNUAL COMPILATION
OF REPORTED MARKET SHARE
DATA ON COMPANIES,
PRODUCTS, AND SERVICES

2 0 0 4

ROBERT S. LAZICH, Editor

GALE®

THOMSON

™

GALE

Detroit • New York • San Diego • San Francisco • Cleveland • New Haven, Conn. • Waterville, Maine • London • Munich

Market Share Reporter 2004
Robert S. Lazich

Project Editor
Amanda Quick

Editorial
Joyce Piwowarski, Susan Turner

Imaging and Multimedia
Michael Logusz

Manufacturing
NeKita McKee

ISBN 0-7876-7219-X
ISSN 0071-0210

Printed in the United States of America
10 9 8 7 6 5 4 3 2 1

TABLE OF CONTENTS

TABLE OF TOPICS

The *Table of Topics* lists all topics used in *Market Share Reporter* in alphabetical order. One or more page references follow each topic; the page references identify the starting point where the topic is shown. The same topic name may be used under different SICs; therefore, in some cases, more than one page reference is provided.

INTRODUCTION

Market Share Reporter (MSR) is a compilation of market share reports from periodical literature. The fourteenth edition covers the period 1998 through 2003; while dates overlap slightly with the thirteenth edition, the fourteenth edition of *MSR* has completely new and updated entries. As shown by reviews of previous editions plus correspondence and telephone contact with many users, this is a unique resource for competitive analysis, diversification planning, marketing research, and other forms of economic and policy analysis. Features of the 2004 edition include—

- More than 2,000 entries, all new or updated.
- SIC classification, with entries arranged under 511 SIC codes.
- Corporate, brand, product, service and commodity market shares.
- Coverage of private and public sector activities.
- North American coverage.
- Comprehensive indexes, including products, companies, brands, places, sources, and SICs.
- Table of Topics showing topical subdivisions of chapters with page references.
- Graphics.
- Annotated source listing—provides publishers' information for journals cited in this edition of *MSR*.

MSR is a one-of-a-kind resource for ready reference, marketing research, economic analysis, planning, and a host of other disciplines.

Categories of Market Shares

Entries in *Market Share Reporter* fall into four broad categories. Items were included if they showed the relative strengths of participants in a market or provided subdivisions of economic activity in some manner that could assist the analyst.

- *Corporate market shares* show the names of companies that participate in an industry, produce a product, or provide a service. Each company's market share is shown as a percent of total industry or product sales for a defined period, usually a year. In some cases, the company's share represents the share of the sales of the companies shown (group total)—because shares of the total market were not cited in the source or were not relevant. In some corporate share tables, brand information appears behind company names in parentheses. In these cases, the tables can be located using either the company or the brand index.

- *Institutional shares* are like corporate shares but show the shares of other kinds of organizations. The most common institutional entries in *MSR* display the shares of states, provinces, or regions in an activity. The shares of not-for-profit organizations in some economic or service functions fall under this heading.

- *Brand market shares* are similar to corporate shares with the difference that brand names are shown. Brand names include equivalent categories such as the names of television programs, magazines, publishers' imprints, etc. In some cases, the names of corporations appear in parentheses behind the brand name; in these cases, tables can be located using either the brand or the company index.

- *Product, commodity, service, and facility* shares feature a broad category (e.g. household appliances) and show how the category is subdivided into components (e.g. refrigerators, ranges, washing machines, dryers, and dishwashers). Entries under this category cover products (autos, lawnmowers, polyethylene, etc.), commodities (cattle, grains, crops), services (telephone, child care), and facilities (port berths, hotel suites, etc.). Subdivisions may be products, categories of services (long-distance telephone, residential phone service, 800-service), types of commodities (varieties of grain), size categories (e.g., horsepower ranges), modes (rail, air, barge), types of facilities (categories of hospitals, ports, and the like), or other subdivisions.

- *Other shares.* MSR includes a number of entries that show subdivisions, breakdowns, and shares that do not fit neatly into the above categorizations but properly belong in such a book because they shed light on public policy, foreign trade, and other subjects of general interest. These items include, for instance, subdivisions of governmental expenditures, environmental issues, and the like.

Coverage

The fourteenth edition of *Market Share Reporter* covers essentially the same range of industries as previous editions. However, all tables are *new* or represent *updated* information (more recent or revised data). Also, coverage in detail is different in certain industries, meaning that more or fewer SICs are covered or product details *within* SICs may be different. For these reasons, it is recommended that previous editions of *MSR* be retained rather than replaced.

Coverage. Beginning with the fifth edition, MSR's geographic area of coverage became North America—Canada, the United States, and Mexico. As in all past editions, the vast majority of entries are for the United States. In the first four editions of MSR, international data were included at greater or lesser intensity depending on availability of space. This necessitated, among other things, frequent exclusion of data organized by states or regions of the United States—which are popular with users.

In order to provide better service to users, a companion publication, called *World Market Share Reporter (WMSR)*, is available. *WMSR* features global market share information as well as country-specific market share and/or market size information outside North America. At the same time, *MSR* features more geographical market shares in the North American area.

MSR reports on *published* market shares rather than attempting exhaustive coverage of the market shares, say, of all major corporations and of all products and services. Despite this limitation, *MSR* holds share information on more than 4,000 companies, more than 2,000 brands, and more than 1,900 product, commodity, service, and facility categories. Several entries are usually available for each industry group in the SIC classification; omitted groups are those that do not play a conventional role in the market, e.g., Private Households (SIC 88).

Variation in coverage from previous editions is due in part to publication cycles of sources and a different mix of brokerage house reports for the period covered (due to shifting interests within the investment community).

As pointed out in previous editions, *MSR* tends to reflect the current concerns of the business press. In addition to being a source of market share data, it mirrors journalistic preoccupations, issues in the business community, and events abroad. Important and controversial industries and activities get most of the ink. Heavy coverage is provided in those areas that are—

- large, important, basic (autos, chemicals)
- on the leading edge of technological change (computers, electronics, software)
- very competitive (toiletries, beer, soft drinks)
- in the news because of product recalls, new product introductions, mergers and acquisitions, lawsuits, and for other reasons
- relate to popular issues (environment, crime), or have excellent coverage in their respective trade press.

In many cases, several entries are provided on a subject each citing the same companies. No attempt was made to eliminate such seeming duplication if the publishing and/or original sources were different and the market shares were not identical. Those who work with such data know that market share reports are often little more than the "best guesses" of knowledgeable observers rather than precise measurements. To the planner or analyst, variant reports about an industry's market shares are useful for interpreting the data.

Publications appearing in the January 2001 to June 2003 period were used in preparing *MSR*. As a rule, material on market share data for 2003 were used by preference; in response to reader requests, we have included historical data when available. In some instances, information for earlier years was included if the category was unique or if the earlier year was necessary for context. In a few other cases, projections for 2004 and later years were also included.

"Unusual" Market Shares

Some reviewers of the first edition questioned—sometimes tongue-in-cheek, sometimes seriously—the inclusion of tables on such topics as computer crime, endangered species of fish, children's allowances, governmental budgets, and weapons system stockpiles. Indeed, some of these categories do not fit the sober meaning of "market share." A few tables on such subjects are present in every edition—because they provide market information, albeit indirectly, or because they are the "market share equivalents" in an industrial classification which is in the public sector or dominated by the public sector's purchasing power.

Organization of Chapters

Market Share Reporter is organized into chapters by 2-digit SIC categories (industry groups). The exception is the first chapter, entitled *General Interest and Broad Topics*; this chapter holds all entries that bridge two or more 2-digit SIC industry codes (e.g. retailing in general, beverage containers, building materials, etc.) and cannot, therefore, be classified using the SIC system without distortion. Please note, however, that a topic in this chapter will often have one or more additional entries later—where the table could be assigned to a detailed industry. Thus, in addition to tables on packaging in the first chapter, numerous tables appear later on glass containers, metal cans, etc.

Within each chapter, entries are shown by 4-digit SIC (industry level). Within blocks of 4-digit SIC entries, entries are sorted alphabetically by topic, then alphabetically by title.

SIC and Topic Assignments

MSR's SIC classifications are based on the coding as defined in the *Standard Industrial Classification Manual* for 1987, issued by the Bureau of the Census, Department of Commerce. This 1987 classification system introduced significant revisions to the 1972 classification (as slightly modified in 1977); the 1972 system is still in widespread use (even by the Federal government); care should be used in comparing data classified in the new and in the old way.

The closest appropriate 4-digit SIC was assigned to each table. In many cases, a 3-digit SIC had to be used because the substance of the table was broader than the nearest 4-digit SIC category. Such SICs always end with a zero. In yet other cases, the closest classification possible was at the 2-digit level; these SICs terminate with double-zero. If the content of the table did not fit the 2-digit level, it was assigned to the first chapter of *MSR* and classified by topic only.

Topic assignments are based on terminology for commodities, products, industries, and services in the SIC Manual; however, in many cases phrasing has been simplified, shortened, or updated; in general, journalistically succinct rather than bureaucratically exhaustive phraseology was used throughout.

Organization of Entries

Entries are organized in a uniform manner. A sample entry is provided below. Explanations for each

part of an entry, shown in boxes, are provided below the sample.

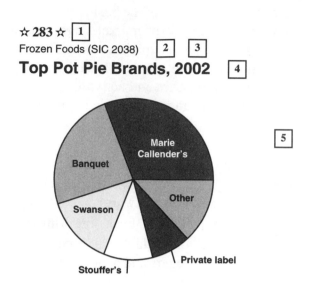

☆ 283 ☆ 1

Frozen Foods (SIC 2038)   2   3

Top Pot Pie Brands, 2002   4

5

Brands are ranked by sales for the 12 weeks ended October 6, 2002.   6

	($ mil.)	Share 7
Marie Callender's	$ 18.19	30.79%
Banquet	14.16	23.97
Swanson	8.17	13.83
Stouffer's	6.14	10.39 8
Private label	4.95	8.38
Other	7.47	12.64

Source: *Frozen Food Age*, January 2003, p. 16, from Information Resources Inc.   9

1   *Entry Number.* A numeral between star symbols. Used for locating an entry from the index.

2   *Topic.* Second line, small type. Gives the broad or general product or service category of the entry. The topic for Top Pot Pie Brands, 2002 is Frozen Foods.

3 *SIC Code.* Second line, small type, follows the topic. General entries in the first chapter do not have an SIC code.

4 *Title.* Third line, large type. Describes the entry with a headline.

5 *Graphic.* When a graphic is present, it follows the title. Some entries will be illustrated with a pie or bar chart. The information used to create the graphic is always shown below the pie or bar chart.

6 *Note Block.* When present, follows the title and is in italic type. The note provides contextual information about the entry to make the data more understandable. Special notes about the data, information about time periods covered, market totals, and other comments are provided. Self-explanatory entries do not have a note block.

7 *Column headers.* Follow the note block. Some entries have more than one column or the single column requires a header. In these cases, column headers are used to describe information covered in the column. In most cases, column headers are years (2002) or indicators of type and magnitude ($ mil.). Column headers are shown only when necessary for clarity of presentation.

8 *Body.* Follows the note block or the column header and shows the actual data in two or more columns. In most cases, individual rows of data in the body are arranged in descending order, with the largest market share holder heading the list. Collective shares, usually labelled "Others" are placed last.

9 *Source.* Follows the body. All entries cite the source of the table, the date of publication, and the page number (if given). In many cases, the publisher obtained the information from another source (original source); in all such cases, the original source is also shown.

Continued entries. Entries that extend over two adjacent columns on the same page are not marked to indicate continuation but continue in the second column. Entries that extend over two pages are marked *Continued on the next page.* Entries carried over from the previous page repeat the entry number, topic (followed by the word *continued*), title, and column header (if any).

Use of Names

Company Names. The editors reproduced company names as they appeared in the source unless it was clearly evident from the name and the context that a name had been misspelled in the original. Large companies, of course, tend to appear in a large number of entries and in variant renditions. General Electric Corporation may appear as GE, General Electric, General Electric Corp., GE Corp., and other variants. No attempt was made to enforce a uniform rendition of names in the entries. In the Company Index, variant renditions were reduced to a single version or cross-referenced.

Use of Numbers

Throughout *MSR*, tables showing percentage breakdowns may add to less than 100 or fractionally more than 100 due to rounding. In those cases where only a few leading participants in a market are shown, the total of the shares may be substantially less than 100.

Numbers in the note block showing the total size of the market are provided with as many significant digits as possible in order to permit the user to calculate the sales of a particular company by multiplying the market total by the market share.

In a relatively small number of entries, actual unit or dollar information is provided rather than share information in percent. In such cases, the denomination of the unit (tons, gallons, $) and its magnitude (000 indicates multiply by 1,000; mil., multiply by 1,000,000) are mentioned in the note block or shown in the column header.

Data in some entries are based on different kinds of currencies and different weight and liquid measures. Where necessary, the unit is identified in the note block or in the column header. Examples are long tons, short tons, metric tons or Canadian dollars, etc.

Graphics

Pie and bar charts are used to illustrate some of the entries. The graphics show the names of companies, products, and services when they fit on the charts. When room is insufficient to accommodate the label, the first word of a full name is used followed by three periods (...) to indicate omission of the rest of the label.

In the case of bar charts, the largest share is always the width of the column, and smaller shares are drawn in proportion. Two bar charts, consequently, should not be compared to one another.

Sources

The majority of entries were extracted from newspapers and from general purpose, trade, and technical periodicals normally available in larger public, special, or university libraries. All told, 1,257 sources were used; of these, 568 were primary print sources, Many more sources were reviewed but lacked coverage of the subject. These primary sources, in turn, used 689 original sources.

In many cases, the primary source in which the entry was published cites another source for the data, the original source. Original sources include other publications, brokerage houses, consultancies and research organizations, associations, government agencies, special surveys, and the like.

Many sources have also been used from the World Wide Web. The citation includes the Web address, the date the article was retrieved, and, if possible, the title of the article or report. In many cases Web pages have no title or author name. As well, it is not uncommon for Web pages to be moved or temporarity out of operation.

Since many primary sources appear as original sources elsewhere, and vice-versa, primary and original sources are shown in a single Source Index under two headings. Primary sources included in *MSR* almost always used the market share data as illustrative material for narratives covering many aspects of the subject. We hope that this book will also serve as a guide to those articles.

Indexes

Market Share Reporter features five indexes and three appendices.

- Source Index. This index holds 1,257 references in two groupings. *Primary sources* (568) are publications where the data were found. *Original sources* (689) are sources cited in the primary sources. Each item in the index is followed by one or more entry numbers arranged sequentially, beginning with the first mention of the source.

- Place Names Index. This index provides references to cities, states, parks and regions in North America. Nearly 300 are included. References are to entry numbers.

- Products, Services, Names and Issues Index. This index holds more than 1,900 references to products, personal names and services in alphabetical order. The index also lists subject categories that do not fit the definition of a product or service but properly belong in the index. Examples include *aquariums*, *counties*, *crime*, *defense spending*, *economies*, *lotteries*, and the like. Some listings are abbreviations for chemical substances, computer software, etc. which may not be meaningful to those unfamiliar with the industries. Wherever possible, the full name is also provided for abbreviations commonly in use. Each listing is followed by one or more references to entry numbers.

- Company Index. This index shows references to more than 4,000 company names by entry number. Companies are arranged in alphabetical order. In some cases, the market share table from which the company name was derived showed the share for a combination of two or more companies; these combinations are reproduced in the index.

- Brand Index. The Brand Index shows references to more than 2,000 brands by entry number. The arrangement is alphabetical. Brands include names of publications, computer software, operating systems, etc., as well as the more conventional brand names (Coca Cola, Maxwell House, Budweiser, etc.)

- Appendix I - SIC Coverage. The first appendix shows SICs covered by *Market Share Reporter*. The listing shows major SIC groupings at the 2-digit level as bold-face headings followed by 4-digit SIC numbers, the names of the SIC, and a *page* reference (rather than a reference to an entry number, as in the indexes). The page shows the first occurrence of the SIC in the book. *MSR*'s SIC coverage is quite comprehensive, as shown in the appendix. However, many 4-digit SIC categories are further divided into major product groupings. Not all of these have corresponding entries in the book.

- Appendix II - NAICS/SIC Conversion Guide. The SIC system is presently being revised, with SIC codes being replaced with North American Industry Classification System (NAICS) codes. NAICS is a six digit classification system that covers 20 sectors and 1,170 industries. The first two digits indicate the sector, the third indicates the subsector, the fourth indicates the industry group, the fifth indicates the NAICS industry, and the sixth indicates the national industry. This book is organized around the "old" SIC system because so many still use it. The appendix has both a SIC to NAICS and a NAICS to SIC look-up facility. More information on NAICS can be obtained form the Census Bureau Web site at: http://www.census.gov/naics.

- Appendix III - Annotated Source List. The third appendix provides publisher names, addresses, telephone and fax numbers, and publication frequency of primary sources cited in *Market Share Reporter*, 14th Edition.

Available in Electronic Formats

Licensing. *Market Share Reporter* is available for licensing. The complete database is provided in a fielded format and is deliverable on such media as disk, CD-ROM or tape. For more information, contact Gale's Business Development Group at 1-800-877-GALE or visit us on our web site at www.galegroup.com/bizdev.

Online. *Market Share Reporter* is accessible online as File MKTSHR through LEXIS-NEXIS and as part of the MarkIntel service offered by Thomson Financial Securities Data. For more information, contact LEXIS-NEXIS, P.O. Box 933, Dayton, OH 45401-0933, phone (937)865-6800, toll-free (800)227-4908,website: http://www.lexis-nexis.com; or Thomson Financial Securities Data, Two Gateway Center, Newark, NJ 07102, phone: (973)622-3100, toll-free: (888)989-8373, website: www.tfsd.com.

Acknowledgements

Market Share Reporter is something of a collective enterprise which involves not only the editorial team but also many users who share comments, criticisms, and suggestions over the telephone. Their help and encouragement is very much appreciated. *MSR* could not have been produced without the help of many people in and outside of The Gale Group. The editors would like to express their special appreciation to Amanda Quick (Coordinating Editor, Gale Group) and to the staff of Editorial Code and Data, Inc.

Comments and Suggestions

Comments on *MSR* or suggestions for improvement of its usefulness, format, and coverage are always welcome. Although every effort is made to maintain accuracy, errors may occasionally occur; the editors will be grateful if these are called to their attention. Please contact:

Editors
Market Share Reporter
The Gale Group
27500 Drake Road
Farmington Hills, Michigan 48331-3535
Phone:(248)699-GALE
or (800)347-GALE
Fax: (248) 699-8069

General Interest and Broad Topics

★ 1 ★

Collectibles

Collectibles Industry, 2000

Sales dropped in 2000 for the second straight year, to $7.1 billion after its peak of $7.9 billion in 1998. Collecting is still quite popular, however, with 35% of the population having one or more collections. One reason for the sales drop is that people collect through the secondary market — such as auctions and eBay.

Figures & sculptures	33.0%
Dolls	13.0
Plush toys	11.0
Ornaments	9.0
Cottages/villages	8.0
Die cast	8.0
Boxes/musicals	5.0
Plates	3.0
Other	11.0

Source: *Research Alert*, June 21, 2002, p. 1, from Unity Marketing.

★ 2 ★

Collectibles

Who Drives the Collectibles Industry

The $6.5 billion (retail) industry is now split evenly between men and women.

	1996	1998	2001
Women	76.0%	68.0%	50.0%
Men	24.0	32.0	50.0

Source: *Gifts & Decorative Accessories*, December 2002, p. 52, from Unity Marketing.

★ 3 ★

Entertainment

Entertainment Dollar Spending

Figures are in billions of dollars.

	2001	2002	Share
Home video sales & rental .	$ 16.80	$ 20.3	39.80%
Prerecorded music	13.70	12.3	24.12
Movie box office	8.41	9.3	18.24
Videogame software	6.35	7.0	13.73
Pop/rock concerts	1.75	2.1	4.12

Source: *Entertainment Marketing Letter*, February 1, 2003, p. 1, from Exhibitor Relations, *Hollywood Reporter*, Interactive Digital Software Association, and Pollstar.

★ 4 ★
Entertainment

U.S. Entertainment Dollar, 2001

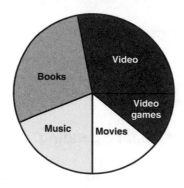

Total spending hit $59 billion.

Video (VHS and DVD)	28.0%
Books	28.0
Music	19.0
Movies	14.0
Video games	11.0

Source: *Business 2.0*, September 2002, p. 38, from A.C. Nielsen, Paul Kagan, and Veronis Suhler.

★ 5 ★
Fasteners

Fastening Demand, 2000

The industry is valued at $17 billion.

Industrial fasteners	47.0%
Lasers	17.0
Welding/brazing	12.0
Structural adhesives	11.0
Soldering	3.0
Nails, staples & tacks	2.0

Source: *Adhesives Age*, December 2002, p. 42, from ChemQuest Group.

★ 6 ★
Freight

How Freight is Shipped in Mexico

Trucking	82.0%
Rail	15.8
Maritime	2.0
Air	0.2

Source: *Business Mexico*, February 2003, p. 42, from Communications and Transportation Secretariat.

★ 7 ★
General Merchandise

Top Mass Market Categories

Sales are shown in billions of dollars for the year ended October 6, 2002. Figures exclude Wal-Mart.

Carbonated beverages	$ 15.23
Milk	10.87
Beer/ale/alcoholic cider	8.46
Fresh bread and rolls	8.08
Cigarettes	7.67
Salty snacks	7.35
Cold cereal	6.85
Frozen dinners/entrees	5.98
Natural cheese	5.07
Ice cream/sherbert	4.95

Source: *MMR*, December 9, 2002, p. 30, from Information Resources Inc.

★ 8 ★
Gifts

Gifts and Decorative Accessory Sales, 2001

The market for gifts and decorations hit $54.6 billion in 2001, down from $55.2 billion from 2000. Candles represent the largest part of the home decor segment with sales of $2 billion. Baby and children's gifts were the top sellers in the general gifts category with $1.8 billion in sales.

	($ bil.)	Share
Home decorative accents	$ 16.89	31.0%
Stationery and paper products . . .	14.07	26.0
General gifts	13.51	25.0
Collectibles	6.40	12.0
Seasonal decorations	3.66	7.0

Source: *Research Alert*, December 6, 2002, p. 5, from Unity Marketing.

★ 9 ★

Licensing

Leaders in Licensing Revenues

The cartoon characters on Nickelodeon, such as Rugrats, Jimmy Neutron and SpongeBob Squarepants, are challenging Disney and Warner Brother's hold on children's categories (SpongeBob Squarepants Band-Aids now outsell Scooby Doo, for example). Companies are ranked by licensing revenue in billions of dollars.

	1998	2002
Disney	$ 10.0	$ 13.0
Warner Brothers	6.0	6.0
Nickelodeon	0.7	2.8

Source: *New York Times*, January 9, 2003, p. C1, from *License Magazine* and company reports.

★ 10 ★

Luxury Goods

Leading Luxury Goods Makers, 2001

Firms are ranked by fiscal year sales in millions of dollars. Gucci, Tiffany & Tommy Hilfiger's fiscal period all end early in the year.

Pinault-Printemps	$ 24,623.9
Christian Dior	11,131.8
LVMH	10,900.0
Swatch	2,731.8
Polo Ralph Lauren	2,363.7
Gucci	2,285.0
Tommy Hilfiger	1,876.7
Tiffany & Co.	1,606.5
Armani	1,126.7
Hermes	1,086.8
Waterford Wedgwood	902.0
Bulgari	678.6

Source: *Brandweek*, April 28, 2003, p. 32, from Unity Marketing.

★ 11 ★

Media

Media Revenues

Gross revenues are shown in billions of dollars. B-to-B stands for business-to-business. The communications industry is expected to rebound but it will no longer be one of the nation's top 3 fastest growing industries.

	2001	2006
Cable and satellite TV	$ 70.2	$ 106.3
Newspapers	61.9	79.4
Filmed entertainment	53.6	74.6
Broadcast TV	38.7	46.7
Consumer Internet	21.5	39.1
B-to-B media	21.0	24.4
Consumer magazines	20.9	24.5
Radio broadcasting	17.9	24.1
Consumer books	17.8	20.5
Recorded music	13.9	12.8

Source: *New York Times*, August 5, 2002, p. C9, from Veronis Suhler Stevenson.

★ 12 ★

Media

Subscription Service Revenues, 2002

Figures are in millions of dollars. Magazine data is for 2001. Many of these media were minor industries a year ago and have seen striking growth.

Wireless voice service	$ 81,800
Cable TV	46,300
Satellite TV	10,800
Cable modem	7,800
Magazines	6,900
Dial up and T-1	3,700
DSL	3,300
Content sites	1,300
SMS messaging	353
Online games	303
Video-on-demand	163

Source: *Business 2.0*, April 2003, p. 34, from In-Stat/MDR, ComScore, Forrester Research, and Insight Research.

★ 13 ★

Natural Products

Natural Products Industry

Sales are shown in millions of dollars.

	($ mil.)	Share
Vitamins	$ 2,307	14.20%
Packaged grocery	1,612	9.92
Personal care (including aromatherapy)	1,147	7.06
Herbs/botanicals	1,067	6.57
Produce	1,052	6.48
Minerals	827	5.09
Frozen/refrigerated	823	5.07
Sports supplements	623	3.84
Dairy	618	3.80
Foodservice	583	3.59
Other	5,585	34.38

Source: *Natural Foods Merchandiser*, June 2002, p. 20, from SPINS.

★ 14 ★

Nutrition

Nutrition Industry Sales

Sales are shown in millions of dollars. Total industry sales grew from $33.1 billion in 1996 to $53.2 billion in 2001.

	1996	2001	Share
Functional foods . . .	$ 12,300	$ 18,600	34.96%
Natural organic foods . .	7,010	12,900	24.25
Vitamins	4,720	6,213	11.68
Herbs/botanicals	2,990	4,337	8.15
Multi-vitamins	2,495	3,169	5.96
Sports nutrition	1,070	1,662	3.12

	1996	2001	Share
Minerals	$ 890	$ 1,451	2.73%
Meal supplements	620	2,246	4.22

Source: *Chemical Market Reporter*, June 17, 2002, p. FR11, from *Nutrition Business Journal* and Health Industry Partners.

★ 15 ★

Packaging

Beverage Packaging Shares, 2006

Data show unit shares.

Cans	42.4%
Plastic	30.3
Glass	17.0
Other	10.4

Source: *Beverage World*, December 15, 2002, p. 72, from Beverage Marketing Corp.

★ 16 ★

Packaging

Case-Ready Packaging by Type, 2001

In 2001, about 1.6 billion packages in the fresh red meat industry were sold in case-ready form, triple the number in 1997. The number could hit 2.8 billion in 2005. Some of the growth is attributable to Wal-Mart's move into the fresh meat segment.

Overwrap trays	54.0%
Lidded trays	35.0
Vacuum packages	11.0

Source: *National Provisioner*, June 2002, p. 12, from *Case Ready Meat Packaging*.

★ 17 ★

Packaging

Fruit Beverage Packaging, 2002

Market shares are shown in percent. Data are for the single-serve market.

Plastic bottles	49.8%
Glass bottles	37.3
Cans	12.9

Source: *Beverage Aisle*, February 15, 2003, p. 18, from Beverage Marketing Corp.

★ 18 ★

Packaging

Packaging Materials Industry, 2005

The market is forecasted to reach $104.8 billion.

Paperboard/molded pulp	39.0%
Plastics	26.0
Metal	16.0
Paper	10.0
Wood	4.0
Glass	4.0
Textile	1.0

Source: *Plastics News*, September 9, 2002, p. 3, from Impact Marketing Consultants.

★ 19 ★

Packaging

Pouches Demand

Figures are shown in millions of dollars. Total demand is expected to increase from 62 million pouches in 2001 to 79 million in 2006.

	2001	2006	Share
Flat	$ 2,805	$ 3,580	44.03%
Pillow	1,725	2,090	25.71
Side seal	1,080	1,490	18.33
Stand-up	450	970	11.93

Source: *Canadian Packaging*, March 2003, p. 7, from Freedonia Group.

★ 20 ★

Pets

Most Popular Pets

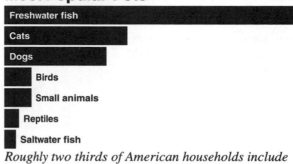

Roughly two thirds of American households include pets. Small animals include guinea pigs, gerbils, hamsters and similar creatures. Figures are in millions.

Freshwater fish	185.0
Cats	77.7
Dogs	65.0
Birds	17.3
Small animals	16.8
Reptiles	8.8
Saltwater fish	7.0

Source: *Christian Science Monitor*, March 11, 2003, p. 20, from American Pet Products Manufacturers Association.

★ 21 ★

Pets

Number of Household Pets, 2002

Figures show percentage of households with pets. Small animals includes rabbits, gerbils and guinea pigs. 62% of households have some sort of pet. The pet product market may hit $31 billion in 2003.

Dogs	39.0%
Cats	34.0
Freshwater fish	13.0
Birds	6.0
Small animals	5.0
Reptiles	4.0
Saltwater fish	0.7

Source: *Pet Product News*, April 2003, p. 49, from American Pet Products Manufacturers Association.

★ 22 ★

Private Label Industry

Leading Private Label Categories, 2002

Supermarket sales are shown in millions of dollars for the year ended June 16, 2002.

Carbonated beverages	$ 15,014.0
Milk	10,987.0
Beer/ale/alcoholic cider	8,277.6
Fresh bread & rolls	8,031.2
Cigarettes	7,675.7
Salty snacks	7,315.5
Cold cereal	6,855.4
Frozen dinners/entrees	5,916.0
Natural cheese	5,026.5
Ice cream/sherbert	4,896.0

Source: *Private Label Buyer*, August 2002, p. 10, from Information Resources Inc.

★ 23 ★

Promotional Industry

Promotional Products Industry, 2001

The industry saw sales of $16.5 billion, a 7.3% decline from 2000. This is the first negative growth in the industry in 40 years.

Wearbales/apparel	29.3%
Writing instruments	10.6
Other	60.1

Source: *Wearables Business*, August 1, 2002, p. NA, from Promotional Products Association International.

★ 24 ★

Teenagers

What Teenagers Want to Buy

Figures show what teenagers were planning to purchase in the coming year, according to a survey. 56% of respondents reported receiving spending money from their parents, 35% got money as gifts, and 30% from doing odd jobs.

Cellular phone	22.0%
CD burner	19.0
Used car	18.0
MP3 player	17.0
DVD player	15.0

Source: *New York Times*, December 1, 2002, p. 10, from Teenage Research Unlimited.

★ 25 ★

Weddings

Where We Get Married

Roughly 2.4 million weddings are held annually, representing $72 billion in spending. Another $8 billion is thought to be spent on honeymoons. Las Vegas is the top spot for weddings, representing about 5% of the market.

	No.	Share
Las Vegas	110,000	4.58%
Hawaii	20,000	0.83
Jamaica	5,000	0.21
U.S. Virgin Islands	5,000	0.21
Bahamas	4,000	0.17
Other	2,256,000	94.00

Source: *Knight Ridder/Tribune Business News*, November 6, 2002, p. NA, from Association of Bridal Consultants.

SIC 01 - Agricultural Production - Crops

★ 26 ★
Grain (SIC 0110)

Largest Grain Handlers in Western Canada

Market shares are as of July 2000.

UGG/Agricore	40.0%
Saskatchewan Wheat Pool	26.0
Cargill	11.0
Other	23.0

Source: "Market Share up for Grabs." available March 28, 2003 from http://www.producer.com.

★ 27 ★
Produce (SIC 0110)

Best-Selling Random Weight Produce

Sales of random weight items are for all outlets. Figures are in millions of dollars.

Bananas	$ 1,636.3
Grapes	1,120.6
Tomatoes (except Plum/Roma)	732.7
Onions	431.5
Cantaloupe	410.8
Sweet peppers	382.2
Oranges	375.3
Apples (except Red Delicious, Gala)	345.8
Potatoes	328.5
Watermelon	326.3

Source: *Supermarket News*, December 30, 2002, p. 24, from A.C. Nielsen Homescan Fresh Produce Service.

★ 28 ★
Seeds (SIC 0110)

Top Seed Producers, 2002

Market shares are as of September 2002.

DuPont (Pioneer)	7.8%
Monsanto	6.9
Syngenta	3.8
Groupe Limagrain	3.1
Grupo Pulsar (Seminis)	1.8
Other	76.6

Source: "Top Seed Companies." available April 7, 2003 from http://www.ilfb.com/viedocument.asp?did3758, from Illinois Farm Bureau.

★ 29 ★
Wheat (SIC 0111)

Largest Wheat Producing States, 2002

Production is shown in thousands of bushels.

	(000)	Share
Kansas	267,300	16.54%
North Dakota	216,610	13.40
Washington	129,695	8.02
Montana	109,895	6.80
Oklahoma	98,000	6.06
Idaho	87,660	5.42
Texas	78,300	4.84

Continued on next page.

7

★ 29 ★ *Continued*
Wheat (SIC 0111)

Largest Wheat Producing States, 2002

Production is shown in thousands of bushels.

	(000)	Share
Minnesota	62,240	3.85%
Other	566,741	35.06

Source: *Crop Production*, National Agricultural Statistics Service, January 2003, p. 14, from U.S. Department of Agriculture.

★ 30 ★
Rice (SIC 0112)

Largest Rice Producing States, 2002

Production is shown in thousands of Cwt (hundredweight).

	(000)	Share
Arkansas	96,752	45.86%
California	42,989	20.38
Louisiana	29,400	13.94
Mississippi	16,192	7.68
Texas	14,616	6.93
Missouri	11,011	5.22

Source: *Crop Production*, National Agricultural Statistics Service, January 2003, p. 14, from U.S. Department of Agriculture.

★ 31 ★
Corn (SIC 0115)

Corn Seed Market

Market shares are shown in percent.

DuPont/Monsanto	73.0%
Other	27.0

Source: *Knight Ridder/Tribune Business News*, December 6, 2002, p. NA.

★ 32 ★
Soybeans (SIC 0116)

Largest Soybean Producing States, 2002

Production is shown in thousands of bushels.

	(000)	Share
Iowa	494,880	18.13%
Illinois	449,780	16.48
Minnesota	308,850	11.31
Indiana	235,750	8.64
Nebraska	176,330	6.46
Missouri	170,000	6.23
Ohio	141,300	5.18
Other	752,819	27.58

Source: *Crop Production*, National Agricultural Statistics Service, January 2003, p. 14, from U.S. Department of Agriculture.

★ 33 ★
Soybeans (SIC 0116)

Soybean Processing in North America

Market shares are shown in percent.

ADM	26.0%
Cargill	21.0
Other	53.0

Source: *Feedstuffs*, July 29, 2002, p. 1.

★ 34 ★
Beans (SIC 0119)

Largest Bean Producing States, 2001- 2002

Production is shown in thousands of Cwt (hundredweight). Figures are for dry edible beans and a clean basis.

	(000)	Share
North Dakota	10,557	35.01%
Michigan	4,903	16.26
Nebraska	3,465	11.49
Minnesota	2,475	8.21

Continued on next page.

★ 34 ★ *Continued*

Beans (SIC 0119)

Largest Bean Producing States, 2001- 2002

Production is shown in thousands of Cwt (hundredweight). Figures are for dry edible beans and a clean basis.

	(000)	Share
Idaho	1,860	6.17%
California	1,807	5.99
Colorado	1,785	5.92
Other	3,298	10.94

Source: *Crop Production*, National Agricultural Statistics Service, December 10, 2002, from U.S. Department of Agriculture.

★ 35 ★

Hay (SIC 0119)

Largest Hay Producing States, 2002

Production is shown in thousands of tons.

	(000)	Share
Texas	13,850	9.17%
California	9,594	6.36
Missouri	7,840	5.19
Kansas	6,965	4.61
Minnesota	6,610	4.38
Nebraska	5,950	3.94
Indiana	5,645	3.74
Kentucky	5,520	3.66
Wisconsin	5,340	3.54
Oklahoma	5,030	3.33
Other	78,618	52.08

Source: *Crop Production*, National Agricultural Statistics Service, January 2003, p. 14, from U.S. Department of Agriculture.

★ 36 ★

Oats (SIC 0119)

Largest Oat Producing States, 2002

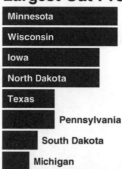

Production is shown in thousands of bushels.

	(000)	Share
Minnesota	15,960	13.40%
Wisconsin	15,000	12.59
Iowa	13,300	11.16
North Dakota	12,760	10.71
Texas	7,040	5.91
Pennsylvania	7,015	5.89
South Dakota	4,500	3.78
Michigan	4,160	3.49
Other	39,397	33.07

Source: *Crop Production*, National Agricultural Statistics Service, January 2003, p. 14, from U.S. Department of Agriculture.

★ 37 ★

Sorghum (SIC 0119)

Largest Sorghum Producing States, 2002

Production is shown in thousands of bushels.

	(000)	Share
Kansas	135,000	36.51%
Texas	130,050	35.17
Arizona	17,710	4.79
Missouri	15,725	4.25
Nebraska	15,000	4.06
Oklahoma	14,850	4.02
Illinois	6,391	1.73
Mississippi	6,237	1.69
Other	28,795	7.79

Source: *Crop Production*, National Agricultural Statistics Service, January 2003, p. 14, from U.S. Department of Agriculture.

★ 38 ★

Cotton (SIC 0131)

Largest Cotton Producing States, 2002

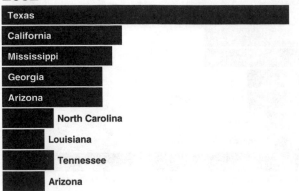

Texas
California
Mississippi
Georgia
Arizona
North Carolina
Louisiana
Tennessee
Arizona

Production is shown in thousands of bales.

	2001	2002	Share
Texas	4,296.4	5,037	28.99%
California	2,409.0	2,010	11.57
Mississippi	2,396.0	1,920	11.05
Georgia	2,220.0	1,750	10.07
Arizona	1,833.0	1,650	9.50
North Carolina	1,673.0	860	4.95
Louisiana	1,034.0	750	4.32
Tennessee	978.0	800	4.60
Arizona	704.5	614	3.53

Source: *Crop Production*, National Agricultural Statistics Service, December 10, 2002, from U.S. Department of Agriculture.

★ 39 ★

Cotton (SIC 0131)

Largest Cottonseed Producing States, 2002

Production is shown in thousands of tons.

	(000)	Share
Texas	1,984.0	30.91%
Mississippi	751.0	11.70
California	720.0	11.22
Arizona	640.0	9.97
Georgia	564.0	8.79

	(000)	Share
Tennessee	309.0	4.81%
Louisiana	275.0	4.28
North Carolina	271.0	4.22
Other	905.3	14.10

Source: *Crop Production*, National Agricultural Statistics Service, January 2003, p. 14, from U.S. Department of Agriculture.

★ 40 ★

Cotton (SIC 0131)

Organic Cotton Production, 2002

A total of 9,897 bales of organic cotton were harvested from 11,316 acres during the year. Production will be lowered in 2002 to 9,044 acres. Figures are in acres.

	Acres	Share
Texas	6,872	75.98%
New Mexico	589	6.51
California	584	6.46
Arizona	578	6.39
Missouri	421	4.66

Source: *PR Newswire*, December 30, 2002, p. NA, from Organic Trade Association and Cotton Incorporated.

★ 41 ★

Tobacco (SIC 0132)

Largest Tobacco Producing States, 2002

Production is shown in thousands of pounds.

	(000)	Share
North Carolina	357,350	40.17%
Kentucky	226,430	25.45
Tennessee	72,540	8.15
Virginia	66,180	7.44
South Carolina	59,475	6.69
Georgia	55,650	6.26
Florida	11,960	1.34
Ohio	9,460	1.06
Indiana	8,000	0.90
Other	22,587	2.54

Source: *Crop Production*, National Agricultural Statistics Service, January 2003, p. 14, from U.S. Department of Agriculture.

★ 42 ★
Sugarbeets (SIC 0133)

Largest Sugarbeet Producing States, 2002

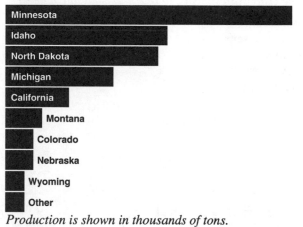

Production is shown in thousands of tons.

	(000)	Share
Minnesota	8,854	32.14%
Idaho	5,040	18.29
North Dakota	4,799	17.42
Michigan	3,204	11.63
California	1,862	6.76
Montana	1,096	3.98
Colorado	794	2.88
Nebraska	760	2.76
Wyoming	659	2.39
Other	482	1.75

Source: *Crop Production*, National Agricultural Statistics Service, January 2003, p. 14, from U.S. Department of Agriculture.

★ 43 ★
Potatoes (SIC 0134)

Largest Potato Producing States, 2002

Production is shown in thousands of Cwt (hundredweight).

	(000)	Share
Idaho	133,385	28.80%
Washington	95,200	20.55
Wisconsin	31,125	6.72
Colorado	30,189	6.52
Oregon	24,936	5.38
North Dakota	23,460	5.06
Minnesota	18,700	4.04
California	17,695	3.82

	(000)	Share
Maine	16,960	3.66%
Nebraska	8,611	1.86
Other	62,953	13.59

Source: *Crop Production*, National Agricultural Statistics Service, January 2003, p. 14, from U.S. Department of Agriculture.

★ 44 ★
Melons (SIC 0161)

Most Harvested Melons

Figures are based on 15,100 acres harvested in the fall.

Cantaloupes	59.0%
Honeydews	35.0
Watermelons	6.0

Source: *USA TODAY*, September 3, 2002, p. D1, from National Agricultural Statistics Service.

★ 45 ★
Vegetables (SIC 0161)

Largest Vegetable Growers

Companies are ranked by acreage.

Grimmaway Farms	47,000
Tanimura & Antle	33,083
Larsen Farms	28,000
D'Arrigo Bros. Co. of California	27,509
Ocean Mist Farms/Boutonnet Farms	17,447
Rio Farms	14,885
Nunes Vegetables Inc.	14,675
Boskovich Farms Inc.	13,500
Dresick Farms Inc.	13,393
AgriNorthwest	13,000

Source: *AVG*, October 2002, p. 12.

★ 46 ★

Vegetables (SIC 0161)

Most Harvested Vegetables, 2001

Data are for the fall.

Lettuce 20.0%
Broccoli 15.5
Tomatoes 13.9
Carrots 10.8
Green beans 10.4
Other 29.4

Source: *USA TODAY*, September 24, 2002, p. D1, from National Agricultural Statistics Board.

★ 47 ★

Berries (SIC 0171)

California's Strawberry Production

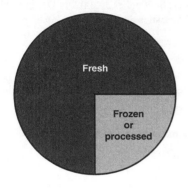

Roughly 1.4 billion pounds of strawberries are produced annually.

Fresh 75.0%
Frozen or processed 25.0

Source: "California Strawberries at a Glance." available March 7, 2003 from http://www.mbsf.com/glance2.html.

★ 48 ★

Berries (SIC 0171)

Cranberry Production by State, 2002

The crop was estimated to reach 572 million pounds.

Wisconsin 51.0%
Massachusetts 31.0
Oregon 8.0
New Jersey 7.0
Washington 3.0

Source: *USA TODAY*, November 26, 2002, p. 1A, from National Agricultural Statistics Service.

★ 49 ★

Berries (SIC 0171)

Fresh Berry Market

Market shares are shown in percent.

Driscoll's 65.0%
Other 35.0

Source: "Driscoll's." available March 7, 2003 from http://www.workshop4.com/cl_driscolls.html.

★ 50 ★

Nuts (SIC 0173)

Largest Peanut Producing States, 2002

Production is shown in thousands of pounds.

	(000)	Share
Georgia	1,313,000	39.54%
Texas	868,000	26.14
Alabama	379,250	11.42
North Carolina	210,000	6.32
Florida	197,800	5.96
Oklahoma	159,600	4.81
Virginia	119,700	3.60
Other	73,140	2.20

Source: *Crop Production*, National Agricultural Statistics Service, January 2003, p. 14, from U.S. Department of Agriculture.

★ 51 ★
Nuts (SIC 0173)

Largest Pecan Producing States, 2002

Production is shown in thousands of pounds.

	(000)	Share
Georgia	45,000	25.61%
Texas	40,000	22.77
New Mexico	36,000	20.49
Oklahoma	14,000	7.97
Arizona	14,000	7.97
Alabama	7,000	3.98
Louisiana	6,000	3.41
Mississippi	3,000	1.71
California	2,800	1.59
Other	7,900	4.50

Source: *Crop Production*, National Agricultural Statistics Service, December 10, 2002, p. 14, from U.S. Department of Agriculture.

★ 52 ★
Nuts (SIC 0173)

Largest Sunflower Producing States, 2002

Production is shown in thousands of pounds.

	(000)	Share
North Dakota	1,710,050	68.48%
South Dakota	373,750	14.97
Kansas	151,590	6.07
Minnesota	86,050	3.45
Colorado	63,000	2.52
Texas	31,800	1.27
Other	80,996	3.24

Source: *Crop Production*, National Agricultural Statistics Service, January 2003, p. 14, from U.S. Department of Agriculture.

★ 53 ★
Oranges (SIC 0174)

Largest Orange Producing States

Production is shown in thousands of boxes. Figures are for 2001-2002.

	(000)	Share
Florida	197,000	75.18%
California	63,000	24.04
Texas	1,580	0.60
Other	450	0.17

Source: *Crop Production*, National Agricultural Statistics Service, December 10, 2002, from U.S. Department of Agriculture.

★ 54 ★
Bananas (SIC 0175)

Top Banana Distributors, 2001

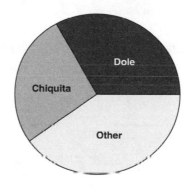

Market shares are for North America.

Dole	33.0%
Chiquita	27.0
Other	40.0

Source: *The Cincinnati Post*, August 3, 2002, p. 10B.

★ 55 ★
Pineapples (SIC 0175)

Fresh Pineapple Market, 2001

The company claims to be the largest marketer of fresh pineapple in the world. Market shares are estimated in percent.

Fresh Del Monte Produce	50.0%
Other	50.0

Source: *BusinessWeek Online*, April 7, 2003, p. NA.

★ 56 ★
Flowers (SIC 0181)

California's Poinsettia Market

Counties are ranked by sales in millions of dollars. The most popular color remains red, with 85% of the market.

San Diego	$ 42.7
San Mateo	4.0
Santa Barbara	1.8

Source: *Knight Ridder/Tribune Business News*, November 27, 2002, p. NA.

★ 57 ★
Flowers (SIC 0181)

Retail Flower Sales, 2001

Flowers are ranked in thousands of stems (figures include imports and domestic). Glads' data are in spikes amd Pompon are in bunches.

Roses	1,420,546
Carnations (Standard)	785,066
Alstroemeria	195,236
Tulips	143,831
Gerbera	125,527
Glads	123,609
Chrysanthemums	104,921
Iris	101,100
Lilies	99,576
PomPon	96,404

Source: *Supermarket News*, December 30, 2002, p. 17, from Society of American Florists, National Agricultural Statistics Service, and United States Department of Agriculture.

★ 58 ★
Flowers (SIC 0181)

Top States for Bedding/Garden Plants, 2002

Sales are shown in thousands of dollars at the whole-sale sales.

	($000)	Share
California	$ 303,533	13.76%
Michigan	189,381	8.58
Texas	187,159	8.48
Ohio	131,759	5.97
Florida	101,597	4.61
North Carolina	101,409	4.60

	($000)	Share
North Carolina	$ 96,818	4.39%
Illinois	75,481	3.42
Pennsylvania	75,447	3.42
New Jersey	75,018	3.40
Other	868,626	39.37

Source: *Floriculture Crops*, National Agricultural Statistics Service, December 2002, p. 4, from U.S. Department of Agriculture.

★ 59 ★
Flowers (SIC 0181)

Top States for Carnations, 2001

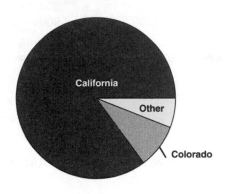

Sales are shown in thousands of dollars, at the wholesale level.

	($000)	Share
California	$ 3,929	85.95%
Colorado	390	8.53
Other	252	5.51

Source: *Floriculture Crops*, National Agricultural Statistics Service, December 2002, p. 4, from U.S. Department of Agriculture.

★ 60 ★
Flowers (SIC 0181)

Top States for Cut Flowers, 2002

Sales are shown in thousands of dollars at the whole-sale sales.

	($000)	Share
California	$ 292,115	68.85%
Florida	23,168	5.46
Washington	18,857	4.44
Hawaii	16,221	3.82
Oregon	10,698	2.52

Continued on next page.

★ **60** ★ *Continued*

Flowers (SIC 0181)

Top States for Cut Flowers, 2002

Sales are shown in thousands of dollars at the whole-sale sales.

	($000)	Share
New Jersey	$ 8,533	2.01%
Michigan	8,119	1.91
Colorado	6,440	1.52
Minnesota	5,184	1.22
Other	34,921	8.23

Source: *Floriculture Crops*, National Agricultural Statistics Service, December 2002, p. 4, from U.S. Department of Agriculture.

★ **61** ★

Flowers (SIC 0181)

Top States for Gladioli, 2001

Sales are shown in thousands of dollars, at the wholesale level.

	($000)	Share
Florida	$ 11,983	49.55%
California	4,209	17.40
New Jersey	1,304	5.39
Illinois	272	1.12
New York	11	0.05
Other	6,404	26.48

Source: *Floriculture Crops*, National Agricultural Statistics Service, December 2002, p. 4, from U.S. Department of Agriculture.

★ **62** ★

Flowers (SIC 0181)

Top States for Lilies, 2001

Sales are shown in thousands of dollars, at the wholesale level.

	($000)	Share
California	$ 45,829	79.77%
Colorado	1,119	1.95
Ohio	949	1.65
Minnesota	484	0.84
Michigan	286	0.50

	($000)	Share
Pennsylvania	$ 211	0.37%
New Jersey	100	0.17
Indiana	12	0.02
Other	8,462	14.73

Source: *Floriculture Crops*, National Agricultural Statistics Service, December 2002, p. 4, from U.S. Department of Agriculture.

★ **63** ★

Flowers (SIC 0181)

Top States for Orchids, 2001

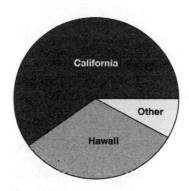

Sales are shown in thousands of dollars, at the wholesale level.

	($000)	Share
California	.$ 5,421	59.81%
Hawaii	2,915	32.16
Other	727	8.02

Source: *Floriculture Crops*, National Agricultural Statistics Service, December 2002, p. 4, from U.S. Department of Agriculture.

★ 64 ★

Flowers (SIC 0181)

Top States for Roses, 2001

Sales are shown in thousands of dollars, at the wholesale level.

	($000)	Share
California	$ 44,648	65.99%
Pennsylvania	2,296	3.39
Colorado	2,213	3.27
Michigan	581	0.86
Other	17,918	26.48

Source: *Floriculture Crops*, National Agricultural Statistics Service, December 2002, p. 4, from U.S. Department of Agriculture.

★ 65 ★

Flowers (SIC 0181)

Top States for Tulips, 2001

Sales are shown in thousands of dollars, at the wholesale level.

	($000)	Share
California	$ 12,723	48.44%
Washington	8,160	31.07
Minnesota	550	2.09
Pennsylvania	41	0.16
Other	4,791	18.24

Source: *Floriculture Crops*, National Agricultural Statistics Service, December 2002, p. 4, from U.S. Department of Agriculture.

★ 66 ★

Lawn & Garden Industry (SIC 0181)

Green Good Sales, 2002

Evergreens made up nearly 36% of the $13.6 billion industry.

Evergreens	35.8%
Bedding plants	18.9
Flowering plants	11.4
Shrubs	11.1
Foliage	10.2
Decidous trees	4.4

Flowering trees	2.9%
Fruit & nut plants	2.3
Bulbs	1.5
Roses	1.5

Source: *Nursery Retailer*, March/April 2003, p. 57, from U.S. Bureau of the Census, *Floriculture and Nursery Crop Situation and Outlook Yearbook*, and *1998 Census & Horticultural Specialties*.

★ 67 ★

Lawn & Garden Industry (SIC 0181)

Green Good Sales in Maryland

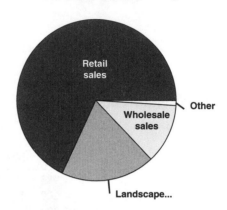

The $1.15 billion industry is the number one segment of the agricultural industry, in terms of value.

Retail sales	68.0%
Landscape installation and maintenance	19.0
Wholesale sales	12.0
Other	1.0

Source: *American Nurseryman*, June 1, 2002, p. 14, from Maryland Agricultural Statistics Service.

★ 68 ★

Lawn & Garden Industry (SIC 0181)

Lawn & Garden Sales by Segment, 2002

Green goods had 40% of the market, or $37.9 billion in sales. Sales are projected to reach $38.7 billion in 2003.

Green goods	40.0%
Trim-a-tree	10.0
Tools	10.0
Chemicals	8.9
Watering equipment	8.0
Fertilizers	8.0

Continued on next page.

★ 68 ★ *Continued*
Lawn & Garden Industry (SIC 0181)

Lawn & Garden Sales by Segment, 2002

Green goods had 40% of the market, or $37.9 billion in sales. Sales are projected to reach $38.7 billion in 2003.

Accessories	7.5%
Power equipment	5.3
Casual furniture	2.3

Source: *Nursery Retailer*, March/April 2003, p. 57, from U.S. Bureau of the Census, *Floriculture and Nursery Crop Situation and Outlook Yearbook*, and *1998 Census & Horticultural Specialties*.

★ 69 ★
Lawn & Garden Industry (SIC 0181)

Lawn & Garden Sales by State, 2002

California
Texas
Illinois
Iowa
Minnesota
Other

Retail sales of lawn & garden goods reached $94.9 billion.

California	9.4%
Texas	6.3
Illinois	6.1
Iowa	4.3
Minnesota	4.3
Other	69.6

Source: *Nursery Retailer*, March/April 2003, p. 57, from U.S. Bureau of the Census, *Floriculture and Nursery Crop Situation and Outlook Yearbook*, and *1998 Census Horticultural Specialties*.

★ 70 ★
Mushrooms (SIC 0182)

Specialty Mushroom Sales, 2001

Figures show value of production for 2000-2001.

	($000)	Share
Shiitake	27,818	65.09%
Oyster	7,499	17.55
Other	7,419	17.36

Source: "Mushrooms." available January 3, 2003 from http://www.usda.mannlib.cornell.edu, from U.S. Department of Agriculture.

★ 71 ★
Farms (SIC 0191)

Top States for Farms, 2002

Figures show number of farms.

	(000)	Share
Texas	230,000	10.66%
Missouri	107,000	4.96
Iowa	92,500	4.29
Tennessee	90,000	4.17
Kentucky	89,000	4.12
Oklahoma	87,000	4.03
California	84,000	3.89
Minnesota	79,000	3.66
Wisconsin	77,000	3.57
Illinois	76,000	3.52
Other	1,146,590	53.13

Source: *Farms and Land in Farms*, National Agricultural Statistics Service, January 2003, p. 4, from U.S. Department of Agriculture.

SIC 02 - Agricultural Production - Livestock

★ 72 ★
Hogs and Pigs (SIC 0213)

Top States for Hogs and Pigs, 2002

Production is shown in thousands of heads.

	(000)	Share
Iowa	15,300	25.96%
North Carolina	9,600	16.29
Minnesota	5,900	10.01
Illinois	4,050	6.87
Indiana	3,150	5.34
Missouri	2,950	5.00
Nebraska	2,900	4.92
Oklahoma	2,490	4.22
Ohio	1,440	2.44
South Dakota	1,290	2.19
Other	9,873	16.75

Source: *Hogs and Pigs*, National Agricultural Statistics Service, December 2002, p. 4, from U.S. Department of Agriculture.

★ 73 ★
Sheeps and Goats (SIC 0214)

Top States for Sheep and Goats, 2002

Figures show thousands of heads.

	(000)	Share
Texas	1,130	16.90%
California	800	11.97
Wyoming	480	7.18
South Dakota	400	5.98
Colorado	370	5.53
Montana	335	5.01
Oregon	285	4.26
Idaho	260	3.89
Iowa	250	3.74
Other	2,375	35.53

Source: *Sheep and Goats*, National Agricultural Statistics Service, January 2003, p. 4, from U.S. Department of Agriculture.

★ 74 ★
Broilers (SIC 0250)

Largest Broiler Processors, 2002

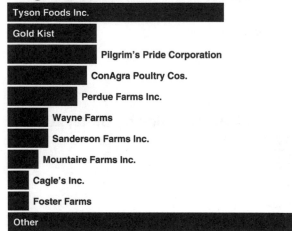

Companies are ranked by ready-to-cook production processed, in millions. Shares are shown based on 663.13 million pounds produced by the top firms over the previous year.

	(mil.)	Share
Tyson Foods Inc.	148.84	22.45%
Gold Kist	61.53	9.28
Pilgrim's Pride Corporation	57.53	8.68
ConAgra Poultry Cos.	51.53	7.77
Perdue Farms Inc.	48.15	7.26
Wayne Farms	29.15	4.40
Sanderson Farms Inc.	25.11	3.79
Mountaire Farms Inc.	19.71	2.97
Cagle's Inc.	16.18	2.44
Foster Farms	15.54	2.34
Other	189.86	28.63

Source: *WATTPoultryUSA*, January 2003, p. 66.

★ 75 ★
Broilers (SIC 0251)

Average Number of Layers by State, 2002

Figures are in thousands.

	(000)	Share
Iowa	36,980	10.97%
Ohio	30,479	9.04
California	23,652	7.01
Pennsylvania	23,641	7.01
Indiana	22,435	6.65
Georgia	20,452	6.07
Texas	18,608	5.52
Arkansas	14,829	4.40
Minnesota	11,729	3.48
Nebraska	11,591	3.44
Other	122,806	36.42

Source: *Egg Industry*, February 2003, p. 10, from United States Department of Agriculture.

★ 76 ★
Eggs (SIC 0252)

Egg Production by State, 2002

Figures are in millions of eggs.

	(mil.)	Share
Iowa	9,910	11.43%
Ohio	7,940	9.16
Pennsylvania	6,520	7.52
California	6,124	7.06
Indiana	5,973	6.89
Georgia	4,961	5.72
Texas	4,774	5.51
Arkansas	3,329	3.84
Minnesota	3,124	3.60
Nebraska	2,977	3.43
Other	31,066	35.83

Source: *Egg Industry*, February 2003, p. 10, from United States Department of Agriculture.

★ 77 ★
Eggs (SIC 0252)

Top Egg Producers, 2002

Firms are ranked by millions of producers as of December 31, 2002.

Cal-Maine Foods Inc.	20.6
Rose Acre Farms Inc.	17.5
Michael Foods Egg Products Co.	14.0
Buckeye Egg Farm	11.0
Decoster Egg Farms	10.5
Sparboe Companies	10.5
Moark LLC	8.4
Dutchland Farms L.P.	7.3
Fort Recovery Equity	6.5
ISE America Inc.	6.0
Daybreak Foods	5.5
Hillandale Farms Inc.	5.4

Source: *Egg Industry*, January 2003, p. 20.

★ 78 ★
Turkeys (SIC 0253)

Largest Turkey Processors, 2002

Companies are ranked by live pounds processed, in millions.

	(mil.)	Share
Cargill	1,210	17.19%
Jennie-O Turkey Store	1,200	17.05
Butterball Turkey Co.	800	11.36
Carolina Turkeys	580	8.24
Pilgrim's Pride	509	7.23
Louis Rich Brand	300	4.26
Bil Mar	273	3.88
House of Raeford	250	3.55
Perdue Farms Inc.	233	3.31
Other	1,685	23.93

Source: *WATTPoultryUSA*, January 2003, p. 66.

★ 79 ★
Turkeys (SIC 0253)

Top States for Turkeys, 2002

Figures show thousands of heads.

	(000)	Share
North Carolina	45,500	15.22%
Arkansas	29,500	9.87
Missouri	25,500	8.53

Continued on next page.

★ 79 ★ *Continued*
Turkeys (SIC 0253)

Top States for Turkeys, 2002

Figures show thousands of heads.

	(000)	Share
Virginia	20,000	6.69%
California	17,700	5.92
Indiana	13,000	4.35
South Carolina	9,900	3.31
Pennsylvania	9,900	3.31
Iowa	6,800	2.27
Ohio	5,400	1.81
Other	115,829	38.74

Source: *Turkeys Raised*, National Agricultural Statistics Service, January 2003, p. 4, from U.S. Department of Agriculture.

★ 80 ★
Horses (SIC 0272)

Largest Breeders

Individuals and partnerships are ranked by earnings in millions of dollars.

Mockingbird Farm Inc.	$ 11.18
Farnsworth Farms	10.12
Adena Springs	9.36
John Franks	8.95
Allen E. Paulson	6.56
Edward P. Evans	6.11
Mr. and Mrs. John C. Mabee	5.72
Charles Nuckols Jr. & Sons	5.62
Juddmonte Farms	5.55

Source: "Leading Breeders 2002." available March 7, 2003 from http://www.equineonline.com.

★ 81 ★
Dogs (SIC 0279)

Top Dog Registrations, 2002

Data show total dog registrations.

Retrievers (Labrador)	154,616
Retrievers (Golden)	56,124
German Shepherds	46,963
Beagles	44,610
Dachshunds	42,571
Yorkshire Terriers	37,277
Boxers	34,340
Poodles	33,917
Chihuahuas	28,466
Shih Tzu	28,294

Source: "Registration Statistics." available February 11, 2003 from http://www.akc.org, from American Kennel Club.

SIC 07 - Agricultural Services

★ 82 ★

Dogs (SIC 0752)

Worker Dog Population

Figures show the number of dogs for certain categories.

Guide dogs	10,000
Hearing dogs	4,000
Service dogs	3,000

Source: *The Nikkei Weekly*, March 10, 2003, p. 17.

SIC 08 - Forestry

★ 83 ★

Christmas Trees (SIC 0811)

Christmas Tree Production

A total of 9.55 million trees were sold in the top 17 states generating $149 million in gross sales.

	(000)	Share
Oregon	3,832	40.23%
Michigan	2,164	22.72
North Carolina	2,060	21.63
Pennsylvania	681	7.15
Washington	458	4.81
Ohio	55	0.58
New York	54	0.57
Illinois	52	0.55
Connecticut	37	0.39
California	32	0.34
Other	101	1.06

Source: ''Nursery Products.'' available April 7, 2003 from http://www.usda.gov, from National Agricultural Service and U.S. Department of Agriculture.

★ 84 ★

Christmas Trees (SIC 0811)

Christmas Tree Production in Oregon, 2001

Oregon's Christmas tree gross sales reached $98.2 million in 2001. The state sold over 6.1 million trees throughout the country and the world. Sales of trees are shown by species.

	(000)	Share
Douglas fir	3,465	56.63%
Noble fir	2,165	35.38
Grand fir	393	6.42
Scotch pine	31	0.51
Nordmann fir	9	0.15
Other	56	0.92

Source: ''Oregon Christmas Tree Survey.'' available April 7, 2003 from http://www.oda.state.or.us/oass/oass.html, from Oregon Agricultural Statistics Service.

SIC 09 - Fishing, Hunting, and Trapping

★ 85 ★

Fishing (SIC 0910)

Fishing Industry Spending, 2001

More than 34 million residents over 16 years of age fished during the year. Spending is shown in billions of dollars.

	($ mil.)	Share
Equipment	$ 17.0	47.49%
Food and lodging	6.0	16.76
Transportation	3.5	9.78
Land leasing and ownership	3.2	8.94
Licenses, stamps, tags, permits	0.6	1.68
Membership dues and contributions	0.1	0.28
Magazines, books	0.1	0.28
Other	5.3	14.80

Source: *Research Alert*, November 1, 2002, p. 5, from U.S. Fish and Wildlife Service.

★ 86 ★

Fishing (SIC 0910)

Largest Fishing Ports, 2001

Ports are ranked by value of fishery landings in millions of dollars.

New Bedford, MA	$ 150.5
Dutch Harbor-Unalaska, AK	129.4
Kodiak, AK	74.4
Dulac-Chauvin, LA	60.9
Brownsville-Port Isabel, TX	59.8
Empire-Venice, LA	59.1
Hampton Roads Area, VA	56.8
Key West, FL	40.0
Honolulu, HI	40.0
Bayou La Batre, AL	38.9

Source: "Leading Ports." available May 7, 2003 from http://www.st.nmfs.gov, from National Marine Fisheries Service.

★ 87 ★

Hunting (SIC 0971)

What We Spend on Hunting

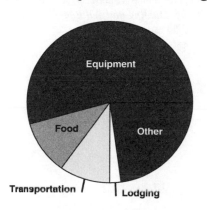

Americans spent $20 billion on hunting in 2001. According to a survey by the Fish and Wildlife Service, 13 million Americans over the age of 16 hunted an average of 17.5 days last year.

Equipment	50.0%
Food	10.0
Transportation	9.0
Lodging	2.0
Other	21.0

Source: *Shooting Industry*, July 2002, p. 8, from U.S. Fish and Wildlife Service.

★ 88 ★
Hunting (SIC 0971)

Who Hunts, 2001

Figures show percentage of each age group that went hunting.

35-44	. . . . 8.0%
25-34	. . . . 7.0
45-54	. . . . 7.0
18-24	. . . . 6.0
55-64	. . . . 6.0
65+	. . . . 3.0

Source: *USA TODAY*, November 1, 2002, p. A1, from *National Survey of Fishing, Hunting and Wildlife-Associated Recreation.*

SIC 10 - Metal Mining

★ 89 ★

Mining (SIC 1000)

Top Mining Firms in Canada

Firms are ranked by revenue in thousands of Canadian dollars.

Noranda Inc.	$ 6,152.0
Suncor Energy Inc.	3,995.0
Agrium Inc.	3,355.2
Syncrude Canada	3,211.0
Potash Corp. of Saskatchewan	3,209.3
Inco Ltd.	3,198.9
Barrick Gold Corp.	3,079.7
Dofasco Inc.	2,962.5
Newmont Mining Corp.	2,576.6
Stelco Inc.	2,561.0

Source: *Canadian Mining Journal*, August 2002, p. 9.

★ 90 ★

Gold (SIC 1041)

Largest Gold Producers in Canada

Companies are ranked by gold equivalent production in thousands of kilograms. Data are for the first nine months of the year.

Barrick Gold	127.5
Placer Dome	59.3
Kinross Gold	20.4
Goldcorp	14.2
Cambior	13.6
Echo Bay Mines	13.0
Iamgold	6.6
Northgate Exploration	6.4
Tech Cominco	6.2
Inmet Mining	6.1

Source: *Canadian Mining Journal*, December 2002, p. 12.

★ 91 ★

Gold (SIC 1041)

Largest Gold Producers in North America, 2001

Companies are ranked by production in thousands of ounces.

	(000)	Share
Ango Gold	6,983	28.21%
Barrick Gold Corporation	6,124	24.74
Newmont Mining	5,430	21.93
Placer Dome Inc.	2,756	11.13
Kinross Gold Corporation	950	3.84
Echo Bay Mines	658	2.66
Cambior	615	2.48
Meridian Gold Inc.	435	1.76
Glamis Gold Inc.	230	0.93
Franco-Nevada	185	0.75
Other	391	1.58

Source: "Mining Statistics." available January 7, 2003 from http://www.nma.org, from National Mining Association.

★ 92 ★

Silver (SIC 1044)

Largest Silver Producers in North America, 2001

Companies are ranked by production in millions of ounces.

Industrias Penoles	51.7
Grupo Mexico	22.1
Homestake Mining	15.5
Coeur d'Alene Mines Corp.	10.9
Noranda Inc.	9.3
Hecla Mining Company	7.4
Pan American Silver	6.9
Placer Dome Inc.	6.8
Echo Bay Mines Ltd.	6.5

Source: "Mining Statistics." available January 7, 2003 from http://www.nma.org, from National Mining Association and Silver Institute.

★ 93 ★

Silver (SIC 1044)

Silver Market by State, 2001

Total production was estimated at 1.7 million metric tons. Total estimated value was placed at $245 million.

	Kilograms	Share
Nevada	544,000	31.36%
California	7,590	0.44
Colorado	2,830	0.16
Other	1,180,000	68.03

Source: "Mineral Statistics." available April 7, 2003 from http://www.usgs.gov, from U.S. Geological Survey.

★ 94 ★

Cobalt (SIC 1061)

Cobalt End Markets, 2002

Total production fell almostly steadily from 3,080 metric tons in 1998 to 2,700 in 2002. Total consumption was thought to be $150 million.

Superalloys, various chemical uses	22.0%
Cemented carbides for cutting and wear-resistant applications	19.0
Aircraft gas turbine engines	8.0
Other	51.0

Source: "Mineral Statistics." available April 7, 2003 from http://www.usgs.gov, from U.S. Geological Survey.

★ 95 ★

Vanadium (SIC 1094)

Vanadium End Markets, 2002

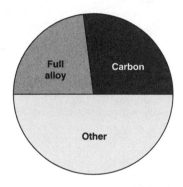

Metallurgical use, such as an alloying agent for iron and steel, accounts for 90% of domestic use.

Carbon	27.0%
Full alloy	23.0
Other	50.0

Source: "Mineral Statistics." available April 7, 2003 from http://www.usgs.gov, from U.S. Department of the Interior and U.S. Geological Survey.

SIC 12 - Coal Mining

★ 96 ★

Coal (SIC 1220)

Largest Coal Producers, 2001

*Shares are shown based on total production of 1.1
billion short tons.*

Peabody Energy Corporation	17.3%
Arch Coal Inc.	10.6
Kennecott Energy Company	10.5
CONSOL Energy Inc.	6.6
RAG American Coal Holding	5.8
AEI Resources Inc.	4.1
Massey Energy Company	4.0
Triton Coal Company	3.8
The North American Coal Corporation . . .	2.8
Westmoreland Coal Company	2.5
Other	32.0

Source: "Mining Statistics." available January 7, 2003
from http://www.nma.org, from National Mining Association.

SIC 13 - Oil and Gas Extraction

★ 97 ★

Oil & Gas (SIC 1311)

Largest Gas Producers, 2001

ExxonMobil Corp.
Chevron Texaco Corp.
Anadarko Petroleum Corp.
El Paso Corp.
Burlington Resources Inc.
Phillips Petroleum Co.
Devon Energy Corp.
Unocal Corp.
Conoco Inc.
Marathon Oil Corp.

Companies are ranked by production in billions of cubic feet.

ExxonMobil Corp.	1,114
Chevron Texaco Corp.	988
Anadarko Petroleum Corp.	573
El Paso Corp.	552
Burlington Resources Inc.	409
Phillips Petroleum Co.	402
Devon Energy Corp.	376
Unocal Corp.	371
Conoco Inc.	291
Marathon Oil Corp.	289

Source: *Oil & Gas Journal*, September 9, 2002, p. 70, from *Oil & Gas Journal 200*.

★ 98 ★

Oil & Gas (SIC 1311)

Largest Oil & Gas Firms in Canada

Companies are ranked by production in barrels of oil equivalent per day.

EnCana Corp.	586,516
Imperial Oil Ltd.	362,333
Canadian Natural Resources	318,000
Husky Energy Inc.	272,642
Devon Energy	253,485
ExxonMobil Canada	222,667
Burlington Resources Canada	222,532
Talisman Energy	200,800
Petro-Canada	196,500
BP Canada Energy Co.	162,407

Source: *Oilweek*, July 8, 2002, p. 19.

★ 99 ★

Oil & Gas (SIC 1311)

Largest Oil Refiners

Companies are ranked by share of total refining capacity. The refining industry has taken hits over the year: jet fuel consumption is down, the possibility of a war in Iraq and the price of crude oil has dropped.

ConocoPhillips	12.0%
Exxon Mobil	10.6
Valero	9.6
BP	8.4
ChevronTexaco	5.4
Other	54.0

Source: *Wall Street Journal*, October 24, 2002, p. B6, from A.G. Edwards.

★ 100 ★

Gas Liquids (SIC 1321)

Largest Gas Liquid Firms in Canada

Companies are ranked by production in barrels per day.

Imperial Oil Ltd.	267,000
EnCana Corp.	195,183
Husky Energy Inc.	177,400
Canadian Natural Resources Ltd.	167,000
Suncor Energy Inc.	127,100
ExxonMobil Canada	103,000
Devon Energy Corp.	83,535

Continued on next page.

★ 100 ★ *Continued*

Gas Liquids (SIC 1321)

Largest Gas Liquid Firms in Canada

Companies are ranked by production in barrels per day.

Petro-Canada	77,400
Anadarko Canada Corp.	77,000
Nexen Inc.	74,100

Source: *Oilweek*, July 8, 2002, p. 19.

★ 101 ★

Gas Liquids (SIC 1321)

Largest Gas Liquid Producers, 2001

Companies are ranked by production in millions of barrels.

ChevronTexaco Corp.	224.0
ExxonMobil Corp.	210.0
Phillips Petroleum Co.	154.0
Anadarko Petroleum Corp.	48.0
Marathon Oil Corp.	46.0
Devon Energy Corp.	32.0
Unocal Corp.	29.0
Burlington Resources Inc.	28.7
Amerada Hess Corp.	28.0
Kerr-McGee Corp.	28.0

Source: *Oil & Gas Journal*, September 9, 2002, p. 70, from *Oil & Gas Journal 200*.

★ 102 ★

Gas Liquids (SIC 1321)

Largest Natural Gas Liquid Producers, 2001

Figures are in millions of barrels per day. The top 10 firms had 72% of the market, up from 52% in 1992.

DEFS	396
BP	199
El Paso	158
Williams	121
ExxonMobil	120
Enterprise	75
ONEOK	74
ConocoPhillips	66
Devon Energy Corp.	62
Dynergy	59

Source: *Gas Processors Report*, April 7, 2003, p. NA.

★ 103 ★

Oil Wells (SIC 1381)

Land Rig Market

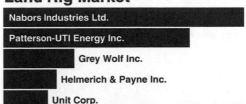

The market is now controlled by a handful of major players after once being a fragmented mom and pop industry. The top 5 firms control nearly 1,500 land rigs in existence.

Nabors Industries Ltd.	27.0%
Patterson-UTI Energy Inc.	21.0
Grey Wolf Inc.	8.0
Helmerich & Payne Inc.	6.0
Unit Corp.	5.0
Other	33.0

Source: *Oil & Gas Journal*, September 23, 2002, p. 60.

★ 104 ★

Oil Wells (SIC 1381)

Leading Drill Operators, 2002

Companies are ranked by total number of wells as of August 15, 2002. Worldwide, rig activity dropped 22% over the previous year to 1,822 active rigs.

	Wells	Share
Dominion Exploration & Production	439	8.8%
BP PLC	340	6.8
EOG Resources Inc.	236	4.7
Occidental Petroleum Corp.	229	4.6
El Paso Corp.	223	4.5
Chevron Texaco Corp.	189	3.8
Devon Energy Corp.	181	3.6
Equitable Production	165	3.3
Phillips Petroleum Co.	154	3.1

Source: *Oil & Gas Journal*, September 23, 2002, p. 43, from Baker Hughes.

★ 105 ★

Oil Wells (SIC 1381)

Oil Well Drilling, 2002

A total of 29,233 wells are estimated to be drilled for the year. States are ranked by the number of wells drilled.

	No.	Share
Texas	8,316	30.32%
Wyoming	4,193	15.29
California	2,030	7.40
Oklahoma	1,934	7.05
Pennsylvania	1,802	6.57
Louisiana	1,186	4.32
Colorado	1,175	4.28
New Mexico	1,170	4.27
Kansas	915	3.34
Gulf of Mexico	911	3.32
Other	3,799	13.85

Source: *World Oil*, August 2002, p. 39.

★ 106 ★

Oil Wells (SIC 1381)

Stripper Well Production

Stripper wells are marginal wells that pump no more than 15 barrels per day. Such wells represent 20% of all oil production. Production is shown in millions of barrels.

Texas	129.0
Oklahoma	47.1
California	35.1
Kansas	25.2
Louisiana	16.1
New Mexico	13.2
Illinois	10.2
Wyoming	8.6
Ohio	4.9

Source: *New York Times*, December 27, 2002, p. C3, from Interstate Oil and Gas Compact Commission.

SIC 14 - Nonmetallic Minerals, Except Fuels

★ 107 ★

Stone (SIC 1420)

Crushed Stone Production, 2001

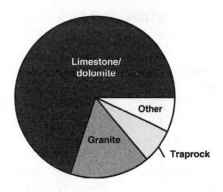

Crushed stone valued at $9 billion was produced by 1,400 companies operating 3,700 active quarries in 49 states. Texas was the top producing state.

Limestone/dolomite	70.0%
Granite	16.0
Traprock	7.0
Other	7.0

Source: "Mineral Statistics." available April 7, 2003 from http://www.usgs.gov, from U.S. Geological Survey.

★ 108 ★

Stone (SIC 1420)

Largest Aggregate Producers, 2002

Firms are ranked by net earnings for the first six months of the year. The third largest firm was Hanson PLC and Lafarge North America; data for these companies was not available.

Vulcan Materials	$ 1,215.9
Martin Marietta	714.7

Source: *Pit & Quarry*, September 2003, p. 20.

★ 109 ★

Granite (SIC 1422)

Granite Market, 2001

The major uses are shown in percent.

Curbing	31.0%
Monumental rough stone	25.0
Monumental dressed stone	13.0
Rough blocks for construction	12.0
Ashlars and partial squared pieces	1.0
Other	18.0

Source: "Mineral Statistics." available April 7, 2003 from http://www.usgs.gov, from U.S. Geological Survey.

★ 110 ★

Limestone (SIC 1422)

Limestone Market, 2001

The major uses are shown in percent.

Rough blocks for building/construction	42.0%
Ashlars and partially squared pieces	14.0
Other	44.0

Source: "Mineral Statistics." available April 7, 2003 from http://www.usgs.gov, from U.S. Geological Survey.

★ 111 ★

Slate (SIC 1429)

Dimension Slate Market, 2001

The major end uses are shown based on tonnage.

Flooring	40.0%
Roofing	34.0
Flagging	10.0
Other	16.0

Source: "Mineral Statistics." available April 7, 2003 from http://www.usgs.gov, from U.S. Geological Survey.

★ 112 ★

Clays (SIC 1450)

Clay Production by Type

Figures are in metric tons.

	1999	2001	Share
Common clay	24,800	23,700	58.50%
Kaolin	9,160	9,030	22.29
Bentonite	4,070	3,820	9.43
Fuller's earth	2,560	2,400	5.92
Ball clay	1,200	1,170	2.89
Fire clay	402	391	0.97

Source: *Ceramic Bulletin*, August 2002, p. 36, from U.S. Geological Survey.

★ 113 ★

Potash (SIC 1474)

Potash Market, 2002

Total production was estimated at 4.2 million metric tons. Figures refer to agricultural potash only.

	m.t.	Share
Illinois	586,000	13.72%
Iowa	418,000	9.79
Indiana	352,000	8.24
Ohio	335,000	7.85
Missouri	289,000	6.77
Minnesota	272,000	6.37
Florida	135,000	3.16
Tennessee	135,000	3.16
Kentucky	121,000	2.83
Other	1,627,000	38.10

Source: "Mineral Statistics." available April 7, 2003 from http://www.usgs.gov, from U.S. Geological Survey.

★ 114 ★

Soda Ash (SIC 1474)

Soda Ash Market, 2002

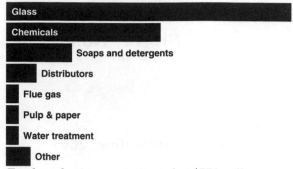

Total production was estimated at $770 million.

Glass	48.0%
Chemicals	26.0
Soaps and detergents	11.0
Distributors	5.0
Flue gas	2.0
Pulp & paper	2.0
Water treatment	2.0
Other	4.0

Source: "Mineral Statistics." available April 7, 2003 from http://www.usgs.gov, from U.S. Geological Survey.

SIC 15 - General Building Contractors

★ 115 ★
Residential Construction (SIC 1521)
Largest Housing Markets

States are ranked by number of housing permits. The top 3 states had 30% of the market.

Florida	177,152
Texas	155,651
California	142,882
Georgia	94,597
North Carolina	78,194
Arizona	61,302
Illinois	55,938
Virginia	54,450
Colorado	50,986
Michigan	50,052

Source: *Mortgage Banking*, January 2003, p. 37, from U.S. Housing Markets.

★ 116 ★
Residential Construction (SIC 1521)
Top Builders, 2001

Firms are ranked by number of closings.

Centex Corp.	26,060
Lennar Corp.	23,899
Pulte Homes	22,915
D.R. Horton	22,772
K.B. Home	21,486
The Ryland Group	12,686
NVR	10,372
Beazer Homes	9,582
M.D.C. Holdings	8,174
K. Hovnanian Enterprises	6,700

Source: *Builder*, May 2002, p. 132.

★ 117 ★
Residential Construction (SIC 1521)
Top Builders in Atlanta, GA

Market shares are shown based on sales.

Pulte Homes	3.5%
Colony Homes	2.8
D.R. Horton/Torrey Dobson Homes	2.8
Bowen Builders Group	1.9
Ryland Homes	1.7
Other	87.3

Source: *Builder*, May 2002, p. 196, from Meyers Group.

★ 118 ★
Residential Construction (SIC 1521)
Top Builders in Charlotte/Gastonia N.C./ Rock Hill S.C.

Market shares are shown based on sales.

NVR/Ryan Homes	7.0%
Ryland Homes	5.0
Mulvaney Homes	4.1
Pulte Homes	3.4
Squire/Beazer Homes	3.1
Other	77.4

Source: *Builder*, May 2002, p. 196, from Meyers Group.

★ 119 ★
Residential Construction (SIC 1521)

Top Builders in Chicago, IL

- Concord Homes
- D.R. Horton/Cambridge Homes
- Neumann Homes
- Ryland Homes
- Pulte Homes
- Other

Market shares are shown based on sales.

Concord Homes	4.4%
D.R. Horton/Cambridge Homes	4.3
Neumann Homes	4.0
Ryland Homes	3.6
Pulte Homes	3.0
Other	80.7

Source: *Builder*, May 2002, p. 196, from Meyers Group.

★ 120 ★
Residential Construction (SIC 1521)

Top Builders in Cincinnati, OH

Market shares are shown based on sales.

Drees Homes	13.8%
Fischer Homes	11.7
NVR/Ryan Homes	10.9
Crossmann Communities	6.1
Erpenbeck Co.	5.2
Other	52.3

Source: *Builder*, May 2002, p. 196, from Meyers Group.

★ 121 ★
Residential Construction (SIC 1521)

Top Builders in Columbus, OH

Market shares are shown based on sales.

M/I Homes	18.7%
Dominion Homes	17.8
Rockford Homes	4.1
Crossman Communities	4.0
Centex Homes	3.3
Other	52.1

Source: *Builder*, May 2002, p. 196, from Meyers Group.

★ 122 ★
Residential Construction (SIC 1521)

Top Builders in Dallas, TX

Market shares are shown based on sales.

Centrex Homes/Fox & Jacobs/CityHomes	7.8%
Lennar Corp./U.S. Home Corp.	6.0
D.R. Horton/Continental	5.9
Choice Homes	5.9
Highland Homes	5.3
Other	69.1

Source: *Builder*, May 2002, p. 196, from Meyers Group.

★ 123 ★
Residential Construction (SIC 1521)

Top Builders in Detroit, MI

Market shares are shown based on sales.

Pulte Homes	8.4%
Crosswinds Communities	3.3
Toll Brothers	2.8
S.R. Jacobson Development Corp.	2.6
MJC Cos.	2.4
Other	80.5

Source: *Builder*, May 2002, p. 196, from Meyers Group.

★ 124 ★
Residential Construction (SIC 1521)

Top Builders in Indianapolis, MD

Market shares are shown based on sales.

Crossmann Communities/Trinity Homes	18.1%
C.P. Morgan	11.4
Davis Homes	8.2
Arbor Homes	5.3
Ryland Homes	4.9
Other	52.1

Source: *Builder*, May 2002, p. 196, from Meyers Group.

★ 125 ★
Residential Construction (SIC 1521)

Top Builders in Las Vegas, NV

Market shares are shown based on sales.

KB Home	13.1%
Pulte Homes	9.7
American West Homes	4.3
Weyerhaeuser Real Estate Co./Pardee Homes	3.8
D.R. Horton	3.5
Other	65.6

Source: *Builder*, May 2002, p. 196, from Meyers Group.

★ 126 ★
Residential Construction (SIC 1521)

Top Builders in Minneapolis/St. Paul, MN

Market shares are shown based on sales.

Lennar Corp./Lundgren Bros./Orrin Thompson Homes	4.4%
Pulte Homes	4.1
Rottlund Homes	3.9
Frana & Sons	3.1
Centex Homes	3.0
Other	81.5

Source: *Builder*, May 2002, p. 196, from Meyers Group.

★ 127 ★
Residential Construction (SIC 1521)

Top Builders in Nashville, TN

- Beazer Homes USA/Phillips Builders
- NVR/Ryan Homes/Fox Ridge Homes
- Ole South Properties
- Pulte Homes
- Butler Builders
- Other

Market shares are shown based on sales.

Beazer Homes USA/Phillips Builders	7.0%
NVR/Ryan Homes/Fox Ridge Homes	4.6
Ole South Properties	4.5
Pulte Homes	3.3
Butler Builders	1.6
Other	79.0

Source: *Builder*, May 2002, p. 196, from Market Graphics.

★ 128 ★
Residential Construction (SIC 1521)

Top Builders in Orange County, CA

Market shares are shown based on sales.

Standard Pacific Homes	9.3%
William Lyon Homes	7.6
Centex Homes	7.6
Brookfield Homes	7.3
KB Home	6.8
Other	61.4

Source: *Builder*, May 2002, p. 196, from Meyers Group.

★ 129 ★
Residential Construction (SIC 1521)

Top Builders in Philadelphia, PA

Market shares are shown based on sales.

NVR/Ryan Homes	7.3%
Orleans Homebuilders	6.1
K. Hovnanian Enterprise	5.6
Toll Brothers	4.8
Pulte Homes	4.1
Other	72.1

Source: *Builder*, May 2002, p. 196, from Meyers Group.

★ 130 ★
Residential Construction (SIC 1521)
Top Builders in Phoenix/Mesa, AZ

Pulte Homes/Del Webb Group

D.R. Horton/Continental/Dietz-Crane

Shea Homes/Shea Homes for Active Adults

KB Home

M.D.C. Holdings/Richmond American Homes

Other

Market shares are shown based on sales.

Pulte Homes/Del Webb Group	10.2%
D.R. Horton/Continental/Dietz-Crane	9.3
Shea Homes/Shea Homes for Active Adults	6.6
KB Home	6.2
M.D.C. Holdings/Richmond American Homes	4.8
Other	62.9

Source: *Builder*, May 2002, p. 196, from Meyers Group.

★ 131 ★
Residential Construction (SIC 1521)
Top Builders in Portland, OR/ Vancouver, WA

Market shares are shown based on sales.

Arbor Homes	4.6%
D.R. Horton/RMP Properties	3.3
Schuler Homes	2.3
Don Morissette Homes	2.0
Legend Homes Corp.	1.9
Other	85.9

Source: *Builder*, May 2002, p. 196, from Meyers Group.

★ 132 ★
Residential Construction (SIC 1521)
Top Builders in Pulaski/Saline Counties, AR

Market shares are shown in percent.

The Janet Jones Co.	9.2%
Real Estate Journal	7.7
McKay & Co. Realty	6.7
Rainey Realty	5.7
Rector Phillips Morse	5.7
Adkins, McNeil Smith & Associates	5.1
Other	59.9

Source: *Arkansas Business*, July 29, 2002, p. 1, from Real Estate Central.

★ 133 ★
Residential Construction (SIC 1521)
Top Builders in Salt Lake City/Ogden, Utah

Market shares are shown based on sales.

Ivory Homes	7.4%
Salisbury Homes	5.8
Woodside Homes	4.1
Hamlet Homes	3.5
Reliance Homes	3.1
Other	76.1

Source: *Builder*, May 2002, p. 196, from Meyers Group.

★ 134 ★
Residential Construction (SIC 1521)
Top Builders in San Antonio, TX

Market shares are shown based on sales.

KB Home	33.0%
D.R. Horton/Continental Homes	12.5
Pulte Homes	5.1
Centex Homes	4.8
Ryland Homes	4.6
Gordon Hartman Homes	4.6
Other	35.4

Source: *Builder*, May 2002, p. 196, from Meyers Group.

★ 135 ★

Residential Construction (SIC 1521)

Top Builders in Seattle/Bellevue/ Everett, WA

Market shares are shown based on sales.

Weyerhaeuser Real Estate Co./Quadrant Homes	7.1%
Polygon Northwest Co.	6.4
Murray Franklyn	3.6
Soundbuilt Homes	3.5
Schuler Homes/Stafford Homes	3.5
Other	75.9

Source: *Builder*, May 2002, p. 196, from Meyers Group.

★ 136 ★

Residential Construction (SIC 1521)

Top Builders in Tampa Bay, FL

Lennar Corp./U.S. Home
Pulte Homes
Ryland Homes
Westfield Homes
M/I Homes
Other

Market shares are shown based on sales.

Lennar Corp./U.S. Home	8.5%
Pulte Homes	5.6
Ryland Homes	5.5
Westfield Homes	4.0
M/I Homes	3.6
Other	72.8

Source: *Builder*, May 2002, p. 196, from Meyers Group.

★ 137 ★

Residential Construction (SIC 1521)

Top Builders in the Twin Cities

Firms are ranked by number of permits.

Centex Homes	421
Rottlund	336
D.R. Horton	324
Orrin Thompson Homes	320
Pulte Homes of Minnesota	259

Source: *Finance and Commerce Daily Newspaper*, March 11, 2003, p. NA, from Builders Association of the Twin Cities.

SIC 16 - Heavy Construction, Except Building

★ 138 ★

Contracting Work (SIC 1600)

Largest Contractors, 2001

Firms are ranked by revenues in billions of dollars.

Bechtel	$ 11.29
Fluor Corp.	7.19
Skanska Inc.	6.67
Centex	6.28
The Turner Corp.	6.26
Halliburton	5.85
Peter Kiewit Sons Inc.	3.85
Washington Group International	3.58
J.A. Jones Inc.	2.86
Bovis Lend Lease	2.80

Source: *ENR*, May 20, 2002, p. 63.

★ 139 ★

Contracting Work (SIC 1600)

Largest Contractors in Detroit, MI

Firms are ranked by revenues in millions of dollars.

Barton Malow Co.	$ 1,350.0
Walbridge Aldinger Co.	925.0
Washington Group International	639.0
Skanska USA Building	384.4
Turner Construction Co.	276.0
JM Olson Corp.	227.3
Black & Veatch	208.5
George W. Auch Co.	151.2

Source: *Crain's Detroit Business*, March 10, 2003, p. 24.

★ 140 ★

Contracting Work - Highways (SIC 1611)

Leading Federal Highway Contractors

The top contractors are ranked by value of contracts awarded during the year. Awards are in millions of dollars.

Peter Kiewit Sons Inc.	$ 527.5
Modern Continental Construction	447.5
Zachry, H.B. Constr. Co.	330.7
Apac Inc.	279.2
Yonkers Contract. Co. Inc.	195.5
Granite Const. Co.	153.9
Williams Bros. Const.	137.7
The Walsh Group Inc.	121.1
Myers, Allan A. Inc.	120.9

Source: *Transportation Builder*, November-December 2002, p. 10, from American Road & Transportation Builders Association.

★ 141 ★

Contracting Work - Utility Work (SIC 1623)

Leading Utility Contractors, 2001

Firms are ranked by revenues in millions of dollars.

MasTec Inc.	$ 1,222.0
Henkels & McCoy Inc.	610.5
InfraSource	459.5
Garney Construction Co.	98.3
UTILX Corp.	96.2
Kearney Development Co. Inc.	64.3
RCI Construction Group	64.0
Grimm Construction Co.	39.3
Ryan Inc. Eastern	39.0
W.A. Chester LLC	35.4

Source: *ENR*, October 7, 2002, p. 48.

★ 142 ★
Horizontal Directional Drilling (SIC 1623)

HDD End Markets

| Telecommunications |
| Oil/gas pipelines |
| Water |
| Gas distribution |
| Electric |
| Sewer |
| Other |

The leading markets for Horizontal Directional Drilling are shown. Contractors in the HDD industry have complained about intense competition for a small number of jobs. According to a survey, contractors expect to purchase 800 rigs in the coming year.

Telecommunications	22.3%
Oil/gas pipelines	17.4
Water	16.0
Gas distribution	15.5
Electric	12.4
Sewer	10.7
Other	5.7

Source: *Underground Construction*, June 2002, p. 30.

SIC 17 - Special Trade Contractors

★ 143 ★
Contracting Work (SIC 1700)

Largest Specialty Firms

Firms are ranked by revenues in millions of dollars.

EMCOR Group	$ 2,718.78
Limbach Facility Services	672.00
Air Conditioning Co.	365.00
Fisk Electric Co.	360.00
Encompass Mechanical Services	258.00
Centimark	226.00
TDIndustries	191.00
Southland Industries	177.00
ISEC Inc.	176.00
Murphy Co.	151.61

Source: *Building Design & Construction*, July 2002, p. 57, from *Building Design & Construction 2002 Giants Survey*.

★ 144 ★
Contracting Work - Painting (SIC 1721)

Leading Painting Contractors, 2001

Firms are ranked by revenues in millions of dollars.

Performance Contracting Group Inc.	$ 356.9
KHS&S Contractors	194.8
National Construction Enterprises Inc.	169.9
Cleveland Construction Inc.	164.3
Ecker Enterprises Inc.	148.7
Acousti Engineering Co. of Florida	141.0
Eliason & Knuth Cos. Inc.	116.3
Midwest Drywall Inc.	100.1
Precision Walls Inc.	85.5
Standard Drywall Inc.	77.1

Source: *ENR*, October 7, 2002, p. 48.

★ 145 ★
Contracting Work - Electrical (SIC 1731)

Leading Electrical Contractors, 2001

Firms are ranked by revenues in millions of dollars.

EMCOR Group	$ 1,709.9
Integrated Electrical Services	1,641.0
Encompass Service Corp.	1,568.3
Quanta Services Inc.	806.0
MYR Group Inc.	627.4
Cupertino Electric Inc.	509.3
Mass. Electric Construction Co.	377.0
Rosendin Electric Inc.	365.0
Fisk Corp.	287.6
Xcelecom Inc.	265.3

Source: *ENR*, October 7, 2002, p. 48.

★ 146 ★
Contracting Work - Masonry (SIC 1741)

Leading Masonry Contractors, 2001

Firms are ranked by revenues in millions of dollars.

The Western Group	$ 48.1
Dee Brown Inc.	46.2
Seedorff Masonry Inc.	40.7
Sun Valley Masonry Inc.	40.6
Pyramid Masonry Contractors Inc.	38.7
Caretti Inc.	36.3
J.D. Long Masonry Inc.	36.1
John J. Smith Masonry Co.	33.7
B.W. Dexter II Inc.	33.5
Masonry Arts Inc.	31.4

Source: *ENR*, October 7, 2002, p. 48.

★ 147 ★
Contracting Work - Windows & Doors (SIC 1751)
Leading Window & Door Firms

Selected firms are shown by estimated sales in millions of dollars.

Jeld-Wen Inc.	$ 2,000
Andersen Corp.	1,800
Masonite International Corp.	1,400
Pella	914
Atrium Companies	500

Source: *Windows & Door*, February 2003, p. 2.

★ 148 ★
Contracting Work - Windows & Doors (SIC 1751)
Residential Window and Door Market

Figures are in millions of units.

	2001	2004	Share
Vinyl	25.5	26.4	46.98%
Wood	23.6	22.5	40.04
Aluminum	6.5	5.9	10.50
Other	0.7	1.4	2.49

Source: *Windows & Door*, June/July 2002, p. NA, from Drucker Research.

★ 149 ★
Contracting Work - Windows & Doors (SIC 1751)
Skylight Market in Canada, 2002

Large manufacturers include Velux-Canada, Columbia Mfg. Co., Sunburst Skylights and Andersen Windows.

British Columbia	50.0%
Atlantic provinces	25.0
Ontario	18.0
Other	7.0

Source: "Skylights." available April 7, 2003 from http://www.usatrade.gov, from United States Department of Commerce and Homecare Building Centers.

★ 150 ★
Contracting Work - Flooring (SIC 1752)
Top Builder Contractors, 2001

The builder market is a significant part of the installed residential flooring market. Total sales reached $9.5 billion: $5.1 billion for installed floorcoverings, $2.4 billion for multi-family housing and $1.95 for manufactured housing.

Floors	$ 205
Peninsula Floors Inc.	162
Coleman Floor Co.	110
Arvada Hardwood Floor Co.	81
Adams Bros.	73
Creative Touch Interactive	73
Floors Inc. (Texas)	72
Leonard's Carpet Service	67
Wisenbaker Builder Services	66
SuperFloors	64

Source: *Floor Focus*, April 2002, p. NA.

★ 151 ★
Contracting Work - Roofing (SIC 1761)

Leading Roofing Contractors, 2001

Firms are ranked by revenues in millions of dollars.

generalRoofing	$ 268.9
Centimark Corp.	241.0
Tecta America Corp.	136.2
The Hartford Roofing Co.	73.0
Birdair Inc.	66.0
Baker Roofing Co.	48.0
Latite Roofing & Sheet Metal Co. Inc.	46.7
The Holland Roofing Group	40.0
W.R. Kelso Co.	38.0
Best Roofing & Waterproofing Inc.	36.0

Source: *ENR*, October 7, 2002, p. 48.

★ 152 ★
Contracting Work - Roofing (SIC 1761)

Roofing Demand

Demand is expected to grow 1.7% annually through 2007 to 256 million squares. This represents an $11 billion market.

	2002	2007	Share
Asphalt shingles	145.5	155.5	67.90%
Metal roofing	18.0	21.5	9.39
Elastomeric roofing	17.0	19.0	8.30
Built-up roofing	15.5	16.5	7.21
Modified bitumen roofing	15.0	16.5	7.21

Source: *Research Studies - Freedonia Group*, February 28, 2003, p. 3, from Freedonia Group.

★ 153 ★
Contracting Work - Sheet Metal (SIC 1761)

Leading Sheet Metal Contractors, 2001

Firms are ranked by revenues in millions of dollars.

Kirk & Blum - Div. Of Ceco Environmental	$ 76.5
EMCOR Group Inc.	68.4
Crown Corr Inc.	60.5
Hill Mechanical Group	53.7
McKinstry Co.	48.8
Independent Sheet Metal Co. Inc.	48.3
Cal-Air Inc.	44.6
Kinetics	43.0

Holaday-Parks Inc.	$ 40.8
Bonland Industries Inc.	38.2

Source: *ENR*, October 7, 2002, p. 48.

★ 154 ★
Contracting Work - Concrete (SIC 1771)

Largest Concrete Contractors, 2001

Firms are ranked by concrete revenues in millions of dollars.

Baker Concrete Construction	$ 384.0
Clayco Construction	328.0
Walsh Group	282.6
Miller & Long	281.6
CECO Concrete Construction	179.5
S&F Concrete Construction	162.0
Structural Group	142.0
Interstate Highway Construction	125.9
McCarthy Building Construction	114.0

Source: *Concrete Construction*, July 2002, p. 32.

★ 155 ★
Contracting Work - Steel (SIC 1791)

Leading Steel Contractors, 2001

Firms are ranked by revenues in millions of dollars.

The Williams Group	$ 82.4
Schuff Steel Co.	81.5
Midwest Steel Inc.	78.5
Derr Construction Co.	60.5
Area Erectors Inc.	58.4
Interstate Iron Works Corp.	48.5
Sowles Co.	47.6
Pittsburgh Tank and Tower Co. Inc.	42.2
Pacific Coast Steel Inc.	41.1
Ben Hur Construction Co.	37.5

Source: *ENR*, October 7, 2002, p. 48.

★ 156 ★
Contracting Work - Glazing/Curtain Wall (SIC 1793)

Leading Glazing/Curtain Wall Contractors, 2001

Firms are ranked by revenues in millions of dollars.

Walters & Wolf	$ 185.3
Harmon Inc.	146.6

Continued on next page.

★ 156 ★ *Continued*
Contracting Work - Glazing/Curtain Wall (SIC 1793)

Leading Glazing/Curtain Wall Contractors, 2001

Firms are ranked by revenues in millions of dollars.

Enclos Corp.	$ 134.5
Architectural Glass & Aluminum Co. Inc.	65.1
Trainor Glass Co.	59.6
W&W Glass Systems Inc.	51.4
APG-America Inc.	35.3
Masonry Arts inc.	32.6
Karas & Karas Glass Co. Inc.	30.6
Architectural Wall Solutions Inc.	25.8

Source: *ENR*, October 7, 2002, p. 48.

★ 157 ★
Contracting Work - Excavation/Foundation (SIC 1794)

Leading Excavation/Foundation Contractors, 2001

Firms are ranked by revenues in millions of dollars.

Hayward Baker Inc.	$ 147.0
Manafort Brothers	137.9
Ryan Inc. Central	95.6
Malcolm Drilling Co. Inc.	90.6
Ryan Inc. Eastern	88.5
Berkel & Co. Contractors Inc.	87.0
Independence Excavating Inc.	73.3
Case Foundation Co.	72.7
McKinney Drilling Co.	72.0
Nicholson Construction Co.	64.2

Source: *ENR*, October 7, 2002, p. 48.

★ 158 ★
Contracting Work - Demolition (SIC 1795)

Leading Demolition Contractors, 2001

Firms are ranked by revenues in millions of dollars.

Penhall Co.	$ 126.6
Brandenburg Industrial Service Co.	66.2
Cleveland Wrecking Co.	47.4
MRP Site Development Inc.	41.8
Mazzochi Wrecking	37.7
Bierlein Demolition Contractors	36.6
North America Site Developers Inc.	35.0
Manafort Brothers Inc.	31.3

Mercer Wrecking Recycling Corp.	$ 26.1
Nuprecon Inc.	23.8

Source: *ENR*, October 7, 2002, p. 48.

★ 159 ★
Spa Industry (SIC 1799)

Leading Spa Pool Installers

Firms are ranked by revenues in thousands of dollars.

Spa & Leisure Inc.	$ 6,287.4
Olympic Hot Tub Co.	6,137.0
Spa Brokers Inc.	4,900.0
Pool & Spa Depot	3,600.0
Great Atlantic	2,416.8
Pools Plus Inc.	2,280.0
Tony V's Sunrooms & Spas	1,950.0
Aqua Quip	1,890.7

Source: *Pool & Spa News*, September 6, 2002, p. 55, from *Pool & Spa News 100*.

★ 160 ★
Swimming Pools (SIC 1799)

Leading Aboveground Pool Installers

Firms are ranked by revenues in thousands of dollars.

B&G Inc.	$ 4,600.0
Leslie's Poolmart	3,017.0
Pool & Spa Depot	2,700.0
Baja Spas	1,260.0
Pool & Patio Center Inc.	1,170.0
Pools Plus Inc.	760.0
Central Iowa Pool & Spa	448.3
Ultra Modern Pool & Patio Inc.	394.4

Source: *Pool & Spa News*, September 6, 2002, p. 55, from *Pool & Spa News 100*.

SIC 20 - Food and Kindred Products

★ 161 ★
Food (SIC 2000)
Best-Selling Private Label Items

Sales are in millions of dollars for the year ended June 16, 2002. Figures exclude Wal-Mart.

Carbonated beverages	$ 15,014.1
Milk	10,987.8
Beer/ale/alcoholic cider	8,277.6
Fresh bread & rolls	8,031.2
Cigarettes	7,675.7
Salty snacks	7,315.5
Cold cereal	6,855.4
Frozen dinners/entrees	5,916.0
Natural cheese	5,026.5
Ice cream/cheese	4,896.0

Source: *Private Label Buyer*, August 2002, p. 4, from Information Resources Inc.

★ 162 ★
Food (SIC 2000)
Healthy Food Industry in Canada

Healthy food sales are shown in millions of dollars. Dollar shares show the percentage of the entire industry this segment represents.

	($ mil.)	Share
Flavored soft drinks	$ 335.6	22.6%
Yogurt	243.1	42.5
Cereal, ready-to-eat	231.4	29.3
Frozen dinners & entrees	80.0	7.5
Cheese, prepackaged specialty	77.0	18.4
Cream cheese	56.2	40.0
Pourable salad dressings	49.0	27.1
Mayonnaise & salad dressing	47.3	30.5
Peanut butter	37.6	29.9
Rice & corn cakes	36.9	56.6

Source: *Globe and Mail*, September 28, 2002, p. 1, from A.C. Nielsen.

★ 163 ★
Food (SIC 2000)
Largest Food Companies

The largest U.S. based food companies are ranked by food sales in millions of dollars.

Kraft Foods Inc.	$ 38.11
ConAgra Inc.	27.63
PepsiCo. Inc.	26.93
Archer Daniels	23.45
Cargill Inc.	21.50
Coca-Cola	20.09
Mars Inc.	15.30
Anheuser-Busch	12.26
Tyson Foods	10.75
Dean Foods	9.70

Source: *Prepared Foods*, December 2002, p. 83.

★ 164 ★
Food (SIC 2000)
Largest Food Companies in Canada

Firms are ranked by food and drink sales in billions of dollars.

McCain Foods Limited	$ 5.3
Maple Leaf Foods Inc.	4.7
George Weston Limited	3.8
Parmalat Canada Limited	2.5
Molson Inc.	2.4
Co-operative Federee de Quebec	2.4
Saputo	2.1
Agropur	1.9
Cott Corporation	1.6
Nestle Canada	1.6

Source: *Food in Canada*, September 2002, p. 24.

★ 165 ★
Food (SIC 2000)

Largest Refrigerated/Frozen Meal Producers, 2002

Companies are ranked by estimated sales in millions of dollars.

Nestle USA	$ 2,500
ConAgra Foods	2,000
Kraft Foods Inc.	1,700
Schwan's Sales Enterprises	1,100
Chef America	600
H.J. Heinz Co.	583
Pinnacle Foods Corp.	496
Kellogg Co.	464
Luigino's Inc.	450

Source: *Refrigerated & Frozen Foods*, February 2002, p. 22.

★ 166 ★
Food (SIC 2000)

Largest Snack/Appetizer/Side Dish Producers, 2002

Companies are ranked by estimated sales in millions of dollars.

McCain Anchor Appetizer Group	$ 550.0
Heinz Frozen Food Co.	534.0
Kraft Foods Inc.	375.0
SCIS Food Services	350.0
Reser's Fine Foods	315.0
ConAgra Foods Inc.	300.0
J&J Snack Foods Corp.	233.8
Rich-SeaPak Corp.	170.0
General Mills Inc.	157.4
Tyson Foods	130.0

Source: *Refrigerated & Frozen Foods*, February 2002, p. 22.

★ 167 ★
Food (SIC 2000)

Top Natural Food Categories, 2003

Sales are in millions of dollars for the year ended January 25, 2003. Figures are for food, drug and mass channels.

Vitamins and minerals	$ 1,507.9
Meal replacements and supplement powders	878.9
Packaged fresh produce	842.0
Energy bars and gels	602.0
Bottled water	593.4
Carbonated beverages and single-serve drinks	560.6
Non-dairy beverages	367.3
Diet formulas	358.4
Teas	350.3
Frozen/refrigerated meat alternatives	328.4

Source: *Supermarket News*, March 3, 2003, p. 22, from A.C. Nielsen SPINS and Spins Naturaltrack.

★ 168 ★
Meat (SIC 2011)

Largest Red Meat Producing States, 2002

Production is shown in millions of pounds. Meat includes beef, veal, pork, lamb and mutton.

	(mil.)	Share
Nebraska	630.3	16.13%
Iowa	541.6	13.86
Kansas	458.5	11.73
Texas	387.2	9.91
Illinois	233.2	5.97
Minnesota	201.0	5.14
North Carolina	178.0	4.56
Colorado	153.4	3.93
Indiana	117.5	3.01
Pennsylvania	109.2	2.79
Other	897.4	22.97

Source: *Livestock Slaughter*, National Agricultural Statistics Service, December 2002, p. 4, from U.S. Department of Agriculture.

★ 169 ★
Meat (SIC 2011)

Top Beef Producers, 2002

Figures show percent of total slaughter as of September 2002.

IBP/Tyson	27.3%
Excel/Cargill	20.8
Swift	16.1
Farmland National	7.8
Smithfield	6.6
Other	21.4

Source: "Top Beef Producers." available April 7, 2003 from http://www.ilfb.com/viedocument.asp?did3756, from Illinois Farm Bureau.

★ 170 ★
Meat (SIC 2011)

Top Meat Producing Provinces in Canada

Sales are shown in millions of dollars. Top players in the country are Better Beef, Burns Foods, Cargill, Hub Meat Packers, Intercontinental, J.M. Schneider, Lakeside Feeders, Maple Leaf Foods and Quality Meat Packers.

	($ mil.)	Share
Ontario	$ 2,100	33.82%
Alberta	2,000	32.21
Quebec	1,000	16.10
British Columbia	419	6.75
Saskatchewan	248	3.99
Manitoba	239	3.85
Atlantic Canada	204	3.29

Source: "Meat Products." available April 7, 2003 from http://www.usatrade.gov, from United States Department of Commerce.

★ 171 ★
Meat (SIC 2011)

Top Refrigerated Uncooked Meat Makers, 2002

Market shares are shown based on supermarket sales for the year ended February 24, 2002.

Jack Frost	19.7%
Moran	10.5
Hormell Foods	10.0
Perdue Farms	6.6
Private label	29.6
Other	23.6

Source: *Refrigerated & Frozen Foods*, June 2002, p. 82, from Information Resources Inc. InfoScan.

★ 172 ★
Meat (SIC 2011)

Top Uncooked Meat Brands, 2002

Market shares are shown based on supermarket sales for the year ended May 19, 2002.

	($ mil.)	Share
Gold'n Plump	$ 106.91	18.41%
Turkey Store	57.06	9.83
Moran	50.61	8.72
Perdue	22.55	3.88
Excel	12.32	2.12
J K Paty	12.30	2.12
Honeysuckle White	12.24	2.11
Perdue Cookin good	11.90	2.05
IBP	8.05	1.39
Private label	178.00	30.65
Other	108.76	18.73

Source: *National Provisioner*, August 2002, p. 62, from Information Resources Inc.

★ 173 ★

Bacon (SIC 2013)

Top Bacon Brands, 2002

Market shares are shown based on supermarket sales for the year ended May 19, 2002. Figures exclude Wal-Mart.

Oscar Mayer	17.4%
Hormel Black Label	7.0
Farmland	3.8
Bar S	3.8
Gwaltney	2.9
Smithfield	2.8
Wright	2.8
Hormel	2.5
Louis Rich	2.2
Private label	19.0
Other	35.8

Source: *National Provisioner*, August 2002, p. 52, from Information Resources Inc.

★ 174 ★

Bacon (SIC 2013)

Top Refrigerated Bacon Makers, 2002

Shares are shown based on dollar sales at grocery, drug and mass market outlets (but not Wal-Mart) for the year ended December 29, 2002.

Kraft/Oscar Mayer	17.6%
Hormel Foods	11.2
Armour Swift-Eckrich Inc.	4.5
Farmland Foods Inc.	4.3
Private label	18.0
Other	44.4

Source: *Grocery Headquarters*, April 2003, p. 43, from Information Resources Inc.

★ 175 ★

Hot Dogs (SIC 2013)

Hot Dog Consumption, 2001

Figures show purchases in retail stores in millions of pounds. Roughly 808 million pounds were sold.

	(mil.)	Share
Los Angeles	36.6	4.53%
New York City, NY	33.3	4.12
Chicago, IL	20.5	2.54
San Antonio/Corpus Christie, TX . .	20.2	2.50
Philadelphia, PA	17.1	2.12
Dallas/Ft. Worth, TX	16.7	2.07
Baltimore, MD/Washington D.C. . . .	15.2	1.88
Birmingham, Montgomery, AL . . .	14.1	1.75
Other	634.3	78.50

Source: *Food Institute Report*, August 5, 2002, p. 5, from DDBC News.

★ 176 ★

Hot Dogs (SIC 2013)

Top Hot Dog Brands, 2002

Market shares are shown based on supermarket sales for the year ended May 19, 2002. Figures exclude Wal-Mart.

Oscar Mayer	18.7%
Ball Park	16.3
Bar S	6.0
Hebrew National	3.9
Bryan	3.1
Nathan	2.7
Armour	2.7
Eckrich	2.3
Kahn	2.1
Private label	6.3
Other	35.9

Source: *National Provisioner*, August 2002, p. 52, from Information Resources Inc.

Hot Dogs (SIC 2013)

Top Hot Dog Producers, 2002

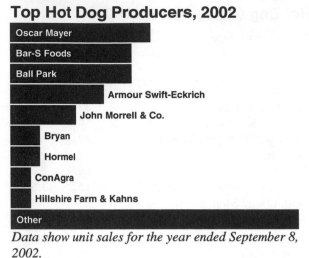

	Oscar Mayer
	Bar-S Foods
	Ball Park
	Armour Swift-Eckrich
	John Morrell & Co.
	Bryan
	Hormel
	ConAgra
	Hillshire Farm & Kahns
	Other

Data show unit sales for the year ended September 8, 2002.

	($ mil.)	Share
Oscar Mayer	125.9	15.21%
Bar-S Foods	109.7	13.26
Ball Park	108.1	13.06
Armour Swift-Eckrich . . .	85.9	10.38
John Morrell & Co. . . .	59.4	7.18
Bryan	23.6	2.85
Hormel	21.2	2.56
ConAgra	18.5	2.24
Hillshire Farm & Kahns	18.2	2.20
Other	257.0	31.06

Source: *Progressive Grocer*, November 15, 2002, p. 59, from Information Resources Inc.

Lunch Meat (SIC 2013)

Leading Sliced Lunch Meat Producers, 2002

Companies are ranked by sales in millions of dollars for the year ended July 14, 2002.

	($ mil.)	Share
Kraft/Oscar Mayer	$ 822.3	15.16%
Armour Swift-Eckrich	375.8	6.93
Kraft/Louis Rich	134.1	2.47
Hillshire Farm & Kahns	126.9	2.34
Carl Buddig	125.0	2.30
Land O'Frost	92.6	1.71
Bryan Foods	85.0	1.57
Hormel Foods	80.3	1.48
Thorn Apple Valley	64.7	1.19

	($ mil.)	Share
Private label	$ 467.5	8.62%
Other	3,050.1	56.23

Source: *Progressive Grocer*, September 15, 2002, p. 49, from Information Resources Inc.

Lunch Meat (SIC 2013)

Top Lunch Meat (Non-Sliced) Brands, 2002

Market shares are shown based on supermarket sales for the year ended May 19, 2002. Figures exclude Wal-Mart.

Hickory Farms	7.4%
Oscar Mayer	5.2
Farmland	4.8
Hillshire Farm	4.7
Schweigert	4.1
Hebrew National	4.1
Kahn	3.6
Johnsonville	3.5
Old Wisconsin	3.4
Private label	4.1
Other	55.1

Source: *National Provisioner*, August 2002, p. 52, from Information Resources Inc.

Lunch Meat (SIC 2013)

Top Lunch Meat (Sliced) Brands, 2002

Market shares are shown based on supermarket sales for the year ended May 19, 2002. Figures exclude Wal-Mart.

Oscar Mayer	27.0%
Butterball	5.0
Hillshire Farm Deli Select	4.0
Louis Rich	3.7
Buddig	3.7
Land O Frost Premium	2.5
Bryan	2.3

Continued on next page.

★ 180 ★ *Continued*
Lunch Meat (SIC 2013)

Top Lunch Meat (Sliced) Brands, 2002

Market shares are shown based on supermarket sales for the year ended May 19, 2002. Figures exclude Wal-Mart.

Eckrich	1.9%
Hormel	1.9
Private label	15.1
Other	32.9

Source: *National Provisioner*, August 2002, p. 52, from Information Resources Inc.

★ 181 ★
Meat Snacks (SIC 2013)

Top Meat Snack Brands, 2002

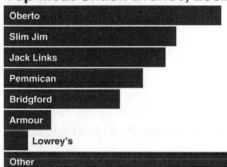

Oberto
Slim Jim
Jack Links
Pemmican
Bridgford
Armour
Lowrey's
Other

Brands are ranked by sales for the year ended April 21, 2002. Figures are for supermarkets, drug stores and discount stores and exclude Wal-Mart.

	($ mil.)	Share
Oberto	$ 47.3	19.23%
Slim Jim	36.4	14.80
Jack Links	33.2	13.50
Pemmican	28.8	11.71
Bridgford	23.9	9.72
Armour	8.9	3.62
Lowrey's	5.2	2.11
Other	62.3	25.33

Source: *MMR*, June 17, 2002, p. 90, from Information Resources inc.

★ 182 ★
Sausage (SIC 2013)

Top Refrigerated Breakfast Sausage/ Ham Brands, 2002

Market shares are shown in percent for the year ended May 19, 2002.

Jimmy Dean	25.8%
Bob Evans	12.2
Odom's Tennessee Pride	5.5
Johnsonville	4.6
Farmer John	3.4
Hormel	3.3
Owens	2.9
Jimmy Dean	2.4
Private label	6.4
Other	33.5

Source: *National Provisioner*, July 2002, p. 26, from Information Resources Inc.

★ 183 ★
Sausage (SIC 2013)

Top Refrigerated Breakfast Sausage/ Ham Makers, 2002

Market shares are shown in percent for the year ended May 19, 2002.

Jimmy Dean Foods	29.1%
Bob Evans Farms Inc.	12.2
Odom's Tennessee Pride	5.5
Hormel Foods	5.3
Johnsonville Foods Inc.	4.6
Clougherty Packing Co.	3.4
Owens Country Sausage	2.9
Private label	6.4
Other	30.6

Source: *National Provisioner*, July 2002, p. 26, from Information Resources Inc.

★ 184 ★
Sausage (SIC 2013)

Top Refrigerated Dinner Sausage Brands, 2002

Market shares are shown in percent for the year ended May 19, 2002.

Hillshire Farms	26.2%
Johnsonville	10.3

Continued on next page.

★ 184 ★ *Continued*
Sausage (SIC 2013)

Top Refrigerated Dinner Sausage Brands, 2002

Market shares are shown in percent for the year ended May 19, 2002.

Eckrich	7.1%
Bryan	3.2
Bar-S	1.4
Thorn Apple Valley	1.3
John Morrell	1.2
Bryan	1.2
Butterball	1.1
Private label	7.2
Other	39.8

Source: *National Provisioner*, July 2002, p. 26, from Information Resources Inc.

★ 185 ★
Sausage (SIC 2013)

Top Refrigerated Dinner Sausage Vendors, 2002

Market shares are shown in percent for the year ended May 19, 2002.

Hillshire Farm & Kahn's	27.9%
Johnsonville Foods Inc.	11.9
Armour-Swift-Eckrich	11.2
Bryan Foods Inc.	4.4
John Morrell & Co.	1.7
Thorn Apple Valley	1.6
Bar-S Foods Co.	1.4
Private label	7.2
Other	32.7

Source: *National Provisioner*, July 2002, p. 26, from Information Resources Inc.

★ 186 ★
Poultry (SIC 2015)

Chicken Sales, 2001

Categories are ranked for random weight sales in millions of dollars.

Chicken breast, boneless	$ 1,583.9
Chicken breast bone-in	751.2
Chicken whole	608.6
Chicken thighs	308.2

Chicken other	$ 247.4
Chicken whole leg	223.4
Chicken wings	219.2
Chicken drumstick	206.4
Chicken cut-up parts	125.3

Source: *Grocery Headquarters*, March 2003, p. 45, from A.C. Nielsen Homescan Consumer Facts, 2001.

★ 187 ★
Poultry (SIC 2015)

How Pork is Consumed, 2001

Ham (incl. lunch meat)	28.0%
Bacon	16.0
Sausage	16.0
Lunchmeat	12.0
Hot dogs	11.0
Pork chops	9.0
Other	8.0

Source: *Meat Retailer*, October-November 2002, p. 28, from NPD and National Pork Board.

★ 188 ★
Poultry (SIC 2015)

Leading Frozen Poultry Makers, 2002

Market shares are shown based on supermarket sales for the year ended February 24, 2002.

Tyson Foods Inc.	23.9%
ConAgra Inc.	14.5
Gold-Kist Inc.	2.7
Barber Foods	2.5
Private label	26.6
Other	29.8

Source: *Refrigerated & Frozen Foods*, June 2002, p. 62, from Information Resources Inc. InfoScan.

★ 189 ★
Poultry (SIC 2015)

Top Frozen Poultry Brands, 2002

Market shares are shown based on supermarket sales for the year ended May 19, 2002.

Tyson	18.9%
Banquet	9.8
Barber	2.5
Gold Kist Young & Tender	2.3

Continued on next page.

★ 189 ★ *Continued*
Poultry (SIC 2015)

Top Frozen Poultry Brands, 2002

Market shares are shown based on supermarket sales for the year ended May 19, 2002.

On Car Redi Serve	2.1%
Advance Fast Fixin	2.0
Tender Bird	1.9
Tyson Chick n Chunks	1.7
Hormel Jennie	1.7
Private label	26.1

Source: *National Provisioner*, August 2002, p. 62, from Information Resources Inc.

★ 190 ★
Poultry (SIC 2015)

Top Pork Producers, 2002

Figures show percent of total slaughter as of September 2002.

Smithfield	21.0%
IBP/Tyson	18.6
Swift	11.3
Excel/Cargill	8.4
Hormel	8.0
Other	32.7

Source: "Top Pork Producers." available April 7, 2003 from http://www.ilfb.com/viedocument.asp?did3756, from Illinois Farm Bureau.

★ 191 ★
Dairy Products (SIC 2020)

Largest Dairy Producers, 2002

Companies are ranked by estimated sales in millions of dollars.

Dean Foods Company	$ 10,000
Kraft Foods Inc.	4,500
Land O'Lakes	2,800
Kroger Co.	2,700
Schreiber Foods	2,000
Dairy Farmers of America	1,704
Leprino Foods	1,501
Prairie Farms Dairy	1,452
Dreyer's Grand Ice Cream	1,426

Source: *Refrigerated & Frozen Foods*, February 2002, p. 38.

★ 192 ★
Butter (SIC 2021)

Top Butter Brands, 2002

Market shares are shown for the year ended May 19, 2002. Figures are for food outlets only and exclude Wal-Mart.

	($ mil.)	Share
Land O'Lakes	$ 432.9	32.40%
Challenge	57.4	4.30
Breakstone	26.2	1.96
Tillamook	24.9	1.86
Crystal Farms	21.0	1.57
Keller's	18.6	1.39
Hotel Bar	17.7	1.32
Cabot	14.6	1.09
Hiland	9.8	0.73
Private label	615.9	46.09
Other	97.3	7.28

Source: *Dairy Field*, August 2002, p. 3, from Information Resources Inc.

★ 193 ★
Butter (SIC 2021)

Top Butter Vendors, 2002

Market shares are shown for the year ended May 19, 2002. Figures are for food outlets only and exclude Wal-Mart.

Land O'Lakes Inc.	32.4%
Challenge Dairy Products	4.7
Sodiaal North America	2.9
Kraft Foods Inc.	2.0
Tillamook County Creamery	1.9
Crystal Farms Inc.	1.6
Cabot Creamery Inc.	1.1

Continued on next page.

★ 193 ★ *Continued*
Butter (SIC 2021)

Top Butter Vendors, 2002

Market shares are shown for the year ended May 19, 2002. Figures are for food outlets only and exclude Wal-Mart.

Hiland Dairy	0.7%
West Farm Foods	0.6
Private label	46.1
Other	6.0

Source: *Dairy Field*, August 2002, p. 3, from Information Resources Inc.

★ 194 ★
Margarine (SIC 2021)

Top Margarine/Butter blend Brands, 2002

Shares are shown based on dollar sales at grocery, drug and mass market outlets (but not Wal-Mart) for the year ended December 29, 2002.

I Can't Believe It's Not Butter	16.5%
Shedd's Country Crock	14.8
Parkay	8.8
Blue Bonnet	7.9
Imperial	5.1
Fleischmann's	5.0
I Can't Believe It's Not Butter Light	4.9
Land O'Lakes	4.5
Private label	8.7
Other	23.8

Source: *Grocery Headquarters*, April 2003, p. 43, from Information Resources Inc.

★ 195 ★
Margarine (SIC 2021)

Top Margarine/Butter blend Makers, 2002

Shares are shown based on dollar sales at grocery, drug and mass market outlets (but not Wal-Mart) for the year ended December 29, 2002.

Van den Bergh Foods Co.	49.8%
ConAgra Inc.	22.6
Land O'Lakes Inc.	4.9
Lever Brothers Co.	3.9
Private label	8.7
Other	10.1

Source: *Grocery Headquarters*, April 2003, p. 43, from Information Resources Inc.

★ 196 ★
Cheese (SIC 2022)

Cheese Sales by Volume, 2002

Distribution is based on supermarket sales for the year ended January 27, 2002.

Chunk/loaf	31.2%
Shredded	22.4
Spreads	3.6
Grated/crumble	3.0
String/sticks	2.9
Cubed	0.7

Source: *Dairy Foods*, July 2002, p. 1, from Information Resources Inc.

★ 197 ★
Cheese (SIC 2022)

Processed Cheese Loaf Market, 2001

The industry had sales of $391 million.

Kraft 87.7%
Other 12.3

Source: "Kraft Sweetens Stock Market." available March 7, 2003 from http://more.abcnews.go.com, from Kraft, A.C. Nielsen, and Information Resources Inc.

★ 198 ★
Cheese (SIC 2022)

Top Natural Cheese Brands, 2002

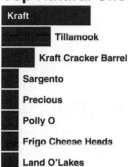

Market shares are shown for the year ended May 19, 2002. Figures exclude Wal-Mart.

Kraft 11.4%
Tillamook 6.2
Kraft Cracker Barrel 3.6
Sargento 2.3
Precious 2.3
Polly O 2.3
Frigo Cheese Heads 2.2
Land O'Lakes 2.0
Athenos 1.8
Private label 35.5
Other 30.4

Source: *Dairy Field*, August 2002, p. 3, from Information Resources Inc.

★ 199 ★
Cheese (SIC 2022)

Top Natural Cheese Producers, 2002

Sales are shown for the year ended August 11, 2002. Figures exclude Wal-Mart.

	($ mil.)	Share
Kraft Foods	$ 431	15.88%
Tillamook	170	6.26
Sorrento	102	3.76
Saputo	90	3.32
Sargento	88	3.24
Kraft Pollio	79	2.91
Kraft Churny	74	2.73
Land O'Lakes	56	2.06
Cabot Creamery	44	1.62
Private label	974	35.89
Other	606	22.33

Source: *Dairy Foods*, October 2002, p. 19, from Information Resources Inc.

★ 200 ★
Cheese (SIC 2022)

Top Natural Shredded Cheese Brands, 2002

Market shares are shown for the year ended May 19, 2002. Figures exclude Wal-Mart.

Kraft 27.1%
Sargento 4.8
Sargento Fancy 3.8
Crystal Farms 3.8
Borden 3.0
Private label 42.6
Other 14.9

Source: *Dairy Field*, August 2002, p. 3, from Information Resources Inc.

★ 201 ★

Frozen Desserts (SIC 2024)

Frozen Dessert Industry, 2001

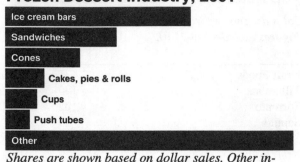

Shares are shown based on dollar sales. Other includes fudge bars, cream bars, fruit and juice bars, Italian ice and frozen yogurt.

Ice cream bars	24.9%
Sandwiches	15.2
Cones	9.8
Cakes, pies & rolls	4.7
Cups	3.9
Push tubes	3.0
Other	38.5

Source: *Dairy Foods*, October 2002, p. 4, from Packaged Facts.

★ 202 ★

Frozen Desserts (SIC 2024)

Top Frozen Novelty Brands, 2002

Market shares are shown based on sales for the year ended May 19, 2002.

Klondike	7.7%
Nestle Drumstick	5.4
Popsicle	4.5
Silhouette	3.5
Haagen Dazs	2.6
Well's Bluebunny	2.5
Blue Bell	2.3
Dole Fruit & Juice	2.1
Fudgesicle	2.1
Private label	16.8
Other	50.5

Source: *Dairy Field*, August 2002, p. 4, from Information Resources Inc.

★ 203 ★

Frozen Desserts (SIC 2024)

Top Frozen Novelty Makers, 2002

Market shares are shown based on sales for the year ended May 19, 2002. Figures exclude Wal-Mart.

Good Humor/Breyers	22.5%
Ice Cream Partners USA	13.4
Mars Inc.	5.6
Well's Dairy Inc.	4.8
Silhouette Brands Inc.	3.5
Dreyer's Grand Ice Cream	3.2
Nestle USA Inc.	2.9
Private label	16.8
Other	27.3

Source: *Dairy Field*, August 2002, p. 4, from Information Resources Inc.

★ 204 ★

Frozen Desserts (SIC 2024)

Top Frozen Yogurt Brands, 2002

Market shares are shown based on sales for the year ended May 19, 2002. Figures exclude Wal-Mart.

Dreyer's/Edy's	19.5%
Ben & Jerry's	14.5
Turkey Hill	7.5
Private label	21.7
Other	36.8

Source: *Dairy Field*, August 2002, p. 4, from Information Resources Inc.

★ 205 ★

Frozen Desserts (SIC 2024)

Top Frozen Yogurt Makers, 2002

Market shares are shown based on sales for the year ended May 19, 2002. Figures exclude Wal-Mart.

Dreyer's Grand Ice Cream	19.5%
Ben & Jerry's Homemade Inc.	14.5
Turkey Hill Dairy Inc.	7.5
Ice Cream Partners USA	6.7
Marigold Foods Inc.	3.9
Morningstar Foods Inc.	2.6
Good Humors/Breyers	2.6
Private label	21.7
Other	21.0

Source: *Dairy Field*, August 2002, p. 4, from Information Resources Inc.

★ 206 ★
Ice Cream (SIC 2024)

Ice Cream Market in Texas

*Blue Bell's share falls somewhere between 50-55%.
It ranks third in the country overall.*

Blue Bell	55.0%
Other	45.0

Source: *Knight Ridder/Tribune Business News*, July 15, 2002, p. NA.

★ 207 ★
Ice Cream (SIC 2024)

Ice Cream Sales by Category

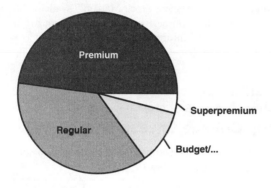

Sales are shown by volume.

Premium	48.0%
Regular	37.0
Budget/economy	11.0
Superpremium	4.0

Source: *Dairy Foods*, March 2003, p. 24, from Smith Dairy Products and Information Resources Inc.

★ 208 ★
Ice Cream (SIC 2024)

Ice Cream Sales by Type, 2002

Sales are for the year ended October 25, 2002.

Ice cream	92.0%
Frozen yogurt	5.0
Ice milk/sherbert	3.0

Source: *Convenience Store News*, February 10, 2003, p. 55, from A.C. Nielsen.

★ 209 ★
Ice Cream (SIC 2024)

Super Premium Ice Cream Market

Market shares are shown in percent.

Unilever	38.0%
Nestle	36.0
Dreyer's	24.0
Other	2.0

Source: *America's Intelligence Wire*, March 6, 2003, p. NA, from Federal Trade Commission.

★ 210 ★
Ice Cream (SIC 2024)

Top Ice Cream Brands, 2002

Brands are ranked by supermarket sales for the year ended May 19, 2002.

	($ mil.)	Share
Dreyer's Grand	$ 795.4	18.4%
Good Humor/Breyers	686.8	15.9
Blue Bell Creameries	253.4	5.8
Ben & Jerry's	199.8	4.6
Ice Cream Partners	192.7	4.4
Wells Dairy	136.9	3.2
Armour Swift-Eckrich	106.7	2.5
Turkey Hill Dairy	105.2	2.4
Marigold Foods	88.2	2.0
Private label	997.2	23.0
Other	769.1	17.8

Source: *New York Times*, June 18, 2002, p. C11, from Information Resources Inc.

★ 211 ★
Ice Cream (SIC 2024)

Top Ice Cream Brands by Unit Sales, 2002

Brands are ranked by sales in millions of units for the year ended November 3, 2002. Figures exclude Wal-Mart.

	(mil.)	Share
Breyers	142.0	16.77%
Blue Bell	71.0	8.39
Dreyers Edys Grand	68.0	8.03
Haagen Dazs	56.0	6.62
Ben & Jerry's	55.0	6.50
Wells Blue Bunny	35.0	4.13

Continued on next page.

★ 211 ★ *Continued*
Ice Cream (SIC 2024)

Top Ice Cream Brands by Unit Sales, 2002

Brands are ranked by sales in millions of units for the year ended November 3, 2002. Figures exclude Wal-Mart.

	(mil.)	Share
Turkey Hill	29.0	3.43%
Healthy Choice	25.0	2.95
Private label	324.0	38.28
Other	41.5	4.90

Source: *Dairy Foods*, December 2002, p. 17, from Information Resources Inc.

★ 212 ★
Ice Cream (SIC 2024)

Top Ice Cream Firms, 2001

Market shares are shown in percent.

Unilever	19.4%
Dreyer's	13.3
Nestle	7.9
Wells Dairy	5.0
Dean Foods	4.8
Other	49.6

Source: *USA TODAY*, June 18, 2002, p. 3B, from Packaged Facts.

★ 213 ★
Pudding (SIC 2024)

Top Pudding/Mousse/Gelatin/Parfait Brands, 2002

Market shares are shown in percent for the year ened December 1, 2002.

Jell-O	51.1%
Jell-O Gelatin Snacks	14.1
Kozy Shack	13.3
Jello-Free	11.5
Swiss Miss	8.8
Jolly Rancher	3.9

Jell-O Extreme	3.5%
Jell-O Creme Savers	2.2
Lakeview Farms	1.6
Private label	5.6

Source: *Dairy Field*, February 2003, p. 45, from Information Resources Inc.

★ 214 ★
Whipped Toppings (SIC 2024)

Whipped Topping Market, 2001

The industry had sales of $368 million.

Kraft	72.7%
Other	27.3

Source: "Kraft Sweetens Stock Market." available March 7, 2003 from http://more.abcnews.go.com, from Kraft, A.C. Nielsen, and Information Resources Inc.

★ 215 ★
Cottage Cheese (SIC 2026)

Top Cottage Cheese Brands, 2002

Market shares are shown based on supermarket sales for the year ended May 19, 2002.

Breakstone	7.8%
Knudsen	7.7
Dean's	2.8
Breakstone Cottage	2.8
Doubles Hiland	2.6
Friendship	2.5
Light'n Lively	2.3
Private label	39.3
Other	32.2

Source: *Dairy Field*, August 2002, p. 42, from Information Resources Inc.

★ 216 ★
Cottage Cheese (SIC 2026)

Top Cottage Cheese Makers, 2002

Market shares are shown based on supermarket sales for the year ended May 19, 2002.

Kraft Foods Inc.	13.8%
Kraft/Knudsen Corp.	10.0
Dean Foods Co.	2.9
Hiland Dairy	2.8
Meadow Gold Dairy Inc.	2.6

Continued on next page.

★ 216 ★ *Continued*
Cottage Cheese (SIC 2026)

Top Cottage Cheese Makers, 2002

Market shares are shown based on supermarket sales for the year ended May 19, 2002.

Friendship Dairies Inc.	2.5%
Private label	39.3
Other	26.1

Source: *Dairy Field*, August 2002, p. 42, from Information Resources Inc.

★ 217 ★
Milk (SIC 2026)

Milk Production by Type

Total milk volume has increased slightly over 30%. Per capita consumption has changed very little.

Low-fat	43.9%
Plain whole	33.2
Fat-free	15.2
Flavored	6.6
Butter	1.1

Source: *Beverage Aisle*, January 15, 2003, p. 24, from Beverage Marketing Corp.

★ 218 ★
Milk (SIC 2026)

Top Flavored Milk Brands, 2002

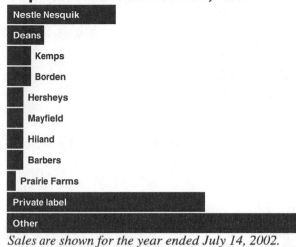

Sales are shown for the year ended July 14, 2002. Figures exclude Wal-Mart.

	($ mil.)	Share
Nestle Nesquik	$ 109	14.61%
Deans	35	4.69
Kemps	22	2.95
Borden	20	2.68
Hersheys	14	1.88
Mayfield	14	1.88
Hiland	13	1.74
Barbers	12	1.61
Prairie Farms	11	1.47
Private label	201	26.94
Other	295	39.54

Source: *Dairy Foods*, September 2002, p. 19, from Information Resources Inc.

★ 219 ★
Milk (SIC 2026)

Top Refrigerated Flavored Milk Makers, 2002

Market shares are shown for the year ended May 19, 2002. Figures exclude Wal-Mart.

Nestle USA Inc.	14.7%
Dean Foods Co.	6.6
Meadow Gold Dairy Inc.	5.2
Marigold Foods Inc.	3.7

Continued on next page.

★ 219 ★ *Continued*

Milk (SIC 2026)

Top Refrigerated Flavored Milk Makers, 2002

Market shares are shown for the year ended May 19, 2002. Figures exclude Wal-Mart.

Land-O-Sun Dairies	2.1%
Hershey Chocolate USA	2.0
Private label	26.6
Other	60.9

Source: *Dairy Field*, August 2002, p. 5, from Information Resources Inc.

★ 220 ★

Milk (SIC 2026)

Top Refrigerated Skim/Lowfat Milk Makers, 2002

Market shares are shown for the year ended May 19, 2002. Figures exclude Wal-Mart.

Marigold Foods Inc.	2.9%
Dean Foods Co.	2.6
McNeil Consumer Products	1.8
Meadow Gold Dairy Inc.	1.3
Parmalat USA Corp.	1.2
Mayfield Dairy Farms Inc.	1.1
Prairie Farms Dairy	1.0
HP Hood Inc.	1.0
Morningstar Foods Inc.	1.0
Private label	64.9
Other	21.2

Source: *Dairy Field*, August 2002, p. 5, from Information Resources Inc.

★ 221 ★

Milk (SIC 2026)

Top Refrigerated Whole Milk Brands, 2002

Shares of the $3.2 billion category are shown for the year ended May 19, 2002. Figures exclude Wal-Mart.

Borden	1.7%
Hiland	1.2
Mayfield	1.1
Prairie Farms	1.1
Dean's	1.0
Farmland Dairies	0.8
Garelick Farms	0.7
Private label	67.2

Source: *Dairy Field*, August 2002, p. 5, from Information Resources Inc.

★ 222 ★

Milk (SIC 2026)

Top Refrigerated Whole Milk Makers, 2002

Shares of the $3.2 billion category are shown for the year ended May 19, 2002. Figures exclude Wal-Mart.

Meadow Gold Dairy Inc.	2.6%
Dean Foods	1.3
Hiland Dairy	1.2
Mayfield Dairy Farms Inc.	1.1
Land-O-Sun Dairies	1.1
Prairie Farms	1.1
Parmalat Farms	1.0
Private label	67.2
Other	23.4

Source: *Dairy Field*, August 2002, p. 5, from Information Resources Inc.

★ 223 ★

Milk (SIC 2026)

Top Selling Flavored Milk Brands, 2002

Brands are ranked by supermarket sales for the year ended June 16, 2002. Private label had sales of $198.7 million.

Nestle Nesquik	$ 100.53
Dean's	34.73
Kemps	21.58
Borden	18.98
Hershey's	14.27
Mayfield	13.51
Hiland	12.58
Barber's	12.11
Prairie Farms	9.77
Hood	9.52

Source: *Supermarket News*, December 30, 2002, p. 27, from Information Resources Inc.

★ 224 ★

Milk (SIC 2026)

Top Skim/Lowfat Milk Brands, 2002

■	Kemps
■	Deans
■	Lactaid 100
■	Mayfield
■	Prairie Farms
■	Land O'Lakes
■	Hiland
■	Horizon Organic
■	Garelick Farms
■	Private label
■	Other

Sales are shown for the year ended June 16, 2002. Figures exclude Wal-Mart.

	($ mil.)	Share
Kemps	$ 117	1.73%
Deans	98	1.45
Lactaid 100	94	1.39
Mayfield	76	1.13
Prairie Farms	66	0.98
Land O'Lakes	59	0.87
Hiland	55	0.82
Horizon Organic	53	0.79

	($ mil.)	Share
Garelick Farms	$ 52	0.77%
Private label	4,374	64.82
Other	1,704	25.25

Source: *Dairy Foods*, September 2002, p. 19, from Information Resources Inc.

★ 225 ★

Milk Substitutes (SIC 2026)

Milk Substitute Market

The $443 million market is shown by company. Hain Celestial is also the leader in the unrefrigerated milk substitutes market. The 40% share includes Rice Dream and Soy Dream brands from Imagine Foods.

Hain Celestial	40.0%
Other	60.0

Source: *New York Times*, December 3, 2002, p. C5, from Information Resources Inc.

★ 226 ★

Sour Cream (SIC 2026)

Top Sour Cream Brands, 2002

Market shares are shown based on supermarket sales for the year ended May 19, 2002.

Breakstone	15.1%
Daisy	12.4
Knudsen Hampshire	6.9
Land O'Lakes	2.5
Friendship	1.8
Dean's	1.7
Knudsen Nice'n Light	1.6
Gandy's	1.5
Meadow Gold	1.5
Private label	33.0
Other	22.0

Source: *Dairy Field*, August 2002, p. 42, from Information Resources Inc.

★ 227 ★
Sour Cream (SIC 2026)

Top Sour Cream Vendors, 2002

Kraft Foods Inc.

Daisy Brand Inc.

Kraft/Knudsen Corp.

Dean Foods Co.

Marigold Foods Inc.

Crowley Foods Inc.

Private label

Other

Market shares are shown based on supermarket sales for the year ended May 19, 2002.

Kraft Foods Inc.	15.3%
Daisy Brand Inc.	12.4
Kraft/Knudsen Corp.	9.0
Dean Foods Co.	4.2
Marigold Foods Inc.	2.2
Crowley Foods Inc.	2.1
Private label	33.0
Other	21.8

Source: *Dairy Field*, August 2002, p. 42, from Information Resources Inc.

★ 228 ★

Yogurt (SIC 2026)

Top Refrigerated Yogurt Makers, 2002

Market shares are shown based on supermarket sales for the year ended May 19, 2002.

Yoplait USA Inc.	34.4%
Dannon Co.	27.9
Kraft Foods Inc.	6.5
Stonyfield Farm Inc.	3.6
Colombo Inc.	2.7
YoFarm Corp.	1.8
Meadow Gold Dairy Inc.	1.3
Private label	13.6
Other	8.2

Source: *Dairy Field*, August 2002, p. 42, from Information Resources Inc.

★ 229 ★

Yogurt (SIC 2026)

Top Yogurt Brands, 2002

Shares are shown based on dollar sales at grocery, drug and mass market outlets (but not Wal-Mart) for the year ended December 29, 2002.

Yoplait	11.3%
Dannon	7.3
Dannon Light 'n Fit	7.1
Yoplait Light	5.7
Yoplait Go-Gurt	4.8
Yoplait Trix	3.7
Yoplait Whips	3.4
Yoplait Custard Style	3.4
Dannon Danimals	3.1
Private label	13.4
Other	36.8

Source: *Grocery Headquarters*, April 2003, p. 43, from Information Resources Inc.

★ 230 ★

Infant Formula (SIC 2032)

Top Baby Formula Brands, 2002

Brands are ranked by sales for the year ended December 29, 2002. Figures are for supermarkets, drug stores and discount stores and exclude Wal-Mart.

	($ mil.)	Share
Enfamil powder	$ 677.4	26.88%
Similac powder	248.7	9.87
Enfamil liquid concentrate	231.7	9.19
Similac liquid concentrate	162.1	6.43
Proobee powder	109.7	4.35
Carnation Good Start powder	95.4	3.79
Isomil powder	93.7	3.72
Isomil liquid concentrate	73.3	2.91
Similac RTD	68.9	2.73
Pedialyte	59.8	2.37
Other	699.3	27.75

Source: *MMR*, February 10, 2003, p. 29, from Information Resources Inc.

★ 231 ★
Baked Beans (SIC 2033)
Baked Beans Market, 2001

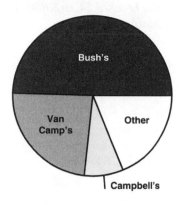

Market shares are shown in percent.

Bush's	50.0%
Van Camp's	24.0
Campbell's	7.5
Other	18.5

Source: "Intentional foul." available March 7, 2003 from http://www.americancynic.com/03192001.html.

★ 232 ★
Canned Food (SIC 2033)
Canned Fruit Sales

Sales are shown in millions of dollars.

Pineapple	$ 241.98
Peaches, cling	241.94
Apple sauces	205.07
Fruit cocktail	112.54
Pears	108.88
Pie & pastry filling	105.64
Cranberries, shelf stable	100.18
Oranges	85.55
Fruit mixes & salad fruits	79.02
Pumpkins	47.48
Cherries, maraschino	43.88

Source: *Progressive Grocer*, September 15, 2002, p. 24, from *Progressive Grocer's 55th Annual Consumers Expenditures Study.*

★ 233 ★
Canned Food (SIC 2033)
Canned Pineapple Market in North America, 2001

Market shares are estimated in percent.

Dole	50.0%
Other	50.0

Source: "Dole." available March 7, 2003 from http://www.dole.com, from company report.

★ 234 ★
Canned Food (SIC 2033)
Canned Vegetable Sales

Supermarket sales are shown in millions of dollars.

	($ mil.)	Share
Green beans	$ 373.21	11.61%
Corn, whole kernel	333.35	10.37
Tomato sauce	243.99	7.59
Peas	167.66	5.22
Mushrooms	164.44	5.12
Beans, kidney and red	114.44	3.56
Tomatoes, whole	98.19	3.05
Tomato paste	97.06	3.02
Tomatoes, stewed	81.54	2.54
Other	1,540.23	47.92

Source: *Food Institute Report*, October 14, 2002, p. 18, from *Progressive Grocer's 55th Consumer Expenditures Survey.*

★ 235 ★
Canned Food (SIC 2033)
Top Canned Pasta Brands, 2002

Brands are ranked by supermarket sales for the year ended December 1, 2002. Figures exclude Wal-Mart.

	Units (mil.)	Share
Chef Boyardee	136.1	37.46%
Franco-American SpaghettiOs . .	94.9	26.12
Franco-American	31.6	8.70
Chef Boyardee Beefaroni	29.9	8.23
Chef Boyardee Overstuffed . . .	19.1	5.26
Chef Boyardee Mini Bites	12.0	3.30

Continued on next page.

★ 235 ★ *Continued*
Canned Food (SIC 2033)

Top Canned Pasta Brands, 2002

Brands are ranked by supermarket sales for the year ended December 1, 2002. Figures exclude Wal-Mart.

	Units (mil.)	Share
Chef Boyardee Homestyle	10.8	2.97%
Chef Boyardee Jr.	10.6	2.92
Chef Boyardee ABCs and 123s	4.8	1.32
Other	13.5	3.72

Source: *Progressive Grocer*, February 15, 2003, p. 39, from Information Resources Inc.

★ 236 ★
Jams and Jellies (SIC 2033)

Top Jam/Jelly Producers

Market shares are shown in percent.

Smucker's	35.0%
Kraft	9.0
Other	56.0

Source: "Their Accountant Might Not Agree." available March 7, 2003 from http://www.marketingprofs.com.

★ 237 ★
Juices (SIC 2033)

Largest Cranberry Juice Makers

Market shares are shown in percent.

Ocean Spray	65.0%
Northland	7.0
Other	28.0

Source: *Knight Ridder/Tribune Business News*, February 28, 2003, p. NA.

★ 238 ★
Juices (SIC 2033)

Refrigerated Juice Flavors, 2002

Total supermarket sales reached $4.31 billion for the period year ended February 24, 2002.

Orange juices	70.7%
Fruit drinks	14.8
Blended fruit juices	6.8
Grapefruit	2.7
Lemonade	2.1
Other	2.9

Source: *Refrigerated & Frozen Foods*, June 2002, p. 41, from Information Resources Inc. InfoScan.

★ 239 ★
Juices (SIC 2033)

Top Juice Flavors, 2001

Shares are for the 100% juice market. Figures are for the year ended January 20, 2001.

Orange & blends	56.0%
Apple & blends	12.0
Grape	6.0
Pineapple	6.0
Vegetable	5.0
Grapefruit	4.0
Cranberry blends	3.0
Other	9.0

Source: *Beverage Aisle*, June 15, 2002, p. 4, from A.C. Nielsen.

★ 240 ★
Juices (SIC 2033)

Top Orange Juice Brands, 2002

Market shares of refrigerated juice brands are shown based on sales volume. Figures are for January 1 - June 15, 2002.

Tropicana	25.6%
Minute Maid	16.0
Tampico	7.9
Sunny Delight	7.8
Florida's Natural	6.1
Private label	21.8
Other	14.8

Source: *Wall Street Journal*, September 3, 2002, p. B6, from *Beverage Digest*.

★ 241 ★

Juices (SIC 2033)

Top Refrigerated Orange Juice Brands, 2002

Market shares are shown based on $3.0 billion in sales.

Tropicana Pure Premium	41.7%
Minute Maid Premium	19.1
Florida's Natural	8.5
Simply Orange	1.5
Tropicana Season's Best	1.3
Citrus World	0.7
Florida's Natural Growers Pride	0.5
Private label	19.0
Other	7.1

Source: *Beverage Industry*, July 2002, p. 44, from Information Resources Inc.

★ 242 ★

Juices (SIC 2033)

Top Refrigerated Orange Juice Companies, 2002

Market shares are shown based on $3.0 billion in sales.

Tropicana Dole Beverages	43.4%
The Minute Maid Co.	20.7
Citrus World Inc.	9.7
Hiland Dairy	0.4
Johanna Foods Inc.	0.4
Marigold Foods	0.3
Odwalla	0.3
Private label	19.6
Other	4.2

Source: *Beverage Industry*, July 2002, p. 44, from Information Resources Inc.

★ 243 ★

Ketchup (SIC 2033)

Ketchup Market Shares

Market shares are shown in percent. The company introduced the Easy Squeeze bottle just before Labor Day, which accounts for 10.3% of their total share.

Heinz	59.0%
Other	41.0

Source: *Knight Ridder/Tribune Business News*, December 13, 2002, p. NA.

★ 244 ★

Ketchup (SIC 2033)

Ketchup Market Shares in Canada

Market shares are shown in percent.

Heinz	76.0%
Other	24.0

Source: *Pittsburgh Post-Gazette*, March 11, 2003, p. NA.

★ 245 ★

Dried Fruit (SIC 2034)

Dried Fruit Sales, 2002

Sales are shown for the year ended June 16, 2002. Figures exclude Wal Mart.

Raisins	40.8%
Plums	18.2
Dates	5.1
Glazed fruit	3.0
Other	32.9

Source: *Grocery Headquarters*, October 2002, p. 51, from Information Resources Inc.

★ 246 ★
Soup (SIC 2034)
Condensed Soup Market, 2002

Shares are shown based on sales for the year ended August 11, 2002. Data do not include Wal-Mart.

	($ mil.)	Share
Campbell Soup	$ 1,200	85.71%
Private label	185	13.21
Other	15	1.07

Source: *Advertising Age*, September 16, 2002, p. 4, from Information Resources Inc.

★ 247 ★
Soup (SIC 2034)
Dry Soup Market, 2002

Figures are in millions of dollars for the year ended November 3, 2002.

	($ mil.)	Share
Lipton Recipe Secrets	$ 112	35.78%
Knorr	39	12.46
Other	162	51.76

Source: *Brandweek*, December 2, 2002, p. 10, from Information Resources Inc.

★ 248 ★
Soup (SIC 2034)
Ready-to-Serve Soup Market, 2002

Shares are shown based on sales for the year ended August 11, 2002. Data do not include Wal-Mart.

	($ mil.)	Share
Campbell Soup	$ 984	57.88%
General Mills (Progresso)	384	22.59
Other	332	19.53

Source: *Advertising Age*, September 16, 2002, p. 4, from Information Resources Inc.

★ 249 ★
Soup (SIC 2034)
Retail Soup Sales

Sales are shown in millions of dollars.

	2000	2002	Share
Ready-to-serve	$ 1,489	$ 1,731	43.93%
Condensed	1,440	1,414	35.89
Dry	776	795	20.18

Source: *Prepared Foods*, January 2003, p. 15, from Information Resources Inc. and Mintel's Global New Products.

★ 250 ★
Soup (SIC 2034)
Top Soup Brands, 2003

Market shares of the ready-to-serve industry are shown for the year ended February 23, 2003. Figures are based on sales at food, drug and mass merchandisers.

Campbell's Chunky	21.1%
Progresso	20.7
Swanson (broth)	12.1
Campbell's Select	9.1
Campbell's	4.7
College Inn (broth)	3.7
Healthy Choice	3.5
Wolfgang Puck's	2.4
Private label	8.8
Other	13.9

Source: *Progressive Grocer*, May 15, 2003, p. 37, from Information Resources Inc.

★ 251 ★
Barbeque Sauce (SIC 2035)
Barbeque Industry Sales

Sales grew 1.1% to $352.5 million for the year ended $229.7 million. Kraft's leading share of the category is shown.

Kraft	44.0%
Other	52.0

Source: *DSN Retailing Today*, October 7, 2002, p. S7, from Information Resources Inc.

★ 252 ★
Dips (SIC 2035)
Top Refrigerated Dip Brands, 2002

Market shares are shown based on supermarket sales for the year ended May 19, 2002.

T. Marzetti	17.9%
Dean's	11.5
Kraft	9.2
Heluva Good	5.9
Classic Guacamole	3.6
Marie's	2.7
Rod's IMO	2.6
Calavo	1.5
Private label	17.4
Other	27.7

Source: *Dairy Field*, August 2002, p. 42, from Information Resources Inc.

★ 253 ★
Hot Sauces (SIC 2035)
Hot Sauce Market, 2002

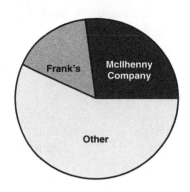

For the year ended October 6, 2002 sales increased 6.5% in the market. McIlhenny makes Tabasco; Frank's makes Frank's Red Hot Cayenne Pepper.

McIlhenny Company	26.5%
Frank's	16.1
Other	57.4

Source: *New York Times*, November 7, 2002, p. C7, from Information Resources Inc.

★ 254 ★
Mayonnaise (SIC 2035)
Top Mayonnaise Producers

Market shares are shown in percent.

Hellman's	42.0%
Kraft	18.0
Other	40.0

Source: "Their Accountant Might Not Agree." available March 7, 2003 from http://www.marketingprofs.com.

★ 255 ★
Mustard (SIC 2035)
Top Mustard Brands, 2001

The $290 million market is shown by brand.

French's	31.8%
Grey Poupon	14.9
Private label	17.6
Other	35.7

Source: *Brandweek*, February 11, 2002, p. 1, from Information Resources Inc.

★ 256 ★

Pasta Sauces (SIC 2035)

Top Pasta Sauce Brands, 2002

Brands are ranked by unit sales for the year ended July 14, 2002. Figures exclude Wal-Mart.

	(mil.)	Share
Prego	121.2	16.23%
Hunt's	96.8	12.96
Ragu Spaghetti/Italian	56.9	7.62
Classico	54.1	7.24
Ragu Chunky Garden Style	54.0	7.23
Ragu Old World Style	53.6	7.18
Ragu Hearty	33.9	4.54
Del Monte Spaghetti	33.1	4.43
Francesco Rinaldi	22.4	3.00
Five Brothers	21.7	2.91
Ragu Cheese Creations	21.6	2.89
Other	177.5	23.77

Source: *Progressive Grocer*, September 15, 2002, p. 44, from Information Resources Inc.

★ 257 ★

Pasta Sauces (SIC 2035)

Top Pasta Sauce Makers, 2002

Shares are shown based on sales at grocery, drug and mass market outlets (but not Wal-Mart) for the year ended December 29, 2002.

Ragu Foods Co.	37.7%
Campbell Soup Co.	21.3
H.J. Heinz Co.	11.1
ConAgra Grocery Headquarters	7.1
Private label	4.7
Other	18.1

Source: *Grocery Headquarters*, April 2003, p. 43, from Information Resources Inc.

★ 258 ★

Pickles (SIC 2035)

Refrigerated Pickle Market

Market shares are shown in percent.

Claussen	85.0%
Other	15.0

Source: *U.S. News & World Report*, November 4, 2002, p. 16.

★ 259 ★

Salad Dressings (SIC 2035)

Top Salad Dressing Brands, 2002

Shares are shown based on dollar sales at grocery, drug and mass market outlets (but not Wal-Mart) for the year ended December 29, 2002.

Kraft	21.8%
Wishbone	15.1
Ken's Steak House	7.2
Hidden Valley	6.7
Hidden Valley Ranch	6.6
Kraft Free	5.9
Newman's Own	3.6
Kraft Light Done Right	3.5
Wishbone Just 2 Good	3.5
Private label	7.9
Other	18.2

Source: *Grocery Headquarters*, April 2003, p. 43, from Information Resources Inc.

★ 260 ★

Salad Dressings (SIC 2035)

Top Salad Dressing Makers, 2002

Shares are shown based on dollar sales at grocery, drug and mass market outlets (but not Wal-Mart) for the year ended December 29, 2002.

Kraft Foods	33.1%
Lipton	18.5
Clorox Co.	13.3
Ken's Foods Inc.	7.2
Newman's Own Inc.	3.6
T. Marzetti Co.	2.0
Agrilink Foods Inc.	1.5
Girard's Fine Foods Inc.	1.4
Western Dressing	1.3
Private label	7.9
Other	10.2

Source: *Grocery Headquarters*, April 2003, p. 43, from Information Resources Inc.

★ 261 ★

Sauces (SIC 2035)

Asian Sauce and Marinade Market

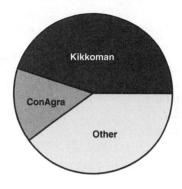

Market shares are shown in percent.

Kikkoman	45.0%
ConAgra	15.0
Other	40.0

Source: *Prepared Foods*, October 2002, p. 11, from Mintel.

★ 262 ★

Sauces (SIC 2035)

Condiment & Sauce Sales

Sales are shown in millions of dollars.

Spaghetti, marinara sauce	$ 1,364.79
Mexican sauces	853.33
Catsup	452.23
Barbecue sauces	323.01
Mustard	294.34
Vinegar	215.60
Gravy, canned	197.68
Oriental sauces	161.60
Gravy mixes, packaged	159.58
Cooking sauce	137.22
Sauce mix, taco	110.67

Source: *Progressive Grocer*, September 15, 2002, p. 24, from *Progressive Grocer's 55th Annual Consumers Expenditures Study.*

★ 263 ★

Steak Sauce (SIC 2035)

Steak Sauce Market, 2001

The industry had sales of $219 million. The company makes the A-1 brand.

Kraft	63.9%
Other	36.1

Source: "Kraft Sweetens Stock Market." available March 7, 2003 from http://more.abcnews.go.com, from Kraft, A.C. Nielsen, and Information Resources Inc.

★ 264 ★

Frozen Fruit (SIC 2037)

Leading Frozen Fruit Brands, 2002

Brands are ranked by sales in millions of dollars for the 12 weeks ended December 1, 2002.

	($ mil.)	Share
Big Valley	$ 4.27	7.65%
Birdseye	2.42	4.33
VIP	1.54	2.76
Cascadian Farm	1.38	2.47
Private label	38.46	68.89
Other	7.76	13.90

Source: *Frozen Food Age*, March 2003, p. 12, from Information Resources Inc.

★ 265 ★

Frozen Vegetables (SIC 2037)

Frozen Vegetable Sales, 2001

Supermarket sales are shown in millions of dollars.

	($ mil.)	Share
Potatoes	$ 1,061.91	35.93%
Mixed vegetables	447.97	15.16
Vegetables in sauce	217.90	7.37
Peas	206.50	6.99
Broccoli	183.80	6.22
Corn	183.19	6.20
Corn on the cob	127.69	4.32
Green beans	114.91	3.89
Lima beans	67.10	2.27
Other	344.16	11.65

Source: *Food Institute Report*, October 14, 2002, p. 18, from *Progressive Grocer's 55th Consumer Expenditures Survey.*

★ 266 ★

Frozen Vegetables (SIC 2037)

Frozen Vegetable Sales in Canada, 2001

Frozen vegetables make up 17% of the entire frozen food market. Sales are in millions of Canadian dollars.

	1998	2001	Share
French fried potatoes	$ 80	$ 110	29.65%
Vegetables & sauce	42	81	21.83
Peas	33	35	9.43
Corn	30	30	8.09
Potatoes, non-fried	28	39	10.51
Beans	6	9	2.43
Onions	6	8	2.16
Broccoli	3	7	1.89
Cauliflower	1	2	0.54
Asparagus	1	1	0.27
Other	38	49	13.21

Source: "Frozen Food Industry." available January 1, 2003 from http://ffas.usda.gov, from A.C. Nielsen.

★ 267 ★

Frozen Vegetables (SIC 2037)

Top Frozen Vegetable Makers, 2002

Market shares are shown for the year ended February 24, 2002.

General Mills	70.9%
Agrilink Foods	25.0
Freezer Queen	2.0
Heinz Frozen Food	1.3
Private label	0.7
Other	1.0

Source: *Refrigerated & Frozen Foods*, June 2002, p. 43, from Information Resources Inc. InfoScan.

★ 268 ★

Frozen Vegetables (SIC 2037)

Top Prepared Vegetable Brands, 2002

Brands are ranked by sales fof the 12 weeks ended October 6, 2002.

	($ mil.)	Share
Green Giant	$ 26.22	70.28%
Birdseye Simply Grillin'	6.09	16.32
Birdseye Side Orders	2.24	6.00
Green Giant Le Sueur	1.75	4.69
Other	1.01	2.71

Source: *Frozen Food Age*, January 2003, p. 16, from Information Resources Inc.

★ 269 ★

Frozen Dinners (SIC 2038)

Top Frozen Dinner Brands, 2002

Brands are ranked by sales in millions of dollars for the year ended June 16, 2002.

	($ mil.)	Share
Healthy Choice	$ 50.33	17.42%
Swanson Hungry-Man	40.93	14.16
Marie Callender's Complete		
Dinners	32.39	11.21
Banquet Select Menu	26.95	9.33
Swanson Homestyle Favorites . .	23.74	8.21
Banquet Value Menu	23.40	8.10
Kid Cuisine	22.91	7.93
Stouffer's Homestyle Dinners . . .	15.38	5.32
Stouffer's Lean Cuisine Cafe		
Classics	6.08	2.10
Other	46.88	16.22

Source: *Frozen Food Age*, September 2002, p. 48, from Information Resources Inc.

★ **270** ★

Frozen Dinners (SIC 2038)

Top Frozen Dinner Makers

Market shares are shown based on supermarket sales for the year ended February 24, 2002.

ConAgra Foods	57.7%
Pinnacle Foods	24.0
Nestle Prepared Food Div.	11.3
Aurora Foods	1.2
Private label	1.2
Other	5.6

Source: *Refrigerated & Frozen Foods*, June 2002, p. 55, from Information Resources Inc. InfoScan.

★ **271** ★

Frozen Dinners (SIC 2038)

Top Frozen Entree Brands, 2002

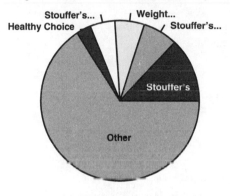

Market shares are shown based on supermarket sales for the year ended February 24, 2002.

	($ mil.)	Share
Stouffer's	$ 473.0	12.88%
Stouffer's Lean Cuisine Cafe		
Classics	259.1	7.06
Weight Watchers Smart Ones . . .	232.7	6.34
Stouffer's Lean Cuisine	167.9	4.57
Healthy Choice	125.5	3.42
Other	2,414.1	65.74

Source: *Refrigerated & Frozen Foods*, June 2002, p. 55, from Information Resources Inc. InfoScan.

★ **272** ★

Frozen Dinners (SIC 2038)

Top Frozen Entree Makers, 2002

Market shares are shown based on supermarket sales for the year ended February 24, 2002.

ConAgra Foods	13.1%
Heinz Frozen Food Co.	12.5
Luigino's	9.1
Uncle Benis	5.1
Nestle Prepared Food Div.	4.2
Other	18.2

Source: *Refrigerated & Frozen Foods*, June 2002, p. 55, from Information Resources Inc. InfoScan.

★ **273** ★

Frozen Foods (SIC 2038)

Frozen Eggroll Market

Sales are in the self-service deli category.

Chung's Foods	50.0%
Other	50.0

Source: *Food Institute Report*, February 27, 2003, p. 2.

★ **274** ★

Frozen Foods (SIC 2038)

Frozen Food Market, 2001

Retail and institutional sales are shown in millions of pounds.

	(mil.)	Share
Potato products	11,140.4	30.45%
Plain vegetables	4,118.7	11.26
Entrees	3,216.4	8.79
Meat	2,999.1	8.20
Pizza/crusts	1,970.7	5.39
Juices	1,944.9	5.32
Fish and seafood	1,825.0	4.99
Dinners	1,479.4	4.04
Dessert pies	1,003.4	2.74
Other	6,893.4	18.84

Source: *Quick Frozen Foods International*, October 2002, p. 150, from U.S. Bureau of the Census and Information Resources Inc.

★ 275 ★
Frozen Foods (SIC 2038)

Leading Frozen Meatless Entree Producers, 2002

Market shares are shown based on supermarket sales for the year ended February 24, 2002.

Kellogg Co.	56.5%
Kraft/Boca Foods	22.8
Wholesome & Hearty Foods	16.5
Lightlife Foods	1.3
Amy's Kitchen	1.0
Other	1.9

Source: *Refrigerated & Frozen Foods*, June 2002, p. 60, from Information Resources Inc. InfoScan.

★ 276 ★

Frozen Foods (SIC 2038)

Top Frozen Appetizer Brands, 2002

Brands are ranked by sales in millions of dollars for the year ended May 19, 2002.

	($ mil.)	Share
Totino's Pizza Rolls	$ 152.25	20.86%
Bagel Bites	97.09	13.30
T.G.I. Friday's	71.10	9.74
Delimex	50.43	6.91
Poppers	37.95	5.20
El Monterey	27.22	3.73
Pagoda Cafe	20.03	2.74
Jose Ole Mexi Minis	19.79	2.71
Hot Bites	17.55	2.40
Private label	30.09	4.12
Other	206.25	28.26

Source: *Frozen Food Age*, August 2002, p. 48, from Information Resources Inc.

★ 277 ★

Frozen Foods (SIC 2038)

Top Frozen Appetizer Makers, 2002

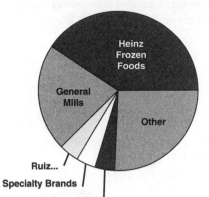

Market shares are shown based on supermarket sales for the year ended February 24, 2002.

Heinz Frozen Foods	41.2%
General Mills	21.8
Ruiz Food Products	3.9
Specialty Brands	3.8
Private label	3.7
Other	25.6

Source: *Refrigerated & Frozen Foods*, June 2002, p. 82, from Information Resources Inc.

★ 278 ★

Frozen Foods (SIC 2038)

Top Frozen Hand-Held Entree Brands, 2002

Brands are ranked by sales in millions of dollars for the year ended May 19, 2002.

	($ mil.)	Share
Hot Pockets	$ 249.18	25.76%
Lean Pockets	133.31	13.78
Croissant Pockets	87.08	9.00
State Fair	59.24	6.12
El Monterey	53.26	5.51
Foster Farms	40.71	4.21
White Castle	36.68	3.79
Tinas	34.19	3.53
Jose Ole	21.05	2.18
Private label	26.84	2.77
Other	225.78	23.34

Source: *Frozen Food Age*, August 2002, p. 48, from Information Resources Inc.

★ 279 ★
Frozen Foods (SIC 2038)

Top Frozen Hand-Held Entree Makers, 2002

Market shares are shown based on supermarket sales for the year ended February 24, 2002.

Chef America	48.8%
Camino Real Foods	6.1
State Fair Foods	5.8
Ruiz Food Products	5.7
Foster Farms	4.2
Other	29.4

Source: *Refrigerated & Frozen Foods*, June 2002, p. 62, from Information Resources Inc. InfoScan.

★ 280 ★
Frozen Foods (SIC 2038)

Top Frozen Potato Makers, 2002

Market shares are shown based on supermarket sales for the year ended February 24, 2002.

Heinz Frozen Food	53.6%
Lamb-Weston	6.6
McCain	2.9
Lynder Earns	1.1
Private label	30.3
Other	5.5

Source: *Refrigerated & Frozen Foods*, June 2002, p. 46, from Information Resources Inc. InfoScan.

★ 281 ★
Frozen Foods (SIC 2038)

Top Frozen Waffle Makers, 2002

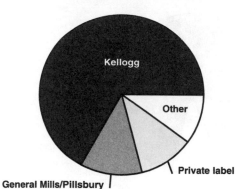

Market shares are shown based on supermarket sales for the year ended February 24, 2002.

Kellogg	67.0%
General Mills/Pillsbury	11.8
Private label	11.4
Other	9.8

Source: *Refrigerated & Frozen Foods*, June 2002, p. 54, from Information Resources Inc. InfoScan.

★ 282 ★
Frozen Foods (SIC 2038)

Top Pizza Makers (Frozen), 2002

Market shares are for the year ended December 29, 2002.

Kraft/Tombstone	32.4%
Tony's Pizza	29.0
Pillsbury	8.6
Kraft/Jack's	6.8
Nestle USA	4.2
Aurora Foods	2.8
Weight Watchers	1.4
McCain Ellio's Foods	1.2
Armour Swift-Eckrich	1.0
Private label	5.9
Other	6.7

Source: *Snack Food & Wholesale Bakery*, February 2003, p. 14, from Information Resources Inc.

★ 283 ★

Frozen Foods (SIC 2038)

Top Pot Pie Brands, 2002

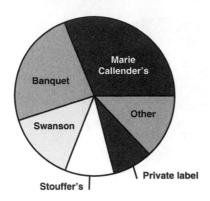

Brands are ranked by sales for the 12 weeks ended October 6, 2002.

	($ mil.)	Share
Marie Callender's	$ 18.19	30.79%
Banquet	14.16	23.97
Swanson	8.17	13.83
Stouffer's	6.14	10.39
Private label	4.95	8.38
Other	7.47	12.64

Source: *Frozen Food Age*, January 2003, p. 16, from Information Resources Inc.

★ 284 ★

Baking Supplies (SIC 2040)

Baking Supply Sales

Sales are shown in millions of dollars.

Stuffing products	$ 253.73
Frosting, ready-to-spread	247.03
Breading products	228.82
Chocolate chips & morsels	199.88
Croutons	133.49
Cake decorations & icing	118.05
Pie & pastry shells-prepared	69.21
Yeast-dry	63.02
Baking chips, non-chocolate	62.31
Baking chocolate	49.17
Baking chips, milk chocolate	49.12
Baking soda	43.51

Source: *Progressive Grocer*, September 15, 2002, p. 24, from *Progressive Grocer's 55th Annual Consumers Expenditures Study*.

★ 285 ★

Flour (SIC 2041)

Flour Sales by Type

Sales are shown in millions of dollars.

	($ mil.)	Share
All purpose, white wheat	$ 264.63	67.33%
Corn meal	80.56	20.50
Single-purpose	28.43	7.23
All purpose, remaining	19.43	4.94

Source: *Progressive Grocer*, September 15, 2002, p. 24.

★ 286 ★

Cereal (SIC 2043)

Top Breakfast Cereal Brands, 2002

Shares are shown for the year ended February 24, 2002. Figures exclude Wal-Mart. The top producers are Kellogg's, General Mills and Post.

Cheerios	5.0%
Frosted Flakes	4.2
Honey Nut Cheerios	3.2
Frosted Mini-Wheats	2.8
Cinnamon Toast Crunch	2.7
Raisin Bran	2.6
Corn Flakes	2.4
Lucky Charms	2.4
Honey Bunches of Oats	2.1
Rice Krispies	2.0
Special K	1.8
Life	1.8
Private label	7.7
Other	59.3

Source: *Progressive Grocer*, May 1, 2002, p. 70, from Information Resources Inc.

★ 287 ★

Cookie Mixes (SIC 2045)

Cookie Mix Market

Market shares are shown in percent.

Betty Crocker	81.0%
Other	19.0

Source: *DSN Retailing Today*, November 11, 2002, p. S10.

★ 288 ★
Dough (SIC 2045)

Best-Selling Biscuit Doughs, 2002

Brands are ranked by sales in millions of dollars for the 12 weeks ended October 6, 2002.

	($ mil.)	Share
Pillsbury Grands	$ 33.74	38.24%
Pillsbury Hungry Jack	11.18	12.67
Pillsbury	8.28	9.38
Pillsbury Big Country	4.98	5.64
Private label	24.34	27.59
Other	5.71	6.47

Source: *Frozen Food Age*, January 2003, p. 19, from Information Resources Inc.

★ 289 ★
Corn Refining (SIC 2046)

High Fructose Corn Syrup Industry

Shares are shown based on North American capacity.

Cargill/Cerestar	32.0%
ADM	26.0
Corn Products/MCP	20.0
AE Stanley	19.0
Roquette	3.0

Source: *Chemical Market Reporter*, July 17, 2002, p. FR3, from Salomon Smith Barney.

★ 290 ★
Pet Food (SIC 2047)

Fish Food Market

Market shares are shown in percent. Hartz Mountain is second in the segment. Tetra has 37% of the market for aquariums and pond-related equipment.

Tetra	48.0%
Other	52.0

Source: *Roanoke Times*, June 9, 2003, p. 14.

★ 291 ★
Pet Food (SIC 2047)

Pet Food Sales

Sales are shown in millions of dollars. Figures are for supermarkets, drug stores and discount stores and exclude Wal-Mart.

	($ mil.)	Share
Dog food, dry	$ 1,610.0	37.05%
Cat food, dry	1,020.0	23.47
Dog & cat treats	711.8	16.38
Dog food, wet	690.2	15.88
Dog food, moist	60.4	1.39
Cat food, moist	14.3	0.33
Other	238.5	5.49

Source: *MMR*, November 4, 2002, p. 25, from A.C. Nielsen.

★ 292 ★
Pet Food (SIC 2047)

Wet Cat Food Market

Market shares are shown in percent. Friskies has 49.3% of the dry cat food market.

Friskies	60.0%
Other	40.0

Source: *Brandweek*, May 5, 2003, p. 4.

★ 293 ★
Bakery Products (SIC 2050)

Largest Baked Goods Producers, 2002

Companies are ranked by estimated sales in millions of dollars.

General Mills	$ 1,700
Sara Lee US Foods	1,300
Mrs. Smith's	608
Rich Products Corp.	580
Otis Spunkmeyer	280
Edwards Fine Foods	210
Aurora Foods Inc.	205
SCIS Food Services Inc.	200
The Bama Cos.	180
Country Home Bakers	170

Source: *Refrigerated & Frozen Foods*, February 2002, p. 38.

★ 294 ★

Bakery Products (SIC 2050)

Top Bakery Product Sales at Wal-Mart, 2002

Sales are shown in millions of dollars for the year ended October 5, 2002.

Fresh bread	$ 596.92
Fresh cakes	429.12
Fresh buns	125.69
Fresh doughnuts	109.21
Fresh breakfast cakes/sweet rolls	98.86
Fresh rolls	72.98
Fresh muffins	69.67
Fresh pies	65.01
Refrigerated biscuits	63.38
Frozen biscuits/rolls/muffins	60.00

Source: *Supermarket News*, December 2, 2002, p. 48, from A.C. Nielsen.

★ 295 ★

Bagels (SIC 2051)

Top Frozen Bagel Brands, 2002

Market shares are shown based on supermarket sales for the year ended July 14, 2002. Figures exclude Wal-Mart.

Lenders	48.9%
Lenders Big'n Crusty	25.0
Private label	13.3
Other	12.8

Source: *Snack Food & Wholesale Bakery*, September 2002, p. 14, from Information Resources Inc.

★ 296 ★

Bagels (SIC 2051)

Top Frozen Bagel Makers, 2002

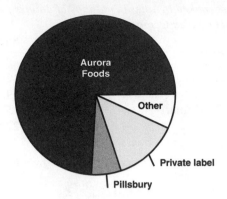

Market shares are shown based on sales for the year ended July 14, 2002. Figures exclude Wal-Mart.

Aurora Foods	73.9%
Pillsbury	6.3
Private label	13.3
Other	6.5

Source: *Snack Food & Wholesale Bakery*, September 2002, p. 14, from Information Resources Inc.

★ 297 ★

Bread (SIC 2051)

Bread Market in the Texas Metroplex Area

Market shares are shown in percent.

Mrs. Baird's	38.0%
Earth Grains	17.0
Other	55.0

Source: *Knight-Ridder/Tribune Business News*, October 16, 2002, p. NA, from Information Resources Inc.

★ 298 ★
Bread (SIC 2051)

Leading Frozen Bread/Roll/Pastry Makers, 2002

Market shares are shown based on supermarket sales for the year ended February 24, 2002.

General Mills	37.6%
Rhodes International	27.7
Hom'ade Foods	8.3
Bridgford Foods	5.3
Private label	6.3
Other	14.8

Source: *Refrigerated & Frozen Foods*, June 2002, p. 30, from Information Resources Inc. InfoScan.

★ 299 ★
Bread (SIC 2051)

Top Bread Makers

Market shares are shown in percent.

Interstate Brands Corp.	14.8%
Sara Lee Bakery Group	10.1
Pepperidge Farm	4.8
General Mills	1.7
Private label	28.4
Other	40.2

Source: *St. Louis Post-Dispatch*, December 12, 2002, p. C14, from Information Resources Inc.

★ 300 ★
Bread (SIC 2051)

Top Fresh Bread Brands, 2002

Market shares are shown based on supermarket sales for the year ended June 23, 2002.

Wonder	5.6%
Oroweat	4.8
Pepperidge Farm	4.7
Nature's Own	4.0
Sunbeam	3.1
Home Pride	3.0
Arnold	2.9

Merita	2.1%
Stroehmann	1.7
Private label	27.0
Other	41.1

Source: *Snack Food & Wholesale Bakery*, August 2002, p. 10, from Information Resources Inc.

★ 301 ★
Bread (SIC 2051)

Top Fresh Bread Brands by Unit Sales, 2002

Market shares are shown based on supermarket sales for the year ended November 11, 2002.

	(mil.)	Share
Wonder	175.0	5.00%
Nature's Own	104.2	2.98
Oroweat	89.0	2.54
Home Pride	82.3	2.35
Sunbeam	74.0	2.11
Arnold	66.4	1.90
Mrs. Baird's	56.6	1.62
Merita	55.3	1.58
Freihofer	41.7	1.19
Pepperidge Farm	36.5	1.04
Brownberry	36.3	1.04
Private label	1,440.0	41.14
Other	1,242.7	35.51

Source: *Progressive Grocer*, February 1, 2003, p. 53, from Information Resources Inc.

★ 302 ★
Bread (SIC 2051)

Top Frozen Bread/Roll Brands, 2001

Market shares are shown in percent.

Pepperidge Farm	23.9%
New York	22.8
Cole's	16.0
Mamma Bella	7.4
Private label	9.7
Other	20.2

Source: *Snack Food & Wholesale Bakery*, June 2002, pp. SI-39, from Information Resources Inc.

★ 303 ★
Buns (SIC 2051)

Top Hamburger/Hot Dog Bun Brands, 2002

Market shares are shown based on supermarket sales for the year ended June 23, 2002.

Wonder	6.0%
Rainbo	3.5
Private label	47.2
Other	43.3

Source: *Snack Food & Wholesale Bakery*, August 2002, p. 10, from Information Resources Inc.

★ 304 ★
Pastries (SIC 2051)

Top Donut Brands, 2002

Brands are ranked by supermarket sales for the year ended September 15, 2002.

	($ mil.)	Share
Entenmann's Donuts	$ 144.9	22.76%
Krispy Kreme Donuts	138.3	21.72
Hostess Donuts	93.1	14.62
Dolly Madison Donuts	38.4	6.03
Little Debbie Donuts	16.9	2.65
Freihofer Donuts	13.8	2.17
Merita Donuts	12.1	1.90
Metz Brands Donuts	9.6	1.51
BreakCake Donuts	9.0	1.41
Private label	93.2	14.64
Other	67.3	10.57

Source: *Baking & Snack*, November 1, 2002, p. NA, from Information Resources Inc.

★ 305 ★
Pastries (SIC 2051)

Top Fresh Coffee Cake Brands, 2001

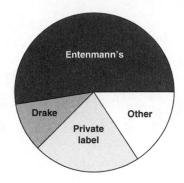

Market shares are shown based on supermarket sales for the year ended December 30, 2001.

Entenmann's	52.7%
Drake	10.0
Private label	21.7
Other	15.6

Source: *Snack Food & Wholesale Bakery*, June 2002, pp. SI-31, from Information Resources Inc.

★ 306 ★
Pastries (SIC 2051)

Top Fresh Danish Brands, 2001

Market shares are shown based on supermarket sales for the year ended December 30, 2001.

Entenmann's	37.5%
Svenhards	26.7
Private label	18.0
Other	17.8

Source: *Snack Food & Wholesale Bakery*, June 2002, pp. SI-31, from Information Resources Inc.

★ 307 ★
Pastries (SIC 2051)

Top Fresh Muffin Brands, 2002

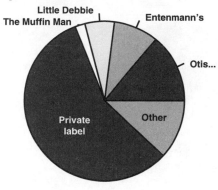

Market shares are shown based on supermarket sales for the year ended October 13, 2002. Figures exclude Wal-Mart.

Otis Spunkmeyer	14.4%
Entenmann's	8.9
Little Debbie	6.2
The Muffin Man	1.6
Private label	56.9
Other	12.0

Source: *Snack Food & Wholesale Bakery*, December 2002, p. 14, from Information Resources Inc.

★ 308 ★
Rolls (SIC 2051)

Top Dinner Roll/Biscuit Brands, 2002

Market shares are shown based on supermarket sales for the year ended June 23, 2002.

Kings Hawaiian	4.3%
Sunbeam	3.4
Private label	33.3
Other	59.0

Source: *Snack Food & Wholesale Bakery*, August 2002, p. 10, from Information Resources Inc.

★ 309 ★
Snack Cakes (SIC 2051)

Top Snack Cake Brands, 2003

Market shares are shown based on supermarket sales for the year ended January 26, 2003.

Little Debbie	31.8%
Hostess	31.4
Tastykake	9.8
Drake	6.1
Dolly Madison	1.9
Entenmann's	1.8
Freeds Bakery	1.5
Marinela	0.8
Blue Bird	0.7
Private label	10.3
Other	3.9

Source: *Snack Food & Wholesale Bakery*, March 2003, p. 12, from Information Resources Inc.

★ 310 ★
Snack Cakes (SIC 2051)

Top Snack Cake Makers in the Northeast

Market shares are shown in percent.

Interstate	45.0%
Tasty Baking	24.9
Other	31.1

Source: *Knight Ridder/Tribune Business News*, August 18, 2002, p. NA.

★ 311 ★
Cookies (SIC 2052)

Top Cookie Brands, 2002

Market shares are shown based on $4 billion in sales across supermarket, drug store and mass merchandiser channels (except for Wal-Mart). Sales are for the year ended December 1, 2002.

Nabisco Oreo	13.6%
Nabisco Chips Ahoy	8.9
Keebler Chips Deluxe	3.9
Nabisco Newtons	3.4
Pepperidge Farm Distinctive Cookies	2.9
Keebler Fudge Shoppe	2.9
Nabisco Teddy Grahams	2.6
Nabisco SnackWell's	2.5

Continued on next page.

★ 311 ★ *Continued*
Cookies (SIC 2052)

Top Cookie Brands, 2002

Market shares are shown based on $4 billion in sales across supermarket, drug store and mass merchandiser channels (except for Wal-Mart). Sales are for the year ended December 1, 2002.

Nabisco Nilla	2.1%
Pepperidge Farm Classics	2.1
Private label	8.3
Other	46.8

Source: *Snack Food & Wholesale Bakery*, January 2003, p. 12, from Information Resources Inc.

★ 312 ★
Cookies (SIC 2052)

Top Cookie Vendors, 2002

Sales are shown for the year ended August 11, 2002. Figures do not include Wal-Mart.

	($ mil.)	Share
Nabisco	$ 1,511.0	38.50%
Keebler	543.1	13.84
Parmalat Bakery Division	303.8	7.74
Pepperidge Farm	255.2	6.50
Little Debbie	196.3	5.00
Murray (Keebler/Kellogg)	186.2	4.74
Voortman	61.5	1.57
Stella D'oro	41.9	1.07
Mrs. Field's	37.8	0.96
Private label	334.3	8.52
Other	453.3	11.55

Source: *Baking & Snack*, October 1, 2002, p. NA, from Information Resources Inc.

★ 313 ★
Crackers (SIC 2052)

Top Cracker Vendors

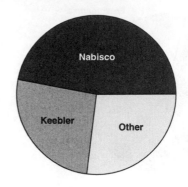

Market shares are shown in percent.

	2001	2002
Nabisco	47.7%	47.1%
Keebler	26.4	26.1
Other	25.9	26.8

Source: *Crain's Chicago Business*, August 5, 2002, p. 1, from Information Resources Inc.

★ 314 ★
Frozen Bakery Products (SIC 2053)

Top Frozen Pie Brands, 2001

Market shares are shown in percent.

Mrs. Smith's	32.6%
Sara Lee	16.0
Edwards	10.9
Marie Callender's	8.8
Mrs. Smith's Special Recipe	6.9
Other	24.8

Source: *Snack Food & Wholesale Bakery*, June 2002, pp. SI-39, from Information Resources Inc.

★ 315 ★
Frozen Bakery Products (SIC 2053)

Top Frozen Pie Makers, 2002

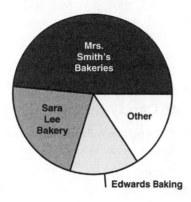

Market shares are shown based on supermarket sales for the year ended February 24, 2002.

Mrs. Smith's Bakeries	48.7%
Sara Lee Bakery	21.5
Edwards Baking	14.3
Other	15.5

Source: *Refrigerated & Frozen Foods*, June 2002, p. 30, from Information Resources Inc. InfoScan.

★ 316 ★
Breath Fresheners (SIC 2064)

Best-Selling Breath Freshener (Spray/ Drop) Brands, 2002

Brands are ranked by sales in millions of units for the year ended February 24, 2002. Figures include supermarkets, drug stores and discount stores but exclude Wal-Mart.

	(mil.)	Share
Tic Tac	94.3	34.62%
Altoids	48.6	17.84
Breathsavers	43.3	15.90
Certs Cool Mint Drops	21.9	8.04
Certs Powerful Mints	11.4	4.19
Breathsavers Ice Breakers	10.2	3.74
Other	42.7	15.68

Source: *MMR*, April 22, 2002, p. 57, from Information Resources Inc.

★ 317 ★
Breath Fresheners (SIC 2064)

Portable Oral Care Industry

The $190.5 million market is shown by company.

Pfizer	70.6%
Wrigley's	12.6
Other	16.8

Source: *Arizona Republic*, February 23, 2003, p. D1, from Information Resources Inc.

★ 318 ★
Breath Fresheners (SIC 2064)

Top Breath Freshener Brands, 2002

Market shares are shown for the year ended April 21, 2002. Figures exclude Wal-Mart.

	($ mil.)	Share
Altoids	$ 95.3	31.03%
Tic Tac	64.8	21.10
Breathsavers	34.9	11.36
Breathsavers Ice Breakers	22.1	7.20
Certs Cool Mint Drops	20.2	6.58
Certs Powerful Mints	17.3	5.63
Smint	7.7	2.51
Mentos Cool Chews	7.3	2.38
Certs	5.2	1.69
Private label	8.2	2.67
Other	24.1	7.85

Source: *Candy Industry*, July 2002, p. 32, from Information Resources Inc.

★ 319 ★
Breath Fresheners (SIC 2064)

Top Breath Freshener Makers, 2002

Shares are shown based on sales at grocery, drug and mass market outlets (but not Wal-Mart) for the year ended October 6, 2002.

Philip Morris Co. Inc.	30.6%
Hershey Foods Corp.	21.4
Ferrero USA Inc.	21.0
Pfizer Inc.	12.2
Chups Chups USA	2.7
Perfetti Van Melle	2.1

Continued on next page.

★ 319 ★ *Continued*

Breath Fresheners (SIC 2064)

Top Breath Freshener Makers, 2002

Shares are shown based on sales at grocery, drug and mass market outlets (but not Wal-Mart) for the year ended October 6, 2002.

Wm. Wrigley Jr. Co.	1.8%
Hampton Assn. & Son Inc.	1.4
Blitz Design Corp.	1.4
Other	5.4

Source: *The Manufacturing Confectioner*, January 2003, p. 24, from Information Resources Inc. InfoScan.

★ 320 ★

Confectionery Products (SIC 2064)

Cordial Cherry Market

The company manufactures the Queen Anne brand of cherries, jubilees and truffles. Market shares are shown in percent.

Gray & Company	71.0%
Other	29.0

Source: "American Marketing Association." available April 7, 2003 from http://www.ama-pdx.org/ event_detail.asp.

★ 321 ★

Confectionery Products (SIC 2064)

Leading Chewy Candy Producers

Masterfoods	
Kraft Confections	
Hershey Foods	
Tootsie Roll Inds.	
Brach's Confections	
Van Melle	
Private label	
Other	

Market shares are shown for the year ended March 24, 2002. Figures exclude Wal-Mart.

Masterfoods	21.1%
Kraft Confections	15.6
Hershey Foods	10.5
Tootsie Roll Inds.	6.9
Brach's Confections	6.0

Van Melle	5.4%
Private label	6.4
Other	28.0

Source: *Candy Industry*, May 2002, p. 34, from Information Resources Inc.

★ 322 ★

Confectionery Products (SIC 2064)

Non-Chocolate Candy Sales, 2002

Total sales reached $2.4 billion for the year ended December 29, 2002. Figures exclude Wal-Mart.

Chewy	26.7%
Hard sugar packaged/roll	13.5
Breath fresheners	12.0
Novelty	11.0
Licorice box/bag > 3.5 oz.	6.5
Plain mints	5.5
Easter	4.7
Christmas	4.2
Valentine	3.3
Caramel and taffy apples/apple kits	2.9
Halloween	2.8
Other	6.9

Source: *Candy Business*, January-February 2003, p. 10, from Information Resources Inc.

★ 323 ★

Confectionery Products (SIC 2064)

Top Candy/Gum Brands in Drug Stores, 2001

Brands are ranked by drug store sales in millions of dollars for the year ended December 30, 2001.

	($ mil.)	Share
Altoids (breath fresheners)	$ 34.2	1.77%
Wrigleys Extra (sugarless gum) . .	29.8	1.54
Hersheys (chocolate candy) . . .	28.7	1.49
M&Ms (chocolate candy)	27.6	1.43
Lifesavers Creme Savers (hard candy)	25.0	1.30
M&Ms (chocolate candy)	21.6	1.12
Trident (sugarless gum)	20.9	1.08

Continued on next page.

★ 323 ★ *Continued*
Confectionery Products (SIC 2064)

Top Candy/Gum Brands in Drug Stores, 2001

Brands are ranked by drug store sales in millions of dollars for the year ended December 30, 2001.

	($ mil.)	Share
Tic Tac (breath fresheners)	$ 18.8	0.97%
Dentyne Ice (sugarless gum) . . .	17.8	0.92
Starburst (non-chocolate candy) . .	16.7	0.87
Other	1,689.2	87.51

Source: *Drug Store News*, May 20, 2002, p. 43, from Information Resources Inc.

★ 324 ★
Confectionery Products (SIC 2064)

Top Candy Makers, 2002

Market shares are shown for the year ended August 11, 2002. Data exclude Wal-Mart.

Hershey	30.0%
Mars	17.1
Wrigley	6.7
Nestle	6.5
Philip Morris	6.3
Russell Stover Candies	4.8
Pfizer	3.5
Other	25.1

Source: *Wall Street Journal*, September 19, 2002, p. B1, from Information Resources Inc.

★ 325 ★
Confectionery Products (SIC 2064)

Top Christmas Candy Brands, 2002

Brands are ranked by sales in millions of dollars for the year ended January 27, 2002. Figures exclude Wal-mart.

	($ mil.)	Share
M&Ms	$ 67.3	20.68%
Hershey's Kisses	47.8	14.69
Reese's	32.3	9.92
Hershey Seasonal Chocolate . . .	31.2	9.59
Snickers	14.1	4.33
York Peppermint Patty	10.1	3.10
Russell Stover Seasonal Candy . .	9.9	3.04
Hershey's Nuggets	7.8	2.40
Other	105.0	32.26

Source: *Professional Candy Buyer*, May-June 2002, p. 38, from Information Resources Inc.

★ 326 ★
Confectionery Products (SIC 2064)

Top Christmas Candy Suppliers, 2002

Shares are for the 52 weeks ended January 27, 2002. Wal-Mart is not included. Figures are for seasonally wrapped products.

	($ mil.)	Share
Hershey Foods Corp.	$ 149.88	46.04%
Masterfoods USA	101.82	31.28
Nestle S.A.	15.71	4.83
Russell Stover Candies	12.73	3.91
R.M. Palmer Co.	12.60	3.87
Frankford Candy & Chocolate . .	4.14	1.27
Thomas Lee Candies	3.95	1.21
Ferrero USA Inc.	3.39	1.04
Other	21.34	6.55

Source: *Professional Candy Buyer*, March/April 2002, p. NA, from Information Resources Inc.

★ 327 ★
Confectionery Products (SIC 2064)

Top Easter Candy Brands, 2001

Shares are for the 52 weeks ended May 19, 2002. Wal-Mart is not included. Figures are seasonally wrapped products.

	($ mil.)	Share
M&M's	$ 56.77	12.42%
Reese's	48.78	10.67
Hershey's	33.20	7.26
Russell Stover	28.61	6.26
Cadbury Creme Egg	19.60	4.29
Cadbury	16.18	3.54
Leaf Robin Eggs	15.83	3.46
Cadbury Mini Eggs	14.96	3.27
Dove	14.76	3.23
Other	208.31	45.58

Source: *Professional Candy Buyer*, July/August 2002, p. NA, from Information Resources Inc.

★ 328 ★
Confectionery Products (SIC 2064)

Top Fruit Snack Brands, 2002

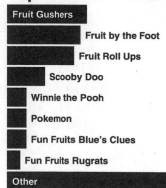

Shares are shown based on sales at grocery, drug and mass market outlets (but not Wal-Mart) for the year ended October 6, 2002.

Fruit Gushers	12.9%
Fruit by the Foot	12.2
Fruit Roll Ups	11.3
Scooby Doo	5.8
Winnie the Pooh	3.4
Pokemon	2.9
Fun Fruits Blue's Clues	2.7
Fun Fruits Rugrats	2.1
Other	46.7

Source: *The Manufacturing Confectioner*, January 2003, p. 24, from Information Resources Inc. InfoScan.

★ 329 ★
Confectionery Products (SIC 2064)

Top Fruit Snack Suppliers, 2002

Shares are shown based on sales for the year ended July 14, 2002. Data exclude Wal-Mart.

	($ mil.)	Share
General Mills	$ 325.02	65.23%
Kraft Foods North America . . .	67.33	13.51
Brach Confections	45.12	9.06
McKee Foods Corp.	8.11	1.63
Stretch Foods Corp.	4.07	0.82
Ferrera Pan Candy Co.	1.73	0.35
Grist Mill Co.	1.40	0.28
Promotion in Motion Cos. Inc. . .	1.31	0.26
Paramount Farms	1.09	0.22
Private label	41.20	8.27
Other	1.90	0.38

Source: *Professional Candy Buyer*, September 2002, p. 13, from Information Resources Inc.

★ 330 ★
Confectionery Products (SIC 2064)

Top Halloween Candies, 2001

The typical household buys 3 to 5 bags around the holidays. Shoppers prefer familiar brands that they like so they can eat the leftovers. Only 8% of households hand out full-size bars. Market shares are shown in percent.

Snickers chocolate candy	14.2%
Reese's Peanut Butter Cups	13.1
Kit Kat Chocolate candy	10.6
Milky Way	6.2
M&Ms	6.0
Other	49.9

Source: *USA TODAY*, October 29, 2002, p. B1, from Information Resources Inc.

★ 331 ★
Confectionery Products (SIC 2064)

Top Halloween Candy Suppliers, 2001

Wal-Mart is not included. Figures are for seasonally wrapped products.

Hershey Chocolate	56.8%
M&M/Mars Inc.	25.6

Continued on next page.

★ 331 ★ *Continued*
Confectionery Products (SIC 2064)

Top Halloween Candy Suppliers, 2001

Wal-Mart is not included. Figures are for seasonally wrapped products.

R.M. Palmer Co.	8.5%
Russell Stover Candies Inc.	3.3
Nestle USA	2.4
Whitman's Chocolates	1.1
Frankford Candy & Chocolate	1.1
Bortz Chocolate Co.	0.3
Archibald Candy Corp.	0.2
Other	0.7

Source: *Professional Candy Buyer*, March/April 2002, p. NA, from Information Resources Inc.

★ 332 ★
Confectionery Products (SIC 2064)

Top Licorice Box/Bag (> 3.5 oz) Brands, 2002

Shares are shown based on sales at grocery, drug and mass market outlets (but not Wal-Mart) for the year ended October 6, 2002.

Y&S Twizzler	61.8%
American Licorice	20.6
Good & Plenty	7.1
Kenny's	3.4
Bassett's	2.1
Private label	0.8
Other	4.2

Source: *The Manufacturing Confectioner*, January 2003, p. 24, from Information Resources Inc. InfoScan.

★ 333 ★
Confectionery Products (SIC 2064)

Top Licorice Box/Bag (> 3.5 oz) Makers, 2002

Shares are shown based on sales at grocery, drug and mass market outlets (but not Wal-Mart) for the year ended October 6, 2002.

Hershey Foods Corp.	70.1%
American Licorice Co.	20.6
KLN Enterprise	3.4
Trebor Bassett Ltd.	2.1
Panda Choc-Finnfoods	0.7
Private label	0.8
Other	2.3

Source: *The Manufacturing Confectioner*, January 2003, p. 24, from Information Resources Inc. InfoScan.

★ 334 ★
Confectionery Products (SIC 2064)

Top Marshmallow Brands, 2002

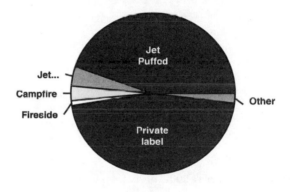

Shares are shown based on sales at grocery, drug and mass market outlets (but not Wal-Mart) for the year ended October 6, 2002.

Jet Puffed	44.5%
Jet Puffed Funmallows	4.1
Campfire	2.8
Fireside	1.3
Private label	45.6
Other	1.7

Source: *The Manufacturing Confectioner*, January 2003, p. 24, from Information Resources Inc. InfoScan.

★ 335 ★

Confectionery Products (SIC 2064)

Top Marshmallow Makers, 2002

Shares are shown based on sales at grocery, drug and mass market outlets (but not Wal-Mart) for the year ended October 6, 2002.

Philip Morris Co. Inc. 49.4%
Conagra Inc. 2.9
Dournak Inc. 1.3
Private label 45.6
Other 0.8

Source: *The Manufacturing Confectioner*, January 2003, p. 24, from Information Resources Inc. InfoScan.

★ 336 ★

Confectionery Products (SIC 2064)

Top Non-Chocolate Candy Producers, 2002

Market shares are shown for the year ended July 14, 2002. Figures exclude Wal-Mart.

Hershey 15.1%
Kraft Foods 13.2
Masterfoods 8.4
Tootsie Roll 7.0
Nestle 5.9
Brach's 5.6
Just Born 2.8
Perfetti Van Melle 1.8
Private label 4.5
Other 35.7

Source: *Confectioner*, October 2002, p. 26, from Information Resources Inc.

★ 337 ★

Confectionery Products (SIC 2064)

Top Novelty Candy Producers, 2002

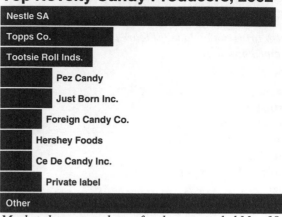

Market shares are shown for the year ended May 19, 2002. Figures exclude Wal-Mart.

Nestle SA 27.1%
Topps Co. 11.3
Tootsie Roll Inds. 9.4
Pez Candy 5.4
Just Born Inc. 4.5
Foreign Candy Co. 4.0
Hershey Foods 3.3
Ce De Candy Inc. 3.3
Private label 3.5
Other 28.2

Source: *Candy Industry*, July 2002, p. 39, from Information Resources Inc.

★ 338 ★

Confectionery Products (SIC 2064)

Top Ready-to-Eat Popcorn/Caramel Corn Brands, 2002

Shares are shown based on sales at grocery, drug and mass market outlets (but not Wal-Mart) for the year ended October 6, 2002.

Smart Food 12.3%
Houston Harvest 10.5
Cracker Jack 10.0
Poppycock 9.8
Crunch 'N Munch 9.5
Jays Oke Doke 4.1

Continued on next page.

★ 338 ★ *Continued*
Confectionery Products (SIC 2064)

Top Ready-to-Eat Popcorn/Caramel Corn Brands, 2002

Shares are shown based on sales at grocery, drug and mass market outlets (but not Wal-Mart) for the year ended October 6, 2002.

Wise	3.4%
Chesters	2.9
Fiddle Faddle	2.8
Other	34.7

Source: *The Manufacturing Confectioner*, January 2003, p. 24, from Information Resources Inc. InfoScan.

★ 339 ★
Confectionery Products (SIC 2064)

Top Ready-to-Eat Popcorn/Caramel Corn Makers, 2002

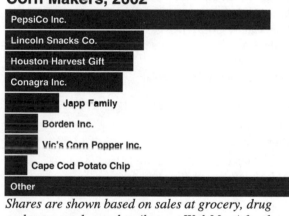

Shares are shown based on sales at grocery, drug and mass market outlets (but not Wal-Mart) for the year ended October 6, 2002.

PepsiCo Inc.	25.2%
Lincoln Snacks Co.	12.7
Houston Harvest Gift	11.8
Conagra Inc.	11.2
Japp Family	4.5
Borden Inc.	3.4
Vic's Corn Popper Inc.	2.8
Cape Cod Potato Chip	1.6
Other	26.8

Source: *The Manufacturing Confectioner*, January 2003, p. 24, from Information Resources Inc. InfoScan.

★ 340 ★
Confectionery Products (SIC 2064)

Top Specialty Nut/Coconut Candy Brands, 2002

Shares are shown based on sales at grocery, drug and mass market outlets (but not Wal-Mart) for the year ended October 6, 2002.

Leaf Pay Day	31.7%
Brach's Maple Nut Goodies	8.4
Pearsons	5.5
Sophie Mae	4.3
Planters	3.3
Brach's	3.2
Annabelle Big Hunk	2.3
Russell Stover	1.9
Boston Baked Beans	1.8
Other	37.6

Source: *The Manufacturing Confectioner*, January 2003, p. 24, from Information Resources Inc. InfoScan.

★ 341 ★
Confectionery Products (SIC 2064)

Top Specialty Nut/Coconut Candy Makers, 2002

Shares are shown based on sales at grocery, drug and mass market outlets (but not Wal-Mart) for the year ended October 6, 2002.

Hershey Foods Corp.	32.4%
Brach's Confections	11.6
Pearson Candy Co.	5.5
Philip Morris Co. Inc.	4.5
Fine Products Co. Inc.	4.3
Annabelle Candy Co. Inc.	2.3
Russell Stover Candies	1.9
Ferrara Pan Candy Co. inc.	1.8
Old Dominion Foods Inc.	1.6
Other	34.1

Source: *The Manufacturing Confectioner*, January 2003, p. 24, from Information Resources Inc. InfoScan.

★ 342 ★
Confectionery Products (SIC 2064)

Top Sugarfree/Sugarless Candy Brands, 2002

Shares are shown based on sales at grocery, drug and mass market outlets (but not Wal-Mart) for the year ended October 6, 2002.

Russell Stover	31.2%
Sweet 'N Low	10.9
Estee	7.0
Life Savers Delites	5.5
Fifty50	5.3
Go Lightly	4.6
Pure Delite	2.2
Sqyntz	2.1
Sorbee	1.7
Private label	7.8
Other	21.7

Source: *The Manufacturing Confectioner*, January 2003, p. 24, from Information Resources Inc. InfoScan.

★ 343 ★
Confectionery Products (SIC 2064)

Top Sugarfree/Sugarless Candy Makers, 2002

Shares are shown based on sales at grocery, drug and mass market outlets (but not Wal-Mart) for the year ended October 6, 2002.

Russell Stover Candies Inc.	32.2%
Simply Lite	11.0
Philip Morris Co. Inc.	7.3
The Hain Celestial Group	7.1
Fifty50	5.3
Hillside Candy Company	4.6

Sorbee International	2.4%
Pure Delite Products	2.2
Hampton Assn. & Son Inc.	2.1
Private label	7.8
Other	18.0

Source: *The Manufacturing Confectioner*, January 2003, p. 24, from Information Resources Inc. InfoScan.

★ 344 ★
Confectionery Products (SIC 2064)

Top Valentine's Day Candy Suppliers, 2002

Shares are for the 52 weeks ended February 24, 2002. Wal-Mart is not included. Figures are for seasonally wrapped products.

	($ mil.)	Share
Hershey Foods Corp.	$ 97.78	32.41%
Russell Stover Candies	70.64	23.42
Masterfoods USA	59.15	19.61
Elmer Candy Corp.	17.95	5.95
Nestle S.A.	15.45	5.12
R.M. Palmer Co.	12.62	4.18
Frankford Candy & Chocolate	4.65	1.54
Ferrero USA Inc.	4.45	1.48
Maxfield Candy	3.23	1.07
Galerie Au Chocolate Inc.	2.21	0.73
Other	13.53	4.49

Source: *Professional Candy Buyer*, March/April 2002, p. NA, from Information Resources Inc.

★ 345 ★
Cough Drops (SIC 2064)

Top Cough Drop Brands, 2002

Brands are ranked by sales in millions of units for the year ended February 24, 2002. Figures include supermarkets, drug stores and discount stores but exclude Wal-Mart.

	($ mil.)	Share
Halls	$ 101.2	28.62%
Ricola	34.7	9.81
Cold Eeze	25.1	7.10
Ludens	24.3	6.87
Halls Defense	22.1	6.25
Robitussin	12.3	3.48
Halls Plus	11.6	3.28
Secrets	11.6	3.28

Continued on next page.

★ 345 ★ *Continued*
Cough Drops (SIC 2064)

Top Cough Drop Brands, 2002

Brands are ranked by sales in millions of units for the year ended February 24, 2002. Figures include supermarkets, drug stores and discount stores but exclude Wal-Mart.

	($ mil.)	Share
Robitussin Honey	$ 11.0	3.11%
Vicks Chloraseptic	8.8	2.49
Private label	44.7	12.64
Other	46.2	13.07

Source: *MMR*, April 22, 2002, p. 57, from Information Resources Inc.

★ 346 ★
Cough Drops (SIC 2064)

Top Cough Drop Makers, 2002

Shares are shown based on sales at grocery, drug and mass market outlets (but not Wal-Mart) for the year ended October 6, 2002.

Pfizer Inc.	38.9%
Ricola Inc.	12.5
American Home Products	8.3
Hershey Foods Corp.	6.9
Quigley Corporation	6.7
Glaxo Smith Kline	4.8
Procter & Gamble	2.9
JB Williams Co.	2.6
Hain Celestial Group	1.8
Other	14.6

Source: *The Manufacturing Confectioner*, January 2003, p. 24, from Information Resources Inc. InfoScan.

★ 347 ★
Energy Bars (SIC 2064)

Energy Bar Segments, 2002

The category has evolved since PowerBar first hit shelves in 1987. It started as a nutritional supplement and is now turning into meal replacement and healthy snacking. Sales reached $580 million for the year ended October 5, 2002.

Diet	41.0%
Lifestyle/wellness	38.0
Athletic	21.0

Source: *Nutraceuticals World*, January 2003, p. 46, from SPINS.

★ 348 ★
Energy Bars (SIC 2064)

Top Energy Bar Makers

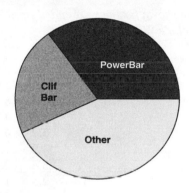

Market shares are shown in percent.

PowerBar	34.5%
Clif Bar	22.2
Other	43.3

Source: *San Francisco Chronicle*, April 27, 2003, p. 14, from A.C. Nielsen.

★ 349 ★
Mints (SIC 2064)

Top Mint Producers, 2002

Market shares are shown for the year ended July 14, 2002. Figures exclude Wal-Mart.

Kraft Foods	35.3%
Ferrero	15.8
Hershey	14.2
Adams	9.0

Continued on next page.

★ **349** ★ *Continued*

Mints (SIC 2064)

Top Mint Producers, 2002

Market shares are shown for the year ended July 14, 2002. Figures exclude Wal-Mart.

Perfetti Van Melle	5.5%
Brach's Confections	3.5
Chupa Chups	1.8
William Wrigley Jr.	1.1
Private label	5.4
Other	8.4

Source: *Confectioner*, October 2002, p. 26, from Information Resources Inc.

★ **350** ★

Mints (SIC 2064)

Top Plain Mint Brands, 2002

Market shares are shown for the year ended April 21, 2002. Figures exclude Wal-Mart.

	($ mil.)	Share
Lifesavers	$ 52.7	39.07%
Mentos	17.6	13.05
Brach's Star Brites	11.2	8.30
Farley's	6.6	4.89
Tic Tac Silvers	5.7	4.23
Brach's	4.9	3.63
Sathers	3.4	2.52
Skittles	2.5	1.85
Richardson	2.4	1.78
Other	27.9	20.68

Source: *Candy Industry*, July 2002, p. 32, from Information Resources Inc.

★ **351** ★

Snack Bars (SIC 2064)

Top Snack/Granola Bar Makers, 2002

Market shares are shown for the year ended March 24, 2002. Figures exclude Wal-Mart.

Kellogg	19.2%
Quaker Oats	17.9
General Mills	10.6
Slim Fast	7.8
McKee	6.3
Nestle USA	5.3
Clif Bar	4.4
Kraft Foods	3.3

Mars Inc.	2.7%
Richardson Labs	2.6
Other	19.9

Source: *Snack Food & Wholesale Bakery*, May 2002, p. 16, from Information Resources Inc.

★ **352** ★

Snack Bars (SIC 2064)

Top Snack/Granola Bars, 2002

Market shares are shown for the year ended October 5, 2002. Figures exclude Wal-Mart.

Quaker Chewy	11.1%
Kelloggs Nutri Grain	8.3
Nature Valley	8.2
Kelloggs Rice Krispie Treats	6.2
Slim Fast	4.2
Quaker Fruit & Oatmeal	4.0
General Mills Milk N Cereal	3.7
Sunbelt	3.6
Kudos	2.8
Clif Luna	2.7
Private label	4.9
Other	40.3

Source: *Candy Industry*, November 2002, p. 42, from Information Resources Inc.

★ **353** ★

Chocolate (SIC 2066)

Chocolate Candy Sales, 2002

Total sales reached $6.6 billion for the year ended December 29, 2002. Figures exclude Wal-Mart.

Box/bag/bar > 3.5 oz.	30.3%
Bar < 3.5 oz.	19.2
Snack size	15.5
Easter	10.9
Christmas	7.7
Valentine	7.4
Gift box chocolates	6.3
Halloween	2.0
All other seasonal	0.4
Novelty	0.2

Source: *Candy Business*, January-February 2003, p. 10, from Information Resources Inc.

★ 354 ★
Chocolate (SIC 2066)

Chocolate Market Leaders

Hershey	
Mars	
Nestle	
Other	

Market shares are shown in percent.

Hershey	. . . .	43.0%
Mars	. . . .	27.0
Nestle	. . . .	9.0
Other	. . . .	21.0

Source: *Financial Times*, September 3, 2002, p. 18, from Thomson Financial, Hershey Foods, and Vontobel Equity Research.

★ 355 ★
Chocolate (SIC 2066)

Top Chocolate Candy Bar (< 3.5 oz) Brands, 2002

Shares are shown based on sales at grocery, drug and mass market outlets (but not Wal-Mart) for the year ended October 6, 2002.

M&Ms	. . . .	12.2%
Hershey's	. . . .	10.4
Reese's	. . . .	6.9
Snickers	. . . .	6.9
Kit Kat	. . . .	5.0
Twix	. . . .	4.0
Butterfinger	. . . .	3.3
York Peppermint Patty	. . . .	3.0
Peter Paul Almond Joy	. . . .	2.9
Reese's Fast Break	. . . .	2.9
Other	. . . .	42.5

Source: *The Manufacturing Confectioner*, January 2003, p. 24, from Information Resources Inc. InfoScan.

★ 356 ★
Chocolate (SIC 2066)

Top Chocolate Candy Bar Snack/Fun Size Brands, 2002

Shares are shown based on sales at grocery, drug and mass market outlets (but not Wal-Mart) for the year ended October 6, 2002.

Snickers	. . . .	14.3%
Reese's	. . . .	13.2
Kit Kat	. . . .	10.5
Milky Way	. . . .	6.4
M&Ms	. . . .	5.8
Butterfinger	. . . .	5.7
Three Musketeers	. . . .	5.3
Nestle Crunch	. . . .	4.2
Peter Paul Almond Joy	. . . .	4.0
Hershey's	. . . .	3.7
Other	. . . .	26.9

Source: *The Manufacturing Confectioner*, January 2003, p. 24, from Information Resources Inc. InfoScan.

★ 357 ★
Chocolate (SIC 2066)

Top Chocolate Candy Box/Bag (> 3.5 oz) Brands, 2002

Shares are shown based on sales at grocery, drug and mass market outlets (but not Wal-Mart) for the year ended October 6, 2002.

M&Ms	. . . .	15.4%
Hershey's	. . . .	12.2
Hershey's Kisses	. . . .	7.2
Hershey's Nuggets	. . . .	4.9
Reese's	. . . .	4.3
Snickers	. . . .	4.1
York Peppermint Patty	. . . .	2.7
Nestle Treasures	. . . .	2.6
Ferrero Rocher	. . . .	2.4
Other	. . . .	44.2

Source: *The Manufacturing Confectioner*, January 2003, p. 24, from Information Resources Inc. InfoScan.

★ 358 ★
Chocolate (SIC 2066)

Top Chocolate Candy Box/Bag (> 3.5 oz) Makers, 2002

Shares are shown based on sales at grocery, drug and mass market outlets (but not Wal-Mart) for the year ended October 6, 2002.

Hershey Foods Corp.	45.9%
Mars Inc.	25.1
Nestle	6.9
Philip Morris Co. Inc.	3.1
Ferrero USA Inc.	2.6
Tootsie Roll Industries	2.5
Storck USA	2.2
Brach's Confections	2.0
Lindt & Sprungli	1.1
Other	8.6

Source: *The Manufacturing Confectioner*, January 2003, p. 24, from Information Resources Inc. InfoScan.

★ 359 ★
Chocolate (SIC 2066)

Top Chocolate Gift Box Makers, 2002

Market shares are shown for the year ended April 21, 2002. Figures exclude Wal-Mart.

	($ mil.)	Share
Russell Stover	$ 127.4	46.28%
Whitman's Sampler	52.2	18.96
Hershey's Pot of Gold	40.4	14.67
Queen Anne	16.0	5.81
Fannie May	9.1	3.31

	($ mil.)	Share
Whitman's	$ 7.8	2.83%
Esther Price	3.5	1.27
Mrs. Field's	3.0	1.09
Other	15.9	5.78

Source: *Candy Industry*, July 2002, p. 32, from Information Resources Inc.

★ 360 ★
Gum (SIC 2067)

Top Gum Makers, 2002

Market shares are shown for the year ended April 21, 2002. Figures exclude Wal-Mart.

William Wrigley Jr. Co.	54.8%
Adams	25.6
Hershey Foods Corp.	16.0
Topps Co.	0.9
Concord Confections Inc.	0.5
Philadelphia Chewing Gum	0.4
Other	1.8

Source: *Candy Industry*, July 2002, p. 32, from Information Resources Inc.

★ 361 ★
Gum (SIC 2067)

Top Oral Care/Cleaner Brands, 2002

Shares are ranked for the year ended August 11, 2002. Figures exclude Wal-Mart.

Listerine Pocketpaks	61.3%
Trident White Chewing Gum	8.3
Trident Advantage Chewing Gum	7.9
Arm & Hammer Dental Care Chewing Gum	6.7
Aquafresh Chewing Gum	5.1
Orbit White Chewing Gum	4.1
Arm & Hammer Advance White Chewing Gum	1.8
Wrigley's Eclipse Flash Strips	1.1
Other	3.7

Source: *Candy Industry*, October 2002, p. 48, from Information Resources Inc.

★ 362 ★

Gum (SIC 2067)

Top Sugarless Gum Brands, 2002

Brands are ranked by sales for the year ended August 11, 2002. Figures exclude Wal-Mart.

Wrigley Extra Sugarless Gum 29.1%
Trident Sugarless Gum 16.7
Dentyne Ice Sugarless Gum 14.2
Wrigley's Eclipse Sugarless Gum 13.7
Orbit Sugarless Gum 6.4
Breathsavers Ice Breakers Sugarless 6.2
Carefree Koolerz Sugarless Gum 3.9
Carefree Sugarless Gum 3.8
Trident for Kids Sugarless Gum 2.2
Other 3.8

Source: *Candy Industry*, October 2002, p. 48, from Information Resources Inc.

★ 363 ★

Smoking Cessation Products (SIC 2067)

Top Smoking Cessation Brands, 2002

Brands are ranked by sales in millions of dollars for the year ended February 24, 2002. Figures include supermarkets, drug stores and discount stores but exclude Wal-Mart.

	($ mil.)	Share
Nicorette	$ 235.3	76.17%
Cigarrest	0.1	0.03
Private label	73.5	23.79

Source: *Chain Drug Review*, June 24, 2002, p. 187, from Information Resources Inc.

★ 364 ★

Snack Nuts (SIC 2068)

Top Snack Nut Brands, 2001

Market shares are shown based on supermarket sales.

Planters 38.0%
Sunkist 3.5
Anns House of Nuts 1.8
Fisher 1.6
Planters Sweet Roast 1.5
Blue Diamond 1.5
Hampton Farms 1.4
Mauna Loa 1.4

Private label 27.2%
Other 22.1

Source: *Snack Food & Wholesale Bakery*, June 2002, p. S65, from Information Resources Inc.

★ 365 ★

Cooking Oil (SIC 2070)

Largest Cooking Oil Makers

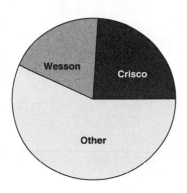

Market shares are shown in percent.

Crisco 24.0%
Wesson 19.0
Other 57.0

Source: "J.M. Smucker Company." available March 7, 2003 from http://www.shareholder.com/Common/Edgar.

★ 366 ★

Beverages (SIC 2080)

Alcoholic Beverage Market in Mexico, 2000

Import shares are shown in percent. Nearly $46 million in alcoholic beverages were sold in the country during the year 2000.

United States 33.0%
Spain 22.0
Great Britain/Ireland 19.0
France 8.0
Chile 6.0
Italy 4.0
Other 8.0

Source: *AgExporter*, August 2002, p. 10, from Mexican statistics.

★ 367 ★
Beverages (SIC 2080)

Beverage Industry Segments

Figures show volume shares. In 1996 to 2001 per capita consumption of milk and coffee fell, according to the source. Bottled water consumption increased.

Soft drinks, carbonated 28.9%
Milk 11.8
Beer 11.7
Coffee 11.4
Bottled water 10.2
Fruit beverages 7.8
Tea 4.7
Wine 1.0
Other 12.4

Source: *Beverage World*, August 2002, p. 24, from Beverage Marketing Corp.

★ 368 ★
Beverages (SIC 2080)

Beverage Sales in Canada, 2002

Sales are shown in millions of dollars for the year ended June 22, 2002.

Milk . . . . $ 1,603.6
Flavored soft drinks 1,478.4
Shelf stable juices, drinks, nectars and iced
 tea (not in cans) 801.1
Chilled juices, drinks, nectars and iced tea
 (not in cans) 533.1
Frozen fruit beverages incl. iced tea 290.9
Roast and ground coffee 252.1
Flat water 200.1
Tea bags 135.3
Instant coffee 133.8
Vegetable juices 109.2
Soya drinks 65.9

Source: *Food in Canada*, September 2002, p. 48, from A.C. Nielsen.

★ 369 ★
Beverages (SIC 2080)

Largest Beverage Firms in North America

Companies are ranked by sales in millions of dollars. The companies are based in North America but figures show global sales.

Coca-Cola Company . . . . $ 20,092.0
Coca-Cola Enterprises 15,700.0
Anheuser-Busch Companies 12,911.0
Pepsi Bottling Group 8,443.0
PepsiCo. 6,424.0
Philip Morris 4,244.0
FEMSA 4,063.2
Pernod Ricard 4,035.0
Southern Wine & Spirits of America . . . 3,450.3
Cadbury Schweppes 3,300.0

Source: *Beverage Aisle*, August 15, 2002, p. 44.

★ 370 ★
Beverages (SIC 2080)

Largest Bottlers in North America, 2001

Firms are ranked by sales in millions of dollars.

Coca-Cola Enterprises . . . . $ 15,700.0
Pepsi Bottling Group 8,443.0
PepsiAmericas 3,200.0
Dr. Pepper/Seven Up Bottling Group . . . 1,820.0
Honickman Affiliates 1,076.0
Coca-Cola Bottling Company
 Consolidated 1,022.7
Coca-Cola Bottling Company United . . . 525.0
Buffalo Rock Company 450.0
Pepsi Bottling Ventures LLC 450.0
Philadelphia Coca-Cola Bottling
 Company 409.0

Source: *Beverage World*, August 2002, p. 33.

★ 371 ★
Beverages (SIC 2080)

Private label Beverage Sales, 2002

Figures show supermarket sales for the year ended October 6, 2002.

Carbonated beverages . . . . $ 854.95
Bottled juices, shelf stable 622.30

Continued on next page.

★ 371 ★ *Continued*
Beverages (SIC 2080)
Private label Beverage Sales, 2002

Figures show supermarket sales for the year ended October 6, 2002.

Bottled water	$ 503.10
Juices, frozen	244.60
Spirits/liquor	114.40
Canned juices, shelf stable	111.30
Wine	15.20
Tea/coffee, ready-to-drink	12.08
Isotonics	11.58
Non-fruit drinks, shelf stable	8.53

Source: *Supermarket News*, November 18, 2002, p. 32, from Information Resources Inc.

★ 372 ★
Beverages (SIC 2080)
Top Beverage Brands in Drug Stores, 2001

Brands are ranked by sales in millions of dollars for the year ended December 30, 2001. Figures exclude Wal-Mart.

	($ mil.)	Share
Coke Classic	$ 205.2	10.21%
Pepsi	146.6	7.30
Budweiser	138.2	6.88
Bud Light	136.9	6.81
Diet Coke	109.8	5.46
Miller Lite	77.8	3.87
Sprite	66.3	3.30
Diet Pepsi	66.2	3.29
Mountain Dew	57.7	2.87
Other	1,004.7	50.00

Source: *Drug Store News*, May 20, 2002, p. 54, from Information Resources Inc.

★ 373 ★
Beer (SIC 2082)
Specialty Beer Market, 2000

Per capita consumption for specialty beer jumped from 4.3 gallons in 1995 to 6.0 gallons in 2000. The industry is expected to see much smaller growth rates as alcohol consumption overall drops. Market shares are shown in percent.

Regional	50.3%
National	26.2
Microbrews	12.4
Brewpubs	11.0

Source: *Beverage Aisle*, July 15, 2002, p. 2, from Beverage Marketing Corp.

★ 374 ★
Beer (SIC 2082)
Top Beer Brands, 2001

Brands are ranked by thousands of 2.25 gallon cases.

	(000)	Share
Bud Light	469,000	18.98%
Budweiser	445,000	18.01
Coors Light	231,700	9.38
Miller Lite	217,000	8.78
Natural Light	113,000	4.57
Busch	105,000	4.25
Busch Light	75,500	3.06
Miller High Life	72,000	2.91
Miller Genuine Draft	70,000	2.83
Michelob Light	40,000	1.62
Other	632,660	25.60

Source: *Beverage Dynamics*, September-October 2002, p. 28, from *Adams Beer Handbook, 2002*.

★ 375 ★
Beer (SIC 2082)
Top Beer Brands, 2002

Market shares are shown in percent.

Bud Light	19.1%
Budweiser	16.3
Coors Light	8.5
Miller Lite	7.9
Natural Lite	4.1
Busch	3.9
Corona Extra	3.4
Miller High Life	2.7

Continued on next page.

★ 375 ★ *Continued*
Beer (SIC 2082)

Top Beer Brands, 2002

Market shares are shown in percent.

Busch Light Draft	2.7%
Miller Genuine Draft	2.5
Other	28.9

Source: *Beverage World*, April 15, 2003, p. 29, from Beverage Marketing Corporation.

★ 376 ★
Beer (SIC 2082)

Top Beer Makers, 2001

Market shares are shown in percent.

Anheuser-Busch	50.9%
Miller Brewing	20.3
Coors	11.7
S&P Industries	4.4
Modelo	4.2
Heineken	2.5
Labatt	2.1
Guinness Bass	0.8
Boston Beer	0.6
D.G. Yeungling	0.5
Other	2.0

Source: *Beverage Aisle*, May 15, 2002, p. 40, from Beverage Marketing Corporation.

★ 377 ★
Beer (SIC 2082)

Top Beer Makers, 2002

Market shares are shown in percent.

Anheuser-Busch	51.6%
Miller Brewing	19.7
Coors	11.5
Modelo	4.2
Pabst Brewing	4.0
Heineken	2.7
Labatt	2.2
Guinness Bass Import	0.8
Boston Beer	0.7
DG Yeungling & Son	0.6
Other	4.2

Source: *Beverage World*, April 15, 2003, p. 29, from Beverage Marketing Corporation.

★ 378 ★
Beer (SIC 2082)

Top Imported Beer Brands, 2002

Market shares are shown in percent.

Corona Extra	29.5%
Heineken	19.4
Labatt's	5.0
Tacate	4.2
Amstel Light	3.2
Guinness	2.9
Foster's	2.8
Beck's	2.6
Bass	2.4
Modelo Especiale	2.3
Other	25.7

Source: *Beverage World*, April 15, 2003, p. 29, from Beverage Marketing Corporation.

★ 379 ★
Malt Beverages (SIC 2082)

Top Malt Beverage Brands, 2002

Market shares are shown for the year ended October 26, 2002.

Smirnoff Ice	29.6%
Mike's Hard Lemonade	15.0
Skyy Blue	11.1
Bacardi Silver	10.6
Zima	8.0
Captain Morgan Gold	2.8
Mike's Hard Iced Tea	2.4
Stolichnaya Citrona	2.3
Diablo	1.6
Other	16.6

Source: *Milwaukee Journal Sentinel*, November 17, 2002, p. NA, from A.C. Nielsen.

★ 380 ★
Wine (SIC 2084)

Largest Wineries, 2002

Companies are ranked by millions of gallons produced.

E&J Gallo Winery	441.0
Canandaigua Wine Co.	157.6
The Wine Group	87.0
JFJ Bronco	62.9
Korbel & Bros.	60.2

Continued on next page.

★ 380 ★ *Continued*
Wine (SIC 2084)

Largest Wineries, 2002

Companies are ranked by millions of gallons produced.

Vie-Del Co.	59.2
Golden State Vntnrs.	54.7
Robert Mondavi	50.1
Delicato Vyds.	43.4
Trinchero Family Estates	43.0

Source: *Wines & Vines*, July 2002, p. 46.

★ 381 ★
Wine (SIC 2084)

Leading Champagne/Imported Sparkling Wine Brands, 2001

Brands are ranked by sales of thousands of 9-liter cases.

	(000)	Share
Martini & Rossi Asti	700	18.12%
Freixenet	590	15.27
Moet & Chandon	565	14.63
Verdi Spumante	393	10.17
Other	1,615	41.81

Source: *Beverage Dynamics*, November-December 2002, p. 30, from *Adams Wine Handbook 2002*.

★ 382 ★
Wine (SIC 2084)

Table Wine Market Shares

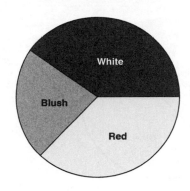

Distribution is shown in percent.

	1991	1995	2001
White	49.0%	41.0%	40.0%
Blush	34.0	34.0	23.0
Red	17.0	25.0	37.0

Source: *Beverage Industry*, July 2002, p. 16, from Wine Institute.

★ 383 ★
Wine (SIC 2084)

Who Drinks Wine

Figures are for the domestic wine market.

35-54	46.5%
55 and over	29.7
21-34	23.8

Source: *Wall Street Journal*, April 24, 2003, p. B1, from *2002 Impact Wine Study*.

★ 384 ★
Wine (SIC 2084)

Wine Bottling Market in Quebec, 2002

Market shares are shown in percent.

Dumont	63.0%
Other	37.0

Source: "Wine." available April 7, 2003 from http://www.usatrade.gov, from United States Department of Commerce.

★ 385 ★
Wine (SIC 2084)
Wine Sales by Type

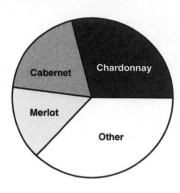

The United States is the fourth largest wine producer in the world. In the past decade red wine consumption has more than doubled. Distribution is shown in percent.

Chardonnay 29.0%
Cabernet 19.0
Merlot 15.0
Other 37.0

Source: *Knight-Ridder/Tribune Business News*, June 3, 2002, p. NA, from Gombert, Fredrikson Report.

★ 386 ★
Liquor (SIC 2085)
Top Canadian Whiskey Brands

Brands are ranked by sales in millions of dollars in supermarkets and drug stores for the year ended September 8, 2002.

Crown Royal . . . . $ 57.3
Canadian Mist 36.0
Black Velvet 28.0

Source: *Beverage Industry*, October 2002, p. 20, from Information Resources Inc.

★ 387 ★
Liquor (SIC 2085)
Top Cordial/Liqeur Brands, 2001

Brands are ranked by sales of thousands of 9-liter cases.

	(000)	Share
DeKuyper	2,565	14.52%
Kahlua	1,380	7.81
Southern Comfort	1,269	7.18
Hiram Walker Cordials	1,035	5.86
Baileys	1,032	5.84
Jagermeister	700	3.96
Alize	600	3.40
E&J Cask & Cream	530	3.00
Jacquin Cordials	490	2.77
Grand Marnier	465	2.63
Other	7,600	43.02

Source: *Beverage Dynamics*, July-August 2002, p. 8, from Adams Handbook Advance, 2002.

★ 388 ★
Liquor (SIC 2085)
Top Gin Brands, 2002

Brands are ranked by sales in millions of dollars in supermarkets and drug stores for the year ended September 8, 2002.

	($ mil.)	Share
Seagrams	$ 26.7	16.71%
Tanqueray	25.4	15.89
Gordons	17.3	10.83
Bombardier	16.1	10.08
Beefeaters	11.4	7.13
Gilbey's	10.9	6.82
Fleischman's	6.2	3.88
Private label	11.6	7.26
Other	34.2	21.40

Source: *Beverage Industry*, October 2002, p. 20, from Information Resources Inc.

★ 389 ★
Liquor (SIC 2085)

Top Rum Brands, 2002

Brands are ranked by sales in millions of dollars in supermarkets and drug stores for the year ended September 8, 2002.

	($ mil.)	Share
Bacardi	$ 135.8	44.42%
Captain Morgan	75.9	24.83
Malibu	18.9	6.18
Ron Rico	9.8	3.21
Myers	8.2	2.68
Castillo	8.0	2.62
Cruzan	3.3	1.08
Private label	22.2	7.26
Other	23.6	7.72

Source: *Beverage Industry*, October 2002, p. 20, from Information Resources Inc.

★ 390 ★
Liquor (SIC 2085)

Top Rum Brands in Mexico

Market shares are shown in percent.

Bacardi	69.0%
Other	31.0

Source: *Daily Business Review*, November 15, 2002, p. A1, from Bacardi.

★ 391 ★
Liquor (SIC 2085)

Top Scotch (Blended) Brands, 2002

Brands are ranked by sales in millions of dollars in supermarkets and drug stores for the year ended September 8, 2002.

Johnnie Walker	$ 24.3
Dewars	23.0
Clan Macgregor	15.1

Source: *Beverage Industry*, October 2002, p. 20, from Information Resources Inc.

★ 392 ★
Liquor (SIC 2085)

Top Single Malt Scotch Brands, 2002

Brands are ranked by sales in thousands of one-liter cases. Market shares are shown in percent.

	Cases	Share
Glenlivet	185	30.1%
Glenfiddich	92	15.0
The Macallan	66	10.7
The Balvenie	34	5.5
Glenmorangie	30	4.9
Other	208	33.8

Source: *Research Alert*, January 3, 2003, p. 10, from Impact Databank.

★ 393 ★
Liquor (SIC 2085)

Top Sparkling Wine Brands, 2001

Brands are ranked by sales of 9-liter cases, in thousands.

	(000)	Share
Andre/Wycliff	2,100	27.18%
Cook's	1,400	18.12
Korbel	1,015	13.14
Ballatore	600	7.77
J. Roget	590	7.64
Other	2,020	26.15

Source: *StateWays*, November-December 2002, p. 28, from *Adams Wine Handbook, 2002*.

★ 394 ★
Liquor (SIC 2085)

Top Tequila Brands, 2002

Brands are ranked by sales in millions of dollars in supermarkets and drug stores for the year ended September 8, 2002.

	($ mil.)	Share
Jose Cuervo	$ 88.3	53.10%
Sauza	33.7	20.26
1800	7.4	4.45
Cazadores	6.5	3.91
Patron	4.4	2.65

Continued on next page.

★ 394 ★ *Continued*
Liquor (SIC 2085)

Top Tequila Brands, 2002

Brands are ranked by sales in millions of dollars in supermarkets and drug stores for the year ended September 8, 2002.

	($ mil.)	Share
Margaritaville	$ 3.0	1.80%
Montezuma	3.0	1.80
Private label	6.9	4.15
Other	13.1	7.88

Source: *Beverage Industry*, October 2002, p. 20, from Information Resources Inc.

★ 395 ★
Liquor (SIC 2085)

Top Vodka Brands, 2001

Brands are ranked by sales of thousands of 9-liter cases.

	(000)	Share
Smirnoff	6,340	16.93%
Absolut	4,450	11.88
Popov Vodka	1,830	4.89
McCormick Vodka	1,700	4.54
Gordon's Vodka	1,590	4.25
Stolichnaya	1,490	3.98
Barton Vodka	1,459	3.90
Skyy	1,295	3.46
Skol Vodka	1,157	3.09
Kamchatka	1,086	2.90
Other	15,055	40.20

Source: *Beverage Dynamics*, May-June 2002, p. 8, from Adams Handbook Advance, 2002.

★ 396 ★
Bottled Water (SIC 2086)

Bottled Water Market in Quebec

Import shares are shown in percent, based on 55 million liters of bottled water.

France	48.0%
Italy	26.0
Spain	6.0
Portugal	5.0
United States	4.0
Other	11.0

Source: *AgExporter*, August 2002, p. 10, from Mexican statistics.

★ 397 ★
Bottled Water (SIC 2086)

Top Bottled Water Brands, 2002

Market shares are shown based on wholesale gallons.

Aquafina	10.8%
Dasani	9.9
Poland Spring	8.0
Arrowhead	5.9
Sparkletts	4.2
Deer Park	4.0
Crystal Geyser	3.5
Ozarka	2.7
Zephyrhills	2.6
Evian	2.5
Other	45.9

Source: *Beverage World*, April 15, 2003, p. 29, from Beverage Marketing Corporation.

★ 398 ★
Bottled Water (SIC 2086)

Top Bottled Water Makers, 2002

Market shares are shown based on wholesale sales of $7.7 billion.

Nestle Waters	31.7%
Pepsico	10.8
Danone Waters	10.0
Coca-Cola	9.9
Suntory Water Group	6.5
Crystal Geyser	3.5
Culligan International	1.6
Vermont Pure	0.9
Glacier Water	0.9
Other	24.2

Source: *Beverage World*, April 15, 2003, p. 29, from Beverage Marketing Corporation.

★ 399 ★
New Age Beverages (SIC 2086)

New Age Beverages Market

- Single-serve water
- Single-serve fruit beverages
- Sports beverages
- RTD teas
- Sparkling water
- Energy drinks
- Premium soda
- RTD coffee
- Other

The $11.6 billion industry is shown in percent. The single-serve water segment grew 26.1%.

Single-serve water	33.8%
Single-serve fruit beverages	20.1
Sports beverages	18.3
RTD teas	12.3
Sparkling water	3.8
Energy drinks	3.6
Premium soda	2.4
RTD coffee	2.1
Other	3.7

Source: *Beverage World*, February 2003, p. 22, from Beverage Marketing Corp.

★ 400 ★
New Age Beverages (SIC 2086)

Top Energy Drink Brands, 2001

Market shares are shown based on retail volume. Total volume sales reached 149.1 million liters in 2001, up from 8.5 million in 1997.

SoBe	35.8%
Snapple Elements	28.2
Red Bull	15.5
Red Devil	2.7
Hansen	2.7
SoBe Adrenaline Rush	2.2
WhoopAss	1.0
Other	11.0

Source: *Beverage Industry*, February 2003, p. 12, from Euromonitor.

★ 401 ★
New Age Beverages (SIC 2086)

Top Sports Drinks, 2001

Market shares are shown in percent.

Gatorade	81.0%
Powerade	14.4
All Sport	2.2
Other	2.3

Source: *Beverage Aisle*, October 15, 2002, p. 1, from Beverage Marketing Corp.

★ 402 ★
Soft Drinks (SIC 2086)

Fountain and Bottle Drinks

The split between the fountain and bottle/can industries is shown in percent.

	1992	2002
Bottles and cans	78.1%	76.8%
Fountain	21.9	23.2

Source: *USA TODAY*, May 28, 2003, p. 2B, from *Beverage Digest*.

★ 403 ★

Soft Drinks (SIC 2086)

Leading Grapefruit Soda Brands in Mexico

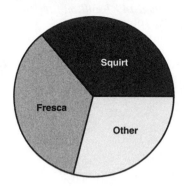

Market shares are shown in percent.

Squirt	36.0%
Fresca	35.0
Other	29.0

Source: *FWN Select*, August 1, 2002, p. NA.

★ 404 ★

Soft Drinks (SIC 2086)

Leading Noncarbonated Drink Makers, 2001

The beverage industry is increasingly under the control under just a handful of companies. Market shares are shown in percent.

	1992	2001
Pepsico	0.4%	40.7%
Coca-Cola	8.1	27.0
Cadbury Schweppes	2.4	18.1
Other	89.1	14.2

Source: *Atlanta Journal-Constitution*, October 20, 2002, p. F1, from *Beverage Digest*.

★ 405 ★

Soft Drinks (SIC 2086)

Lemon-Lime Soft Drinks, 2002

Shares are shown based on sales volume at supermarkets.

Sprite	43.0%
7Up	20.6
Sierra Mist	5.7
Other	30.7

Source: *Advertising Age*, March 10, 2003, p. 15, from Information Resources Inc.

★ 406 ★

Soft Drinks (SIC 2086)

Soft Drink Market in Mexico

Market shares are shown in percent.

Coca-Cola	72.0%
PepsiCo.	20.0
Other	8.0

Source: *FWN Select*, November 6, 2002, p. NA.

★ 407 ★

Soft Drinks (SIC 2086)

Top Diet Soft Drinks, 2002

Total diet drink sales reached 2.75 million cases. The overall soft drink market had sales of 4.13 million cases. Shares of the diet and overall market are shown.

	Market Share	Diet Share
Diet Coke	9.0%	33.2%
Diet Pepsi	5.2	19.2
Caffeine Free Diet Coke	1.7	6.2
Diet Dr. Pepper	1.1	4.0
Diet Mountain Dew	1.0	3.7
Caffeine Free Diet Pepsi	0.9	3.2
Diet Sprite	0.5	2.0
Diet 7Up	0.5	1.9
Pepsi One	0.3	1.1
Fresca	0.3	0.9
Other	6.7	24.6

Source: *Beverage World*, March 15, 2003, p. NA, from Beverage Marketing Corp.

★ 408 ★

Soft Drinks (SIC 2086)

Top Instant Tea Brands, 2002

Market shares are shown for the year ended May 19, 2002. Figures exclude Wal-Mart.

Lipton	36.7%
Nestea	20.7
4C	6.4
Country Time	3.4
Nestea Decaf	2.9
Tetley	1.4
Nestea Free	1.1
Private label	24.8
Other	4.6

Source: *Beverage Industry*, June 2002, p. 48, from Information Resources Inc.

★ 409 ★

Soft Drinks (SIC 2086)

Top Refrigerated Tea Brands, 2002

Market shares are shown for the year ended May 19, 2002. Figures exclude Wal-Mart.

Turkey Hill	21.8%
Nestea	11.5
Arizona	8.9
Milos	6.6
Red Diamond	6.2
Minute Maid Premium	5.4
Galliker	3.8
Clover Farms	2.5
Private label	15.4
Other	17.9

Source: *Dairy Field*, August 2002, p. 3, from Information Resources Inc.

★ 410 ★

Soft Drinks (SIC 2086)

Top Refrigerated Tea Vendors, 2002

Market shares are shown for the year ended May 19, 2002. Figures exclude Wal-Mart.

Turkey Hill Dairy	21.8%
Nestle US Inc.	11.5
Fetolito Vultaggio & Sons	8.9
Milo Restaurant Servicing	6.6
Donovan Coffee Inc.	6.2
The Minute Maid Co.	5.4

Galliker Dairy Co.	4.0%
Private label	15.4
Other	20.2

Source: *Dairy Field*, August 2002, p. 3, from Information Resources Inc.

★ 411 ★

Soft Drinks (SIC 2086)

Top Root Beer Brands, 2001

Market shares are shown in percent.

Barq's	36.5%
Mug's	23.8
A&W	22.9
Other	16.8

Source: *Brandweek*, November 18, 2002, p. 5, from *Beverage Digest*.

★ 412 ★

Soft Drinks (SIC 2086)

Top Seltzer/Tonic/Club Soda Brands, 2002

Market shares are shown for the year ended May 19, 2002.

Canada Dry	23.7%
Schweppes	17.0
Vintage	10.2
Polar	4.2
Diet Schweppes	3.3
Adirondack	3.0
Seagrams	3.0
Canfield	1.6
Shasta	1.0

Continued on next page.

★ 412 ★ *Continued*
Soft Drinks (SIC 2086)

Top Seltzer/Tonic/Club Soda Brands, 2002

Market shares are shown for the year ended May 19, 2002.

Private label	27.2%
Other	5.8

Source: *Beverage Industry*, June 2002, p. 32, from Information Resources Inc.

★ 413 ★
Soft Drinks (SIC 2086)

Top Soft Drink Brands, 2002

Market shares are shown based on 10.08 billion cases.

Coke Classic	19.3%
Pepsi-Cola	12.6
Diet Coke	9.0
Mountain Dew	6.4
Sprite	6.2
Dr. Pepper	5.9
Diet Pepsi	5.5
7Up	1.7
Caffeine Free Diet Coke	1.7
Diet Dr. Pepper	1.1
Other	30.6

Source: *PR Newswire*, February 24, 2003, p. NA, from *Beverage Digest* and Maxwell.

★ 414 ★
Soft Drinks (SIC 2086)

Top Soft Drink Firms, 2002

Market shares are shown based on 10.08 billion cases.

Coca-Cola Co.	44.3%
Pepsi-Cola Co.	31.4
Dr. Pepper/Seven Up	15.0
Cott Corp.	4.2
National Beverage	2.3
Carolina Beverage	0.1

Monarch Co.	0.1%
Big Red	0.1
Private label	2.2
Other	0.3

Source: *PR Newswire*, February 24, 2003, p. NA, from *Beverage Digest* and Maxwell.

★ 415 ★
Seafood (SIC 2091)

Canned Seafood Sales

Sales are shown in millions of dollars.

	($ mil.)	Share
Tuna	$ 1,029.51	70.07%
Salmon	142.22	9.68
Sardines	73.48	5.00
Oysters	44.50	3.03
Clams	43.21	2.94
Crab	36.12	2.46
Shrimp	28.29	1.93
Anchovies	13.23	0.90
Anchovy paste	1.18	0.08
Other	57.46	3.91

Source: *Progressive Grocer*, September 15, 2002, p. 24, from *Progressive Grocer's 55th Annual Consumers Expenditures Study.*

★ 416 ★
Seafood (SIC 2091)

Canned Tuna Market, 2002

Market shares are shown in percent.

StarKist	40.0%
Bumble Bee	24.0
Chicken of the Sea	18.0
Private label	17.0

Source: "Starkist Tuna Sold A New Era?" available January 7, 2003 from http://www.atuna.com.

★ 417 ★
Seafood (SIC 2091)

Largest Seafood Producers, 2001

Firms are ranked by North American sales in millions of dollars.

ConAgra	$ 1,200
StarKist Seafood Co.	1,100

Continued on next page.

★ 417 ★ *Continued*
Seafood (SIC 2091)

Largest Seafood Producers, 2001

Firms are ranked by North American sales in millions of dollars.

Marine Harvest	$ 1,100
Red Chamber Group	680
Trident Seafoods Corp.	650
Nippon Suisan	575
Pacific Seafood	550
Tri-Marine International	460
Fishery Products International	454
Tri-Union Seafoods (Chicken of the Sea)	420

Source: *Seafood Business*, May 2002, p. 1.

★ 418 ★
Seafood (SIC 2091)

Smoked Salmon Market in Canada

Market shares are shown in percent.

Grizzly Sumoir Smoke House	45.0%
Other	55.0

Source: *Food in Canada*, May 2002, p. 33.

★ 419 ★
Seafood (SIC 2092)

Breaded Shrimp Market

The closest competitor in the frozen breaded shrimp market had less than 10% of the market.

ScaPak	50.0%
Other	50.0

Source: *Frozen Food Digest*, December 2002, p. 8.

★ 420 ★
Seafood (SIC 2092)

Shrimp Imports

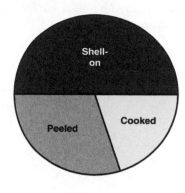

Figures are in thousands of pounds for year to date October. Prices have stabilized and rebounded slightly.

	2001	2002	Share
Shell-on	350,595	367,400	50.10%
Peeled	223,908	219,185	29.89
Cooked	114,669	146,818	20.02

Source: *Quick Frozen Foods International*, January 2003, p. 30, from Urner Barry Publications.

★ 421 ★
Seafood (SIC 2092)

Top Frozen Seafood Brands, 2002

Market shares are shown based on supermarket sales for the year ended May 19, 2002.

Gorton's	11.8%
Van de Kamps	7.3
Mrs. Paul's	3.6
Seapak	3.5
Singleton	3.4
Contessa	2.3
Agua Star	2.2
Mrs. Paul's Select Cuts	2.1
Gorton's Grilled Fillets	1.4
Private label	33.2
Other	29.2

Source: *National Provisioner*, August 2002, p. 74, from Information Resources Inc.

★ 422 ★
Seafood (SIC 2092)

Top Frozen Seafood Producers

Market shares are shown based on supermarket sales for the year ended February 24, 2002.

Aurora Foods	16.4%
Gorton's	14.6
Rich-SeaPak	3.6
ConAgra	3.3
Private label	30.5
Other	31.6

Source: *Refrigerated & Frozen Foods*, June 2002, p. 76, from Information Resources Inc. InfoScan.

★ 423 ★
Coffee (SIC 2095)

Coffee Market in Los Angeles, CA

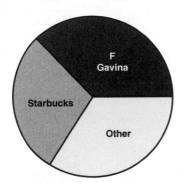

The growth of Starbucks in the 1990s helped bring attention to the gourmet coffee market. Gavina is thought to be in control of the market because of its slightly cheaper price. Shares are shown for the whole bean market.

F Gavina	37.0%
Starbucks	29.0
Other	34.0

Source: *Los Angeles Times*, July 29, 2002, p. C1, from Information Resources Inc.

★ 424 ★
Coffee (SIC 2095)

Top Coffee Brands in Western Canada

Market shares are shown in percent.

Nabob	34.0%
Maxwell House	14.0
MJB	6.0
Other	46.0

Source: *Marketing*, May 20, 2002, p. 2.

★ 425 ★
Coffee (SIC 2095)

Top Ground Coffee Brands, 2002

Brands are ranked by sales in millions of dollars for the year ended April 21, 2002. Figures exclude Wal-Mart.

	($ mil.)	Share
Folgers	$ 337.9	20.61%
Maxwell House	275.7	16.82
Folgers Coffee House	134.8	8.22
Maxwell House Master Blend	129.2	7.88
Starbucks	109.2	6.66
Hills Brothers	47.1	2.87
Yuban	39.6	2.42
Chock Full O Nuts	39.2	2.39
Community	31.4	1.92
Other	495.4	30.22

Source: *MMR*, June 17, 2002, p. 85, from Information Resources Inc.

★ 426 ★
Coffee (SIC 2095)

Top Ground Coffee Makers, 2002

Shares are shown based on dollar sales at grocery, drug and mass market outlets (but not Wal-Mart) for the year ended December 29, 2002. Figures exclude decaf.

Procter & Gamble	32.6%
Kraft Foods Inc.	29.4
Starbucks Coffee	7.4
Sara Lee Corp.	4.4
Community Coffee Co. Inc.	2.2
Chock Full O'Nuts Corp.	2.1
Millstone Coffee Inc.	2.0

Continued on next page.

★ 426 ★ *Continued*
Coffee (SIC 2095)

Top Ground Coffee Makers, 2002

Shares are shown based on dollar sales at grocery, drug and mass market outlets (but not Wal-Mart) for the year ended December 29, 2002. Figures exclude decaf.

F. Gavina & Sons Inc.	1.9%
Rowland Coffee Roasters	1.5
Private label	7.9
Other	8.6

Source: *Grocery Headquarters*, April 2003, p. 43, from Information Resources Inc.

★ 427 ★
Coffee (SIC 2095)

Top Ground Decaffeinated Coffee Brands, 2002

Shares are shown based on sales for the year ended November 3, 2002. Figures exclude Wal-Mart.

Folgers	28.2%
Maxwell House	19.2
Starbucks	7.8
Folgers Coffee Singles	4.4
Millstone	3.2
Chock Full O'Nuts	2.9
Yuban	2.3
Hills Brothers	2.1
Maxwell House Sanka	1.6
Private label	13.4
Other	14.9

Source: *Beverage Industry*, January 2003, p. 11, from Information Resources Inc.

★ 428 ★
Coffee (SIC 2095)

Top Instant Coffee Brands, 2002

Market shares are shown for the year ended February 24, 2002. Figures exclude Wal-Mart.

Folgers	19.4%
General Foods International	18.8
Taster's Choice	12.4
Maxwell House	12.1
Folgers Cafe Latte	5.7
Taster's Choice Original Blend	4.3
Maxwell House Cafe Capuccino	2.8
Nescafe Clasico	2.4

Source: *Beverage Industry*, June 2002, p. 48, from Information Resources Inc.

★ 429 ★
Coffee (SIC 2095)

Top Instant Decaffeinated Coffee Brands, 2002

Shares are shown based on sales for the year ended November 3, 2002. Figures exclude Wal-Mart.

Folgers	25.0%
Tasters Choice Original Blend	21.5
Maxwell House Sanka	13.3
General Foods International Coffee	12.4
Maxwell House	8.1
Caffee D Vita	2.5
Maxwell House Cafe Cappuccino	2.3
Tasters Choice	2.2
Folgers Cafe Latte	1.4
Private label	7.8
Other	3.5

Source: *Beverage Industry*, January 2003, p. 11, from Information Resources Inc.

★ 430 ★
Coffee (SIC 2095)

Top Whole Bean Coffee Brands, 2002

Shares are shown based on sales for the year ended November 3, 2002. Figures exclude Wal-Mart.

Eight O'Clock	31.9%
Starbucks	21.7
Folgers Select	8.1
Millstone	7.8

Continued on next page.

★ 430 ★ *Continued*
Coffee (SIC 2095)

Top Whole Bean Coffee Brands, 2002

Shares are shown based on sales for the year ended November 3, 2002. Figures exclude Wal-Mart.

Seattle's Best	2.3%
Don Francisco	2.2
Brothers	1.8
Green Mountain	1.7
The Roasterie	1.3
Private label	9.8
Other	11.4

Source: *Beverage Industry*, January 2003, p. 11, from Information Resources Inc.

★ 431 ★
Coffee Drinks (SIC 2095)

Bottled Coffee Market

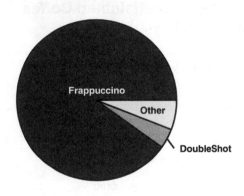

Market shares are in percent.

Frappuccino	90.0%
DoubleShot	4.3
Other	5.7

Source: *Beverage Industry*, October 2002, p. 57, from Information Resources Inc.

★ 432 ★
Coffee Drinks (SIC 2095)

Popular Coffee Drinks

Figures show our favorite types of coffee. In 2000, 54% of the adult population drank coffee daily. There were also 5,850 coffee cafes that drank up $3.95 billion of the total market.

Coffee	58.1%
Espresso	18.1
Cappuccino	14.5
Mocha	8.7
Au lait	0.7

Source: *Restaurant Hospitality*, August 2002, p. 2, from survey.

★ 433 ★
Coffee Drinks (SIC 2095)

Specialty Coffee Drinks

Figures show percent of people drinking each type of specialty coffee drink. Data are from a survey.

Espresso based beverages	49.0%
Gourmet coffee	42.0
Cappuccino	38.0
Cafe mocha	26.0
Late	24.0
Iced coffee	22.0
Espresso	19.0

Source: *Automatic Merchandiser*, February 2003, p. 50, from *National Coffee Association 2002 National Coffee Drinking Trends*.

★ 434 ★
Snacks (SIC 2096)

Snack Industry Sales, 2002

Total sales reached $9.01 billion for the year ended December 1, 2002.

	($ mil.)	Share
Potato chips	$ 2,754.35	30.56%
Tortilla/tostada chips	1,948.90	21.62
Snack bars/granola	1,626.90	18.05
Other salted (no nuts)	954.96	10.60

Continued on next page.

★ 434 ★ *Continued*
Snacks (SIC 2096)

Snack Industry Sales, 2002

Total sales reached $9.01 billion for the year ended December 1, 2002.

	($ mil.)	Share
Pretzels	$ 564.33	6.26%
Cheese snacks	500.13	5.55
Corn snacks (not tortilla)	457.68	5.08
Ready-to-eat popcorn/caramel corn	205.72	2.28

Source: *Baking & Snack*, December 29, 2002, p. 1, from Information Resources Inc.

★ 435 ★
Snacks (SIC 2096)

Top Cheese Snack Brands, 2001

Market shares are shown based on supermarket sales.

Chee-Tos	63.8%
Cheez Doodles	6.3
Planters Cheez Mania	4.4
Golden Flake	2.0
Bachman Jax	1.9
Utz	1.4
Snyder of Berlin	1.0
Old Dutch	0.6
Barrel O Fun	0.6
Private label	8.9
Other	9.1

Source: *Snack Food & Wholesale Bakery*, June 2002, p. S59, from Information Resources Inc.

★ 436 ★
Snacks (SIC 2096)

Top Corn Chip Brands, 2002

Market shares are shown for the year ended October 6, 2002. Figures exclude sales at Wal-Mart.

Fritos	37.8%
Fritos Scoops	27.5
Fritos FlavorTwists	8.0
Bugles	6.9
Doritos 3D	5.1
Other	14.7

Source: *Snack Food & Wholesale Bakery*, November 2002, p. 10, from Information Resources Inc.

★ 437 ★
Snacks (SIC 2096)

Top Potato Chip Brands, 2002

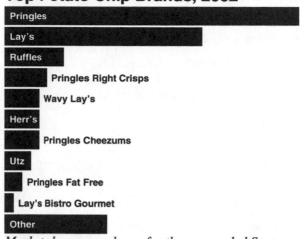

Market shares are shown for the year ended September 8, 2002. Figures exclude Wal-Mart.

Pringles	33.5%
Lay's	23.2
Ruffles	6.9
Pringles Right Crisps	5.2
Wavy Lay's	4.4
Herr's	4.3
Pringles Cheezums	4.1
Utz	3.0
Pringles Fat Free	1.8
Lay's Bistro Gourmet	1.4
Other	12.2

Source: *Chain Drug Review*, November 11, 2002, p. 44, from Information Resources Inc.

★ 438 ★
Snacks (SIC 2096)

Top Potato Chip Brands in Supermarkets

Brands are ranked by sales in millions of dollars.

Lay's	$ 765.31
Ruffles	302.37
Wavy Lay's	298.21
Pringles	177.86
Utz	74.61
Wise	58.82
Ruffles Wow	48.76
Herr's	47.60
Cape Cod	42.41
Jays	39.29

Continued on next page.

★ 438 ★ *Continued*
Snacks (SIC 2096)

Top Potato Chip Brands in Supermarkets

Brands are ranked by sales in millions of dollars.

Lay's Bistro Gourmet . . . .$ 35.71
Private label 133.49

Source: *Supermarket News*, March 10, 2003, p. 20, from Information Resources Inc.

★ 439 ★
Snacks (SIC 2096)

Top Pretzel Brands, 2001

Market shares are shown based on supermarket sales.

Rold Gold 28.8%
Snyder's of Hanover 27.3
Utz 4.2
Combos 2.7
Bachman 2.6
Herr 2.0
Jays 1.6
Anderson 1.5
Old Dutch 1.5
Kraft Handi Snacks 1.5
Quinlan 1.3
Pepperidge Farm Goldfish 1.3
Private label 11.4
Other 12.3

Source: *Snack Food & Wholesale Bakery*, June 2002, p. 10, from Information Resources Inc.

★ 440 ★
Snacks (SIC 2096)

Top Tortilla/Tostada Chip Brands, 2002

Market shares are shown for the year ended October 6, 2002. Figures exclude Wal-Mart.

Doritos 35.1%
Tostitos 28.2
Tostitos Scoops 5.0
Doritos Extremes 3.2
Santitas 3.2
Mission 2.5
Baked Tostitos 1.6

Tostitos Wow 1.2%
Torengos 1.0
Old Dutch 0.9
Doritos Wow 0.9
Other 17.2

Source: *Snack Food & Wholesale Bakery*, November 2002, p. 10, from Information Resources Inc.

★ 441 ★
Snacks (SIC 2096)

Top Tortilla/Tostada Chip Makers, 2002

Market shares are shown for the year ended October 6, 2002. Figures exclude sales at Wal-Mart.

Frito-Lay 79.8%
Mission Foods 2.5
The Hain Celestial Group 1.5
Procter & Gamble 1.1
Private label 4.6
Other 70.5

Source: *Snack Food & Wholesale Bakery*, November 2002, p. 10, from Information Resources Inc.

★ 442 ★
Pasta (SIC 2098)

Macaroni & Cheese Market, 2001

The industry had sales of $766 million.

Kraft 82.6%
Other 17.4

Source: "Kraft Sweetens Stock Market." available March 7, 2003 from http://more.abcnews.go.com, from Kraft, A.C. Nielsen, and Information Resources Inc.

★ 443 ★
Pasta (SIC 2098)

Refrigerated Pasta Market

Market shares are shown in percent.

Nestle 55.0%
Kraft Foods 20.4
Other 24.6

Source: *Refrigerated & Frozen Foods*, June 2002, p. 69, from Information Resources Inc.

★ 444 ★

Pasta (SIC 2098)

Top Frozen Pasta Makers, 2002

Market shares are shown based on supermarket sales for the year ended February 24, 2002.

Rosetta/Heinz Frozen Foods	21.5%
Mrs. Ts/Ateeco Inc.	16.0
Celentano/Rosina Food Products	5.9
Reames Foods	5.7
Private label	20.1
Other	30.8

Source: *Refrigerated & Frozen Foods*, June 2002, p. 55, from Information Resources Inc. InfoScan.

★ 445 ★

Pasta (SIC 2098)

Top Pasta Brands, 2001

Barilla
Ronzoni
Muellers
Creamette
San Giorgio
American Beauty
Skinner
Prince
Golden Grain Mission
Private label

Brands are ranked by sales in millions of dollars for the year ended September 9, 2001.

Barilla	$ 121.5
Ronzoni	82.3
Muellers	73.7
Creamette	70.7
San Giorgio	61.6
American Beauty	51.1
Skinner	31.9
Prince	30.4
Golden Grain Mission	26.7
Private label	208.0

Source: *Food Institute Report*, December 24, 2001, p. 5, from Information Resources Inc. and *Supermarket Business*.

★ 446 ★

Baking Powder (SIC 2099)

Baking Powder Market

The market is estimated at $30 million.

Clabber Girl	55.0%
Other	45.0

Source: *Indianapolis Business Journal*, May 27, 2002, p. 3.

★ 447 ★

Dry Dinners (SIC 2099)

Dry Dinner Market, 2002

The $497 million market is shown in percent for the year ended August 11, 2002.

Betty Crocker	71.1%
Other	28.9

Source: *Brandweek*, October 7, 2002, p. NA, from Information Resources Inc.

★ 448 ★

Dry Mixes (SIC 2099)

Prepared Food Sales

Sales are shown in millions of dollars. Figures are for supermarkets, drug stores and discount stores and exclude Wal-Mart.

	($ mil.)	Share
Dry dinners, pasta	$ 1,390.0	38.71%
Mexican foods, dry	1,110.0	30.91
Rice mixes	535.9	14.92
Dehydrated potatoes	329.6	9.18
Dry dinners, nonpasta	137.0	3.81
Pizza products, shelf stable	32.8	0.91
Other	55.9	1.56

Source: *MMR*, November 4, 2002, p. 25, from A.C. Nielsen.

★ 449 ★

Peanut Butter (SIC 2099)

Top Peanut Butter Brands, 2002

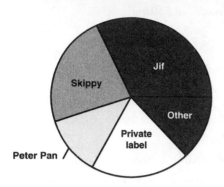

Total sales reached $856.3 million.

Jif	32.0%
Skippy	23.0
Peter Pan	12.0
Private label	20.0
Other	13.0

Source: *The News Journal (Delaware)*, March 3, 2003, p. NA, from Information Resources Inc.

★ 450 ★

Powdered Drinks (SIC 2099)

Powdered Soft Drink Market, 2001

The industry had sales of $756 million.

Kraft	84.7%
Other	15.3

Source: "Kraft Sweetens Stock Market." available March 7, 2003 from http://more.abcnews.go.com, from Kraft, A.C. Nielsen, and Information Resources Inc.

★ 451 ★

Powdered Drinks (SIC 2099)

Top Fruit Drink Brands, 2002

Market shares are shown for the year ended May 19, 2002. Figures exclude Wal-Mart.

Kool Aid	30.1%
Crystal Light Fruit	14.1
Country Time	11.8
Crystal Light Teas	9.6
Kool Aid Magic Twist	4.5
Kool Aid Mega Mountain Twists	4.0
Crystal Light Tropical Passions	3.9%
Wylers	3.0
Kool Aid Island Twists	2.9
Other	16.1

Source: *Beverage Industry*, June 2002, p. 48, from Information Resources Inc.

★ 452 ★

Refrigerated Foods (SIC 2099)

Leading Refrigerated Entree Makers, 2002

Market shares are shown based on supermarket sales for the year ended February 24, 2002.

General Mills	17.2%
Kraft Foods	15.6
Perdue Farms	12.7
Hormel Foods	9.9
Private label	24.3
Other	20.3

Source: *Refrigerated & Frozen Foods*, June 2002, p. 59, from Information Resources Inc. InfoScan.

★ 453 ★

Refrigerated Foods (SIC 2099)

Leading Refrigerated Pizza/Pizza Kit Brands, 2002

Brands are ranked by supermarket sales for the year ended April 21, 2002.

	($ mil.)	Share
MaMa Rosa	$ 72.3	65.97%
Stefano Foods	3.8	3.47
Renos	3.3	3.01
Our Old Italian	3.1	2.83
Pizzeria Uno	3.0	2.74
Nardone Bros.	2.9	2.65
Reser's	1.8	1.64
Home Run Inn	1.4	1.28
Mama Angeline's	1.3	1.19
Private label	9.0	8.21
Other	7.7	7.03

Source: *Baking & Snack*, August 1, 2002, p. NA, from Information Resources Inc.

★ 454 ★
Refrigerated Foods (SIC 2099)
Top Refrigerated Pizza Makers, 2002

Market shares are shown based on supermarket sales for the year ended February 24, 2002.

Gilardi Foods	69.7%
Stefano Foods	3.6
SCIS/I&K Distributors	3.0
Uno Restaurants	2.9
Private label	7.9
Other	12.9

Source: *Refrigerated & Frozen Foods*, June 2002, p. 66, from Information Resources Inc. InfoScan.

★ 455 ★
Refrigerated Foods (SIC 2099)
Top Selling Refrigerated Dinner/ Entrees, 2002

Brands are ranked by supermarket sales for the year ended June 16, 2002. Private label had sales of $136.4 million.

Lloyds	$ 88.54
Louis Rich Carving Board	83.65
Hormel	58.75
Tyson	42.35
Perdue Short Cuts	37.54
Perdue Done It	29.53
Thomas E Wilson	15.67
Kraft Freshmade Creations	11.31
Old El Paso	6.31
Foster Farms Fast Favorites	4.65

Source: *Supermarket News*, December 30, 2002, p. 27, from Information Resources Inc.

★ 456 ★
Salads (SIC 2099)
Top Refrigerated Salad/Cole Slaw Makers, 2002

Market shares are shown based on supermarket sales for the year ended February 24, 2002.

Reser's Fine Foods	13.4%
Fresh Express	6.0
Blue Ridge Farms	4.9
SCIS Foods	3.0
Private label	51.8
Other	20.2

Source: *Refrigerated & Frozen Foods*, June 2002, p. 82, from Information Resources Inc.

★ 457 ★
Salads (SIC 2099)
Top Salad Producers

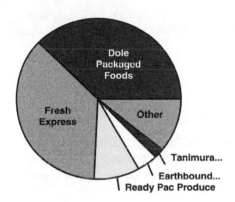

Firms are ranked by sales for the year ended July 14, 2002.

	($ mil.)	Share
Dole Packaged Foods	$ 681.1	37.84%
Fresh Express	671.5	37.31
Ready Pac Produce	154.0	8.56
Earthbound Farm	67.7	3.76
Tanimura & Antle	35.3	1.96
Other	190.4	10.58

Source: *Wall Street Journal*, August 20, 2002, p. B4, from Information Resources Inc.

★ 458 ★

Soy Products (SIC 2099)

Soy Food Industry, 2000-2002

Sales are shown in millions of dollars. Sales grew from $817.1 million to an estimated $1.6 billion in 2002.

	($ mil.)	Share
Soy milk	$ 749.1	45.4%
Meat alternatives	517.9	31.4
Dairy alternatives	117.5	7.1
Other prepared foods	94.0	5.7
Nutrition bars and beverages . . .	92.8	5.6
Soy formula	80.9	4.9

Source: *Research Alert*, October 18, 2002, p. 7, from Mintel Consumer Intelligence.

★ 459 ★

Soy Products (SIC 2099)

Soy Food Sales

The industry saw a 21% growth between 2000 and 2001, hitting sales of $3.2 billion. Soy products are now mainstream products, not just items to be found in health food stores.

Meal replacement beverages & powders . . .	24.0%
Energy bars	21.0
Soymilk beverages	17.0
Meat alternatives	14.0
Tofu	7.0
Cold cereals	4.0
Other	13.0

Source: *Nutraceuticals World*, January 2003, p. 32, from Soyatech/SPINS.

★ 460 ★

Soy Products (SIC 2099)

Top Tofu Producers in Western Canada

Market shares are shown in percent. In Eastern Canada the company has a 55% share.

Sunrise Soya	80.0%
Other	20.0

Source: *Vancouver Sun*, September 25, 2002, p. D2.

★ 461 ★

Spices (SIC 2099)

Retail Spice Production, 2000

Figures are in thousands of pounds (domestic production and imports).

Dehydrated onion/garlic	321,171
Mustard seed	172,494
Red pepper	109,416
Sesame seed	108,133
Black pepper	102,495
Paprika	52,771
Cinnamon	37,022
Cumin seed	17,234
White pepper	16,113
Oregano	14,522

Source: *Supermarket News*, December 30, 2002, p. 17, from American Spice Trade Association.

★ 462 ★

Sugar Substitutes (SIC 2099)

Leading Sugar Substitutes, 2003

Market shares are shown for the 12 weeks ended March 23, 2003.

Splenda	31.5%
Equal	26.1
Sweet 'n Low	18.9
Other	23.5

Source: *Brandweek*, May 12, 2003, p. 22, from Information Resources Inc.

★ 463 ★
Syrup (SIC 2099)

Largest Maple Syrup Producing States, 2002

Production is shown in thousands of gallons.

	(000)	Share
Vermont	495	36.50%
Maine	230	16.96
New York	228	16.81
Wisconsin	79	5.83
New Hampshire	75	5.53
Ohio	75	5.53
Michigan	66	4.87
Pennsylvania	55	4.06
Maine	45	3.32
Connecticut	8	0.59

Source: *Crop Production*, National Agricultural Statistics Service, January 2003, p. 14, from U.S. Department of Agriculture.

★ 464 ★
Tea (SIC 2099)

Powdered Chai Tea Market

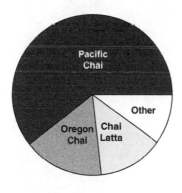

Market shares are shown in percent based on supermarket sales.

Pacific Chai	60.44%
Oregon Chai	16.30
Chai Latta	13.25
Other	10.01

Source: *Knight Ridder/Tribune Business News*, February 24, 2003, p. NA, from A.C. Nielsen.

★ 465 ★
Tea (SIC 2099)

Tea Sales by Type

Sales are shown in millions of dollars.

	($ mil.)	Share
Liquid	$ 609.78	40.44%
Bags	502.42	33.32
Mixes	239.34	15.87
Herbal bags	149.50	9.91
Packaged	6.98	0.46

Source: *Progressive Grocer*, September 15, 2002, p. 24, from *Progressive Grocer's 55th Annual Consumers Expenditures Study*.

★ 466 ★
Tea (SIC 2099)

Top Bagged/Loose Tea Brands, 2002

Market shares are shown for the year ended February 24, 2002. Figures exclude Wal-Mart.

Lipton	29.3%
Bigelow	9.9
Luzianne	6.7
Tetley	4.6
Twinings	4.4
Lipton Soothing Moments	3.0
Stash Tea	2.7
Private label	7.3
Other	32.1

Source: *Beverage Industry*, June 2002, p. 48, from Information Resources Inc.

★ 467 ★
Tortillas (SIC 2099)

Top Hard/Soft Tortilla Brands, 2002

Market shares are shown based on sales for the year ended June 16, 2002. Figures exclude Wal-Mart.

Mission	26.3%
Old El Paso	15.4
Guerrero	11.9
Tia Rosa	4.2
Private label	6.8
Other	35.4

Source: *Snack Food & Wholesale Bakery*, August 2002, p. 14, from Information Resources Inc.

★ 468 ★
Tortillas (SIC 2099)

Top Refrigerated Tortilla Brands, 2002

Market shares are shown based on supermarket sales for the year ended June 16, 2002.

Azteca	15.7%
Pepito	7.2
Private label	6.7
Other	70.4

Source: *Snack Food & Wholesale Bakery*, August 2002, p. 10, from Information Resources Inc.

SIC 21 - Tobacco Products

★ 469 ★
Tobacco (SIC 2100)

Largest Tobacco Firms, 2002

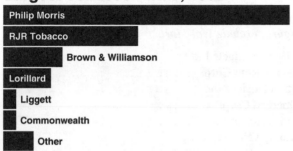

Market shares are shown for the year to date.

	2001	2002
Philip Morris	50.5%	49.3%
RJR Tobacco	23.4	23.2
Brown & Williamson	10.4	10.0
Lorillard (Loews & Carolina) . . .	8.6	8.2
Liggett (Vector)	2.0	2.3
Commonwealth	1.8	2.3
Other	3.4	4.7

Source: *Financial Times*, January 31, 2003, p. 7, from
Thomson Datastream and Prudential Financial Research.

★ 470 ★
Cigarettes (SIC 2111)

Top Cigarette Brands, 2002

Shares are for the second quarter of the year.

Marlboro	37.9%
Newport	7.1
Camel	6.1
Doral	5.9
Basic	5.0
Winston	4.7
Other	33.3

Source: *Wall Street Journal*, September 9, 2002, p. B3,
from Merrill Lynch Tobacco Research.

★ 471 ★
Cigarettes (SIC 2111)

Top Cigarette Makers, 2002

Shares are for the second quarter of the year.

Philip Morris	49.9%
Reynolds	22.9
Brown & Williamson	10.0
Lorillard	8.3
Other	9.0

Source: *Wall Street Journal*, September 6, 2002, p. 1, from
Merrill Lynch Tobacco Research.

★ 472 ★
Cigars (SIC 2121)

Top Sources For Cigar Imports, 2002

Figures are for the first six months of the year.

	($ 000)	Share
Dominican Republic	$ 82,510	66.19%
Honduras	25,190	20.21
Nicaragua	9,896	7.94
Netherlands	1,225	0.98
Mexico	1,031	0.83
Germany	802	0.64
Philippines	516	0.41
Brazil	402	0.32
Switzerland	251	0.20
Ireland	236	0.19
Other	2,606	2.09

Source: *World Tobacco*, November 2002, p. 19.

SIC 22 - Textile Mill Products

★ 473 ★

Fabrics (SIC 2211)

Largest Fabric Makers, 2001

Companies are ranked by estimated interior fabric shipments in millions of dollars.

Joan Fabrics	$ 620
Culp Inc.	369
Quaker Fabric	308
Burlington	268
Microfibres	238
Interface Fabrics Group	209
The Robert Allen Group	200
Richloom Fabrics Group	200
P/Kaufman	175
Hoffman	115

Source: *Furniture Today*, Winter 2002, p. 44.

★ 474 ★

Hosiery (SIC 2250)

Top Hosiery Brands, 2002

Market shares are for the year ended July 14, 2002. Figures exclude Wal-Mart.

L'Eggs Sheer Energy	15.4%
No Nonsense	12.0
L'Eggs Silken Mist	8.4
Just My Size	4.8
Everyday by L'Eggs	4.4
No Nonsense Sheer Endurance	4.2
L'Eggs Sheer Comfort	3.5
Private label	15.0
Other	32.3

Source: *Grocery Headquarters*, October 2002, p. 82, from Information Resources Inc.

★ 475 ★

Hosiery (SIC 2250)

Top Hosiery Makers, 2002

Market shares are for the year ended July 14, 2002. Figures exclude Wal-Mart.

L'Eggs Products Inc.	55.0%
Kayser-Roth Corp.	23.9
Smith Hosiery Inc.	2.1
Americal Corp.	1.3
Hanes Hosiery	0.8
Triumph Hosiery Corp.	0.7
Bossong Hosiery Mills Inc.	0.3
Transmerica Entr. Inc.	0.3
Private label	15.0
Other	0.6

Source: *Grocery Headquarters*, October 2002, p. 82, from Information Resources Inc.

★ 476 ★

Carpets (SIC 2273)

Top Carpet Brands, 2002

Shaw
Mohawk
Coronet
Aladdin
Lees
Beaulieu
Gullistan
Karastan
Other

The top brands are shown based on sales volume.

Shaw	46.0%
Mohawk	30.0
Coronet	5.0
Aladdin	3.0
Lees	3.0

Continued on next page.

★ 476 ★ *Continued*
Carpets (SIC 2273)

Top Carpet Brands, 2002

The top brands are shown based on sales volume.

Beaulieu	2.0%
Gullistan	2.0
Karastan	2.0
Other	7.0

Source: *National Floor Trends*, October 2002, p. 3, from *2002 Carpet and Area Rug Study*.

★ 477 ★
Rugs (SIC 2273)

Leading Area Rug Brands

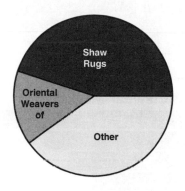

Figures are by sales volume.

Shaw Rugs	45.0%
Oriental Weavers of America	15.0
Other	40.0

Source: *National Floor Trends*, October 2002, p. 8.

★ 478 ★
Rugs (SIC 2273)

Leading Bath Rug Firms, 2002

Firms are ranked by sales in millions of dollars.

Mohawk Home	$ 169
Springs Industries	145
Maples Rugs	59
Pillowtex Corp.	47
Georgia Tufters	35

Source: *Home Textiles Today*, January 6, 2003, p. 1.

★ 479 ★
Rugs (SIC 2273)

Rug Sales by Fiber, 2002

The rug industry saw sales grow 12.5% to $6.3 billion from 2001 to 2002.

Man-made fibers	74.0%
Wool	15.0
Cotton	6.0
Blend of man-made/natural	4.0
Other	1.0

Source: *Home Textiles Today*, January 13, 2003, p. 1.

SIC 23 - Apparel and Other Textile Products

★ 480 ★
Apparel (SIC 2300)

Apparel Market in Canada

Figures show retail sales in millions of dollars.

	2000	2001	2002
Women	$ 9,683	$ 9,926	$ 9,896
Men	6,088	5,992	5,968
Juvenile	2,672	2,709	2,760

Source: "Canadian Apparel Market." available May 6, 2003 from http://www.trendexna.com, from Trendex.

★ 481 ★
Apparel (SIC 2300)

Jeans Sales for Adults

Sales are shown by price range.

	2000	2001
$25 to $49.99	46.0%	43.7%
Under $25	42.7	45.2
$50 to $74.99	8.4	7.0
$75 to $99.99	1.6	2.6
$100 to $124.99	0.6	0.8
$150 and over	0.4	0.4
$125 to $149.99	0.3	0.3

Source: *Daily News Record*, November 18, 2002, p. 30, from NPD Fashionworld.

★ 482 ★
Apparel (SIC 2300)

Largest Apparel Makers

Firms are ranked by sales in millions of dollars. Abercrombie & Fitch ranked 16th in sales but number 1 in profit margins.

Nike Inc.	$ 9,488.8
The Limited Inc.	9,363.0
VF Corp.	5,518.8
Levi Strauss & Co.	4,258.7
Jones Apparel Group	$ 4,073.1
Liz Clairborne	3,448.5
Reebok International	2,992.9
Kellwood Co.	2,281.8
Polo Ralph Lauren	2,225.8
Cintas Corp.	2,160.7
Tommy Hilfiger	1,880.9

Source: *Bobbin*, July 2002, p. 21.

★ 483 ★
Apparel (SIC 2300)

Licensed Sportswear Market

Sales are shown by category. The NCAA has about 30% of licensed sales, with the NFL having 25%.

Jerseys	24.0%
Headwear	19.0
T-shirts	17.0
Tops	15.0
Fleece	6.0
Outerwear	6.0
Other	8.0

Source: *Sporting Goods Business*, January 2003, p. 16, from SportScanINFO.

★ 484 ★
Apparel (SIC 2300)

Popular Brands of Children's Apparel

Figures show the leading responses to this question: "If you were shopping for children's apparel in a discount store or superstore, which brand of men's apparel would you want?"

OshKosh	12.0%
Hanes	9.0
Carter's	8.0
Nike	7.0
Levi's	7.0

Source: *DSN Retailing Today*, October 28, 2002, p. 37, from Leo J. Shapiro.

★ 485 ★
Apparel (SIC 2300)

Retail Activewear Sales, 2001

Shares of dollar sales are shown by segment.

Tees	37.5%
Polo/golf/rugby	12.6
Swimwear	8.7
Tanks/sleeveless	7.5
Sweatshirts	5.0
Shorts	3.8
Outerwear/jackets	3.8
Pants/slacks	2.7
Socks	2.6
Sweatpants	2.3
Other	13.5

Source: *Sporting Goods Business*, May 2002, p. 18, from NPD Group.

★ 486 ★
Apparel (SIC 2300)

Top Golf Shirt Makers, 2002

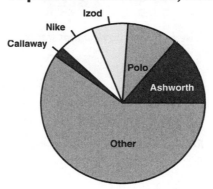

Market shares are shown in percent.

Ashworth	14.0%
Polo	10.1
Izod	7.1
Nike	6.8
Callaway	1.6
Other	60.4

Source: *Knight Ridder/Tribune Business News*, March 29, 2003, p. NA, from Darrell Survey consumer report.

★ 487 ★
Apparel (SIC 2300)

Work Wear Market

Market shares are shown in percent.

Dickies	60.0%
Other	40.0

Source: "Dickies." available March 7, 2003 from http://www.dickiesmedical.com/aboutus.htm.

★ 488 ★
Apparel (SIC 2320)

Leading Casual Sportswear Brands for Men

Shares are shown based on sales at discount stores.

Wrangler	11.6%
Hanes	6.4
Fruit of the Loom	6.1
Cherokee	5.5
Route 66	5.4

Continued on next page.

★ 488 ★ *Continued*
Apparel (SIC 2320)

Leading Casual Sportswear Brands for Men

Shares are shown based on sales at discount stores.

Faded Glory	4.5%
Puritan	3.8
Rustler	2.8
Basic Editions	2.8
Other	51.1

Source: *Daily News Record*, March 10, 2003, p. 20, from STS Market Research.

★ 489 ★
Apparel (SIC 2320)

Popular Brands of Men's Apparel

Figures show the leading responses to this question: "If you were shopping for men's apparel in a discount store or superstore, which brand of men's apparel would you want?"

Hanes	24.0%
Levi's	14.0
Dockers	12.0
Fruit of the Loom	8.0
Wrangler	8.0

Source: *DSN Retailing Today*, October 28, 2002, p. 37, from Leo J. Shapiro.

★ 490 ★
Apparel (SIC 2322)

Leading Men's Underwear Makers

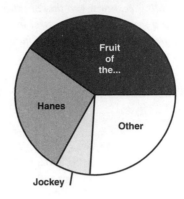

Market shares are shown in percent. Jockey has 35% of the department store channel. Calvin Klein and Joe Boxer each have 13% of the department store channel.

Fruit of the Loom	40.0%
Hanes	27.0
Jockey	7.0
Other	26.0

Source: "Undressing for Success." available March 7, 2003 from http://members.aol.com/mbastyle/web/boxers.html.

★ 491 ★
Apparel (SIC 2325)

Men's Jeans Market

Shares are for men 25-44 years of age.

Levi Strauss & Co.	21.0%
Wrangler	20.7
VF Corp's Rustler	8.0
VF Corp's Lee	6.9
Gap	4.4
Private label	15.0
Other	24.0

Source: *Advertising Age*, August 12, 2002, p. 11, from Wrangler and NPD Fashionworld.

★ 492 ★
Apparel (SIC 2331)

Compression Shirt Market

Market shares are shown in percent.

Under Armour 95.0%
Other 5.0

Source: *Daily News Record*, April 14, 2003, p. 12, from SportScan Info.

★ 493 ★
Apparel (SIC 2341)

Branded Performance Underwear Market

Market shares of the women's sports underwear business are shown in percent.

Under Armour 88.0%
Other 12.0

Source: *Brandweek*, January 27, 2003, p. 9.

★ 494 ★
Apparel (SIC 2341)

Leading Panties Makers

Market shares are shown in percent.

Fruit of the Loom 18.0%
Hanes 16.0
Jockey 3.0
Other 63.0

Source: "Undressing for Success." available March 7, 2003 from http://members.aol.com/mbastyle/web/boxers.html.

★ 495 ★
Apparel (SIC 2341)

Popular Brands of Women's Lingerie

Figures show the leading responses to this question: "If you were shopping for women's intimate apparel in a discount store or superstore, which brand of men's apparel would you want?"

Hanes 43.0%
Victoria's Secret 9.0
Playtex 9.0
Just My Size 9.0
Vanity Fair 8.0

Source: *DSN Retailing Today*, October 28, 2002, p. 37, from Leo J. Shapiro.

★ 496 ★
Golf Hats (SIC 2353)

Golf Hat Market

Several years ago, the company claimed 84% of the hat business for the Professional Golf Association and the Ladies Professional Golf Association. The market share has declined and recently the company shut its doors.

Texace 84.0%
Other 16.0

Source: *Knight Ridder/Tribune Business News*, February 13, 2003, p. NA, from Texace.

★ 497 ★
Window Coverings (SIC 2391)

Leading Curtains/Draperies Makers, 2002

Firms are ranked by sales in millions of dollars.

S. Lichtenberg . . . . $ 135
CHF Industries 130
Springs Industries 92
Croscill Home 88
Miller Curtain Co. 70

Source: *Home Textiles Today*, January 6, 2003, p. 1.

★ 498 ★
Window Coverings (SIC 2391)

Window Coverings Market

32% of window covering sales were sheers and 22% were solids, with the balance composed of prints, lace or jacquards. 46% of sales were blends, 40% were synthetics and 14% cotton or linen.

	($ mil.)	Share
Panels	$ 1,140	30.0%
Pinch-pleat draperies	570	15.0
Top treatments only	456	12.0
Toppers with side panels	342	9.0
Scarves	342	9.0
Pole tops	304	8.0
Kitchen/novelty tiers	228	6.0

Source: *Home Textiles Today*, June 17, 2002, p. 10, from *The Facts: Window Coverings* published annually by source.

★ 499 ★
Homefurnishings (SIC 2392)

Bathroom Product Market, 2001

Domestic has 62% of the market, with imports having the balance.

Bath towels	55.0%
Bath/scatter rugs	24.0
Bath accessories	12.0
Shower curtains	7.0
Tank sets	1.0
Other	1.0

Source: *Home Textiles Today*, June 17, 2002, p. 10, from *The Facts: Bathroom Products* published annually by source.

★ 500 ★
Homefurnishings (SIC 2392)

Home Fashion Sales At Mass Merchandisers

The category saw sales of $14.5 billion at mass merchandisers.

	($ mil.)	Share
Bedding	$ 3,162	21.71%
Bed covers	1,762	12.10
Sewing goods, fabrics	1,758	12.07
Bath goods	1,736	11.92
Shades, blinds	1,363	9.36

	($ mil.)	Share
Yarns	$ 1,199	8.23%
Draperies	740	5.08
Curtains	712	4.89
Rugs	563	3.86
Kitchen textiles	471	3.23
Table linens	352	2.42
Other	749	5.14

Source: *Retail Merchandiser*, July 2002, p. 34, from *Retail Merchandiser Annual Fact Book*.

★ 501 ★
Homefurnishings (SIC 2392)

Ironing Board Cover Market

Market shares are shown in percent.

Magla	80.0%
Other	20.0

Source: "Magla Products Corporate Study." available April 7, 2003 from http://www.magla.com, from Magla.

★ 502 ★
Homefurnishings (SIC 2392)

Kitchen Textile Market Sales, 2002

The category had sales of $466 million.

Kitchen towels	48.0%
Potholders/mitts	21.0
Dishcloths	16.0
Chairpads	14.0
Other	1.0

Source: *Home Textiles Today*, March 3, 2003, p. 6, from *The Facts: Kitchen Textiles 2002* published annually by source.

★ 503 ★
Homefurnishings (SIC 2392)

Leading Bath Towel Makers, 2002

Firms are ranked by sales in millions of dollars.

WestPoint Stevens	$ 550
Pillowtex Corp.	455
Springs Industries	239
Santens	52
1888 Mills	31

Source: *Home Textiles Today*, January 6, 2003, p. 1.

★ 504 ★

Homefurnishings (SIC 2392)

Leading Blanket Makers, 2002

Firms are ranked by sales in millions of dollars.

WestPoint Stevens . . . . $ 160
Sunbeam 105
Charles D. Owen Mfg. 101
Pillowtex Corp. 28
Biddeford Textile 24

Source: *Home Textiles Today*, January 6, 2003, p. 1.

★ 505 ★

Homefurnishings (SIC 2392)

Leading Comforter/Bed Spread Makers, 2002

Firms are ranked by sales in millions of dollars.

Springs Industries . . . . $ 406
WestPoint Stevens 265
Dan River 191
Croscill Home 130
Pillowtex Corp. 114

Source: *Home Textiles Today*, January 6, 2003, p. 1.

★ 506 ★

Homefurnishings (SIC 2392)

Leading Decorative Pillow Makers, 2002

Firms are ranked by sales in millions of dollars.

Brentwood Originals . . . . $ 121
Arlee 69
Mohawk Home 28
Newport 25
Fashion Pillows 22

Source: *Home Textiles Today*, January 6, 2003, p. 1.

★ 507 ★

Homefurnishings (SIC 2392)

Leading Foam Pillow/Topper Makers, 2002

Sleep Innovations	
Carpenter Co.	
Leggett & Platt	
Louisville Bedding	
	Hudson Industries

Firms are ranked by sales in millions of dollars.

Sleep Innovations . . . . $ 52
Carpenter Co. 47
Leggett & Platt 20
Louisville Bedding 17
Hudson Industries 15

Source: *Home Textiles Today*, January 6, 2003, p. 1.

★ 508 ★

Homefurnishings (SIC 2392)

Leading Kitchen Textile Makers, 2002

Firms are ranked by sales in millions of dollars.

Barth and Dreyfuss . . . . $ 60
Franco Mfg. 53
Cecil Saydah 52
John Ritzenthaler Co. 34
Charles Craft 19

Source: *Home Textiles Today*, January 6, 2003, p. 1.

★ 509 ★

Homefurnishings (SIC 2392)

Leading Quilt Makers, 2002

Firms are ranked by sales in millions of dollars.

Sunham Home Fashions . . . . $ 101
Keeco 75
Peking Handicraft 50
Britannica Home 47
American Pacific 45

Source: *Home Textiles Today*, January 6, 2003, p. 1.

★ 510 ★

Homefurnishings (SIC 2392)

Leading Sheet/Pillowcase Makers, 2002

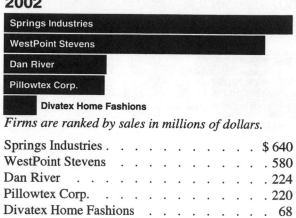

Firms are ranked by sales in millions of dollars.

Springs Industries	$ 640
WestPoint Stevens	580
Dan River	224
Pillowtex Corp.	220
Divatex Home Fashions	68

Source: *Home Textiles Today*, January 6, 2003, p. 1.

★ 511 ★

Homefurnishings (SIC 2392)

Sheet Sales by Thread Count

Mass merchants and club stores have 65% of sales.

180 count	44.5%
200-250 count	43.5
Under 180 count	8.0
250 and above	4.5

Source: *HFN*, March 17, 2003, p. 14, from *HFN's State of the Industry Report*.

★ 512 ★

Homefurnishings (SIC 2392)

Slip Cover Market

Market shares are shown in percent.

Sure Fit	90.0%
Other	10.0

Source: *HFN*, June 17, 2002, p. 15.

★ 513 ★

Homefurnishings (SIC 2392)

Table Linen Market

The $660 million industry is shown in percent. Imported has 89% of the market, with domestic having the balance.

Place mats	39.0%
Tablecloths	36.0
Napkins	18.0
Runners	3.0
Napkin rings	2.0
Other	2.0

Source: *Home Textiles Today*, June 17, 2002, p. 10, from *The Facts: Table Linen* published annually by source.

SIC 24 - Lumber and Wood Products

★ 514 ★
Sawmills (SIC 2421)

Alder Lumber Production, 2001

Alder lumber is used to make backings for Fender Stratocasters, electric guitars made popular by Jimi Hendrix and Eric Clapton.

Weyerhaeuser	75.0%
Other	25.0

Source: *Knight Ridder/Tribune Business News*, April 11, 2003, p. NA.

★ 515 ★
Sawmills (SIC 2421)

Largest Softwood Lumber Producers in Canada

Companies are ranked by production in millions of board feet.

	(mil.)	Share
Canfor	2,817	9.55%
West Fraser Timber	2,065	7.00
Weyerhaeuser Canada	2,001	6.78
Abitibi-Consolidated	1,892	6.41
Slocan Group	1,620	5.49
Tembec	1,155	3.92

	(mil.)	Share
Weldwood	1,142	3.87%
Buchanan Lumber	1,100	3.73
Tolko	1,038	3.52
Domtar	1,016	3.44
Other	13,654	46.28

Source: *Logging and Sawmilling Journal*, March 2003, p. NA.

★ 516 ★
Flooring (SIC 2426)

Top Hardwood Flooring Brands

Figures are based on a survey.

Bruce	31.0%
Mannington	14.0
Hartco	8.0
Robbins	6.0
Harris Tarkett	5.0
Mohawk	5.0
Anderson	4.0
Columbia	4.0
Kahrs	4.0
Other	19.0

Source: *National Floor Trends*, December 2002, p. 8, from *2002 Hardwood Flooring Market Study*.

★ 517 ★
Cabinets (SIC 2430)

Cabinet Demand

Shipments are in millions of dollars. Demand will increase 6.8% during this period.

	2001	2006	Share
Residential	$ 8,660	$ 11,980	76.94%
Nonresidential	2,450	3,470	22.29
Nonbuilding	90	120	0.77

Source: *Wood & Wood Products*, November 2002, p. 13, from Freedonia Group.

★ 518 ★

Cabinets (SIC 2430)

Popular Wood for Cabinets

Total sales exceeded $7 billion.

Red oak	45.0%
Maple	29.8
Cherry	10.9
Hickory	6.0
Birch	2.3
White oak	1.1
Pine	1.0
Other	4.1

Source: *Kitchen & Bath Business*, July 2002, p. 5.

★ 519 ★

Lumber (SIC 2431)

Plastic and Wood Lumber Demand

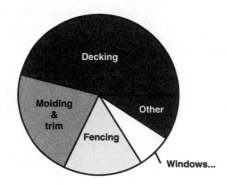

The market is expected to grow from $1.07 billion in 2001 to $1.95 billion in 2006.

	2001	2006
Decking	38.0%	46.0%
Molding & trim	31.0	22.0
Fencing	15.0	16.0
Windows & doors	6.0	7.0
Other	10.0	9.0

Source: *Plastics News*, December 30, 2002, p. 3, from Freedonia Group.

★ 520 ★

Building Components (SIC 2439)

Largest Building Component Producers, 2001

The top manufacturers in North America are ranked by component sales in millions of dollars. Components include roof and floor trusses, wall panels and pre-hung doors. Figures are based on a survey conducted by the source, in which 81 companies responded.

Carpenter Contractors of America	$ 168.0
Stark Truss Co.	90.0
Toll Integrated Syst.	60.0
Raymond Bldg. Sup.	48.5
Boozer Lumber Co.	33.5
Glaize Components	30.0
A.C. Houston	29.0
Fullerton Bldg. Systm.	25.9
Adams Bldg.	25.4
Southern Truss Co.	24.0

Source: "Top Component Producers." available March 7, 2003 from http://www.automatedbuilder.com, p. NA.

★ 521 ★

Pallets (SIC 2448)

Leading Type of Pallets

Figures are based on a survey of 425 respondents representing 15 vertical industries. Pallets are still a widely used material handling tool. According to the survey, 96% of respondents use or plan to use pallets at their location, up from 88% in May2000.

Wood	86.0%
Plastic	8.7
Wood composite	2.1
Cardboard/corrugated	1.7
Metal	1.5

Source: *Material Handling Product News*, July 2002, p. 16, from survey.

★ 522 ★

Manufactured Homes (SIC 2451)

Largest Manufactured Home Makers, 2002

The industry has been suffering from financing issues, high repossessions and large inventories. Industry shipments were down 13% from 2001 and 52% from 1999. Market shares are shown in percent.

Champion Enterprises	17.0%
Fleetwood Enterprises	15.0
Clayton Homes	10.0
Oakwood Homes	10.0
Cavalier Homes	7.0
Other	41.0

Source: *Wall Street Journal*, April 3, 2003, p. B3, from Manufactured Housing Institute.

★ 523 ★

Manufactured Homes (SIC 2451)

Top Modular/Whole-House Panel Builders, 2001

Companies are ranked by units shipped.

Coachmen Housing and Building Systems	2,731
New Era Building Systems	1,622
Muncy Homes	1,450
Excel Homes	1,250
BT Building Systems	1,220
Champion Enterprises	1,090
Genesis Homes	900
Ritz-Craft	788
Horton Homes	750
Crestline Homes	736

Source: "Builder 100." available March 7, 2003 from http://www.builderonline.com.

★ 524 ★

Log Homes (SIC 2452)

Top Log Home Builders, 2001

Honka Log Homes
Jim Barna Log Sytems
Log Homes of America
Gastineau Log Homes
Hearthstone
Wholesale Log Homes
Fall Creek Housing
Town & Country Cedar Homes
Mountaineer Log & Siding

Companies are ranked by units.

Honka Log Homes	3,500
Jim Barna Log Sytems	475
Log Homes of America	150
Gastineau Log Homes	142
Hearthstone	102
Wholesale Log Homes	88
Fall Creek Housing	67
Town & Country Cedar Homes	65
Mountaineer Log & Siding	64

Source: "Builder 100." available March 7, 2003 from http://www.builderonline.com.

★ 525 ★

Decking (SIC 2490)

U.S. Decking Industry, 2001

The figures include only the material used in decking boards, stair treads, balusters, spindles and railings and exclude all structural support. WPC stands for wood-plastic combination.

Treated wood	83.0%
Redwood	6.0
Red cedar	5.0
WPC	4.0
Plastic	1.0

Source: *Wood Markets*, October 2002, p. 1.

★ 526 ★

Wood Composites (SIC 2493)

Wood Composite Market

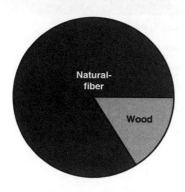

The $860 million market is shown in percent.

Natural-fiber 84.0%
Wood 16.0

Source: *Modern Plastics*, January 2003, p. 25, from
Principia Partners.

SIC 25 - Furniture and Fixtures

★ 527 ★
Furniture (SIC 2500)
Largest Furniture Makers, 2001

Companies are ranked by furniture shipments in millions of dollars. Shares are shown based on shipments of the top 25 companies.

	Shipments ($ mil.)	% of Top 25
La-Z-Boy	$ 2,071.6	16.06%
Furniture Brands International	1,815.6	14.08
LifeStyle Furnishings International	1,258.8	9.76
Ashley Furniture	1,002.6	7.77
Klaussner	826.1	6.40
Ethan Allen	738.9	5.73
Sauder Woodworking	563.0	4.36
Dorel	408.0	3.16
Natuzzi	336.9	2.61
O'Sullivan Inds.	326.5	2.53
Other	3,550.7	27.53

Source: *Furniture Today*, Winter 2002, p. 44.

★ 528 ★
Furniture (SIC 2511)
Wood Furniture Sales in Canada, 1998

Ontario has about 45% of the $3.1 billion home furniture sales and 39% of the $.1 billion office furniture market. Shipments are shown in millions of dollars.

	($ mil.)	Share
Bedding and other	$ 3,406	37.79%
Residential furniture	2,468	27.38
Cabinets and countertops . . .	1,448	16.07
Wood office furniture	1,004	11.14
Institutional furniture	687	7.62

Source: *Wood & Wood Products*, January 2003, p. 49, from *Manufacturing Industries of Canada* and Statistics Canada.

★ 529 ★
Furniture (SIC 2514)
Outdoor Furniture Sales, 2001

California
Texas
Florida
New York
Washington D.C.
Arizona
Georgia
Illinois
Other

Distribution of sales is shown by state.

California	24.4%
Texas	7.1
Florida	5.5
New York	4.6
Washington D.C.	4.3

Continued on next page.

★ 529 ★ *Continued*

Furniture (SIC 2514)

Outdoor Furniture Sales, 2001

Distribution of sales is shown by state.

Arizona	3.9%
Georgia	3.1
Illinois	2.7
Other	44.4

Source: *HFN*, March 24, 2003, p. 48, from *Casual Furniture Report* and American Furniture Manufacturers Association.

★ 530 ★

Bedding (SIC 2515)

Largest Bedding Makers, 2001

Market shares are shown in percent. Wholesale bedding shipments reached $4.59 billion. Figures do not include international sales, royalty shipments, retail sales or sales of non-branded merchandise.

Sealy	23.08%
Serta	15.77
Simmons	14.63
Spring Air	6.99
Therapedic	2.39
King Koil	2.35
Englander	2.20
Restonic	2.18
Kingsdown	2.13
Lady Americana	1.74
Other	26.53

Source: *Furniture Today*, Winter 2002, p. 44, from International Sleep Products Association.

★ 531 ★

Office Furniture (SIC 2520)

Leading Office Furniture Vendors for the Government, 2001

Market shares are shown based on total purchases of $410.7 million.

Herman Miller Inc.	16.63%
Knoll Inc.	12.62
Haworth	9.12
Steelcase Inc.	6.65
UNICOR	5.34
Krueger International	4.20
Kimball Intenational	3.85

Zero Corp.	1.69%
Other	39.90

Source: *Government Executive*, August 15, 2002, p. NA, from Eagle Eye Publishers and Federal Procurement Data Center.

★ 532 ★

Office Furniture (SIC 2520)

Office Furniture Shipments, 2001

Shipments fell 20% to $9.4 billion for the year. Manufacturers are optimistic about shipments in 2003, expecting an increase of 8%, but an unstable economy may stall the plans of some businesses to expand.

Systems	33.9%
Seating	25.2
Files	12.6
Desks	11.5
Tables	7.1
Storage	6.0
Other	3.7

Source: *Purchasing*, December 12, 2002, p. 56, from Business and Institutional Furniture Manufacturers Association.

★ 533 ★

School Furniture (SIC 2531)

School Furniture Market

Market shares are estimated. The company also makes things such as cots and cafeteria trays.

Furniture Focus	50.0%
Other	50.0

Source: *Los Angeles Business Journal*, June 10, 2002, p. 30.

★ 534 ★

Hospital Beds (SIC 2599)

Hospital Bed Market

Market shares are shown in percent.

Hillenbrand	90.0%
Other	10.0

Source: *Knight-Ridder/Tribune Business News*, September 26, 2002, p. NA.

SIC 26 - Paper and Allied Products

★ 535 ★
Paper (SIC 2600)

Pulp & Paper Production

Figures are in thousands of tons for year-to-date April 2000 and 2002.

	2000	2002
Printing/writing	9,030	7,820
Unbleached kraft paperboard	6,989	6,652
Unbleached kraft linerboard	5,652	5,709
Recycled paperboard	5,476	5,120
Uncoated free-sheet	4,738	4,217
Coated papers	3,135	2,716
Newsprint	2,479	1,910
Tissue	2,281	2,290
Coated free-sheet	1,689	1,364
Coated groundwood	1,446	1,352

Source: *Pulp & Paper*, August 2002, p. 32, from American Forest & Paper Association.

★ 536 ★
Paper (SIC 2600)

Pulp & Paper Production in Canada

Figures are in thousands of tons for year-to-date April 2000 and 2002.

	2000	2002	Share
Newsprint	3,081	2,746	42.37%
Printing/writing papers	2,100	2,038	31.45
Linerboard	648	621	9.58
Corrugated medium	392	342	5.28
Boxboard	364	334	5.15
Tissue/specialty papers	218	230	3.55
Kraft paper	181	170	2.62

Source: *Pulp & Paper*, August 2002, p. 32, from Pulp and Paper Products Council.

★ 537 ★
Pulp (SIC 2611)

Largest Pulp Producers in North America

Market shares are shown based on capacity.

Weyerhaeuser	11.3%
Tembec	10.4
Canfor Corp.	6.2
Georgia-Pacific	6.0
International Paper Co.	5.0
Other	61.1

Source: *Pulp & Paper*, August 2002, p. 11.

★ 538 ★
Paper (SIC 2621)

Leading Kraft Paper Producers

Market shares are shown based on North American capacity.

International Paper	18.2%
Smurfit-Stone Container	10.9
Georgia-Pacific	9.3
Inland Paperboard	8.0
Longview Fibre	7.8
Tolko Industries	5.8
Durango-Georgia	5.8
Port Townsend Paper	4.5
Canfor	4.4
West Fraser Timber	4.4
Other	21.0

Source: *Pulp & Paper*, November 2002, p. 11, from American Forest & Paper Association.

★ 539 ★
Paper (SIC 2621)

Leading Newsprint Producers

Market shares are shown based on North American capacity.

Abitibi-Consolidated	31.5%
Bowater Inc.	18.3
Kruger Inc.	6.8
NorskeCanada	6.6
SP Newsprint Co.	5.8
North Pacific Paper	4.5
Tembec Inc.	3.1
Brant-Allen Industries	3.0
Papiers Stadacona	2.6
Boise Cascade	2.5
Other	15.3

Source: *Pulp & Paper*, November 2002, p. 11, from American Forest & Paper Association.

★ 540 ★
Paper (SIC 2621)

Leading Tissue Producers

Market shares are shown based on North American capacity.

Georgia-Pacific	34.8%
Kimberly-Clark	18.8
Procter & Gamble	15.3
Cascades	5.7
SCA Tissue	5.2
Kruger Inc.	3.9
CelluTissue	2.5
J.D. Irving	2.4
Potlatch	2.0

Wausau-Mosinee	1.2%
Other	9.5

Source: *Pulp & Paper*, February 2003, p. 7, from American Forest & Paper Association.

★ 541 ★
Paper (SIC 2621)

Leading Uncoated Groundwood Producers

Top U.S. and Canadian firms are shown by share of capacity.

Abitibi-Consolidated	29.2%
NSI (Norske Canada)	12.8
Bowater	10.4
Stora Enso	10.0
Inexcon (Great Northern Paper)	7.4
Other	30.2

Source: *Pulp & Paper*, September 2002, p. 11, from RISI.

★ 542 ★
Paper (SIC 2621)

Roll Wrap Market

The company controls more than 50% of the North American market. Roll wrap is protective wrapping for paper rolls.

Mosinee Converted	50.0%
Other	50.0

Source: *Knight-Ridder Tribune Business News*, May 4, 2003, p. NA.

★ 543 ★
Paperboard (SIC 2631)

Leading Bleached Paperboard Producers

Market shares are shown based on North American capacity.

International Paper	33.9%
Westvaco	22.2
Potlach	8.5
Georgia-Pacific	7.7
Smurfit-Stone	4.3
Blue Ridge Paper	3.7

Continued on next page.

★ 543 ★ *Continued*

Paperboard (SIC 2631)

Leading Bleached Paperboard Producers

Market shares are shown based on North American capacity.

Gulf States Paper	3.6%
Weyerhaeuser	3.0
Tembec	2.7
Durango-Georgia	2.7
Other	7.6

Source: *Pulp & Paper*, October 2002, p. 11, from American Forest & Paper Association.

★ 544 ★

Paperboard (SIC 2631)

Leading Containerboard Makers

Market shares are shown based on capacity. Figures include Canada and U.S. companies.

Smurfit-Stone	19.2%
Weyerhaeuser	15.2
International Paper	11.5
Temple-Inland	9.9
Georgia-Pacific	9.2
Other	35.0

Source: *Canadian Packaging*, November 2002, p. S9, from *Pulp and Paper North American Fact Book*.

★ 545 ★

Paperboard (SIC 2631)

Leading Kraft Linerboard Producers

Market shares are shown based on North American capacity.

Smurfit-Stone	18.6%
Weyerhaeuser	15.6
International Paper	14.5
Inland Paperboard	10.8
Georgia-Pacific	9.6
PCA	5.1
Norampac Inc.	2.5

Green Bay Packaging	2.2%
Longview Fibre	2.1
Boise Cascade	1.9
Other	17.1

Source: *Pulp & Paper*, January 2003, p. 7, from American Forest & Paper Association.

★ 546 ★

Coated Paper (SIC 2671)

Largest Coated Groundwood Producers

Top U.S. and Canadian firms are shown by share of capacity.

International Paper	22.0%
Stora Enso	17.5
UPM-Kymmene	17.1
MeadWestvaco	10.9
Bowater	7.4
Other	25.1

Source: *Pulp & Paper*, May 2002, p. 11.

★ 547 ★

Coated Paper (SIC 2672)

Largest Coated Freesheet Producers in North America

Companies are ranked by capacity in thousands of tons. MeadWestvaco has a 25% share, Sappi a 22% share.

MeadWestvaco	1,605
Sappi Fine Papers	1,360
International Paper	1,100
Stora Enso	986
Domtar	400
Appleton	270

Continued on next page.

★ 547 ★ *Continued*
Coated Paper (SIC 2672)

Largest Coated Freesheet Producers in North America

Companies are ranked by capacity in thousands of tons. MeadWestvaco has a 25% share, Sappi a 22% share.

West Linn	215
Nexfor Fraser	85
Georgia-Pacific	60
Bowater	60

Source: *Graphic Arts Monthly*, January 2003, p. 36, from American Forest & Paper Association.

★ 548 ★
Tape (SIC 2672)

Duct Tape Market

The Duck brand has over 50% of the market.

Duck	50.0%
Other	50.0

Source: *Fortune*, March 17, 2003, p. 136.

★ 549 ★
Tape (SIC 2672)

Pressure-Sensitive Tape Demand, 2001

Demand is shown by application.

Carton sealing	19.0%
Masking	13.0
Medical/sanitary	12.0
Electrical/electronic	8.0
Stationery	7.0
Bundling & strapping	5.0
Other	36.0

Source: *Label & Narrow Web*, March 2003, p. 42, from Freedonia Group.

★ 550 ★
Tape (SIC 2672)

Pressure-Sensitive Tape Shipments

Shipments are expected to increase 2.8% annually through 2006. Technical and specialty tapes will see the highest growth rates.

	2001	2006	Share
Plastic	$ 2,445	$ 3,025	53.49%
Paper	1,035	1,210	21.40
Adhesive transfer	295	395	6.98
Other	840	1,025	18.13

Source: *Canadian Packaging*, October 2002, p. 30, from Freedonia Group.

★ 551 ★
Trash Bags (SIC 2673)

Largest Trash Bag/Liner Makers

Market shares are shown in percent. Pactiv Corp, Polyethylene Packaging and AEP Industries share another 18% of the market; the top 5 firms have 45% of the market. Consumer trash bags have 39% of the market, institutional has 35% and industrial liners have 26%.

Tyco Plastics	19.0%
Glad Manufacturing	8.0
Other	73.0

Source: *Plastics Technology*, March 2003, p. 67, from Mastio & Company.

★ 552 ★
Diapers (SIC 2676)

Leading Diaper Makers, 2002

Market shares are shown for the year ended November 3. Private label makes up most of the balance of the market.

Procter & Gamble	42.0%
Kimberly-Clark	39.0
Other	19.0

Source: *Star-Ledger*, December 20, 2002, p. 69, from Information Resources Inc.

★ 553 ★
Diapers (SIC 2676)

Private Label Diaper Market

Market shares are shown in percent.

Tyco	95.0%
Other	5.0

Source: *Nonwovens Industry*, May 2003, p. 28.

★ 554 ★
Diapers (SIC 2676)

Top Adult Incontinence Brands, 2002

Brands are ranked by sales in millions of dollars for the year ended February 24, 2002. Figures include supermarkets, drug stores and discount stores but exclude Wal-Mart.

	($ mil.)	Share
Depend	$ 164.0	34.53%
Depend Poise	99.2	20.88
Serenity	43.4	9.14
Sure Care Slip On	4.7	0.99
Attends	4.3	0.91
Entrust Plus	3.3	0.69
Prevail	2.7	0.57
Sure Care	2.7	0.57
Compose	0.9	0.19
Curity	0.6	0.13
Private label	148.3	31.22
Other	0.9	0.19

Source: *Chain Drug Review*, June 24, 2002, p. 187, from Information Resources Inc.

★ 555 ★
Diapers (SIC 2676)

Top Adult Incontinence Brands by Unit Sales, 2002

Brands are ranked by unit sales for the year ended February 24, 2002. Figures include supermarkets, drug stores and discount stores but exclude Wal-Mart.

	(mil.)	Share
Depend Poise	12.2	25.58%
Depend	11.9	24.95
Serenity	5.5	11.53
Prevail	0.3	0.63
Sure Care	0.3	0.63

	(mil.)	Share
Entrust Plus	0.3	0.63%
Sure Care Slip On	0.3	0.63
Other	16.9	35.43

Source: *MMR*, April 22, 2002, p. 57, from Information Resources Inc.

★ 556 ★
Diapers (SIC 2676)

Top Training Pants Makers

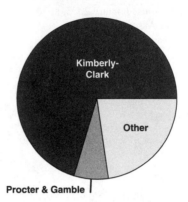

Market shares are shown in percent.

Kimberly-Clark	70.5%
Procter & Gamble	6.7
Other	22.8

Source: *Knight-Ridder/Tribune Business News*, October 23, 2002, p. NA, from Information Resources Inc.

★ 557 ★
Feminine Hygiene Products (SIC 2676)

Tampon Market Leaders

Market shares are shown in percent.

Tampax	40.0%
Playtex	27.0
Kotex	11.0
Other	22.0

Source: *Mergers & Acquisitions Report*, January 20, 2003, p. NA.

★ 558 ★

Feminine Hygiene Products (SIC 2676)

Top Feminine Hygiene Remedies, 2002

Brands are ranked by sales in millions of dollars for the year ended February 24, 2002. Figures include supermarkets, drug stores and discount stores but exclude Wal-Mart.

	($ mil.)	Share
Monistat 3	$ 63.4	15.30%
Summer's Eve	35.2	8.49
Monistat 7	33.8	8.16
Monistat 1	28.1	6.78
Massengill	26.8	6.47
Vagisil	20.8	5.02
K Y	19.2	4.63
Vagistat	17.9	4.32
FDS	12.4	2.99
Gyne Lotrimin 3	10.7	2.58
Private label	62.2	15.01
Other	83.9	20.25

Source: *Chain Drug Review*, June 24, 2002, p. 187, from Information Resources Inc.

★ 559 ★

Feminine Hygiene Products (SIC 2676)

Top Tampon Vendors

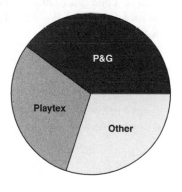

Market shares are shown in percent.

P&G	40.0%
Playtex	30.0
Other	30.0

Source: *Wall Street Journal*, November 13, 2002, p. B2.

★ 560 ★

Sanitary Paper Products (SIC 2676)

Consumer Tissue Market

Market shares are shown in percent.

Bath tissue	56.0%
Paper towels	30.0
Facial tissue	8.5
Napkins	5.5

Source: *Pulp & Paper*, February 2003, p. 7.

★ 561 ★

Sanitary Paper Products (SIC 2676)

Leading Moist Towelette Brands, 2002

Shares are shown for the year ended February 24, 2002. Figures are for supermarkets, drug stores and discount stores and exclude Wal-Mart.

	($ mil.)	Share
Kleenex Cottonelle	$ 48.2	33.61%
Wet Ones	33.7	23.50
Lever 2000	8.2	5.72
Quilted Northern	7.5	5.23
Kleenex Just for Me	7.5	5.23
Pampers Tidy Tykes	7.4	5.16
Splash 'n Go	3.4	2.37
Nice 'n Clean	3.3	2.30
Depend	3.0	2.09
Shower to Shower	2.2	1.53
Private label	9.5	6.62
Other	9.5	6.62

Source: *Chain Drug Review*, June 24, 2002, p. 238, from Information Resources Inc.

★ 562 ★

Sanitary Paper Products (SIC 2676)

Top Baby Wipe Brands, 2002

Brands are ranked by sales in millions of dollars for the year ended December 1, 2002. Figures are for supermarkets, drug stores, and discount stores but exclude Wal-Mart.

	($ mil.)	Share
Huggies Natural Care	$ 111.5	15.13%
Pampers Natural Aloe	43.4	5.89
Huggies	39.0	5.29
Huggies Supreme Care	30.1	4.08

Continued on next page.

★ 562 ★ *Continued*

Sanitary Paper Products (SIC 2676)

Top Baby Wipe Brands, 2002

Brands are ranked by sales in millions of dollars for the year ended December 1, 2002. Figures are for supermarkets, drug stores, and discount stores but exclude Wal-Mart.

	($ mil.)	Share
Pampers Baby Fresh One Ups	$ 26.8	3.64%
Pampers Original Cotton Care	18.9	2.56
Luvs	13.2	1.79
Playtex Baby Magic	8.5	1.15
Pampers Big Wipes	5.5	0.75
Pampers One Ups	5.2	0.71
Other	435.0	59.02

Source: *MMR*, January 27, 2003, p. 21, from Information Resources Inc.

★ 563 ★

Sanitary Paper Products (SIC 2676)

Top Baby Wipe Producers, 2002

Market shares are shown for the year ended November 3, 2002. Figures exclude Wal-Mart.

Kimberly-Clark	41.9%
Procter & Gamble	28.9
Playtex	2.0
Rockline	0.3
Hot Gossip	0.1
Nice-Pak	0.1
Private label	26.7

Source: *Grocery Headquarters*, January 2003, p. 60, from Information Resources Inc.

★ 564 ★

Sanitary Paper Products (SIC 2676)

Top Paper Towel Brands, 2002

Shares are shown based on dollar sales at grocery, drug and mass market outlets (but not Wal-Mart) for the year ended December 29, 2002.

Bounty	36.6%
Brawny	11.5
Scott	10.5
Kleenex Viva	8.6
Sparkle	7.0
Mardi Gras	2.4
Marcal	1.7

Bounty Double Quilted	1.4%
So-Dri	1.4
Private label	17.3
Other	1.6

Source: *Grocery Headquarters*, April 2003, p. 43, from Information Resources Inc.

★ 565 ★

Sanitary Paper Products (SIC 2676)

Top Paper Towel Makers, 2002

Shares are shown based on dollar sales at grocery, drug and mass market outlets (but not Wal-Mart) for the year ended December 29, 2002.

Procter & Gamble	38.1%
Georgia-Pacific Corp.	23.1
Kimberly-Clark Corp.	19.5
Marcal Paper Mills Inc.	1.7
Private label	17.3
Other	0.3

Source: *Grocery Headquarters*, April 2003, p. 45, from Information Resources Inc.

★ 566 ★

Sanitary Paper Products (SIC 2676)

Top Toilet Tissue Brands, 2002

Shares are shown based on dollar sales at grocery, drug and mass market outlets (but not Wal-Mart) for the year ended December 29, 2002.

Charmin	14.8%
Quilted Northern	13.8
Kleenex Cottonelle	10.4
Angel Soft	9.9
Charmin Ultra	8.7
Scott	7.5
Scottissue	4.8
Soft 'n Gentle	3.2
Private label	12.7
Other	14.2

Source: *Grocery Headquarters*, April 2003, p. 43, from Information Resources Inc.

★ 567 ★

Sanitary Paper Products (SIC 2676)

Top Toilet Tissue Makers, 2002

Shares are shown based on dollar sales at grocery, drug and mass market outlets (but not Wal-Mart) for the year ended December 29, 2002.

Georgia-Pacific Corp. 32.5%
Kimberly-Clark Corp. 26.8
Procter & Gamble 25.9
Marcal Paper Mills Inc. 1.5
Private label 12.7
Other 0.6

Source: *Grocery Headquarters*, April 2003, p. 43, from Information Resources Inc.

★ 568 ★

Envelopes (SIC 2677)

Offertory Envelope Industry

American Church is country's largest distributor of monthly mailed and boxed-set church envelopes. It has 35,000 church clients.

American Church 40.0%
Other 60.0

Source: *Knight Ridder/Tribune Business News*, June 19, 2002, p. NA.

★ 569 ★

Wrapping Paper (SIC 2679)

Gift Wrap Market

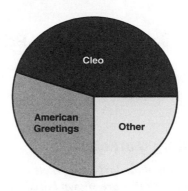

Wrapping paper makes up 45% of Cleo's sales, with 35-40% coming from gift bags. Red and green are still the top colors. Market shares are shown in percent.

Cleo 45.0%
American Greetings 30.0
Other 25.0

Source: *Knight Ridder/Tribune Business News*, December 18, 2002, p. NA, from company reports.

SIC 27 - Printing and Publishing

★ 570 ★
Printing (SIC 2700)

Largest Printing Markets

The printing potential of the largest markets is shown in billions of dollars. Shares are shown based on total printing potential, which is thought to reach $162.4 billion.

	($ bil.)	Share
Non-newspaper publishing	$ 16.1	9.91%
Banking/insurance	12.4	7.64
Telecom	11.3	6.96
Software	9.8	6.03
Medical products/pharmaceuticals	9.4	5.79
Real estate	9.4	5.79
Beverages	8.2	5.05
Automotive	7.9	4.86
Home improvements	7.5	4.62
Packaged goods	7.5	4.62
Other	62.9	38.73

Source: *American Printer*, December 2002, p. 25, from PB/BA International.

★ 571 ★
Printing (SIC 2700)

Leading Printing Firms in North America

Firms are ranked by sales for the most fiscal year in billions of dollars.

Quebecor World	$ 6.30
R.R. Donnelley & Sons	5.29
Moore Corporation	2.20
Vertis Inc.	1.90
Quad/Graphics	1.80

Mail-Well Inc.	$ 1.70
Wallace Computer Services	1.54
Deluxe Corporation	1.46
Standard Register	1.27

Source: *Graphic Arts Monthly*, November 2002, p. 37.

★ 572 ★
Newspapers (SIC 2711)

Largest Newspaper Publishers

Companies are ranked by daily circulation, in millions. Figures are for the six month period ending March 31, 2000.

Gannett Co.	7.3
Knight Ridder	3.9
Tribune Co.	3.7
Advance Publications	2.9
New York Times Co.	2.4
Dow Jones & Co.	2.4
MediaNews Group	1.8
Hearst	1.7
E.W. Scripps	1.5
McClatchy	1.3

Source: *USA TODAY*, June 3, 2003, p. 3B, from *2001NAA Facts About Newspapers*.

★ 573 ★

Newspapers (SIC 2711)

Top Daily Newspaper Markets

Areas are ranked by percentage of adult readership.

Providence, R.I./New Bedford, MA	. 65.3%
Hartford/New Haven, CT	. 65.3
West Palm Beach, FL	. 64.6
Boston, MA	. 64.2
Cleveland, OH	. 63.0
New York City, NY	. 63.0
Pittsburgh, PA	. 63.0
Buffalo, NY	. 62.3
Washington D.C.	. 61.6

Source: *PR Newswire*, May 1, 2002, p. NA, from Newspaper Association of America.

★ 574 ★

Newspapers (SIC 2711)

Top Newspapers, 2003

Figures show average weekday circulation, in thousands, for the six months ended March 31, 2003.

USA Today	2,250
The Wall Street Journal	1,820
The New York Times	1,131
The Los Angeles Times	980
The Washington Post	796
The New York Daily News	737
The Chicago Tribune	621
The New York Post	620
The Denver Post/Rocky Mountain News . . .	602
Newsday	579

Source: *New York Times*, May 6, 2003, p. C4, from Audit Bureau of Circulations.

★ 575 ★

Newspapers (SIC 2711)

Top Sunday Newspaper Markets

Areas are ranked by percentage of adult readership.

West Palm Beach, FL	. 75.6%
Tampa/St. Petersburg/Sarasota, FL	. 75.2
Providence, R.I./New Bedford, MA	. 74.5
Cleveland, OH	. 73.4
Hartford/New Haven, CT	. 73.3
Pittsburgh, PA	. 72.3
Buffalo, NY	. 71.6

Milwaukee, MN	. 70.1%
New York City, NY	. 69.8

Source: *PR Newswire*, May 1, 2002, p. NA, from Newspaper Association of America.

★ 576 ★

Comic Books (SIC 2721)

Comic Industry Leaders, 2003

Marvel Comics
DC Comics
Image Comics
Dark Horse Comics
Crossgen Comics
Dreamwave
Viz Communications
Wizard Communications
Comicsone.com
Tokyopop
Other

Market shares are shown based on sales of comics, graphic novels and magazines for January 2003.

Marvel Comics	. 29.66%
DC Comics	. 25.48
Image Comics	. 6.80
Dark Horse Comics	. 6.54
Crossgen Comics	. 3.61
Dreamwave	. 3.00
Viz Communications	. 2.82
Wizard Communications	. 2.36
Comicsone.com	. 1.95
Tokyopop	. 1.58
Other	. 16.19

Source: "January 2003 Market Share." available February 26, 2003 from http://www.diamondcomics.com, from Diamond Comics.

★ 577 ★
Comic Books (SIC 2721)

Highest-Priced Comics of 2001

Other copies of Captain America No. 1 sold for $166,750 and $95,000. Detective Comics No. 27 featured the first appearance of Batman.

Marvel Comics No. 1	$ 350,000
Detective Comics No. 27	278,190
Captain America Comics No. 1	265,000
More Fun Comics No. 52	207,000
Batman No. 1	150,000
Sensation Comics No. 1	100,000
Amazing Fantasy No. 15	95,000
Amazing Spider-Man No. 1	67,305

Source: *New York Times*, September 15, 2002, p. 9, from *Overstreet Comic Book Pricing Guide*.

★ 578 ★
Comic Books (SIC 2721)

Most Ordered Comic Books

Figures show preorder projections for the month of March 2003 based on orders placed by retailers through Diamond Comic Distributors. Figures show thousands of copies ordered. Only Justice League of America (JLA) and Batman are published by DC Comics; the rest are all Marvel Comics titles.

Batman 613	132
Ultimate Spider-Man 37	114
Ultimate Spider-Man 38	114
New X-Men 138	100
Amazing Spider-Man 51	100
Ultimate X-Men 30	93
Ultimate X-Men 31	93
Uncanny X-Men 420	90
Wolverine 187	65
JLA 79	65
Wolverine 188	65

Source: *Comics Buyers Guide*, March 21, 2003, p. 13, from Diamond Comic Distributors.

★ 579 ★
Comic Books (SIC 2721)

Top Selling Comics

Figures show the average number of copies reported sold per store by retailers reporting to Comics & Games Retailer's Market Beat column for March 2003. This source receives reports from dozens of retailers each month listing their actual sales of the top 30 titles. The reports are averaged and then an algorithm is formed.

Batman	58
Ultimates	52
New X-Men	49
Ultimate Spider-Man	43
Amazing Spider-Man	41
Ultimate X-Men	39
Uncanny X-Men	36
JLA	28
Wolverine	24
Fantastic Four	23
Avengers	22
JSA	20
Incredible Hulk	20

Source: *Comics Buyers Guide*, May 16, 2003, p. 13, from *Comics & Games Retailer*.

★ 580 ★
Magazines (SIC 2721)

Home Planning Magazine Publishers, 2002

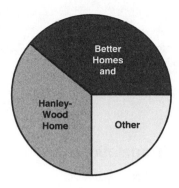

Market shares are shown in percent.

Better Homes and Gardens 39.0%
Hanley-Wood Home Plan 36.0
Other 25.0

Source: ''Hanley-Wood Home Plans Titles Post Big Gains.'' available May 12, 2003 from http://www.hanley-wood.com, from Hanley-Wood and Anderson News Company.

★ 581 ★
Magazines (SIC 2721)

Leading Magazine Publishers, 2002

Shares are shown based on ad pages.

Time Inc. 20.4%
Conde Nast Publications 11.3
Hearst 7.4
Hachette Filipacchi Media 6.7
Primedia 4.6
Other 49.6

Source: *Wall Street Journal*, April 24, 2003, p. 1, from Publishers Information Bureau and Competitive Media Reporting.

★ 582 ★
Magazines (SIC 2721)

Leading Magazines by Revenue, 2001

Magazines are ranked by gross advertising and circulation revenue in millions of dollars.

People . . . . $ 1,119.9
TV Guide 955.6
Time 843.0
Sports Illustrated 841.7
Better Homes & Gardens 641.7
Reader's Digest 580.4
Parade 570.4
Newsweek 517.3
Business Week 454.7
Good Housekeeping 412.2

Source: *Advertising Age*, September 23, 2002, pp. S-2, from Competititive Media Reporting.

★ 583 ★
Magazines (SIC 2721)

Leading Tween/Teenager Magazines, 2001

Paid circulation is shown for the last six months of the year.

Seventeen 2,333,126
YM 2,206,078
Teen People 1,639,107
Teen 1,587,754
Boy's Life 1,224,829

Source: *Youth Markets Alert*, April 2002, p. 2, from Audit Bureau of Circulations.

★ 584 ★
Magazines (SIC 2721)

Magazine Ad Pages, 2002

Figures show the number of ad pages for the full year.

People Weekly 3,697.91
Forbes 3,504.60
Business Week 3,333.12
Fortune 3,331.42
In Style 3,030.54
Vogue 2,889.96
Transworld Skateboarding 2,884.59
Bride's 2,805.44

Continued on next page.

★ 584 ★ *Continued*
Magazines (SIC 2721)
Magazine Ad Pages, 2002

Figures show the number of ad pages for the full year.

New York Magazine 2,512.36
Sports Illustrated 2,498.59

Source: *Advertising Age*, January 13, 2003, p. 17, from Publishers Information Bureau.

★ 585 ★
Magazines (SIC 2721)
Male Fashion Magazine Leaders

Shares are shown based on fashion and retail ads. Through April 2003, Details' total ad pages increased 35% to 299, behind industry leaders GQ at 443 pages and Maxim at 335 pages.

	2000	2002
GQ	36.0%	27.0%
Details	4.0	18.0
Other	60.0	55.0

Source: *Crain's New York Business*, May 5, 2003, p. 6, from Media Industry News.

★ 586 ★
Magazines (SIC 2721)
Top Magazines by Circulation, 2002

Figures show average circulation for the second half of the year.

Modern Maturity 17,183,768
Reader's Digest 11,944,898
TV Guide 9,061,639
Better Homes and Gardens 7,607,832
National Geographic 6,657,424
Good Housekeeping 4,690,508
Family Circle 4,601,708
Woman's Day 4,246,805
Time 4,109,962
Ladies' Home Journal 4,101,414

Source: *Adweek*, March 10, 2003, p. SR22, from Audit Bureau of Circulations.

★ 587 ★
Bibles (SIC 2731)
Bible Publishing Industry

The company has the largest share of the market.

Zondervan 45.0%
Other 55.0

Source: "Corporate Information." available March 7, 2003 from http://www.zondervan.com.

★ 588 ★
Bibles (SIC 2731)
Leading Bible Translations

Shares are shown based on translation.

King International Version 30.0%
King James Version 25.0
Other 45.0

Source: *The Washington Times*, November 25, 2002, p. NA.

★ 589 ★
Books (SIC 2731)
Best-Selling Book Segments, 2002

Total book sales increased 5.5% to $26.87 billion. Adult sales rose 11.9% to $5.09 billion and children's sales rose 1% to $1.83 billion. Figures show estimated sales for the year.

	($ mil.)	Share
Professional	$ 5,140.1	19.13%
El-hi	4,073.3	15.16
Higher education	3,898.2	14.51
Adult hardcover	2,935.5	10.92
Adult paperback	2,160.8	8.04
Mass market paperback	1,726.8	6.43
Book clubs	1,463.3	5.45
Religious	1,262.6	4.70
Children's hardcover	957.2	3.56
Children's paperback	876.3	3.26
Other	2,380.0	8.86

Source: *Publishers Weekly*, March 10, 2003, p. 9, from Association of American Publishers.

★ 590 ★

Books (SIC 2731)

Best-Selling Cliffs Notes Books

Unit sales are shown in millions.

The Scarlet Letter	3.0
The Adventures of Huckleberry Finn	2.6
Hamlet	2.6
Macbeth	2.5
The Great Gatsby	2.0

Source: *USA TODAY*, April 16, 2003, p. D1, from Wiley Publishers.

★ 591 ★

Books (SIC 2731)

Best-Selling Fiction Books, 2002

Rankings are determined by sales figures provided by publishers. Numbers generally reflect report of copies "shipped and billed" in the calendar year 2002 and publishers were instructed to adjust sales figures to include returns through January 31, 2003. Most returns are done after this date, however, so figures should not be perceived as final sales figures. Units are in thousands.

The Summons	2,625.0
Red Rabbit	1,970.9
Remnant	1,880.5
The Lovely Bones	1,841.8
Prey	1,496.8
Skipping Christmas	1,225.0
The Shelters of Stone	1,223.1
Four Blind Mice	1,060.4
Everything's Eventual	925.0
The Nanny Diaries	852.0

Source: *Publishers Weekly*, March 24, 2003, p. 33.

★ 592 ★

Books (SIC 2731)

Best-Selling Harry Potter Titles

Figures show millions of copies in print for paperback and hardcover. The four titles have sold 192 million copies worldwide.

Harry Potter and the Sorcerer's Stone	25.1
Harry Potter and the Chamber of Secrets	22.0
Harry Potter and the Prisoner of Azkaban	16.7
Harry Potter and the Goblet of Fire	16.3

Source: *Wall Street Journal*, January 16, 2003, p. B1, from Scholastic.

★ 593 ★

Books (SIC 2731)

Best-Selling Titles in the "For Dummies" Series

Figures show net sales, in millions, after returns.

Windows for Dummies	10.3
Internet for Dummies	3.5
PCs for Dummies	2.4
Microsoft Office for Dummies	2.3
Word for Dummies	2.0
Excel for Dummies	1.9
Personal Finance for Dummies	1.3
Investing for Dummies	1.2
DOS for Dummies	1.0
Wine for Dummies	1.0

Source: *New York Times*, April 27, 2003, p. 8, from Wiley Publishers.

★ 594 ★

Books (SIC 2731)

Best-Selling Topics in the "For Dummies" Series

Sales are shown in thousands of units.

Personal finance	900
Investing	800
Golf	675
Wine	540
Home buying	420

Source: *USA TODAY*, May 14, 2003, p. D1, from Wiley Publishers.

★ 595 ★
Books (SIC 2731)

Book Purchases by Age, 2001

Figures have been rounded.

45-54	23.0%
35-44	20.0
65 >	19.0
55-64	19.0
25-34	13.0
less than 25	7.0

Source: *Newsweek*, March 3, 2003, p. 43, from Ipsos-NPD.

★ 596 ★
Books (SIC 2731)

Children's Book Sales, 2001

A total of 404 million books are thought to have been sold in 2001. This number will drop slightly in coming years. Paperback sales will be fairly stable, although hardcovers will grow slightly, from 153 million in 2002 to 169 million in 2005. Activity books include painting, pressout books, puzzle and sticker books.

	Units (mil.)	Share
Picture/storybooks	125.5	27.86%
Coloring/activity book	121.5	26.98
Nonfiction	52.5	11.66
Series/chapter	44.0	9.77
Novelty	30.5	6.77
Religious	28.5	6.33
Educational workbooks	24.6	5.46
Leveled readers	7.9	1.75
Classic literature	7.6	1.69
Sound books	5.5	1.22
Reference books	2.3	0.51

Source: *Publishers Weekly*, February 10, 2003, p. 74, from Ipsos BookTrends and Children's Book Council.

★ 597 ★
Books (SIC 2731)

Home Planning Manuals

The company has sold over 30 million home planning books and magazines. Its market share is for traditional and super bookstores.

Hanley-Wood	70.0%
Other	30.0

Source: "Hanley-Wood Expands Newsstand." available May 12, 2003 from http://www.hanley-wood.com, from Hanley-Wood.

★ 598 ★
Books (SIC 2731)

Leading Consumer Book Publishers

Random House

Time Inc.

Scholastic

Penguin Group

HarperCollins

Firms are ranked by revenues in billions of dollars.

Random House	$ 1.85
Time Inc.	1.72
Scholastic	1.22
Penguin Group	1.20
HarperCollins	1.02

Source: *New York Times*, January 17, 2003, p. C1, from Simba Information and Random House.

★ 599 ★
Books (SIC 2731)

Leading Hardcover Publishers, 2002

The figure represents the publisher's share of the 1,530 bestseller positions during the year.

Random House	25.2%
Penguin Putnam Inc.	14.9
Simon & Schuster	13.0
Time Warner	12.7
HarperCollins	11.6
Von Holtzbrinck	7.5
Hyperion	6.1
Regnery	2.0
Other	7.0

Source: *Publishers Weekly*, January 13, 2003, p. 32.

★ 600 ★
Books (SIC 2731)

Leading Softcover Publishers, 2002

The figure represents the publisher's share of the 1,530 bestseller positions during the year.

Random House Inc.	26.5%
Time Warner	16.3
HarperCollins	12.9
Penguin Putnam Inc.	12.7
Simon & Schuster	11.1
Von Holtzbrinck	4.4
Silhouette	3.1
Health Communications	1.9
Hyperion	1.9
Other	9.2

Source: *Publishers Weekly*, January 13, 2003, p. 32.

★ 601 ★
Books (SIC 2731)

Series Romance Market

The company has nearly 100% of the market in North America. For the last 20 years the company has seen revenue and earnings grow 5-6%.

Harlequin	99.0%
Other	1.0

Source: *Maclean's*, March 10, 2003, p. 40.

★ 602 ★
Books (SIC 2731)

Top Book Genres at Food/Drug Stores

Figures show percent of unit sales.

Romance	32.2%
Mystery/thrillers	25.5
General fiction	13.3

Science fiction/occult/fantasy	6.6%
Inspirational	3.1
Cooking/wine	1.8
Reference	1.6
Other	15.9

Source: *Supermarket News*, December 16, 2002, p. 20, from Ipsos NPD BookTrends.

★ 603 ★
Books (SIC 2731)

Who Publishes the Classics

Penguin Classics controls about 70% of the trade paperback classic market. The company recently began a program to give its list of 1,300 titles a facelift. For comparison: Oxford publishes about 800 titles and Modern Library publishes 300.

Penguin Classics	70.0%
Other	30.0

Source: *New York Times*, February 10, 2003, p. C9.

★ 604 ★
Textbooks (SIC 2731)

K-5 Textbook Adoptions in Florida

Shares are estimated.

Harcourt (trophies series)	39.0%
Pearson (Scott Foresman Reading)	28.0
Houghton Mifflin	21.0
Other	12.0

Source: *Educational Marketer*, August 12, 2002, p. NA.

★ 605 ★
Textbooks (SIC 2731)

Math Textbook Market

Market shares are for elementary and middle school books.

Harcourt	40.0%
Houghton Mifflin	40.0
SRA/McGraw-Hill	15.0
Other	5.0

Source: *Educational Marketer*, September 9, 2002, p. NA.

★ 606 ★

Textbooks (SIC 2731)

Top College Publishers, 2001

Market shares are shown based on $3.4 billion in revenues.

Pearson Education	25.7%
Thomson Learning	21.0
McGraw-Hill	14.0
Houghton Mifflin/Vivendi	5.0
John Wiley & Sons	4.0
Bedford, Freeeman & Worth	3.9
W.W. Norton	2.0
Jones & Bartlett	2.0
Other	22.4

Source: *Educational Marketer*, May 20, 2002, p. NA, from Simba Information.

★ 607 ★

Video Game Manuals (SIC 2731)

Video Game Guide Industry, 2001

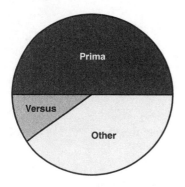

Publishers' shares are shown in percent. Prima published more than 150 guides this year, Versus more than 20.

Prima	50.0%
Versus	10.0
Other	40.0

Source: *San Francisco Chronicle*, October 6, 2002, p. G3.

★ 608 ★

Book Printing (SIC 2732)

Largest Book Printers

Harry Potter has brought life to the category, selling 70 million copies in the country. Firms are ranked by segment sales in millions of dollars.

Quebecor World	$ 693
R.R. Donnelley	688
Banta Corp.	335
Von Hoffmann	305
Bertelsmann Arvato	257
Courier Corp.	211
Phoenix Color	130
Taylor Publishing	114
Walsworth Publishing	84
Webcrafters Inc.	80

Source: *Printing Impressions*, December 2002, p. NA.

★ 609 ★

Printing (SIC 2754)

Largest Catalog Printers

Firms are ranked by segment sales in millions of dollars. R.R. Donelley's figure includes ad inserts.

Quebecor World	$ 1,071
Quad/Graphics	954
R.R. Donnelley	794
Banta Corp.	218
Arandell Corp.	213
Perry Judd's	102
Spencer Press	73
Brown Printing	72
Trend Offset	72
The Dingley Press	69

Source: *Printing Impressions*, December 2002, p. NA.

★ 610 ★

Printing (SIC 2754)

Largest Direct Mail Printers, 2002

Firms are ranked by segment sales in millions of dollars.

Quebecor World	$ 819
Vertis Inc.	370
Moore Corp.	242
Banta Corp.	218
R.R. Donnelley	158

Continued on next page.

★ 610 ★ *Continued*
Printing (SIC 2754)

Largest Direct Mail Printers, 2002

Firms are ranked by segment sales in millions of dollars.

Wallace Computer Services	$ 154
Japs-Olson	97
The Instant Web Cos.	87
The Lehigh Press	83
Clondalkin Group	80

Source: *Printing Impressions*, December 2002, p. NA.

★ 611 ★
Printing (SIC 2754)

Largest Financial Printers

The industry has been affected by corporate scandals, a bear market and the lack of mergers and IPOs, according to the source. Firms are ranked by segment sales in millions of dollars.

Bowne & Co.	$ 717
R.R. Donnelley	476
Merrill Corp.	241
Ennis Business Forms	49
Burrups Packard	25
Applied Printing Technologies	22
Henry Wurst Inc.	16
Scott Printing	16
McNaughton Lithograph/Command Web	14

Source: *Printing Impressions*, December 2002, p. NA.

★ 612 ★
Business Forms (SIC 2761)

Top Forms Manufacturers

Companies are ranked by forms sales in thousands of dollars. Revenue for the top 100 declined to $4.87 billion.

Ennis Business Forms	$ 150,570
PrintXcel	124,550
TST/Impresso	81,448
Printegra	71,625
DSFI	56,000
Highland Computer Forms	44,685
Wise Business Forms	43,200
Paris Business Products	42,000

Vallis Form Service	$ 40,406
Champion Industries	40,032

Source: *Business Forms, Labels & Systems*, October 2002, p. 18.

★ 613 ★
Labels (SIC 2761)

Label Demand

Labels shipments are expected to increase 4.8% annually through 2006.

	2001	2006	Share
Pressure sensitive	$ 7,218	$ 9,645	69.14%
Glue-applied	2,232	2,640	18.92
Other	1,200	1,665	11.94

Source: *Polymers Paint Colour Journal*, January 2003, p. 35, from Freedonia Group.

★ 614 ★
Labels (SIC 2761)

Pressure-Sensitive Label Market

Market shares are estimated in percent.

Avery Dennison	50.0%
Other	50.0

Source: *Los Angeles Business Journal*, April 28, 2003, p. 1.

★ 615 ★
Labels (SIC 2761)

Top Label & Tag Manufacturers

Companies are ranked by label and tag sales in thousands of dollars.

Discount Labels	$ 66,500
Label Art	49,600
Data Label	38,740
Gill Studios	36,600
Lancer Label	36,100
General Data Company	32,000
Stouse	28,207
Diversified Tape & Graphics	25,400
Ennis Business Forms	23,900
Special Service Partners	22,300

Source: *Business Forms, Labels & Systems*, October 2002, p. 18.

★ 616 ★
Greeting Cards (SIC 2771)

Top Greeting Card Producers

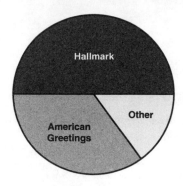

Shares of the $7 billion retail industry are estimated in percent.

Hallmark 50.0%
American Greetings 35.0
Other 15.0

Source: *Knight Ridder/Tribune Business News*, April 15, 2003, p. NA, from McDonald Investments.

★ 617 ★
Greeting Cards (SIC 2771)

Who Purchases Greeting Cards in Canada

Total sales grew from $97.8 million in 1999 to $119.5 million in 2000.

Women 25-64 . . . . 93.0%
Other 7.0

Source: "Greeting Cards." available April 7, 2003 from http://www.usatrade.gov, from United States Department of Commerce.

★ 618 ★
Platemaking (SIC 2796)

CTP Plate Use

The use of digital CTP printing plates in the U.S. and Canada has increased tenfold in the past four years, according to the source. Its market share is in excess of 50%.

Digital CTP plates 50.0%
Other 50.0

Source: *American Printer*, May 1, 2003, p. NA.

SIC 28 - Chemicals and Allied Products

★ 619 ★
Chemicals (SIC 2800)
Beverage Additive Demand

Demand is expected to increase 3.4% per year to $1.7 billion in 2006. Figures are shown in millions of dollars.

	2001	2006	Share
Artificial sweeteners	.$ 559	$ 581	34.79%
Flavors	430	555	33.23
Acidulants	154	184	11.02
Nutraceuticals	98	130	7.78
Other	169	220	13.17

Source: *Research Studies - Freedonia Group*, December 12, 2002, p. 5, from Freedonia Group.

★ 620 ★
Chemicals (SIC 2800)
Chemical Shipments by Year

Figures are in millions of dollars.

	1999	2001	2003
Pharmaceuticals . .	$ 109,249	$ 124,596	$ 132,775
Consumer products .	46,059	48,378	52,850
Coatings	17,091	17,294	18,725
Crop protection . . .	12,821	13,668	14,075
Adhesives & sealants	7,706	8,373	8,675
Electronic chemicals	6,126	6,530	6,725
I&I cleaning chemicals	6,101	6,279	6,650
Industrial gases . . .	5,746	6,251	6,850
Catalysts	1,781	1,828	1,875

Source: *Chemical Market Reporter*, June 24, 2002, p. 14, from American Chemistry Council.

★ 621 ★
Chemicals (SIC 2800)
Membrane Separation Technology

Demand is expected to grow 7.4% a year to 1.3 billion pounds in 2006, valued at $2.1 billion.

Microfiltration	46.0%
Reverse osmosis	23.0
Ultrafiltration	20.0
Pervaporation	3.0
Other	8.0

Source: *Chemical Week*, July 3, 2002, p. 75, from Freedonia Group.

★ 622 ★
Chemicals (SIC 2812)
Chemical Production in Canada

Figures are in thousands of metric tons.

	2000	2001	2002
Ethylene	4,069	4,261	4,793
Ammonia	4,888	4,297	4,446
Sulfuric acid	3,804	3,843	3,990
Polyethylene	2,644	2,986	3,354
Urea	3,887	3,363	3,308
Nitric acid	1,074	1,054	1,174
Ammonium nitrate . . .	1,110	1,174	1,163
Sodium hydroxide	1,094	1,074	1,124
Chlorine	1,079	1,054	1,107
Sodium chlorate	1,107	1,082	1,044

Source: *C&EN*, January 13, 2003, p. 20, from Statistics Canada.

★ 623 ★
Chemicals (SIC 2812)

Concrete Admixture Chemicals

Sales are in millions of dollars by year.

2006 . . . . $ 673.3
2002 . . . . 606.5

Source: *Concrete Products*, March 1, 2003, p. NA, from Hochberg & Co.

★ 624 ★
Chemicals (SIC 2812)

Largest Chemical Companies

Firms are ranked by chemical sales in billions of dollars.

Dow Chemical . . . . $ 27.8
DuPont 26.7
ExxonMobil 15.9
Huntsman Corp. 8.5
General Electric 7.0
BASF 6.8
Chevron Phillips 6.0
PPG Industries 5.9
Equistar Chemicals 5.9
Shell Oil 5.5

Source: *C&EN*, June 24, 2002, p. 46.

★ 625 ★
Chemicals (SIC 2812)

Water Treatment Chemicals

The $3 billion North American market for water treatment chemicals and services is estimated by company.

BetzDearborn 25.0%
Ondeo Nalco 23.0
Chemtreat/Western Chemical/Garratt-
  Callahan 11.0
Drew 4.0
Rohm and Haas 4.0
Dow Chemical 2.0
Calgon Carbon 2.0
Other 6.0

Source: *Chemical Market Reporter*, February 17, 2003, p. 10, from Lake View Associates.

★ 626 ★
Chemicals (SIC 2812)

Wood Plastic Composite Materials

The $30 million market is shown by segment. Trex is the largest producer of wood composite planking with a 70% share.

Colorants 35.0%
Lubricants 30.0
Heat and light stabilizers 20.0
Other 15.0

Source: *Chemical Market Reporter*, January 20, 2003, p. 10, from Eldib Engineering and Research.

★ 627 ★
Industrial Gases (SIC 2813)

Largest Independent Gas Firms

About 52% of the 900 gas distributors nationwide are independent operators. Market shares are shown in percent.

Airgas 19.0%
Praxair 9.0
BOC Group 6.0
Other 66.0

Source: *Crain's Detroit Business*, January 27, 2003, p. 21, from Airgas study.

★ 628 ★
Industrial Gases (SIC 2813)

Packaged Gas Market in Canada

Market shares are shown in percent.

Air Liquide/Praxair 33.0%
BOC 20.0
Other 47.0

Source: *The Morning Call*, March 12, 2003, p. D1.

★ 629 ★

Inorganic Chemicals (SIC 2819)

Largest Ammonia Makers

Shares are shown based on total capacity of 15.8 million metric tons. Fertilizer is the main end market.

	(mil.)	Share
Farmland Industries Inc.	2,490	15.68%
Terra Industries	2,385	15.02
Potash Corporation of Saskatchewan	2,040	12.85
CF Industries Inc.	1,910	12.03
Agrium US Inc.	1,650	10.39
Koch Nitrogen Company	1,095	6.90
Triad Nitrogen	950	5.98
Other	3,360	21.16

Source: *Chemical Market Reporter*, November 25, 2002, p. 31, from ICIS-LOR.

★ 630 ★

Inorganic Chemicals (SIC 2819)

Largest Hydrochloric Acid Producers

Companies are ranked by capacity in thousands of short tons per year.

Dow Chemical	1,495
DuPont Fluroproducts	195
BASF Polymers	176
Vulcan Chemicals	163
Lyondell Chemical	105
Bayer Polyurethanes	100
Pioneer Americas	50

Source: *Chemical Market Reporter*, October 14, 2002, p. 31.

★ 631 ★

Inorganic Chemicals (SIC 2819)

Largest Hydrogen Peroxide Makers, 2001

Shares are shown based on total capacity of 688,000 metric tons.

Degussa	23.0%
FMC	22.0
Atofina	21.0
Solvay	19.0
Eka Chemicals	9.0
Kemira	6.0

Source: *Chemical Week*, December 4, 2002, p. 56, from Atofina Chemicals.

★ 632 ★

Inorganic Chemicals (SIC 2819)

Largest Sulfur Makers

Shares are shown based on total capacity of 12.1 million long tons.

	Tons	Share
ExxonMobil	2,110	18.53%
BP	1,375	12.08
ChevronTexaco	1,190	10.45
Shell	1,065	9.35
Motiva Enterprise	780	6.85
Pursue Energy	580	5.09
ConocoPhillips	485	4.26
Valero Energy	440	3.86
Other	3,360	29.51

Source: *Chemical Market Reporter*, December 9, 2002, p. 35, from ICIS-LOR.

★ 633 ★

Plastics (SIC 2821)

Largest Blow Molders in North America

Companies are ranked by most recent year sales in millions of dollars.

Owens-Illinois Inc.	$ 1,200
Amcor PET Packaging	1,100
Consolidated Container	832
Graham Packaging	744
Plastipak Packaging	715
Kautex Textron	700

Continued on next page.

★ 633 ★ *Continued*
Plastics (SIC 2821)

Largest Blow Molders in North America

Companies are ranked by most recent year sales in millions of dollars.

Crown Cork & Seal/Constar International . . $ 700
Inergy Automotive Systems 540
Siligan Plastics Corp. 441
ABC Group 380

Source: *Plastics News*, October 28, 2002, p. 3.

★ 634 ★
Plastics (SIC 2821)

Largest HDPE Producers

Shares are shown based on North American capacity. HDPE stands for high-density polyethylene.

Chevron Phillips Chemical 24.0%
ExxonMobil Chemical 20.6
Equistar Chemicals 17.5
Solvay Polymers 10.8
Formosa Plastics Corp. 7.7
Other 19.4

Source: *Plastics News*, October 14, 2002, p. 3, from Nexant Chem Systems.

★ 635 ★
Plastics (SIC 2821)

Largest Polycarbonate Producers

Companies are ranked by capacity in thousands of metric tons per year.

GE Plastics 510
Bayer 200
Dow Chemical 170

Source: *Chemical Week*, February 27, 2002, p. 48.

★ 636 ★
Plastics (SIC 2821)

Nylon Resin Industry

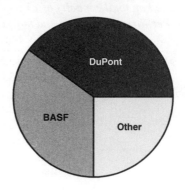

Shares are for North America.

DuPont 40.0%
BASF 35.0
Other 25.0

Source: *Chemical Week*, May 7, 2003, p. 11, from BRO Townsend.

★ 637 ★
Plastics (SIC 2821)

Reinforced Plastics, 2002

The total market reached 2.28 billion pounds.

Automotive 31.0%
Construction 26.0
Marine 12.0
Electronic components 10.0
Appliances 8.0
Consumer products 8.0
Other 5.0

Source: *Plastics News*, August 26, 2002, p. 3, from BCC Inc.

★ 638 ★

Plastics (SIC 2821)

Styrenic Block Copolymer Demand, 2002

The top end markets are shown for North America.

Adhesives/seals	30.0%
Asphalt modification	22.0
Polymer modification	13.0
Roofing	13.0
Fibers	4.0
Other	18.0

Source: *Plastics News*, January 27, 2003, p. 3, from Chemical Market Resources Inc.

★ 639 ★

Rubber (SIC 2822)

Largest Nitrile Rubber Producers

Companies are ranked by capacity in thousands of metric tons per year.

Zeon Chemicals	46
Altamira	40
Bayer	24
DSM Copolymer	15
BASF	10

Source: *Chemical Market Reporter*, June 17, 2002, p. 27.

★ 640 ★

Supplements (SIC 2833)

Dietary Supplement Market, 2000

The $16.8 billion industry is shown by segment.

Vitamins	35.0%
Herbals and botanicals	25.0
Meal supplements	13.0
Specialty supplements	10.0
Sports nutrition products	9.0
Minerals	8.0

Source: *Family Practice News*, December 1, 2002, p. 1, from Dietary Supplement Education Alliance.

★ 641 ★

Supplements (SIC 2833)

Largest Nutritional Supplement Makers, 2003

Companies are ranked by sales in millions of dollars for the year ended February 2, 2003. Figures are based on sales at supermarkets, drug stores and discount stores and exclude Wal-Mart.

	($ mil.)	Share
American Home Products	$ 291.1	18.19%
Pharmavite	169.8	10.61
Bayer	124.2	7.76
Rexall	51.4	3.21
GlaxoSmithKline	44.0	2.75
Nature's Bounty	43.3	2.71
Mission Pharmacal	39.6	2.47
Johnson & Johnson	30.1	1.88
Bausch & Lomb	30.0	1.88
Other	776.5	48.53

Source: *MMR*, March 24, 2003, p. 21, from Information Resources Inc.

★ 642 ★

Supplements (SIC 2833)

Leading Supplement Brands, 2002

Market shares are shown in percent for the year ended September 15, 2002. Figures refer to drug store sales only.

Osteo-Bi-Flex	6.3%
Nature's Resource	5.5
Nature's Bounty	5.3
Nature Made	4.5

Continued on next page.

★ 642 ★ *Continued*

Supplements (SIC 2833)

Leading Supplement Brands, 2002

Market shares are shown in percent for the year ended September 15, 2002. Figures refer to drug store sales only.

Natrol	4.2%
Sundown	2.8
PharmAssure	2.3
Other	69.1

Source: *Chain Drug Review*, October 28, 2002, p. 16, from Information Resources Inc.

★ 643 ★

Supplements (SIC 2833)

Top Supplement Brands, 2002

Market shares are shown for the year ended February 3, 2002. Figures include supermarkets, drug stores and discount stores but exclude Wal-Mart.

Os-Cal	8.8%
Citracal	8.8
Nature Made	6.9
Viactiv	6.4
Caltrate 600	4.4
Slow Fe	3.5
Caltrate Plus	3.3
Caltrate	3.2
Sundown	2.8
Feosol	2.4
Other	49.5

Source: *Chain Drug Review*, May 20, 2002, p. 36, from Information Resources Inc.

★ 644 ★

Supplements (SIC 2833)

Vitamin and Supplement Sales, 2002

The $1.3 billion market is shown in percent for the year ended September 15, 2002. Figures are for drug stores only.

Multivitamins	25.2%
Nonherbals	23.5
Letter vitamins	20.3
Minerals	17.9
Herbals	13.1

Source: *Chain Drug Review*, October 28, 2002, p. 15, from Information Resources Inc.

★ 645 ★

Vitamins (SIC 2833)

Top Letter Vitamin Brands, 2002

Brands are ranked by sales in millions of dollars for the year ended September 15, 2002. Figures are for supermarkets, drug stores, and discount stores but exclude Wal-Mart.

	($ mil.)	Share
Nature Made	$ 119.4	24.44%
Sundown	28.7	5.88
Nature's Bounty	17.3	3.54
Your Life	12.9	2.64
PharmAssure	6.5	1.33
Stresstabs	5.6	1.15
Schiff	5.1	1.04
Windmill	4.9	1.00
Twinlab	3.6	0.74
Private label	191.9	39.28
Other	92.6	18.96

Source: *MMR*, November 4, 2002, p. S2, from Information Resources Inc.

★ 646 ★

Vitamins (SIC 2833)

Top Multivitamin Brands, 2002

Market shares are shown for the year ended February 3, 2002. Figures include supermarkets, drug stores and discount stores but exclude Wal-Mart.

Centrum	16.5%
Centrum Silver	13.3
One-A-Day	8.7
Flintstones	4.8
Centrum Performance	4.4
Theragran M	2.0
Ocuvite	2.0
Centrum kids	1.9
Poly-Vi-Sol	1.4
Geritol Complete	1.1
Other	43.9

Source: *Chain Drug Review*, May 20, 2002, p. 36, from Information Resources Inc.

★ 647 ★
Analgesics (SIC 2834)

Cough and Cold Remedies Market, 2001

The market was valued at $3.3 billion.

Combination products	44.7%
Antihistimines	18.1
Cough remedies	14.3
Decongestants	12.8
Child remedies	10.1

Source: *Datamonitor Industry Market Research*, Annual 2002, p. NA, from Datamonitor.

★ 648 ★
Analgesics (SIC 2834)

Spending on Coughs and Colds, 2002

Figures are in millions of dollars and do not include sales at membership clubs and convenience stores.

Cold remedies	$ 2,190
Cough drops/lozenges	1,880
Nasal products	426
Cough syrup/tablets	423
Sinus remedies	265

Source: *USA TODAY*, February 25, 2003, p. 9D, from A.C. Nielsen.

★ 649 ★
Analgesics (SIC 2834)

Top Acne Treatments, 2002

Brands are ranked by sales in millions of dollars for the year ended February 24, 2002. Figures include supermarkets, drug stores and discount stores but exclude Wal-Mart.

	($ mil.)	Share
Neutrogena Acne Wash	$ 23.9	10.36%
Johnson's Clean & Clear	23.7	10.27
Clearasil	22.5	9.75
Oxy Balance	16.5	7.15
Stridex	13.9	6.02

	($ mil.)	Share
Oxy 10 Balance	$ 12.2	5.29%
Clearasil Stayclear	11.8	5.11
Neutrogena On The Spot	11.2	4.85
Neutrogena	8.3	3.60
Neutrogena Clear Pore	8.2	3.55
Private label	6.1	2.64
Other	72.5	31.41

Source: *Chain Drug Review*, June 24, 2002, p. 187, from Information Resources Inc.

★ 650 ★
Analgesics (SIC 2834)

Top Analgesic (Internal/Liquid) Brands, 2002

Brands are ranked by sales in millions of dollars for the year ended February 24, 2002. Figures include supermarkets, drug stores and discount stores but exclude Wal-Mart.

	($ mil.)	Share
Tylenol	$ 72.8	37.66%
Children's Motrin	68.2	35.28
Children's Advil	13.9	7.19
Advil	4.1	2.12
Infants Motrin	2.3	1.19
Migra Spray	0.7	0.36
Barre	0.6	0.31
Alpharma	0.3	0.16
Private label	30.3	15.68
Other	0.1	0.05

Source: *MMR*, April 22, 2002, p. 57, from Information Resources Inc.

★ 651 ★
Analgesics (SIC 2834)

Top Analgesic (Internal/Tablet) Brands, 2002

Brands are ranked by sales in millions of dollars for the year ended February 24, 2002. Figures include supermarkets, drug stores and discount stores but exclude Wal-Mart.

	($ mil.)	Share
Tylenol	$ 342.8	16.89%
Advil	291.3	14.35
Aleve	147.6	7.27
Bayer	116.3	5.73

Continued on next page.

★ 651 ★ *Continued*

Analgesics (SIC 2834)

Top Analgesic (Internal/Tablet) Brands, 2002

Brands are ranked by sales in millions of dollars for the year ended February 24, 2002. Figures include supermarkets, drug stores and discount stores but exclude Wal-Mart.

	($ mil.)	Share
Tylenol PM	$ 106.5	5.25%
Excedrin	84.7	4.17
Motrin IB	81.6	4.02
Tylenol Arthritis	52.9	2.61
Excedrin Migraine	52.7	2.60
Private label	458.0	22.56
Other	295.6	14.56

Source: *MMR*, April 22, 2002, p. 57, from Information Resources Inc.

★ 652 ★

Analgesics (SIC 2834)

Top Analgesics Makers, 2001

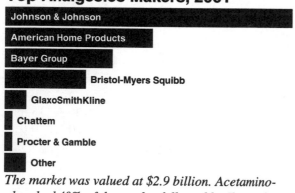

The market was valued at $2.9 billion. Acetaminophen had 40% of the market followed by Ibuprofen with a 22.1% share.

Johnson & Johnson	42.6%
American Home Products	21.6
Bayer Group	15.6
Bristol-Myers Squibb	12.4
GlaxoSmithKline	2.5
Chattem	1.3
Procter & Gamble	1.2
Other	2.8

Source: *Datamonitor Industry Market Research*, Annual 2002, p. NA, from Datamonitor.

★ 653 ★

Analgesics (SIC 2834)

Top Anti-Itch Product Brands, 2002

Brands are ranked by sales in millions of dollars for the year ended February 24, 2002. Figures include supermarkets, drug stores and discount stores but exclude Wal-Mart.

	($ mil.)	Share
Cortizone	$ 30.9	10.88%
Benadryl	28.0	9.86
Cortaid	19.3	6.80
Aveeno	18.2	6.41
Cortizone 10 Plus	12.1	4.26
Lanacane	10.9	3.84
Lotrimin AF	10.6	3.73
Lamisil AT	8.4	2.96
Gold Bond	7.7	2.71
Cortaid Intensive Therapy	6.2	2.18
Private label	53.7	18.92
Other	77.9	27.44

Source: *Chain Drug Review*, June 24, 2002, p. 187, from Information Resources Inc.

★ 654 ★

Analgesics (SIC 2834)

Top Antidiarrheal (Tablet) Brands, 2002

Shares are shown for the year ended February 24, 2002. Figures are for supermarkets, drug stores and discount stores and exclude Wal-Mart.

	($ mil.)	Share
Imodium AD	$ 62.4	45.61%
Imodium Advanced	39.4	28.80
Kaopectate	3.9	2.85
Other	31.1	22.73

Source: *Chain Drug Review*, June 24, 2002, p. 238, from Information Resources Inc.

★ 655 ★
Analgesics (SIC 2834)

Top Cold/Allergy Sinus (Liquid/Powder) Brands, 2002

Brands are ranked by sales in millions of units for the year ended February 24, 2002. Figures include supermarkets, drug stores and discount stores but exclude Wal-Mart.

	($ mil.)	Share
Vicks Nyquil	$ 102.0	16.97%
Tylenol Cold	44.6	7.42
Dimetapp	39.0	6.49
Triaminic	38.2	6.35
Benadryl	32.7	5.44
Robitussin	32.6	5.42
Pediacare	29.1	4.84
Vicks Dayquil	20.9	3.48
Robitussin	20.3	3.38
Motrin	17.5	2.91
Private label	106.6	17.73
Other	117.7	19.58

Source: *MMR*, April 22, 2002, p. 57, from Information Resources Inc.

★ 656 ★
Analgesics (SIC 2834)

Top Cold/Allergy Sinus (Tablet) Brands, 2002

Brands are ranked by sales in millions of units for the year ended February 24, 2002. Figures include supermarkets, drug stores and discount stores but exclude Wal-Mart.

	($ mil.)	Share
Benadryl	$ 122.9	9.68%
Theraflu	57.7	4.54
Sudafed	57.2	4.50
Alka-Seltzer Plus	56.8	4.47
Tylenol Cold	56.5	4.45
Tylenol Sinus	53.1	4.18
Tylenol Allergy Sinus	43.2	3.40
Advil Cold & Sinus	41.4	3.26
Vicks Dayquil	33.6	2.65
Chlor Trimeton	31.6	2.49
Private label	292.6	23.04
Other	423.4	33.34

Source: *MMR*, April 22, 2002, p. 57, from Information Resources Inc.

★ 657 ★
Analgesics (SIC 2834)

Top Cough/Cold Brands in Drug Stores, 2001

Brands are ranked by sales in millions of dollars for the year ended December 30. Figures exclude Wal-Mart.

	($ mil.)	Share
Benedryl	$ 56.5	3.87%
Halls	42.7	2.92
Vicks Nyquil	40.7	2.79
Robitussin DM	38.1	2.61
Theraflu	27.4	1.88
Afrin	25.2	1.73
Tylenol Cold	24.4	1.67
Sudafed	24.4	1.67
Other	1,180.8	80.87

Source: *Drug Store News*, May 20, 2002, p. 54, from Information Resources Inc.

★ 658 ★
Analgesics (SIC 2834)

Top Cough Syrup Brands, 2002

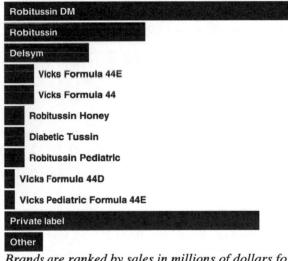

Brands are ranked by sales in millions of dollars for the year ended February 24, 2002. Figures include supermarkets, drug stores and discount stores but exclude Wal-Mart.

	($ mil.)	Share
Robitussin DM	$ 72.3	30.88%
Robitussin	35.1	14.99
Delsym	21.2	9.06
Vicks Formula 44E	7.7	3.29

Continued on next page.

Analgesics (SIC 2834)

Top Cough Syrup Brands, 2002

Brands are ranked by sales in millions of dollars for the year ended February 24, 2002. Figures include supermarkets, drug stores and discount stores but exclude Wal-Mart.

	($ mil.)	Share
Vicks Formula 44	$ 7.7	3.29%
Robitussin Honey	4.9	2.09
Diabetic Tussin	4.4	1.88
Robitussin Pediatric	3.6	1.54
Vicks Formula 44D	3.0	1.28
Vicks Pediatric Formula 44E . . .	2.0	0.85
Private label	63.3	27.04
Other	8.9	3.80

Source: *MMR*, April 22, 2002, p. 57, from Information Resources Inc.

★ 659 ★
Analgesics (SIC 2834)

Top Digestive Brands in Drug Stores, 2001

Brands are ranked by sales in millions of dollars for the year ended December 30. Figures exclude Wal-Mart.

	($ mil.)	Share
Pepcid AC	$ 44.8	4.89%
Zantac 75	39.6	4.33
Metamucil	35.9	3.92
Tums EX	24.5	2.68
Dulcolax	21.7	2.37
Gas X	18.9	2.06
Citrucel	16.7	1.82
Mylanta	15.9	1.74
Other	697.5	76.19

Source: *Drug Store News*, May 20, 2002, p. 54, from Information Resources Inc.

★ 660 ★
Analgesics (SIC 2834)

Top Digestive Remedies Makers, 2001

The market was valued at $3.2 billion. Indigestion/heartburn had a 64.9% share and laxatives with a 21.3% share.

Johnson & Johnson	21.8%
GlaxoSmithKline	15.1
Pfizer	8.2
Procter & Gamble	8.1
Novartis	6.1
Private label	12.8
Other	27.9

Source: *Datamonitor Industry Market Research*, Annual 2002, p. NA, from Datamonitor.

★ 661 ★
Analgesics (SIC 2834)

Top External Analgesic Brands, 2002

Market shares are shown for the year ended December 29, 2002. Figures are based on sales at supermarkets, drug stores, discount stores and exclude Wal-Mart.

Bengay	11.0%
Icy Hot	10.1
Joint-Ritis	9.8
Salonpas	5.0
Aspercreme	4.1
Absorbine Jr.	3.2
Blue Relief	3.2
PK5	2.9
Mineral Ice	2.8
Flex-All 454	2.7
Other	45.2

Source: *Chain Drug Review*, February 17, 2003, p. 27, from Information Resources Inc.

★ 662 ★

Analgesics (SIC 2834)

Top Laxative (Liquid/Powder) Brands, 2002

Brands are ranked by sales in millions of dollars for the year ended February 24, 2002. Figures include supermarkets, drug stores and discount stores but exclude Wal-Mart.

	($ mil.)	Share
Metamucil	$ 79.4	33.62%
Citrucel	33.7	14.27
Fleet	20.3	8.59
Fleet Phospho Soda	11.3	4.78
Perdiem	8.7	3.68
Senokot	4.7	1.99
Konsyl	3.5	1.48
Haleys MO	2.8	1.19
Kletchers Castoria	2.8	1.19
Perdiem Fiber	2.4	1.02
Private label	50.4	21.34
Other	16.2	6.86

Source: *Chain Drug Review*, June 24, 2002, p. 187, from Information Resources Inc.

★ 663 ★

Analgesics (SIC 2834)

Top Laxative (Tablet) Brands, 2002

Brands are ranked by sales in millions of dollars for the year ended February 24, 2002. Figures include supermarkets, drug stores and discount stores but exclude Wal-Mart.

	($ mil.)	Share
Ex-Lax	$ 34.9	9.46%
Dulcolax	34.1	9.24
Fibercon	28.5	7.73
Senokot	24.4	6.61
Correctol	22.1	5.99
Senokot S	20.1	5.45
Colace	19.4	5.26
Fleet	14.3	3.88
Citrucel	10.0	2.71
Metamucil	8.7	2.36
Private label	104.4	28.30
Other	48.0	13.01

Source: *Chain Drug Review*, June 24, 2002, p. 187, from Information Resources Inc.

★ 664 ★

Analgesics (SIC 2834)

Top Lice Treatment Brands, 2002

Brands are ranked by sales in millions of dollars for the year ended February 24, 2002. Figures include supermarkets, drug stores and discount stores but exclude Wal-Mart.

	($ mil.)	Share
Rid	$ 30.0	31.48%
Nix	20.7	21.72
Pronto	5.5	5.77
Clear	2.8	2.94
Acumed	2.7	2.83
Lice Guard Robi Comb	2.2	2.31
Lice Free	1.9	1.99
A 200	1.7	1.78
Lice Meister	1.0	1.05
Pin X	0.9	0.94
Private label	20.1	21.09
Other	5.8	6.09

Source: *MMR*, April 22, 2002, p. 57, from Information Resources Inc.

★ 665 ★

Analgesics (SIC 2834)

Top Nasal Spray Brands, 2002

Brands are ranked by sales in millions of dollars for the year ended June 16, 2002. Figures include supermarkets, drug stores and discount stores but exclude Wal-Mart.

	($ mil.)	Share
Afrin	$ 44.2	14.03%
Primatene Mist	33.5	10.63
Zicam	19.6	6.22
Vicks Sinex	19.6	6.22
Nasalcrom	18.6	5.90
Afrin No Drip	17.7	5.62
Four Way	17.3	5.49
Neo Synephrine	11.2	3.56
Vicks	10.3	3.27
Private label	69.3	22.00
Other	53.7	17.05

Source: *MMR*, August 26, 2002, p. 57, from Information Resources Inc.

★ 666 ★
Analgesics (SIC 2834)

Top Oral Pain Remedy Brands, 2002

Brands are ranked by sales in millions of dollars for the year ended February 24, 2002. Figures include supermarkets, drug stores and discount stores but exclude Wal-Mart.

	($ mil.)	Share
Anbesol	$ 29.5	20.37%
Orajel	22.5	15.54
Baby Orajel	17.2	11.88
Colgate Peroxyl	9.3	6.42
Zilactin	5.9	4.07
Glyoxide	5.0	3.45
Oralbase B	4.5	3.11
Zilactin B	4.1	2.83
Dentek Temparin	3.6	2.49
Orajel PM	3.4	2.35
Private label	5.4	3.73
Other	34.4	23.76

Source: *Chain Drug Review*, June 24, 2002, p. 187, from Information Resources Inc.

★ 667 ★
Analgesics (SIC 2834)

Top Pain Relievers in Drug Stores, 2001

Brands are ranked by drug store sales in millions of dollars for the year ended December 30, 2001.

	($ mil.)	Share
Tylenol (tablets)	$ 143.9	12.86%
Advil (tablets)	111.5	9.96
Aleve (tablets)	60.5	5.40
Bayer (tablets)	48.9	4.37
Tylenol PM (tablets)	43.2	3.86
Motrin 1B (tablets)	34.3	3.06
Tylenol Liquid (liquid)	32.9	2.94
Children's Motrin (liquid)	31.0	2.77
Excedrin (tablets)	30.1	2.69
Tylenol Arthritis (tablets)	23.4	2.09
Other	559.7	50.00

Source: *Drug Store News*, May 20, 2002, p. 43, from Information Resources Inc.

★ 668 ★
Analgesics (SIC 2834)

Top Stomach Remedy (Liquid/Powder) Brands, 2002

Brands are ranked by sales in millions of dollars for the year ended February 24, 2002. Figures include supermarkets, drug stores and discount stores but exclude Wal-Mart.

	($ mil.)	Share
Pepto Bismol	$ 58.9	43.89%
Phillips	38.9	28.99
ExLax	5.1	3.80
Reeses	0.6	0.45
Goldline	0.4	0.30
Rugby	0.3	0.22
Percy Medicine	0.2	0.15
Fleet	0.1	0.07
Other	29.7	22.13

Source: *Chain Drug Review*, June 24, 2002, p. 187, from Information Resources Inc.

★ 669 ★
Analgesics (SIC 2834)

Top Stomach Remedy (Tablet) Brands, 2002

Brands are ranked by sales in millions of dollars for the year ended February 24, 2002. Figures include supermarkets, drug stores and discount stores but exclude Wal-Mart.

	($ mil.)	Share
Pepto Bismol	$ 22.30	74.48%
Phillips	2.20	7.35
Equatactin	1.20	4.01
Handy Solutions Pepto Bismol . .	0.02	0.07
Valet Pepto Bismol	0.02	0.07
Private label	4.20	14.03

Source: *Chain Drug Review*, June 24, 2002, p. 187, from Information Resources Inc.

★ 670 ★
Drugs (SIC 2834)

Anti-Infectives Market Shares

Market shares are estimated in percent. The company produces cefuroxime axetil.

Ranbaxy Laboratories Ltd.	90.0%
Other	10.0

Source: *Asia Africa Intelligence Wire*, December 26, 2002, p. NA.

★ 671 ★
Drugs (SIC 2834)

Antidepressant Market Shares, 2001

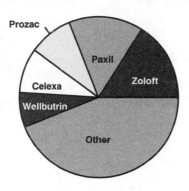

Market shares are shown in percent. A recent survey quoted in the source claims that in any year, 9.5% of Americans met the criteria for a mood disorder.

Zoloft	15.6%
Paxil	14.5
Prozac	9.4
Celexa	9.2
Wellbutrin	7.1
Other	44.2

Source: *New York Times*, June 30, 2002, p. 18, from IMS Health.

★ 672 ★
Drugs (SIC 2834)

Antihistimine Market Shares, 2002

Shares are through September 2002.

Claritin	37.5%
Allegra	28.5
Zyrtec	23.5
Clarinex	8.4
Other	2.1

Source: *New York Times*, November 28, 2002, p. C3, from IMS Health.

★ 673 ★
Drugs (SIC 2834)

Antipsychotic Market Shares

Institutional market shares are shown in percent.

Olanzapine	49.0%
Clozapine	21.0
Quetiapine	18.0
Risperidone	12.0

Source: *Formulary*, July 2002, p. 367.

★ 674 ★
Drugs (SIC 2834)

Drug Delivery System Market, 2001

The market was valued at $3.6 billion.

Oral	61.0%
Inhaled	15.0
Transmucosal	11.0
Injection	6.0
Transdermal	3.0
Other	11.0

Source: *Datamonitor Industry Market Research*, Annual 2002, p. NA, from Datamonitor.

★ 675 ★
Drugs (SIC 2834)

Erectile Dysfunction Market

Viagra first appeared March 1998. 30 million men are thought to have erectile dysfunction. Sales of Viagra hit $1.5 billion in 2001. Market shares are shown in percent.

Viagra	94.0%
Other	6.0

Source: *The Albuquerque Tribune*, March 27, 2003, p. A8, from Pfizer.

★ 676 ★
Drugs (SIC 2834)

Generic Contraceptives Industry

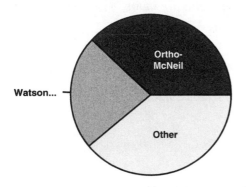

Market shares are shown in percent as of June 2002.

Ortho-McNeil	38.0%
Watson Pharmaceuticals	23.0
Other	39.0

Source: *Knight Ridder/Tribune Business News*, October 29, 2002, p. NA, from Watson Pharmaceuticals.

★ 677 ★
Drugs (SIC 2834)

Hormone Replacement Market

Market shares are shown in percent. Prempro is the leader of the hormone replacement industry containing estrogen and progestin.

Prempro	73.0%
Other	27.0

Source: *Med Ad News*, October 2002, p. 3, from IMS Health.

★ 678 ★
Drugs (SIC 2834)

Hospital Insulin Market

Market shares are shown in percent.

Novo	75.0%
Other	25.0

Source: *Knight Ridder/Tribune Business News*, March 4, 2003, p. NA, from Novo.

★ 679 ★
Drugs (SIC 2834)

Hypertension Drug Market, 2002

Distribution is based on dollar sales through November 30, 2002.

ACE inhibitors	29.0%
Calcium channel blockers	25.0
Beta blockers	23.0
Anglotensin II receptor blockers	12.0
Other	10.0

Source: *Wall Street Journal*, December 18, 2002, p. A7, from NDCHealth.

★ 680 ★
Drugs (SIC 2834)

Injectable Drug Delivery Systems, 2001

The market was valued at $1.9 billion. Cancer had 78% of the market followed by central nervous system with a 14.8% share.

Cancer	70.0%
Takeda and Abbott	13.3
AstraZeneca	9.7
Novartis	7.1

Source: *Datamonitor Industry Market Research*, Annual 2002, p. NA, from Datamonitor.

★ 681 ★

Drugs (SIC 2834)

Multiple Sclerosis Drug

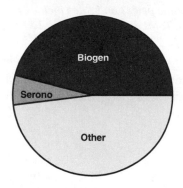

Market shares are shown in percent as of October 2002.

Biogen	46.0%
Serono	6.0
Other	48.0

Source: *The Boston Globe*, November 10, 2002, p. NA.

★ 682 ★

Drugs (SIC 2834)

Nerve Gas Antidote Market

Market shares are shown in percent. The company is the sole supplier of auto injections with nerve gas antidotes to the Department of Defense.

Meridian	95.0%
Other	5.0

Source: *Investor's Business Daily*, October 14, 2002, p. A10.

★ 683 ★

Drugs (SIC 2834)

Organ Transplant Pharmaceuticals

Figures show estimated revenues in billions of dollars by year. The growth spurt will be fueled by new drugs with fewer side effects and new uses for immunosuppressive therapies.

2008	$ 3.26
2001	1.20

Source: *Transplant News*, September 13, 2002, p. 8, from Frost & Sullivan.

★ 684 ★

Drugs (SIC 2834)

Top Antibacterial Drug Makers, 2001

The market was valued at $8.8 billion.

Cipro	43.0%
Augmentin	31.4
Tequin	9.6
Avelox	9.0
Ketek	1.1
Other	5.9

Source: *Datamonitor Industry Market Research*, Annual 2002, p. NA, from Datamonitor.

★ 685 ★

Drugs (SIC 2834)

Top Brand Name Drugs, 2001

Products are ranked by retail sales in billions of dollars.

Lipitor	$ 4.51
Prilosec	3.99
Prevacid	3.19
Zocor	2.73
Celebrex	2.38
Zoloft	2.15
Paxil	2.12
Vioxx	2.02
Prozac	1.99
Augmentin	1.87
Zyprexa	1.82

Source: *Drug Topics*, February 18, 2002, p. 31, from Scott Levin SPA.

★ 686 ★

Drugs (SIC 2834)

Top Cardiovascular Drug Makers, 2001

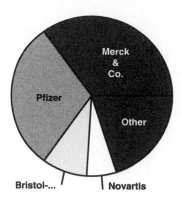

The market was valued at $31.7 billion. Hypertension had the highest share of the market followed by hypocholestrolemia, with 49% and 25.9% shares respectively.

Merck & Co. 34.7%
Pfizer 29.9
Bristol-Myers Squibb 9.1
Novartis 6.4
Other 19.9

Source: *Datamonitor Industry Market Research*, Annual 2002, p. NA, from Datamonitor.

★ 687 ★

Drugs (SIC 2834)

Top CNS Drug Brands, 2001

The market was valued at $20.7 billion. Analgesics had the highest share of the market followed by antipsychotics, with 44% and 18.1% shares respectively.

Imitrex 40.3%
Depakote 39.5
Dilantin 10.4
Sinemet 6.4
Miramex 3.4

Source: *Datamonitor Industry Market Research*, Annual 2002, p. NA, from Datamonitor.

★ 688 ★

Drugs (SIC 2834)

Top Drug Classes, 2002

Figures are wholesale prices and sales include prescription products. Total drug sales reached $192.2 billion.

	($ mil.)	Share
Cholesterol reducers	$ 12.5	6.50%
Proton pump inhibitors	11.9	6.19
SSRI/SNRI	9.9	5.15
Antipsychotics	6.4	3.33
Erythropoietins	6.2	3.23
Seizure disorders	5.5	2.86
COX-2 inhibitors	4.9	2.55
Antihistamines	4.8	2.50
Calcium blockers	4.4	2.29
Ace inhibitors	3.7	1.93
Other	122.0	63.48

Source: *Business Wire*, February 21, 2003, p. NA, from IMS Retail and Provider Perspective.

★ 689 ★

Drugs (SIC 2834)

Top Drug Classes in Canada, 2001

Market shares are shown in percent. Hospitals and retail pharmacies purchased over $11 billion in medicines.

Cardiovasculars 14.2%
Psychotherapeutics 9.8
Cholesterol reducers 8.1
Anti-spasmodic/anti-secretory 7.4
Anti-infectives, systemic 5.9
Other 54.6

Source: ''Aspects of the Canadian Pharmaceutical Market.'' available January 3, 2003 from http://www.imshealthcanada.com, from IMS Health.

★ 690 ★

Drugs (SIC 2834)

Top Drug Firms, 2001

Market shares are shown in percent.

Pfizer 10.0%
GlaxoSmithKline 8.8
Merck 7.1
Johnson & Johnson 6.2
Bristol-Myers Squibb 6.0

Continued on next page.

★ 690 ★ *Continued*
Drugs (SIC 2834)

Top Drug Firms, 2001

Market shares are shown in percent.

AstraZeneca	5.7%
Lilly	4.3
Wyeth	4.0
Novartis	3.9
Pharmacia	3.7
Other	40.3

Source: "Leading 10 Corporations." available from January 7, 2003 from http://www.imshealth.com, from IMS Health.

★ 691 ★
Drugs (SIC 2834)

Top Drug Firms, 2002

Pfizer
GlaxoSmithKline
Merck & Co.
Johnson & Johnson
AstraZeneca
Bristol-Myers Squibb
Novartis
Wyeth
Pharmacia
Lilly
Other

Figures are wholesale prices and sales include prescription products. Total drug sales reached $192.2 billion.

	($ bil.)	Share
Pfizer	$ 19.5	10.15%
GlaxoSmithKline	17.3	9.00
Merck & Co.	12.7	6.61
Johnson & Johnson	12.7	6.61
AstraZeneca	10.9	5.67
Bristol-Myers Squibb	8.8	4.58
Novartis	8.0	4.16
Wyeth	7.4	3.85
Pharmacia	7.2	3.75
Lilly	6.7	3.49
Other	81.0	42.14

Source: *Business Wire*, February 21, 2003, p. NA, from IMS Retail and Provider Perspective.

★ 692 ★
Drugs (SIC 2834)

Top Drugs by Prescriptions, 2002

Top retail drugs are ranked by millions of prescriptions.

	(mil.)	Share
Hydrocordone/APAP	81.26	2.66%
Lipitor	56.41	1.85
Synthroid	40.16	1.32
Atenolol	39.36	1.29
Amoxicillin	34.04	1.11
Premarin tabs	33.32	1.09
Furosemide Oral	31.94	1.05
Norvasc	30.17	0.99
Albuterol Aerosol	29.39	0.96
Alprazolam	29.23	0.96
Other	2,648.36	86.73

Source: *Drug Topics*, March 17, 2003, p. 37, from Verispan Scott-Levin's Source Prescription Audit.

★ 693 ★
Drugs (SIC 2834)

Top Generic Drug Classes, 2001

After stalling slightly in the late 1990s, the industry is starting to spark. Sales grew from roughly $1.1 billion in 2001 top $19 billion in 2006.

Cardiovascular drugs	21.0%
Antiarthritics/analgesics	14.0
Anti-infectives	14.0
Gastrointestinal drugs	10.0
Central nervous systems agents	10.0
Anticancer drugs	8.0
Respiratory drugs	6.0
Hormones	4.0
Other	13.0

Source: *Biomedical Market Newsletter*, August 31, 2002, p. 27, from Business Communications Co.

★ 694 ★

Drugs (SIC 2834)

Top Generic Drug Makers, 2001

The market was valued at $13.7 billion. Central nervous systems drugs led the market with a 45% share, followed by cardiovascular with an 18% share.

Mylan	7.1%
Barr	4.1
Teva	3.7
Watson	3.2
Ivax	2.9
Andrx	2.2
Alphapharmia	1.8
Forest	1.8
Other	73.2

Source: *Datamonitor Industry Market Research*, Annual 2002, p. NA, from Datamonitor.

★ 695 ★

Drugs (SIC 2834)

Top Generic Name Drugs, 2001

Products are ranked by retail sales in billions of dollars.

Hydrocodone	$ 1,196.4
Fluoxetine	730.6
Ranitidine HCI	707.8
Albuterol Aerosol	702.6
Alprazolam	598.9
Atenolol	551.7
Lorazepam	536.4
Propxyphene-N/APAP	476.8
Tamoxifen	443.4
Cephalexin	442.3
Enalapril	432.4
Albuterol Neb Soln	368.8

Source: *Drug Topics*, February 18, 2002, p. 31, from Scott Levin SPA.

★ 696 ★

Drugs (SIC 2834)

Top Prescription Products, 2002

Figures are wholesale prices and sales include prescription products. Total drug sales reached $192.2 billion.

	($ mil.)	Share
Lipitor	$ 6.1	3.17%
Zocor	4.2	2.19
Prevacid	3.7	1.93
Prilosec	3.5	1.82
Procrit	3.1	1.61
Zyprexa	2.9	1.51
Epogen	2.8	1.46
Celebrex	2.6	1.35
Zoloft	2.5	1.30
Paxil	2.3	1.20
Other	158.5	82.47

Source: *Business Wire*, February 21, 2003, p. NA, from IMS Retail and Provider Perspective.

★ 697 ★

Drugs (SIC 2834)

Top Respiratory Drug Makers, 2001

The market was valued at $11.3 billion. Allergic Rhinitis had the highest share of the market with a 49.2%.

Schering-Plough	57.3%
Pfizer	14.7
Aventis	9.8
Glaxo Wellcome	9.6
AstraZeneca	2.2
Whitehall-Robins	1.9
Novartis	1.5
Other	3.0

Source: *Datamonitor Industry Market Research*, Annual 2002, p. NA, from Datamonitor.

★ 698 ★
Drugs (SIC 2834)

Top Statin Drugs

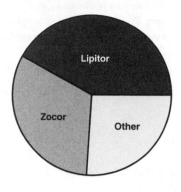

Market shares are shown in percent.

Lipitor 42.0%
Zocor 32.0
Other 26.0

Source: *Fortune*, January 20, 2003, p. 61.

★ 699 ★
Drugs (SIC 2834)

Top Transmucosal Drug Delivery System Makers, 2001

The market was valued at $3.8 billion.

Wyeth 43.0%
GW Pharmaceuticals 22.0
Novartis 4.0
Other 31.0

Source: *Datamonitor Industry Market Research*, Annual 2002, p. NA, from Datamonitor.

★ 700 ★
Weight Control Products (SIC 2834)

Top Diet/Weight Loss Products in Drug Stores, 2001

Brands are ranked by drug store sales in millions of dollars for the year ended December 30, 2001.

	($ mil.)	Share
Metabolife 356 (candy/tablets) . .	$ 70.0	15.19%
Ultra Slim Fast (liquid/powder) . .	46.8	10.15
Ensure (liquid/powder)	29.3	6.36
Ensure Plus (liquid/pwder) . . .	20.3	4.40

	($ mil.)	Share
Slim Fast (snack bars)	$ 13.3	2.89%
Metab O Lite (candy/tablets) . . .	13.3	2.89
Hollywood Celebrity Diet (liquid/ powder)	13.0	2.82
Boost (liquid/powder)	11.7	2.54
Dexatrim Natural (candy/tablets) . .	10.1	2.19
Stacker 2 (candy/tablets)	9.3	2.02
Other	223.8	48.56

Source: *Drug Store News*, May 20, 2002, p. 43, from Information Resources Inc.

★ 701 ★
Weight Control Products (SIC 2834)

Top Weight Control Candy/Tablet Brands, 2002

Brands are ranked by sales in millions of dollars for the year ended December 29, 2002. Figures are based on sales at supermarkets, drug stores, discount stores and exclude Wal-Mart.

Metabolife 356 . . . . 24.5%
Stacker 2 . . . . 9.6
Xenadrine RFAI 9.3
PatentLean 8.6
Dexatrim 4.0
Xenadrine EFX 3.7
Ripped Fuel 3.5
Metab-O-Lite 2.5
Diet Fuel 2.3
Metab-O-Lite Plus 1.6
Other 30.4

Source: *Chain Drug Review*, February 17, 2003, p. 27, from Information Resources Inc.

★ 702 ★
Weight Control Products (SIC 2834)

Top Weight Loss Brands (Liquid/ Powder), 2003

Companies are ranked by sales in millions of dollars for the year ended January 26, 2003. Figures are based on sales at supermarkets, drug stores and discount stores and exclude Wal-Mart.

	($ mil.)	Share
Slim Fast Meal Options	$ 218.5	21.85%
Ultra Slim Fast	165.9	16.59

Continued on next page.

★ 702 ★ *Continued*

Weight Control Products (SIC 2834)

Top Weight Loss Brands (Liquid/Powder), 2003

Companies are ranked by sales in millions of dollars for the year ended January 26, 2003. Figures are based on sales at supermarkets, drug stores and discount stores and exclude Wal-Mart.

	($ mil.)	Share
Ensure	$ 134.8	13.48%
Pedia Sure	88.0	8.80
Ensure Plus	70.4	7.04
Boost	55.5	5.55
Ensure Glucerma	28.3	2.83
Atkins Diet	19.6	1.96
Boost Plus	15.4	1.54
Hollywood Celebrity Diet	14.5	1.45
Private label	62.1	6.21
Other	127.0	12.70

Source: *MMR*, March 24, 2003, p. 21, from Information Resources Inc.

★ 703 ★

Medical Testing Kits (SIC 2835)

Leading Blood Pressure Kit Brands, 2002

Brands are ranked by sales in millions of dollars for the year ended November 3, 2002. Figures include supermarkets, discount stores and drug stores and exclude Wal-Mart.

	($ mil.)	Share
Omron	$ 44.4	53.49%
A&D Medical	8.2	9.88
Mabis	3.4	4.10
Lumiscope	2.8	3.37
Sunmark	1.4	1.69
Samsung	0.8	0.96
Sunbeam	0.7	0.84
Other	21.3	25.66

Source: *MMR*, January 13, 2003, p. 53, from Information Resources Inc.

★ 704 ★

Pregnancy Test Industry (SIC 2835)

Top Home Pregnancy Test Kits, 2003

Brands are ranked by sales in millions of dollars for the year ended January 26, 2003. Figures are for supermarkets, drug stores and discount stores excluding Wal-Mart.

	($ mil.)	Share
EPT	$ 62.7	29.20%
First Response	29.6	13.79
Fact Plus Select	13.7	6.38
Clearblue Easy	12.1	5.64
Selfcare	11.7	5.45
Answer Quick and Simple	10.4	4.84
Inverness Medical	5.5	2.56
Fact Plus Pro	2.5	1.16
Answer	2.4	1.12
Confirm	1.6	0.75
Other	62.5	29.11

Source: *MMR*, March 24, 2003, p. 30, from Information Resources Inc.

★ 705 ★

Blood Testing (SIC 2836)

Blood Supply Screening

Procleix is used to screen the blood supply for AIDS and Hepatitis C. It is supplied by Gen-Probe and Chiron. The companies have an exclusive agreement with the American Red Cross to supply them with Procleix.

Gen-Probe/Chiron	70.0%
Roche	30.0

Source: *Investor's Business Daily*, December 9, 2002, p. A8.

★ 706 ★

Glucose Testing (SIC 2836)

Top Glucose Test Kits, 2002

Brands are ranked by sales in millions of dollars for the year ended February 24, 2002. Figures include supermarkets, drug stores and discount stores but exclude Wal-Mart.

	($ mil.)	Share
ACCU Chek Comfort Curve	$ 88.5	25.50%
Lifescan One Touch	63.3	18.24
Glucometer Elite	35.0	10.08

Continued on next page.

★ 706 ★ *Continued*
Glucose Testing (SIC 2836)

Top Glucose Test Kits, 2002

Brands are ranked by sales in millions of dollars for the year ended February 24, 2002. Figures include supermarkets, drug stores and discount stores but exclude Wal-Mart.

	($ mil.)	Share
Lifescan	$ 32.2	9.28%
Accu Chek Advantage	26.8	7.72
Precision Qid	19.4	5.59
Lifescan Surestep	17.4	5.01
Lifescan Fast Take	17.2	4.96
Therasense Freestyle	13.8	3.98
Glucomter Dex	12.7	3.66
Private label	15.0	4.32
Other	5.8	1.67

Source: *MMR*, April 22, 2002, p. 57, from Information Resources Inc.

★ 707 ★
Bubble Bath (SIC 2841)

Top Bubble Bath Brands, 2002

Brands are ranked by sales for the year ended December 1, 2002. Figures are for supermarkets, drug stores and discount stores and exclude Wal-Mart.

	($ mil.)	Share
Vaseline	$ 7.7	7.13%
Mr. Bubbles	7.4	6.85
Village Naturals	6.8	6.30
Calgon	5.6	5.19
Batherapy	4.3	3.98
Coty Healing Garden	4.0	3.70
Alpha Keri	2.9	2.69
Kid Care Scooby Doo	2.4	2.22
Lauder	2.3	2.13
Hot Gossip Body Care	1.9	1.76
Other	62.7	58.06

Source: *MMR*, February 10, 2003, p. 29, from Information Resources Inc.

★ 708 ★
Detergents (SIC 2841)

Dishwashing Detergent and Rinsing Aids, 2002

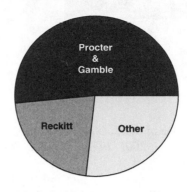

Market shares are shown for the year ended December 1, 2002.

Procter & Gamble	51.6%
Reckitt	21.9
Other	26.5

Source: *Wall Street Journal*, January 13, 2003, p. B4, from Information Resources Inc.

★ 709 ★
Detergents (SIC 2841)

Household Detergent Shipments

Shipments are shown in millions of pounds.

	2001	2006
Laundry detergent	8,120	8,350
Powdered detergent	4,320	4,175
Dishwashing detergents	3,880	4,450
Liquid detergents and presoaks . . .	3,800	4,175

Source: *Soap & Cosmetics*, January 2003, p. 22, from Freedonia Group.

★ 710 ★
Detergents (SIC 2841)

Top Dish Detergent Firms, 2002

The industry had sales of $621.16 million for the year ended December 1, 2002. Figures exclude Wal-Mart.

	($ mil.)	Share
Procter & Gamble	$ 317.60	51.13%
Colgate-Palmolive	235.72	37.95
Lever Brothers	35.88	5.78
Pegasus International	1.47	0.24
Product Concepts	1.18	0.19
USA Detergents	1.11	0.18
Other	28.20	4.54

Source: *Chemical Market Reporter*, January 27, 2003, p. FR3, from Information Resources Inc.

★ 711 ★
Detergents (SIC 2841)

Top Laundry Detergent Brands, 2002

Shares are shown based on dollar sales at grocery, drug and mass market outlets (but not Wal-Mart) for the year ended December 29, 2002.

Tide	36.6%
Purex	9.5
All	8.9
Wisk	6.9
Xtra	5.3
Gain	5.1
Cheer	4.8
Arm & Hammer	4.7
Era	4.3
Private label	2.7
Other	11.2

Source: *Grocery Headquarters*, April 2003, p. 43, from Information Resources Inc.

★ 712 ★
Detergents (SIC 2841)

Top Liquid Laundry Detergent Firms, 2002

The industry had sales of $2.502 billion for the year ended December 1, 2002. Figures exclude Wal-Mart.

	($ mil.)	Share
Procter & Gamble	$ 1,307.15	52.24%
Lever Brothers	470.51	18.81
Dial Corp.	244.37	9.77
USA Detergents	131.17	5.24
Church & Dwight	116.28	4.65
Colgate-Palmolive	111.65	4.46
Huish Detergents	22.30	0.89
Reckitt Benckiser	10.03	0.40
Redox Brands	9.99	0.40
Private label	66.46	2.66
Other	12.09	0.48

Source: *Chemical Market Reporter*, January 27, 2003, p. FR3, from Information Resources Inc.

★ 713 ★
Detergents (SIC 2841)

Top Powdered Laundry Detergent Firms, 2002

The industry had sales of $1.16 billion for the year ended December 1, 2002. Figures exclude Wal-Mart.

	($ mil.)	Share
Procter & Gamble	$ 802.61	68.89%
Lever Brothers	126.15	10.83
Church & Dwight	77.42	6.65
Dial Corp.	42.18	3.62
Huish Detergents	21.48	1.84
Colgate-Palmolive	18.90	1.62
USA Detergents	16.14	1.39
Fabrica De Jabon La Corona . . .	14.97	1.28
Redox Brands	4.62	0.40
Private label	35.79	3.07
Other	4.74	0.41

Source: *Chemical Market Reporter*, January 27, 2003, p. FR3, from Information Resources Inc.

★ 714 ★
Detergents (SIC 2841)

U.S. Detergent Market, 2002

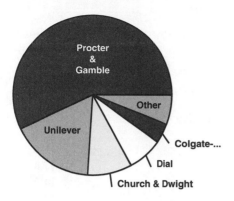

Market shares are shown for the year ended April 21, 2002.

Procter & Gamble	57.0%
Unilever	17.0
Church & Dwight	8.6
Dial	7.4
Colgate-Palmolive	3.9
Other	6.1

Source: *Advertising Age*, May 27, 2002, p. 1, from Information Resources Inc.

★ 715 ★
Fabric Softeners (SIC 2841)

Largest Fabric Softener Makers in Mexico

Market shares are shown in percent.

Procter & Gamble	60.0%
Other	40.0

Source: *South American Business Information*, February 13, 2003, p. NA.

★ 716 ★
Soap (SIC 2841)

Leading Baby Soap Vendors, 2002

Companies are ranked by sales for the year ended May 19, 2002. Figures exclude Wal-Mart.

	Sales	Share
Johnson & Johnson	$ 44,487.3	61.05%
Playtex	12,342.6	16.94
Gerber	8,795.7	12.07

	Sales	Share
Chattem	$ 1,404.1	1.93%
Avent America	356.9	0.49
Lander Co. of Canada	86.0	0.12
Yardley of London	72.4	0.10
Private label	5,327.5	7.31

Source: *Household and Personal Products Industry*, August 2002, p. 42, from Information Resources inc.

★ 717 ★
Soap (SIC 2841)

Leading Bar Soap (Deodorant) Vendors, 2002

Companies are ranked by sales in millions of dollars for the year ended August 11, 2002. Figures exclude Wal-Mart. Shares are estimated.

	($ mil.)	Share
Dial	$ 144.16	32.70%
Colgate-Palmolive	100.59	22.82
Procter & Gamble	97.22	22.05
Lever Bros.	77.68	17.62
Helene Curtis	10.83	2.46
Calderma	2.19	0.50
Garde Intl.	0.75	0.17
Private label	7.41	1.68

Source: *Household and Personal Products Industry*, November 2002, p. 48, from Information Resources Inc.

★ 718 ★
Soap (SIC 2841)

Soap and Bath Market

Figures are for 1996 and 2001. From 1996 to 2001, the bar soap segment fell from 68.5% to 58.8%, while liquid soaps jumped from 31.4% to 41.2%.

	1996	2001
Bar	69.5%	58.8%
Liquid	31.4	41.2

Source: *Cosmetics International*, June 25, 2002, p. 2, from Mintel.

★ 719 ★
Soap (SIC 2841)

Top Bar Brands, 2002

Brands are ranked by sales for the year ended August 11, 2002. Figures are for supermarkets, drug stores, and discount stores but exclude Wal-Mart.

	($ mil.)	Share
Dove	$ 217.1	45.46%
Caress	51.6	10.80
Ivory	47.9	10.03
Oil of Olay	43.4	9.09
Dove Nutrium	20.1	4.21
Jergens	11.7	2.45
Tone Island Mist	10.6	2.22
Tone	6.5	1.36
Cetaphil	6.1	1.28
Aveeno	5.9	1.24
Other	56.7	11.87

Source: *MMR*, October 21, 2002, p. 22, from Information Resources Inc.

★ 720 ★
Soap (SIC 2841)

Top Bar Soap (Nondeodorant) Suppliers, 2002

Market shares are shown based on sales of $477.6 million for the year ended August 11, 2002. Figures include drug stores, supermarkets and discounts stores but exclude Wal-Mart.

Lever Bros.	60.5%
Procter & Gamble	20.3
Dial	5.2
Andrew Jergens	2.7
Yardley of London	1.8
Johnson & Johnson	1.6
Galderma	1.3
Other	6.6

Source: *Chain Drug Review*, September 30, 2002, p. 82, from Information Resources Inc.

★ 721 ★
Soap (SIC 2841)

Top Bath/Body Brands in Drug Stores, 2001

Brands are ranked by sales in millions of dollars for the year ended December 30. Figures exclude Wal-Mart.

	($ mil.)	Share
Dove	$ 29.5	4.30%
Vaseline Intensive Care	28.8	4.20
Nivea	20.2	2.95
Eucerin	19.4	2.83
Lubriderm	17.4	2.54
Jergens	14.3	2.09
Cetaphil	12.9	1.88
Aveeno	12.4	1.81
Curel	11.1	1.62
Other	519.7	75.79

Source: *Drug Store News*, May 20, 2002, p. 54, from Information Resources Inc.

★ 722 ★
Soap (SIC 2841)

Top Liquid Soap Brands, 2002

Brands are ranked by sales in millions of dollars for the year ended February 24, 2002. Figures include supermarkets, drug stores and discount stores but exclude Wal-Mart.

	($ mil.)	Share
Dial	$ 48.1	21.33%
Softsoap	33.7	14.94
Clean & Smooth	17.7	7.85
Softsoap Aquarium Series	16.1	7.14
Purell	15.9	7.05
Softsoap 2 in 1	10.4	4.61
Dial Complete	7.1	3.15
Softsoap Fruit Essentials	6.0	2.66
Softsoap Winter Series	5.9	2.62
Other	64.6	28.65

Source: *MMR*, April 22, 2002, p. 57, from Information Resources Inc.

★ 723 ★

Soap (SIC 2841)

Top Women's Bath Gift Set Brands, 2002

Brands are ranked by sales in millions of dollars for the year ended December 29, 2002. Figures are based on sales at supermarkets, drug stores, discount stores and exclude Wal-Mart.

	($ mil.)	Share
Coty Healing Garden	$ 15.7	9.61%
Calgon	10.5	6.43
Body Image	10.2	6.24
Sarah Michaels	8.3	5.08
Body & Earth	7.0	4.28
Elizabeth Taylor's White Diamonds	3.9	2.39
Annalia's Garden	3.2	1.96
Caress	3.1	1.90
Coty Adidas Moves for Her . .	3.0	1.84
Smith	2.9	1.77
Other	95.6	58.51

Source: *MMR*, February 24, 2003, p. 20, from Information Resources Inc.

★ 724 ★

Cleaning Products (SIC 2842)

Household Cleaner Sales, 2002

Sales are shown in millions of dollars for the year ended December 29, 2002. Figures exclude Wal-Mart, which accoutns for about 25% of all cleaning product sales.

All-purpose cleaners/disinfectants . .	$ 464,838.0
Toilet bowl cleaners/deodorizers . . .	289,895.7
Nonabrasive tub/tile cleaner/degreaser . .	267,711.2
Glass cleaners/ammonia	208,275.7
Drain cleaners	169,844.6
Spray disinfectants	110,816.9
Abrasive tub/tile cleaners	109,200.2
Oven/appliance cleaners/degreasers . . .	49,977.5
Specialty cleaners/polishes	31,830.8

Source: *Household and Personal Products Industry*, December 2002, p. 48, from Information Resources Inc.

★ 725 ★

Cleaning Products (SIC 2842)

Household Cleaner Segments, 2002

The $186 million industry is shown by segment for the year ended August 11, 2002. Figures exclude Wal-Mart.

All purpose cleaners	64.7%
Furniture polish/cleaners	23.5
Glass cleaners	10.8
Metal cleaners	0.9

Source: *Household and Personal Products Industry*, November 2002, p. 48, from Information Resources Inc.

★ 726 ★

Cleaning Products (SIC 2842)

Top Disinfectant Brands, 2002

Brands are ranked by sales in millions of dollars for the year ended March 24, 2002. Figures exclude Wal-Mart.

	($ mil.)	Share
Pine Sol	$ 86.9	18.68%
Lysol	75.1	16.14
Formula 409	46.4	9.97
Mr. Clean	39.6	8.51
Clorox Clean Up	37.6	8.08
Fantastik	36.8	7.91
Murphy's Oil	19.0	4.08
Spic & Span	15.5	3.33
Orange Clean	9.8	2.11
Private label	16.2	3.48
Other	82.3	17.69

Source: *MMR*, May 13, 2002, p. 1, from Information Resources Inc.

★ 727 ★

Baby Care (SIC 2844)

Top Baby Lotion Brands, 2002

Market shares are shown for the year ended August 11, 2002. Figures are for supermarkets, drug stores, and discount stores but exclude Wal-Mart.

Johnson & Johnson	42.1%
Aveeno	16.7
Baby Magic	15.3
Johnson's Bedtime	12.6
Gerber	3.2
J&J Convenience Kit	2.0

Continued on next page.

★ 727 ★ *Continued*

Baby Care (SIC 2844)

Top Baby Lotion Brands, 2002

Market shares are shown for the year ended August 11, 2002. Figures are for supermarkets, drug stores, and discount stores but exclude Wal-Mart.

Burt's Bees	1.3%
Healing Garden	1.0
Other	5.8

Source: *Chain Drug Review*, October 14, 2002, p. 73, from Information Resources Inc.

★ 728 ★

Baby Care (SIC 2844)

Top Baby Oil Brands, 2002

Brands are ranked by sales in millions of dollars for the year ended February 24, 2002. Figures include supermarkets, drug stores and discount stores but exclude Wal-Mart.

	($ mil.)	Share
Johnson's	$ 24.7	57.98%
Johnson & Johnson	1.9	4.46
Playtex Baby Magic	1.2	2.82
Gerber	0.6	1.41
Lander	0.5	1.17
Other	13.7	32.16

Source: *Chain Drug Review*, June 24, 2002, p. 187, from Information Resources Inc.

★ 729 ★

Baby Care (SIC 2844)

Top Baby Ointment/Cream Brands, 2002

Brands are ranked by sales in millions of dollars for the year ended February 24, 2002. Figures include supermarkets, drug stores and discount stores but exclude Wal-Mart.

	($ mil.)	Share
Desitin	$ 28.4	39.28%
A and D	17.3	23.93
Balmex	10.4	14.38
Aveeno	2.6	3.60
Johnson's	2.4	3.32
Johnson's Baby	1.9	2.63
Dr. Smiths	1.5	2.07

	($ mil.)	Share
Gerber	$ 1.1	1.52%
Triple Paste	0.6	0.83
Boudreau's Butt Paste	0.4	0.55
Private label	3.7	5.12
Other	2.0	2.77

Source: *MMR*, April 22, 2002, p. 57, from Information Resources Inc.

★ 730 ★

Baby Care (SIC 2844)

Top Baby Powder Brands, 2002

Brands are ranked by sales in millions of dollars for the year ended February 24, 2002. Figures include supermarkets, drug stores and discount stores but exclude Wal-Mart.

	($ mil.)	Share
Johnson's	$ 36.7	59.97%
Gold Bond	1.8	2.94
Johnson & Johnson	1.7	2.78
Johnson's Baby	1.7	2.78
Caldesene	1.6	2.61
Gerber	1.2	1.96
Desitin	0.6	0.98
Balmex	0.6	0.98
Playtex Baby Magic	0.4	0.65
Lander	0.3	0.49
Other	14.6	23.86

Source: *Chain Drug Review*, June 24, 2002, p. 187, from Information Resources Inc.

★ 731 ★

Cosmetics (SIC 2844)

Top Eye Makeup Brands, 2002

Market shares are shown for the year ended October 6, 2002. Figures include drug stores, supermarkets and discount stores but exclude Wal-Mart.

Expert Eyes	8.0%
Great Lash	6.3
Cover Girl Eye Enhancers	4.0
Voluminous	3.9
Almay One Coat	3.7
Volume Express	3.2
Full 'N Soft	3.2
ColorStay	2.7
Wear Infinite	2.6

Continued on next page.

★ 731 ★ *Continued*
Cosmetics (SIC 2844)

Top Eye Makeup Brands, 2002

Market shares are shown for the year ended October 6, 2002. Figures include drug stores, supermarkets and discount stores but exclude Wal-Mart.

Cover Girl Professional	2.4%
Other	60.0

Source: *Chain Drug Review*, January 20, 2003, p. 16, from Information Resources Inc.

★ 732 ★
Cosmetics (SIC 2844)

Top Face Makeup Brands, 2002

Market shares are shown for the year ended October 6, 2002. Figures include drug stores, supermarkets and discount stores but exclude Wal-Mart.

Cover Girl	7.9%
Cover Girl Smoothers	3.9
ColorStay	3.4
New Complexion	3.2
Visible Lift	3.1
Age Defying	2.9
Neutrogena	2.5
Feel Naturale	2.4
Cover Girl Simply Powder	2.3
Cover Girl Ultimate Finish	2.3
Other	66.1

Source: *Chain Drug Review*, January 20, 2003, p. 16, from Information Resources Inc.

★ 733 ★
Cosmetics (SIC 2844)

Top Lip Makeup Brands, 2002

Market shares are shown for the year ended October 6, 2002. Figures include drug stores, supermarkets and discount stores but exclude Wal-Mart.

Cover Girl Outlast	7.1%
Super Lustrous	6.4
Max Factor Lipfinity	4.2
Wet Shine	4.1
Moisture Whip	3.9
Colour Riche	3.5
ColorStay	3.5
Cover Girl Continuous Color	3.5
Endless	3.0
Moon Drops	2.6
Other	58.2

Source: *Chain Drug Review*, January 20, 2003, p. 16, from Information Resources Inc.

★ 734 ★
Denture Care (SIC 2844)

Top Denture Adhesive Brands, 2002

Brands are ranked by sales in millions of dollars for the year ended February 24, 2002. Figures include supermarkets, drug stores and discount stores but exclude Wal-Mart.

	($ mil.)	Share
Fixodent	$ 67.6	41.81%
Super Poligrip	20.4	12.62
Sea Bond	16.6	10.27
Fixodent Free	16.2	10.02
Poligrip Free	11.1	6.86
Fixodent Fresh	7.1	4.39

Continued on next page.

★ 734 ★ *Continued*

Denture Care (SIC 2844)

Top Denture Adhesive Brands, 2002

Brands are ranked by sales in millions of dollars for the year ended February 24, 2002. Figures include supermarkets, drug stores and discount stores but exclude Wal-Mart.

	($ mil.)	Share
Poligrip Ultra Fresh	$ 4.6	2.84%
Effergrip	4.2	2.60
Super Wernets	2.9	1.79
Rigident	2.4	1.48
Private label	1.6	0.99
Other	7.0	4.33

Source: *Chain Drug Review*, June 24, 2002, p. 187, from Information Resources Inc.

★ 735 ★

Denture Care (SIC 2844)

Top Denture Care (Tablet) Brands, 2002

Brands are ranked by sales in millions of dollars for the year ended February 24, 2002. Figures include supermarkets, drug stores and discount stores but exclude Wal-Mart.

	($ mil.)	Share
Polident	$ 26.2	25.51%
Efferdent	23.2	22.59
Efferdent Plus	16.1	15.68
Polident Overnight	8.9	8.67
Smokers Polident	4.6	4.48
Fixodent	3.9	3.80
Polident for Partials	3.5	3.41
Private label	16.3	15.87

Source: *Chain Drug Review*, June 24, 2002, p. 187, from Information Resources Inc.

★ 736 ★

Deodorants (SIC 2844)

Deodorant Sales by Type

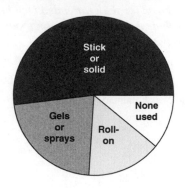

According to the source, 90% of Americans use deodorant at least once a week.

Stick or solid	.52.0%
Gels or sprays	22.0
Roll-on	.15.0
None used	.11.0

Source: *American Demographics*, June 2002, p. 56, from Mediamark Research.

★ 737 ★

Deodorants (SIC 2844)

Top Deodorant Brands, 2002

Market shares of the $1.15 billion category are shown for the year ended December 29, 2002. Figures for Wal-Mart are not included.

Mennen	7.7%
Right Guard	6.7
Degree	6.1
Old Spice Endurance	5.7
Secret	4.7
Secret Sheer Dry	4.6
Dove	4.5
Secret Platinum	3.9
Mitchum	3.6
Ban	3.6
Other	48.9

Source: *Household and Personal Products Industry*, March 2003, p. 1, from Information Resources Inc.

★ 738 ★
Deodorants (SIC 2844)

Top Deodorant Brands by Unit Sales, 2002

Unit shares are shown for the year April 21, 2002.

Mennen Speed Stick	8.0%
Degree	6.5
Right Guard Sport	6.4
Secret Sheer Dry	5.5
Dove	5.5
Secret	5.5
Old Spice High Endurance	5.0
Gillette	3.7
Ban	3.3
Other	50.6

Source: *Progressive Grocer*, July 1, 2002, p. 76, from Information Resources Inc.

★ 739 ★
Deodorants (SIC 2844)

Top Deodorant Brands for Men, 2002

The stagnant category has enjoyed a boost from increased consumer interest in body sprays. Brands are ranked by sales in millions of dollars for the year ended December 1, 2002. Figures include supermarkets, drug stores and discount stores but not Wal-Mart.

	($ mil.)	Share
Mennen Speed Stick	$ 90.0	7.76%
Right Guard Sport	77.8	6.71
Degree	71.1	6.13
Old Spice High Endurance	65.1	5.61
Secret	55.7	4.80
Secret Sheer Dry	54.0	4.66
Dove	51.9	4.47
Secret Platinum	43.8	3.78
Gillette Series	42.2	3.64
Ban	41.9	3.61
Other	566.5	48.84

Source: *MMR*, January 27, 2003, p. 21, from Information Resources Inc.

★ 740 ★
Ear Care (SIC 2844)

Eardrop Market in Nashville, TN

Market shares are shown for July 2001. PNH stands for polymyxin/neomycin/hydrocortisone.

PNH	51.0%
Fluoroquinolones ciprofloxacin	19.0
Ofloxacin	16.0
Other	14.0

Source: *Ear, Nose and Throat Journal*, January 2003, p. S13.

★ 741 ★
Eye Care (SIC 2844)

Top Eye/Lens Care Brands, 2002

Brands are ranked by sales in millions of dollars for the year ended February 24, 2002. Figures include supermarkets, drug stores and discount stores but exclude Wal-Mart.

	($ mil.)	Share
Alcon Opti Free Express	$ 69.2	8.70%
Bausch & Lomb Renu Multiplus	60.2	7.57
Bausch & Lomb Renu	41.1	5.17
Alcon Optl Free	26.1	3.28
Ciba Vision Aosept	24.9	3.13
Allergan Refresh Tears	22.6	2.84
Allergan Refresh Plus	20.9	2.63
Ciba Vision Genteal	18.5	2.33

Continued on next page.

Eye Care (SIC 2844)

Top Eye/Lens Care Brands, 2002

Brands are ranked by sales in millions of dollars for the year ended February 24, 2002. Figures include supermarkets, drug stores and discount stores but exclude Wal-Mart.

	($ mil.)	Share
Visine	$ 18.5	2.33%
Bausch & Lomb Sensitive Type	18.1	2.28
Private label	77.9	9.80
Other	397.2	49.95

Source: *Chain Drug Review*, June 24, 2002, p. 187, from Information Resources Inc.

★ 742 ★

Foot Care (SIC 2844)

Top Foot Care/Athletes Foot Medication Vendors, 2002

Shares are shown for the year ended August 11, 2002.

Schering-Plough	42.9%
Novartis	24.4
Combe Inc.	4.8
Upjohn Co.	2.2
Chattem Inc.	2.1
Alva/Amco Pharmacal Cos. Inc.	1.4
Medtech Labs Inc.	1.2
Kramer Labs	0.9
Private label	11.6
Other	8.5

Source: *Grocery Headquarters*, October 2002, p. 88, from Information Resources Inc.

★ 743 ★

Foot Care (SIC 2844)

Top Foot Care Brands in Drug Stores, 2001

Brands are ranked by drug store sales in millions of dollars for the year ended December 30, 2001.

	($ mil.)	Share
Dr. Scholl's (devices)	$ 42.7	15.02%
Lamisil AT (medications)	21.0	7.39
Litrimin AF (medications)	19.7	6.93
Tinactin (medications)	15.3	5.38

	($ mil.)	Share
Professional Foot Care (devices)	$ 7.0	2.46%
Desenex (medications)	7.0	2.46
Dr. Scholl's Dynastep (devices)	6.5	2.29
Dr. Scholl's (medications)	6.5	2.29
Airplus (devices)	6.0	2.11
Dr. Scholl's Advantage (devices)	4.8	1.69
Other	147.7	51.97

Source: *Drug Store News*, May 20, 2002, p. 43, from Information Resources Inc.

★ 744 ★

Foot Care (SIC 2844)

Top Foot Care Vendors, 2002

Shares are shown for the year ended August 11, 2002.

Schering-Plough	64.6%
ProFoot Care	6.7
Implus Footcare	2.7
PediFix Footcare	2.5
Johnson & Johnson	2.4
Combe Inc.	2.4
Novartis	2.4
Homedics	2.0
W.E. Bassett Co.	1.2
Private label	6.3
Other	6.8

Source: *Grocery Headquarters*, October 2002, p. 88, from Information Resources Inc.

★ 745 ★

Fragrances (SIC 2844)

Leading Fragrance Brands, 2002

Market shares are shown based on sales for the year ended October 6, 2002. Figures are for drug stores, supermarkets and discount stores but exclude Wal-Mart. Top firms include Beckiser (Calgon Coty), Chattem (Gold Bond), Johnson & Johnson (Shower toShower), Elizabeth Arden (Elizabeth Taylor) and Parfums de Couer (Body Fantasies).

Calgon Coty	4.3%
Gold Bond Chattem	4.0
Shower to Shower	3.8

Continued on next page.

★ 745 ★ *Continued*
Fragrances (SIC 2844)

Leading Fragrance Brands, 2002

Market shares are shown based on sales for the year ended October 6, 2002. Figures are for drug stores, supermarkets and discount stores but exclude Wal-Mart. Top firms include Beckiser (Calgon Coty), Chattem (Gold Bond), Johnson & Johnson (Shower toShower), Elizabeth Arden (Elizabeth Taylor) and Parfums de Couer (Body Fantasies).

Elizabeth Taylor White Diamonds	3.6%
Body Fantasies	2.9
Jean Nate	2.0
Jovan Musk for Women	1.9
Vanderbilt	1.8
Adidas Moves for Her	1.7
Jovan White Musk	1.7
Other	72.3

Source: *Chain Drug Review*, January 6, 2003, p. 79, from Information Resources Inc.

★ 746 ★
Fragrances (SIC 2844)

Top Colognes for Men, 2001

- Acqua di Gio pour Homme
- Romance Men
- Polo Ralph Lauren
- Davidoff Cool Water
- Eternity for Men
- Tommy
- Drakkar Noir
- Ralph Lauren Polo Sport
- Curve for Men
- Obsession for Men

The best selling brands in premium outlets. Figures are in millions of dollars.

Acqua di Gio pour Homme	$ 81.1
Romance Men	59.6
Polo Ralph Lauren	58.3
Davidoff Cool Water	53.2
Eternity for Men	50.7
Tommy	46.9
Drakkar Noir	44.4
Ralph Lauren Polo Sport	43.1

Curve for Men	$ 43.1
Obsession for Men	41.8

Source: *Daily News Record*, December 23, 2002, p. 49, from Euromonitor.

★ 747 ★
Fragrances (SIC 2844)

Top Fragrance Brands in Drug Stores, 2001

Brands are ranked by sales in millions of dollars for the year ended December 30. Figures exclude Wal-Mart.

	($ mil.)	Share
Elizabeth Taylor's White Diamonds	$ 11.1	2.19%
Old Spice	9.5	1.87
Calgon	9.3	1.83
Coty Healing Garden	8.5	1.67
Coty Stetson	8.1	1.59
Drakkar Noir	8.0	1.58
Gold Bond	7.6	1.50
Body Fantasy	7.1	1.40
Other	438.7	86.38

Source: *Drug Store News*, May 20, 2002, p. 54, from Information Resources Inc.

★ 748 ★
Fragrances (SIC 2844)

Top Fragrances for Teenage Girls, 2002

Figures are based on a survey of 1,000 male and female teenagers.

Tommy Girl	9.0%
Victoria Secret	8.0
Lucky You	7.0
Happy	7.0

Source: *Retail Merchandiser*, February 2003, p. 48, from Zandl Group.

★ 749 ★
Fragrances (SIC 2844)

Top Fragrances for Women, 2002

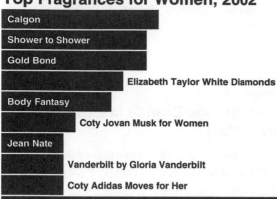

Brands are ranked by sales in millions of dollars for the year ended February 24, 2002. Figures include supermarkets, drug stores and discount stores but exclude Wal-Mart.

	($ mil.)	Share
Calgon	$ 17.3	12.52%
Shower to Shower	16.0	11.58
Gold Bond	15.9	11.51
Elizabeth Taylor White Diamonds	13.9	10.06
Body Fantasy	12.0	8.68
Coty Jovan Musk for Women . . .	7.6	5.50
Jean Nate	7.4	5.35
Vanderbilt by Gloria Vanderbilt . .	7.4	5.35
Coty Adidas Moves for Her . . .	7.2	5.21
Other	33.5	24.24

Source: *MMR*, April 22, 2002, p. 57, from Information Resources Inc.

★ 750 ★

Fragrances (SIC 2844)

Top Men's Gift Set Brands, 2002

Brands are ranked by sales in millions of dollars for the year ended February 24, 2002. Figures include supermarkets, drug stores and discount stores but exclude Wal-Mart.

	($ mil.)	Share
Coty Stetson	$ 6.6	11.46%
Coty Adidas Moves	6.4	11.11
Old Spice	5.0	8.68
Coty Aspen	3.5	6.08
All Coty Products	2.9	5.03

	($ mil.)	Share
Gillette Mach3	$ 2.8	4.86%
Coty Preferred Stock	2.5	4.34
Nautica	2.0	3.47
Coty All Stetson Products . . .	1.9	3.30
Parfums de Coeur Bod Man . . .	1.6	2.78
Other	22.4	38.89

Source: *Chain Drug Review*, June 24, 2002, p. 187, from Information Resources Inc.

★ 751 ★

Hair Care (SIC 2844)

Largest Ethnic Hair Care Product Makers, 2002

The top makers of chemical products are ranked by sales for the year ended February 3, 2002. Sales at Wal-Mart are not included.

	($ mil.)	Share
Pro-line International	$ 11.2	6.44%
Carson Products	9.0	5.17
Luster Products	7.3	4.20
SoftSheen Products	6.3	3.62
Colomer	4.8	2.76
Wella/Johnson	4.7	2.70
A.P. Products	3.4	1.95
Gillette	0.4	0.23
Cheatham Chemical	0.3	0.17
Other	126.6	72.76

Source: *Household & Personal Products Industry*, April 2002, p. 9, from Information Resources Inc.

★ 752 ★

Hair Care (SIC 2844)

Largest Ethnic Hair Dressing Makers, 2002

The top makers of hair dressing products are ranked by sales for the year ended February 3, 2002. Sales at Wal-Mart are not included.

Luster Products	$ 5.0
Pro-Line International	3.6
Namasday Laboratory	3.5
Wella/Johnson	3.1
Bronner Brothers	2.5
Soft Sheen	2.4
J. Strickland	2.4
A.P. Products	1.3

Continued on next page.

★ 752 ★ *Continued*

Hair Care (SIC 2844)

Largest Ethnic Hair Dressing Makers, 2002

The top makers of hair dressing products are ranked by sales for the year ended February 3, 2002. Sales at Wal-Mart are not included.

Imperial Dak	$ 1.2
J.M. Products	1.0

Source: *Household & Personal Products Industry*, April 2002, p. 9, from Information Resources Inc.

★ 753 ★

Hair Care (SIC 2844)

Top Depilatory Brands, 2002

Brands are ranked by sales in millions of dollars for the year ended February 24, 2002. Figures include supermarkets, drug stores and discount stores but exclude Wal-Mart.

	($ mil.)	Share
Nads	$ 30.2	20.84%
Nair	30.1	20.77
Sally Hansen	26.6	18.36
Epil Stop	23.2	16.01
Magic	6.1	4.21
Nair 3 in 1	5.6	3.86
Ardell Surgi Cream	4.1	2.83
Bikini Zone	3.9	2.69
Ardell Surgi Wax	2.6	1.79
Hair Off	2.3	1.59
Other	10.2	7.04

Source: *Chain Drug Review*, June 24, 2002, p. 187, from Information Resources Inc.

★ 754 ★

Hair Care (SIC 2844)

Top Hair Care Brands in Drug Stores, 2001

Brands are ranked by sales in millions of dollars for the year ended December 30. Figures exclude Wal-Mart.

	($ mil.)	Share
L'Oreal Preference	$ 66.2	4.06%
L'Oreal Excellence	48.8	3.00
L'Oreal Feria	45.5	2.79

	($ mil.)	Share
Clairol Nice N Easy	$ 42.6	2.61%
Just for Men	33.6	2.06
Clairol Natural Instincts	30.9	1.90
Garnier Nutrisse	23.7	1.45
Clairol Hydrience	23.3	1.43
Other	1,314.5	80.69

Source: *Drug Store News*, May 20, 2002, p. 54, from Information Resources Inc.

★ 755 ★

Hair Care (SIC 2844)

Top Hair Coloring Brands, 2002

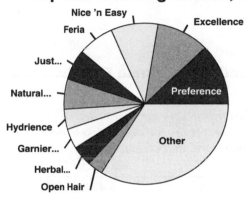

Market shares are shown for the year ended October 6, 2002. Figures include drug stores, supermarkets and discount stores but exclude Wal-Mart.

Preference	12.2%
Excellence	10.2
Nice 'n Easy	8.7
Feria	7.4
Just For Men	6.2
Natural Instincts	6.0
Hydrience	4.1
Garnier Nutrisse	4.1
Herbal Essences	4.0
Open Hair	3.2
Other	33.2

Source: *Chain Drug Review*, January 20, 2003, p. 16, from Information Resources Inc.

★ 756 ★

Hair Care (SIC 2844)

Top Hair Coloring Brands, 2003

Market shares are shown for the year ended February 3, 2003. They exclude Wal-Mart, club and dollar stores.

L'Oreal	48.1%
Clairol	34.7
Combe	8.6
Revlon	6.7
Other	1.9

Source: *Advertising Age*, March 24, 2003, p. 12, from Information Resources Inc.

★ 757 ★

Hair Care (SIC 2844)

Top Hair Conditioner/Rinse Brands, 2002

Brands are ranked by sales for the year ended December 29, 2002. Figures are for supermarkets, drug stores and discount stores and exclude Wal-Mart.

	($ mil.)	Share
Clairol Herbal Essences	$ 47.8	6.04%
Alberto VO5	40.7	5.14
Thermasilk	39.4	4.98
Infusium 23	32.2	4.07
Pantene Smooth and Sleek	31.0	3.92
Finesse	28.3	3.58
Pantene Sheer Volume	22.0	2.78
Pantene Constant Care	20.4	2.58
Pantene Color Revival	17.1	2.16
Suave	16.5	2.08
Other	496.1	62.68

Source: *MMR*, February 10, 2003, p. 29, from Information Resources Inc.

★ 758 ★

Hair Care (SIC 2844)

Top Hair Relaxer Kits, 2002

Brands are ranked by sales in millions of dollars for the year ended February 24, 2002. Figures include supermarkets, drug stores and discount stores but exclude Wal-Mart.

	($ mil.)	Share
Soft Sheen Optimum Care	$ 5.6	10.87%
Dark & Lovely	4.1	7.96
Just for Me	3.6	6.99
Proline Soft & Beautiful	3.5	6.80
African Pride	3.4	6.60
Lusters Scurl	3.4	6.60
Johnson's Gentle Treatment	3.1	6.02
Dark & Lovely Plus	2.9	5.63
Ogilvie	2.6	5.05
Proline	2.0	3.88
Other	17.3	33.59

Source: *Chain Drug Review*, June 24, 2002, p. 187, from Information Resources Inc.

★ 759 ★

Hair Care (SIC 2844)

Top Hair Spray Brands, 2002

Pantene Pro V
Suave Unilever
Herbal Essences
Salon Selectives
Aqua Net
Sebastian Shaper
White Rain Classic Care
Pantene Pro V
Consort
Other

Market shares are shown for the year ended October 6, 2002. Figures include drug stores, supermarkets and discount stores but exclude Wal-Mart.

Pantene Pro V	7.1%
Suave Unilever	6.7
Herbal Essences	4.8
Salon Selectives	4.5
Aqua Net	4.2
Sebastian Shaper	3.6
White Rain Classic Care	3.5

Continued on next page.

★ 759 ★ *Continued*
Hair Care (SIC 2844)

Top Hair Spray Brands, 2002

Market shares are shown for the year ended October 6, 2002. Figures include drug stores, supermarkets and discount stores but exclude Wal-Mart.

Pantene Pro V	3.3%
Consort	3.2
Other	59.1

Source: *Chain Drug Review*, January 20, 2003, p. 16, from Information Resources Inc.

★ 760 ★

Hair Care (SIC 2844)

Top Hair Styling Brands, 2002

Market shares are shown for the year ended October 6, 2002. Figures include drug stores, supermarkets and discount stores but exclude Wal-Mart.

Frizz Ease	7.1%
Pantene Pro V	6.6
L.A. Looks	6.3
Herbal Essences	4.4
Salon Selectives	2.9
Dep	2.6
Got 2B Advanced	2.6
ThermaSilk	2.5
Pro Vitamin	2.1
Suave	2.1
Other	60.8

Source: *Chain Drug Review*, January 20, 2003, p. 16, from Information Resources Inc.

★ 761 ★

Hair Care (SIC 2844)

Top Hair Styling Product Makers, 2002

The top makers of gel and mousse are ranked by sales for the year ended February 24, 2002. Figures exclude Wal-Mart.

	($ mil.)	Share
Helene Curtis	$ 66.9	12.96%
Procter & Gamble	61.6	11.93
Dep	55.7	10.79
John Frieda	50.9	9.86
L'Oreal	50.7	9.82

	($ mil.)	Share
Clairol	$ 28.7	5.56%
Advanced Research Labs	19.4	3.76
Alberto-Culver	14.1	2.73
Chesebrough Pond's	12.5	2.42
Redmond	10.4	2.01
Other	145.3	28.15

Source: *Household & Personal Products Industry*, May 2002, p. 71, from Information Resources Inc.

★ 762 ★

Hair Care (SIC 2844)

Top Shampoo Brands, 2002

Market shares are shown for the year ended October 6, 2002. Figures include drug stores, supermarkets and discount stores but exclude Wal-Mart.

Herbal Essences	7.1%
Suave	3.2
Head & Shoulders	3.2
Pantene Smooth and Sleek	2.8
ThermaSilk	2.8
Pantene Classically Clean	2.6
Pantene Sheer Volume	2.6
Finesse	2.6
Pert Plus	2.5
Pantene Pro V	2.3
Private label	3.1
Other	65.2

Source: *Chain Drug Review*, January 20, 2003, p. 16, from Information Resources Inc.

★ 763 ★

Hair Care (SIC 2844)

Top Shampoo Brands in Supermarkets

Market shares are shown in percent.

Clairol Herbal Essences	6.7%
Suave	3.6
Head & Shoulders Classic Clean	3.5
Pert Plus	3.0
Pantene Classically Clean	3.0
Pantene Smooth and Sleek	2.9
Thermasilk	2.6
Loreal Kids	2.5
Finesse	2.4
Pantene Sheer Volume	2.4
Other	67.4

Source: *Supermarket News*, February 10, 2003, p. 30, from Information Resources Inc.

★ 764 ★

Hair Care (SIC 2844)

Top Shampoo Makers, 2002

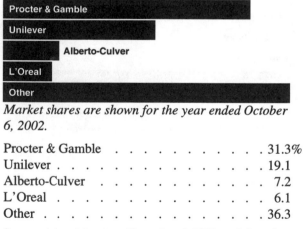

Market shares are shown for the year ended October 6, 2002.

Procter & Gamble	31.3%
Unilever	19.1
Alberto-Culver	7.2
L'Oreal	6.1
Other	36.3

Source: *Advertising Age*, November 4, 2002, p. 3, from Information Resources Inc.

★ 765 ★

Hair Growth Products (SIC 2844)

Top Hair Growing Treatments, 2002

Brands are ranked by sales in millions of dollars for the year ended February 24, 2002. Figures include supermarkets, drug stores and discount stores but exclude Wal-Mart.

	($ mil.)	Share
Rogaine	$ 48.6	63.36%
Nu hair	0.8	1.04
Barre	0.4	0.52
Doo Gro	0.2	0.26
Alpharma	0.1	0.13
Private label	26.6	34.68

Source: *Chain Drug Review*, June 24, 2002, p. 187, from Information Resources Inc.

★ 766 ★

Lip Care (SIC 2844)

Leading Lip Care Brands, 2002

Shares are shown for the year ended February 24, 2002. Figures are for supermarkets, drug stores and discount stores and exclude Wal-Mart.

	($ mil.)	Share
Chapstick	$ 66.5	24.43%
Abreva	38.7	14.22
Blistex	25.9	9.52
Carmex	13.9	5.11
Mentholatum	11.9	4.37
Chapstick Flava Craze	7.8	2.87
Campho Phenique	7.8	2.87
Herpecin	6.3	2.31
Blistex Herbal Answer	5.7	2.09
Kank A	5.4	1.98
Private label	5.9	2.17
Other	76.4	28.07

Source: *Chain Drug Review*, June 24, 2002, p. 238, from Information Resources Inc.

★ 767 ★

Nail Care (SIC 2844)

Top Artificial Nail Brands, 2003

Market shares are for the year ended January 3, 2003. Figures include supermarkets, drug stores and discount stores but exclude Wal-Mart.

Broadway Nails	20.2%
Kiss	17.8
Nailene	8.6
Nailene Color	4.4
IBD 5 Second	3.9
Kiss 1 Easy Step	3.2
California Girl	3.0
Fing'rs	3.0
Cosmar Press & Go	2.9
Pro-10	2.7
Other	30.3

Source: *Chain Drug Review*, March 17, 2003, p. 27, from Information Resources Inc.

★ 768 ★

Nail Care (SIC 2844)

Top Nail Accessory Brands, 2002

Brands are ranked by sales in millions of dollars for the year ended February 24, 2002. Figures include supermarkets, drug stores and discount stores but exclude Wal-Mart.

	($ mil.)	Share
Revlon	$ 35.5	24.43%
Lacross	24.4	16.79
Trim	22.2	15.28
Kiss	7.8	5.37
Gem	4.6	3.17
Joncl	4.2	2.89
Sally Hansen	3.5	2.41
Fing'rs	3.1	2.13
Oleg Cassini	2.4	1.65
Nailene	1.6	1.10
Private label	14.2	9.77
Other	21.8	15.00

Source: *MMR*, April 22, 2002, p. 57, from Information Resources Inc.

★ 769 ★

Nail Care (SIC 2844)

Top Nail Care Brands in Drug Stores, 2001

Brands are ranked by sales in millions of dollars.

	($ mil.)	Share
Revlon (implements)	$ 20.5	5.51%
Maybelline Express Finish (polish)	14.5	3.90
LaCross (implements)	14.0	3.76
Sally Hansen Hard as Nails (polish)	12.6	3.39
Sally Hansen (polish)	12.5	3.36
Revlon (polish)	12.2	3.28
L'Oreal Jet Set (polish)	11.9	3.20
Kiss (artificial/accessories)	10.8	2.90
Other	263.1	70.71

Source: *Drug Store News*, May 20, 2002, p. 54, from Information Resources Inc.

★ 770 ★

Nail Care (SIC 2844)

Top Nail Polish Brands, 2002

Brands are ranked by sales in millions of dollars for the year ended February 24, 2002. Figures include supermarkets, drug stores and discount stores but exclude Wal-Mart.

	($ mil.)	Share
Maybelline Express Finish	$ 26.2	8.18%
Sally Hansen Hard As Nails	21.6	6.74
Sally Hansen	20.3	6.34
Revlon	18.6	5.81
L'Oreal Jet Set	17.8	5.56
Cover Girl Nail Slicks	13.6	4.24
Wet 'n Wild	11.5	3.59
Sally Hansen Teflon Tuff	10.6	3.31
Sally Hansen Chrome	9.8	3.06
Revlon Super Top Speed	9.6	3.00
Other	160.8	50.19

Source: *MMR*, April 22, 2002, p. 57, from Information Resources Inc.

★ 771 ★
Nasal Care (SIC 2844)

Top Nasal Strip Brands, 2002

Brands are ranked by sales in millions of dollars for the year ended February 24, 2002. Figures include supermarkets, drug stores and discount stores but exclude Wal-Mart.

	($ mil.)	Share
Breathe Right	$ 46.30	91.18%
Clear Passage	0.40	0.79
Breathe Right Near Clear	0.08	0.16
Private label	4.00	7.88

Source: *Chain Drug Review*, June 24, 2002, p. 187, from Information Resources Inc.

★ 772 ★
Nasal Care (SIC 2844)

Top Nose Spray Brands, 2002

Brands are ranked by sales in millions of dollars for the year ended February 24, 2002. Figures include supermarkets, drug stores and discount stores but exclude Wal-Mart.

	($ mil.)	Share
Afrin	$ 47.3	14.74%
Primatene Mist	29.6	9.22
Nasalcrom	21.1	6.57
Zicam	20.1	6.26
Vicks Sinex	19.6	6.11
4 Way	17.3	5.39
Afrin No Drip	16.6	5.17
Neo Synephrine	11.5	3.58
Vicks	10.5	3.27
Vicks Vapo Steam	9.1	2.83

	($ mil.)	Share
Private label	$ 72.9	22.71%
Other	45.4	14.14

Source: *MMR*, April 22, 2002, p. 57, from Information Resources Inc.

★ 773 ★
Oral Care (SIC 2844)

Top Dental Floss Brands, 2002

Brands are ranked by sales in millions of dollars for the year ended February 24, 2002. Figures include supermarkets, drug stores and discount stores but exclude Wal-Mart.

	($ mil.)	Share
Glide	$ 26.9	24.66%
Reach	24.0	22.00
Reach Easy Slide	8.1	7.42
Reach Dentotape	7.0	6.42
Reach Gentle Gum Care	5.8	5.32
J&J Reach Whitening	5.4	4.95
Oral B Satinfloss	4.7	4.31
Oral B	4.5	4.12
Oral B Ultra Floss	4.4	4.03
Oral B Satintape	3.1	2.84
Private label	7.6	6.97
Other	7.6	6.97

Source: *Chain Drug Review*, June 24, 2002, p. 187, from Information Resources Inc.

★ 774 ★
Oral Care (SIC 2844)

Top Mouthwash Brands, 2002

Brands are ranked by sales in millions of dollars for the year ended February 24, 2002. Figures include supermarkets, drug stores and discount stores but exclude Wal-Mart.

	($ mil.)	Share
Listerine	$ 238.1	46.60%
Scope	82.2	16.09
Plax	23.7	4.64
Act	17.5	3.43
Targon	8.6	1.68
Act for Kids	7.1	1.39
Biotene	7.0	1.37
Cepacol	6.2	1.21
Rembrandt Age Defying	2.7	0.53

Continued on next page.

★ 774 ★ *Continued*
Oral Care (SIC 2844)

Top Mouthwash Brands, 2002

Brands are ranked by sales in millions of dollars for the year ended February 24, 2002. Figures include supermarkets, drug stores and discount stores but exclude Wal-Mart.

	($ mil.)	Share
Toms of Maine	$ 2.7	0.53%
Private label	94.4	18.48
Other	20.7	4.05

Source: *MMR*, April 22, 2002, p. 57, from Information Resources Inc.

★ 775 ★
Oral Care (SIC 2844)

Top Oral Care Products in Drug Stores, 2001

Brands are ranked by drug store sales in millions of dollars for the year ended December 30, 2001.

	($ mil.)	Share
Listerine (mouthwash/rinse)	$ 65.0	6.44%
Crest (toothpaste)	47.9	4.75
Colgate (toothpaste)	36.4	3.61
Braun Oral B (accessories)	26.4	2.62
Colgate Total (toothpaste)	21.4	2.12
Scope (mouthwash/rinse)	19.5	1.93
Aquafresh (toothpaste)	19.5	1.93
Sensodyne (toothpaste)	18.4	1.82
Listerine Pocketpaks	18.3	1.81
Other	736.3	72.97

Source: *Drug Store News*, May 20, 2002, p. 43, from Information Resources Inc.

★ 776 ★
Oral Care (SIC 2844)

Top Toothpaste Vendors, 2002

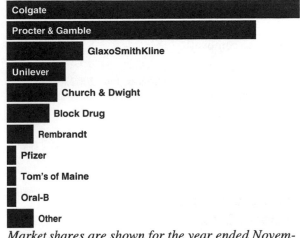

Market shares are shown for the year ended November 29, 2002. Figures exclude Wal-Mart.

Colgate	34.2%
Procter & Gamble	29.4
GlaxoSmithKline	9.4
Unilever	6.9
Church & Dwight	5.9
Block Drug	4.9
Rembrandt	2.9
Pfizer	1.3
Tom's of Maine	1.1
Oral B	0.9
Other	3.1

Source: *Grocery Headquarters*, March 2003, p. 60, from Information Resources Inc.

★ 777 ★
Personal Care Products (SIC 2844)

Toiletries Market in Canada, 2000

Sales are shown in millions of dollars.

	($ mil.)	Share
Hair care	$ 519.0	28.10%
Skin care	357.0	19.33
Bath preparations	218.0	11.80
Color cosmetics	212.0	11.48
Women's fragrances	158.0	8.56
Oral hygiene	107.5	5.82
Men's fragrances	85.0	4.60
Deo/antiperspirants	80.0	4.33
Sun care	48.0	2.60
Nail care	31.5	1.71

Continued on next page.

★ 777 ★ *Continued*

Personal Care Products (SIC 2844)

Toiletries Market in Canada, 2000

Sales are shown in millions of dollars.

	($ mil.)	Share
Shaving/hair removal	$ 12.0	0.65%
Other	18.7	1.01

Source: *European Cosmetic Markets*, June 2002, p. 225, from *Cosmetics* and Canadian Cosmetics, Toiletries and Fragrance Association.

★ 778 ★

Shaving Cream (SIC 2844)

Leading Ethnic Shaving Care Vendors, 2002

Companies are ranked by sales in millions of dollars for the year ended July 21, 2002. Figures exclude Wal-Mart. Shares are estimated based on sales of $26.4 million.

	Sales	Share
Carson Products	$ 6,207,022	23.51%
Pharmoland Research Labs . .	1,165,685	4.42
Biocosmetic Research Labs . .	439,765	1.67
Medtech	141,580	0.54
J. Strickland & Co.	108,922	0.41
Other	18,337,026	69.46

Source: *Household and Personal Products Industry*, October 2002, p. 48, from Information Resources Inc.

★ 779 ★

Shaving Cream (SIC 2844)

Top Shaving Cream Brands, 2002

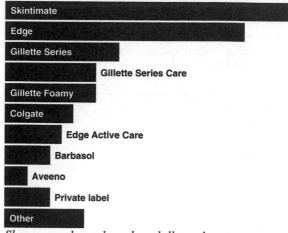

Shares are shown based on dollar sales at grocery, drug and mass market outlets (but not Wal-Mart) for the year ended December 29, 2002.

Skintimate	24.8%
Edge	21.4
Gillette Series	10.0
Gillette Series Care	8.2
Gillette Foamy	7.7
Colgate	5.9
Edge Active Care	4.5
Barbasol	4.1
Aveeno	2.1
Private label	4.1
Other	7.2

Source: *Grocery Headquarters*, April 2003, p. 45, from Information Resources Inc.

★ 780 ★

Skin Care (SIC 2844)

Largest Hand & Body Lotion Makers, 2003

Market shares are shown for the year ended February 22, 2003. Figures exclude Wal-Mart, membership club stores and dollar stores.

Unilever	17.0%
Kao Corp.	15.1
Beiersdorf	12.9
Johnson & Johnson	10.6
Pfizer	8.9
Alberto-Culver	3.7
Galderma	3.3

Continued on next page.

★ **780** ★ *Continued*

Skin Care (SIC 2844)

Largest Hand & Body Lotion Makers, 2003

Market shares are shown for the year ended February 22, 2003. Figures exclude Wal-Mart, membership club stores and dollar stores.

Private label	5.8%
Other	22.7

Source: *Advertising Age*, March 17, 2003, p. 6, from Information Resources Inc.

★ **781** ★

Skin Care (SIC 2844)

Top Facial Cleanser Brands, 2002

Market shares are shown for the year ended October 6, 2002. Figures include drug stores, supermarkets and discount stores but exclude Wal-Mart.

Pond's	10.8%
Olay Daily Facials	7.8
Clean & Clear	5.8
Cetaphil	5.0
Noxzema	4.4
Neutrogena Deep Clean	4.3
St. Ives Swiss Formula	4.2
Olay	4.1
Neutrogena	3.6
Biore	3.5
Other	46.5

Source: *Chain Drug Review*, January 20, 2003, p. 16, from Information Resources Inc.

★ **782** ★

Skin Care (SIC 2844)

Top Facial Moisturizer Vendors, 2002

Market shares are shown based on sales of $257.9 million for the year ended August 11, 2002. Figures include drug stores, supermarkets and discount stores but exclude Wal-Mart.

Procter & Gamble	33.7%
Neutrogena	19.6
L'Oreal	10.0
Chesebrough-Pond's	9.2
Johnson & Johnson	7.2
Beiersdorf	4.2

Galderma	2.5%
Revlon	2.5
Other	11.1

Source: *Chain Drug Review*, September 30, 2002, p. 82, from Information Resources Inc.

★ **783** ★

Skin Care (SIC 2844)

Top Hand & Body Lotion Brands, 2002

Vaseline Intensive Care

Nivea

Jergens

Lubriderm

Curel

Eucerin

Aveeno

St. Ives Swiss Formula

Suave

Cetaphil

Private label

Other

Market shares are shown for the year ended October 6, 2002. Figures include drug stores, supermarkets and discount stores but exclude Wal-Mart.

Vaseline Intensive Care	9.9%
Nivea	6.6
Jergens	6.2
Lubriderm	6.0
Curel	4.8
Eucerin	4.4
Aveeno	4.3
St. Ives Swiss Formula	3.6
Suave	3.6
Cetaphil	3.1
Private label	5.6
Other	41.9

Source: *Chain Drug Review*, January 20, 2003, p. 16, from Information Resources Inc.

★ 784 ★

Skin Care (SIC 2844)

Top Hand & Body Moisturizer Suppliers, 2002

Market shares are shown based on sales of $787.7 million for the year ended August 11, 2002. Figures include drug stores, supermarkets and discount stores but exclude Wal-Mart.

Andrew Jergens	15.3%
Beiersdorf	12.3
Chesebrough-Pond's	11.6
Pfizer	9.2
Neutogena	5.9
Helene Curtis	5.7
Johnson & Johnson	4.3
Alberto-Culver	3.6
Galderma	3.1
Other	29.0

Source: *Chain Drug Review*, September 30, 2002, p. 82, from Information Resources Inc.

★ 785 ★

Sun Care (SIC 2844)

Leading Sunscreen/Insect Repellant Makers, 2002

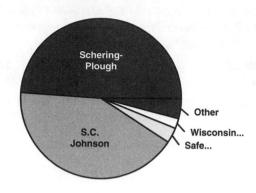

The market is shifting to lotions with higher SPFs as people become more aware of the harmful effects of the sun. Market shares are shown based on sales at drug stores, supermarkets and discount stores for the year ended August 11, 2002. Figures do not include Wal-Mart.

Schering-Plough	48.4%
S.C. Johnson	41.2
Safe Solutions	3.0
Wisconsin Pharmaceuticals	1.9
Other	4.1

Source: *Chain Drug Review*, September 30, 2002, p. S27, from Information Resources Inc.

★ 786 ★

Sun Care (SIC 2844)

Top Sun Care Brands, 2002

Brands are ranked by sales in millions of dollars for the year ended July 14, 2002. Figures exclude Wal-Mart.

	($ mil.)	Share
Banana Boat	$ 49.5	11.82%
Coppertone	48.9	11.68
Neutrogena	39.8	9.50
Hawaiian Tropic	27.6	6.59
Coppertone Sport	26.5	6.33
Coppertone Water Babies	19.6	4.68
Coppertone Endless Summer	16.4	3.92
Banana Boat Sport	15.1	3.61

Continued on next page.

★ **786** ★ *Continued*

Sun Care (SIC 2844)

Top Sun Care Brands, 2002

Brands are ranked by sales in millions of dollars for the year ended July 14, 2002. Figures exclude Wal-Mart.

	($ mil.)	Share
No-Ad	$ 9.5	2.27%
Private label	36.6	8.74
Other	129.3	30.87

Source: *MMR*, August 26, 2002, p. 1, from Information Resources Inc.

★ **787** ★

Sun Care (SIC 2844)

Top Sun Care Vendors, 2002

Companies are ranked by sales in millions of dollars for the year ended December 29, 2002. Figures exclude Wal-Mart.

	($ mil.)	Share
Schering-Plough	$ 149.5	35.28%
Playtex Products	89.4	21.09
Neutrogena	54.1	12.77
Tanning Research Labs	38.1	8.99
Private label	36.9	8.71
Other	55.8	13.17

Source: *Household and Personal Products Industry*, March 2003, p. 48, from Information Resources Inc.

★ **788** ★

Paints and Coatings (SIC 2851)

Thermal Spray Industry

The U.S. market represents $500 million of the roughly $3 billion industry.

Aeronautical/aerospace gas turbine repair . . .	40.0%
Automobile components (not turbines)	14.0
Land-based turbines	12.0
Other	34.0

Source: *Advanced Coatings & Surface Technology*, March 2003, p. 12, from Technical Insights.

★ **789** ★

Paints and Coatings (SIC 2851)

Paints and Coatings Market, 2001

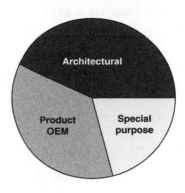

Value shares are shown. OEM stands for original equipment manufacturer.

Architectural	43.2%
Product OEM	36.0
Special purpose	20.8

Source: *Paints and Coatings Industry*, October 2002, p. 146, from U.S. Bureau of the Census.

★ **790** ★

Paints and Coatings (SIC 2851)

Paints and Coatings Market, 2005

Shipments are shown by end market.

Powder	48.6%
High-solids	15.0
Conventional solventborne	11.7
Two-component	10.2
Waterborne	9.5
E-coat	3.5
Radiation cure	1.1

Source: *Industrial Paint & Powder*, January 2003, p. 18, from Freedonia Group.

★ **791** ★

Paints and Coatings (SIC 2851)

Top Coatings Producers, 2002

Shares are for the North American market.

Sherwin-Williams	18.8%
PPG	10.8
ICI	10.7
Valspar	10.0

Continued on next page.

★ 791 ★ *Continued*
Paints and Coatings (SIC 2851)

Top Coatings Producers, 2002

Shares are for the North American market.

Akzo Nobel	8.7%
DPont	7.7
RPM	6.1
Other	27.2

Source: *Coatings World*, November 2002, p. 23, from PGPhillips & Associates Inc.

★ 792 ★
Paints and Coatings (SIC 2851)

Top Luxury Car Colors in North America, 2002

Figures show the preferred colors for vehicles, based on a survey.

Silver	32.1%
White met.	17.7
White	11.8
Medium/dark blue	8.6
Black	8.5
Medium/dark gray	7.2
Medium red	6.0
Gold	3.0
Medium/dark green	1.8

Source: *PR Newswire*, December 13, 2002, p. NA, from *DuPont Automotive Color Popularity Report*.

★ 793 ★
Paints and Coatings (SIC 2851)

Top Sport/Compact Car Colors in North America, 2002

Figures show the preferred colors for vehicles, based on a survey.

Silver	24.6%
Black	14.3
Medium/dark blue	12.9
White	8.8
Bright red	6.9

Medium/dark gray	6.7%
Medium red	5.5
Light brown	4.3
Gold	4.1

Source: *PR Newswire*, December 13, 2002, p. NA, from *DuPont Automotive Color Popularity Report*.

★ 794 ★
Paints and Coatings (SIC 2851)

Top SUV/Truck/Van Colors in North America, 2002

Figures show the preferred colors for vehicles, based on a survey.

White	19.3%
Silver	18.0
Black	12.4
Medium/dark blue	11.4
Medium/dark gray	7.5
Medium red	7.1
Medium/dark green	6.7
Light brown	5.1
Bright red	4.5

Source: *PR Newswire*, December 13, 2002, p. NA, from *DuPont Automotive Color Popularity Report*.

★ 795 ★
Paints and Coatings (SIC 2851)

Top Vehicle Colors in North America, 2002

Figures show the preferred colors for vehicles, based on a survey.

Silver	22.8%
White	15.2
Black	12.0
Medium/dark blue	10.9
Medium/dark gray	7.0
Medium red	6.9
Light brown	6.4
Medium/dark green	5.0
Bright red	3.3

Source: *PR Newswire*, December 13, 2002, p. NA, from *DuPont Automotive Color Popularity Report*.

★ 796 ★
Organic Chemicals (SIC 2865)
Largest Cumene Producers

Companies are ranked by capacity in millions of pounds per year.

Georgia Gulf	1,500
Koch Petroleum	1,500
Sunoco	1,200
Shell Chemical	1,100
Citgo Petroleum	1,100
Chevron Phillips Chemical	990
Marathon Ashland Petroleum	800

Source: *Chemical Market Reporter*, May 13, 2002, p. 31.

★ 797 ★
Organic Chemicals (SIC 2865)
Largest Phenol Producers

Companies are ranked by capacity in millions of pounds per year.

Sunoco	2,040
Shell Chemical	1,180
Ineos Phenol	880
Mount Vernon Phenol	710
Georgia Gulf	660

Source: *Chemical Market Reporter*, May 20, 2002, p. 27, from Blue Johnson & Associates.

★ 798 ★
Organic Chemicals (SIC 2865)
Largest Xylene Producers

Companies are ranked by capacity in thousands of metric tons per year.

BP Chemicals	2,025
ExxonMobil Chemical	1,699
Chevron Phillips Chemical	830
Citgo	562

Koch Industries	547
Valero	545
Atofina Petrochemicals	354
Hess	346
El Paso	285
Sunoco Chemical	197

Source: *Chemical Week*, June 26, 2002, p. 31, from Dewitt & Co.

★ 799 ★
Organic Chemicals (SIC 2869)
How Perchloroethlene is Consumed

Figures show annual end markets.

Refrigerants	50.0%
Dry cleaning/textiles	25.0
Metal cleaning/degreasing	10.0
Cleaning car brakes	10.0
Other	5.0

Source: *Wall Street Journal*, October 1, 2002, p. B1, from Halogenated Solvents Industry.

★ 800 ★
Organic Chemicals (SIC 2869)
Largest Acetone Makers

Shares are shown based on total capacity.

	M.t.	Share
Sunoco Chemicals	555	29.35%
Shell Chemicals	352	18.61
Ineos Phenol	273	14.44
Dow Chemical	260	13.75
Mount Vernon Phenol	211	11.16
Georgia Gulf	186	9.84
JLM Industries	31	1.64
Other	23	1.22

Source: *Chemical Week*, December 4, 2002, p. 35, from Chemical Market Associates Inc.

★ 801 ★

Organic Chemicals (SIC 2869)

Largest Flurocarbon Producers

Companies are ranked by capacity in millions of pounds per year.

DuPont 430
Honeywell 290
Atofina Chemicals 227
Ineos Fluor 68
MDA Manufacturing 40
Solvay 40
Air Products and Chemicals 10

Source: *Chemical Market Reporter*, September 30, 2002, p. 27.

★ 802 ★

Organic Chemicals (SIC 2869)

Largest Methanol Makers

Shares are shown based on total capacity of 1.7 million gallons. Figures are for Canada and the United States.

	M.t.	Share
Beaumont Methanol	280	15.60%
Celanese Canada	255	14.21
Lyondell	250	13.93
Millennium Petrochemicals	210	11.70
Clear Lake Methanol	200	11.14
Celanese	175	9.75
Other	425	23.68

Source: *Chemical Market Reporter*, December 16, 2002, p. 35, from ICIS-LOR.

★ 803 ★

Agrichemicals (SIC 2879)

Pest and Lawn & Garden Industry

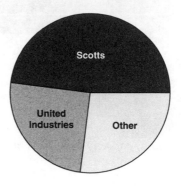

Market shares are shown in percent.

	2000	2002
Scotts	51.0%	48.0%
United Industries	12.0	25.0
Other	27.0	27.0

Source: *Knight Ridder/Tribune Business News*, September 29, 2002, p. NA, from United Industries.

★ 804 ★

Insecticides (SIC 2879)

Insecticide Market Shares, 2001

The market was valued at $330 million.

Herbicides 65.4%
Insecticides 14.0
Fungicides 11.1
Nematricides 9.5

Source: *Datamonitor Industry Market Research*, Annual 2002, p. NA, from Datamonitor.

★ 805 ★
Adhesives (SIC 2891)

Largest Automotive Adhesives Producers

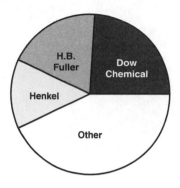

Revenues reached $537 million in 2000. This figure may reach reach $621 million in 2005. Market shares are shown in percent.

Dow Chemical	24.0%
H.B. Fuller	19.0
Henkel	14.0
Other	43.0

Source: *Adhesives Age*, March 2003, p. 12, from Frost & Sullivan.

★ 806 ★
Adhesives (SIC 2891)

U.S. Adhesive Sales

Figures are in millions of dollars.

	2001	2006	Share
Non-rigid bonding . . .	$ 1,305	$ 1,634	23.39%
Packaging	1,322	1,599	22.89
Construction	1,002	1,203	17.22
Other	2,040	2,551	36.51

Source: *Adhesives & Sealants Industry*, July 2002, p. 23, from Business Communications Co.

★ 807 ★
Ink (SIC 2893)

Largest Printing Ink Firms

The top firms in the United States are ranked by global sales of printing inks and colorants. Some figures are estimates.

Sun Chemical	$ 3,300
Flint Ink	1,400
INX International Ink Co.	300
SICPA Management	110
Color Converting Industries	108
Wikoff Color Corporation	81
Central Ink Corporation	73
Toyo Ink International	71
Superior Printing Ink	67
Nazdar	65
Van Son Holland Ink Corporation of America	64
Sensient Technologies	55

Source: *Ink World*, April 2002, p. 25.

★ 808 ★
Carbon Black (SIC 2895)

Largest Carbon Black Producers

Figures are in thousands of metric tons.

	(000)	Share
Cabot	640	28.96%
Degussa Engineered Carbons	465	21.04
Columbian Chemicals	450	20.36
Sid Richardson Carbon	350	15.84
Continental Carbon	305	13.80

Source: *Chemical Week*, February 26, 2003, p. 31, from SRI Consulting.

★ 809 ★
Fly Ash (SIC 2899)

Fly Ash Market Shares

Fly ash are fine particles left behind after coal has burned. It has become an additive to make concrete more durable.

ISG	50.0%
Lafarge North America	11.0
Other	39.0

Source: *Investor's Business Daily*, November 19, 2002, p. A10.

★ 810 ★

Salt (SIC 2899)

Kosher Salt Market

Kosher crystals represent only about 6% of the $100 million market.

Morton 75.0%
Diamond Crystal 25.0

Source: *Detroit Free Press*, July 24, 2002, p. 2F.

SIC 29 - Petroleum and Coal Products

★ 811 ★
Jet Fuel (SIC 2911)

Jet Fuel Sales, 2002

The company had well over 80% of the market for the year.

Jet Center	80.0%
Other	20.0

Source: *Knight Ridder/Tribune Business News*, April 27, 2003, p. NA.

★ 812 ★
Propane (SIC 2911)

How Propane is Used

Usage is shown in billions of gallons. Other includes agricultural uses such as grain drying and flame cultivation.

	(bil.)	Share
Chemical, industrial, utility	9.8	50.0%
Residential/commercial/recreational	8.0	40.8
Internal combustion engine	0.4	2.0
Other	1.4	7.2

Source: *LP Gas*, July 2002, p. 22, from National Propane Gas Association.

★ 813 ★
Lubricants (SIC 2992)

Lubricant Additives Demand

Demand is shown in millions of dollars.

	2001	2006
Deposit control additives	$ 504	$ 556
Viscosity & index improvers	323	357
Antiwear & EP additives	195	216
Antioxidants	191	231
Corrosion inhibitors	130	145
Defoamers	65	75

	2001	2006
Pour point depressants	$ 35	$ 40
Other	102	115

Source: *Lubricants World*, September 2002, p. 5, from Freedonia Group.

★ 814 ★
Motor Oils (SIC 2992)

Motor Oil Market

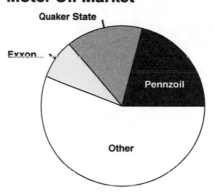

Market shares are shown in percent.

Pennzoil	21.0%
Quaker State	15.0
Exxon Mobil	8.0
Other	56.0

Source: *The Houston Chronicle*, March 27, 2002, p. NA.

★ 815 ★

Motor Oils (SIC 2992)

Motor Oil Market in North Carolina

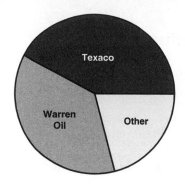

Market shares are shown based on grocery store sales.

Texaco 42.0%
Warren Oil 37.0
Other 21.0

Source: *Knight Ridder/Tribune Business News*, April 4, 2003, p. NA, from Marketing Management.

SIC 30 - Rubber and Misc. Plastics Products

★ 816 ★
Rubber Products (SIC 3000)

Largest Rubber Product Makers in North America, 2001

Firms are ranked by rubber sales in millions of dollars. Figures include tires, hose, belts and similar products.

Goodyear Tire & Rubber Co.	$ 7,700.0
Michelin North America Inc.	5,643.0
Bridgestone/Firestone	5,250.0
Cooper Tire & Rubber Co.	2,618.4
Continental Tire North America Inc.	1,564.0
Parker Hannifin	1,100.0
Tomkins P.L.C.	1,050.0
Federal-Mogul Corp.	846.8
Freudenberg-NOK	776.0
Hutchinson North America	624.1

Source: *Rubber & Plastics News*, July 15, 2002, p. 12, from *Rubber & Plastics News Top 100*.

★ 817 ★
Tires (SIC 3011)

Highway Truck Tire Market, 2002

Market shares are shown in percent.

Goodyear	19.0%
Michelin	18.0
Bridgestone	16.0
Firestone	7.0
General	6.0
Yokohama	5.0
Toyo	4.0
Sumitomo	3.0
Dunlop	3.0
Cooper	3.0
Other	16.0

Source: *Tire Business*, April 28, 2003, p. 16.

★ 818 ★
Tires (SIC 3011)

North American Tire Market, 2002

Market shares are shown based on a $23.9 billion industry.

Goodyear/Dunlop	28.4%
Michelin/Uniroyal Goodrich	23.0
Bridgestone/Firestone	20.5
Cooper	6.6
Continental Tire	6.5
Other	15.0

Source: *Tire Business*, Market Data Book, p. NA.

★ 819 ★
Tires (SIC 3011)

Passenger Tire Market, 2002

Market shares are shown in percent.

Goodyear	15.0%
Michelin	9.0
Firestone	6.0
Cooper	6.0
Bridgestone	6.0
BFGoodrich	6.0
General	4.0
Uniroyal	4.0
Dunlop	3.0
Dayton	3.0
Other	38.0

Source: *Tire Business*, Market Data Book, p. NA.

★ 820 ★
Tires (SIC 3011)

Passenger Tire Market in Canada

Market shares are shown based on 15.7 million tires.

Motomaster	18.5%
Goodyear	15.0

Continued on next page.

★ 820 ★ *Continued*
Tires (SIC 3011)

Passenger Tire Market in Canada

Market shares are shown based on 15.7 million tires.

Michelin	9.5%
Bridgestone	6.0
BFGoodrich	5.0
Dayton	4.0
Cooper	4.0
Uniroyal	3.5
Hankook	3.5
Yokohama	3.0
Toyo	3.0
Firestone	3.0
Other	22.0

Source: *Modern Tire Dealer*, Fact Book 2003, p. 1, from MTD estimates.

★ 821 ★
Tires (SIC 3011)

Small Farm Tire Market

Market shares are shown in percent. Figures cover the original equipment market.

Firestone	36.5%
Goodyear	35.0
Titan	28.0
Kelly	8.0
TBC	6.5
Co-op	6.0
American Farmer	5.0
Denman	3.5
Other	4.5

Source: *Modern Tire Dealer*, Fact Book 2002, p. NA, from MTD estimates.

★ 822 ★
Tires (SIC 3011)

Tire Production by Segment, 2002

Figures are estimates.

	(mil.)	Share
Cars	198.00	80.77%
Light trucks	33.10	13.50
Medium trucks	13.90	5.67
Heavy trucks	0.13	0.05

Source: *Financial Times*, March 3, 2003, p. 8, from Rubber Manufacturers Association.

★ 823 ★
Tires (SIC 3011)

Tire Production in North America, 2002

Figures show daily production.

Oklahoma	141,500
North Carolina	124,700
Alabama	96,000
Tennessee	86,900
South Carolina	80,000
Texas	43,500
Mississippi	42,000
Illinois	41,500
Quebec	41,000
Virginia	40,700

Source: *Tire Business*, Market Data Book, p. NA, from Rubber Manufacturers Association.

★ 824 ★
Tires (SIC 3011)

Top Light Truck Tire Brands, 2002

Market shares are shown based on 34 million units.

Goodyear	12.5%
BFGoodrich	8.5
Michelin	6.5
Cooper	6.5
Bridgestone	6.5
Multi-Mile	6.0
General	6.0
Firestone	5.5
Kelly	4.0
Sears	3.5
Toyo	3.0
Cordovan	3.0
Other	28.5

Source: *Modern Tire Dealer*, Fact Book 2003, p. NA, from MTD estimates.

★ 825 ★
Tires (SIC 3011)

Top Light Truck Tire Brands in Canada

Market shares are shown based on 2.3 million tires.

Motomaster	14.0%
Goodyear	14.0

Continued on next page.

★ **825** ★ *Continued*

Tires (SIC 3011)

Top Light Truck Tire Brands in Canada

Market shares are shown based on 2.3 million tires.

Michelin	10.5%
Bridgestone	7.0
BFGoodrich	7.0
Dayton	7.0
Hankook	5.0
Firestone	4.5
Yokohama	4.0
Toyo	3.0
Uniroyal	3.0
Other	21.0

Source: *Modern Tire Dealer*, Fact Book 2003, p. 1, from MTD estimates.

★ **826** ★

Tires (SIC 3011)

Top Tire Makers, 2002

Market shares are shown in percent.

Goodyear	19.5%
Michelin	16.0
Bridgestone	15.5
Other	49.0

Source: *Modern Tire Dealer*, Fact Book 2003, p. NA, from MTS estimates.

★ **827** ★

Tires (SIC 3011)

Top Tire Replacement Brands, 2002

Market shares are shown based on 190.5 million units.

Goodyear	15.0%
Michelin	8.5
Firestone	7.5
Cooper	5.5
Bridgestone	5.5
BFGoodrich	5.0
General	4.0
Sears	4.0
Multi-Mil	3.0
Uniroyal	2.5
Kumho	2.5

Kelly	2.5%
Dayton	2.5
Other	32.0

Source: *Modern Tire Dealer*, Fact Book 2003, p. NA, from MTD estimates.

★ **828** ★

Tires (SIC 3011)

Truck Tire Market

Market shares are shown in percent.

Goodyear	28.5%
Bridgestone/Firestone	23.5
Michelin	20.0
Continental	8.0
Yokohama	4.0
Toyo	3.5
Treadways	3.0
Cooper	2.0
Kumho	2.0
TBC (Power King)	2.0
Other	5.5

Source: *Modern Tire Dealer*, Fact Book 2002, p. NA, from MTD estimates.

★ **829** ★

Footwear (SIC 3021)

Athletic Footwear Sales

Figures are in billions of dollars for January-June.

	1998	2000	2002
Men's	$ 3.90	$ 3.81	$ 4.19
Women's	1.70	1.87	2.04
Children's	1.17	1.03	1.15

Source: "Spending for Athletic Footwear." available from http://www.sgma.com, from Sporting Goods Manufacturers Association.

★ 830 ★

Footwear (SIC 3021)

Athletic Shoe Market, 2001

Market shares are shown in percent.

Nike	37.6%
Reebok	12.4
New Balance	9.3
Adidas	8.3
Skechers	3.0
Other	29.4

Source: *Wall Street Journal*, July 3, 2002, p. 1, from Wells Fargo.

★ 831 ★

Footwear (SIC 3021)

Athletic Shoe Market, 2002

Market shares are shown in percent.

Nike	39.1%
Reebok	12.0
New Balance	11.6
Adidas	9.6
Other	27.7

Source: *New York Times*, March 6, 2003, p. C1, from Sporting Goods Intelligence.

★ 832 ★

Footwear (SIC 3021)

Top Athletic Footwear Markets, 2001

Spending is shown in millions of dollars.

	($ mil.)	Share
Running	$ 4,548.9	29.5%
Basketball	2,821.9	18.3
Cross-training	2,220.5	14.4

	($ mil.)	Share
Walking	$ 1,218.2	7.9%
Athleisure	971.5	6.3
Recreational	801.8	5.2
Hiking	678.5	4.4
Tennis	570.5	3.7
Sport sandals	354.7	2.3
Aerobics	215.9	1.4

Source: *Footwear News*, July 8, 2002, p. 18, from NPD Fashionworld and Sporting Goods Manufacturers Association.

★ 833 ★

Footwear (SIC 3021)

Women's Footwear Sales

Women's footwear grew 7%, compared to 4% for men. Women's footwear has about 26% of the overall athletic footwear market (men have about 62% with the rest held by children and juveniles).

Running	36.0%
Casual	18.0
XT	13.0
Walking	11.0
Softball	9.0
Outdoor	4.0
Tennis	4.0
Aerobic	2.0
Basketball	2.0
Soccer	1.0

Source: *Sporting Goods Business*, December 2002, p. 38, from SportscanInfo.

★ 834 ★

Belting (SIC 3052)

Top Belting Markets in the Northeast Central States

Figures are in millions of dollars.

Motor vehicles & car bodies	$ 52.4
Internal combustion engines	21.8
Construction machinery	21.3
Paper mills	17.5
Motor vehicles parts & accessories	16.9

Source: *Industrial Distribution*, September 2002, p. 53, from Industrial Market Information.

★ 835 ★

Hose (SIC 3052)

End Markets for Hosing

Distribution is shown for sales at home improvement stores.

Sprinklers 42.0%
Nozzles 34.0
Accessories 24.0

Source: *Do-It-Yourself Retailing*, July 2002, p. 142, from Vista Sales & Marketing.

★ 836 ★

Rubber Products (SIC 3060)

Industrial Rubber Product Sales

Sales are expected to grow from $14.2 billion in 2001 to $18.4 billion in 2006.

	2001	2006	Share
Motor vehicles	$ 4,707	$ 5,735	31.17%
Industrial machinery/ equipment	4,040	5,730	31.14
Construction	1,968	2,335	12.69
Aerospace/other transportation	1,515	2,030	11.03
Other	1,970	2,570	13.97

Source: *Rubber World*, September 2002, p. 12, from Freedonia Group.

★ 837 ★

Condoms (SIC 3069)

Top Condom Brands, 2002

Brands are ranked by sales in millions of dollars for the year ended February 24, 2002. Figures include supermarkets, drug stores and discount stores but exclude Wal-Mart.

	($ mil.)	Share
Trojan	$ 66.1	31.09%
Trojan Enz	39.8	18.72
Durex	31.6	14.86
LifeStyles	24.6	11.57
Trojan Ultra Pleasure	10.5	4.94
Trojan Magnum	8.8	4.14
Kling Tite Naturalamb	8.3	3.90
Trojan Supra	4.8	2.26
Trojan Extended Pleasure	3.7	1.74
LifeStyles Ultra Sensitive	2.5	1.18
Other	11.9	5.60

Source: *Chain Drug Review*, June 24, 2002, p. 187, from Information Resources Inc.

★ 838 ★

Condoms (SIC 3069)

Top Condom Makers, 2003

Companies are ranked by sales in millions of dollars for the year ended January 26, 2003. Sales are at supermarkets, drug stores and discount stores but exclude Wal-Mart.

	($ mil.)	Share
Church & Dwight	$ 153.5	68.71%
Durex Consumer Products	32.2	14.41
Ansell American	31.3	14.01
Okamoto	1.5	0.67
Other	4.9	2.19

Source: *MMR*, March 24, 2003, p. 29, from Information Resources Inc.

★ 839 ★
Inflatable Rides Business (SIC 3069)

Inflatable Bounce House Industry

Inflatable attractions are staples at fairs, festivals and community functions. It is a fairly small market — $50 million — and Cutting Edge is the largest supplier of the industry.

Cutting Edge	15.0%
Other	85.0

Source: *Star Tribune*, February 14, 2003, p. 18E.

★ 840 ★
Plastic Containers (SIC 3080)

Plastic Container Producers

The market includes plastic blow molded drums, intermediate bulk containers and tight-head pails. Hunter Drum is a division of Russell Stanley.

Russell Stanley Holdings Inc.	40.0%
Greif Brothers Corp.	20.0
Other	40.0

Source: *Plastics Technology*, January 2003, p. 61, from Mastio & Company.

★ 841 ★
Plastic Containers (SIC 3080)

Plastic Container Sales

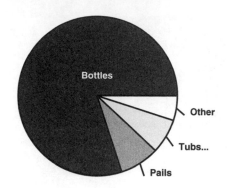

Demand is shown in millions of pounds. Analysts expect the industry to see a 4% growth rate annually to 2006. In dollar terms, the industry should see a 5% growth rate to hit $15 billion in 2006.

	2001	2006	Share
Bottles	8,852	10,945	80.12%
Pails	905	1,075	7.87
Tubs & cups	800	895	6.55
Other	643	745	5.45

Source: *Canadian Packaging*, November 2002, p. 9, from Freedonia Group.

★ 842 ★
Plastic Film and Sheet (SIC 3081)

Largest Film and Sheet Producers

Companies are ranked by most recent year sales in millions of dollars.

Bemis Co.	$ 1,801.9
DuPont	1,279.0
Tyco Plastics and Adhesives	1,250.0
Cryovac Inc.	1,220.0
Printpack Inc.	950.0
Sigma Plastics Group	805.0
Pechiney Plastic Packaging	803.0
Pilant Corp.	722.7
Pactiv Corp.	671.0
Spartech Plastics	630.4

Source: *Plastics News*, September 2, 2002, p. 3.

★ 843 ★
Plastic Film and Sheet (SIC 3081)

Plastic Film and Sheet Production, 2001

Figures show value of shipments.

	($ mil.)	Share
Wisconsin	$ 1,401.4	27.73%
South Carolina	491.2	9.72
Illinois	372.1	7.36
Georgia	304.8	6.03
Texas	228.2	4.52
Other	2,256.3	44.64

Source: *Plastics News*, January 20, 2003, p. 3, from Society of the Plastics Industry.

★ 844 ★
Plastic Pipe (SIC 3084)

Polyethylene Pipe Market

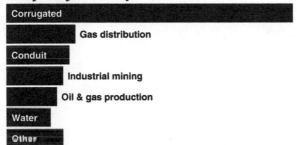

Total demand reached 1.95 billion pounds. Figures are for Canada and the United States.

Corrugated	46.0%
Gas distribution	11.0
Conduit	10.0
Industrial mining	9.0
Oil & gas production	8.0
Water	7.0
Other	9.0

Source: *Plastics News*, November 11, 2002, p. 3, from Walsh Consulting Services Inc.

★ 845 ★
Plastic Bottles (SIC 3085)

PET Bottle End Markets

Figures for PET (polyethylene terephthalate) are shown in millions of units. Data are for North America and estimates. The total falls somewhere between 3,240-3,790 million units. Ketchup is 475-575; juice 1,700-1,900 units; CSD 500-600; Flavored alcoholic beverages 250-300; Beer 240-340.

	(mil.)	Share
Juice & tea	1,900	50.13%
CSD	600	15.83
Ketchup	575	15.17
Beer	340	8.97
Alcoholic beverages, flavored	300	7.92
Water	75	1.98

Source: *Plastics Technology*, March 2003, p. 48, from Business Development Associates.

★ 846 ★
Christmas Trees (SIC 3089)

Artificial Christmas Tree Market

The company has the leading share of the market.

Boto	40.0%
Other	60.0

Source: "Deck the Halls With Boto." available December 11, 2002 from http://www.webb-site.com/articles/boto.htm.

★ 847 ★
Plastic Utensils (SIC 3089)

Eating Utensil Market

Market shares are estimated in percent.

Diamond Brands	50.0%
Other	50.0

Source: *Journal News*, October 29, 2002, p. 1D, from Jarden Corp.

★ 848 ★

Storage Products (SIC 3089)

Leading Household/Kitchen Storage Brands, 2002

Brands are ranked by sales in millions of dollars for the year ended November 3, 2002. Figures include supermarkets, drug stores, discount stores and exclude Wal-Mart.

	($ mil.)	Share
Rubbermaid Rough Tote	$ 75.7	9.19%
Rubbermaid Servin Saver	65.8	7.99
Gladware	65.3	7.93
Sterilite Clearview	63.4	7.70
Sterilite	62.7	7.61
Ziploc	62.7	7.61
Rubbermaid	39.2	4.76
Sterilite Ultra	28.5	3.46
Ziploc Tabletops	23.1	2.81
Style Master	21.2	2.57
Other	315.9	38.36

Source: *MMR*, January 13, 2003, p. 53, from Information Resources Inc.

SIC 31 - Leather and Leather Products

★ 849 ★

Leather Goods (SIC 3100)

Leather Product Sales in Canada, 2001

Figures are for the first two quarters of the year and based on a survey of 6,000 respondents. Figures are in thousands of dollars.

Handbags/evening	$ 92,051
Wallets	24,552
Luggage	21,008
Belts	20,488
Briefcases	1,610
Backpacks	1,603
Credit cards/key case	1,396
Sport bags	790

Source: *LL&A*, February/March 2002, p. NA, from Market Facts Canada.

★ 850 ★

Footwear (SIC 3140)

Golf Shoe Market

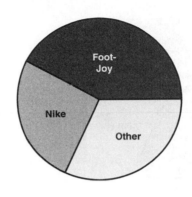

Market shares are shown in percent.

Foot-Joy	42.0%
Nike	26.0
Other	32.0

Source: *Florida Times-Union*, February 2, 2003, p. C12.

★ 851 ★

Footwear (SIC 3143)

Men's Footwear Industry, 2002

Distribution is shown in percent. Figures are for March 2001 - February 2002.

Casual	39.5%
Dress casual	32.3
Dress	14.2
Active casual	9.2
Athletic	4.8

Source: *Footwear News*, May 13, 2002, p. 4, from NPD Fashionworld.

SIC 32 - Stone, Clay, and Glass Products

★ 852 ★
Glass Containers (SIC 3221)

Glass Container Market

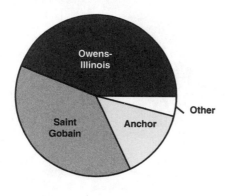

Shares are estimated for the U.S. and Canada.

Owens-Illinois 44.0%
Saint Gobain 38.0
Anchor 14.0
Other 4.0

Source: "North American Industry." available April 1, 2003 from http://www.o-i.com, from Owens-Illinois and Deutsche Bank.

★ 853 ★
Glassware (SIC 3221)

Foodservice Glassware Market

Libbey produces and sells foodservice glassware, which includes various types of tumblers and stemware. Anchor actually has the third largest share of the market but is seen as Libbey's largest direct competitor because of the resemblance between some of their products. (Libbey tried to acquire the company and a suit was filed to block the merger.) Data are as of April 2002.

Libbey Inc. 65.0%
Anchor 7.0
Other 28.0

Source: "Analysis to Aid Public Comment." available January 1, 2003 from http://www.ftc.gov.

★ 854 ★
Cement (SIC 3241)

Masonry Cement Shipments, 2002

Total shipments reached 4.43 million metric tons for the year.

	M.t.	Share
Florida	681,394	15.36%
California, southern	411,491	9.28
North Carolina	294,196	6.63
Georgia	292,349	6.59
Tennessee	210,180	4.74
Ohio	191,733	4.32
Michigan	145,566	3.28
Alabama	145,385	3.28
Other	2,064,201	46.53

Source: "Mineral Statistics." available April 7, 2003 from http://www.usgs.gov, from U.S. Department of the Interior and U.S. Geological Survey.

★ 855 ★

Concrete (SIC 3241)

Cement & Concrete Additives

Figures are in millions of dollars.

	($ mil.)	Share
Chemicals	$ 469	52.05%
Minerals	315	34.96
Fibers	117	12.99

Source: *Do-It-Yourself Retailing*, August 2002, p. 142, from Freedonia Group.

★ 856 ★

Advanced Ceramics (SIC 3250)

Advanced Ceramic Components

Figures are in millions of dollars.

	2001	2006	Share
Electronic ceramics	$ 5,185	$ 8,761	68.66%
Chemical processing/ environmental	1,420	2,036	15.96
Ceramic coatings	780	1,208	9.47
Structural ceramics	450	755	5.92

Source: *Ceramic Industry*, August 2002, p. 17, from Business Communications.

★ 857 ★

Bricks (SIC 3251)

Top Brick Makers

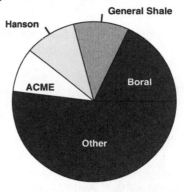

Market shares are shown in percent for 1998. The top companies are strong regional players: ACME in Texas and Hanson in the Carolinas and Texas.

Boral	18.0%
General Shale	11.0
Hanson	10.0
ACME	9.0
Other	52.0

Source: "Hanson Brick America." available January 7, 2003 from http://www.hansonplc.com.

★ 858 ★

Ceramic Tile (SIC 3253)

Ceramic Tile Sales

Figures are based on tiles sold by ceramic tile stores.

	1999	2002
Floor tile	58.0%	64.0%
Wall tile	19.0	17.0
Countertops & backsplashes	9.0	8.0
Trims & decorative tile	8.0	7.0
Exterior	6.0	4.0

Source: *National Floor Trends*, November 2002, p. 8, from *Ceramic Tile Market 2002: A Comprehensive Study*.

★ 859 ★

Clay Refractories (SIC 3255)

Leading Clay Building Material Producers, 2001

The leading manufacturers in the clay building material and refractories segment are shown by market share.

Mohawk Industries	15.0%
Cookson Group	13.0
Boral Limited	7.0
Pacific Coast Building Products	6.0
Wienerberger	5.0
Other	54.0

Source: "Clay Building Materials." available January 7, 2003 from http://www.ibisworld.com, from IBIS.

★ 860 ★

Bathtubs (SIC 3261)

Reasons for Bathtub Purchases

Data refer to purchases made for remodeling.

Conventional	62.0%
Whirlpool	38.0

Source: *Do-It-Yourself Retailing*, April 2003, p. 61, from Info Scan.

★ 861 ★

Burial Vaults (SIC 3281)

Burial Vault Market in Minnesota

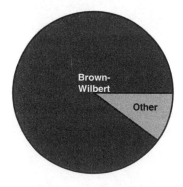

Market shares are estimated in percent.

Brown-Wilbert	90.0%
Other	10.0

Source: *Knight Ridder/Tribune Business News*, November 18, 2002, p. NA.

SIC 33 - Primary Metal Industries

★ 862 ★
Steel (SIC 3312)

Largest Steel Firms, 2002

Firms are ranked by net sales in billions of dollars.

U.S. Steel Corp.	$ 6.94
Nucor Corp.	4.56
AK Steel Corp.	4.28
Bethlehem Steel Corp.	3.57
National Steel Corp.	2.60
The Timken Co.	2.55
Commercial Metals Co.	2.44
Dofasco Inc.	2.35
Ispat Inland	2.22
Alleghany Technologies Inc.	1.90

Source: *Metal Center News*, March 2003, p. 4.

★ 863 ★
Golf Club Shafts (SIC 3317)

Golf Club Shaft Market

Market shares are shown in percent.

True Temper Sports Inc.	65.0%
Other	35.0

Source: *Knight-Ridder Tribune Business News*, January 21, 2003, p. NA.

★ 864 ★
Steel Pipe (SIC 3317)

Steel Pipe and Tube

Suppliers have witnessed 13% decline in purchased tonnage and 12% drop in transaction prices. Figures are in thousands of net tons.

	1999	2002	Share
Mechanical	4,439	3,308	28.51%
Standard pipe	1,999	2,161	18.62
Structural tube	2,743	2,150	18.53
Line pipe	2,093	1,963	16.92

	1999	2002	Share
OCTG pipe	1,344	1,576	13.58%
Stainlesss tube	229	172	1.48
Structural pipe & tube	256	150	1.29
Pressure tube	72	124	1.07

Source: *Purchasing*, March 6, 2003, p. 12B, from Steel Tube Industry.

★ 865 ★
Copper (SIC 3331)

Refined Copper Consumption, 2001

Total shipments reached 2.85 million short tons.

	(mil.)	Share
Wire rod mills	2,127	74.40%
Brass mills	688	24.06
Foundries	14	0.49
Powder plants	8	0.28
Ingot makers	6	0.21
Other	16	0.56

Source: "Annual Data 2002." available April 7, 2003 from http://www.usgs.gov, from Copper Development Association and U.S. Geological survey.

★ 866 ★
Aluminum (SIC 3334)

Aluminum End Markets, 2001

Total shipments reached 21.47 billion pounds.

Transportation	30.9%
Containers & packaging	22.6
Building & construction	13.5
Consumer durables	6.7
Electrical	6.3
Machinery & equipment	6.0
Other	13.8

Source: "Facts at a Glance." available April 7, 2003 from http://www.aluminum.org, from Aluminum Association.

★ 867 ★

Nickel (SIC 3339)

Top End Markets for Nickel, 2002

The United States had no active nickel mines during the year. Value of primary consumption as placed at $775 million.

Transportation	32.0%
Chemical industrry	13.0
Electrical equipment	10.0
Construction	9.0
Fabricated metal products	8.0
Household appliances	7.0
Other	21.0

Source: "Annual Data 2002." available April 7, 2003 from http://www.usgs.gov, from U.S. Geological Survey.

★ 868 ★

Memorials (SIC 3351)

Bronze Memorial Market

Market shares are estimated. Matthews controls 20% of the entire memorial market.

Matthews International Corp.	75.0%
Other	25.0

Source: *Mergers & Acquisitions Report*, November 25, 2002, p. NA, from Johnson Rice & Co.

★ 869 ★

Aluminum (SIC 3353)

Primary Aluminum Production, 2001

Aluminum production was valued at $4 billion. The 11 smelters east of the Mississippi River accounted for 77% of total production. Consumption is shown based on data from 25,000 firms.

Transportation	35.0%
Packaging	25.0
Building	15.0
Consumer durables	8.0
Electrical	7.0
Other	10.0

Source: "Mineral Statistics." available April 7, 2003 from http://www.usgs.gov, from U.S. Geological Survey.

★ 870 ★

Metal Castings (SIC 3360)

Metal Casting Demand, 2003

Total casting demand reached 14.6 million tons.

Gray iron	20.3%
Bronze	18.6
Aluminum diecast	17.8
Aluminum perm. Mold & sand	17.2
Carbon/low-alloy steel	13.6
Ductile iron	8.1
Other	4.4

Source: *Modern Casting*, September 2002, p. 24, from American Foundrymen's Society.

SIC 34 - Fabricated Metal Products

★ 871 ★
Knives (SIC 3421)

Imported Swiss Army Knives

Market shares are shown in percent.

Victorinox 80.0%
Other 20.0

Source: *Sporting Goods Business*, August 2002, p. 40.

★ 872 ★
Razor Blades (SIC 3421)

Disposable Razor Market Shares

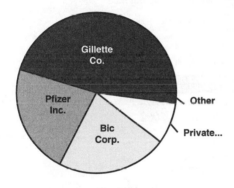

Market shares exclude sales at Wal-Mart.

Gillette Co. 43.4%
Pfizer Inc. (Schick) 21.0
Bic Corp. 21.0
Private label 7.9
Other 2.2

Source: *St. Louis Post-Dispatch*, September 24, 2002, p. C1, from Information Resources Inc.

★ 873 ★
Razor Blades (SIC 3421)

Top Razor Blade Brands, 2002

Market shares are shown for the year ended October 6, 2002. Figures include drug stores, supermarkets and discount stores but exclude Wal-Mart.

Schick Slim Twin 14.1%
Custom Plus 9.6
Good News 8.6
Schick Xtreme3 . . . . 7.7
Daisy Plus 7.2
Good News Plus 6.7
Bic Softwin 6.6
Bic 5.2
Custom Plus for Women 4.3
Good News Pivot 4.2
Private label 8.0
Other 17.8

Source: *Chain Drug Review*, January 20, 2003, p. 16, from Information Resources Inc.

★ 874 ★
Razor Blades (SIC 3421)

Top Razor Blade (Disposable) Brands, 2002

Brands are ranked by sales in millions of dollars for the year ended February 24, 2002. Figures include supermarkets, drug stores and discount stores but exclude Wal-Mart.

	($ mil.)	Share
Schick Slim Twin	$ 59.0	14.82%
Gillette Custom Plus	39.3	9.87
Gillette Good News	37.1	9.32
Schick Xtreme III	35.7	8.97
Gillette Daisy Plus	29.1	7.31
Gillette Good News Plus	28.4	7.13
Bic Softwin	22.4	5.63
Bic	22.2	5.58

Continued on next page.

215

★ 874 ★ *Continued*

Razor Blades (SIC 3421)

Top Razor Blade (Disposable) Brands, 2002

Brands are ranked by sales in millions of dollars for the year ended February 24, 2002. Figures include supermarkets, drug stores and discount stores but exclude Wal-Mart.

	($ mil.)	Share
Gillette Good News Pivot Plus	$ 17.1	4.30%
Gillette Custom Plus for Women	17.1	4.30
Private label	32.1	8.06
Other	58.6	14.72

Source: *MMR*, April 22, 2002, p. 57, from Information Resources Inc.

★ 875 ★

Razor Blades (SIC 3421)

Top Refill Razor Brands, 2002

Market shares are shown for the year ended October 6, 2002. Figures include drug stores, supermarkets and discount stores but exclude Wal-Mart.

Mach3	36.2%
Venus	11.5
Sensor Excel	10.3
Sensor	9.0
Mach3 Turbo	7.2
Atra Plus	3.4
Sensor Excel for Women	3.1
Trac II Plus	2.8
Schick Silk Effects	2.1
Schick Tracer FX	2.0
Private label	4.0
Other	8.4

Source: *Chain Drug Review*, January 20, 2003, p. 16, from Information Resources Inc.

★ 876 ★

Razor Blades (SIC 3421)

Top Refill Razor Makers

Market shares exclude sales at Wal-Mart.

Gillette Co.	87.2%
Pfizer Inc. (Schick)	8.0
Private label	4.0
Other	0.8

Source: *St. Louis Post-Dispatch*, September 24, 2002, p. C1, from Information Resources Inc.

★ 877 ★

Razor Blades (SIC 3421)

Top Women's Razor Brands, 2002

Market shares are shown based on sales for the year ended September 8, 2002.

Gillette Venus	29.4%
Gillette Mach III	20.5
Gillette Mach II Turbo	13.0
Gillette Sensor Excel for Women	5.9
Schick Silk Effects Plus	5.5
Gillette Mach II Cool Blue	4.9
Gillette Sensor Excel	4.6
Gillette Sensor	2.7
Schick Xtreme III	2.4
Other	11.1

Source: *Progressive Grocer*, November 15, 2002, p. 71, from Information Resources Inc.

★ 878 ★
Shovels (SIC 3423)

Shovels and Pushers

Plastic accounts for the lion's share of the market for both shovels and pushers.

Plastic 65.0%
Other 35.0

Source: *Knight Ridder/Tribune Business News*, March 5, 2003, p. NA, from Lenock & Cilek Ace Hardware.

★ 879 ★
Locks (SIC 3429)

Auto Lock Market in North America

The company has the leading share in the market for mechanical and electro-mechanical automobile locks.

Strattec 61.0%
Other 39.0

Source: "Four Promising Small Caps." available January 7, 2003 from http://www.fool.com.

★ 880 ★
Plumbing Fixtures (SIC 3430)

Plumbing Product Demand

Upscale fixtures will help drive demand for plumbing fixtures. Demand is shown in millions of dollars.

	2001	2006
Plumbing fittings	$ 3,687	$ 4,379
Plumbing fixtures	3,174	4,035

Source: *Supply House Times*, October 2002, p. 22, from Freedonia Group.

★ 881 ★
Sanitaryware (SIC 3430)

Largest Sanitaryware Producers

Firms are ranked by sales in millions of dollars.

Toto Ltd. . . . . $ 3,200
Kohler 2,800
INAX Corp. 2,200
American Standard 1,800
Roca 1,400
U.S. Industries 1,100

Dal-Tile International . . . . $ 1,030
Noritake 901
Villeroy & Boch 864

Source: *Ceramic Industry*, August 2002, p. 29, from *2002 Whitewares Giants* and company reports and public information.

★ 882 ★
Faucets (SIC 3432)

Top Faucet Makers

Market shares are shown in percent. Meon is a division of Fortune Brands.

Moen 31.4%
Masco 26.9
Other 41.7

Source: *Forbes*, December 9, 2002, p. NA.

★ 883 ★
Plumbing Fixtures (SIC 3432)

PEX Market Shares, 2001

PEX (cross-linked polyethylene) has been used in radiant heating installations since the early 1980s, according to the source. Its popularity is growing and it is now slowly being used in potable water systems.

Copper 90.0%
PEX 7.0
Other 3.0

Source: *Plumbing & Mechanical*, March 2003, p. 62, from *Reeves Journal*.

★ 884 ★

Boilers (SIC 3443)

Boiler Imports in Canada

Total imports of steam generation boiler equipment reached $64.5 million (C$100 million) in 2001, an increase of 83% over 2000. Canadian companies manufactured $503 million (C$780 million) of such equipment. The top importers from the United States are shown.

Ontario	36.0%
Manitoba	28.0
Alberta	24.0
Other	12.0

Source: "Boilers." available April 7, 2003 from http://www.usatrade.gov, from United States Department of Commerce.

★ 885 ★

Boilers (SIC 3443)

Boiler Market Shares

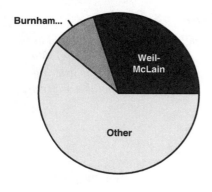

Selected shares are estimated in percent.

Weil-McLain	30.0%
Burnham Boiler	9.0
Other	61.0

Source: *Fuel Oil News*, April 2003, p. 19.

★ 886 ★

Forgings (SIC 3463)

Forging Industry in North America

Figures are in millions of dollars.

	1999	2001	Share
Impression die . . .	$ 4,637.5	$ 4,460.2	75.78%
Open die	725.2	763.1	12.96
Seamless ring	607.1	662.6	11.26

Source: *Forging*, May 2002, p. 13, from Forging Industry Association.

★ 887 ★

Guns (SIC 3484)

Gun Production, 2000

Figures are in millions.

	(mil.)	Share
Pistols	1.96	40.25%
Rifles	1.58	32.44
Shotguns	0.90	18.48
Revolvers	0.32	6.57
Machine guns	0.05	1.03
Other	0.06	1.23

Source: *Wall Street Journal*, October 14, 2002, p. A4, from Bureau of Alcohol, Tobacco and Firearms.

★ 888 ★

Guns (SIC 3484)

Top Handgun Makers, 2000

Companies are ranked by production.

	Units	Share
Ruger	345,711	26.97%
Smith & Wesson	220,992	17.24
Bryco Arms	116,664	9.10
Other	598,494	46.69

Source: *Shooting Industry*, July 2002, p. 32.

★ 889 ★
Guns (SIC 3484)

Top Rifle Makers, 2000

Ruger	
Marlin	
Remington	
Other	

Companies are ranked by production.

	Units	Share
Ruger	309,017	19.52%
Marlin	287,418	18.16
Remington	250,249	15.81
Other	736,358	46.52

Source: *Shooting Industry*, July 2002, p. 32.

★ 890 ★
Guns (SIC 3484)

Top Shotgun Makers, 2000

Companies are ranked by production.

	Units	Share
Remington	355,178	39.53%
Mossberg	352,494	39.23
H&R	162,706	18.11
Other	28,064	3.12

Source: *Shooting Industry*, July 2002, p. 32.

★ 891 ★
Valves (SIC 3491)

Industrial Valve Shipments

Figures are in millions of dollars.

	1999	2001
Automated valves	$ 944.1	$ 980.0
Ball valves	540.0	556.0
Gate, globe and check valves	450.0	465.5
Industrial butterfly valves	272.0	290.5
Plug valves	192.0	209.0
Pressure relief valves	175.0	181.0

Source: *Supply House Times*, January 2003, p. 30, from Valve Manufacturers Association.

★ 892 ★
Wire (SIC 3496)

Insulated Wire and Cable

Demand is shown in millions of dollars.

	2001	2006	Share
Fiber optics	3,870	5,290	20.19%
Building	3,700	4,370	16.68
Electronics	3,580	4,840	18.47
Telephone	2,880	3,750	14.31
Power	2,320	2,720	10.38
Other	4,100	5,230	19.96

Source: *Control Engineering*, September 2002, p. 1, from Freedonia Group.

SIC 35 - Industry Machinery and Equipment

★ 893 ★

Wind Power (SIC 3511)

Wind Power Capacity

Figures are in megawatts. According to the source, a growing number of states are requiring utilities that sell power to include a specific percent of renewable, non-polluting sources in their portfolios. Renewables is responsible for 7% of all electricity generated in the country.

	MW	Share
California	1,714	40.23%
Texas	1,096	25.72
Iowa	324	7.60
Minnesota	319	7.49
Washington	178	4.18
Oregon	158	3.71
Wyoming	141	3.31
Kansas	114	2.68
Colorado	61	1.43
New York	48	1.13
Other	108	2.53

Source: *C&EN*, February 24, 2003, p. 29, from National Renewable Energy Laboratory.

★ 894 ★

Farm Equipment (SIC 3523)

Farm Machinery Sales

Total sales were $6.6 billion for the first three quarters, down nearly $537 million. Figures are for 2 wheel drive unless shown.

	2001	2002
2 wheel drive, under 40 HP	72,419	78,674
40 & under 100 HP	40,765	41,453
100 HP & over	12,391	9,993
Combines	4,551	3,359
4 wheel drive	2,560	1,973

Source: *Ag Lender*, November 2002, p. 4, from Association of Equipment Manufacturers.

★ 895 ★

Farm Equipment (SIC 3523)

Tractor and Combine Sales in Canada

Sales are for the year to date ended August 2002.

	Units	Share
2 WD, 40-100 HP	4,314	40.29%
2 WD, 0-40 HP	3,479	32.49
2 WD, 100+ HP	2,506	23.41
4 WD	408	3.81

Source: *Implement & Tractor*, September/October 2002, p. 4, from Canadian Farm and Industrial Equipment Institute.

★ 896 ★

Lawn & Garden Equipment (SIC 3524)

Lawn and Garden Shipments

Shipments are shown in thousands of units.

	2001	2003
Walk-behind powered motors	5,622	5,963
Front-engine lawn tractors	1,214	1,399
Tillers	322	436
Riding garden tractors	181	167

Source: *Appliance Manufacturer*, January 2003, p. 50, from Outdoor Power Equipment Institute.

★ 897 ★

Lawn & Garden Equipment (SIC 3524)

Top Leaf Blower Makers, 2001

Market shares are shown in percent.

Toro	36.0%
Black & Decker	28.0
Frigidaire Home Products (Weed Eater)	22.0
MTD (Ryobi)	8.0
Other	6.0

Source: *Appliance Manufacturer*, April 2002, p. 1.

★ 898 ★

Lawn & Garden Equipment (SIC 3524)

Top Mower (Walk-behind) Makers, 2001

Market shares are shown in percent.

American Yard Products	30.0%
MTD Products	20.0
Murray	18.0
Toro	6.0
Snapper	1.0
Other	125.0

Source: *Appliance Manufacturer*, April 2002, p. 1.

★ 899 ★

Concrete-Mixing Trucks (SIC 3531)

Concrete-Mixing Truck Market

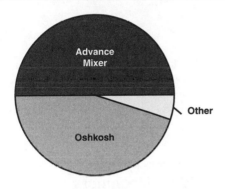

The market is for front discharge vehicles. Advance Mixer's share is slightly over 50%.

Advance Mixer	50.0%
Oshkosh	45.0
Other	5.0

Source: *Knight Ridder/Tribune Business News*, March 3, 2003, p. NA, from Advance Mixer.

★ 900 ★

Construction Equipment (SIC 3531)

Backhoe Market Shares

Market shares are shown in percent.

Case/Deere/Caterpillar/New Holland	85.0%
Other	15.0

Source: *Diesel Progress North American Edition*, February 2003, p. 4.

★ 901 ★

Construction Equipment (SIC 3531)

Construction Equipment Leaders

The leaders in the industry are ranked by equipment replacement value in billions of dollars.

U.S. Army Engineers	$ 3.5
United Rentals	3.2
Martin Marietta Aggregates	2.5
Rental Service Corp.	2.3
Ashland	2.3
Vulcan Materials	2.2
Hertz Equipment Rental	2.1
Hanson Building Materials	2.1
Peter Kiewit Sons	1.9
Peabody Energy	1.7

Source: *Construction Equipment*, September 2002, p. 31.

★ 902 ★

Lift Trucks (SIC 3537)

Largest Lift Truck Suppliers, 2001

Companies are ranked by worldwide revenues in billions of dollars. Top North American brands include Linde, Toyota, Raymond, Hsyter, Yale and Multiton.

Linde	$ 2,800
Toyota	2,700
NACCO/MHG	1,500
Jungheinrich	1,400
Mitsubishi/Caterpillar	1,000
Crown	820
Nissan	705
Manitou	682
Komatsu	676
TCM	600

Source: *Modern Materials Handling*, August 2002, p. 25.

★ 903 ★

Machine Tools (SIC 3540)

Leading Machine Tool Makers in Canada

Market shares are shown in percent.

Haas	23.6%
Mazak	13.6

Continued on next page.

★ 903 ★ *Continued*

Machine Tools (SIC 3540)

Leading Machine Tool Makers in Canada

Market shares are shown in percent.

Okuma	12.6%
Daewoo	9.8
DMG	5.9
Fadal	5.0
Matsuura	4.6
Other	24.9

Source: *Canadian Machinery and Metalworking*, March 2003, p. 14, from Canadian Machine Tool Distributors Association.

★ 904 ★

Machine Tools (SIC 3540)

Leading Machining Centers in Canada

Market shares are shown in percent.

Haas	37.8%
Mazak	13.2
DMG	11.4
Fadal	11.1
Matsuura	10.2
Daewoo	10.2
Other	6.2

Source: *Canadian Machinery and Metalworking*, March 2003, p. 14, from Canadian Machine Tool Distributors Association.

★ 905 ★

Machine Tools (SIC 3540)

Leading Milling Centers in Canada

Market shares are shown in percent.

Milltronics	34.2%
Toshiba	22.9
Trak Mill	17.1
Fidia	5.7
Nicolas-Correa	5.7
Other	14.3

Source: *Canadian Machinery and Metalworking*, March 2003, p. 14, from Canadian Machine Tool Distributors Association.

★ 906 ★

Machine Tools (SIC 3540)

Machine Tool Orders

Figures are for the year to July 2002.

Metalcutting	93.0%
Metalforming	7.0

Source: *Metalworking Insiders Report*, September 17, 2002, p. 8, from U.S. Machine Tool Consumption series.

★ 907 ★

Woodworking Machinery (SIC 3553)

Woodworking Machinery Market in Canada, 2001

Import shares are shown in percent. Total sales reached $220 million.

United States	35.0%
Taiwan	23.0
Germany	19.0
Other	23.0

Source: ''Woodworking Machinery.'' available April 7, 2003 from http://www.usatrade.gov, from United States Department of Commerce.

★ 908 ★

Plastic Molding Technology (SIC 3559)

Plastic Molding Machinery

The company is the worldwide leader of the high volume industry. In the low volume segment, is has no share.

Husky	76.0%
Other	24.0

Source: *Canadian Business*, March 17, 2003, p. 17.

★ 909 ★

Semiconductor Equipment (SIC 3559)

Top Wafer Fab Equipment Makers, 2002

Market shares are shown based on $16.5 billion in total revenues.

Applied Materials	22.2%
Tokyo Electron	10.1
ASML	9.7
KLA-Tencor	7.3

Continued on next page.

★ 909 ★ *Continued*
Semiconductor Equipment (SIC 3559)

Top Wafer Fab Equipment Makers, 2002

Market shares are shown based on $16.5 billion in total revenues.

Novellus Systems	4.8%
Nikon	4.8
Lam Research	3.6
Hitachi	3.2
Canon	3.1
Other	31.1

Source: *Business Wire*, April 7, 2003, p. NA, from Gartner Dataquest Inc.

★ 910 ★
Compressors (SIC 3563)

Portable Air Compressor Market

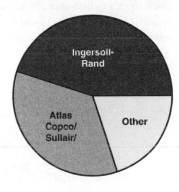

Ingersoll-Rand is the leader in the North American market, with 40-45% of the market. The top four firms have roughly 80% of the industry.

Ingersoll-Rand	45.0%
Atlas Copco/Sullair/Sullivan	35.0
Other	20.0

Source: *Diesel Progress North American Edition*, April 2003, p. 4.

★ 911 ★
Compressors (SIC 3563)

Scroll Compressor Market

Market share is for scroll compressors used in residential and light commercial air conditioner and heat pump systems.

Emerson	80.0%
Other	20.0

Source: *St. Louis Post-Dispatch*, October 29, 2002, p. NA.

★ 912 ★
Packaging Machinery (SIC 3565)

Packaging Machinery Industry

Market shares are shown in percent. The company has a 65% share worldwide.

Better Packages	75.0%
Other	25.0

Source: *Knight Ridder/Tribune Business News*, May 30, 2003, p. NA, from Better Packages.

★ 913 ★
Packaging Machinery (SIC 3565)

Packaging Machinery Spending, 2002

Spending reached $4.99 billion.

Food products	40.1%
Beverage products	18.0
Pharmaceuticals/medical products	11.9
Consumer and commercial	8.2
Soft goods nondurable	6.6
Chemicals	6.1
Personal care products	6.0
Other	3.1

Source: *Frozen Food Digest*, October 2002, p. 54, from *7th Annual PMMI Shipments and Outlook Study* and U.S. Department of Commerce.

★ 914 ★

Computers (SIC 3571)

Educational Handheld Market

Market shares are shown in percent.

TI	80.0%
Other	20.0

Source: *Knight Ridder/Tribune Business News*, November 12, 2002, p. NA, from Texas Instruments.

★ 915 ★

Computers (SIC 3571)

Leading Desktop Computer Makers, 2002

Unit shares are shown for the first three quarters.

Dell	30.1%
Hewlett-Packard	19.3
Gateway	7.0
Apple	4.9
IBM	4.7
Other	34.0

Source: *New York Times*, December 16, 2002, p. C18, from Gartner Dataquest.

★ 916 ★

Computers (SIC 3571)

Leading Notebook Computer Makers, 2002

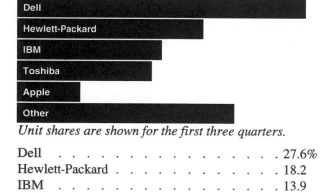

Unit shares are shown for the first three quarters.

Dell	27.6%
Hewlett-Packard	18.2
IBM	13.9
Toshiba	13.1
Apple	5.9
Other	21.3

Source: *New York Times*, December 16, 2002, p. C18, from Gartner Dataquest.

★ 917 ★

Computers (SIC 3571)

PC Industry in the United States

Shipments are in millions of units. Spending is thought to be influenced by security issues and potential war in Iraq.

	2001	2002	2003
Commercial	30.5	30.9	32.9
Consumer	15.5	16.6	17.8

Source: "IDC Sees Solid PC Market." available December 10, 2002 from http://www.idc.com., from International Data Corp.

★ 918 ★

Computers (SIC 3571)

Rugged Computer Market

Rugged computers are designed to withstand more abuse than is typically delivered by the standard clumsy consumer. Such devices started in the military and only recently became available to the public when computer components became more durable. Market shares are shown in percent.

Panasonic	75.0%
Other	25.0

Source: *Arizona Republic*, April 4, 2003, p. D1, from International Data Corp.

★ 919 ★

Computers (SIC 3571)

School Computer Leaders, 2001-2002

Apple had a share around 60% in the early 1990s. Its command of the school market has been declining with competition from lower-priced PCs. Market shares are shown in percent.

Apple	31.0%
Dell	18.0
Compaq	10.0
Gateway	5.0
IBM	4.0
Other	32.0

Source: *New York Times*, February 17, 2003, p. C4, from Quality Education Data.

★ 920 ★
Computers (SIC 3571)

Thin-Client Computer Market

The stripped-down systems offload data processing, storage and applications to server computers. Market shares are shown in percent.

Wyse	49.7%
Neoware	8.4
IBM	5.9
HP/Compaq	5.6
Sun	4.5
Other	25.9

Source: *Investor's Business Daily*, August 12, 2002, p. A4, from International Data Corp.

★ 921 ★
Computers (SIC 3571)

Top PC Firms, 2002

A total of 46.47 million units were thought to be shipped during the year. This includes desk-based PCs, mobile PCs and IA32 servers.

	Units	Share
Dell	12,982.0	27.93%
Hewlett-Packard	9,221.5	19.84
Gateway	2,745.1	5.91
IBM	2,542.3	5.47
Apple	1,708.0	3.68
Other	17,275.1	37.17

Source: "Gartner Dataquest Says PC Market Experienced Slight Upturn." available January 16, 2003 from http://www.gartner.com, from Gartner Dataquest.

★ 922 ★
Computers (SIC 3571)

Top PC Firms in Canada, 2002

Market shares are shown in percent.

Dell	20.3%
Hewlett-Packard	18.0
IBM	14.4
Toshiba Canada	6.3
Other	41.0

Source: *Computing Canada*, December 13, 2002, p. 18, from International Data Corp.

★ 923 ★
Computers (SIC 3571)

Top PDA Vendors, 2001

Market shares are shown in percent.

Palm	49.1%
Handspring	23.0
Compaq	9.4
Hewlett-Packard	5.5
Other	13.0

Source: *Advertising Age*, October 21, 2002, p. 6, from International Data Corp.

★ 924 ★
Computers (SIC 3571)

Top PDA Vendors, 2002

A total of 5.9 million units were thought to be shipped during the year.

Palm	46.0%
Sony	14.7
Hewlett-Packard	11.3
Handspring	8.7
Toshiba	4.0
RIM	3.3
Casio	2.2
Symbol	2.0
Other	7.7

Source: "Gartner Dataquest Says Worldwide PDA Market Suffers." available January 27, 2003 from http://www.gartner.com, from Gartner Dataquest.

★ 925 ★
Computer Data Storage (SIC 3572)

External Storage Market, 2002

Market shares are shown based on revenue.

Hewlett-Packard	21.9%
EMC	17.2
IBM	13.6
Hitachi	7.7
Sun	6.8
Dell	5.0
Network Appliance	3.9
Other	23.9

Source: *Computer Reseller News*, January 27, 2003, p. 22, from International Data Corp. and Thomas Wiesel Partners.

★ 926 ★

Computer Data Storage (SIC 3572)

LTO Library Shipments

Shipments jumped from 700 units in 2000 to 13,000 units in 2001.

DLT libraries	57.0%
LTO Ultrium	21.0
8mm	16.0
Other	6.0

Source: *InfoStar*, May 2002, p. 12, from Freeman Reports.

★ 927 ★

Computer Disk Drives (SIC 3572)

Leading CD-Rewritable Drive Makers, 2002

Unit shares are shown for the year through October.

Cendyne	10.0%
Sony	9.0
I/O Magic	8.6
Universal Buslink	5.6
Pacific Digital	5.3
Other	61.5

Source: *New York Times*, December 16, 2002, p. C18, from Gartner Dataquest.

★ 928 ★

Computer Peripherals (SIC 3577)

Computer Speakers Market

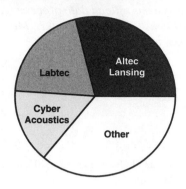

Shares are shown based on unit sales in December 2002.

Altec Lansing	29.4%
Labtec	20.0
Cyber Acoustics	15.1
Other	35.5

Source: *Twice*, March 11, 2002, p. 28, from NPD.

★ 929 ★

Computer Peripherals (SIC 3577)

Cordless Keyboard Market, 2002

Unit shares are shown based on revenues for October 2001-September 2002. The company also has 57% of the cordless mouse market.

Logitech	93.0%
Other	7.0

Source: *Business Wire*, December 11, 2002, p. NA, from NPDTechworld.

★ 930 ★
Computer Peripherals (SIC 3577)

Human-Machine Interface Industry, 2005

The $390.4 million industry is forecasted for North America. The proprietary and PC-based operator terminals sector is expected to see strong growth.

Touchscreen operator panels 42.8%
Graphical operator panels 22.4
PC-based, touchscreen operator panels . . . 19.4
PC-based operator panels 10.7
Other 4.9

Source: *Control Engineering*, August 2002, p. 15, from IMS Research and Control Engineering research.

★ 931 ★
Computer Peripherals (SIC 3577)

Leading MP-3 Player Makers, 2002

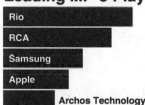

Rio
RCA
Samsung
Apple
Archos Technology
Other

Unit shares are shown for the year through October.

Rio 18.4%
RCA 14.9
Samsung 11.3
Apple 8.8
Archos Technology 7.1
Other 39.5

Source: *New York Times*, December 16, 2002, p. C18, from Gartner Dataquest.

★ 932 ★
Computer Peripherals (SIC 3577)

Printer Cartridge Market

Market shares are shown in percent.

Hewlett-Packard 58.3%
Lexmark 16.4
Epson 15.3
Canon 6.9
Other 3.1

Source: *Investor's Business Daily*, July 16, 2002, p. A4, from International Data Corp.

★ 933 ★
Computer Peripherals (SIC 3577)

Touch Pad Market

The company has somewhere between 60-70% of the market.

Synaptics 70.0%
Other 30.0

Source: *Florida Today*, April 16, 2003, p. 1, from Authentec.

★ 934 ★
Computer Printers (SIC 3577)

Leading Computer Printer Makers, 2002

Market shares are shown in percent.

Hewlett-Packard 52.0%
Lexmark 18.0
Other 30.0

Source: *Financial Times*, March 25, 2003, p. 33, from International Data Corp.

★ 935 ★
Computer Printers (SIC 3577)

Monochrome Printer Market

Market shares are shown in percent.

Hewlett-Packard 70.0%
Other 30.0

Source: *Los Angeles Times*, March 25, 2003, p. C3.

★ 936 ★
Computer Printers (SIC 3577)

Multifunction Printer Market, 2002

Market shares are shown for the first six months of the year.

Hewlett-Packard	38.9%
Lexmark	30.0
Canon	11.6
Brother	7.0
Sharp	3.5
Other	9.0

Source: *Investor's Business Daily*, September 25, 2002, p. A6, from International Data Corp.

★ 937 ★

Computer Printers (SIC 3577)

Standard Printer Market, 2002

Market shares are shown for the first six months of the year.

Hewlett-Packard	47.0%
Lexmark	18.9
Epson	18.2
Canon	9.6
Okidata	1.4
Other	4.9

Source: *Investor's Business Daily*, September 25, 2002, p. A6, from International Data Corp.

★ 938 ★

POS Terminals (SIC 3578)

Largest POS Terminal Makers, 2002

Manufacturers shipped an estimated 1.95 million terminals, up 12.3% from 2001. Market shares are shown for North America.

VeriFone	31.0%
Hypercom	30.5
Other	39.5

Source: *Cardline*, March 7, 2003, p. 1, from *ATM & Debit News*.

★ 939 ★

Liquid Crystal Displays (SIC 3579)

LCD Market Shares, 2002

Shares are for the second quarter.

Dell	8.3%
Samsung	8.0
HP	6.2
NEC-Mitsubishi	4.9
Sony	4.5
Other	68.1

Source: *Investor's Business Daily*, October 29, 2002, p. A7, from DisplaySearch.

★ 940 ★

Office Equipment (SIC 3579)

Leading Office Machine Vendors for the Government, 2001

Market shares are shown based on total purchases of $319.4 million.

SRI International	27.59%
Xerox Corp.	13.49
Berkshire Hathaway	10.03
Lockheed Martin	7.73
Other	41.16

Source: *Government Executive*, August 15, 2002, p. NA, from Eagle Eye Publishers and Federal Procurement Data Center.

★ 941 ★
Postage Meters (SIC 3579)

Postage Meter Market

Market shares are shown in percent.

Pitney Bowes 80.0%
Other 20.0

Source: *National Post*, July 23, 2002, p. IN3.

★ 942 ★
Heating and Cooling (SIC 3585)

Heating and Cooling Shipments

Shipments are shown in thousands of units.

	2001	2003
Water heaters	9,405	9,873
Furnaces	3,240	3,355
Heaters	700	712
Fireplaces	387	387
Boilers	352	329

Source: *Appliance Manufacturer*, January 2003, p. 50, from Air Conditioning and Refrigeration Institute and Gas Appliance Manufacturers Association.

★ 943 ★
Heating and Cooling (SIC 3585)

Packaged Terminal Air Conditioner Industry

The industry is shown by end market. McQuay International claims to be the market leader in new construction and replacement.

Lodging 65.0%
Health care, nursing homes, assisted living . . 25.0
Office space and resid. add ons 10.0

Source: *Air Conditioning, Heating & Refrigeration News*, June 10, 2002, p. 14, from Carrier Corp.

★ 944 ★
Heating and Cooling (SIC 3585)

Top Air Conditioner (Room) Producers, 2001

Market shares are shown based on shipments.

GE/GE Profile 16.5%
Fedders 13.2
Kenmore 12.8

Whirlpool 9.1%
Frigidaire 8.3
LG/Goldstar 8.2
Hampton Bay 5.0
Friedrich 3.3
Sharp 3.0
Amana 2.3
Other 18.3

Source: *HFN*, July 8, 2002, p. 54, from Association of Home Appliance Manufacturers.

★ 945 ★
Heating and Cooling (SIC 3585)

Top Commercial Icemaker Makers, 2001

Market shares are shown in percent.

Manitowoc 43.0%
Welbilt (Ice-O-Matic, Scotsman) 30.0
Hoshizaki 22.0
Cornelius 5.0

Source: *Appliance Manufacturer*, April 2002, p. 1.

★ 946 ★
Heating and Cooling (SIC 3585)

Top Commercial Refrigerator/Freezer Makers, 2001

Market shares are shown in percent.

True 39.0%
UTC/Carrier (Beverage Air) 18.5
ITW (Traulsen, Hobart) 11.5
Enodis (Delfield) 10.0
Glywed (Victory, Williams) 5.0
Continental 4.5
Manitowoc (McCall) 3.5
Dover (Randell) 2.5
Other 5.5

Source: *Appliance Manufacturer*, April 2002, p. 1.

★ 947 ★

Heating and Cooling (SIC 3585)

Top Furnace (Gas Residential) Makers, 2001

Market shares are shown in percent.

United Technologies 33.5%
Goodman 16.0
Lennox 15.0
American Standard 13.0
Rheem/Paloma Industries 10.0
York 6.0
Nordyne 4.5
Other 2.0

Source: *Appliance Manufacturer*, April 2002, p. 1.

★ 948 ★

Heating and Cooling (SIC 3585)

Top Water Heater (Electric) Makers, 2001

Market shares are shown in percent.

Rheem/Paloma Industries 39.0%
State 17.0
A.O. Smith 16.0
Bradford-White 14.0
American Water Heater Co. 13.0
Other 1.0

Source: *Appliance Manufacturer*, April 2002, p. 1.

★ 949 ★

Heating and Cooling (SIC 3585)

Top Water Heater (Gas) Makers, 2001

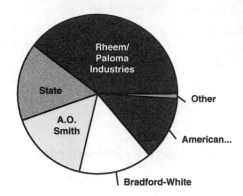

Market shares are shown in percent.

Rheem/Paloma Industries 40.0%
State 16.0
A.O. Smith 16.0
Bradford-White 15.0
American Water Heater Co. 13.0
Other 1.0

Source: *Appliance Manufacturer*, April 2002, p. 1.

★ 950 ★

Filter Pitchers (SIC 3599)

Pitcher Market Shares, 2001

Unit sales declined for the second year in a row, from 4.13 million pitchers sold in 2000 to 4.09 million in 2001. Dollar sales rose slightly, from $71.7 million to $72.49 million.

Brita 80.0%
Other 20.0

Source: "Creative Marketing." available from http://www.wcp.net, from *HomeWorld Business*.

SIC 36 - Electronic and Other Electric Equipment

★ 951 ★

Electronics (SIC 3600)

EMS Market in North America

The total market for electronics manufacturing servi-
ces (EMS) reached $115.5 billion. This figure does
not include system and build box activities. PCB
stands for printed circuit boards.

	($ bil.)	Share
Assembly services	$ 43.9	38.01%
Semiconductors	41.7	36.10
Passive components	15.1	13.07
Design, test, prototype, rework and repair	7.5	6.49
PCB consumption	7.3	6.32

Source: *CircuiTree*, August 2002, p. 65, from North American Market for Electronics Manufacturing Services.

★ 952 ★

Electronics (SIC 3600)

Leading Electronics Makers, 2002

Market shares are shown for the third quarter based
on revenues.

Flextronics	14.8%
Solectron	13.9
Sanmina-SCI	11.6
Celestica	8.7
Foxconn	8.2
Other	42.8

Source: *Computer Reseller News*, January 13, 2003, p. 24,
from International Data Corp.

★ 953 ★

Power Generating Equipment (SIC 3621)

Electric Power Generation

The North American markets are estimated in
millions of dollars.

	2002	2007
Small gas turbines	$ 125	$ 150.0
Microturbines	46	173.1
Fuel cell technologies	45	110.0

Source: *Electric Light & Power*, February 2003, p. 26,
from Venture Development Corp.

★ 954 ★

Appliances (SIC 3630)

Home Appliance Shipments

Shipments are shown in thousands of units.

	2001	2003
Surface cooktops	13,466	13,958
Microwave ovens	12,644	12,749
Refrigerators	9,305	10,023
Dryers	6,501	6,991
Dishwashers	5,627	6,141
Electric ranges	5,066	5,372
Gas ranges	3,036	3,249
Freezers	2,215	2,441
Compactors	117	117

Source: *Appliance Manufacturer*, January 2003, p. 50,
from Association of Home Appliance Manufacturers.

★ 955 ★

Appliances (SIC 3630)

Top Appliance Makers, 2001

Market shares are shown in percent.

Whirlpool	39.2%
GEA	23.2
Maytag	21.6
Electrolux	15.0
Other	1.0

Source: *Appliance Manufacturer*, April 2002, p. 1.

★ 956 ★

Cooking Equipment (SIC 3631)

Top Gas Range Producers, 2001

Market shares are shown based on shipments.

Kenmore	21.9%
GE/GE Profile	21.1
Frigidaire	9.0
Whirlpool	8.5
Maytag	8.5
Magic Chef	5.5
Tappan	5.0
Hotpoint	3.9
Amana	3.8
Jenn-Air	1.6
Other	11.2

Source: *HFN*, July 8, 2002, p. 54, from Association of Home Appliance Manufacturers.

★ 957 ★

Cooking Equipment (SIC 3631)

Top Microwave Producers, 2001

Market shares are shown based on shipments.

Sharp	23.5%
GE/GE Profile	20.6
Panasonic	10.6
Kenmore	8.5
Emerson	7.7
Samsung	6.8
Whirlpool	4.1
Sanyo	2.4
Magic Chef	2.2
Other	11.0

Source: *HFN*, July 8, 2002, p. 54, from Association of Home Appliance Manufacturers.

★ 958 ★

Cooking Equipment (SIC 3631)

Top Range (Electric) Makers, 2001

Market shares are shown in percent.

GEA	41.0%
Whirlpool	26.0
Electrolux	18.0
Maytag	14.0
Other	1.0

Source: *Appliance Manufacturer*, April 2002, p. 1.

★ 959 ★

Cooking Equipment (SIC 3631)

Top Range Hood Makers, 2001

Market shares are shown in percent.

Broan NuTone	85.0%
Watertown Metal Products	6.0
Vent Line	5.0
Other	4.0

Source: *Appliance Manufacturer*, April 2002, p. 1.

★ 960 ★
Freezers (SIC 3632)

Top Freezer Makers, 2001

Market shares are shown in percent.

Electrolux	63.0%
W.C. Wood	24.0
Haier	8.0
Sanyo Fisher	1.0
Other	4.0

Source: *Appliance Manufacturer*, April 2002, p. 1.

★ 961 ★
Refrigerators (SIC 3632)

Top Refrigerator Makers, 2002

Market shares are shown in percent.

Whirlpool	35.0%
GE	25.0
Maytag	20.0
Other	30.0

Source: *The Courier-Journal*, March 19, 2003, p. 1F, from Morgan Keegan.

★ 962 ★
Laundry Equipment (SIC 3633)

Top Automatic Washer Producers, 2001

Market shares are shown based on shipments.

Kenmore	29.9%
Maytag	22.8
Whirlpool	18.2
GE/GE Profile	11.7
Frigidaire	5.1
Amana	3.1

Roper	2.7%
Hotpoint	1.2
Other	5.3

Source: *HFN*, July 8, 2002, p. 54, from Association of Home Appliance Manufacturers.

★ 963 ★
Laundry Equipment (SIC 3633)

Top Dryer Makers, 2001

Market shares are shown in percent.

Whirlpool	50.5%
Maytag	24.0
GEA	19.0
Electrolux	5.5
Other	1.0

Source: *Appliance Manufacturer*, April 2002, p. 1.

★ 964 ★
Personal Care Appliances (SIC 3634)

Top Hair Dryer Makers, 2001

Market shares are shown in percent.

Conair	49.0%
Helen of Troy	33.5
Remington	4.0
Windmere	1.5
Other	12.0

Source: *Appliance Manufacturer*, April 2002, p. 1.

★ 965 ★
Small Appliances (SIC 3634)

Coffee Maker Market, 2002

Shares are shown for the first six months, based on unit sales.

Mr. Coffee	24.2%
Black & Decker	14.9
Proctor Silex	11.1
Other	49.8

Source: *New York Times*, November 21, 2002, p. C10, from NPD Houseworld.

★ 966 ★

Small Appliances (SIC 3634)

Electric Indoor Grills, 2002

Unit shares are shown for June - November 2002.

George Foreman	77.0%
Hamilton Beach	4.0
Black & Decker	2.0
Sunbeam	2.0
Other	15.0

Source: "How Many More Rounds Does the Champ have Left?" available online April 7, 2003 from http://www.npdhouseworld.com, from NPD Consumer Information.

★ 967 ★

Small Appliances (SIC 3634)

Top Electric Can Opener Makers, 2001

Market shares are shown in percent.

Hamilton Beach/Proctor-Silex	33.0%
Applica Consumer Products	25.0
Holmes (Rival)	16.0
Presto	5.0
Salton/Maxim Housewares	2.0
Sunbeam	1.0
Other	18.0

Source: *Appliance Manufacturer*, April 2002, p. 1.

★ 968 ★

Small Appliances (SIC 3634)

Top Iron Makers, 2001

Market shares are shown in percent.

Hamilton Beach/Proctor-Silex	38.0%
Applica Consumer Products (Black & Decker)	32.0
Sunbeam	10.0
Rowenta	5.0
Other	15.0

Source: *Appliance Manufacturer*, April 2002, p. 1.

★ 969 ★

Small Appliances (SIC 3634)

Top Mixer (Hand & Stand) Makers, 2001

Market shares are shown in percent.

Hamilton Beach/Proctor-Silex	32.0%
Whirlpool	16.0
Applica Consumer Products (Black & Decker)	13.0
Sunbeam	8.0
West Bend	5.0
Other	26.0

Source: *Appliance Manufacturer*, April 2002, p. 1.

★ 970 ★

Small Appliances (SIC 3634)

Top Small Electrics Makers, 2001

Market shares are shown in percent.

Hamilton Beach Proctor-Silex	38.0%
Applica Consumer Products (Black & Decker)	18.0
Sunbeam Corp.	14.4
Salton/Maxim Housewares	4.8
West Bend	2.0
Whirlpool	1.8
Braun	1.6
Other	19.4

Source: *Appliance Manufacturer*, April 2002, p. 1.

★ 971 ★

Small Appliances (SIC 3634)

Top Toaster Makers, 2001

Market shares are shown in percent.

Hamilton Beach/Proctor-Silex	48.0%
Salton/Maxim	23.0
Applica Consumer Products	13.0
Sunbeam	4.0
Holmes (Rival)	4.0
Other	8.0

Source: *Appliance Manufacturer*, April 2002, p. 1.

★ 972 ★
Vacuum Cleaners (SIC 3635)

Top Vacuum Cleaner (Hand-Held) Makers, 2001

Market shares are shown in percent.

Applica Consumer Products (Black & Decker)	39.0%
Royal	30.0
EuroPro	14.5
Eureka	7.5
Hoover	4.0
Bissell	2.0
Other	3.0

Source: *Appliance Manufacturer*, April 2002, p. 1.

★ 973 ★
Vacuum Cleaners (SIC 3635)

Top Vacuum Cleaner Makers, 2001

Market shares are shown in percent.

Hoover	26.5%
Eureka	26.0
Royal	17.0
Matsushita	9.0
Bissell	6.5
Oreck	5.0
Iona	3.0
Kirby	2.5
Electrolux	2.0
Rexaire	1.5
Other	1.0

Source: *Appliance Manufacturer*, April 2002, p. 1.

★ 974 ★
Compactors (SIC 3639)

Top Compactor Makers, 2001

Market shares are shown in percent.

Whirlpool	88.0%
Broan nuTone	11.0
Other	1.0

Source: *Appliance Manufacturer*, April 2002, p. 1.

★ 975 ★
Dishwashers (SIC 3639)

Top Dishwasher Producers, 2001

Market shares are shown based on shipments.

Kenmore	25.9%
Maytag	17.8
GE/GE Profile	17.2
Whirlpool	14.9
Frigidaire	7.5
KitchenAid	7.1
Bosch	3.7
Hotpoint	2.0
Amana	1.0
Other	2.9

Source: *HFN*, July 8, 2002, p. 54, from Association of Home Appliance Manufacturers.

★ 976 ★
Garbage Disposals (SIC 3639)

Top Disposal Makers, 2001

Market shares are shown in percent.

In-Sink-Erator	75.0%
Anaheim/Watertown/Water King	25.0

Source: *Appliance Manufacturer*, April 2002, p. 1.

★ 977 ★
Light Bulbs (SIC 3641)

Top Light Bulb Brands, 2003

Market shares show mass merchandiser sales for the year ended February 23, 2003. Figures exclude Wal-mart.

General Electric	52.6%
Sylvania	6.6

Continued on next page.

★ 977 ★ *Continued*

Light Bulbs (SIC 3641)

Top Light Bulb Brands, 2003

Market shares show mass merchandiser sales for the year ended February 23, 2003. Figures exclude Wal-mart.

GE Reveal	5.1%
GE Miser	4.9
GE Long Life	3.7
Philips	2.9
GE Miser Plus	0.9
Private label	14.3
Other	9.0

Source: *Grocery Headquarters*, May 2003, p. 112, from Information Resources Inc.

★ 978 ★

Light Bulbs (SIC 3641)

Top Light Bulb Makers, 2003

Market shares show mass merchandiser sales for the year ended February 23, 2003. Figures exclude Wal-mart.

General Electric	71.0%
Osram Sylvania	7.3
Philips	4.1
Feit Electric	0.6
Private label	14.3

Source: *Grocery Headquarters*, May 2003, p. 112, from Information Resources Inc.

★ 979 ★

Consumer Electronics (SIC 3651)

Consumer Electronics Sales, 2002

Unit shipments are shown. Color TV figure does not include projection. VCR decks does not include digital models.

Projection televisions	2,330,048
Color TV/VCR combinations	2,281,995
Color televisions	599,951
DVD players	409,713
VCR decks	128,072
TV/DVD players	51,117

Source: *Appliance*, March 2003, p. 20, from Consumer Electronics Association.

★ 980 ★

Consumer Electronics (SIC 3651)

Electronics Sales At Mass Merchandisers

The category saw sales of $9.1 billion at mass merchandisers.

	($ mil.)	Share
Computer/home office equipment	$ 2,408	26.40%
Audio equipment	1,910	20.94
Televisions	1,630	17.87
Video equipment	757	8.30
Videocassettes	701	7.68
Videogame software	520	5.70
Audiotapes	506	5.55
Videogame modules, cartridges	415	4.55
Other	275	3.01

Source: *Retail Merchandiser*, July 2002, p. 34.

★ 981 ★

Consumer Electronics (SIC 3651)

Top 8MM Camcorder Brands, 2001

Dollar shares are shown based on retail point-of-sale data for the period January - September 2001.

Sharp	35.1%
Sony	30.5
Canon	13.1
Samsung	10.5
Hitachi	2.9
Other	7.9

Source: *Twice*, January 8, 2002, p. 26, from NPD Techworld.

★ 982 ★

Consumer Electronics (SIC 3651)

Top Audio Brands, 2001

Market shares are shown based on unit sales.

Sony	19.6%
Panasonic/Technics	7.6
Aiwa	7.5
Philips/Magnavox	7.2
Lenoxx Sound	5.8
RCA	5.6
GE	5.5

Continued on next page.

★ **982** ★ *Continued*
Consumer Electronics (SIC 3651)

Top Audio Brands, 2001

Market shares are shown based on unit sales.

GPX	4.2%
Other	37.0

Source: *Dealerscope*, August 2002, p. 18, from Consumer Electronics Association, Electronic Industries Association, and Dealerscope research.

★ **983** ★
Consumer Electronics (SIC 3651)

Top Camcorder Makers, 2002

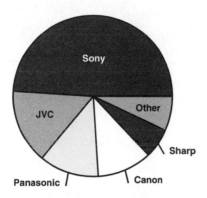

Unit shares are shown for the year through October.

Sony	48.9%
JVC	14.9
Panasonic	12.4
Canon	10.9
Sharp	6.0
Other	6.9

Source: *New York Times*, December 16, 2002, p. C18, from Gartner Dataquest.

★ **984** ★
Consumer Electronics (SIC 3651)

Top Car Amplifiers/Equalizer Brands, 2001

Dollar shares are shown based on retail point-of-sale data for the period January - September 2001.

Rockford Fosgate	19.9%
Kenwood	12.9
MTX	12.2
Jensen	9.2
Sony	8.4
Other	37.4

Source: *Twice*, January 8, 2002, p. 26, from NPD Techworld.

★ **985** ★
Consumer Electronics (SIC 3651)

Top Car CD-Player Brands, 2001

Dollar shares are shown based on retail point-of-sale data for the period January - September 2001.

Pioneer	22.4%
Sony	20.4
Kenwood	13.6
JVC	11.5
Alpine	11.1
Other	21.0

Source: *Twice*, January 8, 2002, p. 26, from NPD Techworld.

★ **986** ★
Consumer Electronics (SIC 3651)

Top Car Mobile Multimedia Brands, 2001

Dollar shares are shown based on retail point-of-sale data for the period January - September 2001.

Alpine	28.5%
Audiovox	26.4
Kenwood	17.4
Steel Horse	11.2
Pioneer	3.9
Other	12.6

Source: *Twice*, January 8, 2002, p. 26, from NPD Techworld.

★ 987 ★
Consumer Electronics (SIC 3651)

Top CD Boombox Brands, 2001

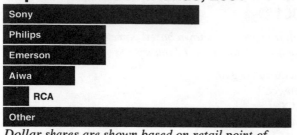

Dollar shares are shown based on retail point-of-sale data for the period January - September 2001.

Sony	25.0%
Philips	13.3
Emerson	12.8
Aiwa	8.8
RCA	2.9
Other	37.2

Source: *Twice*, January 8, 2002, p. 26, from NPD Techworld.

★ 988 ★
Consumer Electronics (SIC 3651)

Top CD Player Brands, 2001

Dollar shares are shown based on retail point-of-sale data for the period January - September 2001.

Sony	47.4%
Technics	8.6
Yamaha	5.7
Kenwood	5.2
Pioneer	4.6
Other	28.5

Source: *Twice*, January 8, 2002, p. 26, from NPD Techworld.

★ 989 ★
Consumer Electronics (SIC 3651)

Top DVD Player Makers, 2002

Unit shares are shown for the year through October.

Sony	16.4%
Apex	11.4
Toshiba	10.3
Samsung	10.3
Panasonic	9.9
Other	41.7

Source: *New York Times*, December 16, 2002, p. C18, from Gartner Dataquest.

★ 990 ★
Consumer Electronics (SIC 3651)

Top Home Theater Audio System Brands, 2001

Dollar shares are shown based on retail point-of-sale data for the period January - September 2001.

Sony	46.1%
Kenwood	10.6
Yamaha	9.5
Panasonic	9.1
Philips	6.3
Other	18.4

Source: *Twice*, January 8, 2002, p. 26, from NPD Techworld.

★ 991 ★
Consumer Electronics (SIC 3651)

Top Personal CD-Player Brands, 2001

Dollar shares are shown based on retail point-of-sale data for the period January - September 2001.

Sony	37.6%
Philips	9.7
Panasonic	9.5
Aiwa	6.2
RCA	5.4
Other	31.6

Source: *Twice*, January 8, 2002, p. 26, from NPD Techworld.

★ 992 ★
Consumer Electronics (SIC 3651)

Top Portable Minidisc Brands, 2001

Dollar shares are shown based on retail point-of-sale data for the period January - September 2001.

Sony	95.7%
Sharp	3.8
Aiwa	0.3
JVC	0.3

Source: *Twice*, January 8, 2002, p. 26, from NPD Techworld.

★ 993 ★
Consumer Electronics (SIC 3651)

Top Receiver/Amp/Tuner Brands, 2001

Dollar shares are shown based on retail point-of-sale data for the period January - September 2001.

Sony	23.1%
Yamaha	23.0
Denon	9.6
Onkyo	8.8
Technics	5.7
Other	29.8

Source: *Twice*, January 8, 2002, p. 26, from NPD Techworld.

★ 994 ★
Consumer Electronics (SIC 3651)

Top Remote Control Brands, 2001

Dollar shares are shown based on retail point-of-sale data for the period January - September 2001.

RCA	36.7%
One For All	16.3
Sony	13.1
Magnavox	7.8
Philips	4.1
Gemini	1.9
Other	20.1

Source: *Twice*, January 8, 2002, p. 26, from NPD Techworld.

★ 995 ★
Consumer Electronics (SIC 3651)

Top Shelf System Brands, 2001

Dollar shares are shown based on retail point-of-sale data for the period January - September 2001.

Aiwa	18.4%
Panasonic	13.5
Sony	13.2
Philips	12.9
RCA	8.4
Other	33.6

Source: *Twice*, January 8, 2002, p. 26, from NPD Techworld.

★ 996 ★
Consumer Electronics (SIC 3651)

Top Stereo Headphone Brands, 2001

Dollar shares are shown based on retail point-of-sale data for the period January - September 2001.

Sony	44.3%
Koss	21.3
Philips	8.7
Jensen	5.7
Aiwa	3.5
Advent	3.5
Other	13.0

Source: *Twice*, January 8, 2002, p. 26, from NPD Techworld.

★ 997 ★
Consumer Electronics (SIC 3651)

Top VCR Brands (2-Head Mono), 2001

Dollar shares are shown based on retail point-of-sale data for the period January - September 2001.

Orion	34.2%
Panasonic	11.6
Symphonic	10.1
Sanyo	9.1
RCA	9.0
Sylvania	7.0
Funai	5.1
Other	13.9

Source: *Twice*, January 8, 2002, p. 26, from NPD Techworld.

★ 998 ★
Consumer Electronics (SIC 3651)

Top VCR Brands (Hi-Fi), 2001

Dollar shares are shown based on retail point-of-sale data for the period January - September 2001.

Sony	26.7%
Panasonic	15.3
Philips	5.9
JVC	5.3
Toshiba	5.1
Other	41.7

Source: *Twice*, January 8, 2002, p. 26, from NPD Techworld.

★ 999 ★
Digital Video Recorders (SIC 3651)

DVR Market Leaders, 2008

Market shares are forecasted.

TiVo	19.0%
Metabyte	17.0
OpenTV	14.0
Digeo (Moxl)	11.0
Ultimate TV/Web TV	9.0
ReplayTV	5.0
Other	26.0

Source: *Wireless Satellite and Broadcasting Newsletter*, July 2002, p. 1, from company sources.

★ 1000 ★
Televisions (SIC 3651)

Digital Television Sales

Total sales reached 1.78 million units.

Projection	74.0%
Direct view	24.0
Plasma flat panel	2.0
LCD flat panel	1.0

Source: *New York Times*, March 31, 2003, p. C3, from NPD Group and Sony.

★ 1001 ★
Televisions (SIC 3651)

LCD Television Market

Market shares are shown in percent.

Sharp	81.0%
Other	19.0

Source: *Consumer Electronics*, August 26, 2002, p. NA.

★ 1002 ★
Televisions (SIC 3651)

Plasma TV Market

Market shares are shown in percent. A cheap model runs about $5,000 but the price is expected to fall.

Sony	48.0%
Panasonic	21.0
Fujitsu	11.0
Pioneer	8.0
Philips	6.0
Other	6.0

Source: *Investor's Business Daily*, September 27, 2002, p. A6, from NPD Techworld and Consumer Electronics Association.

★ 1003 ★
Televisions (SIC 3651)

Top Digital TV Brands, 2001

Market shares are shown based on unit sales.

Sony	25.0%
Mitsubishi	17.8
Hitachi	14.2
Toshiba	11.5

Continued on next page.

★ 1003 ★ *Continued*
Televisions (SIC 3651)
Top Digital TV Brands, 2001

Market shares are shown based on unit sales.

Panasonic	9.5%
RCA	7.5
Philips	3.3
Pioneer	2.4
Other	8.8

Source: *Dealerscope*, August 2002, p. 18, from Consumer Electronics Association, Electronic Industries Association, and Dealerscope research.

★ 1004 ★
Televisions (SIC 3651)
Top Television Makers, 2002

Unit shares are shown for the year through October.

Sony	16.1%
RCA	10.5
Toshiba	8.9
Sharp	8.9
Panasonic	8.5
Other	47.1

Source: *New York Times*, December 16, 2002, p. C18, from Gartner Dataquest.

★ 1005 ★
Music (SIC 3652)
CD Album Sales, 2002

Figures are in millions of units. CD album sales fell from 712 million to 649.5 million in 2002. R&B had the largest fall over the previous year: 17.8%.

	(mil.)	Share
Rock	201.0	30.95%
Rap	85.0	13.09
Christian/gospel	50.0	7.70
Jazz	23.0	3.54
Other	290.5	44.73

Source: *USA TODAY*, January 3, 2003, p. 11D, from SoundScan.

★ 1006 ★
Music (SIC 3652)
Jazz Music Market in Canada

Market shares are shown in percent.

Universal Music Canada	56.0%
Other	44.0

Source: *Billboard*, October 26, 2002, p. 47.

★ 1007 ★
Music (SIC 3652)
Leading Music Publishers in North America, 2002

Shares are shown based on $1.2 billion in revenues.

	($ mil.)	Share
EMI	$ 252	21.0%
Warner Chappell	216	18.0
UMPG	120	10.0
Sony/ATV	78	6.5
BMG	72	6.0
Other	462	38.5

Source: *Music & Copyright*, January 22, 2003, p. 1, from *Music & Copyright* research.

★ 1008 ★
Music (SIC 3652)
Top Albums, 2002

Sales are shown in millions of units. The Eminem Show is by Eminem; Nellyville is by Nelly; Let Go is by Avril Lavigne; Home is by the Dixie Chicks; 8 Mile and O Brother are movie soundtracks; Missundaztood is by Pink; Drive is by Alan Jackson; ComeAway With Me is by Norah Jones; New Day Has Come is by Celine Dion.

The Eminem Show	7.61
Nellyville	4.92
Let Go	4.12
Home	3.69
8 Mile	3.50
Missundaztood	3.14
Ashanti	3.10

Continued on next page.

★ 1008 ★ *Continued*

Music (SIC 3652)

Top Albums, 2002

Sales are shown in millions of units. The Eminem Show is by Eminem; Nellyville is by Nelly; Let Go is by Avril Lavigne; Home is by the Dixie Chicks; 8 Mile and O Brother are movie soundtracks; Missundaztood is by Pink; Drive is by Alan Jackson; ComeAway With Me is by Norah Jones; New Day Has Come is by Celine Dion.

Drive	3.05
O Brother, Where Art Thou	2.74
Come Away With Me	2.66
New Day Has Come	2.65

Source: *Entertainment Weekly*, January 17, 2003, p. 77, from Nielsen SoundScan.

★ 1009 ★

Music (SIC 3652)

Top CD Sellers, 2002

Vivendi
Warner Music Group
Sony Music
BMG
EMI
Other

Market shares are shown in percent. Compact discs sold 649.5 million units through December 29, and made up 94% of music sales overall.

Vivendi	28.8%
Warner Music Group	15.9
Sony Music	15.7
BMG	14.8
EMI	8.4
Other	16.4

Source: *America's Intelligence Wire*, January 3, 2003, p. NA, from SoundScan.

★ 1010 ★

Music (SIC 3652)

Top Country Music Distributors, 2002

Market shares are shown in percent.

Universal	29.2%
BMG	24.3
WEA	18.2
Sony	15.4
Indies	7.0
EMD	6.0

Source: *Billboard*, January 18, 2003, p. 47, from SoundScan.

★ 1011 ★

Music (SIC 3652)

Top Latin Music Distributors, 2002

Market shares are shown in percent.

Indies	24.1%
Sony	23.8
Universal	22.7
WEA	11.2
EMD	9.4
BMG	8.9

Source: *Billboard*, January 18, 2003, p. 47, from SoundScan.

★ 1012 ★

Music (SIC 3652)

Top Music Firms, 2002

Market shares are shown in percent through December 22, 2002.

Universal Music Group	28.9%
Warner Music Group	17.0
Sony Music Entertainment	16.5
Bertelsmann Music Group	14.8
EMI Group	9.3
Other	13.5

Source: *Los Angeles Times*, December 29, 2002, p. C1, from SoundScan.

★ 1013 ★
Music (SIC 3652)

Top Music Firms in Mexico, 2002

Market shares are shown for the first eight months of the year.

WMG	21.2%
SME	20.1
UMG	18.0
BMG	15.4
EMI	14.9
Fonovisa	6.8
Other	3.6

Source: *Music & Copyright*, November 27, 2002, p. 6, from *Music & Copyright* research.

★ 1014 ★
Music (SIC 3652)

Top New Album Distributors, 2002

Market shares are shown in percent.

Universal	31.3%
BMG	17.4
Sony	15.2
Warner Music Group	14.3
EMI	7.3
Other	14.6

Source: *New York Times*, January 11, 2003, p. B1, from Nielsen SoundScan.

★ 1015 ★
Music (SIC 3652)

Top R&B Music Distributors, 2002

Market shares are shown in percent.

Universal	41.9%
Sony	16.7
BMG	15.6
WEA	11.6
Indies	8.6
EMD	6.1

Source: *Billboard*, January 18, 2003, p. 47, from SoundScan.

★ 1016 ★
Music (SIC 3652)

Top Rap Music Distributors, 2002

Market shares are shown in percent.

Universal	51.8%
Indies	12.4
BMG	11.5
Sony	10.9
WEA	8.1
EMD	5.4

Source: *Billboard*, January 18, 2003, p. 47, from SoundScan.

★ 1017 ★
Cable Modems (SIC 3661)

Cable Modem Market Leaders

The 9 million unit industry is shown in percent.

Motorola	36.0%
Toshiba Corp.	17.5
Thompson Multimedia	14.0
Other	32.5

Source: *Electronic Buyers News*, May 13, 2002, p. 3, from In-Stat Group.

★ 1018 ★

Fax Machines (SIC 3661)

Top Fax Machine Producers

Unit shares are for July 2002.

Brother	40.1%
Panasonic	32.7
Sharp	15.3
Hewlett-Packard	11.3
Canon	0.6

Source: *New York Times*, September 16, 2002, p. C8, from NPDTechworld.

★ 1019 ★

Fiber Optics (SIC 3661)

Fiber Optics Demand

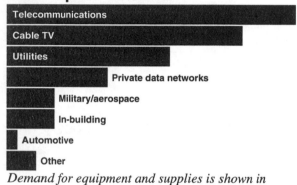

Demand for equipment and supplies is shown in millions of dollars.

	2001	2006	Share
Telecommunications	$ 4,940	$ 7,165	31.99%
Cable TV	3,430	5,825	26.00
Utilities	1,845	3,935	17.57
Private data networks	1,595	2,465	11.00
Military/aerospace	630	1,120	5.00
In-building	700	1,010	4.51
Automotive	20	150	0.67
Other	565	730	3.26

Source: *Lightwave*, October 2002, p. 98, from Freedonia Group.

★ 1020 ★

Telephones (SIC 3661)

Top Cordless Phone Brands, 2001

Dollar shares are shown based on retail point-of-sale data for the period January - September 2001.

General Electric	27.6%
VTech	15.1
Panasonic	13.8
Sony	12.0
Uniden	9.8
AT&T	8.8
BellSouth	4.7
Northwestern Bell	3.8
Other	4.4

Source: *Twice*, January 8, 2002, p. 26, from NPD Techworld.

★ 1021 ★

Two-Way Radios (SIC 3661)

Top Two-Way Radio Brands, 2001

Dollar shares are shown based on retail point-of-sale data for the period January - September 2001.

Motorola	40.6%
Cobra	18.6
Audiovox	12.4
Ranger	12.3
Bellsouth	3.2
Other	12.9

Source: *Twice*, January 8, 2002, p. 26, from NPD Techworld.

★ 1022 ★

Cellular Phones (SIC 3663)

CDMA Phone Leaders

CDMA stands for code division multiple access.

Motorola	23.5%
Kyocera	15.7
Audiovox	15.1
Nokia	14.0
Samsung	13.1
Other	18.6

Source: *Investor's Business Daily*, July 15, 2002, p. A6, from Gartner Inc.

★ 1023 ★
Cellular Phones (SIC 3663)

North American Handset Sales

Distribution is shown by year.

	2000	2003	2006
Replacement	48.0%	55.0%	63.0%
New	52.0	45.0	37.0

Source: *PR Newswire*, June 10, 2002, p. NA, from Strategy Analytics.

★ 1024 ★
Satellites (SIC 3663)

Research Satellite Market

Market shares are shown in percent. Figure refers to small and mid-sized research satellites.

Spectrum Astro	70.0%
Other	30.0

Source: *Knight Ridder/Tribune Business News*, November 17, 2002, p. NA.

★ 1025 ★
Set-Top Boxes (SIC 3663)

Digital Set-Top Box Market, 2002

```
Motorola
Hughes Network Systems
Scientific-Atlanta
Sony
EchoStar
Other
```

Shares are for the third quarter in North America.

Motorola	32.7%
Hughes Network Systems	17.7
Scientific-Atlanta	14.5
Sony	12.9
EchoStar	7.9
Other	14.3

Source: *Investor's Business Daily*, March 7, 2003, p. A4, from Acacia Research Group.

★ 1026 ★
Telecommunications Equipment (SIC 3663)

Leading Telecom Equipment Makers, 2002

Market shares are shown for the $27 billion industry as of June 2002.

Cisco	14.6%
Siemens	11.7
Ericsson	11.3
Alcatel	10.2
Notel	9.8
Lucent	7.8
Other	34.6

Source: *Ottawa Citizen*, September 11, 2002, p. B3, from Synergy Research Group.

★ 1027 ★
Networking Equipment (SIC 3669)

Carrier Voice Packet Market, 2002

Market shares are shown based on port shipments in the fourth quarter. The market includes Voice over IP and Voice over ATM.

Nortel Networks	42.0%
Cisco Systems	25.8
Sonus Networks	16.6

Source: *Internet Wire*, February 19, 2003, p. NA, from Synergy Research.

★ 1028 ★
Networking Equipment (SIC 3669)

Electrical Wiring Devices

Market shares are shown in percent.

Levitron	52.0%
Eagle Electric	15.0
GE	10.0
Broan	7.0
Other	16.0

Source: *Cabling Installation & Maintenance*, April 2003, p. 32, from *Home Builder Executive Survey* published June 2002.

★ 1029 ★

Networking Equipment (SIC 3669)

Enterprise-Class Router Shares, 2002

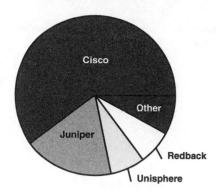

Shares are for the second quarter.

Cisco	60.9%
Juniper	17.7
Unisphere	7.0
Redback	6.7
Other	7.7

Source: *Computer Reseller News*, October 21, 2002, p. 57, from Gartner Dataquest.

★ 1030 ★

Networking Equipment (SIC 3669)

Four-Port Serial-to-Ethernet Devices

The company has a 93% of the four port segment of the multiport serial-to-ethernet device networking edge servers. It has a 69% share of the eight port segment.

Comtrol Corporation	93.0%
Other	7.0

Source: *PR Newswire*, March 12, 2003, p. NA, from company report.

★ 1031 ★

Networking Equipment (SIC 3669)

Home Network Systems

Market shares are shown in percent.

Leviton	31.0%
OnQ Technologies	25.0
USTec	14.0
OpenHouse	8.0
FutureSmart	8.0
Other	13.0

Source: *Cabling Installation & Maintenance*, April 2003, p. 32, from *Home Builder Executive Survey* published June 2002.

★ 1032 ★

Networking Equipment (SIC 3669)

Network Processor Market

Market shares are for fourth quarter 2001 - third quarter 2002.

AMCC	38.0%
IBM	19.0
Motorola	15.0
Intel	11.0
Agere	9.0
Vitesse	6.0
Other	1.0

Source: *EBN*, January 27, 2003, p. 3, from Linley Group.

★ 1033 ★

Networking Equipment (SIC 3669)

Networking Equipment Industry

Market shares are shown in percent.

Cisco	39.7%
Nortel Networks	6.2
Alcatel (Newbridge)	4.5
Lucent Technologies	4.4
3Com	4.3
Other	40.9

Source: *New York Times*, July 8, 2002, p. C7, from InStat/MDR.

★ 1034 ★
Networking Equipment (SIC 3669)

Private Branch Exchange Market, 2002

Market shares are shown in percent.

Avaya	36.1%
Nortel	30.3
Siemens	13.9
NEC	6.7
Fujitsu	3.8
Intecom	2.9
Mitel	1.9
Other	4.4

Source: *The Telecom Manager's Voice Report*, January 13, 2003, p. 3, from *Annual PBX Special Report*.

★ 1035 ★
Networking Equipment (SIC 3669)

Router Market Shares

North American shares are for the third quarter 2001.

Cisco	80.0%
Juniper	11.0
Unisphere	8.0
Ericsson	1.0

Source: *Telephony*, May 27, 2002, p. 20, from RHK.

★ 1036 ★
Networking Equipment (SIC 3669)

Switch-Fabric Market Shares

The switch-fabric interconnect market is valued at $500 million.

Agilent	25.0%
Vitesse	20.0
AMCC	15.0
Conexant	12.0
Other	28.0

Source: *EBN*, February 3, 2003, p. 3, from Fairchild Semiconductor.

★ 1037 ★
Networking Equipment (SIC 3669)

Web Conferencing Market, 2002

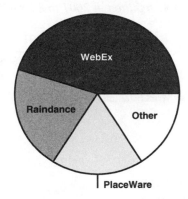

Market shares are shown based on revenues.

WebEx	45.0%
Raindance	21.0
PlaceWare	18.0
Other	16.0

Source: *Computer Reseller News*, January 27, 2003, p. 22, from Yankee Group.

★ 1038 ★
Networking Equipment (SIC 3669)

Wireless LAN Market, 2002

The industry grew 8% in the seond quarter of 2002.

Cisco Systems	17.0%
Linksys Group	13.3
Buffalo Technology	11.4
Other	58.3

Source: *Transport Technology Today*, October 2002, p. 16, from Dell'Oro Group.

★ 1039 ★
Videoconferencing (SIC 3669)

Videoconferencing Market, 2002

Shares are shown based on first quarter.

Polycom	64.0%
Tandberg	18.4
Sony	9.1
VCon	3.5
Other	5.0

Source: *Network World*, June 17, 2002, p. 24.

★ 1040 ★

Lasers (SIC 3674)

Laser Sales by Type

Revenues fell from $5.6 billion in 2001 to $4.8 billion in 2003.

	2001	2002
Diodes	65.0%	56.0%
Nondiodes	35.0	44.0

Source: *Laser Focus World*, January 2003, p. 73, from Strategies Unlimited.

★ 1041 ★

Microprocessors (SIC 3674)

Analog-IC Market

The $23.9 billion industry is shown by company.

ST	14.1%
TI	13.0
Analog Devices	6.4
Philips Semiconductors	6.0
National Semiconductor	5.2
Other	56.3

Source: *EBN*, February 24, 2003, p. 6, from Databeans Inc.

★ 1042 ★

Microprocessors (SIC 3674)

Cable Modem Chip Market, 2002

Market shares are shown in percent.

Broadcom	52.8%
Texas Instruments	24.5
Imedia	9.4
LSI Logic	7.5
Conexant	4.7
Other	0.9

Source: *New York Times*, April 7, 2003, p. C9, from In-Stat/MDR.

★ 1043 ★

Microprocessors (SIC 3674)

Computer Chips for Modems

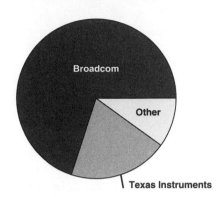

Market shares are estimated in percent.

Broadcom	70.0%
Texas Instruments	20.0
Other	10.0

Source: *Orange Country Register*, December 3, 2002, p. NA, from *Cable Datacom News*.

★ 1044 ★

Microprocessors (SIC 3674)

DRAM Market Shares, 2002

The Dynamic Random Access Memory market is shown. Shares are for fourth quarter. DDR had a 11% share in fourth quarter in 2001. The battle between DDR and Rambus has reportedly divided the industry.

DDR	51.0%
Older memories	44.0
Rambus	5.0

Source: *Investor's Business Daily*, September 26, 2002, p. A6, from International Data Corp.

★ 1045 ★
Microprocessors (SIC 3674)
DSP Chip Market Shares, 2002

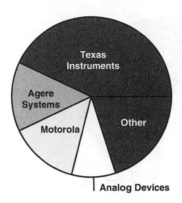

Market shares are shown in percent.

	2001	2002
Texas Instruments	40.0%	43.2%
Agere Systems	16.1	13.9
Motorola	12.0	14.1
Analog Devices	8.2	8.9
Other	23.7	19.9

Source: *Investor's Business Daily*, April 10, 2003, p. A6, from Forward Concepts.

★ 1046 ★
Microprocessors (SIC 3674)
Graphics Chips Market, 2002

Figures are for the second quarter.

Nvidia	36.0%
ATI	23.0
Other	41.0

Source: *Canadian Business*, October 28, 2002, p. 99, from In-Stat.

★ 1047 ★
Microprocessors (SIC 3674)
High End Image Control Chips

Market shares are shown in percent. Figure refers to chips for multimedia projectors.

Pixelworks	90.0%
Other	10.0

Source: *Knight Ridder/Tribune Business News*, March 18, 2003, p. NA.

★ 1048 ★
Microprocessors (SIC 3674)
IC Implementation Tools

Market shares are shown in percent.

Synopsys	41.0%
Magma Design Automation	31.0
Cadence	24.0
Other	4.0

Source: *Electronic Engineering Times*, December 2, 2002, p. 41, from Gartner Dataquest Inc.

★ 1049 ★
Microprocessors (SIC 3674)
IC SPICE Market Shares, 2001

The $59.1 million market is shown in percent. By 2006, the industry is forecasted to reach $99 million.

Synopsys-Avanti	38.0%
Nassda	35.0
Cadence	19.0
Other	8.0

Source: *Electronic News*, November 4, 2002, p. 1, from Gartner Dataquest Inc.

★ 1050 ★
Microprocessors (SIC 3674)
Largest Fabless Chip Producers, 2001

Firms are ranked by worldwide sales in millions of dollars. Of the companies shown, only VIA is not a U.S. firm.

	($ mil.)	Share
Qualcomm	$ 1,235	9.58%
Nvidia	1,206	9.35
Xilinx	1,149	8.91
VIA Technologies	1,009	7.83
Broadcom	962	7.46
Altera	839	6.51
Cirrus Logic	534	4.14
Other	5,958	46.21

Source: *Electronic Business*, February 2003, p. 54, from IC Insights.

★ 1051 ★
Microprocessors (SIC 3674)

Programmable Chip Market, 2002

Shares are for the second quarter.

Xilinx	51.0%
Altera	31.0
Lattice	11.0
Actel	6.0
Quicklogic	1.0

Source: *Investor's Business Daily*, December 16, 2002, p. A4, from company reports.

★ 1052 ★
Microprocessors (SIC 3674)

Wireless Chip Market

Market shares are shown in percent.

Intersil Corp.	51.7%
Agere Systems	24.4
RF Micro Devices	5.6
Atheros Communications Inc.	5.4
Texas Instruments	4.5
Broadcom Corp.	3.9
Other	4.5

Source: *Investor's Business Daily*, April 7, 2003, p. A5, from International Data Corp.

★ 1053 ★
Batteries (SIC 3691)

Medical Equipment Batteries

The company makes batteries for defibrillators, pacemakers and artificial hearts.

Wilson Greatbatch Technologies	90.0%
Other	10.0

Source: *Investor's Business Daily*, October 4, 2002, p. A7.

★ 1054 ★
Batteries (SIC 3691)

Rechargable Battery Market, 2005

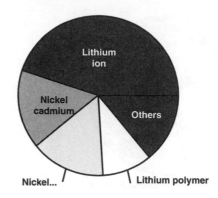

The $4.2 billion market is estimated in percent. Batteries for cellular phones, personal digital assistants and wireless devices are expected to drive the market.

Lithium ion	45.0%
Nickel cadmium	16.0
Nickel metal hydride	15.0
Lithium polymer	10.0
Others	14.0

Source: *Purchasing*, December 12, 2002, p. 50, from Freedonia Group.

★ 1055 ★
Batteries (SIC 3691)

Rechargable Battery Market by Company

Market shares are shown in percent.

Rayovac	75.0%
Other	25.0

Source: *Battery & EV Technology*, April 2002, p. NA.

★ 1056 ★
Batteries (SIC 3691)

Top Battery Brands, 2002

Brands are ranked by sales for the year ended December 1, 2002. Figures are for supermarkets, drug stores, and discount stores but exclude Wal-Mart.

	($ mil.)	Share
Duracell	$ 519.9	38.80%
Energizer	319.0	23.81

Continued on next page.

★ 1056 ★ *Continued*
Batteries (SIC 3691)

Top Battery Brands, 2002

Brands are ranked by sales for the year ended December 1, 2002. Figures are for supermarkets, drug stores, and discount stores but exclude Wal-Mart.

	($ mil.)	Share
Duracell Ultra	$ 119.4	8.91%
Rayovac Maximum	71.7	5.35
Energizer Max	64.7	4.83
Energizer E2 Titanium	46.7	3.49
Rayovac	26.1	1.95
Panasonic	9.1	0.68
Eveready	9.1	0.68
Rayovac Renewal	3.8	0.28
Other	150.5	11.23

Source: *MMR*, January 27, 2003, p. 22, from Information Resources Inc.

★ 1057 ★
Batteries (SIC 3691)

Top Battery Brands by Unit Sales, 2002

Market shares are shown based on unit sales for the year ended November 3, 2002. Figures are for drug stores, supermarkets and discount stores but exclude Wal-Mart.

Duracell	34.1%
Energizer	16.2
Duracell Ultra	8.3
Energizer E2 Titanium	2.3
Energizer Max	2.0
Rayovac	0.6
Panasonic	0.6
Other	35.9

Source: *Chain Drug Review*, January 6, 2003, p. 79, from Information Resources Inc.

★ 1058 ★
Batteries (SIC 3691)

Top Battery Brands in Drug Stores, 2001

Brands are ranked by sales in millions of dollars for the year ended December 30. Figures exclude Wal-Mart.

	($ mil.)	Share
Duracell	$ 159.5	31.00%
Energizer, alkaline	86.2	16.75
Duracell Ultra, alkaline	56.3	10.94
Duracell, zinc air	17.8	3.46
Energizer E2 Titanium, alkaline . .	10.8	2.10
Energizer, zinc air	5.0	0.97
Other	178.9	34.77

Source: *Drug Store News*, May 20, 2002, p. 54, from Information Resources Inc.

★ 1059 ★
Digital Media (SIC 3695)

Leading Blank CD-R Brands, 2002

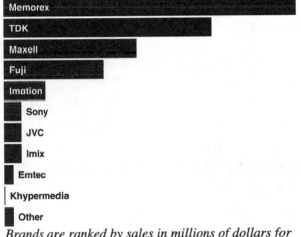

Brands are ranked by sales in millions of dollars for the year ended November 3, 2002. Figures include supermarkets, drug stores, discount stores and exclude Wal-Mart.

	($ mil.)	Share
Memorex	$ 29.5	34.50%
TDK	21.7	25.38
Maxell	13.5	15.79
Fuji	10.5	12.28
Imation	3.9	4.56
Sony	1.7	1.99
JVC	1.6	1.87
Imix	1.4	1.64

Continued on next page.

Digital Media (SIC 3695)

Leading Blank CD-R Brands, 2002

Brands are ranked by sales in millions of dollars for the year ended November 3, 2002. Figures include supermarkets, drug stores, discount stores and exclude Wal-Mart.

	($ mil.)	Share
Emtec	$ 0.7	0.82%
Khypermedia	0.3	0.35
Other	0.7	0.82

Source: *MMR*, January 13, 2003, p. 53, from Information Resources Inc.

★ 1060 ★

Recording Media (SIC 3695)

Blank Recording Media Sales, 2002

Distribution of sales is shown for the year ended September 8, 2002.

Video cassettes	62.2%
CDs	21.3
Audio cassettes	12.1
Minidiscs/DVDs	0.2
Other	4.1

Source: *National Petroleum News*, December 2002, p. 16, from Information Resources Inc. InfoScan.

★ 1061 ★

Video Tapes (SIC 3695)

Leading Blank Video Tape Brands, 2002

Brands are ranked by sales in millions of dollars for the year ended November 3, 2002. Figures include supermarkets, drug stores, discount stores and exclude Wal-Mart.

	($ mil.)	Share
Sony	$ 44.3	17.18%
Fuji HQ	23.8	9.23
Maxell GX Silver	21.5	8.34
TDK Revue	21.5	8.34
Sony V	19.1	7.41
Maxell HGX Gold	13.3	5.16
Fuji	12.7	4.92
TDK HG Ultimate	8.1	3.14

	($ mil.)	Share
RCA	$ 7.7	2.99%
Other	85.9	33.31

Source: *MMR*, January 13, 2003, p. 53, from Information Resources Inc.

★ 1062 ★

Money Recovery Systems (SIC 3699)

Money Recovery Systems, 2002

The company is the world leader in protecting cash. Its products are highly effective in deterring bank robberies, recovering stolen money and identifying thieves. The SecurityPAC Electronic Protection System (SPEPS) is the company's top product. Market shares are for North America.

ICI Security Systems Inc.	75.0%
Other	25.0

Source: "ICI Security Systems." available January 7, 2003 from http://www.american-capital.com.

SIC 37 - Transportation Equipment

★ 1063 ★
Auto Auctioning (SIC 3711)
Auto Auction Market

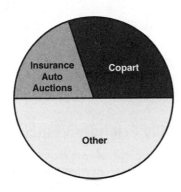

Market shares are shown in percent.

Copart	30.0%
Insurance Auto Auctions	20.0
Other	50.0

Source: *BusinessWeek Online*, Spring 2002, p. NA.

★ 1064 ★
Autos (SIC 3711)
Best-Selling Convertibles, 2002

Total registrations reached 302,320, a drop of 2.7% over 2001. Fort Myers/Naples, FL had the highest share of convertibles. Data show total new registrations.

	No.	Share
Chrysler Sebring	43,809	14.49%
Ford Mustang	42,418	14.03
Ford Thunderbird	19,356	6.40
Mitsubishi Eclipse	15,887	5.26
Lexus SC 430	14,925	4.94
Mazda Miata	14,089	4.66
Mercedes SL	12,415	4.11
Chevrolet Corvette	11,959	3.96
Porsche Boxster	10,300	3.41

	No.	Share
Honda S2000	9,728	3.22%
Other	107,434	35.54

Source: *PR Newswire*, March 24, 2003, p. NA, from R.L. Polk & Co.

★ 1065 ★
Autos (SIC 3711)
Best-Selling Vehicles in Canada, 2002

Figures show unit sales.

Dodge Caravan	83,588
Honda Civic	69,973
Ford F-series	67,809
Chevrolet Cavalier	53,614
Toyota Corolla	52,117
Mazda Protege	48,872
Pontiac Sunfire	46,036
Chevrolet Silverado	42,781
Ford Focus	40,228
GMC Sierra	38,914

Source: *Motor Trend*, May 2003, p. 34, from wardsauto.com.

★ 1066 ★
Autos (SIC 3711)
Best-Selling Vehicles in Los Angeles County, 2002

Sales are from July 2001 - June 2002.

Toyota Camry	22,710
Honda Accord	20,019
Honda Civic	18,451
Ford F-150	13,750
Ford Explorer	13,379
Toyota Corolla	12,673
Chevrolet Silverado	10,079
Toyota Tacoma	9,541

Continued on next page.

★ 1066 ★ *Continued*

Autos (SIC 3711)

Best-Selling Vehicles in Los Angeles County, 2002

Sales are from July 2001 - June 2002.

Ford Expedition	8,344
Nissan Altima	7,809

Source: *Los Angeles Business Journal*, September 2, 2002, p. 21, from R.L. Polk & Co.

★ 1067 ★

Autos (SIC 3711)

Best-Selling Vehicles in Mexico, 2002

Figures show unit sales.

Nissan Tsuru	79,227
Chevrolet Joy/Swing	72,420
Volkswagen Pointer	65,349
Volkswagen Jetta	40,483
Nissan Plantina	36,683
Nissan Sentra	33,069
Chevrolet Silverado	29,839
Ford F-series	28,612
Nissan Pickup	28,197
Dodge Atoz	27,707

Source: *Motor Trend*, May 2003, p. 34, from wardsauto.com.

★ 1068 ★

Autos (SIC 3711)

Best-Selling Vehicles in Mexico (Market Share)

Market shares are shown in percent.

Tsuru/Sentra (Nissan)	21.0%
Joy/Swing (Chevrolet)	12.0
Pointer (VW)	8.0
Jetta (VW)	6.0
Atos (Dodge)	5.0
Other	48.0

Source: *Latin Trade*, October 2002, p. 45, from DRI-WEFA.

★ 1069 ★

Autos (SIC 3711)

Best-Selling Vehicles in Texas, 2002

Data show retail registrations through November.

Ford F-series	102,465
Chevrolet Silverado	67,808
Dodge Ram	63,607
Chevrolet Tahoe	29,215
Honda Accord	25,538
Ford Explorer	24,787
Chevrolet Suburban	24,671
Ford Expedition	23,138
Toyota Camry	19,029

Source: *Automotive News*, February 24, 2003, p. 38, from R.L. Polk & Co.

★ 1070 ★

Autos (SIC 3711)

Environmentally Friendly Vehicles

Electric and gas-electric hybrid cars have seen a 54% increase over the past five years, from 650 registrations in 1997 to nearly 35,000 from January-October 2002. Figures show the most registrations for the first 10 months of the year.

Los Angeles, CA	5,141
San Francisco, CA	3,461
Washington D.C.	1,976
Sacramento, CA	1,459
New York, NY	1,338

Source: *Research Alert*, January 17, 2003, p. 6, from R.L. Polk & Co.

★ 1071 ★

Autos (SIC 3711)

Funeral Coaches and Limo Market

The company's share has been estimated at 65-75% of the market.

Accubilt Inc.	75.0%
Other	25.0

Source: *Knight Ridder/Tribune Business News*, November 6, 2002, p. NA.

★ 1072 ★
Autos (SIC 3711)
Large Pickup Truck Market, 2002

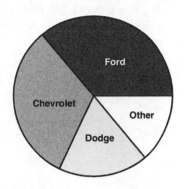

Market shares are shown in percent.

Ford	36.0%
Chevrolet	32.0
Dodge	18.0
Other	14.0

Source: *Knight Ridder/Tribune Business News*, January 5, 2003, p. NA.

★ 1073 ★
Autos (SIC 3711)
Light Truck Sales by Type

Total sales grew from 7.4 million in 1998 to 8.7 million in 2002. Sales of light trucks - SUVs, pickups, minivans - composed 52% of all vehicle sales in 2002.

	1998	2002
Pickup trucks	40.0%	34.7%
Minivans and vans	21.8	16.9
Middle-sized SUVs	19.9	19.6
Large SUVs	9.7	10.0
Cross over utility vehicles	3.3	14.2
Luxury SUVs	2.6	2.6
Small SUVs	2.2	1.9

Source: *New York Times*, February 18, 2003, p. C3, from WardsAuto.com.

★ 1074 ★
Autos (SIC 3711)
Luxury Car Market, 2002

Market shares are shown through October 2002. Cadillac was the leader in 1992 with a 17.8% share.

Lexus	11.6%
BMW	11.4
Mercedes Benz	10.4
Cadillac	9.3
Lincoln	7.5
Other	49.8

Source: *New York Times*, November 21, 2002, p. C8, from Sanford C. Bernstein and Ward's AutoInfoBank.

★ 1075 ★
Autos (SIC 3711)
Luxury Car Market in Michigan

Shares cover Wayne, Oakland and Macomb counties.

Lincoln	29.7%
Cadillac	25.8
Lexus	7.7
Volvo	5.9
BMW	5.6
Mercedes-Benz	4.9
Audi	4.6
Jaguar	4.3
Acura	4.0
Other	7.5

Source: *Detroit News*, July 21, 2002, p. 9a, from R.L. Polk.

★ 1076 ★
Autos (SIC 3711)
Top Auto Makers, 2002

A total of 16.8 million cars and light trucks were sold during the year, down from 17.1 million in 2001. The Big Three had 61.7% of the market, down from 63.3% in 2001. Asians grew from 30.2% to 31.3% for the same period.

GM	28.4%
Ford	20.2
Chrysler	13.1
Toyota	10.4
Honda	7.4
Nissan	4.4

Continued on next page.

★ 1076 ★ *Continued*
Autos (SIC 3711)

Top Auto Makers, 2002

A total of 16.8 million cars and light trucks were sold during the year, down from 17.1 million in 2001. The Big Three had 61.7% of the market, down from 63.3% in 2001. Asians grew from 30.2% to 31.3% for the same period.

Mitsubishi	2.0%
Other	14.1

Source: *Los Angeles Times*, January 4, 2003, p. C1.

★ 1077 ★
Autos (SIC 3711)

Top Auto Makers in Canada

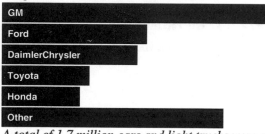

A total of 1.7 million cars and light trucks were sold in the country.

	Units	Share
GM	516,000	30.35%
Ford	258,000	15.18
DaimlerChrysler	246,000	14.47
Toyota	146,000	8.59
Honda	140,000	8.24
Other	394,000	23.18

Source: *Kingston Whig-Standard*, January 4, 2003, p. 17.

★ 1078 ★
Autos (SIC 3711)

Top Car Makers in Michigan

Market shares are shown in percent. The Ford Explorer was the top seller in Michigan with 46,065 units sold.

General Motors	40.3%
Ford	29.3
Chrysler	17.6
Other	12.5

Source: *Detroit News*, July 21, 2002, p. 9a, from R.L. Polk.

★ 1079 ★
Autos (SIC 3711)

Top Cars for Young Buyers, 2002

Market shares are shown based on vehicles sold to buyers 25 and younger.

Ford	17.0%
Chevrolet	14.0
Honda	12.0
Toyota	9.0
Volkswagen	6.0
Other	42.0

Source: *New York Times*, January 16, 2003, p. C1, from Autodata, CNW Marketing Research, and J.D. Power & Associates.

★ 1080 ★
Autos (SIC 3711)

Top Minivans, 2002

A total of 1,134,801 units were sold during the year.

Dodge Caravan	21.6
Honda Odyssey	13.5
Ford Windstar	13.1
Chrysler Town & Country	11.1
Chevrolet Venture	8.3
Other	32.4

Source: *Automotive News*, April 28, 2003, p. 41, from Automotive News Data Center.

★ 1081 ★
Autos (SIC 3711)

Top Passenger Car Producers, 2002

Market shares are shown in percent.

GM	28.7%
Ford	21.1
DaimlerChrysler	14.4
Toyota	10.3
Honda	7.6
Nissan	4.3
Other	13.6

Source: *Financial Times*, January 24, 2003, p. 16, from J.D. Power.

★ 1082 ★
Autos (SIC 3711)

Top Selling SUVs, 2002

Figures are for the first 11 months of the year.

Ford Explorer	433,847
Chevy TrailBlazer	249,568
Jeep Grand Cherokee	224,233
Chevy Tahoe	209,767
Jeep Liberty	171,212
Ford Expedition	163,454
Honda CR-V	146,266
Ford Escape	145,471
Toyota Highlander	131,134
Dodge Durango	106,925

Source: *Advertising Age*, March 10, 2003, p. 12, from *Automotive News*.

★ 1083 ★
Autos (SIC 3711)

Top SUV Producers, 2002

Market shares are shown in percent.

GM	30.9%
Ford	20.7
DaimlerChrysler	15.4
Toyota	11.0
Honda	6.7
Nissan	4.0
Other	11.3

Source: *Financial Times*, January 24, 2003, p. 16, from J.D. Power.

★ 1084 ★
Motor Coaches (SIC 3711)

Motor Coach Industry

Market shares are shown in percent.

Motor Coach Industries	65.0%
Other	35.0

Source: *Daily Herald*, August 28, 2002, p. 1, from Motor Coach Industries.

★ 1085 ★
Police Cars (SIC 3711)

Police Car Market

The company produces the Crown Victoria.

Ford Motor	85.0%
Other	15.0

Source: *Automotive News*, July 8, 2002, p. 10.

★ 1086 ★
Heavy-Duty Vehicles (SIC 3713)

Heavy-Duty Vehicle Industry

Shares for diesel-fueled vehicles are estimates. HEVs stand for hybrid electric vehicles.

	2010	2020
Diesel-fueled vehicles	80.0%	66.0%
HEVs	10.0	17.0
Fuel cell-powered vehicles	2.0	6.0
Other	8.0	11.0

Source: *Electric Vehicle Online Today*, March 11, 2003, p. NA, from Weststart-CALSTART.

★ 1087 ★
Trucks (SIC 3713)

Class 6 Truck Leaders, 2002

Market shares are shown through October 2002.

International	38.8%
Ford	26.1
Freightliner	23.6
General Motors	3.2
Chevrolet	2.2
Hino USA	1.8
Sterling	1.3
Mitsubishi Fuso	1.2
Nissan	1.1
Other	0.7

Source: "U.S. Retail Truck Sales." available January 7, 2003 from http://www.todaystrucking.com, from Ward's Communications.

★ 1088 ★
Trucks (SIC 3713)

Class 6 Truck Leaders in Canada, 2002

Market shares are shown through October 2002.

International	36.5%
General Motors	25.1
Ford	14.8
Freightliner	12.1
Hino Canada	9.6
Sterling	1.9
Other	2.0

Source: "Canadian Truck Sales." available January 7, 2003 from http://www.todaystrucking.com, from Canadian Vehicle Manufacturers Association.

★ 1089 ★
Trucks (SIC 3713)

Class 7 Truck Leaders, 2002

Market shares are shown through October 2002.

International	39.6%
Freightliner	25.4
General Motors	13.2
Chevrolet	5.4
Sterling	4.5
Peterbilt	3.6
Kenworth	3.4
Other	4.9

Source: "U.S. Retail Truck Sales." available January 7, 2003 from http://www.todaystrucking.com, from Ward's Communications.

★ 1090 ★
Trucks (SIC 3713)

Class 7 Truck Leaders in Canada, 2002

Market shares are shown through October 2002.

International	39.3%
General Motors	19.0
Freightliner	9.9
Sterling	9.4
Peterbilt	7.3
Kenworth	6.5
Ford	4.5
Hino Canada	2.7
Other	1.4

Source: "Canadian Truck Sales." available January 7, 2003 from http://www.todaystrucking.com, from Canadian Vehicle Manufacturers Association.

★ 1091 ★
Trucks (SIC 3713)

Class 8 Truck Leaders, 2002

Market shares are shown for year to date.

Freightliner	31.2%
Paccar	23.5
Navistar	16.1
Volvo	7.9
Other	31.3

Source: *Financial Times*, September 16, 2002, p. 20, from *Automotive News*, SSSB, and *Stark's Truck & Highway Ledger*.

★ 1092 ★
Trucks (SIC 3713)
Class 8 Truck Leaders in Canada, 2002

Market shares are shown through October 2002.

Freightliner	22.2%
International	22.2
Kenworth	13.5
Mack	10.6
Peterbilt	9.6
Volvo	8.7
Other	13.2

Source: "Canadian Truck Sales." available January 7, 2003 from http://www.todaystrucking.com, from Canadian Vehicle Manufacturers Association.

★ 1093 ★
Trucks (SIC 3713)
Top Truck Makers, 2002

Market shares are shown based on sales of 69,328 heavy-duty truck sold.

Freightliner	31.0%
International	16.0
Mack	13.0
Peterbilt	12.0
Kenworth	11.0
Volvo	8.0
Sterling	6.0
Other	3.0

Source: *The Roanoke Times*, March 20, 2003, p. 1, from *Heavy Duty Trucking*.

★ 1094 ★
Trucks (SIC 3713)
Truck Sales by Class

Figures show sales by class. Class 1 (0-6,000 lbs.), Class 2 (6,001-10,000 lbs.), Class 3 (10,001-14,000 lbs.), Class 4 (14,001-16,000 lbs.), Class 5 (16,001-19,500 lbs.), Class 6 (19,501-26,000 lbs.), Class 7 (26,001-33,000 lbs.), Class 8 (33,001 and over lbs.).

	2001	2002	Share
Class 1	5,112,837	5,007,304	62.79%
Class 2	2,507,702	2,564,745	32.16
Class 8	139,614	146,031	1.83
Class 3	101,499	80,042	1.00
Class 7	91,651	69,328	0.87
Class 6	42,434	45,095	0.57
Class 4	52,037	37,827	0.47
Class 5	24,362	24,003	0.30

Source: "U.S. Retail Truck Sales." available January 7, 2003 from http://www.ntea.com, from National Truck Equipment Association.

★ 1095 ★
Auto Parts (SIC 3714)
Auto Parts Spending, 2000

Consumers spent $432 billion in 2000 on 17.4 million new autos containing nearly $242 billion worth of components.

	($ mil.)	Share
Engine, transmission	$79.8	33.00%
Steering, suspension	46.0	19.02
Body	43.5	17.99
Exterior, interior	43.5	17.99
Electrical	19.3	7.98
Heat, air	9.7	4.01

Source: *The Indianapolis Star*, April 8, 2003, p. C1, from Center for Automotive Research.

★ 1096 ★

Auto Parts (SIC 3714)

Brake Pad Aftermarket

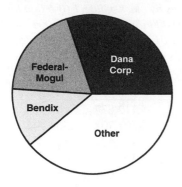

Market shares are shown in percent for North America.

Dana Corp.	30.0%
Federal-Mogul	19.0
Bendix	12.0
Other	39.0

Source: *Aftermarket Business*, March 2003, p. 14, from Frost & Sullivan.

★ 1097 ★

Auto Parts (SIC 3714)

Popular Battery Brands

Data show a survey of technicians of brands they most often install.

Interstate	44.0%
ACDelco	19.0
Exide	16.0
NAPA	10.0

Source: *Aftermarket Business*, October 2002, p. 34, from *Aftermarket Business 8th Annual Do-It-For-Me report.*

★ 1098 ★

Auto Parts (SIC 3714)

Popular Clutch Brands

Data show a survey of technicians of brands they most often install.

Borg-Warner	23.0%
Luk	18.0
Beck/Arnley	10.0
ACDelco	10.0
Perfection Hy-Test	5.0

Source: *Aftermarket Business*, October 2002, p. 34, from *Aftermarket Business 8th Annual Do-It-For-Me report.*

★ 1099 ★

Auto Parts (SIC 3714)

Popular Shock Absorber Brands

Data show a survey of technicians of brands they most often install.

Monroe	52.0%
Gabriel	19.0
NAPA	13.0
ACDelco	12.0
Carquest	11.0
KYB	8.0
Moog	7.0

Source: *Aftermarket Business*, October 2002, p. 34, from *Aftermarket Business 8th Annual Do-It-For-Me report.*

★ 1100 ★

Auto Parts (SIC 3714)

Power Transmission Component Demand

The demand for clutches, brakes and similar parts is expected to increase 4.3% annually to $3.4 billion in 2006.

	2001	2006	Share
Sprockets & chains	$ 680	$ 835	24.78%
Clutches & brakes	610	740	21.96
Couplings & u-joints	550	650	19.29
Pulleys & sheaves	435	565	16.77
Other	460	580	17.21

Source: *Research Studies - Freedonia Group*, May 8, 2002, p. 1, from Freedonia Group.

★ 1101 ★
Auto Parts (SIC 3714)

Suspension Market in Canada

Market shares are shown in percent. The company has 62% of the market in the U.S. and Canada.

Sanluis Rassini 90.0%
Other 10.0

Source: "Sanluis." available April 16, 2003 from http://www.sanluiscorp.com.

★ 1102 ★
Auto Parts (SIC 3714)

Top Airbag Makers, 2000

Market shares are shown in percent.

Autoliv 33.0%
TRW 30.0
Delphi 17.0
Breed 6.0
Takata 5.0
Other 9.0

Source: "Market Consolidation Occupies Airbag Manufacturers." available June 6, 2002 from http://www.just-auto.com, from industry estimates.

★ 1103 ★
Auto Parts (SIC 3714)

Top Seatbelt Makers, 2000

Market shares are shown in percent.

TRW 40.0%
Breed 25.0
Takata 15.0
Autoliv 12.0
Other 8.0

Source: "Market Consolidation Occupies Airbag Manufacturers." available June 6, 2002 from http://www.just-auto.com, from industry estimates.

★ 1104 ★
Auto Parts (SIC 3714)

Transmission Market Shares

Shares are for dealer-installed remanufactured transmissions on cars made by the Big Three.

Aftermarket Technology Corp. 72.0%
Other 28.0

Source: *Wall Street Journal*, May 13, 2003, p. B7, from Aftermarket Technology.

★ 1105 ★
Auto Parts (SIC 3714)

Wiper Blade Market

Shares are shown for the aftermarket.

Anco 41.0%
Champion 10.0
Other 49.0

Source: *Rubber & Plastics News*, November 11, 2002, p. 1, from Federal-Mogul Corp.

★ 1106 ★
Truck Trailers (SIC 3715)

Largest Truck Trailer Manufacturers

Companies are ranked by shipments.

	Units	Share
Wabash National	27,149	19.65%
Utility Trailer Manufacturing . . .	17,574	12.72
Stoughton Trailers	10,000	7.24
Manac	6,900	4.99
Other	76,557	55.40

Source: *Trailer/Body Business*, February 1, 2003, p. NA, from Economic Planning Associates.

★ 1107 ★
Motorhomes (SIC 3716)

Top Class A Motorhome Producers, 2002

Market shares are shown in percent.

Fleetwood 20.8%
Winnebago 18.1
Monaco 18.0
Coachmen 6.3
National RV Holdings 5.5

Continued on next page.

★ 1107 ★ *Continued*
Motorhomes (SIC 3716)

Top Class A Motorhome Producers, 2002

Market shares are shown in percent.

Damon	4.7%
Tifflin	4.6
Thor	3.8
Gulfstream	2.8
Other	9.4

Source: *RV Business*, April 2003, p. 16, from Recreational Vehicle Industry Association.

★ 1108 ★
Motorhomes (SIC 3716)

Top Class C Motorhome Producers, 2002

Market shares are shown in percent.

Winnebago	26.0%
Thor	16.1
Coachmen	13.2
Gulfstream	10.7
Fleetwood	10.1
Jayco Inc.	6.9
Forest River	4.9
R-Vision	3.1
Monaco	2.3
Trail Wagons	1.6
Other	5.1

Source: *RV Business*, April 2003, p. 16, from Recreational Vehicle Industry Association.

★ 1109 ★
Aircraft (SIC 3721)

Leading Aircraft Contractors for the Government, 2001

Market shares are shown based on total purchases of $34.9 billion.

Boeing Co.	27.94%
Lockheed Martin	21.73
United Technologies	10.28
General Electric	4.41
Northrop Grumman	3.68
Raytheon	3.52
General Dynamics	2.87

Honeywell Inc.	1.33%
Veritas Capital Inc.	1.16
Other	23.08

Source: *Government Executive*, August 15, 2002, p. NA, from Eagle Eye Publishers and Federal Procurement Data Center.

★ 1110 ★
Jets (SIC 3721)

Business Jet Market, 2002

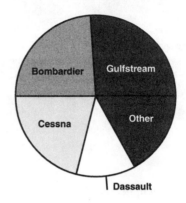

Shares are shown based on $5.9 billion for the first six months. By units delivered, Cessna has 42% of the industry.

Gulfstream	26.0%
Bombardier	24.0
Cessna	21.0
Dassault	12.0
Other	17.0

Source: *Interavia*, September 2002, p. 3, from General Aviation Manufacturers Association.

★ 1111 ★
Jets (SIC 3721)

Fractional Ownership Market

Market shares are shown in percent.

NetJets	49.0%
Flexjet	18.0
Travel Air	17.0
Flight Options	16.0

Source: *Financial Times*, September 10, 2002, p. 2, from Aviation Research Group.

★ 1112 ★
Aircraft Engines (SIC 3724)

Jet Engine Servicing in the Southeast

The market includes repairing and overhauling. The company's Augusta plant has 85% of the Southeastern market.

Garrett Aviation Service	85.0%
Other	15.0

Source: *Knight Ridder/Tribune Business News*, September 8, 2002, p. NA, from Garrett.

★ 1113 ★
Boats (SIC 3732)

Boating Market, 2001

Over 69 million people participated in recreational boating during the year. Figures show unit sales.

Outboard motors	299,000
Outboard boats	224,400
Boat trailers	135,900
Canoes	105,800
Personal watercraft	83,000
Sterndrive boats	74,100
Sailboats	26,200
Inboard boats (runabouts)	13,700
Inboard boats (cruisers)	8,100
Jet boats	6,000

Source: *Research Alert*, May 3, 2002, p. 9, from National Marine Manufacturers Asociation and *2001 Annual Sailing Business Review*.

★ 1114 ★
Boats (SIC 3732)

Powered Vessels to be Built, 2002

43 shipyards delivered or signed contracts to build 469 vessels, down from 544 vessels in 2001. Patrol boats were in the lead (as in 2001), no doubt a response to security concerns.

	Units	Share
Patrol (military and nonmilitary) . .	126	39.50%
Non-self-propelled vessels	57	17.87
Supply	33	10.34
Ferry, water taxi	32	10.03
Tug, AHTS	21	6.58
Research	15	4.70
Boom, spill response	13	4.08

	Units	Share
Pushboat, towboat	12	3.76%
Dinner, excursion, sightseeing . . .	10	3.13

Source: *Workboat*, January 2003, p. 48, from *Workboats 2002 Construction Survey*.

★ 1115 ★
Railroad Equipment (SIC 3743)

Intermodal Double Stack Market in North America

Market shares are shown in percent. The company has held this share for about a decade.

Greenbrier	60.0%
Other	40.0

Source: "Greenbrier Doubles Backlog." available March 7, 2003 from http://www.grbx.xom.

★ 1116 ★
Bicycles (SIC 3751)

Bicycle Industry Sales, 2002

Bicycles have seen a boost in sales from boomers, who are looking to bikes for exercise (riding on pavement as opposed to mountain biking). Distribution of unit sales through July 2002.

Pavement	42.2%
Hardtail & dual suspension MTB	30.4
20 and 24-inch BMX	27.2

Source: *Bicycle Retailer and Industry News*, October 1, 2002, p. 1, from Bicycle Product Suppliers Association.

★ 1117 ★
Bicycles (SIC 3751)

Bicycle Sales by Type, 2001

There are thought to be 43 million bike owners in the United States. An average mountain bike costs $455. A road bike is the most expensive at $1,181.

Mountain	36.8%
Youth	26.1
Comfort	20.8
Hybrid	8.8
Road	4.4
Other	3.1

Source: *New York Times*, July 21, 2002, p. 10, from National Bicycle Dealers Association.

★ 1118 ★
Dirtbikes (SIC 3751)

Leading Dirtbike Makers, 2003

Shares are shown based on total forecasted sales of 273,368 bikes during the calendar year.

Honda	44.79%
Yamaha	29.90
Suzuki	9.10
KTM	5.50
Other	0.11

Source: *Dealernews*, April 2003, p. 90, from Motorcycle Industry Council, SEC filings, and company reports.

★ 1119 ★
Motorcycles (SIC 3751)

Cruiser Market Shares

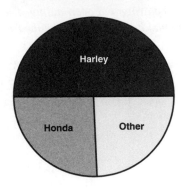

Market shares are shown in percent.

Harley	45.0%
Honda	23.0
Other	22.0

Source: *Fortune*, August 12, 2002, p. 122.

★ 1120 ★
Motorcycles (SIC 3751)

Leading Motorcycle Makers, 2003

Shares are shown based on total forecasted sales of 840,635 two-wheel bikes during the calendar year.

Honda	26.88%
Harley-Davidson	26.83
Yamaha	17.59
Suzuki	11.28
Kawasaki	9.29
BMW	3.00
KTM	2.41
Triumph	0.92
Buell	0.70
Indian	0.37
Ducati	0.23
Polaris/Victory	0.23
Other	0.27

Source: *Dealernews*, April 2003, p. 90, from Motorcycle Industry Council, SEC filings, and company reports.

★ 1121 ★
Motorcycles (SIC 3751)

On-Highway Motorcycle Sales

On-highway motorcycles represent 62% of all motorcycle sales.

Cruisers 56.0%
Sport bike 21.0
Touring 18.0
Other 5.0

Source: *Business Wire*, March 21, 2003, p. NA, from Motorcycle Industry Council.

★ 1122 ★
Aerospace (SIC 3761)

Largest Defense Contractors, 2002

Companies are ranked by fiscal year sales of Department of Defense prime contract in billions of dollars.

Lockheed Martin . . . . $ 17.0
Boeing 16.6
Northrop Grumman 8.6
General Dynamics 7.0
Raytheon 7.0

Source: *USA TODAY*, April 3, 2003, p. A1, from U.S. Department of Defense.

★ 1123 ★
Aerospace (SIC 3761)

Leading Missile Contractors for the Government, 2001

Market shares are shown based on total purchases of $3.1 billion.

Lockheed Martin 46.14%
Raytheon Co. 42.13
Northrop Grumman 4.30
Boeing 2.50
Motorola 0.97
Carlyle Group 0.75
Marvin Group 0.62
Harris Corp. 0.30
Honeywell Inc. 0.27
Other 2.02

Source: *Government Executive*, August 15, 2002, p. NA, from Eagle Eye Publishers and Federal Procurement Data Center.

★ 1124 ★
Travel Trailers (SIC 3792)

Travel Trailer/Fifth-Wheel Market, 2002

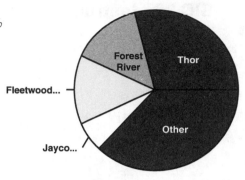

Market shares are shown for the first ten months of the year.

Thor 28.8%
Forest River 14.3
Fleetwood Enterprises Inc. 13.6
Jayco Inc. 6.3
Other 37.0

Source: *RV Business*, March 2003, p. 7, from Statistical Surveys.

★ 1125 ★
Snowmobiles (SIC 3799)

Snomobile Registrations by State, 2002

	Units	Share
Michigan	301,805	18.26%
Minnesota	277,290	16.78
Wisconsin	232,320	14.06
New York	146,662	8.87
Maine	96,600	5.84
New Hampshire	73,625	4.45
Illinois	54,128	3.28
Idaho	50,000	3.03
Pennsylvania	45,270	2.74
Vermont	41,000	2.48
Other	334,054	20.21

Source: "Statistics." available March 7, 2003 from http://www.snowmobile.org, from International Snowmobile Manufacturers Association.

SIC 38 - Instruments and Related Products

★ 1126 ★
Military Training Equipment (SIC 3812)
Flight Simulation Technology

Market shares are shown in percent.

Lockheed Martin	17.1%
L-3 Communications	11.4
CAE	4.1
Other	67.4

Source: *National Defense*, November 2002, p. NA.

★ 1127 ★
Radar Systems (SIC 3812)
Top Radar Producers, 2002-2011

Market shares are shown based on toal production of $19.6 billion.

Raytheon	32.2%
Thales	18.5
Other	50.7

Source: "Raytheon Tops in Radar Market." available January 3, 2003 from http://www.forecast1.com, from Forecast International.

★ 1128 ★
Laboratory Instruments (SIC 3821)
Spectrophotometer End Markets

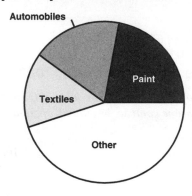

Color spectrophotometry is a process that makes use of ultraviolet/visible spectrophometers to perform colorimetric measurements. Demand is shown by end market.

Paint	22.0%
Automobiles	18.0
Textiles	15.0
Other	45.0

Source: *Spectroscopy*, April 2002, p. 12, from Strategic Directions International.

★ 1129 ★
Environmental Equipment (SIC 3822)

Air Monitoring Equipment and Services

The value of markets are shown in millions of dollars. Mass spectrometers and electrochemical and physical analysis instruments led with sales of $209.1 million.

	2002	2007
Industry	$ 398.7	$ 697.0
Aftermarket	381.1	570.6
Government	288.1	434.5

Source: *American Ceramic Society Bulletin*, March 2003, p. 10, from Business Communications Co.

★ 1130 ★
Automated Meter Readers (SIC 3824)

Largest AMR Shippers, 2001

Firms are ranked by units shipped.

	Units	Share
SchlumbergerSema Convergent Group	2,758,000	34.56%
Itron Systems	2,652,000	33.23
Distribution Control Systems	687,000	8.61
Hunt Technologies Inc.	447,000	5.60
Amco Automated Systems Inc.	403,000	5.05
Other	1,033,000	12.94

Source: *Utility Business*, April 2002, p. 50, from Cognyst Consulting.

★ 1131 ★
Biometrics (SIC 3827)

Biometric Market Technologies, 2001

The industry had revenues of $523.9 million in 2001 and may hit $1.9 billion in 2005. Figures do not include AFIS revenues.

Finger scan	48.8%
Facial scan	15.4
Middleware	11.9
Hand-scan	10.4

Iris-scan	6.2%
Voice-scan	4.3
Signature-scan	2.7
Keystroke-scan	0.4

Source: "Biometric Market Report." available January 7, 2003 online from http://www.biometricgroup.com, from International Biometric Group.

★ 1132 ★
Sensors (SIC 3827)

Chemical Sensor Market, 2006

Demand is forecasted in millions of dollars.

Optical chemical sensors	$ 180
Optical gas-phase	156
Infrared-type optical	115

Source: *Sensor Business Digest*, December 2002, p. NA.

★ 1133 ★
Trace Detection Equipment (SIC 3829)

Trace Detection Industry

Market shares are shown in percent. The company makes systems that detect traces of explosives and illegal drugs.

Ion Track	50.0%
Other	50.0

Source: *Buyouts*, November 4, 2002, p. NA.

★ 1134 ★
First Aid Products (SIC 3841)

Top Antiseptics, 2002

Brands are ranked by sales for the year ended September 8, 2002. Figures exclude Wal-Mart.

	($ mil.)	Share
Neosporin Plus	$ 45.7	12.65%
Neosporin	39.2	10.85
Mederma	13.1	3.63
Solarcaine	11.0	3.05
Bactine	10.8	2.99
Betadine	9.0	2.49
Aquaphor	8.9	2.46
Polysporin	8.5	2.35
Becton Dickinson	7.4	2.05
Fruit of the Earth	5.5	1.52

Continued on next page.

Continued

First Aid Products (SIC 3841)

Top Antiseptics, 2002

Brands are ranked by sales for the year ended September 8, 2002. Figures exclude Wal-Mart.

	($ mil.)	Share
Private label	$ 132.3	36.63%
Other	69.8	19.32

Source: *MMR*, October 21, 2002, p. 48, from Information Resources Inc.

★ 1135 ★

First Aid Products (SIC 3841)

Top First Aid Device (Support/ Braces) Brands, 2002

Brands are ranked by sales in millions of dollars for the year ended February 24, 2002. Figures include supermarkets, drug stores and discount stores but exclude Wal-Mart.

	($ mil.)	Share
Ace	$ 62.6	29.67%
Futuro	46.0	21.80
Tru Fit	18.0	8.53
Bauer & Black	9.2	4.36
Futuro Sport	8.6	4.08
Tru Fit Elasto Preene	6.9	3.27
TED	6.3	2.99
Johnson & Johnson Coach	5.0	2.37
Homedics Thera P	4.2	1.99
Futuro Beyond Support	3.9	1.85
Private label	6.8	3.22
Other	33.5	15.88

Source: *MMR*, April 22, 2002, p. 57, from Information Resources Inc.

★ 1136 ★

First Aid Products (SIC 3841)

Top Heat/Ice Pack Brands, 2002

Market shares are shown for the year ended December 29, 2002. Figures are based on sales at supermarkets, drug stores, discount stores and exclude Wal-Mart.

ThermaCare	36.0%
TheraMed	12.6
Bed Buddy	7.8

Ace	6.2%
Nexcare	4.5
Faultless	3.6
Tru-Fri Polar Preene	3.0
TheraBeads	1.9
Mentholatum Migraine	1.8
Be Koool	1.8
Other	20.8

Source: *Chain Drug Review*, February 17, 2003, p. 27, from Information Resources Inc.

★ 1137 ★

Medical Equipment (SIC 3841)

Counterpulsation Equipment Market

These devices are used primarily in treating the over 6 million people who suffer from angina. The company has no patent on the entire technology, but it does on parts.

Vasomedical	80.0%
Other	20.0

Source: *Long Island Business News*, July 26, 2002, p. 11A.

★ 1138 ★

Medical Equipment (SIC 3841)

Inflation Device Industry

The company's share exceeds 50% of the market. They make devices that inflate like balloons and clear out clogged arteries.

Merit Medical Systems Inc.	50.0%
Other	50.0

Source: *Investor's Business Daily*, October 11, 2002, p. A6.

★ 1139 ★

Medical Equipment (SIC 3841)

Operating Table Market

Market shares are estimated in percent.

STERIS	40.0%
Skytron	35.0
Getinge (Manquet line)	20.0
Other	5.0

Source: *Healthcare Purchasing News*, April 2003, p. 32, from industry estimates.

★ 1140 ★
Medical Equipment (SIC 3841)

Sleep Apnea Market

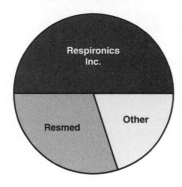

Market shares are estimated in percent. Respironic's share exceeds 50%.

Respironics Inc. 50.0%
Resmed 30.0
Other 20.0

Source: *Investor's Business Daily*, August 27, 2002, p. A8, from Respironic.

★ 1141 ★
Medical Equipment (SIC 3841)

Sterilization and Disinfectant Market, 2001

Suppliers' shares are shown in percent. The disinfection and sterilization market is thought to have been valued at $647 million in 2001.

3M 22.9%
STERIS 21.4
Kimberly Clark 16.4
Advanced Sterilization Products 8.9
Other 30.4

Source: *Healthcare Purchasing News*, February 2003, p. 40, from Frost & Sullivan.

★ 1142 ★
Medical Equipment (SIC 3841)

Surgical Glove Sales, 2002

Dollar shares are for the second quarter of the year.

Powder-free latex 53.0%
Powdered latex 35.0
Synthetic 10.0

Source: *Healthcare Purchasing News*, November 2002, p. 36, from IMS Health's Hospital Supply Index.

★ 1143 ★
Medical Equipment (SIC 3841)

Ultrasound Equipment Industry

Market shares are estimated in percent.

Siemens 50.0%
Philips Medical Systems/General Electric . . . 34.0
Other 16.0

Source: *Hospital Materials Management*, July 2002, p. 19, from Klein Biomedical Consultants.

★ 1144 ★
Medical Equipment (SIC 3841)

Wound Management Market Shares, 2001

The market was valued at $287 million.

Hospitals 50.0%
Nursing homes 35.0
Home health 10.0
Retail distribution 5.0

Source: *Datamonitor Industry Market Research*, Annual 2002, p. NA, from Datamonitor.

★ 1145 ★
Hearing Aids (SIC 3842)

Hearing Aid Sales, 2002

An estimated 1.9 million hearing aids are projected to be sold. DSP stands for digital signal processing.

DSPs 42.0%
Analog non-programmable 30.0
DPA 28.0

Source: *The Hearing Journal*, January 2003, p. 17, from Hearing Industries Association Statistical Reporting Program.

★ 1146 ★

Orthopedic Implants (SIC 3842)

Craniomaxillofacial Fixation Market Shares, 2001

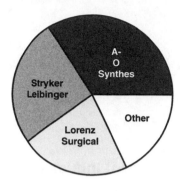

The market is estimated at $130 million.

A-O Synthes 34.0%
Stryker Leibinger 26.0
Lorenz Surgical 22.0
Other 18.0

Source: "Annual 2001 Menu." available January 7, 2003 from http://www.biomet.com, from Biomet.

★ 1147 ★

Orthopedic Implants (SIC 3842)

Leading Orthopedic Implant Makers, 2001

The market was valued at $3.4 billion.

J&J/DePuy/ACE/L-C/Acromed 15.0%
Stryker/Howmedica/Osteonics 11.5
Zimmer 10.2
Sythes/Stratec 6.8
Biomet/Merck 6.6
Other 50.0

Source: *Datamonitor Industry Market Research*, Annual 2002, p. NA, from Datamonitor.

★ 1148 ★

Orthopedic Implants (SIC 3842)

Orthopedic Implant Market Shares, 2001

The market was valued at $3.4 billion.

Knee implants 34.8%
Hip implants 25.4
Spinal implants 20.6
Trauma devices 19.3

Source: *Datamonitor Industry Market Research*, Annual 2002, p. NA, from Datamonitor.

★ 1149 ★

Orthopedic Implants (SIC 3842)

Orthopedic Trauma Market Shares, 2001

The market was valued at $648 million.

Synthes/Stratec/Mathys 43.1%
Smith and Nephew 19.6
Zimmer 8.5
Biomet 8.0
StrykerHowmedicaOsteonics 6.2
J&J/DePuy 5.0
Othofix 2.4
Other 7.2

Source: *Datamonitor Industry Market Research*, Annual 2002, p. NA, from Datamonitor.

★ 1150 ★

Orthopedic Implants (SIC 3842)

Top Knee Implant Makers, 2001

The market was valued at $1.2 billion. Top market segments were femoral cemented with 36% and tibial cemented with 31.4%.

Johnson & Johnson/DePuy 27.5%
Zimmer 21.2
Stryker/Howmedica/Osteonics 18.1
Biomet/Merck 10.2
Smith and Nephew 7.9
Sulzer 6.6
WMT/Cremascoli 5.1
Other 3.3

Source: *Datamonitor Industry Market Research*, Annual 2002, p. NA, from Datamonitor.

★ 1151 ★
Orthopedic Implants (SIC 3842)

Top Shoulder Joint Producers, 2001

The market was valued at $59 million.

Biomet	33.0%
J&J/DePuy	31.0
Tornier	13.0
Sulzer Orthopedics	9.0
Smith & Nephew	8.0
Other	6.0

Source: *Datamonitor Industry Market Research*, Annual 2002, p. NA, from Datamonitor.

★ 1152 ★
Orthopedic Implants (SIC 3842)

Top Spinal Implant Makers, 2001

The market was valued at $622 million.

Medtronic/Sofamor/Danek	31.3%
Sulzer/Spine-Tech	27.6
US Surgical	21.9
J&J/DePuy	9.1
Sythes/Stratec/Mathys	5.5
Other	4.6

Source: *Datamonitor Industry Market Research*, Annual 2002, p. NA, from Datamonitor.

★ 1153 ★
Surgical Implants (SIC 3842)

Cardiovascular Device Market

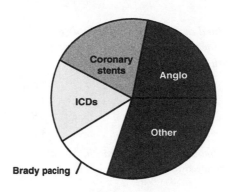

The top 17 firms (those with revenues exceeding $500 million) makes up 65% of all revenues. Market shares are shown in percent. Other includes interventional devices, heart valves, electrophysiology, AAA/vascular grafts, vascular sealing and biventricular pacing.

	($ bil.)	Share
Anglo	$ 3.2	21.77%
Coronary stents	3.0	20.41
ICDs	2.5	17.01
Brady pacing	1.6	10.88
Other	4.4	29.93

Source: *Healthcare Purchasing News*, April 2003, p. 30, from Frost & Sullivan.

★ 1154 ★
Surgical Implants (SIC 3842)

Finger Products Market

Market shares are estimated in percent.

Wright Medical Group	75.0%
Other	25.0

Source: *Investor's Business Daily*, September 26, 2002, p. A7.

★ 1155 ★
Surgical Implants (SIC 3842)

Leading Maxillofacial Implant Makers, 2001

The market was valued at $133 million. Plates & screws had 86% of the market, followed by specialty instrumentation with an 8.3% share.

Synthes	47.6%
StrykerHowmedica/Osteonics	39.3
KLS-Martin	9.5
Other	3.6

Source: *Datamonitor Industry Market Research*, Annual 2002, p. NA, from Datamonitor.

★ 1156 ★
Surgical Implants (SIC 3842)

Leading Reconstructive Device Makers, 2001

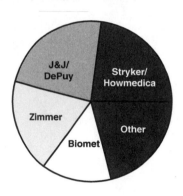

The reconstructive device market is valued at $2.5 billion.

Stryker/Howmedica	23.0%
J&J/DePuy	23.0
Zimmer	19.0
Biomet	14.0
Other	21.0

Source: "Annual 2001 Menu." available January 7, 2003 from http://www.biomet.com, from Biomet.

★ 1157 ★
Surgical Implants (SIC 3842)

Mastectomy Products Industry

Market shares are shown in percent.

Coloplast	60.0%
Other	40.0

Source: *Home Care Magazine*, October 1, 2002, p. NA.

★ 1158 ★
Surgical Implants (SIC 3842)

Musculoskeletal Market Shares, 2002

The market is valued at $7.6 billion.

	($ mil.)	Share
Reconstructive devices	$ 3,085	40.49%
Spinal products	1,425	18.70
Fixation	990	12.99
Arthroscopy	700	9.19
Softgoods & bracing	485	6.36
O.R. supplies	285	3.74
Dental reconstructive implants	285	3.74
Powdered surgical equipment	195	2.56
Bone cements & accessories	170	2.23

Source: "Annual 2001 Menu." available January 7, 2003 from http://www.biomet.com, from Biomet.

★ 1159 ★
Surgical Implants (SIC 3842)

Revision Market Shares, 2002

The reconstructive device market is valued at $382.2 million.

Hips/knees	75.0%
Cerdage cables & instruments	12.0
Cement removal	5.0
Custom implants	3.0
Accessories	3.0
Shoulders/others	2.0

Source: "Annual 2001 Menu." available January 7, 2003 from http://www.biomet.com, from Biomet.

★ 1160 ★
Surgical Implants (SIC 3842)

Stent Market Leaders

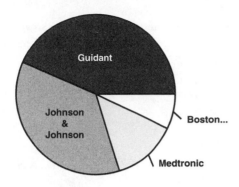

Market shares are shown in percent.

Guidant	43.0%
Johnson & Johnson	36.0
Medtronic	13.0
Boston Scientific	7.0

Source: *Wall Street Journal*, October 3, 2002, p. B6.

★ 1161 ★
Dental Equipment (SIC 3843)

Dental Industry Market Shares

Companies are expected to benefit from the dental needs of aging baby boomers. Market shares are shown in percent.

Patterson Dental	30.0%
Schein	30.0
Other	40.0

Source: *Milwaukee Journal Sentinel*, December 29, 2002, p. NA.

★ 1162 ★
Dental Equipment (SIC 3843)

Leading Dental Implant Makers, 2001

The dental reconstructive implant market is valued at $250 million.

3i	31.0%
Nobel Biocare	29.0
Sulzer Dental	19.0
ITI Straumann	14.0
Other	17.0

Source: "Annual 2001 Menu." available January 7, 2003 from http://www.biomet.com, from Biomet.

★ 1163 ★
Dental Equipment (SIC 3843)

Prophy Angles and Cups

Prophy angles and cups are the drill-like instruments used to clean and polish teeth.

Young Innovations	60.0%
Other	40.0

Source: *Investor's Business Daily*, October 10, 2002, p. A10.

★ 1164 ★
Electromedical Equipment (SIC 3845)

Defibrillator Market Shares

Market shares are shown for hospitals. In the pre-hospital market Physio has a 60% share.

Physio	36.0%
Zoll	35.0
Philips	29.0

Source: *Investor's Business Daily*, February 28, 2003, p. A8, from company reports and First Call.

★ 1165 ★
Electromedical Equipment (SIC 3845)

Ear Implant Market

The market was evenly split between Cochlear and Advanced Bionics. The latter company has withdrawn from the market, so Cochlear's share is now estimated.

Cochlear 80.0%
Other 20.0

Source: *Australasian Business Intelligence*, August 20, 2002, p. NA.

★ 1166 ★
Electromedical Equipment (SIC 3845)

EEP Equipment Market

The electroencephalography diagnostic and monitoring market is shown by segment. Revenues are expected to grow from $177.1 million in 2002 to $309.6 million in 2009.

Sleep disorders 49.0%
Other 51.0

Source: *PR Newswire*, March 18, 2003, p. NA, from Frost & Sullivan.

★ 1167 ★
Electromedical Equipment (SIC 3845)

ICD Market Shares, 2001

The $1.5 billion market is shown in percent. ICD stands for implantable cardiac defibrillator.

Medtronic 50.0%
Guidant 37.0
St. Jude Medical 11.0
Other 2.0

Source: *Electronic Business*, July 2002, p. 66, from U.S. Bancorp Piper Jaffray.

★ 1168 ★
Electromedical Equipment (SIC 3845)

Leading Echocardiography System Makers, 2001

The market was valued at $306 million. Systems make up 95.8% of the echocardiograph market, with the balance held by contrast agents.

Philips ATL/Agilent 60.0%
Siemens/Acuson 25.0
GE Medical Systems 10.0
Toshiba 3.0
Biosound Esaote 2.0

Source: *Datamonitor Industry Market Research*, Annual 2002, p. NA, from Datamonitor.

★ 1169 ★
Electromedical Equipment (SIC 3845)

Pacemaker Market Shares, 2001

The $1.7 billion market is shown in percent.

Medtronic 50.0%
St. Jude Medical 25.0
Guidant 22.0
Other 3.0

Source: *Electronic Business*, July 2002, p. 66, from U.S. Bancorp Piper Jaffray.

★ 1170 ★
Surgical Lighting (SIC 3845)

Fixed, Focused Lighting Market

Market shares are estimated in percent.

Skytron 30.0%
STERIS and Getinge's ALM brand 25.0
Berchtold 20.0
Other 25.0

Source: *Healthcare Purchasing News*, April 2003, p. 32, from industry estimates.

★ **1171** ★
Contact Lenses (SIC 3851)

Lens Market by Type, 2003

Figures are projections.

Plastic 56.6%
Polycarbonates 31.9
Hi-index/mid index 10.0
Glass 1.5

Source: "The State of the U.S. Optical Retail Market." available December 2002 from http://www.optistock.com/ Jobson-som-2002-12.ppf, from Jobson Research.

★ **1172** ★
Contact Lenses (SIC 3851)

Top Soft Contact Lens Producers, 2001

Companies are ranked by sales in millions of dollars.

	($ mil.)	Share
Johnson & Johnson	$ 420	35.0%
CIBA Vision	330	28.0
Ocular Sciences	150	13.0
Bausch & Lomb	120	10.0
Cooper Companies	120	10.0

Source: "Contact Lens Market." available April 7, 2003 from http://www.optistock.com, from Robert Baird & Co.

★ **1173** ★
Contact Lenses (SIC 3851)

Top Toric Lens Producers

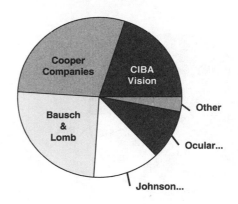

Market shares are shown in percent.

	2001	2002
CIBA Vision	26.5%	20.0%
Cooper Companies	26.5	29.0
Bausch & Lomb	24.5	25.0
Johnson & Johnson	12.0	13.0
Ocular Sciences	8.5	10.0
Other	2.0	3.0

Source: "Contact Lens Market." available April 7, 2003 from http://www.optistock.com, from Robert Baird & Co.

★ **1174** ★
Optical Goods (SIC 3851)

Optical Market Shares, 2002

Dollar shares are shown based on product categories.

Lenses (inc. treatments) 52.2%
Frames 32.0
Contact lenses 12.0
Plano sunglasses/clips 3.8

Source: "The State of the U.S. Optical Retail Market." available December 2002 from http://www.optistock.com/ Jobson-som-2002-12.ppf, from Jobson Research.

★ 1175 ★
Optical Goods (SIC 3851)

Top Excimer Laser Producers, 2002-03

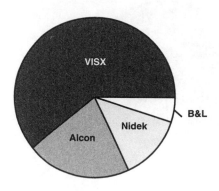

Market shares are estimated in percent. Roughly 1.3 million procedures are conducted annually.

VISX	61.0%
Alcon	21.0
Nidek	13.0
B&L	5.0

Source: "Refractive Eye Surgery." available April 7, 2003 from http://www.optistock.com, from SG Cowen.

★ 1176 ★
Optical Goods (SIC 3851)

Top IOL Producers, 2001

Market shares are shown in percent. IOL stands for interocular lenses.

	1994	2001
Bausch & Lomb	32.0%	11.0%
Alcon	28.0	50.0
Allergan/AMO	20.0	26.0
STARR Surgical	6.0	7.0
Pharmacia	5.0	3.0
Other	4.0	2.0

Source: "Cataract Market." available April 7, 2003 from http://www.optistock.com, from SG Cowen.

★ 1177 ★
Optical Goods (SIC 3851)

Vision Related Sales, 2002

Figures are in billions of dollars.

	($ bil.)	Share
Optical retail	$ 16.2	71.05%
Exams	3.6	15.79
SG/clips	1.8	7.89
Refractive surgery	0.6	2.63
OTC readers	0.4	1.75
Contact lenses	0.2	0.88

Source: "The State of the U.S. Optical Retail Market." available December 2002 from http://www.optistock.com/Jobson-som-2002-12.ppf, from Jobson Research.

★ 1178 ★
Sunglasses (SIC 3851)

Top Brands of Sunglasses, 2001

Top-tier sunglass sales hit about $490 million annually; the average pair costs $82.

	($ mil.)	Share
Ray-Ban	$ 113.5	23.16%
Oakley	90.5	18.47
Nike	40.0	8.16
Tommy Hilfiger	25.0	5.10
Gucci	23.5	4.80
Polo Sport	22.5	4.59
Kenneth Cole	22.0	4.49
DKNY	14.2	2.90
Bolle	14.2	2.90
Other	124.6	25.43

Source: *DNR*, August 5, 2002, p. 24, from Dioptics Market Research Division.

★ 1179 ★
Copiers (SIC 3861)

High-End Digital Copier Market, 2001

Market shares are shown in percent.

Canon	22.6%
Xerox	16.8
Other	60.6

Source: *Fortune*, October 14, 2002, p. 218, from International Data Corp.

★ 1180 ★
Copiers (SIC 3861)

Leading Duplicating Machine Vendors for the Government, 2001

Market shares are shown based on total purchases of $267.4 million.

Xerox	26.84%
Verizon Communications	9.70
Canon USA Inc.	6.66
Oce-Van der Grinten	5.98
Minolta Corp.	3.70
Danka Holding Co.	2.29
Sharp Electronics	2.29
National Micrographics Systems	2.03
Other	40.51

Source: *Government Executive*, August 15, 2002, p. NA, from Eagle Eye Publishers and Federal Procurement Data Center.

★ 1181 ★
Photographic Equipment (SIC 3861)

Digital Camera Households by Year

Figures show the share of households with a digital camera. The 2003 figure is estimated.

2003	30.0%
2002	20.0
2001	15.0
1999	6.0
1997	2.0

Source: *U.S. News & World Report*, March 23, 2003, p. 70, from InfoTrends Research Group.

★ 1182 ★
Photographic Equipment (SIC 3861)

Digital Minlab Market

Market shares are shown in percent. Fuji has about 5,000 labs in place.

Fuji Photo Film	60.0%
Other	40.0

Source: *BusinessWeek*, March 24, 2003, p. 80.

★ 1183 ★
Photographic Equipment (SIC 3861)

Leading Digital Camera Makers, 2002

Unit shares are shown for the year through October.

Sony	18.2%
Olympus	13.1
Logitech	9.4
Canon	8.8
Kodak	7.9
Other	42.6

Source: *New York Times*, December 16, 2002, p. C18, from Gartner Dataquest.

★ 1184 ★
Photographic Equipment (SIC 3861)

Top Conventional Film Brands, 2002

Market shares are shown for the year ended December 1, 2002.

Kodak Gold	28.2%
Kodak Advantix	16.1
Kodak Max	13.1
Kodak Gold Max	10.1
Fuji Super HQ	8.7
Fuji Fujicolor Superia	6.6
Kodak Max Zoom 800	2.6
Fuji Fujicolor Superia X-TRA	2.6
Fuji Nexia for Advanced Photo System Camera	1.6
Private label	6.3
Other	4.1

Source: *Grocery Headquarters*, February 2003, p. 72, from Information Resources Inc.

★ 1185 ★
Photographic Equipment (SIC 3861)

Top Conventional Film Makers, 2002

Market shares are shown for the year ended December 1, 2002.

Eastman Kodak Co.	73.8%
Fuji Photo Film USA Inc.	19.7
Konishiroku Photo	0.2
Private label	6.3

Source: *Grocery Headquarters*, February 2003, p. 72, from Information Resources Inc.

★ 1186 ★

Photographic Equipment (SIC 3861)

Top Disposable Camera Brands, 2002

Brands are ranked by sales in millions of dollars for the year ended December 29, 2002. Figures are based on sales at supermarkets, drug stores, discount stores and exclude Wal-Mart.

	($ mil.)	Share
Kodak Max Flash	$ 212.0	30.41%
Kodak Max HQ	94.8	13.60
Fuji Quicksnap Flash	92.9	13.33
Kodak Fun Saver	55.5	7.96
Kodak Max	31.3	4.49
Fuji Quicksnap	23.1	3.31
Kodak Advantix Switchable . . .	14.1	2.02
Kodak Advantix Access	8.8	1.26
Fuji Quicksnap Waterproof	6.6	0.95
Kodak Max Sport	6.3	0.90
Other	151.7	21.76

Source: *MMR*, February 24, 2003, p. 20, from Information Resources Inc.

★ 1187 ★

Photographic Equipment (SIC 3861)

Top Photo Brands in Drug Stores, 2001

Brands are ranked by sales in millions of dollars for the year ended December 30. Figures exclude Wal-Mart.

	($ mil.)	Share
Kodak Max Flash	$ 114.2	14.02%
Kodak Gold	113.5	13.94
Polaroid 600 Platinum	86.1	10.57
Kodak Advantix	67.2	8.25

	($ mil.)	Share
Kodak Gold Max	$ 66.2	8.13%
Fuji Super HQ	26.6	3.27
Kodak Max	25.9	3.18
Fuji Quicksnap Flash	25.1	3.08
Other	289.5	35.55

Source: *Drug Store News*, May 20, 2002, p. 54, from Information Resources Inc.

★ 1188 ★

Aquatic Timing Equipment (SIC 3873)

Aquatic Timing and Scoring Industry

Market shares are shown in percent.

Colorado Time Systems	80.0%
Other	20.0

Source: "Sponsors." available January 7, 2003 from http://www.usdiving.org.

SIC 39 - Miscellaneous Manufacturing Industries

★ 1189 ★

Jewelry (SIC 3911)

Jewelry Industry Sales

| Diamond jewelry |
| Karat gold jewelry |
| Watches |
| Other |

Diamond jewelry sales grew from 2000 to 2001, while other categories are declining.

Diamond jewelry	29.6%
Karat gold jewelry	17.8
Watches	8.8
Other	53.8

Source: *JCK's High-Volume Retailer*, November 2002, p. 9, from Unity Marketing.

★ 1190 ★

Jewelry (SIC 3911)

Retail Jewelry Sales, 2001

Jewelry sales were at $40.6 billion in 2001. They fell for the second straight year. The industry is expected to recover in 2002.

Diamond jewelry	32.4%
Loose diamonds	15.1
Karat gold	11.1
Colored stones	9.3
Repairs	8.6
Watches	4.7
Tabletop gifts/silver	2.3
Cultured pearls	2.0
Estate jewelry	2.0
Other	12.5

Source: *National Jeweler*, September 1, 2002, p. 50, from Jewelers of America.

★ 1191 ★

Jewelry (SIC 3911)

Top Markets for Jewelry and Watches, 2002

Sales are shown in millions of dollars.

	($mil.)	Share
New York City, NY	$ 2,300	4.41%
Chicago, IL	2,000	3.84
Los Angeles, CA	1,800	3.45
Boston, MA	1,600	3.07
Washington D.C.	1,500	2.88
Philadelphia, PA	1,100	2.11
Atlanta, GA	979	1.88
Detroit, MI	970	1.86
Houston, TX	922	1.77
Dallas, TX	869	1.67
Other	38,060	73.05

Source: *Research Alert*, April 18, 2003, p. 5, from Claritas, U.S. Bureau of Labor Statistics, and JCK International Publishing Group.

★ 1192 ★

Flatware (SIC 3914)

Tabletop Sales, 2001-02

Sales are shown in millions of dollars.

	2001	2002	Share
Glassware	$ 1,160.0	$ 1,200.0	25.86%
Houseware dinnerware .	1,080.0	1,080.0	23.28
Upstairs dinnerware . .	818.2	794.5	17.12
Crystal	724.6	710.9	15.32
Stainless-steel flatware .	683.8	680.0	14.66
Sterling-silver flatware .	131.4	125.5	2.70

Source: *HFN*, March 17, 2003, p. 32, from *HFN's State of the Industry Report*.

★ 1193 ★
Musical Instruments & Supplies (SIC 3931)

Cymbal Market, 2002

The company sells more than 500,000 cymbals a year.

Zildjian	65.0%
Other	35.0

Source: *Los Angeles Times*, May 12, 2003, p. C6.

★ 1194 ★
Musical Instruments & Supplies (SIC 3931)

Electronic Music Market, 2002

Figures are in millions of dollars.

Keyboard synthesizers	$ 103.94
Electronic pianos/professional organs	68.20
Electronic drums	40.30
Sound modules	18.05
Drum machines	10.98
Controller keyboards	8.99
Rack-mounted samplers	8.39
Sequencers	1.75

Source: *Music Trades*, April 2003, p. 112, from U.S. Department of Commerce, industry reports and associations.

★ 1195 ★
Musical Instruments & Supplies (SIC 3931)

Largest Musical Product Suppliers, 2002

Companies are ranked by estimated revenues in millions of dollars.

Yamaha Corporation of America	$ 693.76
Harman Intl.	424.70
Steinway Musical Instruments	332.20
Shure Corporation	267.50
Fender Musical Instruments	244.10
Telex Communications	218.90
Roland Corp.	200.00
Peavey Electronics	190.00

Mackie Designs	$ 187.40
Digidesign	136.00
Gibson Guitar	135.00
Kaman Music Corp.	127.70

Source: *Music Trades*, April 2003, p. 112, from U.S. Department of Commerce, industry reports and associations.

★ 1196 ★
Musical Instruments & Supplies (SIC 3931)

Musical Instruments and Product Market, 2002

Figures are in millions of dollars.

Fretted instruments	$ 921.0
Sound reinforcement	850.6
Acoustic pianos	693.0
School music products	571.8
Printed music	497.0
Percussion	475.3
Microphones	369.1
Instrument amplifiers	359.0
Electronic music products	260.7
Signal processing	213.6

Source: *Music Trades*, April 2003, p. 112, from U.S. Department of Commerce, industry reports and associations.

★ 1197 ★
Musical Instruments & Supplies (SIC 3931)

Piano Market in Concert Halls

Market shares are shown in percent.

Steinway	95.0%
Other	5.0

Source: *Fortune*, March 17, 2003, p. 96.

★ 1198 ★
Musical Instruments & Supplies (SIC 3931)

School Music Market, 2002

Figures show unit sales.

Clarinets	138,955
Violins/violas/cellos	124,950
Trumpets	117,177
Flutes	112,155
Alto saxs	55,732

Continued on next page.

★ **1198** ★ *Continued*
Musical Instruments & Supplies (SIC 3931)

School Music Market, 2002

Figures show unit sales.

Trombones	55,100
Euphoniums	19,776
Tenor saxs	11,995
French horns	11,055
Coronets	3,887

Source: *Music Trades*, April 2003, p. 112, from U.S. Department of Commerce, industry reports and associations.

★ **1199** ★
Musical Instruments & Supplies (SIC 3931)

Trombone Market

The companies Conn and Selmer recently merged and one company exec claimed this share of the market.

Conn-Selmer	91.0%
Other	9.0

Source: "Trombone Digest." available April 9, 2003 from http://www.trombone.org.

★ **1200** ★
Toys and Games (SIC 3944)

Largest Toy Makers

No other company has more than 2% of the market.

Mattel/Hasbro	34.0%
Other	66.0

Source: *The Cincinnati Post*, December 20, 2002, p. B10.

★ **1201** ★
Toys and Games (SIC 3944)

Preschool Electronic Toy Market, 2002

Market shares are shown in percent. The company has 3.7% of the entire toy market.

LeapFrog	78.8%
Other	21.2

Source: *Electronic Education Report*, February 28, 2003, p. NA, from NPD.

★ **1202** ★
Toys and Games (SIC 3944)

Retail Toy Sales, 2002

Spending is estimated in millions of dollars. Video games are not included and would represent another $10 billion.

	($ mil.)	Share
Infant/preschool	$ 2,807	15.43%
Dolls	2,429	13.36
Arts and crafts	2,183	12.00
Vehicles	2,101	11.55
Plush	1,555	8.55
Action figures and accessories . .	1,258	6.92
Sports toys	987	5.43
Building sets	751	4.13
Ride-ons	566	3.11
Pretend play	554	3.05
Learning and exploration	371	2.04
Trading cards	285	1.57
Models/accessories	253	1.39
Other	2,086	11.47

Source: *Research Alert*, March 7, 2003, p. 7, from NPD Group and Toy Industry Association.

★ **1203** ★
Toys and Games (SIC 3944)

Top Role Playing Game Firms, 2003

Market shares are shown for February 2003.

Wizards of the Coast	42.38%
White Wolf	28.17
Fantasy Flight	7.48
Decipher	3.96
Kenzer	3.60
Palladium	3.55
Alderac	3.51
Steve Jackson	1.68
Mongoose	1.54
Other	7.73

Source: "Top Ten Lists." available April 7, 2003 from http://www.hubhobbyshop.com.

★ 1204 ★
Toys and Games (SIC 3944)

Top Trading Card Game Firms, 2003

Market shares are shown for February 2003.

Wizards of the Coast	37.30%
Upper Deck	33.37
Decipher	19.26
Score	7.25
White Wolf	0.92
Sabretooth	0.62
Interactive Imagination	0.51
Alderac	0.44
Comic Images	0.20
Other	0.13

Source: "Top Ten Lists." available April 7, 2003 from http://www.hubhobbyshop.com.

★ 1205 ★
Toys and Games (SIC 3944)

Toy Car and Action Figure Market in Mexico

Mattel has more than 50% of the market.

Mattel	50.0%
Other	50.0

Source: *South American Business Information*, May 26, 2003, p. NA.

★ 1206 ★
Toys and Games (SIC 3944)

Toy Train Market

The market for wooden trains is thought to be about $200 million annually. Thomas the Tank Engine is manufactured by The Learning Curve.

Thomas the Tank Engine	70.0%
Other	30.0

Source: *Crain's Chicago Business*, April 7, 2003, p. 3.

★ 1207 ★
Video Game Consoles (SIC 3944)

Top Video Game Console Makers in Canada

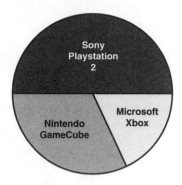

Market shares are estimated in percent. Playstation's share is between 48-50%.

Sony Playstation 2	50.0%
Nintendo GameCube	32.0
Microsoft Xbox	18.0

Source: *Marketing Magazine*, October 14, 2002, p. 2, from Nintendo of Canada.

★ 1208 ★
Video Game Consoles (SIC 3944)

Video Game Consoles and the Internet

Online gaming is seen as the newest wave in the video game industry. Figures show the millions of consoles projected to be connected to the Internet.

2007	16.0
2006	12.1
2005	8.2
2004	5.0
2003	2.1

Source: *USA TODAY*, April 15, 2003, p. 3B, from Jupiter Research.

★ 1209 ★
Video Game Consoles (SIC 3944)

Video Game Hardware Market, 2002

Sony claims 21.5 million games in North America (50.3 million worldwide), and Microsoft saw 5.4 million Xboxes sold (8.0 million worldwide). Market shares are shown in percent.

Sony PlayStation 2	60.0%
Microsoft Xbox	23.0
Nintendo Gamecube	17.0

Source: *Knight Ridder/Tribune Business News*, January 24, 2003, p. NA, from NPD Funworld.

★ 1210 ★
Video Games (SIC 3944)

Best-Selling Video Games, 1995-2002

Data show units sold, in millions, from 1995 through September 2002.

Super Mario 64	5.9
Pokemon Yellow	5.1
GoldenEye007	5.0
Pokemon Blue	5.0
Mario Kart 64	4.8
Pokemon Red	4.8
Grand Theft Auto III	4.2
Pokemon Silver	3.9
Pokemon Gold	3.8
Zelda: Ocarina of Time	3.5

Source: *USA TODAY*, October 30, 2002, p. 4D, from NPD Funworld TRSTS service.

★ 1211 ★
Video Games (SIC 3944)

Football Video Game Market

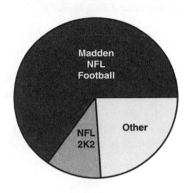

Market shares are shown in percent. Madden NFL Football leads across seven game platforms and is manufactured by Electronic Arts.

Madden NFL Football	65.0%
NFL 2K2	11.0
Other	24.0

Source: *Knight-Ridder/Tribune Business News*, August 19, 2002, p. NA, from SoundView Technology Group.

★ 1212 ★
Video Games (SIC 3944)

Mobile Game Revenues in North America

Figures show estimated millions of revenues of the market for playing games on mobile devices. The global market may hit $4.4 billion by 2006.

	2001	2002	2006
Social gamers	$ 0.98	$ 3.62	$ 228.98
Casual gamers	0.06	0.74	217.39
Dedicated gamers	2.67	8.03	151.74

Source: *Games Analyst*, April 19, 2002, p. 5, from Ovum.

★ 1213 ★
Video Games (SIC 3944)

PC Game Sales, 2002

Market shares are shown based on genre.

Strategy	27.4%
Children's	15.9

Continued on next page.

★ 1213 ★ *Continued*

Video Games (SIC 3944)

PC Game Sales, 2002

Market shares are shown based on genre.

Shooter	11.5%
Family entertainment	9.6
Role-playing	8.0
Sports	6.3
Racing	4.4
Other	16.9

Source: *Investor's Business Daily*, May 16, 2003, p. A4, from Interactive Digital Software Association.

★ 1214 ★

Video Games (SIC 3944)

Top Video Game Brands, 2001

Titles are ranked by sales in millions of dollars.

Tony Hawk	$ 216.9
Mario	206.8
Pokemon	197.3
Madden NFL	196.9
GTA	106.1
The Sims	104.6
Harry Potter	79.2
Final Fantasy	78.8
Gran Turismo	77.2
NBA Live	77.2

Source: *Games Analyst*, November 1, 2002, p. 5, from NPD.

★ 1215 ★

Video Games (SIC 3944)

Top Video Game Publishers, 2001

Market shares are shown in percent.

Electronic Arts	16.0%
Nintendo	15.6
ActiVision	8.0
Sony	7.8
THQ	6.2
Take-Two	4.5
Konami of America	3.8
Infogrames	3.5
Sega of America	3.5
Acclaim	3.3
Capcom USA	2.7

Namco	2.7%
Other	23.4

Source: *Screen Digest*, August 2002, p. 254, from NPD Group.

★ 1216 ★

Video Games (SIC 3944)

Top Video Game Publishers, 2002

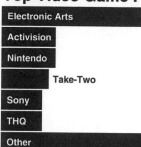

Market shares are shown in percent. Grand Theft Auto 3 was the top seller on Playstation 2; Halo was the top seller on XBox; Super Mario Sunshine was tops on Gamecube and WarCraft III on the PC.

Electronic Arts	20.8%
Activision	8.3
Nintendo	7.7
Take-Two	7.2
Sony	6.4
THQ	6.3
Other	43.2

Source: *Business 2.0*, December 2002/January 2003, p. 112, from NPD Techworld and NPD Funworld.

★ 1217 ★

Video Games (SIC 3944)

Top Video Game Rentals, 2002

An estimated 39% of TV households own a video game console. $721.6 million was spent on renting video games for the year. Titles are ranked by revenues in millions of dollars.

Grand Theft Auto III	$ 11.57
Spider-Man: The Movie	9.46
Grand Theft Auto: Vice City	9.09
Medal of Honor Frontline	8.39
Stuntman	7.40
Max Payne	6.65
State of Emergency	5.95
Madden NFL 2003	5.74

Continued on next page.

★ 1217 ★ *Continued*
Video Games (SIC 3944)

Top Video Game Rentals, 2002

An estimated 39% of TV households own a video game console. $721.6 million was spent on renting video games for the year. Titles are ranked by revenues in millions of dollars.

007 Agent Under Fire	.$ 5.22
Test Drive	4.49

Source: *Video Business*, January 27, 2003, p. 26, from Video Software Dealers Association VidTrac.

★ 1218 ★
Video Games (SIC 3944)

Video Game Players by Age, 2002

Figures are based on a survey of 1,500 households. Of the top 10 games in 2001, 2 were rated mature, 3 teen and 5 for everyone.

18 and under	45.0%
18 to 35	36.0
36 and up	19.0

Source: *Wall Street Journal*, October 14, 2002, p. B1, from Interactive Digital Software Association, NPD Funworld, and Entertainment Software Ratings Board.

★ 1219 ★
Video Games (SIC 3944)

Video Game Rental Market, 2002

Market shares are shown in percent.

Infogrames	17.6%
Midway	8.8
THQ	7.7
Acclaim	5.9
Take Two	5.8
Nintendo	4.8
Activision	4.8
Electronic Arts	4.5
Other	40.1

Source: *Video Business*, January 27, 2003, p. 26, from Video Software Dealers Association VidTrac.

★ 1220 ★
Video Games (SIC 3944)

Video Game Sales by Genre, 2002

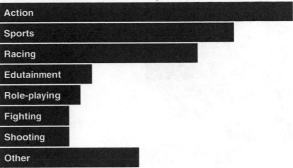

Market shares are shown based on genre.

Action	25.1%
Sports	19.5
Racing	16.6
Edutainment	7.6
Role-playing	7.4
Fighting	6.4
Shooting	5.5
Other	11.9

Source: *Investor's Business Daily*, May 16, 2003, p. A4, from Interactive Digital Software Association.

★ 1221 ★
Sporting Goods (SIC 3949)

Basketball Market Shares

Spalding has more than half the market.

Spalding	50.0%
Other	50.0

Source: *Brandweek*, January 27, 2003, p. 9.

★ 1222 ★
Sporting Goods (SIC 3949)

Best-Selling Sporting Equipment, 2001

Spending is shown in billions of dollars.

	($ mil.)	Share
Exercise equipment machines . . .	$ 3.61	25.30%
Golf	2.59	18.15
Firearms/hunting	1.80	12.61
Camping	1.69	11.84
Team/institutional	1.54	10.79
Fishing	1.00	7.01
Other	2.04	14.30

Source: "U.S. Sports Products Sales Show Slight Dip." available from http://www.sgma.com, from Sporting Goods Manufacturers Association.

★ 1223 ★
Sporting Goods (SIC 3949)

Bicycle Helmet Market

Market shares are shown in percent.

Bell	69.0%
Other	31.0

Source: *Bicycle Retailer and Industry News*, August 15, 2002, p. 24.

★ 1224 ★
Sporting Goods (SIC 3949)

Children's Snow Shoe Market

Market shares are shown in percent.

Little Bear Snowshoes	90.0%
Other	10.0

Source: *ColoradoBiz*, December 2002, p. 45.

★ 1225 ★
Sporting Goods (SIC 3949)

Golf Glove Market

Market shares are shown based on unit sales.

FootJoy	50.0%
Other	50.0

Source: *Golf World*, March 28, 2003, p. S1, from Golf Datatech.

★ 1226 ★
Sporting Goods (SIC 3949)

NFL Helmet Market

Market shares are shown in percent. Riddell has just under half of the collegiate market and less than that of the high school and youth markets.

Riddell	85.0%
Other	15.0

Source: *Crain's Chicago Business*, August 5, 2002, p. 4, from Sporting Goods Manufacturers Association.

★ 1227 ★
Sporting Goods (SIC 3949)

Putter Market Shares

Market shares are shown in percent.

Callaway Golf's Odyssey	48.7%
Other	51.3

Source: *Canadian Corporate News*, March 7, 2003, p. NA, from Golf Datatech.

★ 1228 ★
Sporting Goods (SIC 3949)

Sporting Goods Industry, 2002

Figures are in billions of dollars.

	($ bil.)	Share
Sports apparel	$ 21.8	44.40%
Sporting goods equipment	17.8	36.25
Athletic footwear	9.5	19.35

Source: "U.S. Sporting Goods Industry." available April 10, 2003 from http://www.sgma.com, from Sporting Goods Manufacturers Association.

★ 1229 ★
Sporting Goods (SIC 3949)
Wooden Bat Market

The company has 60% of the Major League market and 80% of the minor leagues.

Hillerich & Bradsby	80.0%
Other	20.0

Source: *Forbes*, April 14, 2003, p. 220.

★ 1230 ★
Markers (SIC 3953)
Permanent Marker Market

Shares are estimated.

Sharpie	50.0%
Other	50.0

Source: *PR Newswire*, July 24, 2002, p. NA, from A.C. Nielsen.

★ 1231 ★
Toothbrushes (SIC 3991)
Electric Toothbrush Market

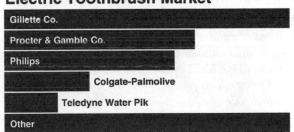

Sales hit $417.7 million for the year ended August 11, 2002. Data do not include Wal-Mart. Gillette makes Braun and Oral B.

Gillette Co.	26.5%
Procter & Gamble Co.	18.3
Philips	15.6
Colgate-Palmolive	7.7
Teledyne Water Pik	4.7
Other	27.2

Source: *Advertising Age*, September 9, 2002, p. 3, from Information Resources Inc.

★ 1232 ★
Toothbrushes (SIC 3991)
Toothbrush Sales by Type

Figures are in millions of dollars. Figures refer to food and drug stores but exclude Wal-Mart.

	1999	2001
Manual	$ 545	$ 477
Power	151	316

Source: *Retail Merchandiser*, March 2003, p. 28, from Information Resources Inc.

★ 1233 ★
Toothbrushes (SIC 3991)
Top Toothbrush Vendors, 2002

The $3.6 billion industry is shown for the year ended April 21, 2002.

Oral-B	27.8%
Colgate Oral	21.8
Johnson & Johnson	13.1
Procter & Gamble	9.0
Unilever	5.9
GlaxoSmithKline	4.4
John O. Butler	3.9
Zooth	2.1
Radius	0.4
Other	11.6

Source: *Grocery Headquarters*, July 2002, p. 48, from Information Resources Inc.

★ 1234 ★
Signs (SIC 3993)
Sign Industry

Figures show the preferred types of electric signs, based on a survey conducted by the source. Neon represents roughly 30% of overall sign sales. Channel letters represent the largest share of neon signs, although the figure dropped from 64% to 58%. The average electric sign company sells $631,710.

	2000	2001
Neon	57.0%	41.0%
Fluroescent	41.0	47.0

Source: "Neon Sign Industry Survey." available April 15, 2003 from http://www.signweb.com, from *Neon Sign Industry Survey, 2001*.

★ 1235 ★
Caskets (SIC 3995)
Casket Market in North America

Market shares are shown based on a $1.5 billion wholesale market.

Batesville 64.0%
Other 36.0

Source: *Canadian Business*, October 28, 2002, p. 50.

★ 1236 ★
Flooring (SIC 3996)
Laminate Flooring Brands

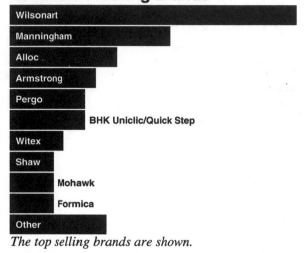

The top selling brands are shown.

Wilsonart 27.0%
Manningham 15.0
Alloc 10.0
Armstrong 8.0
Pergo 7.0
BHK Uniclic/Quick Step 7.0
Witex 5.0
Shaw 4.0
Mohawk 4.0
Formica 4.0
Other 9.0

Source: *National Floor Trends*, August 2002, p. 18, from *2002 National Floor Trends Laminate Flooring Market Study*.

★ 1237 ★
Flooring (SIC 3996)
Linoleum Sales in North America

The share has been estimated at 85-90%.

Forbo 90.0%
Other 10.0

Source: *Knight Ridder/Tribune Business News*, February 2, 2003, p. NA.

★ 1238 ★
Artificial Turf (SIC 3999)
Artificial Turf Market

Market shares are estimated in percent.

Field Turf/SRI Sports 80.0%
Other 20.0

Source: *Crain's Detroit Business*, April 14, 2003, p. 3, from General Sports Turf.

★ 1239 ★
Baby Products (SIC 3999)
Largest Infant Gear Producers

Firms are ranked by estimated infant gear sales in millions of dollars. Safety and convenience are the chief desired features of shoppers in this industry (a segment of the $5.75 billion juvenile products industry). Graco makes products under the Little Tikes/ Graco division.

Graco Children's Products . . . . $ 375
Dorel Juvenile Group 300
Evenflo 200

Source: *Home Textiles Today*, February 10, 2003, p. S6, from Juvenile Products Manufacturers Association.

★ 1240 ★

Baby Products (SIC 3999)

Top Nursing/Feeding Accessory Brands, 2002

Playtex
Gerber
Playtex Drop Ins
Avent
Johnson's Healthflow
Playtex Spill Proof
Evenflo Sensitive Response
Luv 'n Care
Munchkin
First Years
Private label
Other

Brands are ranked by sales in millions of dollars for the year ended February 24, 2002. Figures include supermarkets, drug stores and discount stores but exclude Wal-Mart.

	($ mil.)	Share
Playtex	$ 40.2	12.65%
Gerber	32.5	10.22
Playtex Drop Ins	21.6	6.79
Avent	16.8	5.28
Johnson's Healthflow	15.3	4.81
Playtex Spill Proof	12.2	3.84
Evenflo Sensitive Response . . .	9.3	2.93
Luv 'n Care	8.5	2.67
Munchkin	8.5	2.67
First Years	8.5	2.67
Private label	10.2	3.21
Other	134.3	42.25

Source: *MMR*, April 22, 2002, p. 57, from Information Resources Inc.

★ 1241 ★

Baby Products (SIC 3999)

Top Safety Accessory Brands, 2002

Brands are ranked by sales in millions of dollars for the year ended February 24, 2002. Figures include supermarkets, drug stores and discount stores but exclude Wal-Mart.

	($ mil.)	Share
Safety 1st	$ 37.9	12.50%
Cosco	37.2	12.27
Century	25.2	8.31
First Years	18.9	6.23
Playtex Diaper Genie	17.4	5.74
Graco	14.0	4.62
Gerry	13.8	4.55
Evenflo	13.0	4.29
Fisher Price	7.7	2.54
Kids	7.3	2.41
Private label	5.9	1.95
Other	104.9	34.60

Source: *MMR*, April 22, 2002, p. 57, from Information Resources Inc.

★ 1242 ★

Candles (SIC 3999)

Top Candle Producers

Market shares are shown in percent.

Candle-lite	19.2%
S.C. Johnson & Son	12.6
American Greetings	6.1
Lancaster Colony	4.3
Dial	3.9
Reed Candle	3.0
Signature Brands	2.8
Yankee Candle	2.4
Other	45.7

Source: *Chain Drug Review*, September 2, 2002, p. 30, from Information Resources Inc.

★ 1243 ★

Candles (SIC 3999)

Top Scented Candle Brands, 2002

Brands are ranked by sales in millions of dollars for the year ended April 21, 2002. Figures exclude Wal-Mart.

	($ mil.)	Share
Glade Candle Scents	$ 88.6	12.84%
Candle Lite	45.7	6.62
Fragrance De Lite	37.0	5.36
Gildhouse	35.5	5.14
Colony	35.0	5.07
Reeds	19.8	2.87
Mood Makers	19.2	2.78
Renuzit Longlast Aromaessence	15.5	2.25
Martha Stewart	15.0	2.17
Other	378.8	54.89

Source: *MMR*, July 29, 2002, p. 45, from Information Resources Inc.

★ 1244 ★

Coinless Tickets (SIC 3999)

Coinless Ticket Market, 2002

Coinless slot machines use a bar-coded coupon or slot ticket as a payout of proceeds. According to the source, "the secure and coded ticket can either be cashed or inserted into another machine's bill acceptor crediting the same value."

LaserLock	90.0%
Other	10.0

Source: "Laserlock Signs Agreement." available January 7, 2003 from http://www.immedia.it.

★ 1245 ★

Fire Logs (SIC 3999)

Leading Firelog/Firestarter Brands, 2002

Market shares are shown in percent for the year ended April 21, 2002.

Duraflame	26.8%
Pine Mountain	12.7
Duraflame Crackleframe	5.1
Chimney Sweep Log	3.1
Duraflame Colorlog	2.8
Pine Mountain Cracklelog	2.7%
Quick Start	1.9
Gold Arrow	1.5
Private label	27.7
Other	15.7

Source: *Grocery Headquarters*, July 2002, p. 50, from Information Resources Inc.

★ 1246 ★

Flashlights (SIC 3999)

Top Flashlight Brands, 2002

Brands are ranked by sales in millions of dollars for the year ended May 19, 2002. Figures exclude Wal-Mart.

	($ mil.)	Share
Mag Light	$ 8.9	10.65%
Mini Mag Lite	8.1	9.69
Energizer	7.0	8.37
Coleman	6.5	7.78
Eveready	5.3	6.34
Garrity	3.5	4.19
Eveready Bright Light	2.4	2.87
Ray O Vac Prodigy	2.3	2.75
Other	39.6	47.37

Source: *MMR*, July 29, 2002, p. 45, from Information Resources Inc.

★ 1247 ★

Hair Accessories (SIC 3999)

Top Hair Accessory Brands, 2002

Brands are ranked by sales in millions of dollars for the year ended May 19, 2002. Figures exclude Wal-Mart.

	($ mil.)	Share
Scunci	$90.2	22.59%
Goody	57.8	14.48
Cosmopolitan	26.0	6.51
Scunci No Damage	16.1	4.03
Seventeen	15.4	3.86
Ace	10.9	2.73
Conair	9.2	2.30
Karina	8.5	2.13
Vidal Sassoon	7.9	1.98
Scunci Kids	7.8	1.95
Other	149.5	37.44

Source: *MMR*, July 29, 2002, p. 42, from Information Resources Inc.

★ 1248 ★

Pet Products (SIC 3999)

Top Dog/Cat Product Makers, 2002

Market shares are shown for the year ended November 3, 2002. Figures refer to supermarkets and drug stores.

Hartz Mountain Corp.	52.5%
Sergeant's Pet Products	5.6
Ethical Products	3.4
Van Ness Plastics	3.0
Clorox	2.5
Doskocil Mfg. Co.	2.1
Combe Inc.	2.0
Aspen Pet	1.8
Other	27.1

Source: *Grocery Headquarters*, February 2003, p. 72, from Information Resources Inc.

★ 1249 ★

Pet Products (SIC 3999)

Top Rawhide Dog Chew Makers, 2002

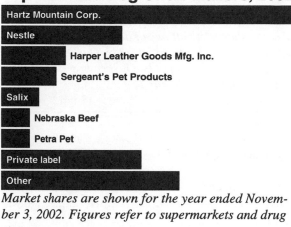

Market shares are shown for the year ended November 3, 2002. Figures refer to supermarkets and drug stores.

Hartz Mountain Corp.	30.6%
Nestle	13.0
Harper Leather Goods Mfg. Inc.	7.3
Sergeant's Pet Products	5.6
Salix	4.4
Nebraska Beef	2.9
Petra Pet	2.5
Private label	14.7
Other	19.0

Source: *Grocery Headquarters*, February 2003, p. 72, from Information Resources Inc.

★ 1250 ★

Swimming Pools (SIC 3999)

Inground Pool Market

Market shares are shown by region.

Southeast	28.0%
Southwest	25.0
South Central	20.0
Northeast	15.0
East Central	6.0
West Central	4.0
Northwest	2.0

Source: *Pool & Spa Marketing*, Annual 2002, p. 19, from National Swimming Pool Institute.

★ 1251 ★

Swimming Pools (SIC 3999)

Swimming Pool Market in Canada, 2001

Sales are shown in millions of dollars. Ontario has 65% of inground pools, followed by Quebec with 27%. In above-ground pools, Quebec has 79% of all such pools and Ontario has 15%.

	($ mil.)	Share
Inground pools	$ 183.3	21.80%
Chemicals	155.8	18.53
Replacement equipment & products	65.0	7.73
Service contracts	63.0	7.49
Above-ground pools	58.2	6.92
Accessories	55.0	6.54
Gas/oil heaters	13.5	1.61
Heat pumps	3.0	0.36
Solar heaters	2.5	0.30
Other	241.5	28.72

Source: *Pool & Spa Marketing*, Spring 2002, p. 32, from Statistics Canada and national building permit data.

★ 1252 ★

Umbrellas (SIC 3999)

Umbrella Market, 2002

Market shares are shown for department stores. The company claims that 75% of its purchases are as gifts.

Totes	90.0%
Other	10.0

Source: *New York Times*, November 22, 2002, p. C6.

SIC 40 - Railroad Transportation

★ 1253 ★
Railroads (SIC 4011)

Leading Intermodal Railroads

Market shares are shown based on revenues.

BNI	29.0%
CP	22.0
UNP	18.0
NSC	18.0
CNI	16.0
CSX	15.0

Source: *Transportation & Distribution*, January 2003, p. 64, from Morgan Stanley.

★ 1254 ★
Railroads (SIC 4011)

Rail Traffic, 2002

Figures show the number of carloads for the 46 weeks ended November 16, 2002.

	No.	Share
Coal	138,185	44.34%
Agricultural products	44,414	14.25
Nonmetallic min. & prod.	36,095	11.58
Chemicals	35,492	11.39
Motor vehicles & equipment . . .	24,986	8.02
Forest products	18,042	5.79
Other	14,432	4.63

Source: *Railway Age*, December 2002, p. 1, from American Railway Car Institute Committee and Railway Progress Institute.

★ 1255 ★
Railroads (SIC 4011)

Railroad Market Shares, 2002

Shares are shown for the 52 weeks ended December 28, 2002.

UNP	34.4%
BNSF	30.8
CSX	26.6
NSC	25.3

Source: ''2002 Summary Report.'' available from http://www.railmatch.com, from *Railfax Carloading Report*.

SIC 41 - Local and Interurban Passenger Transit

★ 1256 ★
Mass Transit (SIC 4111)

Boston-New York Air/Rail Market

Amtrak claims 40% of this market, larger than any single airline.

Amtrak	40.0%
Other	60.0

Source: *Railway Age*, March 2003, p. G4, from Amtrak.

★ 1257 ★
Mass Transit (SIC 4111)

Commuter Traffic from New York to D.C.

Amtrak's share of this market is shown in percent. As of September 30, 2001 it also had 53% of the New York-Washington commuting market through its Acela Express service.

Amtrak	65.0%
Other	35.0

Source: *Crain's New York Business*, September 16, 2002, p. 29.

★ 1258 ★
Mass Transit (SIC 4111)

Largest Rail Systems, 2001

Agencies are ranked by value of cost of projects, in millions.

MTA New York City Transit	9,200
MTA Long Island Rail Road	2,747
Washington Metropolitan Area Transit Authority	2,433
New York Transit Corp.	2,410
Amtrak	2,400
Dallas Area Rapid Transit	2,248
Southeastern Pennsylvania Transportation Authority	2,000
Metropolitan Atlanta Rapid Transit Authority	1,820

Source: *Metro Magazine*, Annual Fact Book, p. NA.

★ 1259 ★
Luxury Transportation (SIC 4119)

Largest Luxury Transportation Operators in North America

Companies are ranked by size of fleet.

Carey New York	524
Mears Transporation Group	472
Empire International	390
Bell Transportation	376
Carey Chicago	297

Continued on next page.

294

★ 1259 ★ *Continued*
Luxury Transportation (SIC 4119)

Largest Luxury Transportation Operators in North America

Companies are ranked by size of fleet.

Dave El	258
BostonCoach	257
A-1 Limousine	240
Boston Coach (Boston)	226
Connecticut Limousine	190

Source: *Limousine & Chauffered Transportation*, July 2002, p. 46, from survey of companies.

★ 1260 ★
Taxi Industry (SIC 4121)

Taxi Industry in Pennsylvania

Market shares are shown in percent. The region covers Harrisburg, Carlisle, York and Gettysburg.

Yellow Cab	80.0%
Other	20.0

Source: *Knight Ridder/Tribune Business News*, March 13, 2003, p. NA.

★ 1261 ★
Buses (SIC 4131)

Intercity Bus Transportation

Market shares are estimated in percent.

Greyhound	60.0%
Other	40.0

Source: *Knight Ridder/Tribune Business News*, December 11, 2002, p. NA.

★ 1262 ★
Buses (SIC 4131)

Largest Bus Fleets in North America, 2002

Contractors are ranked by size of fleet. Laidlaw Education Services remains in the top spot with a 5% increase in its fleet size. Laidlaw is now nearly three times as large as the number two company.

Laidlaw Education Services	42,790
First Student Inc.	15,000
National Express Corp.	8,649
Atlantic Express Corp.	6,998
Stock Transportation	2,210
Student Transportation of America	2,163
Cardinal Coach Lines	1,450
Cook-Illinois Corp.	1,200
Baumann and Sons	1,030
WE Transport Inc.	927

Source: *School Bus Fleet*, June/July 2002, p. NA, from *School Bus Fleet's Top 50 Contractor Survey*.

SIC 42 - Trucking and Warehousing

★ 1263 ★
Trucking (SIC 4210)
Top Refrigerated Trucking Firms

Firms are ranked by revenues in millions of dollars.

C R England Inc.	$ 438.6
Prime Inc.	396.4
Frozen Food Express Industries	392.3
Rocor International	269.9
Marten Transport	260.7
KLLM Inc.	234.2
Dick Simon Trucking Inc.	231.4
Stevens Transport Inc.	219.5
Grojean Transportation	175.9
Midwest Coast Transport	126.0

Source: *Refrigerated Transporter*, September 2002, p. 18.

★ 1264 ★
Trucking (SIC 4210)
Top Trucking Firms

Firms are ranked by revenues in billions of dollars.

United Parcel	$ 20.30
FedEx Ground	2.71
Roadway Express	2.64
Yellow Freight	2.46
Schneider National	2.38
Sirva Inc.	2.24
J.B. Hunt Transport	2.10
Consolidated Freightways	2.05
FedEx Freight	1.96

Source: *Commercial Carrier Journal*, August 2002, p. 36.

★ 1265 ★
Express Delivery Services (SIC 4215)
Overnight Ground Delivery Market

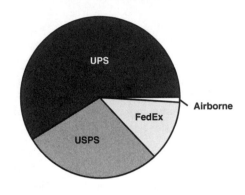

Market shares are shown in percent.

UPS	58.4%
USPS	28.1
FedEx	12.4
Airborne	1.2

Source: *Wall Street Journal*, March 25, 2003, p. B4, from Salomon Smith Barney Inc.

★ 1266 ★
Warehouse Space (SIC 4220)
Warehouse Space in North America, 2002

60% of the firms on the list were managing more warehousing and distribution space. Shares are shown based on the 810.7 million square feet managed by the top 50 firms. Figures are in millions of square feet.

	(mil.)	Share
Defense Logistics Agency	74.3	9.16%
United Parcel Service	70.4	8.68
Wal-Mart Stores	62.0	7.65
Excel	46.7	5.76
General Motors	32.0	3.95

Continued on next page.

★ 1266 ★ *Continued*

Warehouse Space (SIC 4220)

Warehouse Space in North America, 2002

60% of the firms on the list were managing more warehousing and distribution space. Shares are shown based on the 810.7 million square feet managed by the top 50 firms. Figures are in millions of square feet.

	(mil.)	Share
Fleming Co.	32.0	3.95%
APL Logistics	23.0	2.84
Tibbett & Britten Group NA	22.0	2.71
Target	20.0	2.47
Kmart	20.0	2.47
AmeriCold Logistics	19.0	2.34
Sysco	18.2	2.24
Other	371.1	45.78

Source: *Warehousing Management*, October 2002, p. 16.

★ 1267 ★

Warehousing Services (SIC 4225)

Storage Services for Businesses

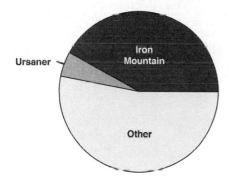

The company primarily retains and manages paper records for companies. It also offers electronic storage services.

Iron Mountain	42.0%
Ursaner	5.0
Other	53.0

Source: *Investor's Business Daily*, March 17, 2003, p. A6.

SIC 43 - U.S. Postal Service

★ 1268 ★
Postal Service (SIC 4311)

Postal Deliveries

Figures show the millions of delivery points for both businesses and homes.

	Residence	Business
City	77.0	7.10
Rural	32.1	1.10
P.O. Box	15.7	4.00
Highway contract	2.0	0.05

Source: "Operating Statistics." available April 22, 2003 from http://www.usps.com, from U.S. Postal Service.

★ 1269 ★
Postal Service (SIC 4311)

Who Sorts Our Mail

The Postal Service sorts 90% of the nation's letters. Future automation will save 2.4 million working hours.

U.S. Postal Service	90.0%
Other	10.0

Source: *Forbes*, September 16, 2002, p. 72.

SIC 44 - Water Transportation

★ 1270 ★
Shipping (SIC 4412)

Domestic Freight Transportation, 2008

Rail intermodal refers to shared container/truck movements.

Trucking	68.2%
Rail	13.4
Pipeline	9.3
Water passage	7.6
Rail intermodal	1.4
Air deliveries	0.2

Source: *Refrigerated Transporter*, February 1, 2003, p. NA, from American Trucking Association and U.S. Freight Transportation Forecast.

★ 1271 ★
Shipping (SIC 4412)

Largest Export Carriers, 2001

Market shares are shown for the the first 8 months of the year. Figures are based on twenty-foot equivalent units.

Maersk Sealand	12.6%
APL	6.8
Evergreen	6.0
Hanjin Shipping	5.7
Cosco	4.6
OOCL	4.3
P&O Nedlloyd	4.3
Hapag-Lloyd	4.0
Hyundai Merchant Marine	3.9
Other	47.8

Source: *Journal of Commerce*, December 9, 2002, p. 32, from U.S. Global Container Report and PIERS.

★ 1272 ★
Shipping (SIC 4412)

Largest Import Carriers, 2001

Market shares are shown for the the first 8 months of the year. Figures are based on twenty-foot equivalent units.

Maersk Sealand	13.3%
Evergreen	7.7
APL	6.6
Hanjin Shipping	6.2
Cosco	5.4
P&O Nedlloyd	4.5
K Line	4.1
NYK Line	4.1
Hyundai Merchant Marine	4.0
OOCL	4.0
Other	40.1

Source: *Journal of Commerce*, December 9, 2002, p. 32, from U.S. Global Container Report and PIERS.

★ 1273 ★
Shipping (SIC 4412)

Largest Import-Export Handlers

Carriers are ranked by volume, in thousands of TEUS (twenty-foot equivalent units).

Maersk Sealand	2,552.9
Evergreen	1,187.3
APL	1,145.9
Hanjin Shipping	1,056.9
Cosco	880.2
P&O Nedlloyd	731.5
Hyundai	711.6
OOCL	686.5
K Line	655.1

Source: *JoC Week*, June 17, 2002, p. 19, from Port Import/Export Reporting Service.

★ 1274 ★

Shipping (SIC 4412)

Shipping Market in Hawaii

Market shares are shown in percent. Nationally, the industry has $1.5 trillion in sales and generates 13 million jobs.

Matson Navigation Co.	70.0%
CSX Lines	30.0

Source: *Hawaii Business*, February 2003, p. 23, from U.S. Department of Transportation Maritime Administration.

★ 1275 ★

Cruise Lines (SIC 4481)

Cruise Line Industry, 2005

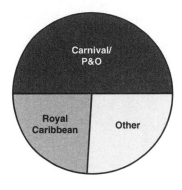

Shares are shown based on a Carnival/P&O merger.

Carnival/P&O	50.0%
Royal Caribbean	24.0
Other	26.0

Source: *Los Angeles Times*, December 13, 2002, p. C14, from Salomon Smith Barney.

★ 1276 ★

Ports (SIC 4491)

Largest Ports

Ports are ranked by volume, in millions of TEUS (twenty-foot equivalent units).

Los Angeles	5.18
Long Beach	4.46
New York & New Jersey	3.32
Oakland	1.64
Charleston, SC	1.53
Tacoma	1.32

Seattle	1.32
Hampton Roads, VA	1.30

Source: *JoC Week*, July 8, 2002, p. 19, from Port Import/Export Reporting Service.

★ 1277 ★

Ports (SIC 4491)

West Coast Tonnage

The top ports are shown by share of total tonnage.

Los Angeles	29.0%
Long Beach, CA	27.0
Tacoma, WA	9.0
Oakland, CA	8.0
Portland, OR	7.0
Seattle, WA	7.0
Other	12.0

Source: *USA TODAY*, July 3, 2002, p. 3B, from Pacific Maritime Association.

★ 1278 ★

Ports (SIC 4491)

Who Gets Imports From Asia

The nation received more than 7.9 million 20-foot containers for the year ended July 2002.

Los Angeles	35.0%
Long Beach, CA	30.0
New York City	8.0
Seattle, WA	6.0
Tacoma, WA	5.0
Savannah, GA	4.0
Oakland, CA	4.0
Other	8.0

Source: *New York Times*, October 1, 2002, p. A22, from *Journal of Commerce's Port Import/Export Reporting Service* and U.S. Bureau of the Census.

SIC 45 - Transportation by Air

★ 1279 ★
Air Routes (SIC 4512)
JFK Airport to Orlando, FL

Market shares are shown in percent.

JetBlue 56.6%
Delta Express 26.8

Source: *USA TODAY*, January 29, 2003, p. 3B, from Unisys R2A Transportation Management Consultants.

★ 1280 ★
Air Routes (SIC 4512)
JFK Airport to Tampa, FL

Market shares are shown in percent.

JetBlue 69.7%
Delta Express 29.4

Source: *USA TODAY*, January 29, 2003, p. 3B, from Unisys R2A Transportation Management Consultants.

★ 1281 ★
Air Routes (SIC 4512)
U.S. and Caribbean Market

Shares are shown for January 2003.

American 45.0%
Continental 10.0
US Airways 10.0
Delta 7.0
Air Jamaica 7.0
Other 21.0

Source: *USA TODAY*, February 4, 2003, p. 5B, from OAG data and Back Aviation Solutions.

★ 1282 ★
Airlines (SIC 4512)
Airline Market in Salt Lake City, NV

The market share of the lead carrier is shown.

Delta 54.0%
Other 46.0

Source: *USA TODAY*, January 21, 2003, p. 3B, from OAG data and Back Aviation Solutions.

★ 1283 ★
Airlines (SIC 4512)
Airline Market in Atlanta, GA

The market share of the lead carrier is shown.

Delta 67.0%
Other 33.0

Source: *USA TODAY*, January 21, 2003, p. 3B, from OAG data and Back Aviation Solutions.

★ 1284 ★
Airlines (SIC 4512)
Airline Market in Charlotte, N.C.

The market share of the dominant carrier is shown for the city.

US Airways 82.0%
Other 18.0

Source: *Rocky Mountain News*, November 30, 2002, p. 5C, from *Aviation Daily*.

★ 1285 ★
Airlines (SIC 4512)

Airline Market in Houston, TX

The market share of the dominant carrier is shown for the city.

Continental 73.0%
Other 27.0

Source: *Rocky Mountain News*, November 30, 2002, p. 5C, from *Aviation Daily*.

★ 1286 ★
Airlines (SIC 4512)

Airline Market in Minneapolis, MN

The market share of the lead carrier is shown.

Northwest 68.0%
Other 32.0

Source: *USA TODAY*, January 21, 2003, p. 3B, from OAG data and Back Aviation Solutions.

★ 1287 ★
Airlines (SIC 4512)

Airline Market in Pittsburgh, PA

The market share of the dominant carrier is shown for the city.

US Airways 73.0%
Other 27.0

Source: *Rocky Mountain News*, November 30, 2002, p. 5C, from *Aviation Daily*.

★ 1288 ★
Airlines (SIC 4512)

Airline Market in San Francisco, CA

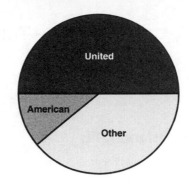

Market shares are shown in percent.

United 50.3%
American 10.5
Other 39.2

Source: *Wall Street Journal*, December 6, 2002, p. B4, from Salomon Smith Barney.

★ 1289 ★
Airlines (SIC 4512)

Leading Airline Groups

Market shares are shown based on total domestic revenue passenger miles.

Delta-Northwest-Continental 35.0%
United-U.S. Airways 23.0
Northwest-Continental 18.0
Other 23.0

Source: *Aviation Week & Space Technology*, January 27, 2003, p. 41, from U.S. Department of Transportation.

★ 1290 ★
Airlines (SIC 4512)

Leading Airlines for Federal Travelers, 2001

Market shares are shown based on sales of $2.3 billion.

United 22.2%
Delta 20.4
U.S. Airways 14.5
American 10.8
Northwest 7.5

Continued on next page.

★ 1290 ★ *Continued*
Airlines (SIC 4512)

Leading Airlines for Federal Travelers, 2001

Market shares are shown based on sales of $2.3 billion.

Continental	5.2%
Trans World Airlines	4.5
Southwest	2.9
Other	12.0

Source: *Government Executive*, August 15, 2002, p. NA, from Eagle Eye Publishers and Federal Procurement Data Center.

★ 1291 ★
Airlines (SIC 4512)

Private Jet Market

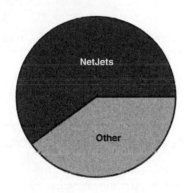

Market shares are shown in percent.

NetJets	60.0%
Other	40.0

Source: *Business Record (Des Moines)*, December 30, 2002, p. 11.

★ 1292 ★
Frequent Flier Programs (SIC 4512)

Frequent Flier Programs, 2001

Data show how people earned points in 2001.

Flying	57.0%
Flight bonuses	13.0
Credit card	11.0
Telephone	7.0
Car rental	3.0
Other	9.0

Source: *New York Times*, December 10, 2002, p. C5, from WebFlyer.com.

★ 1293 ★
Frequent Flier Programs (SIC 4512)

Largest Frequent Flier Programs

Membership is shown in millions.

American	43.0
United	40.0
Delta	29.0
Continental	23.2
US Airways	21.2

Source: *New York Times*, December 10, 2002, p. C5, from WebFlyer.com.

★ 1294 ★
Air Cargo (SIC 4513)

Air Cargo Leaders, 2002

Airlines are ranked by revenues for the first three quarters of the year.

Northwest	$ 504
United	474
American	415
Delta	332
Continental	192
US Airways	104
Southwest	63
Alaska	59
America West	21

Source: *Air Cargo World*, December 2002, p. 7, from company reports.

★ 1295 ★

Air Courier Services (SIC 4513)

Express Delivery Industry, 2002

The market is for domestic and export air and ground delivery.

UPS	43.0%
FedEx	22.0
USPS	19.0
DHL	7.0
Airborne	5.0
Emery	4.0

Source: *World Trade*, November 2002, p. 62, from Colography Group and Armstrong & Associates.

★ 1296 ★

Air Courier Services (SIC 4513)

Leading Air Courier Vendors for the Government, 2001

Market shares are shown based on total purchases of $609.5 million.

Wallenius Wilhelmsen	33.41%
Federal Express Corp.	29.65
Air Transport International	11.47
CNF Transportation	6.56
Lynden Air Cargo	4.04
Other	14.87

Source: *Government Executive*, August 15, 2002, p. NA, from Eagle Eye Publishers and Federal Procurement Data Center.

★ 1297 ★

Air Courier Services (SIC 4513)

Overnight Air Delivery Market

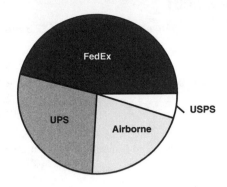

Market shares are shown in percent.

FedEx	45.9%
UPS	28.1
Airborne	20.6
USPS	5.4

Source: *Wall Street Journal*, March 25, 2003, p. B4, from Salomon Smith Barney Inc.

★ 1298 ★

Airports (SIC 4581)

Airline Market at Albany International Airport

Shares are shown for the first nine months.

Southwest	23.1%
US Airways	22.8
Delta	12.2
Other	31.9

Source: *The Business Review - Serving New York's Capital Region*, October 18, 2002, p. NA, from *Aviation Daily*.

★ 1299 ★
Airports (SIC 4581)

Airline Market at Boston International Airport

Market shares are shown in percent.

Delta/Continental/Northwest 27.0%
United/U.S. Airways 25.3
American 22.5
Other 25.2

Source: *Knight Ridder/Tribune Business News*, February 4, 2003, p. NA.

★ 1300 ★
Airports (SIC 4581)

Airline Market at Buffalo Niagara International Airport

Market shares are shown based on enplanements.

US Airways 27.0%
Southwest Airlines 16.0
JetBlue 12.0
Other 45.0

Source: *Knight Ridder/Tribune Business News*, February 7, 2003, p. NA.

★ 1301 ★
Airports (SIC 4581)

Airline Market at Hartsfield International Airport, 2002

Airlines shares of the Georgia hub are shown for the first seven months of the year.

Delta 71.0%
AirTran 11.0
Other 18.0

Source: *Atlanta Journal-Constitution*, September 19, 2002, p. G1, from airport statistics.

★ 1302 ★
Airports (SIC 4581)

Airline Market in Chicago O'Hare

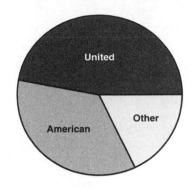

Market shares are shown in percent.

United 47.2%
American 34.6
Other 18.2

Source: *Wall Street Journal*, December 6, 2002, p. B4, from Salomon Smith Barney.

★ 1303 ★
Airports (SIC 4581)

Airline Market in Washington D.C./ Dulles

Market shares are shown in percent.

United 60.7%
Delta 6.7
Other 32.6

Source: *Wall Street Journal*, December 6, 2002, p. B4, from Salomon Smith Barney.

★ 1304 ★
Airports (SIC 4581)

Top Cargo Airports in the Central States, 2001

Airports are ranked by tonnage.

Memphis, TN 2,631,239
Louisville 1,469,013
Chicago 1,284,822
Indianapolis 1,151,105
Dallas/Ft. Worth 793,974
Dayton 550,721

Continued on next page.

★ 1304 ★ *Continued*

Airports (SIC 4581)

Top Cargo Airports in the Central States, 2001

Airports are ranked by tonnage.

Minneapolis/St. Paul	339,924
Cincinnati	338,364
Toledo	320,565

Source: *Air Cargo World*, August 2002, p. 26, from Airports Council International.

SIC 46 - Pipelines, Except Natural Gas

★ 1305 ★

Pipelines (SIC 4619)

Largest Pipeline Firms

Firms are ranked by revenue in millions of dollars.

Williams	$ 9,391
Plains All Amer. Pipeline	8,384
Enterprise Products	3,624
Western Gas Resources	2,490

Source: *Fortune*, April 14, 2003, p. F60, from *Fortune Top 500*.

SIC 47 - Transportation Services

★ 1306 ★

Tourism (SIC 4720)

Largest Tourist Events in Canada

Figures show average attendance at non-sporting events. The economic impact is $267 million.

Canadian National Exhibition	1,400,000
Calgary Stampede	1,200,000
Winter Carnivale	1,000,000
Pacific National Exhibition	1,000,000
Winterlude	700,000

Source: *Canadian Underwriter*, June 2002, p. 16.

★ 1307 ★

Travel (SIC 4720)

International Arrivals to the United States, 2001

The number of visitors is shown, in thousands.

	(000)	Share
Canada	13,507.0	30.08%
Mexico	9,558.0	21.29
United Kingdom	4,097.2	9.13
Japan	4,082.6	9.09
Germany	1,313.7	2.93
Republic of Korea	617.8	1.38
Venezuela	555.2	1.24
Brazil	551.4	1.23
Italy	472.3	1.05
Other	10,143.1	22.59

Source: "Outbound to the U.S." available March 25, 2003 from http://www.ita.org, from U.S. Department of Commerce and Office of Tourism and Travel.

★ 1308 ★

Travel (SIC 4720)

Top Spring Break Spots

Figures show estimated number of student visitors.

Panama City, FL	450,000
South Padre Island, TX	150,000
Daytona Beach, FL	150,000
Lake Havasu City, AZ	40,000
Cancun, Mexico	40,000

Source: *USA TODAY*, February 14, 2003, p. D1.

★ 1309 ★

Travel (SIC 4720)

Traveling Abroad for U.S. Residents, 2001

The top destinations are shown, in thousands. The number of resident travelers fell from 60.8 million to 57.9 million.

	(000)	Share
Mexico	17,153	29.59%
Canada	15,561	26.85
U.K.	3,383	5.84
France	2,626	4.53
Italy	1,944	3.35
Germany	1,894	3.27
Dominican Republic	1,338	2.31

Continued on next page.

★ **1309** ★ *Continued*

Travel (SIC 4720)

Traveling Abroad for U.S. Residents, 2001

The top destinations are shown, in thousands. The number of resident travelers fell from 60.8 million to 57.9 million.

	(000)	Share
Jamaica	1,313	2.27%
Japan	1,060	1.83
Spain	1,010	1.74
Other	10,681	18.43

Source: "Latest Statistics." available March 25, 2003 from http://www.ita.org, from U.S. Department of Commerce and Office of Tourism and Travel.

★ **1310** ★

Travel Agencies (SIC 4724)

Corporate Travel Leaders

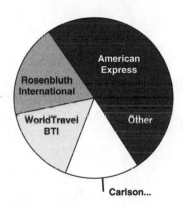

Figures show the estimated share of accounts in the source's list of the top 100 spenders on corporate travel. IBM was the top spender on the list, followed by General Electric and then Accenture.

American Express	36.8%
Rosenbluth International	19.6
WorldTravel BTI	16.7
Carlson Wagonlit Travel	16.0
Other	16.9

Source: *Business Travel News*, August 26, 2002, p. 3.

★ **1311** ★

Travel Agencies (SIC 4724)

Largest Travel Agencies, 2001

Firms are ranked by sales in millions of dollars.

American Express Travel Related Services	$ 17,200
Carlson Wagonlit Travel	9,000
Navigant International	6,200
Rosenbluth International	5,000
Worldtravel	4,500
Travelocity	3,100
AAA Travel	3,086
Expedia	2,900
TQ3 Maritz Travel	1,720
Liberty Mutual	1,390

Source: *Travel Weekly*, June 24, 2002, p. 86.

★ **1312** ★

Travel Reservations (SIC 4724)

How We Book Travel Plans, 2002

The table shows the split between offline and online travel bookings. Overall, 15% of all bookings are done online.

	Offline	Online
Cruises/vacation plans	96.0%	4.0%
Hotels	91.0	9.0
Airlines	80.0	20.0

Source: *Travel Weekly*, March 31, 2003, p. 10, from PhoCusWright.

★ **1313** ★

Travel Reservations (SIC 4724)

Travel Distribution Business

Shares are shown based on total bookings.

Sabre	42.0%
Worldspan	29.0
Galileo	20.5
Other	8.5

Source: *Knight Ridder/Tribune Business News*, March 5, 2003, p. NA, from Worldspan.

★ 1314 ★

Travel Reservations (SIC 4724)

Travel Reservation Systems

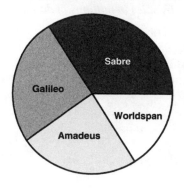

Market shares are shown in percent.

	1998	2001
Sabre	32.0%	34.0%
Galileo	31.0	26.0
Amadeus	25.0	24.0
Worldspan	12.0	16.0

Source: *New York Times*, July 8, 2002, p. C1, from *Travel Distribution Report.*

SIC 48 - Communications

★ 1315 ★
Wireless Services (SIC 4812)

Largest Wireless Firms, 2002

Market shares are shown in percent.

Verizon	26.0%
Cingular	19.0
AT&T Wireless	17.0
Nextel	8.0
Sprint PCS	8.0
VoiceStream	7.0
Other	15.0

Source: *Financial Times*, January 15, 2003, p. 18, from CIBC World Markets.

★ 1316 ★
Wireless Services (SIC 4812)

Largest Wireless Firms in Mexico, 2003

The total number of mobile users is expected to hit 28 million in 2003. Market shares are shown in percent.

Telcel	75.0%
Other	25.0

Source: *Latin America Telecom*, March 2003, p. 11.

★ 1317 ★
Wireless Services (SIC 4812)

Largest Wireless Service Firms in Canada, 2001

Shares are shown based on $6.6 billion in revenues.

Telus Mobility	30.4%
Rogers AT&T Wireless	27.6
Bell Mobility	25.0
Microcell	8.8
Aliant Mobility	4.0
SaskTel Mobility	2.3
MTS Mobility	1.9

Source: "Wireless Service Revenues." available March 7, 2003 from http://www.strategis.ic.gc/ca/ssI/sf/rt-0702f2-16e.pdf, from Industry Canada.

★ 1318 ★
Wireless Services (SIC 4812)

Largest Wireless Service Firms in Ontario

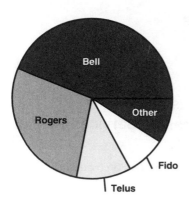

Market shares are shown in percent.

Bell	44.0%
Rogers	28.0
Telus	11.0
Fido	8.0
Other	9.0

Source: *Marketing Magazine*, October 14, 2002, p. 33.

★ 1319 ★
Wireless Services (SIC 4812)

Mobile Phone Penetration

53% of the population in major metropolitan areas subscribe to a mobile phone service.

Greenville, SC	71.0%
St. Louis	69.0
Orlando, FL	65.0
Raleigh, NC	65.0
Washington D.C.	64.0
Atlanta, GA	64.0
Boston, MA	63.0

Source: *Business Wire*, February 11, 2003, p. NA, from *Telephia Report*.

★ 1320 ★
Telephone Services (SIC 4813)

Dial Around Market in Canada

The long-distance dial-around market is shown by company. YAK processes 4.5 million calls a month and 38 million minutes for over 350,000 recurring monthly customers.

YAK	60.0%
Other	40.0

Source: *Canadian Corporate News*, December 3, 2002, p. NA.

★ 1321 ★
Telephone Services (SIC 4813)

Local Phone Market in Mexico

Market shares are shown in percent.

Telemex	96.0%
Other	4.0

Source: *Wall Street Journal*, November 26, 2002, p. A22, from Pyramid Research.

★ 1322 ★
Telephone Services (SIC 4813)

Local Phone Market in New Mexico

Shares are shown based on number of lines.

Qwest	85.0%
Other	15.0

Source: *Albuquerque Journal*, April 16, 2003, p. B4, from Federal Communications Commission.

★ 1323 ★
Telephone Services (SIC 4813)

Local Phone Service Leaders

All figures are for the end of September 2002.

Verizon	27.4%
SBC	24.7
BellSouth	11.5
Qwest	8.6
Other	27.9

Source: *The Boston Globe*, January 12, 2003, p. E1, from TNS Telecoms and Leichtman Research Group.

★ 1324 ★
Telephone Services (SIC 4813)
Long-Distance Households, 2002

Market shares are shown based on households. Figures are for third quarter.

AT&T	33.8%
MCI	15.8
Verizon	10.6
Sprint	8.3
VarTec	6.3
Other	34.5

Source: *USA TODAY*, January 8, 2003, p. 2B, from TNS Telecom.

★ 1325 ★
Telephone Services (SIC 4813)
Long-Distance Market in Mexico

Market shares are shown in percent.

Telemex	73.0%
Other	27.0

Source: *Wall Street Journal*, November 26, 2002, p. A22, from Pyramid Research.

★ 1326 ★
Telephone Services (SIC 4813)
Long-Distance Service Market

Market shares are shown in percent.

AT&T	38.0%
WorldCom	26.0
Sprint	12.0
Other	24.0

Source: *USA TODAY*, June 27, 2002, p. A1, from Giga Information Group.

★ 1327 ★
Telephone Services (SIC 4813)
Outbound International Calls

Figures show the countries that receive the most phone calls from the United States. Total minutes increased from 8.81 million minutes in 1991 to 37.27 million in 2001.

	1991	2001
Canada	1,929	5,106
Mexico	1,038	5,193
Great Britain	660	2,066
Germany	560	1,214
Japan	338	1,004
Dominican Republic	196	994
Philippines	183	1,627
India	59	1,445

Source: *New York Times*, February 3, 2003, p. C7, from TeleGeography.

★ 1328 ★
Telephone Services (SIC 4813)
Phone Market in California

SBC PacBell has 95% of the residential phone market, which translates into more than 7.8 million customers. Market shares are shown in percent.

SBC PacBell	95.0%
Other	5.0

Source: *Los Angeles Times*, July 24, 2002, p. C1, from FCC.

★ 1329 ★
Telephone Services (SIC 4813)
Phone Market in Indiana

Shares are shown based on lines owned.

SBC Ameritech/Verizon	90.0%
Other	10.0

Source: *Knight-Ridder/Tribune Business News*, June 23, 2002, p. NA.

★ 1330 ★

Telephone Services (SIC 4813)

Phone Market in New Jersey

Market shares are shown in percent.

Verizon Communications	97.0%
Other	3.0

Source: *The Record*, August 22, 2002, p. NA, from Verizon.

★ 1331 ★

Electronic Commerce (SIC 4822)

Holiday Internet Sales

Spending is shown for November 2 - December 13, 2002.

Books, music, video/DVD	17.8%
Apparel/clothing	17.5
Travel	14.7
Consumer electronics	11.6
Toys & video games	11.4
Other	27.0

Source: *PR Newswire*, December 20, 2002, p. NA, from Goldman, Sachs & Co., Harris Interactive, and Nielsen/NetRatings.

★ 1332 ★

Electronic Commerce (SIC 4822)

Leading E-Retailers

Firms are ranked by estimated online revenue in millions of dollars.

Amazon.com	$ 3,422
Office Depot	1,600
Staples	950
Gateway	775
Costco Wholesale	450
Barnes & Noble.com	405
Buy.com	395
QVC.com	350
Spiegel Group	332
J.C. Penney	324

Source: *Shopping Center World*, September 2002, p. 4, from Retail Forward.

★ 1333 ★

Electronic Commerce (SIC 4822)

Online Auction Market

Market shares are shown in percent.

eBay	85.0%
Other	15.0

Source: *Fortune*, May 26, 2003, p. 90.

★ 1334 ★

Electronic Commerce (SIC 4822)

Online Payment Systems

Market shares are shown in percent. Other includes Billpoint, C2it and Yahoo!PayDirect.

PayPal	85.0%
Other	15.0

Source: *New York Times*, July 9, 2002, p. C6, from Celent Communications.

★ 1335 ★

Electronic Commerce (SIC 4822)

Online Spending by Content, 2001-2002

Figures are in millions of dollars.

	2001	2002
Business/investing content	$ 214.3	$ 292.0
Entertainment	112.0	227.5
Personals/dating	72.0	302.1
Research	57.9	106.6
General news	51.8	70.0
Games	46.5	72.0
Community directories	46.1	91.1
Credit help	32.4	40.4

Continued on next page.

★ 1335 ★ *Continued*
Electronic Commerce (SIC 4822)

Online Spending by Content, 2001-2002

Figures are in millions of dollars.

	2001	2002
Personal growth	$ 24.7	$ 4.3
Greeting cards	2.1	36.2

Source: *Investor's Business Daily*, March 7, 2003, p. A4, from comScore Networks Inc. and Online Publishers Association.

★ 1336 ★
Electronic Commerce (SIC 4822)

Top Auction Categories on eBay, 2002

Distribution is shown for the first quarter of the year.

Collectibles, antiques, jewelry	48.0%
Books, music, video	24.0
Clothing, accessories	12.0
Consumer electronics	9.0
Home & garden	5.0
Business supplies	2.0

Source: *Investor's Business Daily*, April 18, 2002, p. A4, from U.S. Bancorp Piper Jaffray Inc., Merrill Lynch & Co., and comScore Networks Inc.

★ 1337 ★
Internet (SIC 4822)

Largest Online Music Services

Figures show millions of users for January 2003.

Kazaa	15.9
AOL Music Channel	11.5
MusicMatch Jukebox	9.0
Launch	7.2
VUNet USA Music & Media	4.7
MTV Networks Music	4.4
Sony Music	3.9
BMG Music Service	3.9
Lyrics.com	2.7

Source: *Investor's Business Daily*, March 19, 2003, p. A4, from Nielsen/NetRatings Inc.

★ 1338 ★
Internet (SIC 4822)

Top Online Dating Sites

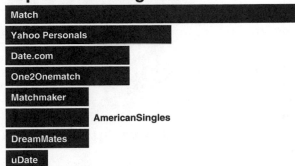

Nearly 25 million people visited dating Web sites in November 2002. Figures show millions of unique visitors.

Match	6.7
Yahoo Personals	3.8
Date.com	3.1
One2Onematch	2.8
Matchmaker	2.4
AmericanSingles	2.2
DreamMates	1.8
uDate	1.4

Source: *New York Times*, January 19, 2003, p. 9, from Media Metrix.

★ 1339 ★
Internet (SIC 4822)

Top Search Engines

Figures show millions of unique visitors for January 2003.

Google	39.4
Yahoo	38.6
MSN	36.8
AOL	22.0
Ask Jeeves	13.3
Overture	6.4
InfoSpace	6.0
Netscape	5.9
AltaVista	5.4
Xupiter.com	3.4

Source: *The Boston Globe*, February 23, 2003, p. 1, from Nielsen/NetRatings.

★ 1340 ★
Internet (SIC 4822)

Top Tax Sites

Figures show unique number of visitors per week, in thousands.

www.irs.gov	1,600
Intuit.com	1,200
TurboTax.com	857
HRBlock.com	554
TaxAct.com	308

Source: *BusinessWeek*, March 10, 2003, p. 14, from Nielsen/NetRatings.

★ 1341 ★
Internet (SIC 4822)

Top Web Sites, 2002

Unique visitors are shown, in millions, for the year through October.

Yahoo.com	60.0
MSN.com	54.7
AOL.com	47.7
Microsoft.com	45.8
Google.com	22.3

Source: *New York Times*, December 16, 2002, p. C18, from Gartner Dataquest.

★ 1342 ★
Internet Service Providers (SIC 4822)

Consumer Broadband Lines

Figures show the estimated number of lines.

	2002	2004	2006
Cable modem	6.37	19.99	32.11
DSL	3.57	14.78	31.77

Source: *Telephony*, May 6, 2002, p. 30, from Ovum Research.

★ 1343 ★
Internet Service Providers (SIC 4822)

High-Speed Internet Access

Figures show thousands of subscribers. Other refers to satellite and fixed wireless.

	(000)	Share
Cable modem	9,400	62.49%
DSL	5,400	35.90
Fiber	22	0.15
Other	220	1.46

Source: *Washington Post*, February 7, 2003, p. 1, from industry surveys.

★ 1344 ★
Internet Service Providers (SIC 4822)

High-Speed Internet Connections in the Valley, AZ

Market shares are shown in percent.

Cox Communications	75.0%
Other	25.0

Source: *Arizona Republic*, December 19, 2002, p. D1, from Cox.

★ 1345 ★
Internet Service Providers (SIC 4822)

Internet Backbone Services

Shares are shown based on capacity.

WorldCom	29.0%
Qwest	8.0
Level 3	7.0
Cogent	7.0
Sprint	6.0
Genuity	6.0
XO	5.0
France Telecom	5.0
Cable & Wireless	4.0
AT&T	4.0
Other	19.0

Source: *USA TODAY*, July 17, 2002, p. 3B, from TeleGeography.

★ 1346 ★
Internet Service Providers (SIC 4822)

Largest DSL Providers

Firms are ranked by millions of customers. DSL had 35.1% of the connections at the end of the year; cable had 61.7%.

SBC	2.2
Verizon	1.7
BellSouth	1.0
Qwest	0.5
Covad	0.4

Source: *USA TODAY*, April 29, 2003, p. B1, from analysts.

★ 1347 ★
Internet Service Providers (SIC 4822)

Leading Internet Service Providers, 2002

Figures show millions of subscribers as of December 2002.

America Online	26.5
MSN	9.0
EarthLink	4.8
Comcast	3.2
Road Runner	2.6
SBC	2.2
United Online	1.9
Verizon	1.8
SBC-Prodigy	1.4
Cox	1.3

Source: *New York Times*, February 3, 2003, p. C7, from ISP-Planet.

★ 1348 ★
Internet Service Providers (SIC 4822)

Number of Broadband Subscribers

Figures are in millions of households.

2005	38.8
2004	29.8
2003	22.1
2002	16.0

Source: *EContent*, March 2003, p. 15, from Parks Associates.

★ 1349 ★
Radio Broadcasting (SIC 4832)

Leading Radio Formats

Market shares are shown in percent.

Country	19.8%
News talk	11.3
Oldies	7.5
Adult contemporary	6.4
Spanish	5.9
Other	49.1

Source: *New York Times*, February 23, 2003, p. 10, from *Inside Radio*.

★ 1350 ★
Radio Broadcasting (SIC 4832)

Radio Firm Market Shares, 2001

Market shares are shown based on $16.2 billion in revenues.

Clear Channel	20.2%
Viacom	12.7
Cox	2.7
ABC Radio	2.5
Entercom	2.5
Citadel	2.0
Radio One	1.8
Emmis	1.6
Cumulus	1.6
Univision	1.6
Other	50.8

Source: *Fortune*, March 3, 2003, p. 120.

★ 1351 ★
Radio Broadcasting (SIC 4832)

Radio Market in Charlotte, NC

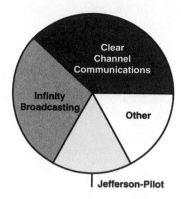

Shares are shown based on station ownership.

Clear Channel Communications 38.0%
Infinity Broadcasting 29.0
Jefferson-Pilot 16.0
Other 17.0

Source: *Media Week*, January 13, 2003, p. 14, from BIA Financial Network.

★ 1352 ★
Radio Broadcasting (SIC 4832)

Radio Market in Dayton, OH

Shares are shown based on station ownership.

Clear Channel Communications 44.2%
Cox Radio 25.8
Radio One 14.3
Hawes-Sauders Broadcast Prop. 7.7
WPFB Inc. 1.3
Johnson Communications 1.3
Other 5.4

Source: *Media Week*, August 19, 2002, p. 14, from BIA Financial Network.

★ 1353 ★
Radio Broadcasting (SIC 4832)

Radio Market in Hartford-New Haven, CT

Shares are shown based on station ownership.

Infinity Broadcasting 48.3%
Clear Channel Communications 31.3
Buckley Broadcasting 10.7
Marlin Broadcasting 5.8
Other 3.9

Source: *Media Week*, February 24, 2003, p. 14, from BIA Financial Network.

★ 1354 ★
Radio Broadcasting (SIC 4832)

Radio Market in Los Angeles, CA

Figures show share of ownership of the radio market.

Clear Channel 29.6%
Infinity Broadcasting 27.4
Hispanic Broadcasting 8.2
Emmis Communications 6.8
ABC Radio 5.4
Radio One 4.2
Liberman Broadcasting 3.2
Other 15.2

Source: *Media Week*, October 7, 2002, p. 4, from Arbitron.

★ 1355 ★
Radio Broadcasting (SIC 4832)

Radio Market in New Orleans, LA

Shares are shown based on station ownership.

Entercom Communications 45.8%
Clear Channel Communications 35.4
Wilks Broadcasting 10.4
222 Corp. 2.9
Other 5.7

Source: *Media Week*, March 3, 2003, p. 16, from Arbitron.

★ 1356 ★

Radio Broadcasting (SIC 4832)

Radio Market in Rochester, NY

Shares are shown based on station ownership.

Infinity Broadcasting	38.9%
Clear Channel Communications	32.0
Entercom	17.1
Other	12.0

Source: *Media Week*, January 13, 2003, p. 14, from BIA Financial Network.

★ 1357 ★

Radio Broadcasting (SIC 4832)

Radio Market in San Diego, CA

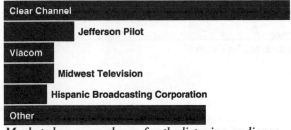

Market shares are shown for the listening audience.

Clear Channel	40.8%
Jefferson Pilot	10.0
Viacom	7.4
Midwest Television	6.7
Hispanic Broadcasting Corporation	6.2
Other	28.9

Source: *Wall Street Journal*, October 4, 2002, p. 1, from Arbitron and the companies.

★ 1358 ★

Radio Broadcasting (SIC 4832)

Satellite Radio Distribution

XM is the leader in the industry with 76,000 subscribers as of March 2002. 53% of their subscribers are under 40 years of age. Data show subscribers by distribution channel.

	2002	2004	2006
Aftermarket, light vehicle	478	3,087	6,263
RV & truck	184	1,186	2,407
Factory installed, light vehicle	35	322	940
In-home	33	957	2,307

Source: *Satellite News*, May 6, 2002, p. NA, from Tellus Venture Associates.

★ 1359 ★

Radio Broadcasting (SIC 4832)

Satellite Radio Services

Market shares are estimated in percent.

XM	69.0%
Sirius	31.0

Source: *Investor's Business Daily*, July 24, 2002, p. A6, from Salomon Smith Barney.

★ 1360 ★

Radio Broadcasting (SIC 4832)

Top Radio Firms, 2001

Firms are ranked by estimated revenues in millions of dollars. Clear Channel owns one-tenth of all radio stations in the nation.

Clear Channel	$ 3.25
Infinity Broadcasting	2.08
Cox	0.43
Entercom	0.40
ABC Radio	0.40
Citadel	0.31
Radio One	0.29
Hispanic Broadcasting	0.26
Cumulus	0.26
Emmis	0.25

Source: *New York Times*, June 19, 2002, p. C1, from *Inside Radio*.

★ 1361 ★

Television Broadcasting (SIC 4833)

Largest TV Groups

Groups are ranked by percentage of household coverage.

Viacom VIA	39.5%
Fox TV Stations	38.1
Paxson	33.4
NBC GE	30.4
Tribune	28.7
ABC	23.8
Univision	21.0
Gannett	17.5
Hearst-Argyle	15.9
Trinity Broadcasting Network	15.8

Source: *Broadcasting & Cable*, April 8, 2002, p. 48, from Federal Commmunication Commission.

★ 1362 ★

Television Broadcasting (SIC 4833)

Leading TV Broadcasters in Canada

Market shares are shown for September - November 2002.

Global Television Network (CanWest)	36.0%
CTV	28.0
Canadian Broadcasting Corp.	26.0
Other	10.0

Source: *Hollywood Reporter*, March 18, 2003, p. S7, from BBM Canada Meter Service.

★ 1363 ★

Television Broadcasting (SIC 4833)

Leading TV Broadcasters in Mexico

Market shares are shown for February 6 -9, 2003.

Televisa	74.64%
TV Azteca	25.36

Source: *Hollywood Reporter*, March 18, 2003, p. S7, from IBOPE AGB Mexico.

★ 1364 ★

Television Broadcasting (SIC 4833)

Top Shows on Network Television, 2002- 2003

Figures show average millions of viewing households. Data are for the season through May 11, 2003.

CSI	17.4
Friends	14.7
Joe Millionaire	14.2
E.R.	14.0
American Idol (Tuesday)	13.2
Survivor: Thailand	12.9
Everybody Loves Raymond	12.6
American Idol (Wednesday)	12.5
Law and Order	12.5
Survivor: Amazon	12.5

Source: *New York Times*, May 19, 2003, p. C1, from Nielsen Media Research.

★ 1365 ★

Television Broadcasting (SIC 4833)

Top Syndicated Shows, 2002

Figures show millions of viewers. They are first run averages for August 26 - December 1, 2002.

Wheel of Fortune	13.0
Jeopardy!	10.0
Entertainment Tonight	7.8
Oprah Winfrey Show	7.2
Judge Judy	6.7
Dr. Phil	5.4
Judge Joe Brown	4.4
Inside Edition	4.2
Live With Regis and Kelly	4.1

Source: *USA TODAY*, December 17, 2002, p. 3D, from Nielsen Media Research.

★ 1366 ★

Television Broadcasting (SIC 4833)

Top TV Networks

Figures show millions of total viewers for the season September 23, 2002 - May 21, 2003.

CBS	12.56
NBC	11.65
Fox	9.98
ABC	9.97
WB	4.10
UPN	3.52

Source: *USA TODAY*, May 27, 2003, p. 3D, from Nielsen Media Research.

★ 1367 ★

Television Broadcasting (SIC 4833)

TV Market in Quebec, 2002

Market shares are shown for the 46 weeks ended July 14, 2002. Data are for those 2 and over. In the 18 to 49 segment, TVA had a 26.5% and TQS is 15.9%.

TVA	28.5%
TQS	14.8
Radio-Canada	14.3
Other	42.3

Source: *Marketing*, August 26, 2002, p. 17.

★ 1368 ★

Cable Broadcasting (SIC 4841)

Cable Broadcasting in Canada, 2002

Canada has 12 million television households. DTH stands for direct to home.

Cable	61.0%
No multichannel	18.0
DTH	16.0
Grey DTH	5.0

Source: *Deal Memo*, December 16, 2002, p. 3, from Dominion Bond Rating Service.

★ 1369 ★

Cable Broadcasting (SIC 4841)

Cable Market in Massachusetts

Market shares are shown in percent.

AT&T Broadband	77.06%
Other	22.94

Source: *Boston Herald*, November 14, 2002, p. 46.

★ 1370 ★

Cable Broadcasting (SIC 4841)

Cable TV Market Shares

Cable was in 68.8 million homes in June 2002, up less than 1% from June 2001. Meanwhile, the number of satelite homes increased over 9% for the same period. Market shares are shown in percent.

AT&T	24.0%
AOL Time Warner	14.0
DirecTV	12.0
EchoStar Communications	8.3
Other	41.7

Source: *Los Angeles Times*, January 1, 2003, p. C9, from Federal Commmunications Commission.

★ 1371 ★

Cable Broadcasting (SIC 4841)

Top Cable Networks, 2002-03

Figures show millions of prime time viewers for the season September 23, 2002 - May 21, 2003.

TNT	2.25
Nickelodeon/Nick at Nite	2.06
Fox News Channel	1.93
USA	1.87
Lifetime	1.85
ESPN	1.76
Cartoon Network	1.70
CNN	1.31
TLC	1.22
TBS	1.00

Source: *USA TODAY*, May 27, 2003, p. 3D, from Nielsen Media Research.

★ 1372 ★

Cable Broadcasting (SIC 4841)

Top News Channels, 2002

Shares are shown for the first quarter of 2002.

Fox News Channel	33.0%
CNN	27.0
MSNBC	15.0
CNBC	14.0
Headline News	11.0

Source: *USA TODAY*, April 4, 2002, p. 2A, from Nielsen Media Research.

★ 1373 ★

Cable Broadcasting (SIC 4841)

Top Shows for Kids

The shows with the most viewers ages 2-11 are shown for September 30, 2002-February 2003. Figures are for the highest rated time period.

SpongeBob SquarePants	2.7
Fairly Odd Parents	2.7
Jimmy Neutron	2.4
Rugrats	2.3
Wonderful Word of Disney	2.2
Hey Arnold!	2.1
The Simpsons	2.1
Rocket Power	1.9
Survivor	1.9
Yu-Gi-Oh!	1.8

Source: *USA TODAY*, March 6, 2003, p. 5D, from Nielsen Media Research.

★ 1374 ★

Cable Broadcasting (SIC 4841)

What We Watch on Cable

Entertainment includes comedies, drama and movies.

Entertainment	36.6%
Children	21.1
News	14.1
Nature/education	11.1
Women	7.0
Music	5.4
Sports	4.7

Source: *The Economist*, April 13, 2002, p. 9, from Nielsen Media Research and Booz Allen Hamilton.

★ 1375 ★

Pay Television (SIC 4841)

Largest Cable/Satellite Providers, 2002

Companies are ranked by millions of subscribers as of September 2002.

AT&T	13.1
DirecTV	10.9
Time Warner	10.9
Comcast	8.5
Echostar	7.8
Charter Comm.	6.7
Cox Comm.	6.3
Adelphia Comm.	5.8
Cablevision	3.0

Source: *New York Times*, April 10, 2003, p. C6, from Kagan World Media.

★ 1376 ★

Pay Television (SIC 4841)

Pay TV Market, 2002

Market shares are shown in percent.

Cable	73.0%
DirecTV	13.0
EchoStar	9.0
Other	5.0

Source: *Wall Street Journal*, October 9, 2002, p. A1, from Carmel Group.

★ 1377 ★

Pay Television (SIC 4841)

Satellite TV Market in Canada, 2002

Market shares are shown in percent.

Bell ExpressVu/Star Choice 61.0%
Cable 37.0

Source: *Canada NewsWire*, January 6, 2003, p. NA.

★ 1378 ★

Video-On-Demand (SIC 4841)

Video-on-Demand Industry

The service is available in 7.1 million homes.

AOL TW 42.0%
Cablevision 21.0
Cox 10.0
Charter 8.0
AT&T B-Band 7.0
Insight 5.0
Adelphia 3.0
Other 4.0

Source: *Hollywood Reporter*, June 3, 2002, p. 1, from Nielsen/NetRatings.

SIC 49 - Electric, Gas, and Sanitary Services

★ 1379 ★
Electricity (SIC 4911)

U.S. Electricity Sources, 2000

Coal	52.0%
Nuclear	20.0
Fossil fuels (not coal)	19.0
Renewable energy	10.0

Source: *New York Times*, August 27, 2002, p. D1.

★ 1380 ★
Power Marketing (SIC 4911)

Largest Power Marketers in North America

Firms are ranked by sales for the fourth quarter of 2002. Figures are expressed in millions of megawatt hours.

Duke Energy	141.1
American Electric Power	119.8
El Paso Merchant Energy	116.0
Mirant	93.3
Williams	59.1
Reliant Resources	56.2
Sempra Energy Trading	54.3
Entergy-Koch	42.5
Cinergy	39.1

Source: *Natural Gas Week*, April 14, 2003, p. 1, from direct inquiries, company sources, Federal Energy Regulatory Commission and Securities and Exchange Commission.

★ 1381 ★
Utilities (SIC 4911)

Largest Utilities in Canada

Firms are ranked by revenues in millions of dollars.

Hydro-Quebec	$ 12.6
B.C. Hydro & Power	8.0
Ontario Power Generation	$ 6.2
TransAlta Corp.	4.9
Epcor Utilities	3.7
Canadian Utilities	3.5
Manitoba Hydro-Electric Board	1.9
Saskatchewan Power Corp.	1.1

Source: *Globe and Mail's Report on Business*, Annual 2002, p. NA.

★ 1382 ★
Natural Gas Marketing (SIC 4920)

Largest Natural Gas Marketers in North America

Mirant
BP Energy
Duke Energy
American Electric Power
Sempra Energy Trading
Coral Energy
El Paso Merchant Energy
ConocoPhillips
Dynergy
Oneok

Firms are ranked by sales for the fourth quarter of 2002. Figures are expressed in billions of cubic feet per day and include physical volumes only.

Mirant	18.7
BP Energy	18.2
Duke Energy	14.7
American Electric Power	11.8
Sempra Energy Trading	11.7
Coral Energy	9.4

Continued on next page.

★ 1382 ★ *Continued*
Natural Gas Marketing (SIC 4920)

Largest Natural Gas Marketers in North America

Firms are ranked by sales for the fourth quarter of 2002. Figures are expressed in billions of cubic feet per day and include physical volumes only.

El Paso Merchant Energy	8.2
ConocoPhillips	7.4
Dynergy	6.4
Oneok	6.0

Source: *Natural Gas Week*, April 14, 2003, p. 1, from corporate financial statements, direct inquiries and government data.

★ 1383 ★
Natural Gas Distribution (SIC 4922)

Largest Gas Distribution Utilities

Companies are ranked by millions of customers.

Southern California Gas Co.	5.10
Pacific Gas & Electric Co.	3.90
Keyspan Energy Delivery	2.00
Nicor Gas	2.00
AGL Resources Inc.	1.79
Xcel Energy	1.70
Dominion	1.69
Public Service Electric & Gas	1.64
Consumers Energy Co.	1.62
Centerpoint Energy Houston/Entex	1.53

Source: *Pipeline & Gas Journal*, November 2002, p. 25, from *Pipeline & Gas Journal's 500 Report.*

★ 1384 ★
Natural Gas Distribution (SIC 4922)

Largest Gas Pipeline Operators, 2001

Companies are ranked by miles of pipeline operated.

Duke Energy Field Services	57,000
Northern Natural Gas Co.	16,733
Tennessee Gas Pipeline Co.	14,100
Columbia Gas Transmission	10,550
Transcontinental Gas Pipe Line Corp.	10,338

El Paso Natural Gas Co.	9,942
Natural Gas Pipeline Co. of America	9,769
ANR Pipeline Co.	9,610
Texas Eastern Transmission	9,014

Source: *Pipeline & Gas Journal*, November 2002, p. 25, from *Pipeline & Gas Journal's Annual 500 Report.*

★ 1385 ★
Waste Disposal Industry (SIC 4953)

Rollover Business in Alabama

Construction companies use large dumpsters that require special ''rollover'' trucks to empty. Company's share of this service is shown.

Alabma Dumpster	65.0%
Other	35.0

Source: *Montgomery Advertiser*, November 16, 2002, p. C8.

★ 1386 ★
Waste Disposal Industry (SIC 4953)

Solid Waste Management

The big three have two thirds of the market. In 1996, the top 3 firms (Waste Management, Browning-Ferris and USA Waste Services) held 35% of the market.

Waste Management/Allied Waste/Republic Services	66.0%
Other	34.0

Source: *Waste News*, November 25, 2002, p. 10, from Raymond James & Associates.

SIC 50 - Wholesale Trade - Durable Goods

★ 1387 ★

Wholesale Trade - Tires (SIC 5014)

Replacement Tire Shipments, 2001

Distribution of manufacturers' shipments are shown in percent.

Local dealerships	44.0%
General merchandise distribution	19.0
National chains	19.0
Tire makers outlet	10.0
Regional dealerships	3.0
Other	5.0

Source: *Tire Business*, Market Data Book, p. NA.

★ 1388 ★

Wholesale Trade - Tires (SIC 5014)

Top Passenger Tire Marketers, 2002

Market shares are shown in percent.

	2000	2002
TBC	7.5%	8.0%
Treadways Corp.	3.0	3.0
Hercules	2.5	2.5
Del-Nat	2.5	2.5
American Tire Distributors	1.5	1.5
SURE Tire	1.0	1.0
Other	82.0	81.5

Source: *Modern Tire Dealer*, Fact Book 2003, p. NA, from MTD estimates.

★ 1389 ★

Wholesale Trade - Office Supplies (SIC 5040)

Largest Office Supply Stores

Stores are ranked by number of outlets.

Staples	1,400
Office Depot	1,038
OfficeMax	969

Source: *Crain's Cleveland Business*, March 17, 2003, p. 1.

★ 1390 ★

Medical Product Distribution (SIC 5047)

Medical/Surgical Product Distributor Shares

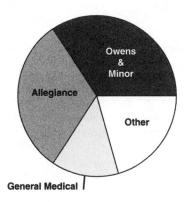

The market is estimated at $12-14 billion.

Owens & Minor	35.0%
Allegiance (Cardinal)	32.0
General Medical	14.0
Other	21.0

Source: *Healthcare Purchasing News*, November 2002, p. 32, from Goldman Sachs and company data.

★ 1391 ★
Optical Labs (SIC 5048)

Largest Optical Laboratories, 2002

The top wholesale labs are ranked by sales in millions of dollars. The top 25 firms outperformed the retail sector, with sales of $1,108.3 billion compared to $16.2 billion. The sales increase over 2001 is largely from the labs growing their Rx business or maintaining it at the same level.

Essilor Laboratories of America	$ 388.4
Hoya Optical Laboratories	134.6
Walman Optical	53.8
Soderberg	32.1
ICare Industries	23.5
Nova Optical Laboratory	21.0
Pech Optical	20.7
Luzerne Optical	20.2
SOLA Optical	20.0
Rite-Style Optical	15.3

Source: "Top 25." available January 7, 2002 from http://www.visionmonday.com, from Jobson Research.

★ 1392 ★
Wholesale Trade - Electrical Goods (SIC 5060)

Largest Electrical Goods Distributors in North America

Companies are ranked by sales in millions of dollars.

Avnet	$ 6,500
Arrow	6,211
Pioneer-Standard	2,540
Future	1,900
Bell	1,207
Memec	1,030
TTI	650
Newark	534
Reptron	399
All American	381

Source: *EBN*, May 13, 2002, p. NA, from EBN research.

★ 1393 ★
Wholesale Trade - Pool Supplies (SIC 5091)

Pool Supply Wholesaling

SCP is the top wholesaler in the country. Fort Wayne Pools is the number two competitor.

SCP	40.0%
Other	60.0

Source: *Investor's Business Daily*, December 24, 2002, p. A6.

SIC 51 - Wholesale Trade - Nondurable Goods

★ 1394 ★
Wholesale Trade - Business Forms (SIC 5112)

Largest Business Form Distributors

Companies are ranked by sales in millions of dollars.

SFI	$ 284.0
Proforma	227.7
American Solutions for Business	214.7
Global DocuGraphix	110.3
GBS	96.7
Data Supplies	76.7
Merrill Corp. Emerging Markets	60.6
Source4	59.4
Allied Office Products	51.0

Source: *Business Forms, Labels & Systems*, November 2002, p. 38.

★ 1395 ★
Drug Distribution (SIC 5122)

Drug Distribution Channels, 2001

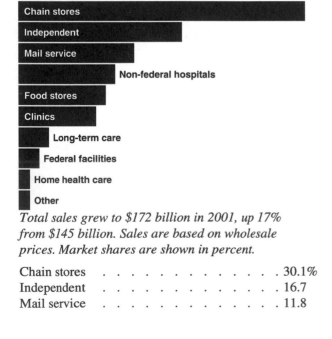

Total sales grew to $172 billion in 2001, up 17% from $145 billion. Sales are based on wholesale prices. Market shares are shown in percent.

Chain stores	30.1%
Independent	16.7
Mail service	11.8
Non-federal hospitals	10.1%
Food stores	9.1
Clinics	7.7
Long-term care	3.3
Federal facilities	1.7
Home health care	1.1
Other	1.2

Source: "IMS Reports 16.9% in 2001." available January 3, 2003 from http://www.imshealth.com, from IMS Health and Retail and Provider Perspective.

★ 1396 ★
Wholesale Trade - Food (SIC 5140)

Foodservice Market in Canada

The $13.2 billion industry is estimated as of April 2002. The retail segment is 78% of the market and foodservice is the rest.

Sysco	20.0%
Gordon Food Service	11.0
Other	69.0

Source: *Food in Canada*, May 2002, p. 20, from A&W Revenue Royalties Income Fund.

★ 1397 ★
Wholesale Trade - Groceries (SIC 5141)

Largest Grocery Wholesalers

Firms are ranked by sales of supplies stores in millions of dollars.

	($ mil.)	Share
Supervalu	$ 21,133	17.36%
Fleming	19,288	15.84
C&S Wholesale Grocers	11,901	9.78
Unified Western Grocers	7,102	5.83
Wakefern Food Corp.	7,102	5.83
Associated Wholesale Grocers	4,925	4.05
Nash Finch	4,534	3.72
Super Store Industries	4,432	3.64

Continued on next page.

★ 1397 ★ *Continued*
Wholesale Trade - Groceries (SIC 5141)

Largest Grocery Wholesalers

Firms are ranked by sales of supplies stores in millions of dollars.

	($ mil.)	Share
Roundy's	$ 3,515	2.89%
Grocers Supply Co.	3,177	2.61
White Rose	2,830	2.32
Spartan Stores	2,270	1.86
Other	29,533	24.26

Source: *Food Institute Report*, February 3, 2003, p. 5, from *Progressive Grocer* and Trade Dimensions.

★ 1398 ★
Wholesale Trade - Alcohol (SIC 5181)

Beer Market in Tallahassee, FL

Tri-Eagle Sales is a locally owned and operated Anheuser Busch distributor for a nine-country area. Shares are for 2002.

Tri-Eagle Sales	71.0%
Other	29.0

Source: *Knight Ridder/Tribune Business News*, April 26, 2003, p. NA.

★ 1399 ★
Wholesale Trade - Alcohol (SIC 5181)

Largest Beer Distributors

Firms are ranked by volume of sales in millions of cases.

The Reyes Family	40.0
Ben E. Keith	31.5
Manhattan Beer Distributors	27.5
JJ Taylor Companies Inc.	23.2
Silver Eagle Distributors	23.2
The Sheehan Family	22.5
Pearce Beverage Company	22.3
Hensley & Company	22.1
Topa Equities Ltd. Inc.	21.0
Gold Coast Beverage Dist.	20.1

Source: *Beverage World*, September 2002, p. 42.

★ 1400 ★
Wholesale Trade - Alcohol (SIC 5182)

Leading Wine and Liquor Wholesalers, 1999

Market shares are shown for 1999.

Southern Wine & Spirits of America	11.8%
Charner Industries Ind./Sunbelt Beverage Corp.	6.6
National Distributing Company Inc.	5.7
Other	75.9

Source: *American Business Review*, June 2002, p. 128, from Impact Databank.

★ 1401 ★
Wholesale Trade - Alcohol (SIC 5182)

Wine Distribution in North Carolina

Market shares are shown in percent.

	1995	2003
Mutual/Mims/Classic Wines/Empire Distributors	75.0%	50.0%
Other	25.0	50.0

Source: *Knight Ridder/Tribune Business News*, February 11, 2003, p. NA, from The Wine Merchant.

SIC 52 - Building Materials and Garden Supplies

★ 1402 ★

Home Improvement Stores (SIC 5231)

Home Improvement Market Shares in Canada, 2001

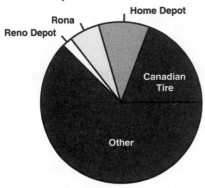

Market shares are shown in percent.

Canadian Tire	19.2%
Home Depot	10.0
Rona	6.4
Reno Depot	2.2
Other	62.2

Source: *Home Channel News*, June 17, 2002, p. 1, from *Hardlines* and industry estimates.

★ 1403 ★

Home Improvement Stores (SIC 5231)

Home Improvement Retailing

Market shares are shown in percent.

Home Depot	20.0%
Lowe's	12.0
Menard's	3.0
Other	65.0

Source: *The Indianapolis Star*, November 30, 2002, p. NA, from A.G. Edwards.

★ 1404 ★

Home Improvement Stores (SIC 5231)

Leading Home Improvement Retailers in Canada

Firms are ranked by sales in millions of Canadian dollars.

Canadian Tire	$ 5,374.8
Home Depot Canada	2,800.0
Rona	1,800.0
Reno Depot	618.0
ICI Canada	272.0
Totem Building Supplies	165.0
Kent Building Supplies	165.0
Windsor Building Supplies	138.1

Source: *Home Channel News*, May 20, 2002, p. 82.

★ 1405 ★

Home Improvement Stores (SIC 5231)

Leading Home Improvement Stores

Firms are ranked by sales in millions of dollars.

Home Depot	$ 53,553.0
Lowe's Cos.	22,111.1
Wal-Mart	11,042.9
Menard	5,200.0
Sears	3,900.0
Kmart	3,341.1
Sherwin-Williams	3,206.0
Carolina Holdings	2,560.0
84 Lumber	1,864.0
ICI Paints	1,700.0

Source: *Home Channel News*, May 20, 2002, p. 73.

SIC 53 - General Merchandise Stores

★ 1406 ★
Retailing (SIC 5300)

Largest Retail Companies

Firms are ranked by sales in billions of dollars.

Wal-Mart	$ 219.8
Home Depot	53.5
Kroger	50.0
Sears	41.0
Target	39.3
Albertson's	37.9
Kmart	37.0
Costco	34.7
Safeway	34.3
J.C. Penney	32.0

Source: *Stores*, July 2002, p. S5.

★ 1407 ★
Retailing (SIC 5300)

Leading Frequent Shopper Markets, 2001

Figures show the percent of households participating in at least one program.

Chicago, IL	96.0%
Baltimore/Washington D.C.	96.0
Denver, CO	95.0
Buffalo/Rochester NY	95.0
Philadelphia, PA	94.0
Columbus, OH	90.0
New York City, NY	89.0
Los Angeles, CA	89.0
San Francisco, CA	89.0
Boston, MA	88.0

Source: *Supermarket News*, December 30, 2002, p. 16, from A.C. Nielsen Homescan.

★ 1408 ★
Retailing (SIC 5300)

Leading Mass Merchandisers in Boston, MA

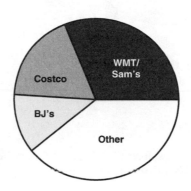

Market shares are shown for 2001.

WMT/Sam's	31.0%
Costco	18.4
BJ's	11.7
Other	38.9

Source: *Drug Store News*, June 17, 2002, p. 147, from *Metro Market Studies 2002 Distribution Guide*.

★ 1409 ★
Retailing (SIC 5300)

Leading Mass Merchandisers in Chicago, IL

Market shares are shown for 2001.

WMT/Sam's	38.8%
Target	19.8
Kmart	13.6
Other	27.8

Source: *Drug Store News*, June 17, 2002, p. 147, from *Metro Market Studies 2002 Distribution Guide*.

★ 1410 ★
Retailing (SIC 5300)

Leading Mass Merchandisers in Dallas, TX

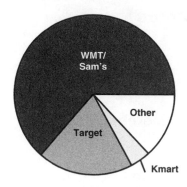

Market shares are shown for 2001.

WMT/Sam's	63.2%
Target	19.4
Kmart	4.0
Other	13.4

Source: *Drug Store News*, June 17, 2002, p. 147, from *Metro Market Studies 2002 Distribution Guide*.

★ 1411 ★
Retailing (SIC 5300)

Leading Mass Merchandisers in Detroit, MI

Market shares are shown for 2001.

Meijer	33.1%
Kmart	19.9
WMT/Sam's	17.2
Other	29.8

Source: *Drug Store News*, June 17, 2002, p. 147, from *Metro Market Studies 2002 Distribution Guide*.

★ 1412 ★
Retailing (SIC 5300)

Leading Mass Merchandisers in Los Angeles, CA

Market shares are shown for 2001.

Costco	39.7%
Target	21.2
WMT/Sam's	20.3
Other	18.8

Source: *Drug Store News*, June 17, 2002, p. 147, from *Metro Market Studies 2002 Distribution Guide*.

★ 1413 ★
Retailing (SIC 5300)

Leading Mass Merchandisers in New York City, NY

Market shares are shown for 2001.

Costco	45.0%
Kmart	16.6
WMT/Sam's	9.0
BJ's	8.2

Source: *Drug Store News*, June 17, 2002, p. 147, from *Metro Market Studies 2002 Distribution Guide*.

★ 1414 ★
Retailing (SIC 5300)

Mass Merchandiser Retail Shares

The year started off badly, with retail sales off still from the end of 2000. Holiday sales were dampened by the attacks of September 11, 2001. Total retail sales — including autos and foodservice — hit $2.3 trillion. Figures show distribution of $720.7 billion in sales.

	($ bil.)	Share
Broadline mass	$ 265.6	36.85%
Category dominant specialty . . .	191.6	26.59
Chain drug stores	101.8	14.13
Wholesale clubs	69.5	9.64
Mid-tier chains	53.2	7.38
Off-price apparel apparel	19.6	2.72
Variety/closeout chains	19.4	2.69

Source: *Retail Merchandiser*, July 2002, p. 34.

★ 1415 ★

Retailing (SIC 5300)

Retailing Industry, 2001

Sales for the top 150 companies reached $555.3 billion in 2001, up from $517.2 billion in 2000.

	2000	2001
Discount department stores . . .	$ 130.9	$ 134.3
Supercenters	85.2	102.5
Membership warehouse clubs . . .	65.7	71.4
Mid-tier department stores	54.1	54.0
Consumer electronics retailers . . .	38.7	43.2
Off-price apparel chains	28.9	30.9
Office supply chains	18.5	17.2
Automotive aftermarket chains . . .	13.2	12.7
Dollar stores	10.2	11.9
Military exchange posts	10.0	10.5
Other	61.8	66.7

Source: *DSN Retailing Today*, July 8, 2002, p. 17, from company reports and DSN research.

★ 1416 ★

Department Stores (SIC 5311)

Top Department Stores in Canada

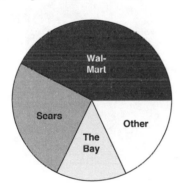

Market shares are shown in percent.

	2000	2002
Wal-Mart	36.3%	42.4%
Sears	23.5	25.2
The Bay	12.4	14.3
Other	27.8	18.1

Source: *National Post*, December 18, 2002, p. F3, from DRBS.

★ 1417 ★

Convenience Stores (SIC 5331)

Best-Selling Convenience Store Items

The top 10 items in convenience stores were relatively stable from 2001 to 2002. Cigaretttes and non-alcoholic beverages continue to make up nearly half of in-store sales. Foodservice sales were down by $1 billion among survey respondents.

	2001	2002
Cigarettes	38.7%	35.8%
Packaged beverages (non-alcohol) . .	11.7	12.3
Foodservice	11.4	13.3
Beer	9.9	10.9
General merchandise	3.6	2.7
Candy	3.4	3.9
Fluid milk products	3.0	2.8
Other tobacco	2.7	1.5
Salty snacks	2.3	3.4
Publications	2.0	1.4
Other	11.3	12.0

Source: *Convenience Store News*, June 17, 2002, p. 28, from *2002 NACS/CSNews Industry Databank*.

★ 1418 ★

Convenience Stores (SIC 5331)

Largest Convenience Store Operators

Companies are ranked by units operated.

Shell/Motiva	6,530
7-Eleven Stores	5,219
BP	3,959
Exxon Mobil Corp.	3,700
Phillips Petroleum	2,722
Speedway SuperAmerica	2,081
Valero Co.	1,813
The Pantry Inc.	1,292
Casey's General Stores Inc.	1,129

Source: *National Petroleum News*, October 2002, p. 1, from *2002 GECFF/NPN C-Store Survey*.

★ 1419 ★
Discount Merchandising (SIC 5331)

Leading Dollar Stores

Firms are ranked by sales in millions of dollars.

Dollar General	$ 5,323
Family Dollar Stores	3,665
Dollar Tree Stores	1,987
99 Cents Only	522
Bills Dollar Stores	360

Source: *DSN Retailing Today*, July 8, 2002, p. 32, from company reports and DSN research.

SIC 54 - Food Stores

★ 1420 ★
Grocery Stores (SIC 5411)
Largest Grocery Markets

Supermarket sales are shown in millions of dollars. Figures are for chain stores, which accounted for 82% of supermarket dollar volume.

	($ mil.)	Share
California	.$ 47,060	11.82%
Texas	29,715	7.46
Florida	25,015	6.28
New York	21,191	5.32
Pennsylvania	16,889	4.24
Ohio	15,723	3.95
Illinois	15,308	3.84
North Carolina	12,857	3.23
Michigan	12,494	3.14
Georgia	12,329	3.10
Other	189,638	47.62

Source: *Progressive Grocer*, November 1, 2002, p. 10, from Trade Dimensions.

★ 1421 ★
Grocery Stores (SIC 5411)
Top Grocery Stores, 2001

The $458 billion industry is shown in percent.

Wal-Mart	12.0%
Kroger	11.0
Safeway	8.0
Albertson's	8.0
Ahold USA	5.0
Sam's	4.0
Other	52.0

Source: *Financial Times*, August 28, 2002, p. 18, from *Supermarket News* and Bernstein Research.

★ 1422 ★
Grocery Stores (SIC 5411)
Top Grocery Stores, 2002

$728.7 billion in food sales took place over the year.

Wal-Mart	13.0%
Kroger	7.2
Costco Wholesale	5.2
Albertsons	4.9
Safeway	4.8
Sam's Clubs	4.4
Ahold Retail	3.4
Supervalu	2.7
Publix	2.2
Fleming	2.1
Other	50.1

Source: *Supermarket News*, January 13, 2003, p. 12, from U.S. Bureau of the Census, U.S. Department of Commerce, and SN research and other sources.

★ 1423 ★
Grocery Stores (SIC 5411)
Top Grocery Stores in Arkansas

Market shares are shown in percent.

Wal-Mart	28.55%
Kroger	14.73
Harp's Food Stores	8.59
Supermarket Investors	6.20
Brookshire Grocery	3.71
Wal-Mart Neighborhood Market	2.81
Ellison Enterprises	1.88
C.V.'s Foodliner	1.59
Sexton Food Inc.	1.57
Other	30.37

Source: *Arkansas Business*, May 6, 2002, p. 17, from Shelby Report Southwest, Market Scope 2002, and Trade Dimensions of Connecticut.

★ 1424 ★

Grocery Stores (SIC 5411)

Top Grocery Stores in Atlanta, GA

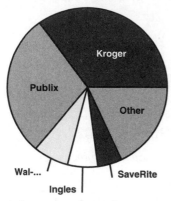

Market shares are shown in percent.

Kroger	34.73%
Publix	28.72
Wal-Mart Supercenters	7.07
Ingles	6.24
SaveRite	5.39
Other	17.85

Source: *Atlanta Journal-Constitution*, September 5, 2002, p. E1, from *Shelby Report*.

★ 1425 ★

Grocery Stores (SIC 5411)

Top Grocery Stores in Boise, ID

Market shares are shown in percent.

Albertson's	46.2%
Fred Meyer/WinCo	35.0
Wal-Mart	10.0
Other	8.8

Source: *Seattle Times*, October 10, 2002, p. E3, from Trade Dimensions.

★ 1426 ★

Grocery Stores (SIC 5411)

Top Grocery Stores in Buffalo, NY

Market shares are shown in percent.

Tops	55.0%
Wegmans	31.0
Other	14.0

Source: *Buffalo Business First*, February 17, 2003, p. NA, from Business First-Goldhaber Research Associates Poll.

★ 1427 ★

Grocery Stores (SIC 5411)

Top Grocery Stores in Charlotte, NC

Market shares are shown in percent for 2002.

Food Lion	31.3%
Harris Teeter	27.3
Other	41.4

Source: *Charlotte Business Journal*, February 7, 2003, p. NA, from Shelby Report.

★ 1428 ★

Grocery Stores (SIC 5411)

Top Grocery Stores in Chicago, IL

Market shares are shown in percent for 2001. Jewel had a 42.6% share in 1999.

Jewel	38.7%
Dominick's	22.8
Other	38.5

Source: *Crain's Chicago Business*, June 17, 2002, p. 1, from *Chain Store Guide*.

★ 1429 ★

Grocery Stores (SIC 5411)

Top Grocery Stores in Chittenden County, VT

Market shares are shown in percent.

Hannaford	31.0%
Shaw's	12.0
Price Chopper	8.0
Other	49.0

Source: *The Burlington Free Press*, May 30, 2003, p. A6, from Griffin Report of Food Marketing.

★ 1430 ★

Grocery Stores (SIC 5411)

Top Grocery Stores in Cincinnati, OH

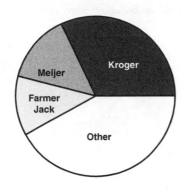

Market shares are shown in percent.

Kroger	32.0%
Meijer	14.0
Farmer Jack	12.0
Other	42.0

Source: *Knight-Ridder/Tribune Business News*, August 11, 2002, p. NA, from Trade Dimensions.

★ 1431 ★

Grocery Stores (SIC 5411)

Top Grocery Stores in Cleveland, OH

Market shares are shown in percent.

Giant Eagle	28.0%
Tops	26.0
Other	46.0

Source: *MMR*, June 17, 2002, p. 1.

★ 1432 ★

Grocery Stores (SIC 5411)

Top Grocery Stores in Dallas, TX

Market shares are shown in percent.

Albertsons	19.4%
Tom Thumb	17.4
Other	63.2

Source: *Knight Ridder/Tribune Business News*, February 11, 2003, p. NA, from Trade Dimensions.

★ 1433 ★

Grocery Stores (SIC 5411)

Top Grocery Stores in Denver, CO

Market shares are shown based on area volume for 2001.

King Soopers	39.0%
Safeway	20.0
Albertson's	12.0
Other	29.0

Source: *MMR*, June 17, 2002, p. 157.

★ 1434 ★

Grocery Stores (SIC 5411)

Top Grocery Stores in Detroit, MI

Market shares are shown in percent.

Farmer Jack	26.1%
Kroger	23.1
Other	50.8

Source: *Crain's Detroit Business*, July 22, 2002, p. 18, from Trade Dimensions.

★ 1435 ★

Grocery Stores (SIC 5411)

Top Grocery Stores in El Paso, TX

Market shares are shown in percent.

Big 8 Foods	27.86%
Wal-Mart Supercenters	15.67
Albertsons	10.61
Rainbow's	10.46
Other	35.40

Source: *El Paso Times*, February 13, 2003, p. 1, from Shelby Report.

★ 1436 ★
Grocery Stores (SIC 5411)

Top Grocery Stores in Fort Worth-Arlington, TX

Market shares are shown in percent.

Albertsons 20.3%
Kroger 18.0
Wal-Mart 17.3
Other 44.4

Source: *Knight Ridder/Tribune Business News*, February 11, 2003, p. NA, from Trade Dimensions.

★ 1437 ★
Grocery Stores (SIC 5411)

Top Grocery Stores in Fresno, CA

Market shares are shown based on area volume for 2001.

Save Mart 30.0%
Safeway/Von's 14.0
Albertson's 10.0
Other 46.0

Source: *MMR*, June 17, 2002, p. 157.

★ 1438 ★
Grocery Stores (SIC 5411)

Top Grocery Stores in Greenville/ Spartanburg/ Anderson, SC

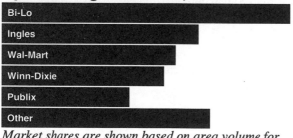

Market shares are shown based on area volume for 2001.

Bi-Lo 25.0%
Ingles 17.0
Wal-Mart 15.0
Winn-Dixie 14.0
Publix 11.0
Other 18.0

Source: *MMR*, June 17, 2002, p. 157.

★ 1439 ★
Grocery Stores (SIC 5411)

Top Grocery Stores in Hartford, CT

Market shares are shown based on area volume for 2001.

Stop & Shop 39.0%
Shaw's 14.0
Big Y 10.0
Other 37.0

Source: *MMR*, June 17, 2002, p. 157.

★ 1440 ★
Grocery Stores (SIC 5411)

Top Grocery Stores in Honolulu, Hawaii

Market shares are shown based on area volume for 2001.

Foodland 23.0%
Safeway 14.0
Costco 13.0
Times 12.0
Daiei 11.0
Other 24.0

Source: *MMR*, June 17, 2002, p. 157.

★ 1441 ★
Grocery Stores (SIC 5411)

Top Grocery Stores in Houston, TX

Market shares are shown based on area volume for 2001.

Kroger 21.0%
H.E.B. 16.0
Randalls 12.0
Fiesta Mart 10.0
Other 51.0

Source: *MMR*, June 17, 2002, p. 157.

★ 1442 ★

Grocery Stores (SIC 5411)

Top Grocery Stores in Indianapolis, MD

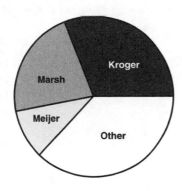

Market shares are shown based on area volume for 2001.

Kroger	31.0%
Marsh	22.0
Meijer	10.0
Other	37.0

Source: *MMR*, June 17, 2002, p. 157.

★ 1443 ★

Grocery Stores (SIC 5411)

Top Grocery Stores in Knoxville, TN

Market shares are shown based on area volume for 2001.

Kroger	30.0%
Food City	16.0
Wal-Mart	12.0
Other	42.0

Source: *MMR*, June 17, 2002, p. 157.

★ 1444 ★

Grocery Stores (SIC 5411)

Top Grocery Stores in Lancaster, PA

Market shares are shown based on area volume for 2001.

Weis Markets	26.0%
Giant	24.0
Other	50.0

Source: *MMR*, June 17, 2002, p. 157.

★ 1445 ★

Grocery Stores (SIC 5411)

Top Grocery Stores in Las Vegas, NV

Market shares are shown based on area volume for 2001.

Albertson's	23.0%
Smith's Food & Drug	20.0
Safeway/Von's	13.0
Raley's	10.0
Other	34.0

Source: *MMR*, June 17, 2002, p. 157.

★ 1446 ★

Grocery Stores (SIC 5411)

Top Grocery Stores in Los Angeles/ Long Beach, 2001

Market shares are shown based on area volume.

Ralph's	22.0%
Safeway/Von's	17.0
Albertson's	12.0
Costco	9.0
Other	30.0

Source: *MMR*, June 17, 2002, p. 157.

★ 1447 ★

Grocery Stores (SIC 5411)

Top Grocery Stores in New York, 2001

Market shares are shown based on area volume.

A&P	22.0%
Pathmark	17.0
Other	61.0

Source: *MMR*, June 17, 2002, p. 157.

★ 1448 ★
Grocery Stores (SIC 5411)

Top Grocery Stores in Newark, NJ

Market shares are shown based on area volume for 2001.

Pathmark	19.0%
A&P	14.0
Shop Rite	12.0
Other	55.0

Source: *MMR*, June 17, 2002, p. 157.

★ 1449 ★
Grocery Stores (SIC 5411)

Top Grocery Stores in Nova Scotia

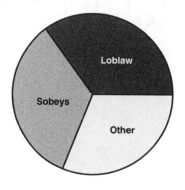

Market shares are shown in percent.

Loblaw	35.0%
Sobeys	34.0
Other	31.0

Source: *Edmonton Journal*, September 11, 2002, p. G3.

★ 1450 ★
Grocery Stores (SIC 5411)

Top Grocery Stores in Nussau/ Suffolk, NY

Market shares are shown based on area volume for 2001.

A&P/Waldbaum	22.0%
Pathmark	19.0
Stop & Shop	15.0
King Kullen	14.0
Other	30.0

Source: *MMR*, June 17, 2002, p. 157.

★ 1451 ★
Grocery Stores (SIC 5411)

Top Grocery Stores in Oakland, CA

Market shares are shown based on area volume for 2001.

Albertson's	29.0%
Safeway	26.0
Costco	12.0
Other	33.0

Source: *MMR*, June 17, 2002, p. 157.

★ 1452 ★
Grocery Stores (SIC 5411)

Top Grocery Stores in Philadelphia, PA

Market shares are shown in percent.

Acme	26.49%
ShopRite	12.61
Genuardis	12.55
Other	48.35

Source: *Knight-Ridder/Tribune Business News*, June 19, 2002, p. NA, from *Food Trade News*.

★ **1453** ★

Grocery Stores (SIC 5411)

Top Grocery Stores in Phoenix/Mesa, AZ

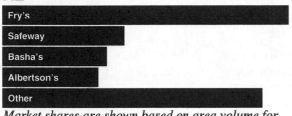

Market shares are shown based on area volume for 2001.

Fry's	33.0%
Safeway	14.0
Basha's	12.0
Albertson's	11.0
Other	30.0

Source: *MMR*, June 17, 2002, p. 157.

★ **1454** ★

Grocery Stores (SIC 5411)

Top Grocery Stores in Pittsburgh, PA

Market shares are shown based on area volume for 2001.

Giant Eagle	38.0%
Super Valu	26.0
Other	36.0

Source: *MMR*, June 17, 2002, p. 157.

★ **1455** ★

Grocery Stores (SIC 5411)

Top Grocery Stores in Portsmouth/Rochester, NH

Market shares are shown based on area volume for 2001.

DeMoulas	43.0%
Shaw's	23.0
Hannaford	13.0
Other	21.0

Source: *MMR*, June 17, 2002, p. 157.

★ **1456** ★

Grocery Stores (SIC 5411)

Top Grocery Stores in Rochester, NY

Market shares are shown based on area volume for 2001.

Wegman's	60.0%
Tops Markets	11.0
Other	29.0

Source: *MMR*, June 17, 2002, p. 157.

★ **1457** ★

Grocery Stores (SIC 5411)

Top Grocery Stores in Sacramento, CA

Market shares are shown based on area volume for 2001.

Raley's	31.0%
Albertson's	14.0
Ralph's	9.0
Other	46.0

Source: *MMR*, June 17, 2002, p. 157.

★ **1458** ★

Grocery Stores (SIC 5411)

Top Grocery Stores in St. Louis, MO

Market shares are shown based on area volume for 2001.

Shnuck Markets	41.0%
Dierberg's	14.0
Super Valu	11.0
Other	34.0

Source: *MMR*, June 17, 2002, p. 157.

★ 1459 ★
Grocery Stores (SIC 5411)

Top Grocery Stores in San Antonio, TX

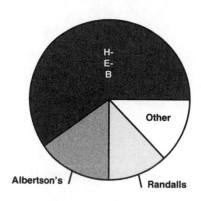

Market shares are shown in percent.

H-E-B	60.0%
Albertson's	15.0
Randalls	12.0
Other	13.0

Source: *Austin American-Statesman*, July 20, 2002, p. F1, from Trade Dimensions.

★ 1460 ★
Grocery Stores (SIC 5411)

Top Grocery Stores in Santa Fe, NM

Market shares are shown in percent.

Smith's	33.23%
Albertson's	29.80
Independents	11.80
Whole Food Markets	9.77
Food Town	9.08
Lowe's Pay N Save	3.90
Wild Oats	1.95
Southwest Cash & Carry	1.32

Source: *Knight Ridder/Tribune Business News*, June 16, 2002, p. NA, from Trade Dimensions.

★ 1461 ★
Grocery Stores (SIC 5411)

Top Grocery Stores in Sarasota/ Bradenton, FL

Market shares are shown based on area volume for 2001.

Publix	44.0%
Kash n' Karry	15.0
Winn-Dixie	10.0
Other	31.0

Source: *MMR*, June 17, 2002, p. 157.

★ 1462 ★
Grocery Stores (SIC 5411)

Top Grocery Stores in Springfield, MA

Market shares are shown based on area volume for 2001.

Big Y	40.0%
Stop & Shop	33.0
Other	27.0

Source: *MMR*, June 17, 2002, p. 157.

★ 1463 ★
Grocery Stores (SIC 5411)

Top Grocery Stores in Syracuse, NY

Market shares are shown based on area volume for 2001.

Wegman's	31.0%
P&C	21.0
Other	48.0

Source: *MMR*, June 17, 2002, p. 157.

★ 1464 ★
Grocery Stores (SIC 5411)
Top Grocery Stores in Tacoma, WA

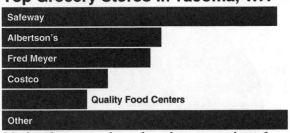

Market shares are shown based on area volume for 2001.

Safeway	26.0%
Albertson's	15.0
Fred Meyer	14.0
Costco	10.0
Quality Food Centers	8.0
Other	27.0

Source: *MMR*, June 17, 2002, p. 157.

★ 1465 ★
Grocery Stores (SIC 5411)
Top Grocery Stores in the Cape Cod Area

The leaders in the area's $1.4 billion retail food business are shown. Figures are estimates. Shaw's share is placed at somewhere between 20-25%.

Stop & Shop	50.0%
Shaw's/Star Market	25.0
Other	25.0

Source: *Knight Ridder/Tribune Business News*, January 21, 2003, p. NA, from Trade Dimensions.

★ 1466 ★
Grocery Stores (SIC 5411)
Top Grocery Stores in Toledo, OH

Marekt shares are shown in percent for 2003. Figures are for Lucas, Wood and Fulton counties.

Kroger	35.4%
Food Town	21.5
Meijer	17.9
Farmer Jack	9.7
Giant Eagle	1.7
Other	13.8

Source: *The Blade*, April 13, 2003, p. D1, from Trade Dimensions.

★ 1467 ★
Grocery Stores (SIC 5411)
Top Grocery Stores in Tulsa, OK

Market shares are shown based on area volume for 2001.

Wal-Mart	21.0%
Albertson's	16.0
Reasor's	15.0
Wearhouse Markets	10.0
Other	38.0

Source: *MMR*, June 17, 2002, p. 157.

★ 1468 ★
Grocery Stores (SIC 5411)
Top Grocery Stores in Washington D.C., 2001

Market shares are shown based on area volume.

Giant Food	38.0%
Safeway	20.0
Other	42.0

Source: *MMR*, June 17, 2002, p. 157.

★ 1469 ★
Grocery Stores (SIC 5411)

Top Grocery Stores in West Palm Beach/ Boca Raton, FL

Market shares are shown based on area volume for 2001.

Publix 52.0%
Winn-Dixie 19.0
Costco 9.0
Other 20.0

Source: *MMR*, June 17, 2002, p. 157.

★ 1470 ★
Grocery Stores (SIC 5411)

Top Grocery Stores in Worchester/ Fitchburg/ Leominster, MA

Market shares are shown based on area volume for 2001.

Stop & Shop 20.0%
Shaw's 15.0
Big D 11.0
Victory 10.0
Price Chopper 9.0
Other 35.0

Source: *MMR*, June 17, 2002, p. 157.

★ 1471 ★
Health Food Stores (SIC 5411)

Leading Health Food Chains

Stores are ranked by number of outlets.

GNC 4,200
Vitamin World 500
Whole Foods 133
Wild Oats 107
Vitamin Shoppe 100

Source: *Health Product Business*, March 2003, p. 28.

★ 1472 ★
Retailing - Beverages (SIC 5411)

Carbonated Beverage Sales

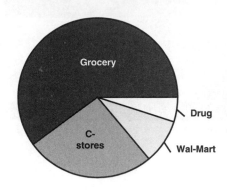

The $21 billion market is shown by channel. C-stores are convenience stores.

Grocery 60.0%
C-stores 26.0
Wal-Mart 9.0
Drug 5.0

Source: *Retail Merchandiser*, January 2003, p. 14, from Spectra Research and Scarborough.

★ 1473 ★
Retailing - Candy (SIC 5441)

Valentine's Day Candy Sales

Total sales of Valentine's Day candy, excluding Wal-Mart, reached $378 million, up 9%. Sales are shown by outlet.

Mass merchants 42.2%
Drug stores 30.5
Other 27.3

Source: *Supermarket News*, February 17, 2003, p. 50, from A.C. Nielsen.

SIC 55 - Automotive Dealers and Service Stations

★ 1474 ★
Auto Dealerships (SIC 5511)
Leading New Car Dealerships

Dealerships are ranked by new car revenues, in millions of dollars. Locations are shown in parentheses.

Longo Toyota (CA)	$ 424.5
Galpin Ford (CA)	294.1
Fletcher Jones Motorcars (CA)	257.0
JM Lexus (FL)	243.6
Ricart (OH)	242.9

Source: *Ward's Dealer Business*, June 2002, p. 34, from *Ward's Dealer 500*.

★ 1475 ★
Auto Dealerships (SIC 5521)
Largest Used Car Groups

Firms are ranked by number of outlets. The top 100 groups sold 1.59 million vehicles.

AutoNation	258,000
Carmax	151,185
Sonic Automotive	81,122
V.T.	76,823
UnitedAuto Group	69,302
Group 1 Automotive	67,927
Ashbury Automotive	65,000
Bill Heard Enterprises	40,875
Lithia Motors	36,960

Source: *Automotive News*, May 20, 2002, p. 32, from Automotive News Data Center.

★ 1476 ★
Auto Dealerships (SIC 5521)
Leading Used Car Dealerships

Dealerships are ranked by new car revenues, in millions of dollars. Locations are shown in parentheses.

Ricart (OH)	$ 128.0
Fletcher Jones Motorcars (CA)	80.7
Earnhardt Ford Sales Co. (AZ)	62.8
Longo Toyota (CA)	60.2
Bill Heard - Landmark Chevrolet (TX)	56.0

Source: *Ward's Dealer Business*, June 2002, p. 34, from *Ward's Dealer 500*.

★ 1477 ★
Retailing - Auto Supplies (SIC 5531)
Dash Cover Sales

Market shares are shown by type of chain.

Automotive chains	73.0%
Discount store chains	24.0
Non-automotive chains	2.0
Department store chains	1.0

Source: *Aftermarket Business*, April 2003, p. 44.

★ 1478 ★
Tire Stores (SIC 5531)
Largest Tire Chains in North America, 2001

Companies are ranked by sales in millions of dollars.

Bridgestone/Firestone	$ 2,600
Sears/NTB	2,200
Discount Tire	1,495
Wal-Mart/Sam's Club	1,200
Les Schwab	1,053
TBC Corp.	875

Continued on next page.

★ 1478 ★ *Continued*

Tire Stores (SIC 5531)

Largest Tire Chains in North America, 2001

Companies are ranked by sales in millions of dollars.

Goodyear	$ 800
Pep Boys	790
Canadian Tire Corp.	265
Ampac Tire Distributors/Tire Pros	250

Source: *Tire Business*, Market Data Book, p. NA.

★ 1479 ★

Tire Stores (SIC 5531)

Leading Tire Stores in Omaha, NE

Figures come from a survey and show preferred places to shop.

Jensen Tire	21.0%
Tires Plus	12.0
Sears	9.0
Firestone	9.0

Source: *Knight Ridder/Tribune Business News*, July 5, 2002, p. NA, from *2002 World-Herald Consumer Preference Study*.

★ 1480 ★

Tire Stores (SIC 5531)

Tire Dealerships by State, 2002

States are ranked by number of retail outlets.

	No.	Share
California	3,870	9.39%
Texas	3,393	8.24
Florida	2,438	5.92
Ohio	1,709	4.15
Pennsylvania	1,697	4.12
North Carolina	1,645	3.99
New York	1,588	3.85
Illinois	1,325	3.22
Michigan	1,157	2.81
Missouri	1,114	2.70
Tennessee	1,085	2.63
Other	20,181	48.98

Source: *Tire Business*, Market Data Book, p. NA, from Federal Highway Administration.

★ 1481 ★

Gas Stations (SIC 5541)

Largest Gas Retailers in El Paso/ Teller Counties, CO

Colorado is among 28 states where the top 4 retailers control 60% of the market. Companies are ranked by number of outlets.

Conoco	49
7-Eleven	45
Diamond Shamrock	36
Shell	15
Sinclair	14
Phillips	8
BP	8

Source: *Knight-Ridder/Tribune Business News*, November 25, 2002, p. NA, from U.S. Senate's Permanent Subcommittee on Investigations.

★ 1482 ★

Gas Stations (SIC 5541)

Top Gasoline Retailers

Market shares are shown in percent.

Shell	14.3%
ExxonMobil	11.8
BP	11.7
ConocoPhillips	11.3
Other	50.9

Source: *Knight-Ridder Tribune Business News*, March 18, 2003, p. NA, from *Lundberg Letter*.

SIC 56 - Apparel and Accessory Stores

★ 1483 ★
Retailing - Apparel (SIC 5600)

Largest Apparel Retailers

Firms are ranked by estimated revenue in billions of dollars.

Wal-Mart	$ 14.96
Target	8.85
J.C. Penney	8.29
May Department Stores	8.15
Gap	7.78
Kmart Corp.	6.74
Federated Department Stores	6.60
Sears, Roebuck & Co.	5.31
Limited Brands	4.73
Dillard's	4.72

Source: *WWD*, December 26, 2002, p. 11, from NPD.

★ 1484 ★
Retailing - Apparel (SIC 5611)

Retail Men's Activewear Sales, 2001

Shares of dollar sales are shown by segment.

Specialty stores	21.4%
Mass merchants	17.1
Sports specialty	14.9
Department stores	14.4
National chains	9.7
Off-price retailers	7.6
Direct mail/e-tail pureplays	4.8
Factory outlets	3.4
Other	6.7

Source: *Sporting Goods Business*, May 2002, p. 18, from NPD Group.

★ 1485 ★
Retailing - Apparel (SIC 5611)

Top Men's Wear Retailers

Wal-Mart
Sears, Roebuck & Co.
Target Corp.
Kmart Corp.
J.C. Penney Co.
Federated Department Store
The Gap
May Department Stores Co.
TJX Cos.
Dillard's

Companies are ranked by sales in billions of dollars.

Wal-Mart	$ 218.0
Sears, Roebuck & Co.	41.0
Target Corp.	39.9
Kmart Corp.	36.1
J.C. Penney Co.	32.0
Federated Department Store	15.6
The Gap	14.4
May Department Stores Co.	14.2
TJX Cos.	10.7
Dillard's	8.7

Source: *Daily News Record*, December 23, 2002, p. 32.

★ 1486 ★
Retailing - Apparel (SIC 5621)

Retail Women's Activewear Sales, 2001

Shares of dollar sales are shown by segment.

Specialty stores	27.3%
Mass merchants	21.5
Department stores	14.5
National chains	9.3

Continued on next page.

★ 1486 ★ *Continued*
Retailing - Apparel (SIC 5621)

Retail Women's Activewear Sales, 2001

Shares of dollar sales are shown by segment.

Sports specialty	7.2%
Off-price retailers	7.0
Factory outlets	1.9
Other	11.3

Source: *Sporting Goods Business*, May 2002, p. 18, from NPD Group.

★ 1487 ★
Retailing - Apparel (SIC 5641)

Top Children's Apparel Categories, 2001

The $25.4 billion industry is shown in percent.

	($ mil.)	Share
Bottoms	$ 6,733.4	26.5%
Tops	6,459.8	25.4
Children's/infant's sets	1,890.9	7.4
Special infants wear	1,721.4	6.8
Tailored clothing	1,641.5	6.5
Outerwear	1,202.5	4.7
Sleepwear	1,167.4	4.6
Hosiery	1,090.1	4.3
Fleecewear	1,064.5	4.2

Source: *Children's Business*, May 2002, p. 27, from NPDFashionworld.

★ 1488 ★
Retailing - Apparel (SIC 5641)

Top Children's Apparel Retailers

Firms are ranked by sales in millions of dollars.

Wal-Mart	$ 6,700
Kmart	2,200
Target	2,050
Sears	1,830
J.C. Penney	1,480
Federated	1,100
Old Navy	1,020
Gap Kids/Baby Gap	1,000
Kohl's	974
Sam's Club	970

Source: *Children's Business*, May 2002, p. 32.

★ 1489 ★
Retailing - Apparel (SIC 5651)

Largest Off-Price Apparel Retailers

Firms are ranked by sales in millions of dollars.

T.J. Maxx/Marshalls/A.J. Wright	$ 9,020
Old Navy	5,100
Ross Stores	2,987
Burlington Coat Factory	2,400
Charming Shoppes	1,994
Stein Mart	1,320
The Men's Wearhouse	1,273
Goody's Family Clothing	1,193
Dress Barn	695

Source: *DSN Retailing Today*, July 8, 2002, p. 32.

★ 1490 ★
Retailing - Apparel (SIC 5651)

Retail Activewear Leaders, 2001

Shares of dollar sales are shown by segment.

Specialty stores	23.5%
Mass merchants	22.6
Department stores	13.9
National chains	10.4
Sports specialty	9.4
Off-price retailers	7.0
Direct mail/e-tail pureplays	5.0
Factory outlets	2.6
Other	5.5

Source: *Sporting Goods Business*, May 2002, p. 18, from NPD Group.

★ 1491 ★
Retailing - Apparel (SIC 5651)

Retail Jeans Market

Market shares are shown in percent. Mass merchandisers include Wal-Mart, Kmart and Target. National chains include J.C. Penney, Mervins and Sears. Family department stores include Goody's and Fred Meyer.

Mass	32.0%
National chains	23.0
Specialty stores	18.0
Department stores	10.0
Family department stores	4.0
Other	13.0

Source: *America's Intelligence Wire*, March 3, 2003, p. NA, from VF Corp.

★ 1492 ★
Retailing - Shoes (SIC 5661)

Top Footwear Retailers, 2002

Figures show percentage of dollar sales of men's, women's, kids', fashion and athletic footwear. Figures are from July 2001-June 2002 and based on survey results.

Payless ShoeSource	6.06%
Wal-Mart	5.71
Foot Locker	3.75
Kmart	3.02
J.C. Penney	2.99
Nordstrom	2.14
Famous Footwear	2.07
Sears, Roebuck & Co.	1.81
Dillard's	1.79
Target	1.75
Other	68.91

Source: *Footwear News*, August 19, 2002, p. 30, from NPD Fashionworld.

★ 1493 ★
Retailing - Shoes (SIC 5661)

Top Shoe Stores in Canada

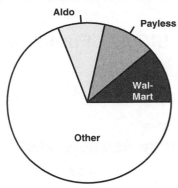

Market shares are shown for the $1.8 billion Canadian shoe industry.

Wal-Mart	9.9%
Payless	8.8
Aldo	8.0
Other	61.0

Source: *National Post*, December 1, 2002, p. 52.

SIC 57 - Furniture and Homefurnishings Stores

★ 1494 ★

Furniture Stores (SIC 5712)

Largest Furniture Retailers, 2001

Companies are ranked by furniture, bedding and accessories sales in millions of dollars.

Rooms To Go	$ 1,260.0
Ethan Allen	1,170.5
Levitz Home Funishings	900.0
Pier 1 Imports	857.9
La-Z-Boy Furniture Galleries	836.2
Berkshire Hathaway	832.7
IKEA	826.0
Havertys	678.1
Value City	675.0
Art Van	575.0
Rhodes	515.8
Thomasville Home Furnishings Stores	475.0

Source: *Furniture Today*, Winter 2002, p. 40.

★ 1495 ★

Furniture Stores (SIC 5712)

Largest Furniture Retailers in Canada, 2001

Companies are ranked by furniture, bedding and accessories sales in millions of dollars.

Sears Canada	$ 684
Leon's Furniture Ltd.	409
Ikea Canada	359
The Brick Warehouse Corp.	350
Groupe BMTC	265
United Furniture Warehouse	201
The Bay	200
Furniture Plus	138
Sleep Country Canada	100
Countrywide Stores	67

Source: *Furniture Today*, Winter 2002, p. 40.

★ 1496 ★

Retailing - Homefurnishings (SIC 5719)

Bedding Market Sales, 2002

Market shares are shown in percent.

Sheets/pillowcases	36.0%
Comforters	20.0
Bed pillows	11.0
Bed-in-the bag	7.0
Mattress pads	5.0
Blankets	5.0
Duvet covers	4.0
Quilts	3.0
Decorative pillows	3.0
Bed spreads	3.0
Other	3.0

Source: *Home Textiles Today*, February 17, 2003, p. 6, from *The Facts: Bedding 2002* publication by source.

★ 1497 ★

Retailing - Homefurnishings (SIC 5719)

Largest Bedding Markets, 2007

Markets are ranked by furniture and bedding sales in millions of dollars.

Chicago, IL	$ 2,638.7
New York, NY	2,592.5
Los Angeles-Long Beach, CA	2,074.3
Boston, MA-N.H.	2,064.4
Washington D.C./MD/VA/WVA	2,002.9
Atlanta, GA	1,391.6
Philadelphia, PA-NJ	1,368.8
Houston, TX	1,260.7
Detroit, MI	1,250.9
Dallas, TX	1,229.7

Source: *Furniture Today*, December 30, 2002, p. 40.

★ 1498 ★
Retailing - Homefurnishings (SIC 5719)
Largest Bedding Retailers, 2001

Companies are ranked by bedding sales in millions of dollars. Bedding includes conventional mattresses/ boxsprings, foam bedding, futons, air beds and waterbeds.

Select Comfort	$ 242.1
Federated Department Stores	235.0
The Mattress Firm	220.0
Mattress Discounters	218.0
Sam's Club	200.0
Sleepy's	199.0
Mattress Giant	174.0
May Department Stores	130.0
Berkshire Hathaway	120.0
Rooms To Go	120.0

Source: *Furniture Today*, Winter 2002, p. 40.

★ 1499 ★
Retailing - Homefurnishings (SIC 5719)
Leading Luxury Home Good Retailers

Companies are ranked by sales in millions of dollars.

Williams-Sonoma	$ 780.30
International Design Guild	286.90
Thomasville	237.50
Dillard's	231.66
Robb & Stucky	220.65
Macy's West	212.67
Boyles	192.50
Expo Design Centers (Home Depot)	158.00
Macy's East	149.02
Marshall Field's	145.13

Source: *HFN*, December 23, 2002, p. 53.

★ 1500 ★
Retailing - Homefurnishings (SIC 5719)
Retail Accessory Sales

Sales are shown in millions of dollars.

	($ mil.)	Share
Gift specialty stores/chains	$ 3,950	34.37%
Discount department stores	1,556	13.54
Home accent specialty	1,436	12.50
Mail order/Internet/TV	1,197	10.42
Department stores	718	6.25
Furniture stores/chains	599	5.21
Home improvement centers . . .	479	4.17
Other	1,556	13.54

Source: *Home Accents Today*, December 2002, p. S8.

★ 1501 ★
Retailing - Homefurnishings (SIC 5719)
Retail Bedding Sales

Distribution is shown in percent.

Furniture stores	42.0%
Specialty bedding stores	38.0
Dept. stores	13.0
Mass merchants	5.0
Other	2.0

Source: *HFN*, August 26, 2002, p. 1.

★ 1502 ★
Retailing - Homefurnishings (SIC 5719)
Retail Massagers Sales

Sales are shown by outlet.

Mass	45.0%
Department	25.0
Other	30.0

Source: *HFN*, March 17, 2003, p. 39, from *HFN's State of the Industry Report*.

★ 1503 ★

Retailing - Homefurnishings (SIC 5719)

Retail Table Linen Market

Mass merchants/clubs	40.0%
Department stores	23.0
Catalogs	5.0
Other	22.0

Source: *HFN*, March 17, 2003, p. 14, from *HFN's State of the Industry Report*.

★ 1504 ★

Retailing - Appliances (SIC 5722)

Leading Appliance Retailers, 2002

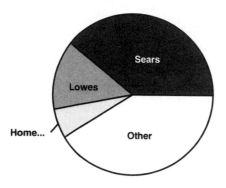

Market shares are shown in percent.

Sears	38.5%
Lowes	13.7
Home Depot	6.4
Other	41.4

Source: *Knight Ridder/Tribune Business News*, February 1, 2003, p. NA.

★ 1505 ★

Retailing - Appliances (SIC 5722)

Retail Coffeemaker Sales, 2002

The automatic drip coffeemaker market had sales of $780 million and 27 million units in 2002. Sales are shown by channel for the last six months of the year.

Traditional mass merchandiser	29.5%
Kitchen/home specialty	28.4
Department stores	26.6
General merchandiser	12.9
Drug stores	2.7

Source: "Some Like it Hot." available online April 7, 2003 from http://www.npdhouseworld.com, from NPD Group/NPD Houseworld/POS Information.

★ 1506 ★

Retailing - Appliances (SIC 5722)

Retail Espresso Machine Sales, 2002

The espresso machine market grew nicely in the 1990s, with a peak household penetration rate of 9%. In 2001, total retail sales exceeded $100 million. For the last six months of 2002, however, sales were down 27.1% over the same period in 2001. Salesare shown by channel for the year.

Kitchen/home specialty	26.0%
Non brick & mortar	23.0
Department stores	16.0
Traditional mass merchandiser	13.0
General merchandiser	10.0
Other	12.0

Source: "Is the Home Espresso Market Losing Steam?" available online April 7, 2003 from http://www.npdhouseworld.com, from NPD Group/NPD Houseworld/POS Information.

★ 1507 ★

Retailing - Appliances (SIC 5722)

Retail Floor Care

Sales are shown by outlet.

Mass merchants	48.0%
Department stores	19.0
Door-to-door	6.0
Appliance stores	5.0
Home improvement centers	5.0
Vacuum stores	4.0

Continued on next page.

★ 1507 ★ *Continued*
Retailing - Appliances (SIC 5722)
Retail Floor Care

Sales are shown by outlet.

Catalogs 1.0%
Other 12.0

Source: *HFN*, July 29, 2002, p. 28.

★ 1508 ★
Retailing - Consumer Electronics (SIC 5731)
Retail DVD Player Market, 2001

Market shares are shown based on unit sales.

Best Buy 21.6%
Wal-Mart 18.5
Circuit City 11.6
Sears 6.3
Kmart 4.6
Target 4.4
Cosco 4.1
Sam's Club 4.0
Other 24.9

Source: *Dealerscope*, August 2002, p. 18, from Consumer Electronics Association, Electronic Industries Association, and Dealerscope research.

★ 1509 ★
Retailing - Videos and DVDs (SIC 5732)
Online VHS/DVD Sales, 2001

Firms are ranked by estimated VHS/DVD revenues in millions of dollars.

Amazon.com . . . . $ 259
Netflix 74
DVDExpress.com 65
Buy.com 59
Wal-Mart 37
CDNow Online 36
Best Buy 20
Target Stores 18
Costco 17
DVDEmpire 16

Source: *Video Store*, April 28, 2002, p. 27.

★ 1510 ★
Retailing - Computer Peripherals (SIC 5734)
Retail MP-3 Player Market, 2001

Market shares are shown based on unit sales.

Best Buy 19.6%
Wal-Mart 11.3
Circuit City 9.4
Target 3.9
Sears 3.8
Kmart 2.7
Radio Shack 2.4
Cosco 1.4
Other 45.5

Source: *Dealerscope*, August 2002, p. 18, from Consumer Electronics Association, Electronic Industries Association, and Dealerscope research.

★ 1511 ★
Retailing - Computers (SIC 5734)
Computer Sales Channels, 2002

Shares are for the last six months of the year.

Retail 65.2%
Direct 34.8

Source: *Investor's Business Daily*, March 10, 2003, p. A4, from NPD Group.

★ 1512 ★
Retailing - Video Games (SIC 5734)
Retail Video Game Market

Through November 2002, video game sales reached $7.4 billion. The industry is booming, due largely to the expanding audience for such entertainment.

Mass merchants 34.0%
Toy stores 20.0
Consumer electronics stores 19.0
Specialty retailers 7.0
Warehouse stores 6.0
Other 14.0

Source: *USA TODAY*, December 23, 2002, p. 3B, from Interactive Software Dealers Association consumer survey.

★ 1513 ★

Retailing - Video Games (SIC 5734)

Top Video Game Retailers, 2002

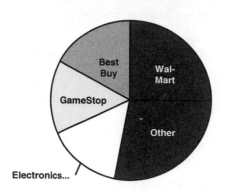

Sales of video game software and hardware reached $10.2 billion. Wal-Mart's share estimates between 20%-25%.

Wal-Mart	25.0%
Best Buy	17.0
GameStop	15.0
Electronics Boutique	15.0
Other	28.0

Source: *Seattle Times*, February 17, 2003, p. C5, from NPD Group.

★ 1514 ★

Retailing - Music (SIC 5735)

Largest Music Retailers, 2001

Data show number of outlets. Many of these companies sell related electronic merchandise.

Musicland Stores	1,336
Circuit City	632
Trans World	584
Best Buy	478
Wherehouse	414
Borders	337
Family Christian Stores	335
Hastings Entertainment	143
Tower Records/Video	101

Source: *Video Store*, April 28, 2002, p. 24, from *Video Store Top 100*.

★ 1515 ★

Retailing - Music (SIC 5735)

Leading Music Retailers

The industry has been suffering. They are facing increased competition from other retailers. Downloading music from the Internet is increasingly popular. CD sales actually fell in 2001, the first declien in a decade, according to the source. Firms are ranked by sales in millions of dollars.

Trans World Entertainment	$ 1,388
Tower Records/Video	631
Wherehouse Music	600
Hastings Entertainment	379

Source: *DSN Retailing Today*, July 8, 2002, p. 35.

★ 1516 ★

Retailing - Musical Products (SIC 5736)

Largest Music Product Retailers

Firms are ranked by estimated revenues in millions of dollars.

Guitar Center	$ 938.0
Sam Ash Music Corp.	351.0
Mars Inc.	340.0
Brook Mays/H&H	160.0
Hermes Music	86.0
Victor's House of Music	61.8
Music and Arts	60.0
Schmitt Music Company	58.0
Sweetwater Sound	56.1
J.W. Pepper	55.0

Source: *Music Trades*, August 2002, p. 86, from *Music Trades Top 200*.

SIC 58 - Eating and Drinking Places

★ 1517 ★
Foodservice (SIC 5812)

Foodservice Industry in Canada, 2001

Market shares are shown in percent.

Restaurants, full-service	38.1%
Restaurants, limited-service	28.2
Social and contract caterers	6.4
Institutional	5.8
Pubs and nightclubs	5.5
Retail	1.7
Other	3.7

Source: "Vending Machine Food." available January 1, 2003 from http://ffas.usda.gov, from Canadian Restaurant and Foodservice Association Foodservice Facts.

★ 1518 ★
Foodservice (SIC 5812)

Leaders in Noncommercial Sectors

The top three contractors in the foodservice arena are Sodexho/Sodexho-Marriott, Aramark and Compass Group. They have about 15% of the overall market. Their market share in selected sectors is shown in the chart.

Healthcare	80.0%
K-12	56.0
Highed education	35.0
B&I	28.0
Recreation	10.0

Source: *Food Management*, February 3, 2003, p. 34, from Technomic.

★ 1519 ★
Foodservice (SIC 5812)

Leading Contract Management Firms, 2001

Firms are ranked by food & beverage sales in millions of dollars.

Sodexho USA	$ 4,900.0
Aramark Corp.	4,782.0
Compass Group North America	4,000.0
Delaware North Companies	1,500.0
HMSHost Corp.	1,262.0
Volume Services America	543.1
Fine Host Corp.	311.0
Bon Appetit Management	279.0
HDS Services	259.0

Source: *Restaurants & Institutions*, September 15, 2002, p. 57, from individual companies.

★ 1520 ★
Foodservice (SIC 5812)

Leading Self-Operated Foodservice Universities, 2001- 2002

College and university foodservice at $9.3 billion segment of the $100 billion noncommercial market. Schools are ranked by food & beverage sales in millions of dollars. Data are for the academic year.

Brigham Young University	$ 37.7
Pennsylvania State University	21.5
Michigan State University	12.5
University of Notre Dame	12.1
Harvard University	10.3
Purdue University	10.1
Rutgers	9.4
University of Illinois	9.4
University of Southern California	8.9

Source: *Restaurants & Institutions*, September 15, 2002, p. 57, from individual universities.

★ 1521 ★

Restaurants (SIC 5812)

Largest Independent Restaurants, 2002

Restaurants are ranked by food and beverage sales in millions of dollars.

Tavern on the Green	$ 36.28
Hilltop Steak House	23.52
Joe's Stone Crab	22.43
Bob Chinn's Crab House	21.31
Spark's Steakhouse	18.60
Old Ebbitt Grill	17.02
21 Club	16.91
Fulton's Crab House	15.63
Gibsons Bar Steakhouse	15.57
Le Cirque	15.13

Source: *Restaurants & Institutions*, April 10, 2003, p. 133.

★ 1522 ★

Restaurants (SIC 5812)

Popular Types of Sandwiches

Figures show the types of sandwiches ordered in commercial restaurants.

Burgers	40.0%
Breakfast	12.0
Fried chicken	6.0
Heroes/subs	5.0
Broiled chicken	5.0
Hot dog	5.0
Turkey	4.0
Roast beef	4.0
Fried fish	2.0
Steak	2.0
Ham	2.0
Other	13.0

Source: *School Foodservice & Nutrition*, August 2002, p. 62, from NPD Foodworld and CREST Research.

★ 1523 ★

Restaurants (SIC 5812)

Quick Service and Fast Food Chains

Figures show the number of outlets for selected chains. Chipotle saw a 70% increase over 2000 figures and Panera Bread saw a 41% growth.

McDonald's	13,099
Burger King	8,248
Wendy's	5,315
Fazoli's	392
Panera Bread	369
Chipotle Mexican Grill	177
Corner Bakery	69

Source: *Wall Street Journal*, November 11, 2002, p. B1, from Technomic.

★ 1524 ★

Restaurants (SIC 5812)

Top Asian Concept Leaders, 2001

Firms are ranked by sales in millions of dollars. Shares are shown based on sales of $1.08 billion.

	($ mil.)	Share
Panda Express	$ 345.8	31.81%
P.F. Chang's China Bistro	312.9	28.78
Benihana	218.5	20.10
Yoshinoya Beef Bowl	56.0	5.15
Pick Up Stix	53.0	4.87
Leeann Chin	53.0	4.87
Other	48.0	4.42

Source: *Restaurants & Institutions*, July 15, 2002, p. S5, from *Restaurants & Institutions Top 400*.

★ 1525 ★

Restaurants (SIC 5812)

Top Breakfast Restaurants, 2001

Chains are ranked by estimated sales in millions of dollars.

Cracker Barrel	$ 895
IHOP	730
Bob Evans	340
Eat 'n Park	55
Mimi's Cafe	35

Source: *Restaurant Business*, September 1, 2002, p. 47, from Technomic.

★ 1526 ★
Restaurants (SIC 5812)

Top Chicken Chains, 2001

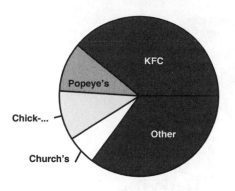

Market shares are estimated based on sales of $12 billion.

KFC	39.0%
Popeye's	10.0
Chick-Fil-A	10.0
Church's	6.0
Other	35.0

Source: *New York Times*, July 9, 2002, p. C2, from Technomic.

★ 1527 ★
Restaurants (SIC 5812)

Top Chili Restaurants in Cincinnati, OH

Market shares are estimated in percent. Gold Star, which actually has more stores in the Cincinnati area, is a strong challenger to Skyline.

Skyline	65.0%
Other	35.0

Source: *The Cincinnati Post*, February 18, 2003, p. C5, from Skyline.

★ 1528 ★
Restaurants (SIC 5812)

Top Coffee/Snack Leaders, 2001

Firms are ranked by sales in millions of dollars. Shares are shown based on sales of $13.54 billion.

	($ mil.)	Share
Dairy Queen	$ 2,790.0	20.60%
Dunkin' Donuts	2,375.0	17.53

	($ mil.)	Share
Starbucks	$ 2,047.0	15.11%
Tim Hortons	1,462.0	10.79
Baskin-Robbins	820.0	6.05
Krispy Kreme Doughnuts . . .	621.7	4.59
Haagen-Dazs Ice Cream Cafe . . .	280.0	2.07
Braum's Ice Cream & Dairy . . .	233.0	1.72
Auntie Anne's Soft Pretzels . . .	220.0	1.62
Carvel	220.0	1.62
Other	2,476.2	18.28

Source: *Restaurants & Institutions*, July 15, 2002, p. S5, from *Restaurants & Institutions Top 400*.

★ 1529 ★
Restaurants (SIC 5812)

Top Dinnerhouse Chains, 2002

Market shares are shown based on aggregate sales of dinnerhouse chains on the source's top 100 list.

Applebee's Neighborhood Grill	15.70%
Red Lobster	12.50
Outback Steakhouse	11.80
Chili's Grill & Bar	10.94
Olive Garden	10.04
T.G.I. Friday's	9.18
Ruby Tuesday	6.21
Bennigan's Irish American	3.56
Other	20.07

Source: *Nation's Restaurant News*, June 24, 2002, p. 3, from Technomic.

★ 1530 ★
Restaurants (SIC 5812)

Top Family Dining Chains, 2002

Market shares are shown based on aggregate sales of family chains on the source's top 100 list.

Denny's	23.75%
Cracker Barrel Old Country Store	14.12
Intl. House of Pancakes/IHOP	14.09
Bob Evans Restaurants	9.01
Perkins Restaurant and Bakery	8.55
Waffle House	7.54

Continued on next page.

★ 1530 ★ *Continued*
Restaurants (SIC 5812)

Top Family Dining Chains, 2002

Market shares are shown based on aggregate sales of family chains on the source's top 100 list.

Shoney's	6.64%
Friendly's Ice Cream	6.50
Steak'n Shake	5.67
Other	4.13

Source: *Nation's Restaurant News*, June 24, 2002, p. 3, from Technomic.

★ 1531 ★
Restaurants (SIC 5812)

Top Family Seafood Leaders, 2001

Firms are ranked by sales in millions of dollars. Shares are shown based on sales of $4.76 billion.

	($ mil.)	Share
Red Lobster	$ 2,200.0	46.13%
Long John Silver's	812.0	17.03
Captain D's	486.0	10.19
Joe's Crab Shack	330.0	6.92
McCormick & Shmick's	188.0	3.94
Legal Son Foods	141.0	2.96
Landry's Seafood House	135.0	2.83
Pappadeaux Seafood Kitchen	78.0	1.64
Bubba Gump Shrimp Co.	70.0	1.47
Other	328.8	6.89

Source: *Restaurants & Institutions*, July 15, 2002, p. S5, from *Restaurants & Institutions Top 400*.

★ 1532 ★
Restaurants (SIC 5812)

Top Grill-Buffet Chains, 2002

Market shares are shown based on aggregate sales of family chains on the source's top 100 list.

Golden Corral	37.96%
Ryan's Family Steak House	28.93
Ponderosa Steakhouse	20.80
Sizzler	12.31

Source: *Nation's Restaurant News*, June 24, 2002, p. 3, from Technomic.

★ 1533 ★
Restaurants (SIC 5812)

Top Hamburger Chains, 2001

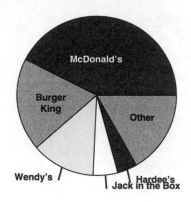

Market shares are estimated based on sales of $46.5 billion.

McDonald's	43.0%
Burger King	19.0
Wendy's	13.0
Jack in the Box	5.0
Hardee's	4.0
Other	17.0

Source: *New York Times*, July 26, 2002, p. C5, from Technomic.

★ 1534 ★
Restaurants (SIC 5812)

Top Hamburger Chains by Sales

Firms are ranked by sales in millions of dollars.

McDonald's	$ 1,270.0
Whataburger	613.4
Jack in the Box	585.6
Sonic	583.8
Wendy's	576.0
Burger King	487.8

Source: *Chain Leader*, August 2002, p. 47, from company reports.

★ 1535 ★
Restaurants (SIC 5812)

Top Italian Concept Leaders, 2001

Firms are ranked by sales in millions of dollars.
Shares are shown based on sales of $5.09 billion.

	($ mil.)	Share
Olive Garden	$ 1,700.0	33.35%
Sbarro	570.6	11.19
Romano's Macaroni Grill	550.6	10.80
Fazoli's	404.7	7.94
Carrabba's Italian Grill	276.0	5.41
Buca di Beppo	176.0	3.45
Bertucci's Brick Oven Pizzeria . .	150.8	2.96
Mazzio's Pizza	144.0	2.82
Maggiano's Little Italy	139.7	2.74
Papa Gino's	123.0	2.41
Other	862.0	16.91

Source: *Restaurants & Institutions*, July 15, 2002, p. S5, from *Restaurants & Institutions Top 400*.

★ 1536 ★
Restaurants (SIC 5812)

Top Pizza Chains

Market shares are shown in percent.

Pizza Hut 13.4%
Domino's 8.4
Little Caesar's 5.3
Papa John's 4.6
Other 68.3

Source: *Advertising Age*, August 26, 2002, p. 5, from Technomic.

★ 1537 ★
Restaurants (SIC 5812)

Top Quick-Service Restaurants

Market shares are shown in percent.

Boston Market 18.6%
Panera Bread 15.7
Fazoli's 12.0
Fuddrucker's 7.8
Au Bon Pain 6.1
Other 39.8

Source: *Knight Ridder/Tribune Business News*, January 6, 2003, p. NA, from Technomic.

★ 1538 ★
Restaurants (SIC 5812)

Top Sandwich Chains, 2001

Market shares are shown in percent. Figures do not include hamburgers.

Subway 30.8%
Arby's 17.6
Other 51.6

Source: *Knight Ridder/Tribune Business News*, March 24, 2003, p. NA, from Technomic.

★ 1539 ★
Restaurants (SIC 5812)

Top Steak/Barbecue Concept Leaders, 2001

Firms are ranked by sales in millions of dollars.
Shares are shown based on sales of $7.05 billion.

	($ mil.)	Share
Outback Steakhouse	$ 2,287.0	32.44%
Lone Star Steakhouse & Saloon . .	466.0	6.61
Tony Roma's Famous for Ribs . .	440.0	6.24
LongHorn Steakhouse	375.7	5.33
Ruth's Chris Steak House	332.0	4.71
Texas Roadhouse	328.5	4.66
Stuart Anderson's Black Angus . .	302.2	4.29
Damon's Grill	285.0	4.04
Other	2,234.3	31.69

Source: *Restaurants & Institutions*, July 15, 2002, p. S5, from *Restaurants & Institutions Top 400*.

★ 1540 ★

Restaurants (SIC 5812)

Where We Get a Quick Bite, 2002

The quick service market is estimated based on averages for the last 18 quarters.

Burgers	43.4%
Pizza	17.9
Sandwiches	7.7
Chicken	7.4
Mexican	7.2
Other	16.4

Source: *Chain Leader*, October 2002, p. 2, from Sandelman & Associates.

★ 1541 ★

Coffeehouses (SIC 5813)

Leading Coffeehouse Chains

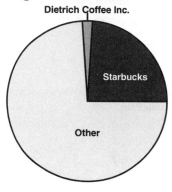

Dietrich Coffee Inc.

Starbucks

Other

The number of coffeehouses doubled between 1996 and 2001, reaching 13,3000 outlets. Mom and Pop operations control 61% of the market.

	Outlets	Share
Starbucks	3,167	23.81%
Dietrich Coffee Inc.	237	1.78
Other	9,896	74.41

Source: *Food Institute Report*, September 30, 2002, p. 3, from Mintel Consumer Intelligence.

SIC 59 - Miscellaneous Retail

★ 1542 ★

Drug Stores (SIC 5912)

Top Drug Stores, 2001

Firms are ranked by sales in billions of dollars.

Walgreens	$ 24.6
CVS	22.2
Rite Aid	15.1
Eckerd	13.8
Albertson's	12.0
Longs Drug Stores	4.3
Medicine Shoppe International	2.0
Phar-Mor	1.2
Duane Reade	1.1

Source: *Drug Store News*, April 29, 2002, p. 60.

★ 1543 ★

Drug Stores (SIC 5912)

Top Drug Stores in Albuquerque, NM

Market shares are shown based on area volume for 2001.

Walgreens	61.0%
Wal-Mart	10.0
Albertson's	9.0
Other	20.0

Source: *Chain Drug Review*, October 14, 2002, p. 35, from Racher Press.

★ 1544 ★

Drug Stores (SIC 5912)

Top Drug Stores in Allentown/ Bethlehem/ Easton, PA

Market shares are shown based on area volume for 2001.

CVS	31.0%
Eckerd	20.0
Rite Aid	11.0
Walgreens	9.0
Other	29.0

Source: *MMR*, June 17, 2002, p. 161.

★ 1545 ★

Drug Stores (SIC 5912)

Top Drug Stores in Ann Arbor, MI

Market shares are shown based on area volume for 2001.

CVS	36.0%
Rite Aid	20.0
Meijer	9.0
Other	35.0

Source: *Chain Drug Review*, October 14, 2002, p. 35, from Racher Press.

★ 1546 ★

Drug Stores (SIC 5912)

Top Drug Stores in Atlanta, GA

Market shares are shown based on area volume for 2001.

CVS	29.0%
Eckerd	24.0
Kroger	12.0
Other	35.0

Source: *MMR*, June 17, 2002, p. 161.

★ 1547 ★
Drug Stores (SIC 5912)

Top Drug Stores in Baltimore, MD

Market shares are shown based on area volume for 2001.

Rite Aid	38.0%
CVS	19.0
Giant Food	9.0
Other	34.0

Source: *Chain Drug Review*, October 14, 2002, p. 35, from Racher Press.

★ 1548 ★
Drug Stores (SIC 5912)

Top Drug Stores in Buffalo/Niagara Falls, NY

Market shares are shown based on area volume for 2001.

Rite Aid	30.0%
Eckerd	19.0
Walgreens	13.0
CVS	8.0
Snyder's	7.0
Other	23.0

Source: *MMR*, June 17, 2002, p. 161.

★ 1549 ★
Drug Stores (SIC 5912)

Top Drug Stores in Canton/Massillon, OH

Market shares are shown based on area volume for 2001.

Rite Aid	32.0%
Marc's	27.0
Discount Drug Mart	15.0
Walgreens	10.0
Other	16.0

Source: *MMR*, June 17, 2002, p. 161.

★ 1550 ★
Drug Stores (SIC 5912)

Top Drug Stores in Chicago, IL

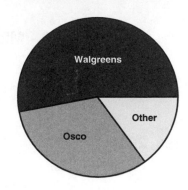

Market shares are shown based on area volume for 2001.

Walgreens	53.0%
Osco	32.0
Other	15.0

Source: *Chain Drug Review*, October 14, 2002, p. 35, from Racher Press.

★ 1551 ★
Drug Stores (SIC 5912)

Top Drug Stores in Cincinnati, OH

Market shares are shown based on area volume for 2001.

Walgreens	36.0%
CVS	18.0
Kroger	13.0
Other	33.0

Source: *MMR*, June 17, 2002, p. 161.

★ 1552 ★
Drug Stores (SIC 5912)

Top Drug Stores in Cleveland/Lorain/ Elyria, OH

Market shares are shown based on area volume for 2001.

CVS 22.0%
Marc's 19.0
Discount Drug Mart 14.0
Walgreens 13.0
Rite Aid 11.0
Medic Drug 8.0
Other 13.0

Source: *Chain Drug Review*, October 14, 2002, p. 35, from Racher Press.

★ 1553 ★
Drug Stores (SIC 5912)

Top Drug Stores in Dallas, TX

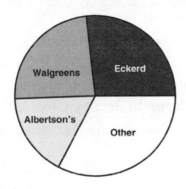

Market shares are shown for 2001.

Eckerd 26.7%
Walgreens 23.7
Albertson's 17.0
Other 32.6

Source: *Drug Store News*, June 17, 2002, p. 147, from *Metro Market Studies 2002 Distribution Guide*.

★ 1554 ★
Drug Stores (SIC 5912)

Top Drug Stores in Detroit, MI

Market shares are shown based on area volume for 2001.

CVS 37.0%
Rite Aid 21.0
Walgreens 14.0
Other 28.0

Source: *Chain Drug Review*, October 14, 2002, p. 35, from Racher Press.

★ 1555 ★
Drug Stores (SIC 5912)

Top Drug Stores in Flint, MI

Market shares are shown based on area volume for 2001.

Rite Aid 59.0%
Walgreens 11.0
Other 30.0

Source: *MMR*, June 17, 2002, p. 161.

★ 1556 ★
Drug Stores (SIC 5912)

Top Drug Stores in Fort Lauderdale, FL

Market shares are shown based on area volume for 2001.

Walgreens 54.0%
Eckerd 27.0
Other 19.0

Source: *Chain Drug Review*, October 14, 2002, p. 35, from Racher Press.

★ 1557 ★

Drug Stores (SIC 5912)

Top Drug Stores in Ft. Worth/ Arlington, TX

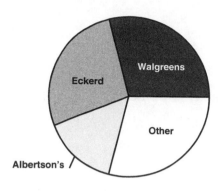

Market shares are shown based on area volume for 2001.

Walgreens	29.0%
Eckerd	27.0
Albertson's	15.0
Other	29.0

Source: *MMR*, June 17, 2002, p. 161.

★ 1558 ★

Drug Stores (SIC 5912)

Top Drug Stores in Gary, IN

Market shares are shown based on area volume for 2001.

Walgreens	63.0%
CVS	9.0
Osco	8.0
Other	20.0

Source: *MMR*, June 17, 2002, p. 161.

★ 1559 ★

Drug Stores (SIC 5912)

Top Drug Stores in Hartford, CT

Market shares are shown based on area volume for 2001.

CVS	47.0%
Walgreens	13.0
Other	40.0

Source: *MMR*, June 17, 2002, p. 161.

★ 1560 ★

Drug Stores (SIC 5912)

Top Drug Stores in Honolulu

Market shares are shown based on area volume for 2001.

Longs	74.0%
Times	12.0
Other	14.0

Source: *Chain Drug Review*, October 14, 2002, p. 35, from Racher Press.

★ 1561 ★

Drug Stores (SIC 5912)

Top Drug Stores in Indianapolis, MD

Market shares are shown in percent.

CVS	37.0%
Walgreens	25.0
Other	38.0

Source: *The Indianapolis Star*, February 2, 2003, p. D8, from *Chain Drug Review*.

★ 1562 ★

Drug Stores (SIC 5912)

Top Drug Stores in Jersey City, NJ

Market shares are shown based on area volume for 2001.

Rite Aid	29.0%
CVS	26.0
Walgreens	17.0
Other	28.0

Source: *MMR*, June 17, 2002, p. 161.

★ 1563 ★

Drug Stores (SIC 5912)

Top Drug Stores in Long Island, NY

Market shares are shown in percent.

CVS	40.0%
Eckerd	29.0
Other	31.0

Source: *MMR*, June 17, 2002, p. 2.

★ 1564 ★
Drug Stores (SIC 5912)

Top Drug Stores in Los Angeles/ Long Beach, CA

Market shares are shown based on area volume for 2001.

Sav-on 41.0%
Rite Aid 25.0
Other 34.0

Source: *Chain Drug Review*, October 14, 2002, p. 35, from Racher Press.

★ 1565 ★
Drug Stores (SIC 5912)

Top Drug Stores in Minneapolis/St. Paul, MN

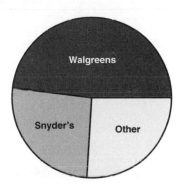

Market shares are shown based on area volume for 2001.

Walgreens 48.0%
Snyder's 26.0
Other 26.0

Source: *Chain Drug Review*, October 14, 2002, p. 35, from Racher Press.

★ 1566 ★
Drug Stores (SIC 5912)

Top Drug Stores in Nashville, TN

Market shares are shown based on area volume for 2001.

Walgreens 38.0%
CVS 17.0
Kroger 14.0
Eckerd 12.0
Other 19.0

Source: *Chain Drug Review*, October 14, 2002, p. 35, from Racher Press.

★ 1567 ★
Drug Stores (SIC 5912)

Top Drug Stores in New Orleans, LA

Market shares are shown based on area volume for 2001.

Walgreens 44.0%
Eckerd 16.0
Wal-Mart 8.0
Rite Aid 1.0
Other 31.0

Source: *Chain Drug Review*, October 14, 2002, p. 35, from Racher Press.

★ 1568 ★
Drug Stores (SIC 5912)

Top Drug Stores in New York, NY

Market shares are shown based on area volume.

Duane Reade 31.0%
CVS 21.0
Rite Aid 20.0
Other 28.0

Source: *Chain Drug Review*, October 14, 2002, p. 35, from Racher Press.

★ 1569 ★
Drug Stores (SIC 5912)

Top Drug Stores in Newark, NJ

Market shares are shown based on area volume for 2001.

CVS	28.0%
Rite Aid	14.0
Walgreens	11.0
Drug Fair	10.0
Pathmark	9.0
Other	28.0

Source: *Chain Drug Review*, October 14, 2002, p. 35, from Racher Press.

★ 1570 ★
Drug Stores (SIC 5912)

Top Drug Stores in Orange County, CA

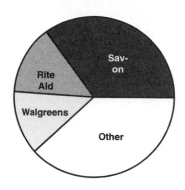

Market shares are shown based on area volume for 2001.

Sav-on	35.0%
Rite Aid	14.0
Walgreens	13.0
Other	38.0

Source: *Chain Drug Review*, October 14, 2002, p. 35, from Racher Press.

★ 1571 ★
Drug Stores (SIC 5912)

Top Drug Stores in Orlando, FL

Market shares are shown based on area volume for 2001.

Walgreens	43.0%
Eckerd	27.0
Other	30.0

Source: *MMR*, June 17, 2002, p. 161.

★ 1572 ★
Drug Stores (SIC 5912)

Top Drug Stores in Philadelphia, PA

Market shares are shown based on area volume for 2001.

CVS	28.0%
Rite Aid	22.0
Eckerd	17.0
Other	33.0

Source: *Chain Drug Review*, October 14, 2002, p. 35, from Racher Press.

★ 1573 ★
Drug Stores (SIC 5912)

Top Drug Stores in Phoenix/Mesa, AZ

Market shares are shown based on area volume for 2001.

Walgreens	55.0%
Osco	15.0
Fry's	10.0
Other	20.0

Source: *Chain Drug Review*, October 14, 2002, p. 35, from Racher Press.

★ 1574 ★
Drug Stores (SIC 5912)

Top Drug Stores in Pittsburgh, PA

Market shares are shown based on area volume for 2001.

Eckerd	30.0%
Rite Aid	16.0
CVS	13.0
Phar-Mor	11.0
Giant Eagle	10.0
Other	20.0

Source: *Chain Drug Review*, October 14, 2002, p. 35, from Racher Press.

★ 1575 ★
Drug Stores (SIC 5912)

Top Drug Stores in Richmond/ Petersburg, VA

Market shares are shown based on area volume for 2001.

CVS	30.0%
Walgreens	17.0
Rite Aid	14.0
Eckerd	9.0
Other	30.0

Source: *MMR*, June 17, 2002, p. 161.

★ 1576 ★
Drug Stores (SIC 5912)

Top Drug Stores in Rochester, NY

Market shares are shown based on area volume for 2001.

Eckerd	27.0%
CVS	19.0
Rite Aid	18.0
Wegman's	13.0
Other	23.0

Source: *Chain Drug Review*, October 14, 2002, p. 35, from Racher Press.

★ 1577 ★
Drug Stores (SIC 5912)

Top Drug Stores in St. Louis, MO

Market shares are shown based on area volume for 2001.

Walgreens	61.0%
Schnuck Markets	11.0
Wal-Mart	10.0
Other	18.0

Source: *Chain Drug Review*, October 14, 2002, p. 35, from Racher Press.

★ 1578 ★
Drug Stores (SIC 5912)

Top Drug Stores in San Diego, CA

Market shares are shown based on area volume for 2001.

Sav-On	28.0%
Rite Aid	21.0
Longs	20.0
Other	31.0

Source: *MMR*, June 17, 2002, p. 161.

★ 1579 ★
Drug Stores (SIC 5912)

Top Drug Stores in San Francisco, CA

Market shares are shown based on area volume for 2001.

Walgreens	51.0%
Longs	24.0
Rite Aid	12.0
Other	13.0

Source: *Chain Drug Review*, October 14, 2002, p. 35, from Racher Press.

★ 1580 ★
Drug Stores (SIC 5912)

Top Drug Stores in Seattle/Bellevue/Everett, WA

Market shares are shown based on area volume for 2001.

Rite Aid 26.0%
Bartell 16.0
Walgreens 13.0
Safeway 11.0
Other 34.0

Source: *Chain Drug Review*, October 14, 2002, p. 35, from Racher Press.

★ 1581 ★
Drug Stores (SIC 5912)

Top Drug Stores in Springfield, MA

Market shares are shown based on area volume for 2001.

CVS 50.0%
Walgreens 16.0
Brooks 13.0
Other 21.0

Source: *Chain Drug Review*, October 14, 2002, p. 35, from Racher Press.

★ 1582 ★
Drug Stores (SIC 5912)

Top Drug Stores in Syracuse, NY

Market shares are shown based on area volume for 2001.

Eckerd 49.0%
Rite Aid 16.0
Kinney Drug 14.0
Other 21.0

Source: *Chain Drug Review*, October 14, 2002, p. 35, from Racher Press.

★ 1583 ★
Drug Stores (SIC 5912)

Top Drug Stores in Toledo, OH

Market shares are shown based on area volume for 2001.

Rite Aid 35.0%
Seaway Foodtown 20.0
Kroger 10.0
Walgreens 9.0
Other 26.0

Source: *Chain Drug Review*, October 14, 2002, p. 35, from Racher Press.

★ 1584 ★
Drug Stores (SIC 5912)

Top Drug Stores in Tulsa, OK

Market shares are shown based on area volume for 2001.

May's Drug 24.0%
Walgreens 20.0
Med-X 14.0
Albertson's 10.0
Other 32.0

Source: *MMR*, June 17, 2002, p. 161.

★ 1585 ★
Drug Stores (SIC 5912)

Top Drug Stores in Washington D.C.

Market shares are shown based on area volume for 2001.

CVS 57.0%
Rite Aid 12.0
Giant Food 11.0
Other 20.0

Source: *Chain Drug Review*, October 14, 2002, p. 35, from Racher Press.

★ 1586 ★
Drug Stores (SIC 5912)

Top Drug Stores in Wilmington/ Newark, DE

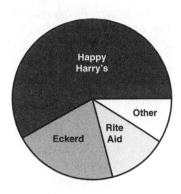

Market shares are shown based on area volume for 2001.

Happy Harry's	58.0%
Eckerd	21.0
Rite Aid	12.0
Other	9.0

Source: *Chain Drug Review*, October 14, 2002, p. 35, from Racher Press.

★ 1587 ★
Drug Stores (SIC 5912)

Top Drug Stores in Youngstown/ Warren, OH

Market shares are shown based on area volume for 2001.

Rite Aid	27.0%
Phar-Mor	20.0
CVS	12.0
Giant Eagle	9.0
Other	32.0

Source: *MMR*, June 17, 2002, p. 161.

★ 1588 ★
Prescriptions (SIC 5912)

Prescription Drug Market, 2002

Market shares are shown in percent.

Chain stores	29.2%
Independents	16.3

Mail service	12.9%
Non-federal hospitals	9.6
Food stores	9.0
Clinics	8.3
Mass merchandisers	7.2
Long-term care	3.4
Federal facilities	1.8
Other	2.3

Source: "IMS Reports 11.8% Dollar Growth in 2002." available March 7, 2003 from http:// www.businesswire.com, from IMS Retail and Provider Perspective.

★ 1589 ★
Prescriptions (SIC 5912)

Who Fills Prescriptions

Data show share of total prescriptions filled.

Walgreen	8.9%
CVS	8.6
Wal-Mart	7.4
Rite Aid	5.6
Eckerd	4.9
Medco Health Solutions	4.0
Other	60.6

Source: *USA TODAY*, September 25, 2002, p. 3B, from Ipsos-NPD.

★ 1590 ★
Retailing - Alcohol (SIC 5921)

Largest Alcohol Retailers in California

Groups are ranked by number of stores.

Albertsons	471
Ralphs Grocery Co.	353
Vons (Safeway)	305
Safeway (No. CA. Division)	229
Smart & Final	161
Stater Bros.	155
Food 4 Less	131
Save Mart Supermarkets	96
Trader Joe's	91

Source: *Progressive Grocer*, March 1, 2003, p. 57, from Trade Dimensions.

★ 1591 ★
Pawn Shops (SIC 5932)

Pawn Shop Industry

Firms are ranked by estimated sales in millions of dollars. Cash America has more than 400 stores across the country, while EZ Pawn has about 280.

Cash America	$ 355
EZ Pawn	186

Source: *Knight-Ridder/Tribune Business News*, September 18, 2002, p. NA.

★ 1592 ★
Retailing - Sporting Goods (SIC 5941)

Golf Shop Sales

The tables compares the sources of revenue for public and private courses.

	Private	Public
Apparel, men's	26.0%	38.0%
Balls	18.0	11.0
Clubs	16.0	7.0
Apparel, women's	9.0	16.0
Shoes	6.0	4.0
Gloves	6.0	4.0
Bags & acccessories	6.0	4.0
Gifts	4.0	5.0

Source: *Golf World Business*, August 2002, p. 12, from AGM/Golf Digest Companies Resource Center.

★ 1593 ★
Retailing - Sporting Goods (SIC 5941)

Top Sporting Goods Retailers

Firms are ranked by sales in millions of dollars.

Foot Locker	$ 1,800
The Sports Authority	1,400
L.L. Bean	1,140
Dick's Sporting Goods	1,050
Famous Footwear	1,044
Cabela's	875
Bass Pro Shops	850
Nike	800
Champs Sports	800
Academy Sports & Outdoors	775

Source: *Sporting Goods Business*, June 2002, p. 26.

★ 1594 ★
Retailing - Sporting Goods (SIC 5941)

Top Sports Goods Retailers in Canada, 2001

Market shares are shown in percent. Sporting goods market is valued at $6.2 billion, with $3.7 billion from equipment.

Canadian Tire	9.3%
Sport Chek	7.4
Sears	6.2
Wal-Mart	4.4
Sports Experts	4.1
Zellers	3.3
Footlocker	2.4
Athlete's World	2.1
Other	60.8

Source: "Annual Market Overview." available December 11, 2002 from http://wwww.sportsvision.info/ annual_stats.html, from Trendex North America.

★ 1595 ★
Retailing - Books (SIC 5942)

Children's Book Sales, 2002

Sales are shown for the first six months of the year. Consumers purchased 201.1 million books for children age 14 and under during the first six months of 2002, up 4% from 2001.

	2001	2002
Special markets	31.0%	26.0%
Bookstores	16.0	17.0
Mass merchandisers	14.0	14.0
Dollar stores	11.0	15.0
Variety stores	6.0	6.0
Supermarkets	3.0	3.0
Drug stores	3.0	3.0
Supermarkets	2.0	2.0
Toy stores	2.0	2.0
Warehouse clubs	2.0	2.0
Other	10.0	10.0

Source: "Children's Book Sales Up." available January 7, 2003 from http://www.npd-ipsos.com, from NPD.

★ 1596 ★
Retailing - Books (SIC 5942)

Leading Book Store Chains, 2002

Barnes & Noble	
Borders Group	
Books-A-Million	

Chains are ranked by sales for the first nine months of the year.

Barnes & Noble	$ 2,585.0
Borders Group	2,265.1
Books-A-Million	303.0

Source: *Publishers Weekly*, November 25, 2002, p. 9.

★ 1597 ★
Retailing - Books (SIC 5942)

Where Adult Books Are Purchased, 2001

Americans purchased 1.09 billion adult trade books in 2001. 56% of all households purchased at least one book during the year, up from 56% in 2000.

Large chain bookstores	23.3%
Book clubs	20.0
Independent/small chain bookstores	14.7
Internet	7.5
Warehouse/price clubs	6.6
Mass merchandisers	5.7
Food/drug stores	3.3
Used bookstores	3.3
Mail order/catalog	3.1
Discount stores	2.1
Multimedia	0.7
Other	9.3

Source: *Research Alert*, October 4, 2002, p. 6, from Ipsos-NPD.

★ 1598 ★
Retailing - Writing Instruments (SIC 5943)

Retail Writing Instrument Sales, 2002

The $750 million industry is shown by channel for the year ended October 5, 2002. Sales grew 4% over the previous year and do not include coloring pencils.

Discount stores	31.0%
Superstores	16.0
Drug stores	14.0
Grocery stores	11.0
Dollar stores	3.0
Warehouse clubs	3.0
Other	22.0

Source: *DSN Retailing Today*, November 11, 2002, p. 39, from A.C. Nielsen.

★ 1599 ★
Retailing - Jewelry (SIC 5944)

Gold Jewelry Sales

Market shares are shown in percent.

Independent stores	49.0%
Discount stores	22.0
Department stores	20.0
Non-store retail	9.0

Source: *National Jeweler*, September 1, 2002, p. 50, from Jewelers of America.

★ 1600 ★
Retailing - Jewelry (SIC 5944)

High-Priced Jewelry Retailing

Shares refer to the market for jewelry priced at $50,000 and higher. Figures are estimates.

Tiffany & Co.	19.0%
Cartier	11.0
Bulgari	3.5
Other	66.5

Source: *Forbes*, November 11, 2002, p. 76.

★ 1601 ★
Retailing - Jewelry (SIC 5944)

Leading Jewelry/Watch Retailers, 2001

Firms are ranked by estimated sales in millions of dollars. Figures show fiscal year sales.

Wal-Mart	$ 2,300.0
Zale Corp.	2,068.0
Sterling	1,599.0
J.C. Penney	1,000.0
Sears, Roebuck & Co.	1,000.0
Finlay Fine Jewelry	952.7
QVC	950.0
Tiffany & Co.	786.7
Helzberg Diamond Shops	500.0
Kmart	500.0
Target	450.0
Fred Meyer Jewelers	450.0

Source: *National Jeweler*, June 2002, p. S3, from Jewelry Industry Research.

★ 1602 ★
Retailing - Toys (SIC 5945)

Top Toy & Game Retailers, 2001

Firms are ranked by sales in millions of dollars.

	($ mil.)	Share
Wal-Mart	$ 8,300	28.04%
Toys R Us	6,747	22.79
KB Toys	2,000	6.76
Kmart	1,999	6.75
Target	1,995	6.74
GameStop	1,121	3.79
Electronics Boutique	868	2.93
Best Buy	750	2.53
Circuit City	350	1.18
Mattel	337	1.14
FAO	332	1.12
Meijer	330	1.11
Other	4,471	15.10

Source: *Playthings*, January 2003, p. 18, from U.S. Department of Commerce.

★ 1603 ★
Retailing - Toys (SIC 5945)

Top Toy Retailers

Market shares of the $30 billion industry are shown in percent.

Wal-Mart	20.0%
Toys R Us	17.0
Target	8.0
Kmart	6.0
K-B	5.0
Other	44.0

Source: *Promo*, January 1, 2003, p. NA, from Gerard Klauer Mattison.

★ 1604 ★
Retailing - Cameras (SIC 5946)

Retail Digital Camera Market, 2001

Market shares are shown based on unit sales.

Best Buy	13.5%
Wal-Mart	11.2
Circuit City	10.5
Staples	3.9
Sears	3.3
Comp USA	2.8
Office Max	2.8
Kmart	2.5
Target	2.4
Other	47.1

Source: *Dealerscope*, August 2002, p. 18, from Consumer Electronics Association, Electronic Industries Association, and Dealerscope research.

★ 1605 ★
Craft Stores (SIC 5949)

Leading Crafts Retailers

The industry spiked in the second half of the year, when Americans were spending more time at home. Firms are ranked by sales in millions of dollars.

Michaels Stores	$ 2,531
Jo Ann Stores	1,570
Hobby Lobby	1,015
Hancock Fabrics	412
Frank's Nursery & Crafts	371

Source: *DSN Retailing Today*, July 8, 2002, p. 35, from DSN research.

★ 1606 ★
Catalogs (SIC 5961)

Leading General Merchandise Catalogs, 2001

Companies are ranked by sales in billions of dollars.

J.C. Penney	$ 3.3
Lands' End	1.6
Spiegel	1.5
Brylane	1.5
Federated Department Stores	1.2
L.L. Bean	1.1
Blair	0.6
Hanover Direct	0.5
Sears	0.5
Neiman Marcus	0.4

Source: *USA TODAY*, December 2, 2002, p. 2B, from *Catalog Age*.

★ 1607 ★
Catalogs (SIC 5961)

School Catalog Market

The company is a cataloger of planners and school agendas for students.

Premier Agenda	70.0%
Other	30.0

Source: *Catalog Age*, February 12, 2003, p. NA.

★ 1608 ★
Home Shopping Industry (SIC 5963)

Home Shopping Leaders, 2001

Networks are ranked by revenues in millions of dollars. The home shopping industry is thought to be worth $7 billion.

QVC	$ 3,920.0
HSN	1,930.0
ShopNBC	463.3
Shop at Home	177.6

Source: *Broadcasting & Cable*, July 15, 2002, p. 24.

★ 1609 ★
Telemarketing (SIC 5963)

Telemarketing Phone Calls

Revenues from telemarketing calls increased 250% from 1990 to 2002, hitting $295 billion. Figures show the millions of phone calls to homes and businesses each day. 2003 figure is projected.

2003	104
1991	18

Source: *Time*, April 28, 2003, p. 56, from industry estimates.

★ 1610 ★
Propane Dealers (SIC 5983)

Largest Propane Retailers, 2002

Companies are ranked by millions of retail gallons sold.

AmeriGas Partners	932.8
Ferrellgas Partners	871.6
Cenex Propane Partners	567.6
Suburban Propane Partners	456.0
Heritage Propane Partners	329.6
CornerStone Propane	238.6
Star Gas Propane	140.0
Inergy L.P.	112.0
Agway Energy Products	88.5
MFA Oil Co.	86.2

Source: *LP/Gas*, February 2003, p. NA.

★ 1611 ★
Propane Dealers (SIC 5983)

Propane Cylinder Industry

There has been a recent trend of consumers exchanging old tanks for new ones. The exchange market is shown by company.

Blue Rhino	50.0%
AmeriGas	20.0
Other	30.0

Source: *Investor's Business Daily*, September 19, 2002, p. A10, from Stephens Inc. and company reports.

★ 1612 ★
Fuel Oil Dealers (SIC 5984)

Petroleum Product Sales

Distribution is shown based on total volume.

Kerosene	54.4%
Gasoline	15.9
Lube	5.5
Diesel	1.5

Source: *Fuel Oil News*, December 2002, p. 14.

★ 1613 ★
Retailing - Flowers (SIC 5992)

Flowers-by-Wire Industry

The entire floral industry is valued at $15 billion a year. It is fiercely competitive as well, with Internet firms competing with standard retail florists. Shares are estimates of the electronic industry.

Teleflora	33.0%
FTD	33.0
American Floral Services	33.0

Source: "Darwin Executive Guides." available April 7, 2003 from http://www.guide.darwinmag.com/lifestyle/shopping/flowers, from American Floral Services.

★ 1614 ★
Retailing - Flowers (SIC 5992)

Retail Flower Sales, 2001

Distribution is shown based on consumer expenditures.

Florist shop	27.1%
Garden centers	21.4
Supermarkets	14.1
Home centers	8.9
Discount stores	7.5
Internet retailers	3.3
Craft/art/specialty stores	2.3
Warehouse clubs	1.5
Other	13.8

Source: *Progressive Grocer*, April 15, 2002, p. 12, from American Floral Endowment and Ipsos-NPD Inc.

★ 1615 ★
Duty-Free Shops (SIC 5999)

Duty-Free Shops in Canada, 2002

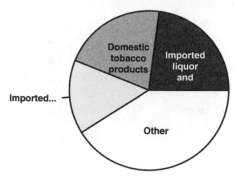

Total sales rose 12.7% over 2001 to hit $144.7 million. The top categories are shown.

Imported liquor and wines	23.14%
Domestic tobacco products	21.00
Imported fragrances and cosmetics	15.00
Other	40.86

Source: *Duty-Free News International*, March 1, 2003, p. 5, from Frontier Duty Free Association.

★ 1616 ★
Military Exchange Posts (SIC 5999)

Leading Military Exchange Posts

The category had over $10 billion in sales. Fastest-growing categories include gasoline, soft drinks, and photo items. Organizations are ranked by sales in millions of dollars.

Army & Air Force Exchange	$ 7,409
Navy Exchange Service Command	2,137
Marine Corps Exchange	620
Veterans Canteen Service	230
Coast Guard Exchange	145

Source: *DSN Retailing Today*, July 8, 2002, p. 32, from DSN research.

★ 1617 ★
Retailing - Personal Products (SIC 5999)

Beauty Care Market in Canada

Sales are shown by channel.

	2000	2002
Department stores	24.1%	21.9%
Drug stores	23.1	25.0
Home/direct sales	18.2	18.4
Cosmetic/beauty care stores	11.0	8.4
Discount stores	10.9	10.5
Other	16.5	12.8

Source: *Cosmetics Magazine - Newsletter*, May 2003, p. NA, from Trendex.

★ 1618 ★
Retailing - Personal Products (SIC 5999)

Retail Soap Market, 2001

Soap sales reached $1.69 billion.

Discount stores	40.0%
Food/drug	33.0
Chain drug stores	15.0
Supermarkets	9.0
Independent drug stores	3.0

Source: *Global Cosmetic Industry*, December 2002, p. 24, from Racher Press.

★ 1619 ★
Retailing - Personal Products (SIC 5999)

Retail Toothpaste Market

Sales are shown for the year ended November 29, 2002. Figures exclude Wal-Mart.

	($ mil.)	Share
Food	$ 731.9	59.04%
Mass	348.1	28.08
Drug stores	159.6	12.88

Source: *Grocery Headquarters*, March 2003, p. 60, from Information Resources Inc.

★ 1620 ★
Retailing - Swimming Pools (SIC 5999)

Leading Pool Retailers

Companies are ranked by revenues in millions of dollars.

Leslie's Poolmart Inc.	$ 301.7
Anthony & Sylvan Pools	14.0
Tony V's Sunrooms & Spas	13.0
Classic Spas & Hot Tubs Inc.	12.0
B&G Inc.	10.0
Spa Brokers Inc.	9.8
Pool & Spa Depot	9.0
Spa & Leisure Inc.	7.8
Long Island Hot Tubs	7.0
Olympic Hot Tub Co.	6.4

Source: *Pool & Spa News*, September 6, 2002, p. 68.

SIC 60 - Depository Institutions

★ 1621 ★
Banking (SIC 6020)

Top Banks in Alabama, 2002

- Regions Bank
- SouthTrust Bank
- AmSouth Bank
- Compass Bank
- Colonial Bank
- New South Federal Savings Bank
- First Commercial Bank
- Other

Market shares are shown based on deposits.

Regions Bank	16.68%
SouthTrust Bank	14.76
AmSouth Bank	12.14
Compass Bank	8.74
Colonial Bank	6.28
New South Federal Savings Bank	1.68
First Commercial Bank	1.63
Other	38.09

Source: "Market Share Report." available January 7, 2003 from http://www.fdic.gov, from Federal Deposit Insurance Corp.

★ 1622 ★
Banking (SIC 6020)

Top Banks in Alaska, 2002

Market shares are shown based on deposits as of June 30, 2002.

Wells Fargo Bank Alaska, National Association	44.00%
First National Bank Alaska	23.02
Northrim Bank	11.00
Keybank National Association	7.64
First Bank	5.00
Mt. McKinley Mutual Savings Bank	3.04

Denali State Bank	2.93%
Other	3.37

Source: "Market Share Report." available January 7, 2003 from http://www.fdic.gov, from Federal Deposit Insurance Corp.

★ 1623 ★
Banking (SIC 6020)

Top Banks in American Samoa, 2002

Market shares are shown based on deposits as of June 30, 2002.

American Samoa Bank	58.38%
Bank of Hawaii	41.62

Source: "Market Share Report." available January 7, 2003 from http://www.fdic.gov, from Federal Deposit Insurance Corp.

★ 1624 ★
Banking (SIC 6020)

Top Banks in Arizona, 2002

Market shares are shown based on deposits as of June 30, 2002.

Bank One	27.53%
Bank of America	21.15
Wells Fargo Bank Arizona	20.35
National Bank of Arizona	4.61
Compass Bank	3.31
World Savings Bank	3.27
Direct Merchants Credit Card Bank	2.71
M&I Marshall and Ilsley Bank	2.28
Other	14.79

Source: "Market Share Report." available January 7, 2003 from http://www.fdic.gov, from Federal Deposit Insurance Corp.

★ 1625 ★
Banking (SIC 6020)

Top Banks in Arkansas

Regions Financial

Arvest Bank Group

Bank of America

BancorpSouth

Simmons First National Corp.

First Security Bancorp

U.S. Bancorp

Other

Market shares are shown based on deposits.

Regions Financial (First Commercial)	10.99%
Arvest Bank Group	6.02
Bank of America (NationsBank)	5.81
BancorpSouth (First United)	4.70
Simmons First National Corp.	4.64
First Security Bancorp	3.37
U.S. Bancorp (Firstar/Mercantile)	2.94
Other	61.53

Source: *Arkansas Business*, December 9, 2002, p. 1, from Federal Deposit Insurance Corp.

★ 1626 ★
Banking (SIC 6020)

Top Banks in Augusta, GA

Market shares are shown based on deposits for June 20, 2002.

Wachovia Bank	24.96%
Regions Bank	15.35
Bank of America	13.06
SunTrust Bank	13.06
Georgia Bank & Trust Co.	9.19
SouthTrust Bank	8.50
Security Federal Bank	6.27
Other	9.61

Source: *Knight-Ridder/Tribune Business News*, December 11, 2002, p. NA, from Federal Deposit Insurance Corp.

★ 1627 ★
Banking (SIC 6020)

Top Banks in Broward County, FL

Market shares are shown based on deposits.

Bank of America	26.0%
Wachovia	14.8
Ohio Savings Bank	8.2
SunTrust	7.2
BankAtlantic	5.9
Other	37.9

Source: *Investor's Business Daily*, February 11, 2002, p. A10, from Federal Deposit Insurance Corp.

★ 1628 ★
Banking (SIC 6020)

Top Banks in California, 2002

Market shares are shown based on deposits as of June 30, 2002.

Bank of America	20.72%
Wells Fargo Bank	14.56
Washington Mutual Bank	13.53
Union Bank of California	5.03
California Federal Bank	4.12
World Savings Bank	4.00
Bank of the West	2.96
Comerica Bank-California	2.55
Other	32.53

Source: "Market Share Report." available January 7, 2003 from http://www.fdic.gov, from Federal Deposit Insurance Corp.

★ 1629 ★
Banking (SIC 6020)

Top Banks in Charlotte, NC

Market shares are shown in percent.

Bank of America	45.71%
Wachovia	32.00
BB&T	4.90
Other	17.39

Source: *Charlotte Observer*, December 4, 2002, p. NA, from Federal Deposit Insurance Corp.

★ 1630 ★

Banking (SIC 6020)

Top Banks in Chicago, IL (Retail)

Market shares are shown in percent.

Bank One Corp.	17.0%
ABN AMRO	13.0
Business Harris Bankcorp Inc.	9.0
Other	61.0

Source: *National Post*, December 12, 2002, p. F4.

★ 1631 ★

Banking (SIC 6020)

Top Banks in Colorado

Market shares are shown in percent.

Wells Fargo	18.0%
U.S. Bank	11.0
FirstBank	9.0
Bank One	5.5
KeyBank	1.4
Compass	1.4
Other	53.7

Source: *Rocky Mountain News*, November 9, 2002, p. 3C, from Federal Deposit Insurance Corp.

★ 1632 ★

Banking (SIC 6020)

Top Banks in Connecticut, 2002

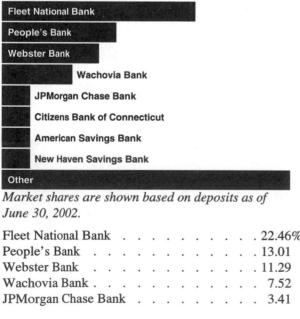

Market shares are shown based on deposits as of June 30, 2002.

Fleet National Bank	22.46%
People's Bank	13.01
Webster Bank	11.29
Wachovia Bank	7.52
JPMorgan Chase Bank	3.41

Citizens Bank of Connecticut	3.35%
American Savings Bank	3.14
New Haven Savings Bank	2.84
Other	32.98

Source: ''Market Share Report.'' available January 7, 2003 from http://www.fdic.gov, from Federal Deposit Insurance Corp.

★ 1633 ★

Banking (SIC 6020)

Top Banks in Delaware, 2002

Market shares are shown based on deposits as of June 30, 2002.

MBNA America Bank	30.74%
Discover Bank	15.77
Chase Manhattan Bank	12.99
ING Bank	7.82
Wilmington Trust Company	7.04
First USA Bank	6.01
Lehman Brothers Bank	3.30
PNC Bank	2.88
Travelers Bank & Trust	1.52
Other	11.93

Source: ''Market Share Report.'' available January 7, 2003 from http://www.fdic.gov, from Federal Deposit Insurance Corp.

★ 1634 ★

Banking (SIC 6020)

Top Banks in Florida, 2002

Market shares are shown based on deposits as of June 30, 2002.

Bank of America	20.44%
Wachovia Bank	14.98
SunTrust Bank	11.85
SouthTrust Bank	3.99
Washington Mutual Bank	3.93
AmSouth Bank	2.19
Ohio Savings Bank	2.17
Citibank, Federal Savings Bank	2.11
Other	38.34

Source: ''Market Share Report.'' available January 7, 2003 from http://www.fdic.gov, from Federal Deposit Insurance Corp.

★ 1635 ★
Banking (SIC 6020)

Top Banks in Guam, 2002

Market shares are shown based on deposits as of June 30, 2002.

Bank of Guam	25.20%
First Hawaiian Bank	22.95
Bank of Hawaii	20.84
Citibank, National Association	13.89
Citizens Security Bank (Guam) Inc.	6.92
First Savings and Loan Association of America	4.84
Other	5.36

Source: "Market Share Report." available January 7, 2003 from http://www.fdic.gov, from Federal Deposit Insurance Corp.

★ 1636 ★
Banking (SIC 6020)

Top Banks in Guilford County, NC

Wachovia	
BB&T	
CCB	
Bank of America	
High Point Bank & Trust	
Other	

Market shares are shown based on deposits. Figures are mid-year 2002.

Wachovia	28.8%
BB&T	21.5
CCB	13.5
Bank of America	12.8
High Point Bank & Trust	8.1
Other	15.3

Source: *Knight Ridder/Tribune Business News*, December 16, 2002, p. NA, from Federal Deposit Insurance Corp.

★ 1637 ★
Banking (SIC 6020)

Top Banks in Hawaii, 2002

Market shares are shown based on deposits as of June 30, 2002.

First Hawaiian Bank	29.73%
Bank of Hawaii	29.43
American Savings Bank	19.44
Central Pacific Bank	8.08
City Bank	5.95
Territorial Savings and Loan Association	2.87
Finance Factors	2.16
Hawaii National Bank	1.69
Other	0.65

Source: "Market Share Report." available January 7, 2003 from http://www.fdic.gov, from Federal Deposit Insurance Corp.

★ 1638 ★
Banking (SIC 6020)

Top Banks in Idaho, 2002

Market shares are shown based on deposits as of June 30, 2002.

Wells Fargo Bank Northwest	27.69%
U.S. Bank National Association	19.37
Keybank National Association	4.93
Bank of America	4.42
Washington Federal Savings and Loan Association	4.13
Bank of Commerce	3.36
Zions First National Bank	2.63
Home Federal Savings and Loan Association	2.30
Other	31.17

Source: "Market Share Report." available January 7, 2003 from http://www.fdic.gov, from Federal Deposit Insurance Corp.

★ 1639 ★
Banking (SIC 6020)

Top Banks in Illinois, 2002

Market shares are shown based on deposits as of June 30, 2002.

Bank One	11.18%
LaSalle Bank National Association	9.53
Harris Trust and Savings Bank	3.77

Continued on next page.

★ 1639 ★ *Continued*

Banking (SIC 6020)

Top Banks in Illinois, 2002

Market shares are shown based on deposits as of June 30, 2002.

Citibank, Federal Savings Bank	3.12%
Northern Trust Company	3.02
American National Bank and Trust Company of Chicago	2.69
Fifth Third Bank	2.42
Charter One Bank, National Association	2.32
Other	61.95

Source: "Market Share Report." available January 7, 2003 from http://www.fdic.gov, from Federal Deposit Insurance Corp.

★ 1640 ★

Banking (SIC 6020)

Top Banks in Indiana, 2002

Market shares are shown based on deposits as of June 30, 2002.

Bank One, Indiana, National Association	12.24%
National City Bank of Indiana	9.88
Old National Bank	5.96
Fifth Third Bank	5.38
1st Source Bank	3.53
Irwin Union Bank and Trust Company	2.51
Union Planters Bank, National Association	2.46
Keybank National Association	2.19
Other	55.85

Source: "Market Share Report." available January 7, 2003 from http://www.fdic.gov, from Federal Deposit Insurance Corp.

★ 1641 ★

Banking (SIC 6020)

Top Banks in Iowa, 2002

Market shares are shown based on deposits as of June 30, 2002.

Wells Fargo Bank Iowa	12.15%
U.S. Bank National Association	9.02
Principal Bank	2.78
Commercial Federal Bank	2.15
Bankers Trust Company	1.97
Hills Bank and Trust Company	1.58
Bank of America	1.56

First American Bank	1.23%
Other	67.56

Source: "Market Share Report." available January 7, 2003 from http://www.fdic.gov, from Federal Deposit Insurance Corp.

★ 1642 ★

Banking (SIC 6020)

Top Banks in Kansas, 2002

Market shares are shown based on deposits as of June 30, 2002.

Capitol Federal Savings Bank	10.59%
Bank of America	6.52
Intrust Bank, National Association	4.22
U.S. Bank National Association	2.68
Gold Bank	2.52
First National Bank of Kansas	2.19
Commerce Bank, National Association	2.19
World Savings Bank	2.14
Other	66.95

Source: "Market Share Report." available January 7, 2003 from http://www.fdic.gov, from Federal Deposit Insurance Corp.

★ 1643 ★

Banking (SIC 6020)

Top Banks in Kentucky, 2002

Market shares are shown based on deposits as of June 30, 2002.

National City Bank of Kentucky	9.13%
Bank One, Kentucky, National Association	7.16
U.S. Bank National Association	5.81
PNC Bank, National Association	4.23
Fifth Third Bank	3.67
Community Trust Bank, National Association	3.58
Area Bank	3.57
Bank of Louisville	2.23
Other	64.20

Source: "Market Share Report." available January 7, 2003 from http://www.fdic.gov, from Federal Deposit Insurance Corp.

★ 1644 ★
Banking (SIC 6020)

Top Banks in Louisiana, 2002

Market shares are shown based on deposits as of June 30, 2002.

Hibernia National Bank	21.41%
Bank One	18.43
Whitney National Bank	8.57
Regions Bank	6.61
AmSouth Bank	2.75
Hancock Bank of Louisiana	2.42
Iberiabank	2.40
Union Planters Bank	1.42
Other	34.99

Source: "Market Share Report." available January 7, 2003 from http://www.fdic.gov, from Federal Deposit Insurance Corp.

★ 1645 ★
Banking (SIC 6020)

Top Banks in Madison, WI

Market shares are shown for 2002.

AnchorBank	16.09%
M&I	15.50
U.S. Bank	12.02
Other	56.39

Source: *Knight Ridder/Tribune Business News*, December 2, 2002, p. NA, from Federal Deposit Insurance Corp.

★ 1646 ★
Banking (SIC 6020)

Top Banks in Maine, 2002

Market shares are shown based on deposits as of June 30, 2002.

BankNorth	19.30%
Keybank National Association	12.68
Fleet National Bank	7.85
Bangor Savings Bank	7.04
Camden National Bank	3.76

Norway Savings Bank	3.31%
Gardiner Savings Institution	2.93
Kennebunk Savings Bank	2.73
Other	59.70

Source: "Market Share Report." available January 7, 2003 from http://www.fdic.gov, from Federal Deposit Insurance Corp.

★ 1647 ★
Banking (SIC 6020)

Top Banks in Maryland, 2002

Market shares are shown based on deposits as of June 30, 2002.

Bank of America	16.57%
Allfirst Bank	10.61
Chevy Chase Bank	8.10
SunTrust Bank	7.95
Wachovia Bank	6.66
Provident Bank of Maryland	4.60
Branch Banking and Trust Company	4.18
Mercantile-Safe Deposit and Trust Company	3.98
Other	37.35

Source: "Market Share Report." available January 7, 2003 from http://www.fdic.gov, from Federal Deposit Insurance Corp.

★ 1648 ★
Banking (SIC 6020)

Top Banks in Massachusetts, 2002

Market shares are shown based on deposits as of June 30, 2002.

Fleet National Bank	22.66%
State Street Bank and Trust Company	12.20
Citizens Bank of Massachusetts	8.86
Sovereign Bank	5.04
Boston Safe Deposit and Trust Company	3.45
BankNorth	3.24
Eastern Bank	2.21
Investors Bank & Trust Company	1.75
Other	40.59

Source: "Market Share Report." available January 7, 2003 from http://www.fdic.gov, from Federal Deposit Insurance Corp.

★ 1649 ★

Banking (SIC 6020)

Top Banks in Michigan, 2002

Market shares are shown based on deposits as of June 30, 2002.

Comerica Bank	16.50%
Standard Federal Bank	14.55
Bank One	13.05
Fifth Third Bank	8.97
National City Bank of Michigan/Illinois	7.07
Charter One Bank	3.86
Huntington National Bank	3.68
Citizens Bank	3.06
Other	29.26

Source: "Market Share Report." available January 7, 2003 from http://www.fdic.gov, from Federal Deposit Insurance Corp.

★ 1650 ★

Banking (SIC 6020)

Top Banks in Minnesota, 2002

Market shares are shown based on deposits as of June 30, 2002.

Wells Fargo Bank Minnesota	30.04%
U.S. Bank National Association	17.03
TCF National Bank	4.13
Associated Bank Minnesota	1.68
Bremer Bank	1.59
M&I Marshall and Ilsley Bank	1.33
Marquette Bank	1.21
Community First National Bank	0.90
Other	42.33

Source: "Market Share Report." available January 7, 2003 from http://www.fdic.gov, from Federal Deposit Insurance Corp.

★ 1651 ★

Banking (SIC 6020)

Top Banks in Mississippi, 2002

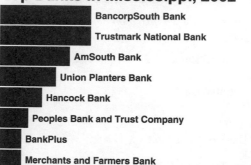

BancorpSouth Bank

Trustmark National Bank

AmSouth Bank

Union Planters Bank

Hancock Bank

Peoples Bank and Trust Company

BankPlus

Merchants and Farmers Bank

Other

Market shares are shown based on deposits as of June 30, 2002.

BancorpSouth Bank	13.29%
Trustmark National Bank	13.15
AmSouth Bank	9.63
Union Planters Bank	7.88
Hancock Bank	6.43
Peoples Bank and Trust Company	3.54
BankPlus	2.70
Merchants and Farmers Bank	2.64
Other	40.74

Source: "Market Share Report." available January 7, 2003 from http://www.fdic.gov, from Federal Deposit Insurance Corp.

★ 1652 ★

Banking (SIC 6020)

Top Banks in Missouri, 2002

Market shares are shown based on deposits as of June 30, 2002.

U.S. Bank	15.50%
Bank of America	10.91
Commerce Bank	9.04
UMB Bank	4.68
Union Planters Bank	3.14
First Bank	2.05
Southwest Bank of St. Louis	1.84
Bank Midwest	1.81
Other	51.03

Source: "Market Share Report." available January 7, 2003 from http://www.fdic.gov, from Federal Deposit Insurance Corp.

★ 1653 ★

Banking (SIC 6020)

Top Banks in Montana, 2002

First Interstate Bank

Wells Fargo Bank Montana

U.S. Bank

Stockman Bank of Montana

First Security Bank of Missoula

Glacier Bank

Mountain West Bank

First Security Bank

Other

Market shares are shown based on deposits as of June 30, 2002.

First Interstate Bank	15.46%
Wells Fargo Bank Montana	11.84
U.S. Bank	7.52
Stockman Bank of Montana	5.95
First Security Bank of Missoula	3.30
Glacier Bank	3.16
Mountain West Bank	2.89
First Security Bank	2.47
Other	47.41

Source: "Market Share Report." available January 7, 2003 from http://www.fdic.gov, from Federal Deposit Insurance Corp.

★ 1654 ★

Banking (SIC 6020)

Top Banks in Nebraska, 2002

Market shares are shown based on deposits as of June 30, 2002.

First National Bank of Omaha	11.76%
Wells Fargo Bank Nebraska	9.81
U.S. Bank	6.46
Pinnacle Bank	4.36
Commercial Federal Bank	4.16
TierOne Bank	3.12
Union Bank and Trust Company	3.06
American National Bank	2.22
Other	55.05

Source: "Market Share Report." available January 7, 2003 from http://www.fdic.gov, from Federal Deposit Insurance Corp.

★ 1655 ★

Banking (SIC 6020)

Top Banks in Nevada, 2002

Market shares are shown based on deposits as of June 30, 2002.

Wells Fargo Bank Nevada	20.41%
Bank of America	19.48
Citibank	19.34
Nevada State Bank	8.23
U.S. Bank National Association	5.97
California Federal Bank	3.51
Colonial Bank	2.23
BankWest of Nevada	2.23
Other	18.60

Source: "Market Share Report." available January 7, 2003 from http://www.fdic.gov, from Federal Deposit Insurance Corp.

★ 1656 ★

Banking (SIC 6020)

Top Banks in New Hampshire, 2002

Market shares are shown based on deposits as of June 30, 2002.

Providian National Bank	41.90%
Citizens Bank New Hampshire	15.17
BankNorth	13.00
Fleet National Bank	5.84
Granite Bank	2.60
Laconia Savings Bank	1.94
First Essex Bank	1.71
Sovereign Bank	1.64
Other	16.20

Source: "Market Share Report." available January 7, 2003 from http://www.fdic.gov, from Federal Deposit Insurance Corp.

★ 1657 ★

Banking (SIC 6020)

Top Banks in New Jersey, 2002

Market shares are shown based on deposits as of June 30, 2002.

Fleet National Bank	19.11%
Wachovia Bank	10.28
PNC Bank	7.20
Merrill Lynch Bank and Trust	6.98
Hudson City Savings Bank	4.73

Continued on next page.

Banking (SIC 6020)

Top Banks in New Jersey, 2002

Market shares are shown based on deposits as of June 30, 2002.

Sovereign Bank	3.76%
Commerce Bank	3.41
Valley National Bank	3.12
Other	41.41

Source: "Market Share Report." available January 7, 2003 from http://www.fdic.gov, from Federal Deposit Insurance Corp.

★ 1658 ★
Banking (SIC 6020)

Top Banks in New Mexico, 2002

Market shares are shown based on deposits as of June 30, 2002.

Wells Fargo Bank	23.75%
Bank of America	15.57
First State Bank of Taos	4.94
Los Alamos National Bank	4.29
Bank of Albuquerque	4.05
First National Bank of Santa Fe	2.21
Charter Bank	2.09
Citizens Bank	1.94
Other	41.16

Source: "Market Share Report." available January 7, 2003 from http://www.fdic.gov, from Federal Deposit Insurance Corp.

★ 1659 ★
Banking (SIC 6020)

Top Banks in New York, 2002

Market shares are shown based on deposits as of June 30, 2002.

JPMorgan Chase Bank	23.59%
Citibank	20.03
HSBC Bank USA	7.27
Bank of New York	5.02
Fleet National Bank	3.37
Manufacturers and Traders Trust Company	2.96
North Fork Bank	2.30
Astoria Federal Savings	2.18
GreenPoint Bank	2.18
Other	31.10

Source: "Market Share Report." available January 7, 2003 from http://www.fdic.gov, from Federal Deposit Insurance Corp.

★ 1660 ★
Banking (SIC 6020)

Top Banks in North Carolina, 2002

Market shares are shown based on deposits as of June 30, 2002.

Wachovia Bank	25.78%
Bank of America	21.11
Branch Banking and Trust Company	15.38
First Citizens Bank & Trust Company	6.85
National Bank of Commerce	6.00
RBC Centura Bank	5.35
First Charter Bank	1.88
First Bank	0.83
Other	16.82

Source: "Market Share Report." available January 7, 2003 from http://www.fdic.gov, from Federal Deposit Insurance Corp.

★ 1661 ★
Banking (SIC 6020)

Top Banks in North Dakota, 2002

Market shares are shown based on deposits as of June 30, 2002.

Wells Fargo	10.86%
U.S. Bank National Association ND	9.89
U.S. Bank	8.82

Continued on next page.

★ 1661 ★ *Continued*

Banking (SIC 6020)

Top Banks in North Dakota, 2002

Market shares are shown based on deposits as of June 30, 2002.

Gate City Bank	4.84%
State Bank of Fargo	3.29
BNC National Bank	3.04
Alerus Financial	2.98
First International Bank & Trust	2.89
Other	53.39

Source: "Market Share Report." available January 7, 2003 from http://www.fdic.gov, from Federal Deposit Insurance Corp.

★ 1662 ★

Banking (SIC 6020)

Top Banks in Ohio, 2002

Market shares are shown based on deposits as of June 30, 2002.

Fifth Third Bank	11.11%
National City Bank	10.09
Keybank National Association	9.61
Bank One	8.18
U.S. Bank	6.55
Huntington National Bank	5.04
Provident Bank	4.73
Charter One Bank	3.98
Other	40.71

Source: "Market Share Report." available January 7, 2003 from http://www.fdic.gov, from Federal Deposit Insurance Corp.

★ 1663 ★

Banking (SIC 6020)

Top Banks in Oklahoma, 2002

Market shares are shown based on deposits as of June 30, 2002.

Bank of Oklahoma	11.94%
BancFirst	5.81
Bank One, Oklahoma	5.05
MidFirst Bank	5.04
Bank of America	5.02
Local Oklahoma Bank	4.61
Arvest Bank	4.01
Stillwater National Bank	2.45
Other	56.07

Source: "Market Share Report." available January 7, 2003 from http://www.fdic.gov, from Federal Deposit Insurance Corp.

★ 1664 ★

Banking (SIC 6020)

Top Banks in Oregon, 2002

Market shares are shown based on deposits as of June 30, 2002.

U.S. Bank	24.77%
Washington Mutual Bank	13.08
Wells Fargo Bank Northwest	11.45
Bank of America	10.66
Keybank National Association	6.00
Umpqua Bank	3.79
Klamath First Federal Savings	3.37
West Coat Bank	2.73
Other	24.15

Source: "Market Share Report." available January 7, 2003 from http://www.fdic.gov, from Federal Deposit Insurance Corp.

★ 1665 ★

Banking (SIC 6020)

Top Banks in Pennsylvania, 2002

*Market shares are shown based on deposits as of
June 30, 2002.*

PNC Bank	12.94%
Wachovia Bank	11.44
Citizens Bank of Pennsylvania	7.58
National City Bank of Pennsylvania . . .	5.57
Mellon Bank, National Association	4.56
Sovereign Bank	3.26
Manufacturers and Traders Trust	2.38
Allfirst Bank	1.93
Northwest Savings Bank	1.82
Other	48.52

Source: "Market Share Report." available January 7, 2003
from http://www.fdic.gov, from Federal Deposit Insurance
Corp.

★ 1666 ★

Banking (SIC 6020)

Top Banks in Puerto Rico, 2002

*Market shares are shown based on deposits as of
June 30, 2002.*

Banco Popular de Puerto Rico	31.48%
Banco Santander Puerto Rico	12.43
FirstBank of Puerto Rico	11.85
Westernbank Puerto Rico	9.70
Banco Bilbao Vizcaya Argentaria	8.24
Citibank	7.53
R-G Premier Bank of Puerto Rico	5.40
Other	13.37

Source: "Market Share Report." available January 7, 2003
from http://www.fdic.gov, from Federal Deposit Insurance
Corp.

★ 1667 ★

Banking (SIC 6020)

Top Banks in Rhode Island, 2002

*Market shares are shown based on deposits as of
June 30, 2002.*

Citizens Bank of Rhode Island	42.34%
Fleet National bank	21.75
Sovereign Bank	12.13
Washington Trust Company	6.46
Bank Rhode Island	4.47
Bank of Newport	3.58
Centreville Savings Bank	3.08
Other	6.19

Source: "Market Share Report." available January 7, 2003
from http://www.fdic.gov, from Federal Deposit Insurance
Corp.

★ 1668 ★

Banking (SIC 6020)

Top Banks in South Carolina, 2002

*Market shares are shown based on deposits as of
June 30, 2002.*

Wachovia Bank	19.80%
Bank of America	12.46
Branch Banking and Trust Company of SC . .	11.12
First-Citizens Bank and Trust Company . . .	7.16
Carolina First Bank	7.15
National Bank of South Carolina	4.30
National Bank of Commerce	3.38
First Federal Savings and Loan	2.39
Other	32.24

Source: "Market Share Report." available January 7, 2003
from http://www.fdic.gov, from Federal Deposit Insurance
Corp.

★ 1669 ★
Banking (SIC 6020)

Top Banks in South Dakota, 2002

Market shares are shown based on deposits as of June 30, 2002.

Wells Fargo Bank	14.91%
Citibank (South Dakota)	7.91
Citibank USA	6.91
First Premier Bank	4.55
U.S. Bank	4.07
Dacotah Bank	3.98
Home Federal Bank	3.83
First National Bank in Sioux Falls	3.09
Other	50.75

Source: "Market Share Report." available January 7, 2003 from http://www.fdic.gov, from Federal Deposit Insurance Corp.

★ 1670 ★
Banking (SIC 6020)

Top Banks in Tennessee, 2002

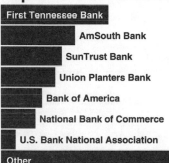

Market shares are shown based on deposits as of June 30, 2002.

First Tennessee Bank	15.65%
AmSouth Bank	11.03
SunTrust Bank	8.61
Union Planters Bank	7.69
Bank of America	6.15
National Bank of Commerce	5.42
U.S. Bank National Association	2.37
Other	43.08

Source: "Market Share Report." available January 7, 2003 from http://www.fdic.gov, from Federal Deposit Insurance Corp.

★ 1671 ★
Banking (SIC 6020)

Top Banks in Texas, 2002

Market shares are shown based on deposits as of June 30, 2002.

JPMorgan Chase Bank	12.38%
Bank of America	12.29
Wells Fargo Bank Texas	7.71
Bank One	7.58
USAA Federal Savings Bank	3.61
Washington Mutual Bank	3.09
Frost National Bank	2.69
Guaranty Bank	2.62
Other	48.03

Source: "Market Share Report." available January 7, 2003 from http://www.fdic.gov, from Federal Deposit Insurance Corp.

★ 1672 ★
Banking (SIC 6020)

Top Banks in Utah, 2002

Market shares are shown based on deposits as of June 30, 2002.

Merrill Lynch Bank	66.42%
Zions First National Bank	6.97
Wells Fargo Bank Northwest	5.77
American Express Centurion Bank	3.35
Conseco Bank	2.46
Providian Bank	2.08
Bank One	2.01
Other	10.94

Source: "Market Share Report." available January 7, 2003 from http://www.fdic.gov, from Federal Deposit Insurance Corp.

★ 1673 ★
Banking (SIC 6020)

Top Banks in Vermont, 2002

Market shares are shown based on deposits as of June 30, 2002.

Chittenden Trust Company	28.10%
BankNorth	18.30
Charter One Bank	11.01
Merchants Bank	8.59
Keybank National Association	5.35
Northfield Savings Bank	3.50

Continued on next page.

★ 1673 ★ *Continued*
Banking (SIC 6020)

Top Banks in Vermont, 2002

Market shares are shown based on deposits as of June 30, 2002.

Passumpsic Savings Bank	2.95%
Other	22.20

Source: "Market Share Report." available January 7, 2003 from http://www.fdic.gov, from Federal Deposit Insurance Corp.

★ 1674 ★
Banking (SIC 6020)

Top Banks in Virginia, 2002

Market shares are shown based on deposits as of June 30, 2002.

Wachovia Bank	15.55%
SunTrust Bank	10.58
Bank of America	9.54
Capital One	8.83
Branch Banking and Trust Company of Virginia	7.63
E*Trade Bank	7.17
Capital One Bank	4.37
Other	36.33

Source: "Market Share Report." available January 7, 2003 from http://www.fdic.gov, from Federal Deposit Insurance Corp.

★ 1675 ★
Banking (SIC 6020)

Top Banks in Washington D.C., 2002

Riggs Bank National Association
Wachovia Bank
Bank of America
SunTrust Bank
Citibank, Federal Savings Bank
Branch Banking and Trust Company
Chevy Chase Bank
Allfirst Bank
Other

Market shares are shown based on deposits as of June 30, 2002.

Riggs Bank National Association	22.88%
Wachovia Bank	18.74
Bank of America	17.38
SunTrust Bank	11.17
Citibank, Federal Savings Bank	9.55
Branch Banking and Trust Company	5.97
Chevy Chase Bank	2.40
Allfirst Bank	1.95
Other	9.96

Source: "Market Share Report." available January 7, 2003 from http://www.fdic.gov, from Federal Deposit Insurance Corp.

★ 1676 ★
Banking (SIC 6020)

Top Banks in Wichita, KS

Market shares are shown based on deposits as of June 30, 2001.

Intrust Bank	19.25%
Bank of America	13.08
Commerce Bank	7.45
Capitol Federal Savings Bank	7.05
Fidelity Bank	6.45
Other	46.72

Source: *Wichita Business Journal*, October 11, 2002, p. 1, from Federal Deposit Insurance Corp.

★ 1677 ★
Credit Unions (SIC 6060)

Largest Credit Unions

Credit unions are ranked by assets in millions of dollars.

U.S. Navy	$ 15,107
State Employees	8,187
Pentagon	4,270
Boeing Employees	3,958
The Golden 1	3,772
United Airlines Employees	3,612
American Airlines	3,396
Orange Country Teachers	3,352
Suncoast Schools	2,998
Kinecta	2,442

Source: *Retailer Banker International*, July 31, 2002, p. 6, from National Credit Union Administration.

★ 1678 ★
Credit Unions (SIC 6062)

Draft Processing in Colorado

The company performs the majority of draft processing for credit unions.

Colleague Services Corp.	80.0%
Other	20.0

Source: "Colleague Services Corporation." available January 7, 2003 from http://www.wausaufs.com.

★ 1679 ★
Bill Payment (SIC 6090)

Corporate Bill Payment

Figures show shares of the business-to-business payment market.

Check	91.0%
ACH	5.0
Credit card	2.0
FedWire	1.0
Other	1.0

Source: *Credit Card Management*, July 2002, p. 40, from Cement Communications.

★ 1680 ★
Bill Payment (SIC 6090)

E-Bill Payment Leaders, 2002

The market leaders in electronic bill-payment are shown for the second quarter of the year. The top five firms processed 92% of the payments in 2001, up from 76% in 1996.

CheckFree Corp.	54.0%
Metavente Corp./Princeton eCom Corp.	18.0
Other	28.0

Source: *American Banker*, December 17, 2002, p. 18, from Financial DNA LLC.

★ 1681 ★
Electronic Fund Transfers (SIC 6090)

Electronic Fund Transfers

Market shares are shown based on transactions.

Star (Concord)	56.0%
Interlink (Visa)	14.0
NYCE (First Data)	9.0
Pulse Pay	8.0
Other	13.0

Source: *Financial Times*, May 15, 2003, p. 20, from *The Nilson Report*.

★ 1682 ★

Credit Cards (SIC 6141)

Credit Card Market, 2002

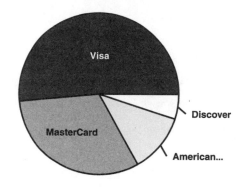

Shares are for both credit and debit cards.

	2Q 2002	3Q 2002
Visa	51.6%	51.5%
MasterCard	31.3	31.7
American Express	12.2	11.8
Discover	4.9	4.9

Source: "Shift Happens." available online January 7, 2003 from http://www.cardweb.com, from CardData.

★ 1683 ★

Credit Cards (SIC 6141)

Federal Credit Card Program, 2001

Market shares are shown in percent.

Citibank	39.0%
Bank of America	29.8
U.S. Bank	26.7
Bank One	4.4

Source: *Credit Card Management*, June 2002, p. 6, from General Services Administration and Anderson & Associates.

★ 1684 ★

Credit Cards (SIC 6141)

IRS Credit Card Payments

Official Payments is a company that allows consumers to pay taxes, fees and fines with their credit card over the phone or through the Internet. In 2001, the firm processed more than 22,500 federal tax payments vlaued at nearly $800 million.

Official Payments	87.0%
Other	13.0

Source: *Fairfield County Business Journal*, June 10, 2002, p. 11.

★ 1685 ★

Credit Cards (SIC 6141)

Largest Credit Card Issuers, 2001

Figures are in billions of dollars. The top 10 firms have 80% of the business.

Citigroup	$ 99.51
MBNA America	74.90
First USA/Bank One	68.20
Chase	40.90
Providian Financial	32.85
Capital One Financial	31.97
Bank of America	28.34
Household Bank	16.10
Fleet	15.64
Direct Merchants	11.90

Source: *Bank Systems & Technology*, March 2003, p. 8, from *The Nilson Report*.

★ 1686 ★
Credit Cards (SIC 6141)

Top Bank Card Issuers in Canada, 2002

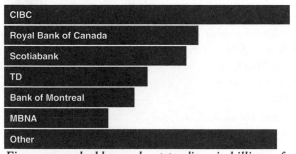

Firms are ranked by card outstandings in billions of Canadian dollars. Data are for the year ended October 31, 2002.

	($ bil.)	Share
CIBC	$ 9.5	21.59%
Royal Bank of Canada	6.4	14.55
Scotiabank	6.0	13.64
TD	5.0	11.36
Bank of Montreal	4.2	9.55
MBNA	3.6	8.18
Other	9.3	21.14

Source: *Cards International*, April 23, 2003, p. 23, from Canadian Bankers Association and company sources.

★ 1687 ★
Debit Cards (SIC 6141)

Debit Card Market Shares

Market shares are shown based on number of cards.

Visa Check Card	74.1%
Debit Mastercard	25.9

Source: *Credit Card Management*, June 2002, p. 33, from *ATM & Debit News*.

★ 1688 ★
Agricultural Loans (SIC 6150)

Leading Agricultural Loan Providers, 2002

Associations are ranked by value of total loans, in billions, for the fiscal year ended September 30, 2002. Commercial banks had 41% of agricultural lending, followed by farm credit systems with 26% of lending.

Mid-America ACA	$ 6.68
FCS of America ACA	6.53
Northwest FCS, ACA	3.98
Farm Credit West ACA	2.19
GreenStone ACA	2.14
AgStar ACA	2.08
American AgCredit ACA	1.76
First Pioneer ACA	1.56
1st Farm Credit Services, ACA	1.50
Badgerland ACA	1.23
MidAtlantic ACA	1.23

Source: *Ag Lender*, December 2002, p. 8, from Farm Credit Administration.

★ 1689 ★
Mortgage Loans (SIC 6162)

Leading Residential Servicers, 2002

Market shares are shown based on servicing volume as of December 31, 2002.

	($ mil.)	Share
Washington Mutual	$ 723.1	11.47%
Wells Fargo Home Mortgage . . .	570.3	9.05
Chase Home Finance	452.4	6.80
Countrywide Financial Corp. . . .	429.0	7.18
Bank of America	264.5	4.20
GMAC Mortgage	198.6	3.15
ABN Amro Mortgage	184.4	2.93
National City Mortgage	123.0	1.95
Cendant Mortgage	115.8	1.84
CitiMortgage	115.4	1.83

Source: *National Mortgage News*, March 2003, p. 10, from NMN-Quarterly Data Report.

★ 1690 ★

Mortgage Loans (SIC 6162)

Leading Subprime Servicers, 2002

Market shares are shown based on servicing volume as of December 31, 2002.

	($ mil.)	Share
Fairbanks Capital Corp.	$ 49,313	9.74%
CitiFinancial	47,313	9.34
Household Financial	47,000	9.28
Ocwen Financial	30,414	6.01
Option One Mortgage Corp.	28,071	5.54
Homecomings/GMAC-RFC	27,353	5.40
Countrywide Financial Corp.	25,181	4.97
Homeq Servicing Corp.	16,749	3.31
Chase Home Finance	16,167	3.19

Source: *Mortgage Servicing News*, March 2003, p. 10, from NMN-Quarterly Data Report.

★ 1691 ★

Loan Arrangers (SIC 6163)

Farm Business Debt

Total debt is shown in percent.

Commercial banks	41.0%
Farm Credit System	28.0
Individuals and others	21.0
Life insurance companies	6.0
Farm Service Agency	4.0

Source: *Ag Lender*, April 2002, p. 1, from United States Department of Agriculture.

★ 1692 ★

Loan Arrangers (SIC 6163)

Leading Investment Grade Lenders

Market shares are shown in percent.

Morgan Chase	28.9%
Citi's Salomon Smith Barney	19.8
Bank One	16.6
Other	34.7

Source: *American Banker*, April 1, 2003, p. 1, from Thomson Financial.

★ 1693 ★

Loan Arrangers (SIC 6163)

Leading Syndicated Lenders

Market shares are shown in percent.

Morgan Chase	26.8%
Bank of America	17.0
Salomon Smith Barney	16.4
Bank One Corp.	9.3
Deutsche Bank	3.5
Other	27.0

Source: *American Banker*, April 1, 2003, p. 1, from Thomson Financial.

SIC 62 - Security and Commodity Brokers

★ 1694 ★
Investment Banking (SIC 6211)
Corporate Security Underwriting, 2002

Market shares are shown in percent.

Citigroup	12.1%
Merrill Lynch	9.7
Credit Suisse First Boston	9.2
Lehman Brothers	8.6
J.P. Morgan Chase	8.3
Morgan Stanley	8.0
UBS Warburg	6.7
Goldman, Sachs	6.7
Bank of America Securities	5.7
Other	25.0

Source: *New York Times*, January 3, 2003, p. C5, from Thomson Financial.

★ 1695 ★
Investment Banking (SIC 6211)
Largest Brokers in North America

Brokers are ranked by number of reps. UBS PaineWebber's figure is an estimate.

Merrill Lynch & Co. Inc.	14,600
Morgan Stanley	13,590
Smith Barney	12,700
American Express Financial Advisors	9,900
Charles Schwab Corp.	8,959
Edward Jones	8,334
UBS PaineWebber Inc.	8,300
Wachovia Securities Inc.	8,105
A.G. Edwards Inc.	7,332

Source: *Investment News*, November 4, 2002, p. 14.

★ 1696 ★
Investment Banking (SIC 6211)
Largest Equity Underwriters

Market shares are shown in percent.

	2001	2002
Goldman	22.2%	16.3%
Salomon	11.2	16.1
Other	66.6	67.6

Source: *PR Newswire*, April 9, 2003, p. NA, from *Bloomberg Markets*.

★ 1697 ★
Investment Banking (SIC 6211)
Leading Money Managers, 2001

Fidelity Investment
Barclays Global Investors
State Street Global
J.P. Morgan Fleming
Capital Group
Mellon Financial Corp.
Merrill Lynch Investment
Citigroup
Axa Financial
Morgan Stanley

Firms are ranked by assets under management in millions of dollars as of January 31, 2001.

Fidelity Investment	$ 853.54
Barclays Global Investors	786.70
State Street Global	785.42
J.P. Morgan Fleming	604.60
Capital Group	589.25
Mellon Financial Corp.	537.29

Continued on next page.

★ 1697 ★ *Continued*

Investment Banking (SIC 6211)

Leading Money Managers, 2001

Firms are ranked by assets under management in millions of dollars as of January 31, 2001.

Merrill Lynch Investment	$ 528.70
Citigroup	502.64
Axa Financial	480.99
Morgan Stanley	414.99

Source: *Institutional Investor*, July 2002, p. 43.

★ 1698 ★

Investment Banking (SIC 6211)

Leading Money Managers in Los Angeles, 2001

Groups are ranked by assets under management in billions of dollars, as of December 31, 2001.

Capital Research & Management Co.	$ 367.1
Capital Guardian	120.1
Western Asset Management Co.	94.2
The TCW Group	88.0
Payden & Rygel	38.1
Dimensional Fund Advisors	35.0
Primecap Management Co.	29.3
Oaktree Capital Management	22.8
Boston Co. Management LLC	21.5

Source: *Los Angeles Business Journal*, June 10, 2002, p. 28, from Financial Research.

★ 1699 ★

Investment Banking (SIC 6211)

Leading Separate-Account Program Sponsors, 2002

Market shares are shown in percent as of September 30, 2002.

Merrill Lynch	24.8%
Salomon Smith Barney Inc.	24.3
UBS PlainWebber Inc.	9.4
Morgan Stanley	9.2
Prudential Securities Inc.	5.1
Charles Schwab & Co. Inc.	2.7
Wachovia Securities	2.7%
A.G. Edwards & Sons Inc.	2.6
Lockwood Financial Services Inc.	2.4
Other	16.8

Source: *Investment News*, December 23, 2002, p. 38, from Cerulli Associates Inc.

★ 1700 ★

Personal Investing (SIC 6211)

Retirement Market Assets

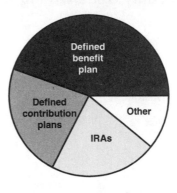

The $10.9 trillion industry is shown by segment. Defined benefit plan assets include those in private and federal defined benefit plans and the vast majority of those in state and loal government retirement funds.

	($ trillion)	Share
Defined benefit plan assets	$ 4.9	45.0%
Defined contribution plans	2.5	23.0
IRAs	2.4	22.0
Other	1.2	11.0

Source: *PR Newswire*, June 28, 2002, p. NA, from Investment Company Institute.

★ 1701 ★
Electronic Communications Networks (SIC 6231)

Nasdaq Trade Volume, 2002

Market shares are shown in percent for June 2002.

Instinet/Island	26.9%
Archipelago/RediBook	10.4
Brut Llc	2.7
MarketXT	2.3
Track	0.7
Other	57.0

Source: *Securities Industry News*, July 22, 2002, p. NA.

★ 1702 ★
Electronic Trading (SIC 6231)

Electronic Interdealer Market for U.S. Treasuries

Market shares are shown in percent. Broker-Tec's Icap has the second largest share.

e-Speed	40.0%
Other	60.0

Source: *Securities Industry News*, June 17, 2002, p. NA.

★ 1703 ★
Electronic Trading (SIC 6231)

Exchange Traded Funds

Market shares are shown in percent.

State Street	40.0%
Barclays Global	29.6
Bank of New York	29.3
Vanguard	1.2

Source: *Investor's Business Daily*, August 15, 2002, p. A10, from Indexfunds.com and Investment Company Institute.

★ 1704 ★
Electronic Trading (SIC 6231)

Online Trading Market

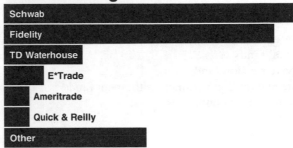

Shares are shown based on $920 billion online account assets.

Schwab	37.2%
Fidelity	33.7
TD Waterhouse	10.1
E*Trade	4.9
Ameritrade	3.4
Quick & Reilly	2.7
Other	18.0

Source: *BusinessWeek*, June 3, 2002, p. 66.

★ 1705 ★
Securites Exchanges (SIC 6231)

Leading Equities Exchanges

ISE has grabbed a 25% market share since it started trading in May 2000. It has proven so popular it is even receiving orders from CBOE. Figures are for July 2002.

Chicago Board Options Exchange	27.0%
International Securities Exchange	25.0
American Stock Exchange	25.0
Pacific Exchange	12.0
Philadelphia Stock Exchange	11.0

Source: *BusinessWeek*, September 2, 2002, p. 88, from Options Cleaning Corp. and ISE.

★ 1706 ★
Securites Exchanges (SIC 6231)

Who Owns Stock, 2002

Figures are at the end of the third quarter.

Household sector 36.7%
Mutual funds 18.3
Private pension funds 12.9
State and local government retirement funds . . 8.5
Life insurance companies 6.4
Other 17.2

Source: *USA TODAY*, March 3, 2003, p. 8B, from Federal Reserve.

★ 1707 ★
Financial Information (SIC 6282)

Real-Time Financial Information Market

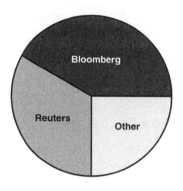

Providers' shares are shown in percent. Figures calculated based on estimated revenue post discount to list price.

	1996	2001
Bloomberg	18.0%	40.0%
Reuters	36.0	32.0
Other	46.0	24.0

Source: *Wall Street Journal*, October 14, 2002, p. B3, from UBS Warburg.

SIC 63 - Insurance Carriers

★ 1708 ★
Insurance (SIC 6300)

Mexico's Insurance Industry, 2002

Figures are in billions of pesos for the first quarter. The market share of foreign companies is 39%.

	(bil.)	Share
Damage	11.790	42.83%
Life	9.456	34.35
Pension	3.130	11.37
Accident/illness	2.971	10.79
Health	0.180	0.65

Source: *Business Mexico*, October 2002, p. 38, from National Insurance and Bonding Commission.

★ 1709 ★
Insurance (SIC 6300)

Voluntary Benefits Market

Distribution is based on sales.

Nonspecialists/employee benefits brokers . . .	39.0%
Brokers	36.0
Career agents	25.0

Source: *National Underwriter*, March 24, 2003, p. 6, from Eastbridge Consulting Group.

★ 1710 ★
Life Insurance (SIC 6311)

Largest Life Insurance Firms, 2001

Market shares are shown based on direct premiums written.

Metropolitan Life Insurance	8.69%
American International Group	8.51
Prudential Insurance Company of America . .	5.93
Northwestern Mutual Life Insurance	4.56
New York Life Insurance Co.	4.01
Netherlands Insurance (W.I.)	3.70
Aegon USA Inc.	3.51

Massachusetts Mutual Life	3.40%
The Hartford Financial Services Group . . .	2.67
John Hancock Mutual Life	2.12
Other	52.90

Source: *Investment News*, December 23, 2002, p. 46, from National Association of Insurance Commissioners.

★ 1711 ★
Life Insurance (SIC 6311)

Top Life Insurers in Utah, 2001

Market shares are shown in percent.

Liberty Life Ins Co.	43.13%
American Natl. Ins Co.	22.28
American Ge Life & Acc Ins Co.	21.25
Fortis Benefits	8.04
Monumental Life Ins Co.	3.18
Other	2.12

Source: "Industrial Life." available January 1, 2003 from http://www.insurance.ut.us, from Utah state government statistics.

★ 1712 ★
Auto Insurance (SIC 6321)

Top Auto Insurers, 2001

Market shares are shown in percent.

State Farm Group	16.6%
Allstate Ins Group	9.9
Zurich/Farmers Group	5.9
Progressive Group	4.7
Nationwide Group	4.4
Berkshire Hathaway	4.0
USAA Group	2.9

Continued on next page.

★ 1712 ★ *Continued*
Auto Insurance (SIC 6321)

Top Auto Insurers, 2001

Market shares are shown in percent.

Travelers/Citigroup	2.6%
Liberty Mutual Ins Cos.	2.4
Amer Intern Group Inc.	2.1
Other	44.5

Source: *Best's Review*, August 2002, p. 52, from A.M. Best & Co.

★ 1713 ★
Auto Insurance (SIC 6321)

Top Auto Insurers in Alabama, 2001

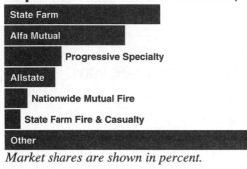

State Farm
Alfa Mutual
Progressive Specialty
Allstate
Nationwide Mutual Fire
State Farm Fire & Casualty
Other

Market shares are shown in percent.

State Farm	22.11%
Alfa Mutual	16.70
Progressive Specialty	7.85
Allstate	6.72
Nationwide Mutual Fire	2.92
State Farm Fire & Casualty	2.36
Other	41.34

Source: "Market Share Report." available April 10, 2003 from http://www.state.al.us, from Alabama government statistics.

★ 1714 ★
Auto Insurance (SIC 6321)

Top Auto Insurers in California, 2001

Market shares are shown in percent.

State Farm Group	12.0%
Zurich/Farmers Group	11.5
California State Auto Group	10.6
Allstate Insurance Group	10.6
Automobile Club of Southern California	9.1
Other	46.2

Source: *A.M. Best Newswire*, December 11, 2002, p. NA, from A.M. Best & Co.

★ 1715 ★
Auto Insurance (SIC 6321)

Top Auto Insurers in Colorado, 2002

Market shares are shown in percent.

State Farm	23.5%
Farmers	15.6
American Family	9.3
Allstate	8.3
U.S. Auto Association	6.4
Progressive	5.3
Geico	3.9
Hartford	2.8
Other	24.9

Source: *Rocky Mountain News*, May 15, 2003, p. 1B, from A.M. Best & Co.

★ 1716 ★
Auto Insurance (SIC 6321)

Top Auto Insurers in Florida, 2001

Market shares are shown in percent.

State Farm Group	22.2%
Allstate Group	17.0
Berkshire Hathaway Insurance Group	11.4
Progressive Insurance Group	8.0
USAA Group	4.6
Other	36.8

Source: *A.M. Best Newswire*, December 11, 2002, p. NA, from A.M. Best & Co.

★ 1717 ★
Auto Insurance (SIC 6321)

Top Auto Insurers in Louisiana

Market shares are shown in percent.

State Farm	33.5%
Allstate Insurance Group	17.8
Progressive Insurance Group	7.8
Southern Farm Bureau Group	6.7
Berkshire Hathaway Insurance Group	5.5
Other	28.7

Source: *A.M. Best Newswire*, June 21, 2002, p. NA, from A.M. Best & Co.

★ 1718 ★
Auto Insurance (SIC 6321)

Top Auto Insurers in Maryland, 2001

Market shares are shown in percent.

State Farm Group	20.0%
Berkshire Hathaway Insurance Group	16.0
Allstate Insurance Group	16.0
Nationwide Group	10.2
Erie Insurance Group	5.9
Other	31.9

Source: *A.M. Best Newswire*, August 21, 2002, p. NA, from A.M. Best & Co.

★ 1719 ★
Auto Insurance (SIC 6321)

Top Auto Insurers in Massachusetts, 2000

Commerce Group Inc.
Arbella Insurance Group
Safety Group
MetLife Auto & Home Group
Liberty Mutual Insurance
Other

Market shares are shown in percent.

Commerce Group Inc.	22.0%
Arbella Insurance Group	11.8
Safety Group	9.8
MetLife Auto & Home Group	7.7
Liberty Mutual Insurance	7.0
Other	8.3

Source: *A.M. Best Newswire*, June 24, 2002, p. NA, from A.M. Best & Co.

★ 1720 ★
Auto Insurance (SIC 6321)

Top Auto Insurers in New Jersey, 2001

Market shares are shown in percent.

State Farm Group	16.3%
Allstate Insurance Group	12.1
New Jersey Manufacturers Group	11.9
Liberty Mutual Insurance Cos.	10.3
Prudential of America Group	7.0
Other	42.4

Source: *A.M. Best Newswire*, January 16, 2003, p. NA, from A.M. Best & Co.

★ 1721 ★

Auto Insurance (SIC 6321)

Top Auto Insurers in New York, 2001

Market shares are shown in percent.

Allstate Insurance Group	17.2%
Berkshire Hathaway Insurance	12.0
State Farm Group	11.8
Travelers/Citigroup	6.7
Progressive Insurance Group	5.0
Other	47.3

Source: *A.M. Best Newswire*, January 22, 2003, p. NA, from A.M. Best & Co.

★ 1722 ★

Auto Insurance (SIC 6321)

Top Auto Insurers in North Carolina, 2000

Market shares are shown in percent.

Nationwide Group	19.0%
State Farm Group	13.0
Allstate Insurance Group	11.0
North Carolina Farm Bureau Group	8.0
GMAC Insurance Group	8.0
Other	41.0

Source: *A.M. Best Newswire*, March 18, 2002, p. NA, from A.M. Best & Co.

★ 1723 ★

Auto Insurance (SIC 6321)

Top Auto Insurers in South Dakota, 2002

Market shares are shown in percent.

State Farm	16.06%
American Family Mutual	10.19
Farmers Mutual	5.05
Farmers Ins. Exchange	4.20
Progressive Northern	4.05
Farm Bureau Mutual	3.41
Other	57.04

Source: "Market Share Report." available April 10, 2003 from http://www.state.sd.us, from South Dakota Division of Insurance.

★ 1724 ★

Auto Insurance (SIC 6321)

Top Auto Insurers in Washington, 2001

State Farm Group

Zurich/Farmers Group

Allstate Insurance Group

Other

Market shares are shown in percent.

State Farm Group	15.0%
Zurich/Farmers Group	13.3
Allstate Insurance Group	12.5
Other	59.2

Source: *A.M. Best Newswire*, January 29, 2003, p. NA, from A.M. Best & Co.

★ 1725 ★

Health Insurance (SIC 6321)

Leading Noncancelable Health Insurers, 2001

Market shares are shown in percent.

UnumProvident Corp.	31.3%
Amer International Group	24.6
Northwestern Mutual Group	11.2
Aon Corp.	7.5
MassMutual Financial Group	7.1
Other	18.3

Source: *Best's Review*, March 2003, p. 78, from A.M. Best & Co.

★ 1726 ★

Health Plans (SIC 6324)

HMO Enrollment by Type

Commercial	77.0%
Medicaid	15.0
Medicare	7.0
Other	1.0

Source: "Free Data Summaries." available March 7, 2003 from http://www.aishealth.com, from *AIS HMO Directory Health, 2002*.

★ 1727 ★
Health Plans (SIC 6324)

Largest Health Programs in Polk County, Iowa

Groups are ranked by number of members as of March 2002. Data refer to HMOS/IPAs/ODSs and PPOs.

Wellmark Bluecross/Blueshield of Iowa . .	566,000
Coventry Health Care of Iowa	90,000
John Deere Health	55,341
Wellmark Health Plan	23,188
Outcomes Pharmaceutical Health Care . .	14,000

Source: *Business Record (Des Moines)*, Annual 2003, p. 122.

★ 1728 ★
Health Plans (SIC 6324)

Largest HMO Markets, 2001

Penetration rate is shown for the leading areas as of January 2001.

Jackson, TN	72.2%
Sacramento, CA	71.7
San Francisco, CA	70.0
Rochester, NY	68.2
Oakland, CA	68.2
Vallejo-Fairfield-Napa, CA	65.5
Buffalo-Niagara Falls, NY	64.0
Madison, WI	62.5
Stockton-Lodi, CA	61.3
New Haven-Meriden, CA	61.3

Source: *Managed Healthcare Executive*, April 2002, p. 56, from *InterStudy Competitive Edge*.

★ 1729 ★
Health Plans (SIC 6324)

Largest HMO Plans

Market shares are shown in percent.

HealthNet Inc.	5.16%
Blue Cross Blue Shield of Tennessee	4.82
UnitedHealth Group Inc.	4.37
WellPoint Health Networks	3.40
Amerigroup	3.24
Other	79.01

Source: *Managed Medicare & Medicaid*, April 22, 2002, p. 7, from *AIS HMO Directory, 2002*.

★ 1730 ★
Health Plans (SIC 6324)

Largest HMOs by Enrollment, 2002

Groups are ranked by number of members as of December 1, 2002.

Kaiser Foundation Health Plan (N. Cal.) .	3,178,028
Kaiser Foundation Health Plan (South Cal.)	3,126,305
Blue Cross of California	2,348,358
HealthNet of California	2,344,529
PacifiCare of California	2,145,166
Keystone Health Plan East Inc.	1,237,277
Oxford Health Plans of New York . . .	1,085,258
Blue Shield of California Access	998,175
Health Options Inc.	963,619
HMO Blue	941,963

Source: *Managed Healthcare Executive*, February 2003, p. 44.

★ 1731 ★
Health Plans (SIC 6324)

Largest HMOs in California

Market shares are shown in percent.

	(000)	Share
Kaiser Foundation Health Plan . . .	3,124	17.92%
Blue Cross of California	1,202	6.90
PacifiCare	1,058	6.07
Health Net of California	950	5.45
L.A. Care Health Plan	824	4.73
Blue Shield of California	445	2.55
CIGNA Healthcare of California . .	443	2.54
Aetna Inc.	351	2.01
Universal Care	319	1.83
Other	8,716	50.00

Source: *Los Angeles Business Journal*, February 24, 2003, p. 33, from companies.

★ 1732 ★
Health Plans (SIC 6324)

Largest HMOs in Florida

Market shares are shown in percent.

United Healthcare	18.4%
Health Options	17.8
Aetna-Prucare	16.3
Florida Health Plan holdings	9.5
Humana Medical Pan	8.8
Other	29.1

Source: *A.M. Best Newswire*, May 21, 2002, p. NA, from A.M. Best & Co.

★ 1733 ★
Health Plans (SIC 6324)

Largest HMOs in New Jersey

Market shares are shown in percent as of September 30, 2002.

Aetna Health	23.6%
Horizon	22.8
HealthNet of NJ	15.5
Americhoice	8.2
AmeriHealth	7.9
Oxford	7.3
Amerigroup	4.3
Cigna	3.8
Other	16.6

Source: "Market Share." available March 25, 2003 from http://www.state.nj.us, from New Jersey state insurance.

★ 1734 ★
Health Plans (SIC 6324)

Largest HMOs in Rochester, NY

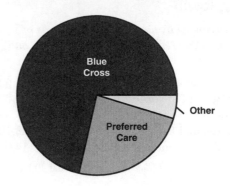

Market shares are shown in percent.

Blue Cross	75.0%
Preferred Care	25.0
Other	5.0

Source: *Rochester Democrat and Chronicle*, April 22, 2003, p. 12d, from New York State Insurance department.

★ 1735 ★
Health Plans (SIC 6324)

Largest HMOs in San Diego, CA

Groups are ranked by number of members as of December 1, 2002.

Kaiser Permanente	502,200
American Specialty Health Plans	498,840
PacifiCare/Secure Horizons	300,000
Aetna US Healthcare	170,333
Blue Cross of California	162,084
Health Net of California	140,012
Sharp Health Plan	124,026

Source: *San Diego Business Journal*, January 20, 2003, p. A20, from companies.

★ 1736 ★
Health Plans (SIC 6324)

Largest Managed Care Organizations

Figures show thousands of members.

United Healthcare	16,500
Aetna U.S. Healthcare	13,700
CCIGNA Healthcare	13,100

Continued on next page.

★ 1736 ★ *Continued*
Health Plans (SIC 6324)

Largest Managed Care Organizations

Figures show thousands of members.

Anthem Blue Cross and Blue Shield	11,100
Kaiser Foundation Health Plan	8,100
Blue Cross of California	6,800
Humana Inc.	6,600
Blue Cross Blue Shield of Michigan	4,800
Empire Blue Cross and Blue Shield	4,600

Source: *Employee Benefit News*, April 1, 2003, p. NA, from *Health Plan Almanac*.

★ 1737 ★
Health Plans (SIC 6324)

Largest Managed Care Providers in Louisiana, 2002

Groups are ranked by number of members as of January 1, 2002.

Blue Cross and Blue Shield Louisiana	151,439
American LIFECARE	100,070
BestCare Inc.	90,005
UnitedHealthCare of Louisiana	73,000
Ochsner Health Plan	62,063
Family Managed Care	39,420
Coventry Health Care of Louisiana	20,000
CIGNA Healthcare of Louisiana	17,836

Source: *Greater Baton Rouge Business Report*, February 4, 2003, p. 39.

★ 1738 ★
Health Plans (SIC 6324)

Largest Medicare Plans

Market shares are shown in percent.

PacifiCare Inc.	16.0%
Kaiser Foundation Health Plan	13.0
Humana Inc.	7.0
UnitedHealth Group Inc.	6.0
Aetna Inc.	4.0
Other	54.0

Source: *Managed Medicare & Medicaid*, April 22, 2002, p. 7, from *AIS HMO Directory, 2002*.

★ 1739 ★
Health Plans (SIC 6324)

Largest PPO Plans

Figures show thousands of members.

Beech Street Corp.	16,000
Galaxy Health Network	3,500
InterGroup Services	1,000
Primary Health Services Inc.	1,000
PPOM	1,000
Health Management Network	1,000
MedCost	896
American LIFECARE	690
Midlands Choice	600

Source: *Employee Benefit News*, April 1, 2003, p. NA, from *Health Plan Almanac*.

★ 1740 ★
Health Plans (SIC 6324)

Largest PPOs in Florida

Groups are ranked by number of members.

Beech Street Corp.	3,756,273
MultiPlan Inc.	1,857,634
CompBenefits	1,500,000
Preferred Patient Care Inc.	1,400,000
BayCare Health Network Inc.	893,741
ProAmerica	691,930
United Healthcare of Florida	652,099
Bradman/Unipsych Companies	650,000
AnciCare PPO Inc.	600,010
Dimension Health	472,698

Source: *Florida Trend*, October 15, 2002, p. 9.

★ 1741 ★
Homeowners Insurance (SIC 6331)

Homeowners Insurance in Hurricane States

Market shares are shown in hurricane prone states. The industry in hurricane-prone states hit $8.7 billion.

State Farm Group	25.8%
Allstate Insurance Group	13.8
Zurich Financial Services Group	8.6
Nationwide Group	5.7
USAA Group	5.5
Citigroup	3.8

Continued on next page.

★ 1741 ★ *Continued*
Homeowners Insurance (SIC 6331)

Homeowners Insurance in Hurricane States

Market shares are shown in hurricane prone states. The industry in hurricane-prone states hit $8.7 billion.

Chubb & Son Inc. 1.9%
Hartford Fire & Casualty Group 1.6
Other 33.2

Source: *Business Wire*, August 14, 2002, p. NA, from Weiss Ratings.

★ 1742 ★
Homeowners Insurance (SIC 6331)

Top Home Insurers in Alabama

Alabama is the 20th largest homeowner insurance market in the country. Market shares are shown in percent.

State Farm Group 30.6%
Alfa Ins Group 20.0
Other 49.4

Source: *Best's Review*, November 2002, p. 56, from A.M. Best & Co.

★ 1743 ★
Homeowners Insurance (SIC 6331)

Top Home Insurers in California, 2001

Market shares are shown in percent.

State Farm Group 22.2%
Zurich/Farmers Group 19.1
Allstate Insurance Group 14.0
California State Auto Group 5.0
Nationwide Group 4.2
Other 45.5

Source: *A.M. Best Newswire*, December 10, 2002, p. NA, from A.M. Best & Co.

★ 1744 ★
Homeowners Insurance (SIC 6331)

Top Home Insurers in Connecticut, 2001

Market shares are shown in percent.

Allstate Insurance Group 10.8%
Travelers/Citigroup Cos. 10.4
Chubb Group 8.3
Hartford Insurance 6.3
Nationwide Group 6.0
Other 59.2

Source: *A.M. Best Newswire*, January 28, 2003, p. NA, from A.M. Best & Co.

★ 1745 ★
Homeowners Insurance (SIC 6331)

Top Home Insurers in Maryland, 2001

Market shares are shown in percent.

State Farm Group 23.0%
Allstate Insurance Group 15.0
Nationwide Group 11.0
Travelers/Citigroup 8.2
Erie Insurance Group 8.0
Other 34.8

Source: *A.M. Best Newswire*, March 20, 2003, p. NA, from A.M. Best & Co.

★ 1746 ★
Homeowners Insurance (SIC 6331)

Top Home Insurers in Mississippi, 2001

Market shares are shown in percent.

State Farm Group 30.3%
Southern Farm Bureau Group 20.7
Allstate Insurance Group 8.9
Nationwide Group 6.1
St. Paul Cos. 5.1
Other 28.9

Source: *A.M. Best Newswire*, January 13, 2003, p. NA, from A.M. Best & Co.

★ 1747 ★
Homeowners Insurance (SIC 6331)

Top Home Insurers in New Mexico

New Mexico is the 37th largest homeowner insurance market in the country. Market shares are shown in percent.

State Farm Group 25.8%
Zurich/Farmers Group 19.9
Other 54.3

Source: *Best's Review*, November 2002, p. 56, from A.M. Best & Co.

★ 1748 ★
Homeowners Insurance (SIC 6331)

Top Home Insurers in Tennessee

Tennessee is the 18th largest homeowner insurance market in the country. Market shares are shown in percent.

State Farm Group 25.6%
Tenn Farmers Cos. 16.6
Other 57.8

Source: *Best's Review*, November 2002, p. 56, from A.M. Best & Co.

★ 1749 ★
Homeowners Insurance (SIC 6331)

Top Home Insurers in Texas, 2001

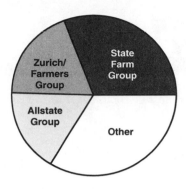

Market shares are shown in percent.

State Farm Group 30.5%
Zurich/Farmers Group 19.2
Allstate Group 16.7
Other 33.6

Source: *A.M. Best Newswire*, August 14, 2002, p. NA, from A.M. Best & Co.

★ 1750 ★
Homeowners Insurance (SIC 6331)

Top Home Insurers in Washington, 2001

Market shares are shown in percent.

State Farm Group 17.4%
Zurich/Farmers Group 17.0
Safeco Insurance Cos. 13.9
Allstate Insurance Group 11.7
Pemco Insurance Cos. 6.7
Other 33.3

Source: *A.M. Best Newswire*, August 21, 2002, p. NA, from A.M. Best & Co.

★ 1751 ★

Homeowners Insurance (SIC 6331)

Top Home Insurers in Washington D.C.

State Farm Group

Travelers/Citigroup

Other

Washington D.C. is the 50th largest homeowner insurance market in the country. Market shares are shown in percent.

State Farm Group	23.6%
Travelers/Citigroup	20.2
Other	56.2

Source: *Best's Review*, November 2002, p. 56, from A.M. Best & Co.

★ 1752 ★

Homeowners Insurance (SIC 6331)

Top Homeowners Firms, 2001

Market shares are shown in percent.

State Farm Group	21.9%
Allstate Ins. Group	11.4
Zurich/Farmers Group	8.6
Nationwide Group	4.6
USAA Group	3.6
Travelers/Citigroup	3.6
Chubb Group of Ins. Cos.	2.6
American Family Ins Group	2.2
Safeco Ins Cos.	2.0
Liberty Mutual Ins Co.	2.0
Other	37.5

Source: *Best's Review*, August 2002, p. 52, from A.M. Best & Co.

★ 1753 ★

Marine Insurance (SIC 6331)

Top Inland Marine Insurers, 2001

Market shares are shown based on premiums written.

American Intern Group	9.5%
Zurich/Farmers Group	6.5
Kemper Ins. Cos.	6.0
State Farm Group	5.1
Travelers/Citigroup	5.0
Hartford Ins. Group	4.5

Allianz of Amer	4.5%
Assurant Group	4.3
Chubb Group of Ins. Cos.	3.7
Other	50.9

Source: *Best's Review*, December 2002, p. 67, from A.M. Best & Co.

★ 1754 ★

Marine Insurance (SIC 6331)

Top Ocean Marine Insurers, 2001

Market shares are shown based on premiums written.

CNA Ins. Cos.	13.5%
American Intern Group	11.1
Ace INA Group	6.3
Allianze of America	6.1
White Mountains Insurance Group	5.5
XL America Group	5.4
St. Paul Cos.	4.8
Royal & SunAlliance	4.1
Zurich/Farmers Group	3.8
Other	39.4

Source: *Best's Review*, December 2002, p. 67, from A.M. Best & Co.

★ 1755 ★

Property Insurance (SIC 6331)

Largest Property Insurers in South Dakota, 2002

Market shares are shown in percent.

United Fire & Casualty	12.38%
North Star Mutual	5.73
St. Paul Fire & Marine	4.65
Acuity A Mutual	4.46
Federated Mutual	4.41
Milbank	4.14
Factory Mutual	4.11
Other	60.12

Source: "Market Share Report." available April 10, 2003 from http://www.state.sd.us, from South Dakota Division of Insurance.

★ 1756 ★

Property Insurance (SIC 6331)

Leading Property & Casualty Firms in the Midwest

Market shares are shown in percent.

State Farm Mutual Auto Insurance	7.5%
American Family Mutual Insurance	3.5
State Farm Fire and Casualty Co.	3.4
Allstate Insurance Co.	2.9
Community Insurance Co.	2.6
Cincinnati Insurance Co.	1.8
Anthem Insurance Cos. Inc.	1.6
Medical Mutual of Ohio	1.2
Other	75.5

Source: *American Banker*, May 23, 2002, p. 12.

★ 1757 ★

Property Insurance (SIC 6331)

Leading Property & Casualty Firms in the Northeast

Market shares are shown in percent.

Allstate Insurance Co.	4.4%
State Farm Mutual Auto Insurance	3.3
Liberty Mutual Fire Insurance	2.1
State Farm Fire and Casualty Co.	1.7
Erie Insurance Exchange	1.7
Nationwide Mutual Insurance Co.	1.6
Commerce Insurance Co.	1.3
Federal Insurance Co.	1.3
National Union Fire Ins. of Pittsburgh	1.3
Other	81.3

Source: *American Banker*, May 23, 2002, p. 12.

★ 1758 ★

Property Insurance (SIC 6331)

Leading Property Catastrophe Risk Writers, 2001

Market shares are shown in percent.

State Farm	15.0%
Allstate	8.3
Zurich/Farmers Group	7.1
Nationwide Group	3.8
Travelers/Citigroup	3.4
Other	62.4

Source: *Best's Review*, September 2002, p. 36, from A.M. Best & Co.

★ 1759 ★

Workers Comp Insurance (SIC 6331)

Top Workers Comp Firms in California, 2001

Market shares are shown in percent.

State Compensation Insurance Fund of California	42.9%
Zurich/Farmers Group	3.9
Liberty Mutual Insurance Cos.	3.8
American Intl Group	3.4
Other	46.0

Source: *A.M. Best Newswire*, August 22, 2002, p. NA, from A.M. Best & Co.

★ 1760 ★

Workers Comp Insurance (SIC 6331)

Top Workers Comp Firms in Colorado, 2001

Market shares are shown in percent.

Pinnacol Assurance Co.	47.0%
Zurich Farmers Group	10.0
Liberty Mutual Insurance Cos.	5.0
CNA Insurance Cos.	4.0
Hartford Insurance Group	3.0
Other	31.0

Source: *A.M. Best Newswire*, August 12, 2002, p. NA, from A.M. Best & Co.

★ 1761 ★
Workers Comp Insurance (SIC 6331)

Top Workers Comp Firms in Florida, 2001

Liberty Mutual Insurance Cos.
FCCI Insurance Group
CNA Insurance Cos.
Hartford Insurance
Associated Industries Insurance Co.
Other

Market shares are shown in percent.

Liberty Mutual Insurance Cos.	12.5%
FCCI Insurance Group	11.7
CNA Insurance Cos.	8.9
Hartford Insurance	6.1
Associated Industries Insurance Co.	5.9
Other	54.9

Source: *A.M. Best Newswire*, December 17, 2002, p. NA, from A.M. Best & Co.

★ 1762 ★
Workers Comp Insurance (SIC 6331)

Top Workers Comp Firms in Nevada, 2000

Market shares are shown in percent.

St. Paul	39.5%
Health Care Indemnity	13.9
Doctors Co. Insurance Group	11.6
CNA Insurance	7.1
Allianz of America Inc.	5.9
Other	22.0

Source: *A.M. Best Newswire*, June 7, 2002, p. NA, from A.M. Best & Co.

★ 1763 ★
Boiler Insurance (SIC 6351)

Largest Boiler/Machinery Insurers in Utah, 2001

Market shares are shown in percent.

Continental Cas.	3.38%
Affiliated Fm Insurance	2.86
American Guarantee	1.50
Allianz Ins.	1.23
American Home	1.06
Cincinnati Ins Co.	1.05
Other	71.08

Source: "Market Share Report." available April 10, 2003 from http://www.insurance.stat.ut.us, from Utah government statistics.

★ 1764 ★
Liability Insurance (SIC 6351)

D&O Insurance Market

The market for directors and officers insurance is shown based on premiums.

AIG	35.0%
Lloyd's/London	14.0
Chubb	13.0
Genesis	5.0
Aegis	5.0
Admiral	3.0
Great American	3.0
Other	22.0

Source: *Wall Street Journal*, July 12, 2002, p. C1, from Tillinghast-Towers Perrin.

★ 1765 ★
Medical Malpractice Insurance (SIC 6351)

Top Medical Malpractice Firms, 2001

Market shares are shown in percent.

MLMIC Group	9.7%
St. Paul Cos.	8.0
GE Global Ins. Group	5.6
ProAssurance Group	4.7
Zurich/Farmers Group	4.3
Health Care Indemnity	3.9
Doctors Co. Ins. Group	3.7
CNA Ins. Cos.	3.4
Norcal Group	3.4

Continued on next page.

★ **1765** ★ *Continued*
Medical Malpractice Insurance (SIC 6351)

Top Medical Malpractice Firms, 2001

Market shares are shown in percent.

Allianz of America	3.2%
Other	50.1

Source: *Best's Review*, August 2002, p. 52, from A.M. Best & Co.

★ **1766** ★
Medical Malpractice Insurance (SIC 6351)

Top Medical Malpractice Insurers in California, 2001

Norcal Group
SCPIE Cos.
Doctors Company Insurance Group
Zurich/Farmers Group
MIEC Group
Other

Market shares are shown in percent.

Norcal Group	23.5%
SCPIE Cos.	18.4
Doctors Company Insurance Group	13.5
Zurich/Farmers Group	7.1
MIEC Group	4.1
Other	33.4

Source: *A.M. Best Newswire*, December 11, 2002, p. NA, from A.M. Best & Co.

★ **1767** ★
Medical Malpractice Insurance (SIC 6351)

Top Medical Malpractice Insurers in Florida, 2001

Market shares are shown in percent.

FPIC Insurance Group Inc.	18.8%
Health Care Indemnity	13.7
ProAssurance Group	9.3
Zurich/Farmers Group	8.1
HDI U.S. Group	5.2
Other	44.9

Source: *A.M. Best Newswire*, January 29, 2003, p. NA, from A.M. Best & Co.

★ **1768** ★
Medical Malpractice Insurance (SIC 6351)

Top Medical Malpractice Insurers in Georgia

Market shares are shown in percent.

Medical Association of Georgia Mutual Insurance Co.	40.9%
St. Paul Cos.	14.6
GE Global Insurance Group	8.1
Health Care Indemnity Inc.	5.3
CNA Insurance	5.1
Other	26.0

Source: *A.M. Best Newswire*, November 19, 2002, p. NA, from A.M. Best & Co.

★ **1769** ★
Medical Malpractice Insurance (SIC 6351)

Top Medical Malpractice Insurers in Kentucky, 2001

Market shares are shown in percent.

GE Global Insurance Group	25.8%
APCapital Group	17.0
Reciprocal Group	10.5
St. Paul	8.4
State Volunteer Mutual Insurance	5.8
Other	33.5

Source: *A.M. Best Newswire*, January 2, 2003, p. NA, from A.M. Best & Co.

★ **1770** ★
Medical Malpractice Insurance (SIC 6351)

Top Medical Malpractice Insurers in Massachusetts, 2001

Market shares are shown in percent.

ProMutual Group	65.8%
MLMIC Group	7.6
American International Group	5.3
Eastern Dentists Insurance Co.	2.8
Allianz of America	2.3
Other	16.2

Source: *A.M. Best Newswire*, April 11, 2003, p. NA, from A.M. Best & Co.

★ 1771 ★

Medical Malpractice Insurance (SIC 6351)

Top Medical Malpractice Insurers in Mississippi, 2001

Market shares are shown in percent.

Medical Assurance Company of Mississippi Inc.	33.7%
Reciprocal Group	29.7
St. Paul	11.3
Doctors Company Insurance Group	6.2
ProAssurance Group	3.8
Other	15.3

Source: *A.M. Best Newswire*, April 11, 2003, p. NA, from A.M. Best & Co.

★ 1772 ★

Medical Malpractice Insurance (SIC 6351)

Top Medical Malpractice Insurers in New Jersey, 2001

Market shares are shown in percent.

Miix Group	35.2%
MLMIC Group	34.4
Zurich/Farmers Group	7.4
ProMutual Group	4.0
GE Global Insurance Group	3.1
Other	15.9

Source: *A.M. Best Newswire*, January 13, 2003, p. NA, from A.M. Best & Co.

★ 1773 ★

Medical Malpractice Insurance (SIC 6351)

Top Medical Malpractice Insurers in Pennsylvania, 2001

Market shares are shown in percent.

Norcal Group	22.5%
Miix Group	17.1
GE Global Insurance Group	10.4
American International Group	9.6
MLMIC	6.1
Other	34.3

Source: *A.M. Best Newswire*, December 10, 2002, p. NA, from A.M. Best & Co.

★ 1774 ★

Medical Malpractice Insurance (SIC 6351)

Top Medical Malpractice Insurers in Virginia, 2001

Market shares are shown in percent.

Reciprocal Group	20.6%
St. Paul Cos.	15.2
Medical Mutual Group of North Carolina	6.8
Medical Mutual Group of Maryland	6.3
GE Global Insurance Group	5.9
Other	45.2

Source: *A.M. Best Newswire*, January 29, 2003, p. NA, from A.M. Best & Co.

★ 1775 ★

Medical Malpractice Insurance (SIC 6351)

Top Medical Malpractice Insurers in Washington, 2001

Market shares are shown in percent.

Physicians Insurance Mutual Group	45.7%
Washington Casualty Co.	16.4
Doctors Company Insurance Group	7.8
Zurich/Farmers Group	7.3
St. Paul Cos.	6.3
Other	16.5

Source: *A.M. Best Newswire*, March 8, 2003, p. NA, from A.M. Best & Co.

★ 1776 ★

Medical Malpractice Insurance (SIC 6351)

Top Medical Malpractice Insurers in West Virginia, 2001

Market shares are shown in percent.

St. Paul Cos.	43.2%
ProAssurance Group	28.6
Health Care Indemnity Inc.	5.6
NCRIC Group	3.7
American International Group	2.7
Other	16.2

Source: *A.M. Best Newswire*, January 23, 2003, p. NA, from A.M. Best & Co.

★ 1777 ★

Multiple Peril Insurance (SIC 6351)

Top Multiple Peril Insurance Firms, 2001

Market shares are shown based on premiums written.

Zurich/Farmers Group	8.2%
Travelers/Citigroup	7.4
CNA Ins Cos.	5.5

Hartford Ins Group	5.4%
Chubb Group of Ins Cos.	4.0
State Farm Group	3.8
Nationwide Group	3.6
Allianz of America	3.4
Liberty Mutual Ins Cos.	3.2
White Mountains Ins. Group	3.0
Other	56.5

Source: *Best's Review*, August 2002, p. 52, from A.M. Best & Co.

★ 1778 ★

Title Insurance (SIC 6361)

Largest Title Insurers in Los Angeles

The volume of mortgages increased 54% over 2001, largely because of low interest rates. The top 25 firms had volume of $155.7 billion. Market shares are shown in percent.

Fidelity National Title	14.40%
First American Title	12.45
Chicago Title	10.19
Southland Title	6.27
American Title	5.48
Stewart Title	5.27
Equity Title	5.24
Lawyers Title	4.57
Investors Title	3.97
Other	32.16

Source: *Los Angeles Business Journal*, March 10, 2003, p. 24.

★ 1779 ★

Pensions (SIC 6371)

Group Pension Market

Manulife announced plans for a hostile takeover of Canada Life Financial Corp. Market shares are estimated in percent.

Manulife	27.0%
Sunlife	25.0
Other	48.0

Source: *Calgary Herald*, December 10, 2002, p. C1.

★ 1780 ★

Pensions (SIC 6371)

Largest Pension Funds

Sponsors are ranked by assets in billions of dollars.

California Public Employees . . . . . . $ 143.0
New York State Common 106.0
California State Teachers 95.5
Federal Retirement Thrift 93.2
Florida State Board 88.5
General Motors 82.5
Texas Teachers 75.1
New York State Teachers 74.9
General Electric 68.7
New Jersey 66.7

Source: *Investor's Business Daily*, January 9, 2003, p. A5.

SIC 64 - Insurance Agents, Brokers, and Service

★ 1781 ★

Reinsurance (SIC 6411)

Largest Life Reinsurers, 2001

Market shares are shown in percent.

Swiss Re	28.0%
Reinsurance Group of America	11.0
Transamerica Re	10.0
ERC	9.0
ING Re	9.0
Munich Re	9.0
Allianz Re	5.0
BMA/Generali Re	4.0
American United Life	4.0
Other	11.0

Source: *Reinsurance Magazine*, July 1, 2002, p. 26, from 2001 Society of Actuaries survey.

SIC 65 - Real Estate

★ 1782 ★
Office Space (SIC 6512)

Serviced Office Market

The defining features of this sector include individual office suites where tenants share access to reception, meeting rooms, utility rooms and high tech infrastructures. Shares are shown based on total number of centers.

HQ Global	7.4%
Regus	2.5
American Office Centers	0.3
Your Office USA	0.3
Others	89.5

Source: *Property Week*, June 14, 2002, p. 57, from OBCAI.

★ 1783 ★
Real Estate (SIC 6512)

Office Space Occupation, 2002

Figures show the business districts with the lowest share of vacant office space. Figures are for the first quarter.

Houston	10.0%
New York	9.7
Portland	9.6
Reno	9.2
San Diego	8.7
Washington D.C.	7.8
Bakersfield	7.4
Sacramento	7.0
Raleigh-Durham	6.3
Charlotte	6.0

Source: *Detroit Free Press*, July 9, 2002, p. 6C, from Grubb & Ellis Co.

★ 1784 ★
Shopping Centers (SIC 6512)

Mall Space by State

Figures show millions of square feet.

California	116.0
Texas	80.0
Florida	64.6
New York	56.4
Ohio	52.4
Pennsylvania	50.8
Illinois	44.9
Michigan	36.4

Source: *Michigan Retailer*, March 2003, p. 1, from International Council of Shopping Centers.

★ 1785 ★
Apartments (SIC 6513)

Largest Apartment Managers, 2002

Firms are ranked by number of apartment units in which they managed as of January 1, 2002.

Apartment Investment and Management Company	303,805
Equity Residential Properties Trust	232,505
Pinnacle Realty Management Company . .	113,546
Lincoln Property Company	103,255
Archstone-Smith	103,000
United Dominion Realty Trust	77,567
Trammell Crow Residential	65,409

Continued on next page.

414

★ 1785 ★ *Continued*
Apartments (SIC 6513)

Largest Apartment Managers, 2002

Firms are ranked by number of apartment units in which they managed as of January 1, 2002.

Sentinel Real Estate Corporation	62,737
Whitehall Funds	58,000
Alliance Holdings	52,691

Source: *National Real Estate Investor*, July 1, 2002, p. NA, from National Multi Housing Council.

★ 1786 ★
Apartments (SIC 6513)

Largest Apartment Owners, 2002

Firms are ranked by number of apartment units in which they had ownership interest as of January 1, 2002.

Apartment Investment and Management	251,201
Related Capital Company	246,918
Equity Residential Properties	226,314
Lend Lease Real Estate Investments	129,962
Boston Capital	110,000
SunAmerica Affordable Housing Partners	107,000
Archstone-Smith Headquarters	99,000
United Dominion Realty Trust	77,567
Whitehall Funds	76,000
Lefrak Organization	71,000

Source: *National Real Estate Investor*, July 1, 2002, p. NA, from National Multi Housing Council.

★ 1787 ★
Master-Planned Communities (SIC 6515)

Largest Master-Planned Communities

Sales were up slightly over 2000, with sales jumping from 23,372 to 23,863. The top 10 saw a decrease in their sales because of reduced lot inventories. Figures show annual sales. Developer's name shown in parentheses.

Summerlin (Howard Hughes Corp.)	2,976
The Villages	2,074
Irvine Ranch (Irvine Community Dev.)	1,975
Poinciana (Avatar Properties)	1,622
The Woodlands	1,601
Anthem Las Vegas (Del Webb)	1,418
Anthem Phoenix (Del Webb)	1,285

Sun City Grand (Sun City)	1,218
Sun City Lincoln Hills (Del Webb)	1,122

Source: *Urban Land*, May 2002, p. 48, from Robert Charles Lesser & Company.

★ 1788 ★
Real Estate (SIC 6531)

Largest Real Estate Brokers

Market shares are shown in percent. Brokers represent sellers in deals of $20 million or more.

	2001	2002
Eastdil Realty	13.3%	12.3%
Cushman & Wakefield	12.3	17.9
CB Richard Ellis	10.8	11.8
Goldman Sachs	6.8	4.2
Jones Lang LaSalle	5.3	5.9
Insignia/ESG	4.3	4.0
Secured Capital	3.6	6.1
Holliday Fenoglio Fowler	1.1	4.7
Salomon Smith Barney	0.4	5.5
Other	42.1	27.6

Source: *Real Estate Alert*, February 5, 2003, p. 1, from Real Estate Alert's Database.

★ 1789 ★
Real Estate (SIC 6531)

Largest Real Estate Brokers in Boston, MA

Market shares are shown in percent.

Cushman	30.0%
Trammell	20.0
Other	50.0

Source: *Real Estate Alert*, February 12, 2003, p. NA, from Real Estate Alert's Deal Database.

★ 1790 ★

Real Estate (SIC 6531)

Real Estate Equity Market

The $402.8 billion market is shown by segment.

REITs	42.5%
Pension funds	36.9
Foreign investors	11.6
Life insurance companies	8.0
Commercial banks	0.6
Savings associations	0.2

Source: *National Real Estate Investor*, February 2003, p. 38, from Lend Lease Real Estate Investments.

★ 1791 ★

Real Estate (SIC 6531)

Who Buys U.S. Property

Germany

Middle East

Other Europe

Canada

Australia

Other

Germany saw changes in its pension fund laws which allowed investments in the U.S. to surge. The Middle East saw boosts from Arab and Israeli investment. Figures show percent of total.

	2001	2002
Germany	51.0%	54.0%
Middle East	15.0	23.0
Other Europe	17.0	8.0
Canada	4.0	6.0
Australia	1.0	5.0
Other	12.0	4.0

Source: *New York Times*, January 1, 2003, p. C3, from Real Capital Analytics.

★ 1792 ★

Real Estate Agencies (SIC 6531)

Largest Real Estate Companies, 2001

Sales of existing single and family homes hit 5.25 million in 2001, up nearly 3% from 2000. Firms are ranked by number of transaction sides. Shares are shown based on sales of 993,656 for the top 20 firms.

	Sales	% of Top 20
NRT Inc.	397,049	39.96%
HomeServices of America	106,740	10.74
Weichert Realtors	85,500	8.60
Long & Foster Real Estate	83,747	8.43
Arvida Realty Services	40,377	4.06
Prudential California	37,413	3.77
Realty Executives	30,000	3.02
GMAC Homeservices Inc.	29,148	2.93
Prudential Fox & Roach	27,863	2.80
The DeWolfe Companies Inc.	25,898	2.61
Other	129,921	13.08

Source: *Realtor Magazine*, July 1, 2002, p. NA, from Realtor questionnaires.

★ 1793 ★

Real Estate Agencies (SIC 6531)

Leading Real Estate Agents in Atlanta, GA

Market shares are shown based on listings sold in 2001.

Re/MAX	51.2%
Coldwell Banker	12.1
Northside Realty	8.5
Harry Norman Realtors	7.9
Prudential	5.7
Other	14.6

Source: "Market Share." available March 1, 2003 from http://www.remax.com, from Remax.

★ 1794 ★

Real Estate Agencies (SIC 6531)

Leading Real Estate Agents in Aurora, CO

Market shares are shown based on listings sold in 2001. Figures are based on information from Local Board or Multiple Listing Service for the time period. Figures combine all listings sold and closed of all office locations and independent offices ofeach multi-office or franchise organization identified, which listings were sold by such organization itself or with the aid of a cooperating broker.

Re/Max	32.6%
Metro Brokers	16.7
Coldwell Banker	10.3
Keller Williams	5.5
Cherry Creek	4.4
Other	30.5

Source: "Market Share." available March 1, 2003 from http://www.remax.com, from Remax.

★ 1795 ★

Real Estate Agencies (SIC 6531)

Leading Real Estate Agents in Chicago, IL

Market shares are shown based on listings sold in 2001. Figures are based on information from Local Board or Multiple Listing Service for the time period. Figures combine all listings sold and closed of all office locations and independent offices ofeach multi-office or franchise organization identified, which listings were sold by such organization itself or with the aid of a cooperating broker.

Re/Max	25.8%
Coldwell Banker	17.7
Century 21	11.2
Baird & Warner	5.0
Prudential	3.3
Other	37.0

Source: "Market Share." available March 1, 2003 from http://www.remax.com, from Remax.

★ 1796 ★

Real Estate Agencies (SIC 6531)

Leading Real Estate Agents in Columbus, OH

Market shares are shown based on listings sold for June 30, 2001-June 30, 2002. Figures are based on information from Local Board or Multiple Listing Service for the time period. Figures combine all listings sold and closed of all office locations and independent offices of each multi-office or franchise organization identified, which listings were sold by such organization itself or with the aid of a cooperating broker.

Re/Max	23.7%
HER	22.0
Coldwell Banker	18.3
Century 21	4.1
Prudential	3.6
Other	28.3

Source: "Market Share." available March 1, 2003 from http://www.remax.com, from Remax.

★ 1797 ★

Real Estate Agencies (SIC 6531)

Leading Real Estate Agents in Dallas, TX

Market shares are shown based on listings sold in the first six months of 2002.

Re/Max	21.5%
Coldwell Banker	16.3
Ebby Halliday	11.6
Century 21	11.3
Keller Williams	8.3
Other	31.0

Source: "Market Share." available March 1, 2003 from http://www.remax.com, from Remax.

★ 1798 ★
Real Estate Agencies (SIC 6531)

Leading Real Estate Agents in Denver, CO

Market shares are shown based on listings sold from June 30, 2001-June 30, 2002. Figures are based on information from Local Board or Multiple Listing Service for the time period. Figures combine all listings sold and closed of all office locations and independent offices of each multi-office or franchise organization identified, which listings were sold by such organization itself or with the aid of a cooperating broker.

Re/Max	31.6%
Metro Brokers	16.7
Coldwell Banker	10.2
Keller Williams	5.3
Cherry Creek	3.5
Other	32.7

Source: "Market Share." available March 1, 2003 from http://www.remax.com, from Remax.

★ 1799 ★
Real Estate Agencies (SIC 6531)

Leading Real Estate Agents in Iowa

Market shares are estimated in percent.

Iowa Realty/First Realty GMAC	65.0%
Other	35.0

Source: *Des Moines Register*, March 30, 2003, p. 1, from *Realty Times*.

★ 1800 ★
Real Estate Agencies (SIC 6531)

Leading Real Estate Agents in Louisville, KY

Market shares are shown based on listings sold in the first three quarters of 2001. Figures are based on information from Local Board or Multiple Listing Service for the time period. Figures combine all listings sold and closed of all office locations and independent offices of each multi-office or franchise organization identified, which listings were sold by such organization itself or with the aid of a cooperating broker.

Re/Max	26.2%
Paul Semonin	20.0
Coldwell Banker	10.7
Century 21	4.4
Prudential	3.3
ERA	3.2
Other	32.2

Source: "Market Share." available March 1, 2003 from http://www.remax.com, from Remax.

★ 1801 ★
Real Estate Agencies (SIC 6531)

Leading Real Estate Agents in Portland, OR

Market shares are shown based on listings sold in 2001.

Re/Max	19.61%
The Hasson Company	10.60
John L. Scott	10.05
Windemere/C&C RGI	9.22
CB Barbara Sue Seal	6.36
Other	44.16

Source: "Market Share." available March 1, 2003 from http://www.remax.com, from Remax.

★ 1802 ★

Real Estate Agencies (SIC 6531)

Leading Real Estate Agents in Sarasota, FL

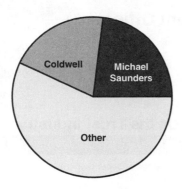

Market shares are shown for year to date.

Michael Saunders	23.0%
Coldwell	20.0
Other	57.0

Source: *Sarasota Herald Tribune*, July 7, 2002, p. D1, from Real Trends.

★ 1803 ★

Real Estate Agencies (SIC 6531)

Leading Real Estate Agents in Southwestern Pennsylvania

Market shares are estimated in percent.

Howard Hanna	29.2%
Coldwell Banker	18.2
Prudential Realty	15.4
Northwood Realty	11.1
Other	26.1

Source: *Pittsburgh Business Times*, January 17, 2003, p. NA, from *West Penn Multi-List Ranking Report*.

★ 1804 ★

Real Estate Agencies (SIC 6531)

Leading Real Estate Agents in Victoria, British Columbia

Market shares are shown based on listings sold in 2001.

Re/Max	24.0%
DFH Real Estate	12.3
Coast Capital	11.3
Royal LePage	9.3
Sutton Group	7.8
Pemberton	6.6
Other	28.7

Source: "Market Share." available March 1, 2003 from http://www.remax.com, from Remax.

SIC 67 - Holding and Other Investment Offices

★ 1805 ★

Bank Holding Companies (SIC 6712)

Largest Bank Holding Companies in Florida

Market shares are shown in percent baed on deposits as of September 30, 2002.

Bank of America	20.40%
Wachovia Corp.	15.22
SunTrust Banks of Florida	12.07
Southtrust of Alabama	3.77
AmSouth Bancorporation	2.25
Ocean Bankshares	1.52
Union Planters Holding Corp.	1.47
Colonial Bancgroup	1.30
Other	42.00

Source: *Florida Trend*, May 2003, p. 88, from Florida Bankers Association.

★ 1806 ★

Bank Holding Companies (SIC 6712)

Top Holding Companies in Florida

Market shares are shown in percent.

Bank of America	21.13%
First Union Trust of Florida	14.26
SunTrust Banks of Florida	10.31
SouthTrust of Alabama Inc.	4.03
AmSouth Bancorporation	2.44
Other	47.83

Source: *Florida Trend*, September 2002, p. 92, from Florida Bankers Association.

★ 1807 ★

Trusts (SIC 6730)

Who Makes Up the Trust Industry

Figures are based on a survey.

Bank or savings & loan	40.0%
Brokerage or securities firm	11.7
Law firm	9.0
Insurance company	8.3
Investment adviser or financial planner	7.2
Independent trust company	3.9

Source: *American Banker*, March 27, 2003, p. 1, from Diversified Services Group.

★ 1808 ★

Franchising (SIC 6794)

Largest Franchisers in Los Angeles County

Companies are ranked by total units.

Merle Norman Cosmetics	1,881
Hilton Hotels Corp.	1,724
IHOP Corp.	1,026
Gold's Gym	648
World Gym International	265
Wetzel's Pretzels	200
Sizzler Restaurants	182
Baja Fresh Mexican Grill	180
My Gym Enterprises	104
Body Balance for Performance	91

Source: *Los Angeles Business Journal*, February 3, 2003, p. 22.

★ **1809** ★

Patents (SIC 6794)

Colleges and Patents

Schools are ranked by number of patents received.

University of California	431
Mass. Institute of Technology	135
California Institute of Technology	109
Stanford University	104
University of Texas	83
University of Wisconsin	81
John Hopkins University	81
State University of New York	55
Penn State University	50
Michigan State University	49

Source: *Christian Science Monitor*, March 21, 2003, p. 24, from U.S. Patent and Trademark Office.

★ **1810** ★

Patents (SIC 6794)

Largest Patent Holders, 2001

Data show preliminary numbers.

IBM	3,411
NEC	1,953
Canon Kabushiki Kaisha	1,877
Micron Technology	1,643
Samsung Electronics	1,450
Matsushita Electrical	1,440
Sony Corporation	1,363
Hitachi Ltd.	1,271
Mitsubishi	1,184

Source: *Technology Access Report*, January 2002, p. 3, from U.S. Patent and Trademark Office.

★ **1811** ★

Patents (SIC 6794)

Largest Patent Holders, 2002

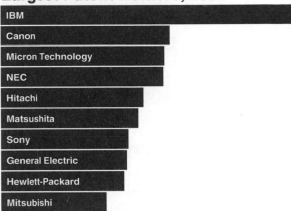

Figures show number of patents awarded.

IBM	3,288
Canon	1,893
Micron Technology	1,833
NEC	1,821
Hitachi	1,602
Matsushita	1,544
Sony	1,434
General Electric	1,416
Hewlett-Packard	1,385
Mitsubishi	1,184

Source: *New York Times*, January 13, 2003, p. C3, from United States Patent and Trademark Office.

★ **1812** ★

Real Estate Investment Trusts (SIC 6798)

REIT Debt Counsel, 2002

Issuer's counsel are shown by market share (shares are based on issuers). The top four firms worked on 22 equity issuances with a combined value of $1.6 billion, down from the 24 issuances worth $3.7 billion in 2001. Figures include registered debt offerings by REITs in the U.S. marketplace.

Latham & Watkins	11.2%
Hogan & Hartson	9.0
Locke Liddell & Sapp	7.9
Goodwin Procter	7.9
Sullivan & Worcester	5.6
Other	58.4

Source: *American Lawyer*, April 2003, p. 123, from Thomson Financial.

SIC 70 - Hotels and Other Lodging Places

★ 1813 ★
Hotels (SIC 7011)

Extended Stay Industry

Total rooms are thought to grow from 229,852 rooms in 2002 to 294,361 rooms in 2007.

	2002	2007
Mid-price	39.0%	36.0%
Upscale	37.0	43.0
Economy	24.0	21.0

Source: *Lodging Hospitality*, March 15, 2003, p. 32, from The Highland Group.

★ 1814 ★
Hotels (SIC 7011)

Largest Hotel Companies, 2002

Cendant Corp.

Six Continents Hotels

Marriott International

Choice Hotels International

Hilton Hotels Corp.

Best Western International

Starwood Hotels & Resorts Worldwide

VIP International

Carlson Hospitality Worldwide

Accor North America

Companies are ranked by number of guestrooms.

Cendant Corp.	552,528
Six Continents Hotels	515,082
Marriott International	448,004
Choice Hotels International	361,674
Hilton Hotels Corp.	333,897
Best Western International	304,664
Starwood Hotels & Resorts Worldwide	225,208
VIP International	176,400
Carlson Hospitality Worldwide	136,653
Accor North America	134,341

Source: *Hotel & Motel Management*, September 16, 2002, p. 38, from survey conducted by the source July 2002.

★ 1815 ★
Hotels (SIC 7011)

Largest Limited-Service Chains

Limited-service chains are economy and midscale without food/drink services. Chains are ranked by guestrooms.

Days Inn Worldwide	161,949
Super 8 Motels	128,108
Hampton Inn/Inn & Suites	122,431
Comfort Inn	106,838
Holiday Inn Express	96,000
Motel 6	85,906
Fairfield Inn	47,971
Travelodge Hotels	46,648
Econo Lodge	42,610
La Quinta Inn/Inn & Suites	41,708

Source: *Hotel & Motel Management*, February 3, 2003, p. 22, from *2002 Limited-Service Hotel Chain Survey*.

★ 1816 ★
Hotels (SIC 7011)

Leading Hotel Firms for Federal Travelers, 2001

Market shares are shown based on sales of $1.6 billion.

Holiday Inn	8.2%
Marriott	4.6
Residence Inn	3.8

Continued on next page.

★ 1816 ★ *Continued*

Hotels (SIC 7011)

Leading Hotel Firms for Federal Travelers, 2001

Market shares are shown based on sales of $1.6 billion.

Hilton	3.3%
Sheraton	3.0
Hampton Inn	2.7
Best Western	2.5
Embassy Suites	2.5
Comfort	2.2
Other	66.3

Source: *Government Executive*, August 15, 2002, p. NA, from Eagle Eye Publishers and Federal Procurement Data Center.

★ 1817 ★

Time Share Industry (SIC 7011)

Cancun Timeshare Industry

Figures are based on a survey of 38 resorts.

Hotel room/studio or efficiencies	50.0%
Two-bedroom units	40.0
One bedrooms	9.0
3 or more rooms	1.0

Source: *Hotel & Motel Management*, January 13, 2003, p. 30, from Interval International.

★ 1818 ★

Time Share Industry (SIC 7011)

Time Share Market

For the past decade, time shares have grown 15% annually. The U.S. has about 1,600 of the world's 5,000 properties and accounts for more than $4 billion in sales.

Florida	25.0%
California	7.0
Other	68.0

Source: *Knight Ridder/Tribune Business News*, July 22, 2002, p. NA, from American Resort Development Association.

★ 1819 ★

Mobile Home Parks (SIC 7033)

Mobile Homes in South Florida

The number of mobile homes is decreasing across South Florida even as the total rises in the state. The article points out that trailer parks are now starting to look like typical neighborhoods or even upscale developments because the land on which they are built is so valuable.

	1990	2000
Broward	27,918	26,834
Palm Beach	21,573	20,083
Miami-Dade	18,543	15,338

Source: *Daily Business Review*, March 13, 2003, p. A2.

SIC 72 - Personal Services

★ 1820 ★
Dry Cleaning Industry (SIC 7216)

Dry Cleaning Market

There are an estimated 45,000 dry cleaners in the country. The industry is highly fragmented.

Top 50 chains 5.0%
Other 95.0

Source: *Business Week Online*, April 25, 2002, p. NA.

★ 1821 ★
Carpet Cleaners (SIC 7217)

Where Carpet Cleaners Buy Their Chemicals

Figures are based on a survey.

Local distributor 65.0%
Direct from manufacturer 25.0
Other 10.0

Source: *ICS Cleaning Specialist*, February 2003, p. 18.

★ 1822 ★
Funerals (SIC 7261)

Funeral Industry in Colorado

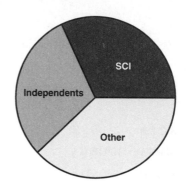

Market shares are shown in percent. SCI owns 40 mortuaries and cemeteries.

SCI 32.0%
Independents 30.0
Other 38.0

Source: *Denver Post*, August 26, 2002, p. NA.

★ 1823 ★
Tax Preparation (SIC 7291)

Tax Preparation in Canada

Figures show the split between paper and electronic returns. Over 23 million returns are expected to be filed.

Paper 60.0%
Electronic 40.0

Source: *Vancouver Province*, March 16, 2003, p. A56, from Canada Customs and Revenue Agency.

★ 1824 ★
Spas (SIC 7299)

Spas in the United States

Day spas are shown as a percent of the total industry. The number of such spas has more than doubled between 1995 and 1999. There are currently 4,500. The industry generates $3.5 billion annually in sales and the average client spends $100.

Day	77.0%
Other	23.0

Source: *Knight-Ridder/Tribune Business News*, May 23, 2002, p. NA, from International Spa Association.

SIC 73 - Business Services

Advertising (SIC 7311)

Largest Agencies, 2001

Firms are ranked by billings in millions of dollars.

BBDO	$ 5.93
DDB	4.31
J. Walter Thompson	4.16
Foote, Cone & Belding	3.93
Ogilvy & Mather	3.73
McCann-Erickson	3.50
Young & Rubicam	3.25
Leo Burnett	3.10
Grey	2.33
Saatchi & Saatchi	2.22

Source: *Adweek*, April 15, 2002, p. 50.

★ 1826 ★

Advertising (SIC 7311)

Largest Agencies in New England

Firms are ranked by billings in millions of dollars.

Arnold (Havas)	$ 950.0
Hill, Holliday, Connors	527.0
Cosmopulos	430.0
Allen & Gerritsen	110.0
Mullen (IPG)	94.0

Toth Brand Imaging	.$ 80.0
Gearon Hoffman	75.0
RDW Group	72.5
North Castle Partners	70.0

Source: *Adweek*, April 15, 2002, p. 56.

★ 1827 ★

Advertising (SIC 7311)

Largest Agencies in the Midwest

Firms are ranked by billings in millions of dollars.

Leo Burnett	$ 3,100.0
PentaMark	2,400.0
Campbell-Ewald	1,850.0
J. Walter Thompson	1,625.0
Foote, Cone & Belding	1,445.0
DDB (OMC)	1,350.0
Campbell Mithun	1,070.0
D'Arcy Masius Benton & Bowles	894.5
Doner	840.0

Source: *Adweek*, April 15, 2002, p. 56.

★ 1828 ★

Advertising (SIC 7311)

Largest Agencies in the Southeast

Firms are ranked by billings in millions of dollars.

Zimmerman & Partners Advertising . . .	$ 702.0
BBDO South	384.6
The Martin Agency	369.4
McKinney & Silver	275.1
Eisner Communications	248.0
WestWayne	230.0
J. Walter Thompson	220.0
Arnold	172.0

Source: *Adweek*, April 15, 2002, p. 56.

★ 1829 ★
Advertising (SIC 7311)

Largest Agencies in the Southwest

Firms are ranked by revenues in millions of dollars.

The Richards Group	$ 84.5
GSD&M	81.1
Temerlin McClain	73.0
Ackerman McQueen	34.0
DDB	29.0
Fogarty Klein Monroe	24.7
Publicis in Mid America	23.0
Dieste, Harmel & Partners	17.1
Moroch-Leo Burnett	16.9

Source: *Adweek*, April 15, 2002, p. 56.

★ 1830 ★
Advertising (SIC 7312)

Billboard/Poster Market in Greater Vancouver

The outdoor advertising market is growing increasingly comptitive, but Viacom Outdoors is taking a bite out of the market. The company claims its share is in excess of 60%.

Pattison Outdoor	60.0%
Other	40.0

Source: *Vancouver Sun*, December 21, 2002, p. D3, from Pattison Outdoor.

★ 1831 ★
Advertising (SIC 7312)

Outdoor Advertising Industry

The industry generated $5.2 billion in revenues. Outdoor advertising represents 2.2% of the industry but has been growing 6.7% annually over the last five years.

Billboards	60.0%
Street furniture	17.0
Transit	17.0
Alternative outdoor	6.0

Source: *American Demographics*, December 2002-January 2003, p. 25, from Outdoor Advertising Association of America.

★ 1832 ★
Advertising (SIC 7319)

Advertising and the Military

Figures show the ad budgets, in millions, for each branch.

Army	$ 85.3
Air Force	41.1
Navy	20.5
Marines	15.9

Source: *USA TODAY*, March 20, 2003, p. 3B, from Competitive Media Reporting and TNS Media Intelligence.

★ 1833 ★
Advertising (SIC 7319)

Advertising in Gay Media, 2001

Between 1997 and 2001, total ad dollars in gay and lesbian publications doubled from $100 million to $208 million. Circulation of such such publications is small — currently about 3.7 million — but growing steadily.

Restaurant/food/beverages	15.4%
Retail/home	8.1
Financial services	7.8
Arts & entertainment	7.3
Medical/health	6.5
Other	54.9

Source: *American Demographics*, February 2003, p. 19, from *2002 Gay Press Report*, Prime Access Inc., and Rivendell Marketing.

★ 1834 ★

Advertising (SIC 7319)

Advertising Market in Canada, 2002

Retail businesses made up 24% of the market, while other types (large multinationals) had 61% of the ad pie. The balance was held by the government, foreign consumers and households/individuals.

Television	38.5%
Newspapers	38.1
Radio	12.7
Magazines	7.3
Outdoor	3.2
Cinema	0.1

Source: "Advertising." available April 7, 2003 from http://www.usatrade.gov, from United States Department of Commerce.

★ 1835 ★

Advertising (SIC 7319)

Advertising Spending, 2001-2002

Spending is shown in millions of dollars.

	2001	2002	Share
Network TV	$ 18.63	$ 20.02	17.07%
Newspapers (local)	18.42	20.09	17.13
Consumer magazines	16.50	16.79	14.32
Spot TV	14.34	16.35	13.94
Cable TV	10.29	10.59	9.03
B-to-B magazines	8.39	7.22	6.16
Internet	6.51	5.74	4.89
Local radio	5.05	5.59	4.77
Syndication - national broadcast	3.19	2.94	2.51

Source: *Business Wire*, March 10, 2003, p. NA, from CMR/TNS Media Intelligence.

★ 1836 ★

Advertising (SIC 7319)

Largest Business-to-Business Advertisers

Companies are ranked by spending in millions of dollars.

Verizon Communications	$ 336.3
Microsoft Corp.	243.4
SBC Communications	240.4
Sprint Corp.	229.9
AT&T Wireless	215.4

Hewlett-Packard	$ 201.7
IBM Corp.	149.6
General Motors Corp.	100.3
AT&T Corp.	98.9

Source: *BtoB*, September 9, 2002, p. 22, from Competitive Media Reporting.

★ 1837 ★

Advertising (SIC 7319)

Largest Cable Advertisers, 2001

Spending is shown in millions of dollars.

AOL Time Warner	$ 294.0
Procter & Gamble	253.9
General Motors	249.2
Philip Morris	221.9
AT&T	158.0
General Mills	150.3
Pfizer	145.6
Glaxosmithkline	124.2
Walt Disney	122.8
Worldcom	121.8

Source: *Adweek*, April 15, 2002, p. 26, from Competitive Media Reporting.

★ 1838 ★

Advertising (SIC 7319)

Largest Medical Advertisers, 2002

Market shares are shown in percent.

Pfizer	9.67%
GlaxoSmithKline	5.62
Wyeth	4.90
Forest Laboratories	4.21
Aventis	3.83
AstraZeneca	3.35
Novartis	2.76
Ortho/McNeil	2.61
Merck	2.46
Abbott Laboratories	2.32
Other	58.27

Source: *Medical Marketing & Media*, March 2003, p. 58, from PERQ/HCI.

★ 1839 ★
Advertising (SIC 7319)

Leading Dental Advertisers, 2002

Figures show share of total ad expenditures for the first six months of the year.

Dentsply	5.94%
Ultradent Products	3.83
Discus Dental Inc.	3.11
Ivoclar Vivadent	3.10
Den-Mat Corporation	2.16
3M-ESPE	2.09
Kerr Manufacturing Co.	2.08
Bisco Dental Products	1.74
Procter & Gamble	1.74
Oral-B Laboratories	1.67
Other	72.54

Source: *Medical Marketing & Media*, October 2002, p. 78, from PERQ/HCI.

★ 1840 ★
Advertising (SIC 7319)

Leading Hospital Advertisers, 2002

Figures show share of total ad expenditures for the first six months of the year.

Cerner Corp.	4.78%
Siemens Medical Systems Inc.	3.44
Multiplan Inc.	1.64
Sodexho	1.63
GE Medical Systems	1.60
Hunter Group	1.47
IDX Corporation	1.46
McKesson Information Solutions	1.46
Alaris Medical System	1.44
Other	81.08

Source: *Medical Marketing & Media*, October 2002, p. 78, from PERQ/HCI.

★ 1841 ★
Advertising (SIC 7319)

Leading Laboratory Advertisers, 2002

Figures show share of total ad expenditures for the first six months of the year.

Bayer Diagnostics	5.23%
Roche Diagnostic Systems	4.71
Beckman Coulter	4.20
Ortho-Clinical Diagnostics	3.33
Abbott Diagnostics	3.26
Olympus America	2.70
Other	23.43

Source: *Medical Marketing & Media*, October 2002, p. 78, from PERQ/HCI.

★ 1842 ★
Advertising (SIC 7319)

New Car Advertising, 2001

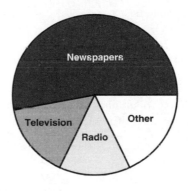

Distribution is shown in percent.

Newspapers	53.0%
Television	15.0
Radio	14.0
Other	18.0

Source: *Austin American-Statesman*, March 10, 2003, p. D1, from auto dealers association.

★ 1843 ★
Advertising (SIC 7319)

Rolling Stock Ad Market in New York

Rolling stock ads are commercials shown in movie theaters. Market shares are shown in percent.

Screenvision 54.0%
Other 46.0

Source: *Business Wire*, September 26, 2002, p. NA.

★ 1844 ★
Advertising (SIC 7319)

Rolling Stock Cinema Advertising

Rolling stock ads are commercials shown in movie theaters. Screenvision services 13,500 movie screens.

Screenvision 54.0%
Other 46.0

Source: *Daily Variety*, September 24, 2002, p. 6.

★ 1845 ★
Advertising (SIC 7319)

Top Ad Spenders, 2002

Figures are in millions of dollars. Shares are shown based on total ad spending of $117.3 billion.

	($ mil.)	Share
General Motors Corp.	$ 2,520.8	2.15%
Procter & Gamble	2,160.3	1.84
AOL Time Warner	1,844.7	1.57
Ford Motor Co.	1,451.1	1.24
Daimler Chrysler	1,401.2	1.19
Walt Disney Co.	1,160.2	0.99
Verizon Communications	1,073.2	0.91
Johnson & Johnson	1,053.2	0.90
Toyota Motor Corp.	937.4	0.80
Altria Group Inc.	920.4	0.78
Other	102,777.5	87.62

Source: *Business Wire*, March 10, 2003, p. NA, from CMR/TNS Media Intelligence.

★ 1846 ★
Photocopying Services (SIC 7334)

Largest Quick Print Firms, 2002

Firms are ranked by calendar year revenues in millions of dollars.

Kinko's . . . . $ 2,000.00
St. Joseph's Digital Solutions 54.50
The Superior Group 23.00
Original Impressions 18.50
JKG Group 18.10
Ginny's & Merit 14.60
Econoprint 13.91
LazerQuick 13.25
IST Management Services 10.70
Copy Craft Printers 10.60
Triangle 10.00
Pel Hughes Printing 9.00

Source: *Graphic Arts Monthly*, February 2003, p. 43, from Reed Research and *2002 Quick Prints Giants Survey*.

★ 1847 ★
School Photography Services (SIC 7335)

Who Selects School Portraits, 2002

Figures show percent of households with the greatest influence in selecting K-11 school portrait packages.

Mother 85.0%
Student photographed 7.0
Father 3.0
Other 5.0

Source: ''Competing for Classroom Sales.'' available from http://www.pmai.org, from Photographic Marketing Association International.

★ 1848 ★
Pest Control Services (SIC 7342)

Leading Types of Pest Control Services

Figures show percent of companies offering each service, based on a survey.

Ants 89.0%
Rodents 89.0
Roaches 88.0
Termites 70.0
Stored product pests 66.0
WDO inspection 62.0

Continued on next page.

★ 1848 ★ *Continued*
Pest Control Services (SIC 7342)

Leading Types of Pest Control Services

Figures show percent of companies offering each service, based on a survey.

Birds	39.0%
Wildlife	28.0

Source: *Pest Control Magazine*, September 2002, p. S4.

★ 1849 ★
Pest Control Services (SIC 7342)

Pest Control Market

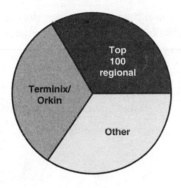

Market shares are shown in percent. There are an estimated 18,250 companies that remove pests from buildings.

Top 100 regional firms	30.0%
Terminix/Orkin	29.0
Other	31.0

Source: *Crain's Chicago Business*, October 14, 2002, p. S1, from National Pest Management Association.

★ 1850 ★
Temp Agencies (SIC 7363)

Leading Temp Agencies, 2002

Firms are ranked by revenues in billions of dollars.

Manpower	$ 10.61
Kelly Services	4.32
Spherion	2.14
Robert Half Intl.	1.90
Volt Info Ssciences	1.49
CDI	1.20
MPS Group	1.15

Source: *Fortune*, April 14, 2003, p. 63.

★ 1851 ★
Software (SIC 7372)

Accounting Software Market

The $1.3 billion market is shown by company.

Microsoft	5.5%
Intuit	4.0
Sage	4.0
Other	86.5

Source: *Computer Reseller News*, January 27, 2003, p. 43, from International Data Corp.

★ 1852 ★
Software (SIC 7372)

Business Intelligence Software, 2002

Market shares are shown based on revenue.

SAS Institute	21.0%
Cognos	10.0
Hyperion	9.0
Business Objects	8.0
Other	52.0

Source: *Investor's Business Daily*, August 27, 2002, p. A4, from AMR Research.

★ 1853 ★
Software (SIC 7372)

Content Management Market

Market shares are shown in percent.

FileNet	8.9%
Documentum	5.2
Interwoven	4.7
IBM	4.6
Other	76.6

Source: *Investor's Business Daily*, August 6, 2002, p. A4, from International Data Corp.

★ 1854 ★
Software (SIC 7372)

Copy Protection Technology

Content owners are turning to an array of technologies to prevent illegal copying. Market shares are shown in percent.

Macrovision	85.0%
Other	15.0

Source: *Tape-Disc Business*, September 2002, p. 22.

★ 1855 ★
Software (SIC 7372)

Database Management Market, 2001

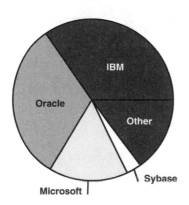

Shares are shown based on license sales.

IBM	34.6%
Oracle	32.0
Microsoft	16.3
Sybase	2.6
Other	14.5

Source: *Network World*, January 13, 2003, p. 14, from Gartner Dataquest.

★ 1856 ★
Software (SIC 7372)

Desktop Productivity Suite Market

Market shares are shown in percent.

Microsoft Office/Works	94.0%
IBM Lotus SmartSuite	3.0
Corel WordPerfect	1.0
Other	2.0

Source: *eWeek*, September 2, 2002, p. 14, from Giga Information Group.

★ 1857 ★
Software (SIC 7372)

Dictation Software Market

The industry refers to software that allows the user to create documents by speaking to a computer. Market shares are shown in percent.

Dragon Systems	65.0%
Other	35.0

Source: *Knight Ridder/Tribune Business News*, March 3, 2003, p. NA.

★ 1858 ★
Software (SIC 7372)

Education Internet Filtering Software, 2002

The education segment has 25% of the entire filtering market, or $53 million. Market shares are shown in percent.

N2H2	17.0%
SurfControl	13.0
Other	70.0

Source: *Electronic Education Report*, May 10, 2002, p. NA, from Simba Information.

★ 1859 ★
Software (SIC 7372)

ERP Software Market, 2002

ERP stands for enterprise resource management.

SAP	35.0%
Oracle	13.0
PeopleSoft	10.0
J.D. Edwards	4.0
Other	38.0

Source: *Infoworld*, September 30, 2002, p. 1, from AMR Research.

★ 1860 ★
Software (SIC 7372)

Firewall/VPN Software Market

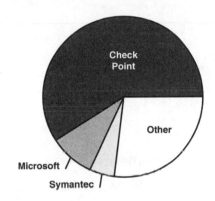

Market shares are shown in percent.

Check Point	59.0%
Microsoft	9.0
Symantec	5.0
Other	27.0

Source: *Infoworld*, August 26, 2002, p. 1, from International Data Corp.

★ 1861 ★
Software (SIC 7372)

Instant Messaging Software

Millions of users are shown for July 2002.

AOL Instant Messenger service	52.5
Microsoft	29.4
Yahoo	21.6

Source: *USA TODAY*, September 18, 2002, p. 3B, from ComScore Media Metrix.

★ 1862 ★
Software (SIC 7372)

Largest Instructional Software Vendors

The market rose from $1.44 billion in 2001 to $1.47 billion in 2002. The market is seeing a slowdown after growing 20% in 2001.

Pearson	15.5%
Riverdeep	8.4
Renaissance Learning	7.9
Other	68.2

Source: *Educational Marketer*, January 6, 2002, p. NA, from Simba Information.

★ 1863 ★
Software (SIC 7372)

Media Player Users

Figures show millions of users for June 2002.

Real One	30.8
Windows Media Player	30.1
QuickTime	12.3
Winamp	7.9
MusicMatch	7.3

Source: *USA TODAY*, September 5, 2002, p. 7D, from ComScore.

★ 1864 ★
Software (SIC 7372)

Messaging Market Shares, 2001

Shares are shown based on number of users.

Microsoft	39.4%
IBM	35.2
Novell	16.0
Other	9.4

Source: *Network World*, January 13, 2003, p. 14, from Gartner Dataquest.

★ 1865 ★
Software (SIC 7372)

Network and Systems Management Market, 2001

Shares are shown based on license sales.

IBM	18.8%
BMC	8.0
CA	6.8
HP	5.4
Other	61.0

Source: *Network World*, January 13, 2003, p. 14, from Gartner Dataquest.

★ 1866 ★
Software (SIC 7372)

Online DIY Tax Market

According to the IRS, nearly 132 million returns were filed in 2002, with 47 million filed electronically and 9.4 million of those self-prepared. Intuit claims to have 85% of the do-it-yourself market and 70% of the desktop tax market.

TurboTax	85.0%
Other	15.0

Source: *Sarasota Herald Tribune*, February 24, 2003, p. E1, from Intuit.

★ 1867 ★
Software (SIC 7372)

Personal Finance Software

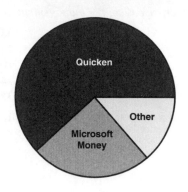

Shares are shown based on unit sales.

Quicken	68.0%
Microsoft Money	27.0
Other	15.0

Source: *Knight Ridder/Tribune Business News*, October 14, 2002, p. NA, from NPD Techworld.

★ 1868 ★
Software (SIC 7372)

Server Software Shipments

Market shares are shown in percent.

	2001	2002
Windows	65.0%	64.0%
Unix	13.0	12.0
Linux	9.0	13.0
Other	12.0	9.0

Source: *USA TODAY*, February 27, 2003, p. 2B, from Gartner Dataquest.

★ 1869 ★
Software (SIC 7372)

Web Browser Shares, 2002

Shares are for August 2002. Other includes Mozilla and Opera. Internet Explorer's share stood at 87% a year ago, and Netscape's share stood at 13%.

Internet Explorer	96.0%
Netscape	3.4
Other	0.6

Source: *Telecomworldwire*, August 29, 2002, p. NA, from StatMarket.

★ 1870 ★
Software (SIC 7372)

Web Site Analytics Services

Market shares are shown in percent.

WebSideStory	.35.0%
Webtrends	.12.0
IBM Global Services	.11.0
Coremetrics	.9.0
Other	.33.0

Source: *Investor's Business Daily*, February 11, 2002, p. A8, from Aberdeen Group.

★ 1871 ★
Software (SIC 7372)

What Types of Spam Do We Receive

Categories are shown for October 2002.

Financial	.36.0%
Products	.31.0
Adult	.12.0
Scams	.4.0
Health	.4.0
Spiritual	.2.0
Internet	.2.0
Lesiure	.2.0
Other	.7.0

Source: *Wall Street Journal*, November 13, 2002, p. 1, from Brightmail.

★ 1872 ★
Servers (SIC 7373)

Application Server Market

The $1.8 billion market is shown in percent.

BEA	.34.0%
IBM	.31.0
Sun	.9.0
Iona	.3.0
Sybase	.1.0
Others	.22.0

Source: *Infoworld*, June 10, 2002, p. 1, from Gartner Dataquest Inc.

★ 1873 ★
Servers (SIC 7373)

U.S. Server Market, 2002

Shares are shown for the second quarter of the year.

	Units	Share
HP	129,499	26.8%
Dell	115,877	24.0
IBM	57,715	12.0
Sun	36,319	7.5
Gateway	5,500	1.1
Other	137,737	28.5

Source: *VARBusiness*, September 30, 2002, p. 34, from Gartner Dataquest Inc.

★ 1874 ★
Information Technology (SIC 7375)

Bank I.T. Spending in North America

According to the source, banks are thought to have spent too much money on technologies — what is called the "me too" trend — as opposed to what customers demanded or what were deemed profitable. Spending is shown in billions of dollars.

	2001	2005	Share
Branch	$ 3.4	$ 4.8	40.68%
ATM/kiosk	1.8	2.0	16.95
Call centers	1.6	2.0	16.95
Personal sales	1.3	1.9	16.10
Internet	0.5	0.9	7.63
Wireless	0.0	0.2	1.69

Source: *Banking Strategies*, July/August 2002, p. 14, from Towers Group.

★ 1875 ★

Information Technology (SIC 7375)

Largest Federal I.T. Contractors

Companies are ranked by contracts in millions of dollars.

Lockheed Martin	$ 3,839.2
Northrop Grumman Corp.	1,457.9
Boeing Co.	1,371.4
Science Applications	1,329.6
General Dynamics Corp.	1,322.3
Computer Sciences Corp.	1,260.4
Raytheon Co.	774.4
TRW Inc.	650.2
Booz Allen Hamilton	577.6
Unisys Corp.	524.7

Source: *Washington Technology*, May 6, 2002, p. 26, from Federal Sources Inc. and General Services Administration's Federal Procurement Data Center.

★ 1876 ★

Computer Services (SIC 7378)

Apple Computer Upgrading

The leader in this industry is shown. XLR8 Inc., one of Sonnet Technologies' competitors, recently ceased business.

Sonnet	90.0%
Other	10.0

Source: *Knight Ridder/Tribune Business News*, August 13, 2002, p. NA.

★ 1877 ★

Computer Services (SIC 7378)

Computer Services Industry

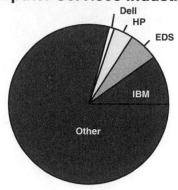

Market shares are shown in percent.

IBM	10.0%
EDS	6.0
HP	4.0
Dell	1.0
Other	79.0

Source: *Time*, December 2, 2002, p. 36, from International Data Corp.

★ 1878 ★

Computer Services (SIC 7378)

Federal Computer Systems

Spending is shown in billions of dollars. The server segment will see the highest growth.

	2003	2004	2005
Civilian	$ 6.3	$ 6.9	$ 7.7
Defense	5.9	6.2	6.8

Source: *Washington Technology*, September 23, 2002, p. 10, from Input.

★ 1879 ★

Computer Services (SIC 7378)

Who Services Macs in Hawaii

The company services 78-80% of the Macs in Hawaii.

Mac Made Easy	80.0%
Other	20.0

Source: *Hawaii Business*, November 2002, p. 52.

★ 1880 ★
Security Industry (SIC 7382)

Security Industry Market Shares

Shares are estimated for 2000.

Securitas	19.0%
Wackenhut	8.0
Allied	2.0
Guardsmark	2.0
Initial (Rentokil)	1.0
Argenbright (Securitor)	1.0
Other	67.0

Source: ''Security Industry.'' available January 7, 2003 from http://www.drkwresearch.com, from Dresdner Kleinwort Wasserstein.

★ 1881 ★
Security Industry (SIC 7382)

Top Security Service Firms In North America, 2001

Firms are ranked by revenues in millions of dollars. The top 100 integrators saw revenues of $2.4 billion. The major revenue sources are integrated systems with 42%, 19% for access control and 18% for closed circuit television.

	($ mil.)	Share
Siemens Building Tech. Inc.	$ 444.0	18.50%
ADT Security Services	375.2	15.63
Diebold	351.8	14.66
NetVersant Solutions	139.0	5.79
SimplexGrinnell	124.0	5.17
Pinkerton Sytems Integration	55.1	2.30
Electronic Technologies Corp.	55.0	2.29
ISR Solutions Inc.	51.6	2.15
Kastle Systems	39.5	1.65
NAVCO Security Systems	32.0	1.33
Other	732.8	30.53

Source: *SDM*, July 2002, p. 46, from *SDM's Top Systems Integrators*.

★ 1882 ★
Earnings Release Industry (SIC 7383)

Earnings Release Market, 2002

Market shares are shown in percent.

PR Newswire	51.0%
Other	49.0

Source: ''Pre-Close Season Update.'' available January 7, 2002 from http://www.unitedbusinessmedia.com, from PR Newswire.

★ 1883 ★
Photofinishing (SIC 7384)

Where Film is Processed

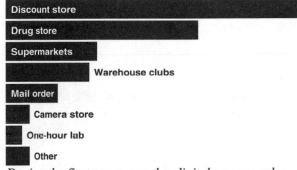

During the first seven months, digital camera sales increased 35% and analog-camera sales fell 25%. Film processing fell 8%. Figures are for the year ended July 2000 and July 2002.

	2000	2002
Discount store	34.6%	37.5%
Drug store	23.1	25.1
Supermarkets	12.8	11.7
Warehouse clubs	9.7	11.0
Mail order	8.8	6.8
Camera store	4.2	3.1
One-hour lab	2.8	1.7
Other	3.8	3.0

Source: ''U.S. Photo Retail Markets.'' available online January 7, 2003 from http://www.pmai.org, from Photo Marketing Association International.

★ 1884 ★

Conventions (SIC 7389)

Where Associations Held Their Meetings

After a dip in 1999, total spending on conventions (associations and the attendee) increased in 2001. Spending rose from $16.3 billion in 1999 to $16.6 billion in 2001. There were 11,800 conventions in 2001.

Chicago	21.0%
Washington D.C.	19.0
Orlando	13.0
Los Angeles	12.0
Atlanta	12.0
Phoenix/Scottsdale	11.0
New York City	11.0
Dallas/Ft. Worth	10.0
San Diego	9.0
New Orleans	9.0
Denver	9.0

Source: *Meetings & Conventions*, August 2002, p. 9, from *Meetings & Conventions 2002 Meetings Market Report.*

★ 1885 ★

Conventions (SIC 7389)

Where People Held Meetings

There was a small jump from 2001 to 2002 in the number of meetings. Spending hit $10.3 billion. There were 844,000 events with over 51 million in attendance. Where these meetings were held is shown in the table. Figures are based on a survey.

Downtown hotels	74.0%
Suburban hotels	54.0
Resort hotels (excl. golf resorts)	50.0
Convention centers	47.0
Airport hotels	39.0
Golf resorts	39.0
Suite hotels	27.0
Gaming facilities	19.0
Residential conference centers	15.0

Source: *Meetings & Conventions*, August 2002, p. 8, from *Meetings & Conventions 2002 Meetings Market Report.*

★ 1886 ★

Mergers & Acquisitions (SIC 7389)

Largest PR Corporate Merger Firms, 2002

Market shares are shown in percent.

Kekst & Co.	50.0%
Joele Frank	16.0
Citigate Sard Verbinnen	12.0
Abernathy MacGregor Group	9.0
Brunswick Group	7.0
Edelman	7.0

Source: *PR Week*, March 3, 2003, p. 3, from Corporate Control Alert.

★ 1887 ★

Mergers & Acquisitions (SIC 7389)

Leaing Energy Merger Advisers

Market shares add up to more than 100% because deals had more than one adviser.

Morgan Stanley	48.2%
Credit Suisse First Boston	36.1
Goldman Sachs	33.2
Merrill Lynch	29.3
Citigroup/Salomon Smith Barney	27.7
Lehman Brothers	22.2
J.P. Morgan	17.6

Source: *New York Times*, August 20, 2002, p. C1, from Thomson Financial Securities Data.

★ 1888 ★

Trade Shows (SIC 7389)

Leading Trade Show Operators

Shares are shown based on total number of shows. The industry saw declines in most measurable standards: exhibition space, number of firms and professional attendance.

Reed Exhibitions	7.5%
VNU Expositions	7.5

Continued on next page.

★ 1888 ★ *Continued*

Trade Shows (SIC 7389)

Leading Trade Show Operators

Shares are shown based on total number of shows. The industry saw declines in most measurable standards: exhibition space, number of firms and professional attendance.

George Little Management	5.0%
VS&A Communications Partners	3.0
Advanstar Communications	2.5
dmg World media	2.0
Hall-Erickson Inc.	1.5
Key 3Media Events Inc.	1.5
Smith, Bucklin & Associates	1.5
Society of Manufacturing Engineers	1.5
Other	66.5

Source: *Tradeshow Week*, April 2, 2002, p. 7, from TSW research.

★ 1889 ★

Trade Shows (SIC 7389)

Leading Trade Show Organizers in Canada

Market shares are shown in percent based on number of shows in the top 50.

dmg world media	22.0%
George Little Management	14.0
Reed Exhibitions	8.0
Other	56.0

Source: *Tradeshow Week*, April 2, 2002, p. 4, from Tradeshow Week Database of Tradeshows.

★ 1890 ★

Trade Shows (SIC 7389)

Trade Show Market By Ownership

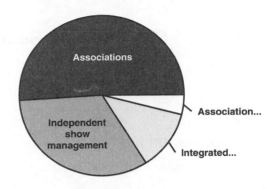

There are 3,568 shows planned for 2003. Shares are shown based on type of ownership.

Associations	50.7%
Independent show management companies (pure plays)	33.0
Integrated BIB media companies	12.1
Association management firms	4.2

Source: *Tradeshow Week*, April 14, 2003, p. 3, from TSW research.

★ 1891 ★

Training (SIC 7389)

Largest Training Budgets

Companies are ranked by the size of their training budgets in millions of dollars.

IBM	$ 700
Accenture	453
Intel	315
Lockheed Martin	309
Delta Air Lines	184
Continental Airlines	113
Prudential Financial	99
Wells Fargo	92
Wachovia Corp.	81
BMO Financial	71

Source: *Training*, March 2003, p. 18.

SIC 75 - Auto Repair, Services, and Parking

★ 1892 ★

Auto Rental (SIC 7514)

Airport Car Rental Market, 2002

Shares are for the first quarter of 2002.

Hertz	28.4%
Avis	21.1
Budget	11.4
Alamo	9.7
Dollar	7.9
Enterprise	3.3
National	3.2
Other	15.0

Source: *Advertising Age*, July 15, 2002, p. 29, from Abrams Travel Data Service.

★ 1893 ★

Auto Rental (SIC 7514)

Auto Rental Market, 2001

Shares are shown based on total revenues. ANC Rental includes National and Alamo.

Enterprise	27.4%
Hertz	19.9
ANC Rental	16.1
Avis	11.5
Budget	8.6
Dollar	4.6
Thrifty	2.9
Other	1.7

Source: *New York Times*, November 28, 2002, p. C1, from *Auto Rental News*.

★ 1894 ★

Auto Rental (SIC 7514)

Car Rental Industry at Palm Springs International Airport

Market shares refer to on-airport rental car gross receipts.

Hertz	30.20%
Avis	23.07
Budget	13.04
Dollar	12.30
National	10.57
Alamo	5.70
Enterprise	5.10

Source: "Palm Springs International Airport." available March 7, 2003 from http://www.palmspringsairport.com.

★ 1895 ★

Auto Rental (SIC 7514)

Car Rental Industry in Atlanta, GA

Shares are shown for the airport market and based on reported revenues for May 2001 - June 2002. Figures include on-airport and off-airport concessionaires and operators to airport authorities.

Hertz	33.64%
Avis	21.15
National	16.10
Alamo	9.56
Budget	8.94
Dollar	5.64
Thrifty	4.41
Other	0.57

Source: *Auto Rental News*, Annual 2002, p. 6.

★ 1896 ★
Auto Rental (SIC 7514)

Car Rental Industry in Los Angeles, CA

Shares are shown for the airport market and based on reported revenues for May 2001 - June 2002. Figures include on-airport and off-airport concessionaires and operators to airport authorities.

Hertz	28.53%
Avis	17.34
Alamo	14.21
National	12.12
Budget	10.43
Dollar	7.39
Thrifty	5.45
Enterprise	4.52

Sourcc: *Auto Rental News*, Annual 2002, p. 6.

★ 1897 ★
Auto Rental (SIC 7514)

Car Rental Industry in Miami, FL

Shares are shown for the airport market and based on reported revenues for May 2001 - June 2002. Figures include on-airport and off-airport concessionaires and operators to airport authorities.

Hertz	29.17%
Alamo	23.77
Avis	15.49
Dollar	10.55
Budget	8.17
National	6.24
Enterprise	1.89
Other	1.68

Source: *Auto Rental News*, Annual 2002, p. 6.

★ 1898 ★
Auto Rental (SIC 7514)

Car Rental Industry in Newark, NJ

Shares are shown for the airport market and based on reported revenues for May 2001 - June 2002. Figures include on-airport and off-airport concessionaires and operators to airport authorities.

Hertz	34.84%
Avis	27.19
National	17.23
Budget	8.65
Dollar	5.83
Alamo	3.98
Enterprise	2.28

Source: *Auto Rental News*, Annual 2002, p. 6.

★ 1899 ★
Auto Rental (SIC 7514)

Car Rental Industry in Orlando, FL

Shares are shown for the airport market and based on reported revenues for May 2001 - June 2002. Figures include on-airport and off-airport concessionaires and operators to airport authorities.

Alamo	20.44%
Dollar	16.01
Hertz	15.84
Avis	14.54
National	12.19
Budget	10.49
Thrifty	2.68
Other	5.56

Source: *Auto Rental News*, Annual 2002, p. 6.

★ 1900 ★
Auto Rental (SIC 7514)

Car Rental Industry in Phoenix, AZ

Shares are shown for the airport market and based on reported revenues for May 2001 - June 2002. Figures include on-airport and off-airport concessionaires and operators to airport authorities.

Hertz	24.92%
Avis	20.43
Alamo	13.18
Budget	13.04
National	11.35

Continued on next page.

★ 1900 ★ *Continued*
Auto Rental (SIC 7514)

Car Rental Industry in Phoenix, AZ

Shares are shown for the airport market and based on reported revenues for May 2001 - June 2002. Figures include on-airport and off-airport concessionaires and operators to airport authorities.

Dollar	6.19%
Enterprise	3.99
Thrifty	3.96
Other	2.92

Source: *Auto Rental News*, Annual 2002, p. 6.

★ 1901 ★
Auto Rental (SIC 7514)

Car Rental Industry in Seattle, WA

Shares are shown for the airport market and based on reported revenues for May 2001 - June 2002. Figures include on-airport and off-airport concessionaires and operators to airport authorities.

Hertz	26.51%
Avis	21.39
National	14.43
Alamo	12.53
Budget	9.64
Dollar	5.40
Thrifty	4.54
Enterprise	4.46
Other	1.10

Source: *Auto Rental News*, Annual 2002, p. 6.

★ 1902 ★
Auto Rental (SIC 7514)

Largest Car and Truck Rental Firms in Baton Rouge, LA

Companies are ranked by number of units in fleet.

Avis Rent-A-Car	425
Budget Rent A Car	180
National Car Rental	148
Gerry Lane Chevrolet	148
Avis-Suburban	100
U-Save Auto Rental	80
Hollingsworth Richards Ford	72
All Star Ford Lincoln Mercury	45

Source: *Greater Baton Rouge Business Report*, Annual 2003, p. 50.

★ 1903 ★
Auto Rental (SIC 7514)

Leading Car Rental Firms for Federal Travelers, 2001

Market shares are shown based on sales of $340 million.

Hertz	14.6%
Avis	14.2
Budget	12.0
National	10.6
Dollar	10.4
Enterprise	10.0
Thrifty	8.8
Alamo	8.6
Other	10.8

Source: *Government Executive*, August 15, 2002, p. NA, from Eagle Eye Publishers and Federal Procurement Data Center.

★ 1904 ★
Auto Repair Services (SIC 7530)
Auto Repair Industry, 2002

Figures show the share of the repair market for light trucks and cars. Service stations and garages saw their share fall from 39.1% in 1992 to 29.5%, while vehicle dealers saw their share increase from 21.6% to 26.6% in the same period.

Service stations, garages	29.5%
Vehicle dealers	26.6
Repair specialists	16.2
Tire stores	8.9
Part stores with bays	6.4
Foreign specialists	6.0
Other	6.4

Source: *Wall Street Journal*, June 3, 2003, p. B4, from Lang Marketing.

★ 1905 ★
Auto Repair Services (SIC 7530)
Auto Service/Repair Market in Salt Lake City, UT

Market shares are shown in percent.

Jiffy Lube	60.0%
Goodyear	17.0
Pep Boys	14.0
David Early Tires	12.0
Firestone	12.0

Source: "Automotive Parts and Services." available March 1, 2003 from http://www.nacorp.com, from Belden Continuing Market Study.

★ 1906 ★
Auto Repair Services (SIC 7530)
Collision Shops in North America

The table compares the number of body repair shops in each country.

United States	53,000
Canada	8,500

Source: *BSB*, January 2003, p. 30, from Diagon Reports GAP 2001.

★ 1907 ★
Tire Retreading (SIC 7534)
Largest North America Retreaders, 2001

Companies are ranked by millions of pounds of rubber used for the year. Figures are for off-the-road tires. Wingfoot was created in November 2000 by the merger of Goodyear and Treadco.

NRI Inc.	7.20
Wingfoot Commercial Tire Systems	6.46
Purcell Tire	6.30
J&M Tire International	3.52
Shrader's Inc.	3.40
B.R. Retreading	3.30
Goodyear Canada	3.00
RDH Tire & Retread	2.71
H&H Industries	2.10
Community Tire Co.	1.50

Source: *Tire Business*, Market Data Book, p. NA, from Rubber Manufacturers Association.

★ 1908 ★
Tire Retreading (SIC 7534)
Largest Truck Tire Retreaders, 2001

Companies are ranked by millions of pounds of rubber used for the year. Figures are for off-the-road tires. Wingfoot was created in November 2000 by the merger of Goodyear and Treadco.

Wingfoot Commercial Tire Systems	37.80
Tire Distribution Systems	25.10
Tire Centers	16.20
GCR Truck Tire/Bridgestone/Firestone	9.60
Les Schwab Tire Centers	9.09
Premier Bandag Inc.	8.50
Kal Tire	7.50

Continued on next page.

Tire Retreading (SIC 7534)

Largest Truck Tire Retreaders, 2001

Companies are ranked by millions of pounds of rubber used for the year. Figures are for off-the-road tires. Wingfoot was created in November 2000 by the merger of Goodyear and Treadco.

Pomp's Tire Service Inc.	7.10
Snider Tire Inc.	7.00
Purcell Tire & Rubber Co.	7.00

Source: *Tire Business*, Market Data Book, p. NA, from Rubber Manufacturers Association.

★ **1909** ★

Carwashes (SIC 7542)

Leading Carwashes

Individual stations are ranked by highest volume for the year.

Car Wash Partners (AZ)	284,000
Urus Management Corporation (Manhattan, NY)	260,000
Wash Depot Holdings (Kansas City, MO)	200,000
Octopus Car Wash (Albu., MN)	168,000
Rain Tunnel (St. Louis, MO)	165,000
Wilshire West (Santa Monica, CA)	140,000
Zax Auto Wash (Auburn Hills, MI)	120,000
Hallmark Car Wash (Houston, TX)	117,842
Mace Security International	110,000
King Car Wash (Westmont, IL)	106,000

Source: *Professional Carwashing & Detailing Online*, December 2002, p. NA.

SIC 76 - Miscellaneous Repair Services

Parts Cleaning Industry (SIC 7620)

Parts Cleaning Industry

Market shares are shown in percent.

Safety-Kleen 85.0%
Other 15.0

Source: *Waste Treatment Technology News*, February
2003, p. NA.

SIC 78 - Motion Pictures

★ 1911 ★
DVDs and Videos (SIC 7812)

DVDs Shipped by Year

Shipments are shown in millions of units.

2002 . . . . 425.6
2001 . . . . 364.4
2000 . . . . 182.4
1999 . . . . 98.0

Source: *PR Week*, March 10, 2003, p. 17, from Ernst & Young for the DVD Entertainment Group.

★ 1912 ★
DVDs and Videos (SIC 7812)

Fitness Video Market, 2003

Market shares are shown for the first quarter of the year.

GoodTimes 25.7%
Anchor Bay 18.5
Gaiam 11.5
PPI Entertainment 10.6
Artisan Home Entertainment 10.4
Goldhil Home Media 6.0
Ventura Distribution 5.9
Warner Home Video 3.4

Sony Music/Sony Wonder 3.3%
Koch 1.7
Other 3.0

Source: *Video Store*, April 27, 2003, p. 6, from Nielsen VideoScan.

★ 1913 ★
DVDs and Videos (SIC 7812)

Top DVD and VHS Distributors, 2002

Market shares are shown in percent. The $20.6 billion industry covers both sales and rentals.

Warner Home Video 21.7%
Buena Vista 18.2
Universal Home Video 11.8
Columbia 11.8
Fox Home Video 10.3
Other 26.2

Source: *Daily News*, January 9, 2003, p. B1, from Video Software Dealers Association.

★ 1914 ★
DVDs and Videos (SIC 7812)

Top DVD Vendors, 2002

Market shares are shown in percent.

Warner 24.4%
Disney 16.3
Universal 11.6
Columbia 11.6
Fox 10.5
Paramount 8.1
MGM 5.8
Artisan 2.4
Other 9.3

Source: *USA TODAY*, January 20, 2003, p. 3B, from *Video Business*.

★ 1915 ★
DVDs and Videos (SIC 7812)

Top Films on DVD and VHS

Films are ranked by DVD and VHS revenues in millions of dollars.

Monsters, Inc.	$ 384.8
The Lord of the Rings	380.2
Spider-Man	347.7
Harry Potter	343.9
Star Wars II: Attack of the Clones	212.5
Ice Age	211.1
Lilo & Stitch	207.6
The Fast and the Furious	199.7
Ocean's Eleven	192.2
Training Day	179.5

Source: *Daily Variety*, January 9, 2003, p. 1, from *Video Business* and Video Software Dealers Association.

★ 1916 ★
DVDs and Videos (SIC 7812)

Top Movie and DVD Firms, 2002

Revenues generated by sales of DVD and VHS hit $12.1 billion for 2002.

Warner Home Video	21.7%
Buena Vista Home Ent.	18.2
Columbia TriStar Home Ent.	11.9
Universal Studios Home Ent.	11.8
20th Century Fox Home Ent.	10.3
Paramount Home Ent.	8.4
MGM Home Ent.	5.4
Other	12.3

Source: *Hollywood Reporter*, January 10, 2003, p. 1, from independent survey of all major Hollywood studios and video distributors.

★ 1917 ★
DVDs and Videos (SIC 7812)

Top Renting Movie Titles, 2002

Consumers spent $8.2 billion renting 2.9 billion VHS cassettes and DVDs. Films are ranked by millions of national turns (DVD and VHS rentals).

Don't Say A Word	25.30
Ocean's Eleven 2001	24.47
Training Day	23.71
The Fast and the Furious	22.10
The Others	19.53

American Pie 2	18.92
Domestic Disturbance	18.34
Rat Race	18.07
Shallow Hal	18.06
Vanilla Sky	17.99

Source: *Business Wire*, January 8, 2003, p. NA, from Video Software Dealers Association VidTrac.

★ 1918 ★
DVDs and Videos (SIC 7812)

Top Selling DVD Titles, 2002

Films are ranked by revenues in millions of dollars.

The Lord of the Rings	$ 257.3
Spider-Man	215.3
Monsters, Inc.	202.0
Harry Potter	166.7
Star Wars II: Attack of the Clones	144.8
The Fast and the Furious	132.0
Ice Age	124.8
Lilo & Stitch	116.1
Goldmember	92.7
Band of Brothers	84.4

Source: *Video Business*, January 13, 2003, p. 48, from Video Business research based on studio data.

★ 1919 ★
DVDs and Videos (SIC 7812)

Top Selling DVD/VHS Titles, 2002

Revenues are in millions of dollars.

Monsters, Inc.	$ 347
The Lord of the Rings	330
Spider-Man	299
Harry Potter	298
Ice Age	203
Lilo & Stitch	198
Star Wars II: Attack of the Clones	188
The Fast and the Furious	146
Atlantis: The Lost Empire	130
Goldmember	121

Source: *Video Business*, January 13, 2003, p. 48, from Video Business research based on studio data.

★ 1920 ★
DVDs and Videos (SIC 7812)

Top VHS Vendors, 2002

Market shares are shown in percent.

Buena Vista	20.5%
Warner Bros.	19.3
Universal	11.4
Columbia	11.4
Fox	10.2
Paramount	8.0
MGM	4.5
Other	14.7

Source: *Video Business*, January 13, 2003, p. 48, from Video Business research based on studio data.

★ 1921 ★
Motion Pictures (SIC 7812)

Box Office Losers, 2002

The films with the lowest domestic box office grosses are shown, ranked by millions of dollars.

Imposter	$ 6.2
Deuces Wild	6.1
The Truth About Charlie	5.3
Slackers	5.2
Formula 51	5.2
Birthday Girl	5.0
Hollywood Ending	4.9
Extreme Ops	4.8
The Adventures of Pluto Nash	4.4
Pinocchio	3.7

Source: *Entertainment Weekly*, January 13, 2003, p. 55, from *Variety* and EDI.

★ 1922 ★
Motion Pictures (SIC 7812)

Box Office Winners, 2002

The highest grossing films in North America are shown by box office receipts through December 29. Figures are in millions. More than $9 billion worth of tickets were sold.

Spider-Man	$ 404
Star Wars Episode 2: Attack of the Clones	310
Harry Potter and the Chamber of Secrets	240
Signs	227
My Big Fat Greek Wedding	218
Austin Powers in Goldmember	213

The Lord of the Rings: The Two Towers	$ 200
Men in Black 2	192
Ice Age	176
Scooby-Doo	153

Source: *New York Times*, December 30, 2002, p. B1, from Exhibitor Relations.

★ 1923 ★
Motion Pictures (SIC 7812)

Top Animated Films, 1994-2002

Pixar and Dreamworks are challenging Disney's control of the animated film industry. Box office receipts are in millions of dollars.

The Lion King	$ 313
Shrek	268
Monsters Inc.	256
Toy Story 2	246
Toy Story	192
Tarzan	171
A Bug's Life	163
Lilo & Stitch	146
Dinosaur	138
Mulan	121

Source: *New York Times*, February 10, 2003, p. C1, from Nielsen EDI.

★ 1924 ★
Television Broadcasting (SIC 7812)

Spanish Television Market

Market shares are shown in percent for March 2002.

Univision	81.0%
Telemundo	19.0

Source: *New Mexico Business Weekly*, April 8, 2002, p. NA.

★ 1925 ★
Film Distribution (SIC 7822)

Independent Film Distribution, 2003

Market shares are shown based on box office receipts for January 2, 2002- January 5, 2003.

New Line Cinema	47.9%
Miramax	20.7
IFC Films	12.7
Focus Features	4.3

Continued on next page.

★ 1925 ★ *Continued*

Film Distribution (SIC 7822)

Independent Film Distribution, 2003

Market shares are shown based on box office receipts for January 2, 2002- January 5, 2003.

Lions Gate Films	3.6%
Artisan Ent.	2.7
Imax Film	2.1
Sony Classics	1.2
Other	4.8

Source: *Deal Memo*, January 27, 2003, p. 6, from Nielsen EDI.

★ 1926 ★

Film Distribution (SIC 7822)

Top Box Office Film Distributors, 2002

Total grosses hit roughly $9.2 billion, with nearly 1.6 billion Americans going to the movies. Market shares are shown in percent.

Sony	17.30%
Disney	13.10
Warner Bros.	11.70
20th Century Fox	10.20
Universal	9.60
New Line	9.40
Paramount	7.50
DreamWorks	5.17
MGM	4.00
Miramax	4.00
Other	8.03

Source: *Daily Variety*, December 31, 2002, p. 1, from Nielsen/EDI.

★ 1927 ★

Entertainers (SIC 7829)

Wealthiest Rock Stars, 2002

Entertainers are ranked net earnings in millions of dollars. Figures include touring, recording and publishing.

Paul McCartney	$ 72.1
The Rolling Stones	44.0
Dave Matthews Band	43.4
Celine Dion	31.1
Eminem	28.9
Cher	26.7
Bruce Springsteen	24.8

Mariah Carey	$ 23.3
Jay-Z	22.7
Ozzy Osbourne/The Osbournes	22.5

Source: *Rolling Stone*, April 3, 2002, p. 57, from interviews with record company executives, lawyers, agents, and publicists, SoundScan, *Yellow Pages of Rock*, and ArtistDirect.

★ 1928 ★

Movie Theaters (SIC 7832)

Imax Movie Settings

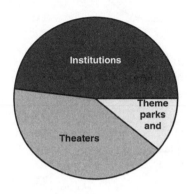

Imax films are shown on 8-story tall screens. The industry is out to change its image from a producer of science films to a displayer of Hollywood films in unique format (Apollo 13 and Beauty and the Beast recently enjoyed runs in Imax theaters across the country).

	1994	2001	Share
Institutions	72	110	48.03%
Theaters	22	93	40.61
Theme parks and other . . .	26	26	11.35

Source: *USA TODAY*, December 17, 2002, p. 3B, from Imax.

★ 1929 ★

Movie Theaters (SIC 7832)

Largest Exhibitors in Canada

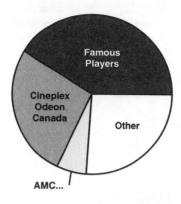

Total admissions hit 107.5 million in 2001, and receipts grew to $732.2 million in Canadian dollars. Companies are ranked by number of screens.

	Screens	Share
Famous Players	882	40.57%
Cineplex Odeon Canada	597	27.46
AMC Theaters Canada	122	5.61
Other	573	26.36

Source: *Hollywood Reporter*, May 11, 2002, p. 26, from AlexFilms and Canadian Film and Television Production Association.

★ 1930 ★

Movie Theaters (SIC 7832)

Largest Movie Theater Chains, 2002

Circuits are ranked by number of screens as of June 1, 2002.

	Screens	Share
Regal Entertainment Group . . .	5,850	16.44%
AMC Entertainment	3,308	9.29
Carmike Cinemas	2,333	6.55
Cinemark USA	2,241	6.30
Loews Cineplex Ent. Corp.	2,161	6.07
National Amusements	1,087	3.05
Hoyts Cinemas	922	2.59
Famous Players Inc.	841	2.36
Century Theatres	822	2.31
Kerasotes Theatres	532	1.49
Other	15,495	43.54

Source: "National Association of Theatre Owners." available January 7, 2003 from http://www.natoonline.org, from National Association of Theatre Owners.

★ 1931 ★

Movie Theaters (SIC 7832)

Leading Movie Theaters in Chicago, IL

Companies shares' are estimated based on box office receipts.

Loews	35.0%
AMC	25.0
Other	40.0

Source: *Knight-Ridder/Tribune Business News*, October 22, 2002, p. NA.

★ 1932 ★

Movie Theaters (SIC 7832)

Theater Exhibition Industry in Mexico

Company's share exceeds 50% of the market. It has 31 theaters and 349 screens.

Cinemex	50.0%
Other	50.0

Source: *Business Wire*, June 19, 2002, p. NA.

★ 1933 ★

Movie Rental Industry (SIC 7841)

Leading Genres for Rentals

Figures are for the first six months of the year. The comedy genre earned more than $1 billion in a six month period which, according to the source, is the first time this has ever happened.

Comedy	27.6%
Drama	24.6
Action	17.6
Thriller	12.5
Horror	6.5
Sci-fi	5.3
Family	3.7
Animation	2.2

Source: *Screen Digest*, September 2002, p. 287.

★ 1934 ★
Movie Rental Industry (SIC 7841)

Leading Movie Rental Chains, 2001

Market shares are shown in percent.

Blockbuster	33.3%
Hollywood Video	10.2
Movie Gallery	3.9
Family Video	1.4
Other	51.2

Source: *The Indianapolis Star*, February 20, 2003, p. C1, from *Video Star*.

★ 1935 ★
Movie Rental Industry (SIC 7841)

Leading Video Specialty Chains, 2002

Blockbuster
Hollywood Entertainment
Movie Gallery
Suncoast Motion Pictures Co.
Netflix
Family Video
DVD.com
Video Warehouse
Mr. Movies
TLA Entertainment Group
DVD Empire
Total Entertainment Center
West Coast Entertainment

Firms are ranked by estimated DVD/VHS revenues in millions of dollars.

Blockbuster	$ 3,917.0
Hollywood Entertainment	1,224.1
Movie Gallery	420.1
Suncoast Motion Pictures Co.	275.6
Netflix	154.0
Family Video	151.2
DVD.com	49.0
Video Warehouse	26.8
Mr. Movies	25.0

TLA Entertainment Group	$ 18.3
DVD Empire	16.9
Total Entertainment Center	16.6
West Coast Entertainment	15.5

Source: *Video Store*, April 13, 2003, p. 20, from *Video Store Top 100*.

★ 1936 ★
Movie Rental Industry (SIC 7841)

Leading Video Specialty Chains in Canada, 2002

Firms are ranked by estimated DVD/VHS revenues in millions of dollars.

Blockbuster	$ 255.0
Rogers Video	130.8
Le Superclub Videotron	60.3
Future Shop	49.1
Movie Gallery	33.7
Jumbo Video	16.0
VHQ Entertainment	14.3
Le Club International	13.0
Best Buy	9.5
Superior Video	6.9

Source: *Video Store*, April 13, 2003, p. 20, from *Video Store Top 100*.

★ 1937 ★
Movie Rental Industry (SIC 7841)

Online Movie Rentals

The company has an estimated share in excess of 90%.

Netflix	90.0%
Other	10.0

Source: *Video Store*, January 19, 2003, p. 1.

★ 1938 ★
Movie Rental Industry (SIC 7841)

Video Rental Market in Mexico

Blockbuster's share is 40-45% of the market.

Blockbuster	45.0%
Other	55.0

Source: *South American Business Information*, September 19, 2002, p. NA.

SIC 79 - Amusement and Recreation Services

Ticketing Services (SIC 7922)

Third-Party Ticketing Services

Ticketmaster is the leader but controls a small part of the industry. Market shares are shown in percent.

Ticketmaster 10.0%
Other 90.0

Source: *The Houston Chronicle*, January 19, 2003, p. 4, from Ticketmaster.

Theatrical Entertainment (SIC 7922)

Broadway Shows

Revenues are for the week ending March 23, 2003.

The Lion King . . . . $ 1,093,754
The Producers 1,016,423
Hairspray 984,732
Mamma Mia 952,655
Thoroughly Modern Millie 746,447

Source: *Variety*, March 31, 2003, p. 2.

Concert Promotions (SIC 7929)

Top Concert Promoters in North America, 2002

Groups are ranked by total gross in millions of dollars.

Clear Channel Entertainment . . . . . $ 1,106.1
House of Blues Concerts 164.6
Concerts West 145.9
Nederlander Organizations 52.1
Metropolitan Entertainment 49.4
Jam Productions 48.0
Jack Utsick Presents 44.1
CIE Events 31.6

OCESA Presents . . . . $ 24.5
Fantasma Productions 22.9

Source: *Amusement Business*, December 23, 2002, p. 8.

Bowling (SIC 7933)

Top States for Bowling

Data show states with the most sanctioned bowlers.

Michigan 303,233
New York 239,951
Ohio 239,010
California 196,154
Illinois 187,166

Source: *USA TODAY*, October 15, 2002, p. C1, from American Bowling Congress, Women's International Bowling Congress, and Young American Bowling Alliance.

Horse Racing (SIC 7948)

Horse Racing Industry, 2002

The top 3 companies manage 80% of the $15.8 billion wagered during the year.

Churchill Downs/Magna/New York Racing
  Association 80.0%
Other 20.0

Source: *The Washington Times*, May 4, 2003, p. A1.

★ 1944 ★

Exercise (SIC 7991)

Working Out by Age Group

Figures show the percentage of Americans by age group that plays a sport or exercise at least once a week.

12-17	71.3%
18-24	57.0
25-34	47.9
35-44	45.2
45-54	39.1
55-64	27.6
65+	24.5

Source: *USA TODAY*, October 14, 2002, p. C1, from ESPN Sports Poll.

★ 1945 ★

Golf Courses (SIC 7992)

Golf Courses by Type

	No.	Share
Public	12,910	72.46%
Private	4,906	27.54

Source: *USA TODAY*, October 4, 2002, p. A1, from National Golf Foundation.

★ 1946 ★

Slot Machines (SIC 7993)

Slot Machine Market in North America, 2001

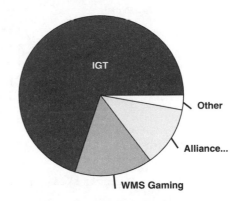

Market shares are estimated in percent. IGT has 65-70% of the market; WMS Gaming has 12-15% and Alliance Gaming 8-12%.

IGT	70.0%
WMS Gaming	15.0
Alliance Gaming Corp.	12.0
Other	3.0

Source: "Antitrust Probe for Slot Deal." available March 7, 2003 from http://www.gamblingmagazine.com.

★ 1947 ★

Amusement Parks (SIC 7996)

Top Amusement Parks in North America, 2002

Attendance is shown in millions.

The Magic Kingdom	14.04
Disneyland	12.72
Epcot	8.28
Disney MGM Studios	8.03
Disney's Animal Kingdom	7.30
Universal Studios	6.85
Islands of Adventure	6.07
Universal Studios Hollywood	5.20
Seaworld Florida	5.00
Disney's California Adventure	4.70

Source: *Amusement Business*, December 23, 2002, p. 8.

★ 1948 ★
Amusement Parks (SIC 7996)

Top Water Parks in North America, 2002

Attendance is shown in thousands.

Blizzard Beach	1,723
Typhoon Lagoon	1,556
Wet'N Wild	1,246
Schlitterbahn	810
Water Country	700
Raging Waters	650
Adenture Island	600
Six Flags Hurricane Harbor	575
Noah's Ark	566

Source: *Amusement Business*, December 23, 2002, p. 8.

★ 1949 ★
Sports (SIC 7997)

Extreme Sports Participation

Figures show the estimated number of participants, in thousands.

	2000	2001	2002
Skate	11.64	13.0	13.4
Snow	7.15	8.0	8.4
BMX	3.97	4.2	4.4
Wake boarding	3.58	4.5	4.7
Surf	2.18	3.1	3.6

Source: *American Demographics*, June 2002, p. 29, from American Sports Data and Fuse Integrated Marketing.

★ 1950 ★
Sports (SIC 7997)

Favorite Spectator Sports, 2002

Figures are based on a poll. Spectator sports include any sport attended, watched on TV, listened to on the radio or followed on some form of media.

National Football League	21.1%
Major League Baseball	12.6
National Basketball Association	10.0
College football	6.3
College basketball	5.3

Source: *USA TODAY*, August 20, 2002, p. C1, from ESPN.

★ 1951 ★
Sports (SIC 7997)

Leading Basketball Teams

Teams are ranked by current value in millions of dollars. Current value of team is based on current arena deal (unless new arena is pending) without deduction for debt (other than arena debt). See source for details.

Los Angeles Lakers	$ 426
New York Knicks	398
Chicago Bulls	323
Dallas Mavericks	304
Philadelphia 76ers	298
Washington Wizards	278
Boston Celtics	274
Phoenix Suns	272
Portland Trail Blazers	270
Sacramento Kings	259

Source: *Forbes*, February 17, 2003, p. 99.

★ 1952 ★
Sports (SIC 7997)

Leading Football Teams

Teams are ranked by current value in millions of dollars. Current value of team is based on current arena deal (unless new arena is pending) without deduction for debt (other than arena debt). See source for details.

Washington Redskins	$ 845
Dallas Cowboys	784
Cleveland Browns	618
Carolina Panthers	609
Baltimore Ravens	607
Tampa Bay Buccaneers	606
Denver Broncos	604
New England Patriots	571
Pittsburgh Steelers	555
Miami Dolphins	553

Source: *Forbes*, December 2, 2002, p. 99.

★ 1953 ★

Sports (SIC 7997)

Leading Hockey Teams

Teams are ranked by current value in millions of dollars. Current value of team is based on current arena deal (unless new arena is pending) without deduction for debt (other than arena debt). See source for details.

Detroit Red Wings	$ 266
New York Rangers	263
Philadelphia Flyers	262
Dallas Stars	254
Colorado Avalanche	250
Boston Bruins	243
Toronto Maple Leafs	241
Chicago Blackhawks	218
Los Angeles Kings	205
Montreal Canadiens	187

Source: *Forbes*, December 23, 2002, p. 99.

★ 1954 ★

Sports (SIC 7997)

Leading Sports Leagues, 2002

Leagues are ranked by revenues in billions of dollars.

NFL	$ 4.8
MLB	3.5
NBA	3.0
NHL	2.0

Source: *BusinessWeek*, January 27, 2003, p. B8.

★ 1955 ★

Sports (SIC 7997)

Leading Sports/Recreational Activities, 2002

Figures refer to millions of participants age 6 and above.

Bowling	53.2
Treadmill exercise	43.4
Freshwater fishing (not fly)	42.6
Tent camping	40.3
Billiards/pool	39.5
Stretching	38.4
Fitness walking	38.0
Day hiking	36.8

Basketball	36.6
Running/jogging	35.9

Source: "Top 30 Participation Activities." available April 10, 2003 from http://www.sgma.com, from Sporting Goods Manufacturers Association.

★ 1956 ★

Sports (SIC 7997)

Number of Avid Golfers

100% of the courses in Alaska and the District of Columbia are public. In Delaware, 50.6% of courses are private, the highest percentage for any state.

Chicago	193,136
Los Angeles-Long Beach	123,669
Detroit, MI	114,282
Washington D.C.-MD-VA-WVA	113,381
Philadelphia, PA-NJ	112,556
Minneapolis-St. Paul, MN-WI	94,656
New York City	93,528
Atlanta, GA	93,395
Phoenix-AZ	89,452
Boston, MA-N.H.	85,653

Source: *Golf World Business*, January 2003, p. 55, from Golf 20/20 and National Golf Foundation.

★ 1957 ★

Sports (SIC 7997)

Ski Industry by Region

Figures show the millions of skier visits to each region. The nation saw a 5.5% decrease over the 2000-2001 season, when 57.3 million visits were reported (the highest ever). But it was also the third busiest season in history.

	(mil.)	Share
Rocky Mountains	18.2	33.58%
Northeast	12.3	22.69
Pacific Northwest	11.8	21.77
Other	11.9	21.96

Source: *Knight-Ridder/Tribune Business News*, May 24, 2002, p. NA, from RRC Associates.

★ 1958 ★
Sports (SIC 7997)

Top Sports for Women

Figures show the millions of women who participated in each activity.

Exercise walking 44.8
Swimming 29.6
Exercising with equipment 22.5
Camping 21.4
Aerobic exercising 17.8
Bicycle riding 17.2
Hiking 12.4
Running/jogging 11.1
Roller skating (in-line) 10.1
Basketball 9.1

Source: *Sporting Goods Business*, November 2002, p. 29, from National Sporting Goods Association.

★ 1959 ★
Carnivals (SIC 7999)

Top Carnivals in North America, 2002

Attendance is shown in thousands.

Conklin Shows 7,751,177
Ray Cammack Shows 5,820,396
Wade Shows 2,950,919
Mighty Blue Grass 2,451,328
Reithoffer Shows 2,322,972
Strates Shows 2,116,583
Murphy Bros. Exposition 1,904,577
Farrow Shows 1,792,348
Amusements of America 1,658,378

Source: *Amusement Business*, December 23, 2002, p. 8.

★ 1960 ★
Fairs (SIC 7999)

Top State Fairs in North America, 2002

Attendance is shown in thousands.

State Farm of Texas 3,000
Minnesota State Fair 1,693
Houston Livestock Show 1,563
Canadian National Exhibition 1,465
Los Angeles County Fair 1,288
Illinois State Fair 1,265

Western Washington Fair 1,185
San Diego County Fair 1,169
Eastern States Exhibition 1,165

Source: *Amusement Business*, December 23, 2002, p. 8.

★ 1961 ★
Gambling (SIC 7999)

Gambling Industry in Kansas City, MO

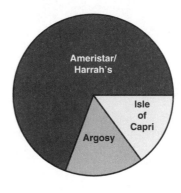

Market shares are shown in percent.

Ameristar/Harrah's 70.00%
Argosy 15.76
Isle of Capri 14.93

Source: *Knight-Ridder/Tribune Business News*, August 21, 2002, p. NA.

★ 1962 ★
Gambling (SIC 7999)

Gambling Market Shares

Market shares are estimated based on gaming revenues.

Las Vegas 26.0%
Atlantic City 15.0
Ledyard, CT 8.2
Chicago, IL 8.2
Other 42.6

Source: "Gambling Market Grows Vegas Shares Slip Slightly." available March 7, 2003 from http://www.gamblingmagazine.com, from American Gaming Association.

★ 1963 ★

Gambling (SIC 7999)

Sports Wagers in Nevada, 2002

Total bets hit $2 billion for the fiscal year ended June 30, 2002.

Football 43.0%
Basketball 26.0
Baseball 22.0
Parlay cards 3.0
Other 6.0

Source: *USA TODAY*, August 30, 2002, p. 6A, from Nevada Gaming Control Board.

★ 1964 ★

Gambling (SIC 7999)

Top Casino Markets, 2001

Annual revenues are shown in millions of dollars.

Las Vegas . . . . $ 4,700.0
Atlantic City, NJ 4,300.0
Chicagoland, (IL and IN) 2,200.0
Connecticut (Indian) 2,000.0
Detroit/Windsor Canada 1,400.0
Tunica/Coahoma, MS 1,200.0
Mississippi Gulf Coast 1,150.0
Reno/Sparks, NV 961.3
Shreveport, LA 806.2

Source: ''AGA Fact Sheet.'' available from http://www.americangaming.org, from Bear Stearns.

SIC 80 - Health Services

★ 1965 ★
Orthopedic Services (SIC 8041)

Orthopedic Services Market in Northern Illinois

The two physician groups Orthopedic and Arthritis Clinic of Rockford are planning to merge, giving it 40% of the market.

Lundholm Orth. Surgery/Rockford Orth.
  Association 60.0%
Orth. and Arthritis Clinic of Rockford/Orth.
  Assoc. of N. Illinois 40.0

Source: *Rockford Register Star*, December 24, 2002, p. 1C, from area doctors.

★ 1966 ★
Nursing Homes (SIC 8050)

Senior Care Arrangements

Figures show the millions of people using each type of care.

	1991	1995	2000
Nursing home	1,427	1,385	1,050
Home health care	1,284	1,284	2,200
Assisted-living facility	303	690	1,200

Source: *Best's Review*, April 2003, p. 70, from American Council of Life Insurers.

★ 1967 ★
Nursing Homes (SIC 8050)

Top Nursing Home Chains

Chains are shown by share ot total beds. Many facilities have struggled or failed after the Medicare cuts of the 1990s. Others have been forced to compete with assisted living chains.

Beverly Enterprises 3.4%
Mariner Health Care 2.4
Manor Care 2.2

Integrated Health Services 2.1%
Kindred Healthcare 2.1
Sun Healthcare 1.8
Genesis Health Ventures 1.6
Life Care Centers 1.1
Extendicare 1.0
Other 82.3

Source: *New York Times*, July 7, 2002, p. 10, from Center for Medicaid and State Operations, Bloomberg Financial Markets, and company reports.

★ 1968 ★
Nursing Homes (SIC 8051)

Largest Nursing Homes on Long Island

Homes are ranked by number of beds.

A. Holly Patterson Extended Care 889
United Presbyterian Residence 672
Parker Jewish Institute for Health Care &
  Rehab 527
Gurwin Jewish Geriatric Center 460
Our Lady of Consolation Nursing 450
Lutheran Center for the Aging 353
L.I. State Veterans Home 350

Source: *Long Island Business News*, February 21, 2003, p. 5B.

★ 1969 ★

Hospitals (SIC 8060)

Hospital Market in Montgomery County, OH

Market shares are shown based on admissions in 2001.

Premier Health Partners 54.6%
Ketterling Medical Center 39.1
VA Medical Center 6.3

Source: *Dayton Daily News*, October 15, 2001, p. E1.

★ 1970 ★

Hospitals (SIC 8060)

Hospital Network in Rochester, NY

Market shares are shown in percent.

Mayo Clinic 96.0%
Other 4.0

Source: *Boston Herald*, September 16, 2002, p. 23.

★ 1971 ★

Hospitals (SIC 8060)

Leading Inpatient Procedures, 2001

Figures show total of all taxpayers.

Manually assisted delivery 1,387,170
Packed cell transfusion 1,341,017
Coronary arteriography using two
   catheters 1,297,160
Left heart cardiac catheterization 1,252,815
Left heart angiocardiogram 1,157,861
Circumcision 1,146,407
Venous catheterizations 1,099,470
Repair of current obstetric laceration . . 1,061,319
Low cervical cesarean section 886,813
Insertion of endotracheal tube 691,039

Source: *Managed Healthcare Executive*, December 2002, p. 39, from Solucient.

★ 1972 ★

Organ Transplants (SIC 8060)

Largest Transplant Centers

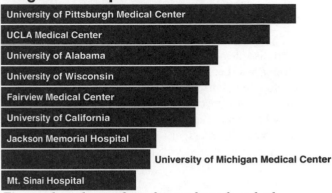

Figures show the number of transplants from both deceased and live donors from January 1, 1988 - December 31, 2002.

University of Pittsburgh Medical Center . . . 8,055
UCLA Medical Center 7,361
University of Alabama 5,945
University of Wisconsin 5,703
Fairview Medical Center 5,398
University of California 5,328
Jackson Memorial Hospital 4,254
University of Michigan Medical Center . . . 4,096
Mt. Sinai Hospital 3,704

Source: *Transplant News*, March 31, 2003, p. NA.

★ 1973 ★

Surgeries (SIC 8060)

Leading Types of Reconstructive Surgeries, 2001

More than 5.7 million patients had some form of reconstructive surgery performed. 44% of the procedures were performed in hospitals and 35% in free-standing ambulatory surgical facilities.

Tumor removal 70.0%
Laceration repair 8.0
Hand surgery 4.0
Scar revision 4.0
Breast reduction 2.0
Other 12.0

Source: *Cosmetic Surgery Times*, October 2002, p. 4, from American Society of Plastic Surgeons.

★ 1974 ★

Mental Health (SIC 8063)

Mental Health Office Visits, 2005

The millions of doctor visits are forecasted for 2005.

	(mil.)	Share
Mood disorders	36.34	37.09%
Anxiety disorders	23.31	23.79
Developmental disorders	7.08	7.23
Schizophrenia/psychotic disorders	5.38	5.49
Sleep disorders	5.18	5.29
Adjustment disorders	2.64	2.69
Substance abuse	2.48	2.53
Personality disorders	1.68	1.71
Delirium dementia	1.67	1.70
Other	12.22	12.47

Source: *Behavioral Health Business News*, July 4, 2002, p. 6, from Caredata.com cited in AIS's *Psychiatric Drug Pipeline Report.*

★ 1975 ★

Diagnostic-Tesing Labs (SIC 8071)

Diagnostic-Testing Lab Market, 2001

Market shares are shown in percent. Hospitals and independents (such as Quest and LabCorp.) each have 39% share.

Hospitals	39.0%
Quest	10.0
LabCorp.	6.0
Other	45.0

Source: *BusinessWeek Online*, April 14, 2002.

★ 1976 ★

Home Care Services (SIC 8082)

Home Care Industry in Seattle, WA

Market shares are shown based on a total of 141,517 clients in September 2002.

Armstrong Uniserve	22.65%
Catholic Community Services	16.36
Chesterfield Health Services	13.67
Sea-Mar	8.98
Elite International	8.10
Fremont Public Association	7.00
Amicable Healthcare Inc.	5.90
Millennia Healthcare Inc.	3.67

Kin On Homecare	3.04%
Other	10.63

Source: "Homecare Market Share." available April 7, 2003 from http://www.cityofseattle.net/humanservices/ads.

★ 1977 ★

Medical Tissue Preservation (SIC 8099)

Blood Vessel and Heart Tissue Preservation

The company holds more than 90% of the market for preserved human blood vessels and heart tissue. It holds 70% of the heart valve market.

CryoLife	90.0%
Other	10.0

Source: *Knight Ridder/Tribune Business News*, September 1, 2002, p. NA.

★ 1978 ★

Nuclear Pharmacy Industry (SIC 8099)

Nuclear Pharmacy Business

A nuclear pharmacy is a highly specialized, licensed facility that supplies radioactive compounds that are used to diagnose, monitor and treat cancer and heart disease. The market is estimated at $1.1 billion.

Syncor	52.0%
Other	48.0

Source: *Mergers & Acquisitions Journal*, August 1, 2002, p. NA.

SIC 81 - Legal Services

★ 1979 ★

Legal Services (SIC 8111)

Highest Grossing Law Firms, 2001

Firms are ranked by gross revenues in millions of dollars.

Skadden, Arps, Slate, Meagher & Flom
  New York . . . . $ 1,225.0
Baker & McKenzie International 1,000.0
Jones, Day, Reavis & Pogue 790.0
Latham & Watkins National 769.5
Sidley, Austin Brown & Wood 715.0
Shearman & Sterling 619.5
White & Case 603.0
Weil, Gotshal & Manges 581.0
Morgan, Lewis & Bockius 574.5
Mayer, Brown & Platt 573.0

Source: *American Lawyer*, July 2002, p. S1.

★ 1980 ★

Legal Services (SIC 8111)

Why Floridians Seek Lawyers

The top reasons are shown based on a survey.

Real estate 16.0%
Child support custody 13.0
Lawsuit 11.0
Bankruptcy 9.0
Divorce 9.0
Draft will 8.0
Other 34.0

Source: *Florida Bar News*, October 15, 2002, p. 1, from Florida Bar.

SIC 82 - Educational Services

★ 1981 ★

Schools (SIC 8211)

For-Profit School Companies

The revenue of for-profit charter operators should increase 10% from 2001 and reach $890 million, according to Eduventures Inc.

Edison Schools	$ 525
Nobel Learning Communities	160
National Heritage Academies	100
Mosaica Education	70

Source: *BusinessWeek*, June 3, 2002, p. 44.

★ 1982 ★

Schools (SIC 8211)

Largest School Districts

Figures show school enrollment.

New York City	1,098,832
Los Angeles	746,831
Chicago	442,000
Miami-Dade County, FL	364,162
Broward County, FL	263,271
Clark County, NV	255,316
Houston, TX	211,148
Philadelphia, PA	204,851
Hawaii	182,798
Hillsborough County, FL	175,021

Source: *American School & University*, January 2003, p. 8, from individual districts.

★ 1983 ★

Universities (SIC 8221)

Largest College and University Enrollments, 1999- 2000

Figures show enrollment.

The University of Texas at Austin	49,009
Ohio State University	48,003
Miami-Dade Community College	47,152
University of Minnesota, Twin Cities . . .	45,361
Arizona State University	44,215
Texas A&M University	43,817
University of Florida	43,382
Michigan State University	43,038
Pennsylvania State University	40,658

Source: *American School & University*, January 2003, p. 8, from *Digest of Education Statistics, 2001*.

★ 1984 ★

Universities (SIC 8221)

Largest University Endowments, 2002

College endowments saw their worst year since 1974. On average, colleges saw their endowments shrink 6%. Schools are ranked by endowments, in billions of dollars. Figures are based on a survey.

Harvard University	$ 17.2
Yale University	10.5
University of Texas System	8.6
Princeton University	8.3
Stanford University	7.6
Massachusetts Institute of Technology	5.4
Emory University	4.6
Columbia University	4.2
University of California	4.2
Texas A&M System and Foundations	3.7

Source: *USA TODAY*, January 21, 2003, p. 6D, from National Association of College and University Business Officers.

★ 1985 ★

Libraries (SIC 8231)

Largest Libraries

Institutions are ranked by millions of volumes held.

Library of Congress	24.61
Harvard University	14.43
Chicago Public Library	10.99
New York Public Library	10.60
Yale University	10.49
Queens Borough Public Library	10.35
The Public Library of Cincinnati & Hamilton County	9.95
University of Illinois - Urbana-Champaign	9.46
University of California - Berkeley	9.10
County of Los Angeles Public Library	8.25

Source: "Fact Sheet." available online March 7, 2003 from http://www.ala.org, from American Library Association.

★ 1986 ★

Libraries (SIC 8231)

Visits to Presidential Libraries

Annual visitors are shown. The Bill Clinton library opens Fall 2004.

John Kennedy (MA)	199,630
Ronald Reagan (CA)	196,699
Lyndon Johnson (TX)	181,629
George Bush (TX)	153,247
Richard Nixon (CA)	147,000
Franklin Roosevelt (NY)	112,755
Gerald Ford (MI)	96,619
Dwight Eisenhower (KA)	77,220
Jimmy Carter (GA)	68,448

Source: *USA TODAY*, April 30, 2002, p. 3A, from National Archives and Records Administration.

★ 1987 ★

Flight Training (SIC 8299)

Who Conducts Pilot Training

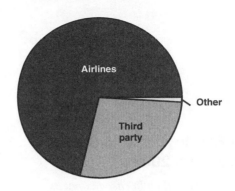

FlightSafety Boeing is the world's largest aviation training firm. Airlines are expected to shed more of their training duties.

Airlines	71.57%
Third party	27.83
Other	0.59

Source: *Air Transport World*, March 2003, p. 43, from FlightSafety Boeing.

★ 1988 ★

Testing Services (SIC 8299)

Largest Test Prep/College Service Firms, 2002

Firms are ranked by revenues in millions of dollars.

Kaplan	$ 621
Sylvan Learning	363
Princeton Review	89

Source: *Educational Marketer*, March 17, 2003, p. NA.

★ 1989 ★

Testing Services (SIC 8299)

Test Design Industry

Market shares are shown in percent.

Harcourt Educational Measurement	40.0%
CTB McGraw-Hill	40.0
Riverside Publishing	20.0

Source: "Testing Industry's Big Four." available from http://www.pbs.org.

SIC 83 - Social Services

★ 1990 ★

Child Care (SIC 8351)

Largest Employer Child Care Organizations, 2002

Companies are ranked by licensed capacity.

Bright Horizons Family Solutions	53,500
Knowledge Beginnings	17,536
KinderCare Learning Centers	9,594
Childtime Learning Centers	6,930
ARAMARK Educational Resources	3,400
La Petite Academy	3,323
New Horizon Child Care	2,695
The Children's Courtyard	2,220
Easter Seals Child Development Center	1,943
The Sunshine House	1,540

Source: *Child Care Information Exchange*, September 2002, p. 60.

★ 1991 ★

Charities (SIC 8399)

Largest Non-Profit Institutions, 2001

Organizations are ranked by income in millions of dollars.

Lutheran Services in America	$ 7,654.95
National Council of YMCAs	4,123.08
American Red Cross	2,711.60
Catholic Charities	2,621.24
United Jewish Communities	2,230.57
Goodwill Industries	1,940.90
Salvation Army	1,914.87
Fidelity Investments Charitable Gift Fund	1,250.65
Boys & Girls Club of America	997.70
American Cancer Society	922.80

Source: *The Non-Profit Times*, November 1, 2002, p. 30, from *NPT Top 100*.

★ 1992 ★

Charities (SIC 8399)

Where Charitable Dollars Went, 2001

A total of $212 billion was given to individuals, foundations and corporations.

Religious causes	38.2%
Health, social services	18.5
Education	15.0
Gifts to foundations	12.1
Arts	5.7
Other	10.5

Source: *BusinessWeek*, July 29, 2002, p. 14, from American Association of Fundraising Counsel Trust for Philanthropy.

★ 1993 ★

Charities (SIC 8399)

Who Gives to Charities, 2001

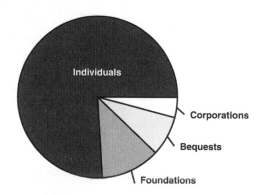

Total charitable giving declined to $212 billion, the first inflation-adjusted decline in 7 years.

Individuals	76.0%
Foundations	12.0
Bequests	8.0
Corporations	4.0

Source: *Newsweek*, December 2, 2002, p. 40, from American Association of Fundraising Counsel.

SIC 84 - Museums, Botanical, Zoological Gardens

★ 1994 ★

Art Exhibitions (SIC 8412)

Selected Art Exhibit Attendance

Figures show the attendance at some of the leading shows in the United States over the previous year. Most shows ran for several months.

Van Gogh and Gauguin	690,951
Treasures of Ancient Egypt	430,772
Gerhard Richter	333,695
Oldenburg and Van Bruggen on the Roof	320,935
Rome on the Grand Tour	290,802
Goya: Images of Women	262,558
Directions: Ernesto Neto	236,206
Directions: Ron Mueck	219,519

Source: *Forbes*, February 11, 2003, p. NA, from *Art Newspaper*.

★ 1995 ★

Museums (SIC 8412)

Leading Museums in Los Angeles, 2001

Figures show attendance.

J. Paul Getty Museum	1,331,546
Los Angeles County Museum of Art	764,696
Natural History Museum of Los Angeles	662,440
Huntington Library, Art Collections	530,157
Travel Town Museum	350,000
Museum of Contemporary Art	315,000
Autry Museum of Western Heritage	282,380
Norton Simon Museum of Art	200,380
California African American Museum	200,000
Petersen Automotive	158,000

Source: *Los Angeles Business Journal*, January 6, 2003, p. 3.

SIC 86 - Membership Organizations

★ 1996 ★
Unions (SIC 8631)

Largest Unions, 2000

Data show number of members.

National Education Association	2,530,000
International Brotherhood of Teamsters	1,402,000
Service Employees International Union	1,374,000
United Food & Commercial Workers	1,308,722
American Fed. Of State, County & Municipal Employees	1,300,000
Laborers' International Union of North America	818,412
Intl. Assoc. of Machinists & Aerospace Workers	730,673
Intl. Brotherhood of Electrical Workers	727,836
American Federation of Teachers	706,973
UAW (International Union, United Automobile...)	671,853

Source: "Unions in U.S." available April 7, 2003 from http://www.laborresearch.org, from U.S. Department of Labor.

★ 1997 ★
Unions (SIC 8631)

Largest Unions in Canada, 2002

Membership is shown, in thousands.

Canadian Union of Public Employees	521.6
National Union of Public and General Employees	325.0
National Auto., Aerospace, Transp. And General Workers	238.0
United Food and Commercial Workers Intl. Union	220.0
United Steelworkers of America	180.0
Public Service Alliance of Canada	150.0
Comm., Energy and Paperworkers Union of Canada	150.0
Intel. Brotherhood of Teamsters	102.0

Source: "Union Membership in Canada." available March 7, 2003 from http://labour.hrdc-drhc.gc.ca.

★ 1998 ★
Political Organizations (SIC 8651)

Largest PACs, 2002

PACs (political action committees) are ranked by federal receipts in millions of dollars.

Emily's List	$ 16.70
NRA Political Vicotry Fund	10.48
Democrat Republican Independent Voter Education	9.80
Intl. Brotherhood of Electr. Workers Comm. On Polit. Education	9.16
UAW-V-Cap	9.04
Amer. Federation of State County & Muni. Employees	8.88
Service Employees Intl. Union	8.37
Voice of Teachers	7.42
Assoc. of Trial Lawyers of America	7.41
NEA Fund for Children and Public Education	6.85

Source: "Top 50 Pacs." available April 7, 2003 from http://www.fec.gov, from Federal Election Committee.

★ 1999 ★
Political Organizations (SIC 8651)

Leading Lobbying Firms, 2002

Groups are ranked by revenues in millions of dollars.

Cassidy & Associates	$ 28.9
Patton Boggs	26.3
Akin Gump Strauss Hauer & Feld	22.2
Piper Rudnick	20.2

Continued on next page.

★ **1999** ★ *Continued*

Political Organizations (SIC 8651)

Leading Lobbying Firms, 2002

Groups are ranked by revenues in millions of dollars.

Greenberg Traurig	$ 17.6
Van Scoyoc Associates	16.9
Barbour, Griffith & Rogers	12.8
Williams & Jensen	12.3
Washington Council Ernst & Young	12.1

Source: *Christian Science Monitor*, April 30, 2003, p. 20, from *National Journal*.

★ **2000** ★

Political Organizations (SIC 8651)

PAC Activity for 2002 Elections

Contributions are shown for current candidates, in millions of dollars. Total spending for federal candidates: $219.9 million in 1998, $259.8 million in 2000 and $282 million in 2002.

	1998	2000	2002
House	$ 158.7	$ 193.4	$ 206.9
Senate	48.1	51.9	59.2

Source: "PAC Activity Increases for 2002 Elections." available April 7, 2003 from http://www.fec.gov, from Federal Election Committee.

★ **2001** ★

Religious Organizations (SIC 8661)

Largest Churches in Atlanta, GA

The membership of churches is shown. Figures are for 2000.

Southern Baptist	666,557
United Methodist Church	279,431
Catholic Church	271,538
Jewish	85,900
Presbyterian Church	70,993
Church of God	57,169
Episcopal Church	43,055
Independent Charismatic	39,580
Christian Churches/Churches of Christ	32,615
Muslims	32,469

Source: *Atlanta Journal-Constitution*, September 18, 2002, p. A1, from Associations of Statisticians of American.

★ **2002** ★

Religious Organizations (SIC 8661)

Largest U.S. Churches, 2002

Roman Catholic
South Baptist
United Methodist
Islam
Church of God
Evan. Lutherans
Mormons
National Baptists
Presybterian USA
National Baptist Convention

Figures are in millions of members. According to the source, church membership grew 7.16% during the decade of 1990-2000, but population grew 13.9%.

Roman Catholic	62.39
South Baptist	15.85
United Methodist	8.37
Islam	5.78
Church of God	5.49
Evan. Lutherans	5.14
Mormons	5.11
National Baptists	4.50
Presybterian USA	3.56
National Baptist Convention	3.50

Source: *Free Inquiry*, Winter 2002, p. 57, from *World Almanac*.

SIC 87 - Engineering and Management Services

★ 2003 ★

Engineering Services (SIC 8711)

Largest Engineering Firms

Firms are ranked by revenues in millions of dollars.

Fluor Corp.	$ 294.8
BE&K	286.3
Washington Group International	190.6
Parsons Brinckerhoff Inc.	182.4
Syska Hennessy Group	66.7
Vanderweil Engineers	62.6
John A. Martin & Associates	50.3
Cosentini Associates	50.0
Flack + Kurtz Inc.	46.0
KPFF Consulting Engineers	39.9

Source: *Building Design & Construction*, July 2002, p. 57, from *Building Design & Construction 2002 Giants Survey*.

★ 2004 ★

Architectural Services (SIC 8712)

Largest Architectural Firms

Firms are ranked by revenues in millions of dollars.

Gensler	$ 232.0
NBBJ	95.4
Kohn Pedersen Fox Associates	86.0
Perkins & Will Inc.	65.3
Kaplan McLaughlin Diaz	64.5
Callison Architecture Inc.	63.0
Hillier	51.2
Zimmer Gunsul Frasca Partnership	46.0
Perkins Eastman Architects	43.0
Thompson, Ventulett, Stainback & Assoc.	40.3

Source: *Building Design & Construction*, July 2002, p. 57, from *Building Design & Construction 2002 Giants Survey*.

★ 2005 ★

Accounting Services (SIC 8721)

Leading Accounting Firms

Firms are ranked by revenues in billions of dollars.

Pricewaterhouse	$ 8.06
Deloitte & Touche	6.13
Ernst & Young	4.49
Arthur Andersen	4.30
KPMG	3.17

Source: *BusinessWeek*, June 3, 2002, p. 75, from *Public Accounting Report*.

★ 2006 ★

Accounting Services (SIC 8721)

Leading CPA Firms, 2002

RSM McGladrey/McGladrey & Pullen
Deloitte & Touche
Pricewaterhouse
Coopers LLP
KPMG

Firms are ranked by fiscal year revenues in millions of dollars.

RSM McGladrey/McGladrey & Pullen	$ 585.0
Deloitte & Touche	6.0
Pricewaterhouse	5.2
Coopers LLP	4.5
KPMG	3.4

Source: *The Practical Accountant*, April 2003, p. 24, from *Annual Regional Survey of Accounting Firms*.

★ 2007 ★

Accounting Services (SIC 8721)

Leading Non CPA Firms, 2002

Firms are ranked by fiscal year revenues in millions of dollars.

H&R Block	$ 3,300
American Express Tax	368
Century Business Services	360
Jackson Hewitt Inc.	330
Centerprise Advisors	168
Fiducial Inc.	101
Gilman + Ciocia Inc.	92

Source: *The Practical Accountant*, April 2003, p. 24, from *Annual Regional Survey of Accounting Firms*.

★ 2008 ★

Payroll Processing (SIC 8721)

Payroll Processing Market

The top firms in the business are ranked by estimated annual sales. The industry sees revenues of about $5 billion annually.

ADP	$ 1,500
Ceridian	1,200
ProBusiness	175

Source: *Mergers & Acquisitions Report*, January 13, 2003, p. NA, from industry sources.

★ 2009 ★

Research (SIC 8730)

Who Conducts Research, 2003

Spending is shown in billions of dollars.

	2002	2003	Share
Industry	$ 213.1	$ 216.2	71.68%
Academia/nonprofit	57.0	61.3	20.32
Federal government	21.6	24.1	7.99

Source: *R&D*, January 2003, p. F3, from Battelle.

★ 2010 ★

Research (SIC 8730)

Who Funds Research, 2003

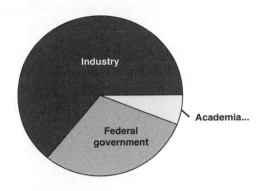

Spending is shown in billions of dollars.

	2002	2003	Share
Industry	$ 193.4	$ 193.7	64.22%
Federal government	81.4	89.5	29.68
Academia, nonprofit	17.2	18.4	6.10

Source: *R&D*, January 2003, p. F3, from Battelle.

★ 2011 ★

Research (SIC 8732)

Largest Contract Research Groups

Companies are ranked by revenue in thousands of dollars. Total revenue is expected to grow from $9.8 billion in 2001 to $16.1 billion in 2005.

Quintiles Transnational Corp.	$ 881.8
Covance Inc.	800.2
Pharmaceutical Product Development	403.7
Parexel International Corp.	379.4
MDS Inc.	277.6
ICON	156.5
Inveresk Research Group	156.2
Kendle International	146.8
Omnicare Inc.	125.3

Source: *Med Ad News*, October 2002, p. S14, from Frost & Sullivan.

★ 2012 ★
Research (SIC 8732)

Largest Corporate R&D Spenders

Firms are ranked by research spending in billions of dollars.

General Motors Corp.	$ 6.5
Ford Motor	6.3
Pfizer	5.7
IBM	5.4
Intel	4.9
Johnson & Johnson	4.4
Microsoft	4.3
Abbott Laboratories	3.7
Hewlett-Packard	3.7
Motorola	3.6

Source: *R&D*, January 2003, p. F3, from *2003 Battelle Research Funding Report*.

★ 2013 ★
Medical Laboratories (SIC 8734)

Esoteric Test Market

Esoteric tests have roughly half of the clinical testing market. Such tests are used when information from routine tests are incomplete or inconclusive. The market is valued at $2.4 billion.

Infectious disease testing	59.0%
Toxicology	17.0
Genetic testing	12.0
Endocrinology	7.0
Oncology	2.0
Immunology	2.0

Source: *Research Alert*, July 5, 2002, p. 10, from Marketdata Enterprises.

★ 2014 ★
Management Services (SIC 8741)

Largest Contingency Search Firms in Los Angeles, CA

Revenues fell for the second time in the last years. 2002 revenues fell 18% over 2001, which were down 16% from 2000.

Sprague & Associates	$ 4.9
Scott-Thaler Associates	4.6
DNA Search Inc.	4.5
Independent Resource Systems	3.7
Carson-Thomas Personnel	3.5
Search Associates Inc.	3.4
Century Group	3.2
AccountPros/Human Resources	3.1
SoftEx Corp.	3.1

Source: *Los Angeles Business Journal*, March 24, 2003, p. 18.

★ 2015 ★
Management Services (SIC 8742)

Leading Management Consultant Firms

Market shares are shown among major firms.

McKinsey	40.6%
Booz, Allen & Hamilton	19.1
A.T. Kearney	14.4
Boston Consulting Group	12.5
Bain	9.7
Other	3.7

Source: *BusinessWeek*, July 8, 2002, p. 71, from *Consultants News*.

★ 2016 ★
Public Relations Services (SIC 8743)

Largest PR Firms, 2001

Firms are ranked by revenue in millions of dollars.

Weber Shandwick Worldwide	$ 283.08
Fleishman-Hillard	263.34
Hill & Knowlton	190.93
Ketchum	161.42
Edelman Public Relations Worldwide	152.38
Burson-Marsteller	150.41
Porter Novelli	116.76
Ogilvy Public Relations Worldwide	94.90

Continued on next page.

★ **2016** ★ *Continued*

Public Relations Services (SIC 8743)

Largest PR Firms, 2001

Firms are ranked by revenue in millions of dollars.

GCI Group/APCO Worldwide . . . .$ 85.43
Golin/Harris International 81.89

Source: *PR Week*, May 13, 2002, p. 13, from Council of
Public Relations Firms.

★ **2017** ★

Marketing Services (SIC 8748)

Largest Marketing Service Firms

*Agencies are ranked by marketing service revenue in
millions of dollars.*

Carlson Marketing Group . . . . $ 274.7
DraftWorldwide 240.9
Digitas 235.5
Rapp Collins Worldwide 202.2
Aspen Marketing Group 189.2
Wunderman 173.0
OgilvyOne Worldwide 169.6
Euro RSCG Impact 142.1
GMR Marketing 132.6
Momentum Worldwide 122.0

Source: *Advertising Age*, May 20, 2002, p. S4.

SIC 92 - Justice, Public Order, and Safety

★ 2018 ★

Internet Fraud (SIC 9220)

Types of Internet Fraud, 2002

For the first six months of the year total reported losses reached $7.2 million. The average loss was $484.

Online auctions	87.0%
General merchandise	6.0
Nigerian money orders	5.0
Hardware/software	1.0
Other	1.0

Source: *Financial Times*, January 27, 2003, p. 18, from National Consumers League.

★ 2019 ★

Police (SIC 9221)

Largest Police Forces, 2000

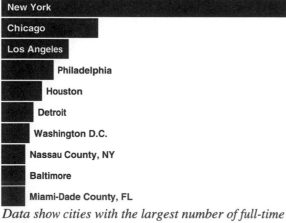

New York
Chicago
Los Angeles
Philadelphia
Houston
Detroit
Washington D.C.
Nassau County, NY
Baltimore
Miami-Dade County, FL

Data show cities with the largest number of full-time sworn officers (those who may carry firearms and make arrests).

New York	40,435
Chicago	13,466
Los Angeles	9,341
Philadelphia	7,024
Houston	5,343
Detroit	4,154
Washington D.C.	3,612
Nassau County, NY	3,038
Baltimore	3,034
Miami-Dade County, FL	3,008

Source: *Census of State and Law Enforcement*, June 2000, p. 6, from U.S. Department of Justice.

★ 2020 ★

Prisons (SIC 9223)

Leading Prison Managers

Market shares are shown based on contracts.

Correctional Corporation of America	52.28%
Wackenhut Corrections Corporation	22.44
Management & Training Corporation	8.88
Cornell Companies	7.08
Correctional Services Corporation	3.27
CiviGenics	1.88
Other	4.17

Source: "Market Share." available January 7, 2003 from http://web.crim.ufl.edu/pcp/census/2001/Market.html.

SIC 93 - Finance, Taxation, and Monetary Policy

★ 2021 ★

Taxation (SIC 9311)

State Tax Revenues

The sources of revenues are shown.

Personal income tax	42.9%
Sales tax	35.4
Corporate income tax	6.2
Other	15.5

Source: *New York Times*, June 5, 2002, p. C1, from Nelson A. Rockefeller Institute of Government.

SIC 95 - Environmental Quality and Housing

★ 2022 ★

Environmental Services (SIC 9511)

Leading Environmental Firms

Firms are ranked by revenues in millions of dollars.

U.S. Filter Corp.	$ 5,400.0
The ERM Group	300.8
Duratek	282.2
Weston Solutions Inc.	275.3
Malcolm Pirnie	216.0
ENSR Intl.	161.0
LVI Services Inc.	151.7
Brown and Caldwell	151.0
Danis Environmental Industries	150.7

Source: *ENR*, July 8, 2002, p. 38.

★ 2023 ★

Housing Programs (SIC 9531)

Leading Housing Grant Recipients

The firms received the largest grants for housing and shelter. Figures are in millions of dollars.

The McKnight Foundation	$ 27.6
Fannie Mae Foundation	11.2
The Blandin Foundation	7.4
The Columbus Foundation and Affiliated Organizations'	6.2
Marin Community Foundation	5.7
The Bush Foundation	5.3
El Pomar Foundation	5.2
John D. and Catherine T. MacArthur Foundation	4.8
Citigroup Foundation	4.0

Source: *Community Banker*, March 2003, p. 37, from Foundation Center.

SIC 96 - Administration of Economic Programs

★ 2024 ★

Roads (SIC 9621)

The State of Our Roads

Unpaved	61.0%
Paved-flexible	22.0
Paved-intermediate type	6.0
Paved-composite	4.0
Paved-low type	4.0
Paved-rigid	3.0

Source: *Pit & Quarry*, January 2002, p. 49, from Federal Highway Administration.

★ 2025 ★

U.S. Department of Energy (SIC 9631)

Leading Government Purchasers in the Energy Dept., 2001

Market shares are shown based on total purchases of $18.6 billion.

University of California System	20.59%
Bechtel Group	14.16
Lockheed Martin Corp.	12.15
BNFL Inc.	9.29
McDermott Inc.	5.45
Fluor Corp.	4.91
Battelle Memorial Institute	4.15
Kaiser Hill Co. LLC	3.38
University of Chicago	2.68
Other	23.24

Source: *Government Executive*, August 15, 2002, p. NA, from Eagle Eye Publishers and Federal Procurement Data Center.

★ 2026 ★

Defense (SIC 9661)

Leading Government Purchasers in NASA, 2001

Market shares are shown based on total purchases of $11.6 billion.

Boeing Co.	21.89%
Lockheed Martin	20.14
California Institute of Technology	13.16
Alliant Techsystems Inc.	3.39
Northop Grumman	3.29
Raytheon	2.45
SAIC	1.47
United Technologies Corp.	1.36
Computer Sciences Corp.	1.13
QSS Group	1.13
Other	30.59

Source: *Government Executive*, August 15, 2002, p. NA, from Eagle Eye Publishers and Federal Procurement Data Center.

★ 2027 ★

Technology Funding (SIC 9661)

Funding of Nanotechnology Research, 2003

Nanotechnology deals with matter in dimensions from 0.1 to 100 nanometers, a technology that applies from farming and food to basic industrial uses. Total funding was $200 million in 2000 and is $710.2 million in 2003.

Grand challenges	37.6%
Fundamental research	32.0
Centers and networks of excellence	15.2
Research infrastructure	12.9
Societal implications and workforce education	2.3

Source: *Electronic Business*, November 2002, p. 42, from National Science and Technology Council's Subcommittee on Nanoscale Science.

SIC 97 - National Security and International Affairs

★ 2028 ★

Defense (SIC 9711)

Leading Government Purchasers in the Air Force, 2001

Market shares are shown based on total purchases of $39.5 billion.

Lockheed Martin	24.18%
Boeing Co.	17.69
United Technologies Corp.	4.67
Northrop Grumman Corp.	4.63
Raytheon Co.	4.56
TRW Inc.	2.92
General Electric Co.	1.47
SAIC	1.29
Aerospace Corp.	1.12
Other	37.47

Source: *Government Executive*, August 15, 2002, p. NA, from Eagle Eye Publishers and Federal Procurement Data Center.

★ 2029 ★

Defense (SIC 9711)

Leading Government Purchasers in the Navy, 2001

Market shares are shown based on total purchases of $41.5 billion.

Northrop Grumman Corp.	20.00%
Boeing Co.	8.49
Lockheed Martin	7.38
General Dynamics	5.80
Raytheon Co.	4.75
General Electric	1.61
Bechtel Group	1.59
BAE Systems	1.18
United Technologies	1.17
Other	48.03

Source: *Government Executive*, August 15, 2002, p. NA, from Eagle Eye Publishers and Federal Procurement Data Center.

SOURCE INDEX

This index is divided into *primary sources* and *original sources*. Primary sources are the publications where the market shares were found. Original sources are sources cited in the primary sources. Numbers following the sources are entry numbers, arranged sequentially; the first number refers to the first appearance of the source in *Market Share Reporter*. All told, 1260 organizations are listed.

Primary Sources

"Mushrooms." available January 3, 2003 from http://www.usda.mannlib.cornell.edu, 70

Music & Copyright, 1007, 1013

Music Trades, 1194-1196, 1198, 1516

"National Association of Theatre Owners." available January 7, 2003 from http://www.natoonline.org, 1930

National Defense, 1126

National Floor Trends, 476-477, 516, 858, 1236

National Jeweler, 1190, 1599, 1601

National Mortgage News, 1689

National Petroleum News, 1060, 1418

National Post, 941, 1416, 1493, 1630

National Provisioner, 16, 172-173, 176, 179-180, 182-185, 189, 421

National Real Estate Investor, 1785-1786, 1803

National Underwriter, 1709

Nation's Restaurant News, 1529-1530, 1532

Natural Foods Merchandiser, 13

Natural Gas Week, 1380, 1382

"Neon Sign Industry Survey." available April 15, 2003 from http://www.signweb.com, 1234

Network World, 1039, 1855, 1864-1865

New Mexico Business Weekly, 1924

New York Times, 9, 11, 24, 106, 210, 225, 253, 574, 577, 593, 598, 603, 671-672, 831, 915-916, 919, 927, 931, 965, 983, 989, 1000, 1004, 1014, 1018, 1033, 1042, 1073-1074, 1079, 1117, 1183, 1252, 1278, 1292-1293, 1314, 1327, 1334, 1338, 1341, 1347, 1349, 1360, 1364, 1375, 1379, 1526, 1533, 1694, 1804, 1811, 1887, 1893, 1922-1923, 1967, 2021

The News Journal (Delaware), 449

Newsweek, 595, 1993

The Nikkei Weekly, 82

The Non-Profit Times, 1991

Nonwovens Industry, 553

"North American Industry." available April 1, 2003 from http://www.o-i.com, 852

"Nursery Products." available April 7, 2003 from http://www.usda.gov, 83

Nursery Retailer, 66, 68-69

Nutraceuticals World, 347, 459

Oil & Gas Journal, 97, 101, 103-104

Oilweek, 98, 100

"Operating Statistics." available April 22, 2003 from http://www.usps.com, 1268

Orange County Register, 1043

"Oregon Christmas Tree Survey." available April 7, 2003 from http://www.oda.state.or.us/oass/oass.html, 84

Ottawa Citizen, 1026

"Outbound to the U.S." available March 25, 2003 from http://www.ita.org, 1307

"PAC Activity Increases for 2002 Elections." available April 7, 2003 from http://www.fec.gov, 2000

Paints and Coatings Industry, 789

"Palm Springs International Airport." available March 7, 2003 from http://www.palmspringsairport.com, 1894

Pest Control Magazine, 1848

Pet Product News, 21

Pipeline & Gas Journal, 1383-1384

Pit & Quarry, 108, 2024

Pittsburgh Business Times, 1799

Pittsburgh Post-Gazette, 244

Plastics News, 18, 519, 633-634, 637-638, 842-844

Plastics Technology, 551, 840, 845

Playthings, 1602

Plumbing & Mechanical, 883

Polymers Paint Colour Journal, 613

Pool & Spa Marketing, 1250-1251

Pool & Spa News, 159-160, 1620

PR Newswire, 40, 413-414, 573, 575, 792-795, 1023, 1030, 1064, 1166, 1230, 1331, 1696, 1700

PR Week, 1886, 1911, 2016

The Practical Accountant, 2006-2007

"Pre-Close Season Update." available January 7, 2002 from http://www.unitedbusinessmedia.com, 1882

Prepared Foods, 163, 249, 261

Printing Impressions, 608-611

Private Label Buyer, 22, 161

Professional Candy Buyer, 325-327, 329, 331, 344

Professional Carwashing & Detailing Online, 1909

Progressive Grocer, 177-178, 232, 235, 250, 256, 262, 284-286, 301, 415, 465, 738, 877, 1420, 1590, 1614

Promo, 1603

Property Week, 1782

Publishers Weekly, 589, 591, 596, 599-600, 1596

Pulp & Paper, 535-541, 543, 545-546, 560

Purchasing, 532, 864, 1054

Quick Frozen Foods International, 274, 420

R&D, 2009-2010, 2012

Railway Age, 1254, 1256

"Raytheon Tops in Radar Market." available January 3, 2003 from http://www.forecast1.com, 1127

Real Estate Alert, 1801-1802

Realtor Magazine, 1788

The Record, 1330

"Refractive Eye Surgery." available April 7, 2003 from http://www.optistock.com, 1175

Refrigerated & Frozen Foods, 165-166, 171, 188, 191, 238, 267, 270-272, 275, 277, 279-281, 293, 298, 315, 422, 443-444, 452, 454, 456

Refrigerated Transporter, 1263, 1270

"Registration Statistics." available February 11, 2003 from http://www.akc.org, 81

Reinsurance Magazine, 1781

Research Alert, 1, 8, 85, 392, 458, 1070, 1113, 1191, 1202, 1597, 2013

Original Sources

Source Index: Original

PLACE NAMES INDEX

This index shows countries, political entities, states and provinces, regions within countries, parks, airports, and cities. The numbers that follow listings are entry numbers; they are arranged sequentially so that the first mention of a place is listed first. The index shows references to more than 280 places.

Santa Fe, NM, 1460
Sarasota, FL, 575, 1461, 1798
Saskatchewan, Canada, 170
Savannah, GA, 1278
Seattle, WA, 135, 1276-1278, 1580, 1901, 1976
Shreveport, LA, 1964
South Carolina, 41, 79, 118, 823, 843, 1319, 1438, 1668
South Central United States, 1250
South Dakota, 36, 52, 72-73, 1669, 1723, 1755
South Padre Island, TX, 1308
Southeast United States, 1112, 1250, 1828
Southwest United States, 1250, 1829
Spain, 366, 396, 1309
Spartanburg, SC, 1438
Springfield, MA, 1462, 1581
Stockton-Lodi, CA, 1728
Switzerland, 472
Syracuse, NY, 1582
Tacoma, WA, 1276-1278
Taiwan, 907
Tallahassee, FL, 1398
Tampa Bay, FL, 136, 575, 1280
Tennessee, 38-39, 41, 71, 127, 740, 823, 854, 1304, 1443,
    1480, 1566, 1670, 1728, 1748
Texas, 29-30, 35-40, 50-53, 58, 69, 71, 73, 75-76, 86,
    105-106, 115, 122, 168, 175, 206, 297, 529, 823, 843,
    893, 1069, 1285, 1304, 1410, 1420, 1435-1436, 1459,
    1480, 1497, 1553, 1557, 1671, 1749, 1783-1784, 1793,
    1982, 2019
Toledo, OH, 1304, 1466, 1583
Tulsa, OK, 1467, 1584
Tunica/Coahoma, MS, 1964
United Kingdom, 1307, 1309
U.S. Virgin Islands, 25
Utah, 133, 1672, 1711, 1763, 1905
Vallejo-Fairfield-Napa, CA, 1728
Valley, AZ, 1344
Vancouver, Canada, 1830
Vancouver, WA, 131
Venezuela, 1307
Verizon, 1347
Vermont, 463, 1125, 1429, 1673
Victoria, British Columbia, 1800
Virginia, 41, 50, 79, 86, 115, 823, 1276, 1497, 1674, 1774,
    1956
Warren, OH, 1587
Washington, 29, 43, 48, 60, 65, 83, 131, 135, 893, 1276,
    1278, 1580, 1724, 1750, 1775, 1901, 1976
Washington D.C., 529, 573, 1070, 1191, 1257, 1319, 1468,
    1497, 1585, 1675, 1751, 1783, 1884, 1956, 2019
Washington D.C. Dulles Airport, 1303
Wayne County, MI, 1075
West Central United States, 1250

West Palm Beach, FL, 573, 575, 1469
West Virginia, 1497, 1776, 1956
Wichita, KS, 1676
Wilmington, DE, 1586
Wisconsin, 35-36, 43, 48, 71, 463, 843, 1125, 1645, 1728
Worcester, MA, 1470
Wyoming, 42, 73, 105-106, 893
Youngstown, OH, 1587

PRODUCTS, SERVICES, NAMES, AND ISSUES INDEX

This index shows, in alphabetical order, references to products, services, personal names, and issues covered in *Market Share Reporter*, 14th Edition. More than 1,950 terms are included. Terms include subjects not readily categorized as products and services, including such subjects as *counties* and *crime*. The numbers that follow each term refer to entry numbers and are arranged sequentially so that the first mention is listed first.

Products, Services, Names, and Issues Index

Products, Services, Names, and Issues Index

COMPANY INDEX

The more than 4,000 companies and institutions in this book are indexed here in alphabetical order. Numbers following the terms are entry numbers. They are arranged sequentially; the first entry number refers to the first mention of the company in *Market Share Reporter*. Although most organizations appear only once, some entities are referred to under abbreviations in the sources and these have not always been expanded.

Company Index

Company Index

Centreville Savings Bank, 1667
Centrex Homes, 122
Century 21, 1791-1793, 1796
Century Business Services, 2007
Century Group, 2014
Century Theatres, 1930
Ceridian Corp., 2008
Cerner Corp., 1840
Cessna, 1110
CF Industries Inc., 629
Chai Latta, 464
Challenge Dairy Products, 193
Champion Enterprises, 522-523
Champion Industries, 612
Champs Sports, 1593
Charles Craft, 508
Charles D. Owen Mfg., 504
Charles Schwab, 1695, 1699
Charming Shoppes, 1489
Charner Industries Ind./Sunbelt Beverage Corp., 1400
Charter Comm., 1375, 1378
Charter One Bank, 1639, 1649, 1658, 1662, 1673
Chase Home Finance, 1685, 1689-1690
Chase Manhattan Bank, 1633
Chattem, 652, 716, 742, 745
Cheatham Chemical, 751
Check Point, 1860
CheckFree Corp., 1680
Chef America, 165, 279
Chemtreat/Western Chemical/Garratt-Callahan, 625
Cherry Creek, 1790, 1794
Chesebrough-Pond's, 761, 782, 784
Chesterfield Health Services, 1976
Chevrolet, 1065, 1068, 1072, 1079-1080, 1087, 1089
Chevron Phillips Chemical, 624, 634, 796, 798
Chevron Texaco Corp., 97, 99, 101, 104, 632
Chevy Chase Bank, 1647, 1675
CHF Industries, 497
Chicago Blackhawks, 1953
Chicago Board Options Exchange, 1705
Chicago Bulls, 1951
Chicago Public Library, 1985
Chicago Title, 1778
Chick-Fil-A, 1526
The Children's Courtyard, 1990
Childtime Learning Centers, 1990
Chili's Grill & Bar, 1529
Chipotle Mexican Grill, 1523
Chiquita, 54
Chiron, 705
Chittenden Trust Company, 1673
Chock Full O'Nuts Corp., 426
Choice Homes, 122

Choice Hotels International, 1814
Christian Dior, 10
Chubb & Son Inc., 1741
Chubb Group of Ins. Cos., 1744, 1752-1753, 1764, 1777
Chung's Foods, 273
Chupa Chups, 319, 349
Church & Dwight, 712-714, 776, 838
Church of God, 2001-2002
Churchill Downs, 1943
Church's, 1526
CIBA Vision, 1172-1173
CIBC, 1686
CIE Events, 1941
CIGNA, 1733
CIGNA Healthcare of California, 1731
CIGNA Healthcare of Louisiana, 1737
Cincinnati Insurance Co., 1756, 1763
Cinemark USA, 1930
Cinemex, 1932
Cineplex Odeon Canada, 1929
Cinergy, 1380
Cingular, 1315
Cintas Corp., 482
Circuit City, 1508, 1510, 1514, 1602, 1604
Cirrus Logic, 1050
Cisco, 1026-1027, 1029, 1033, 1035, 1038
Citadel, 1350, 1360
Citgo Petroleum, 796, 798
Citibank, 1634-1635, 1639, 1655, 1659, 1666, 1669, 1675, 1683
CitiFinancial, 1690
Citigate Sard Verbinnen, 1886
Citigroup, 1685, 1694, 1697, 1741, 1887
Citigroup Foundation, 2023
CitiMortgage, 1689
Citizens Bank, 1649, 1658
Citizens Bank of Connecticut, 1632
Citizens Bank of Massachusetts, 1648
Citizens Bank of New Hampshire, 1656
Citizens Bank of Pennsylvania, 1665
Citizens Bank of Rhode Island, 1667
Citizens Security Bank (Guam) Inc., 1635
Citrus World Inc., 242
City Bank, 1637
CityHomes, 122
CiviGenics, 2020
Clairol, 761
Classic Spas & Hot Tubs Inc., 1620
Classic Wines, 1401
Claussen, 258
Clayco Construction, 154
Clayton Homes, 522
Clear Channel Communications, 1350-1355, 1357, 1360

Company Index

Company Index

Company Index

Company Index

Company Index

BRANDS INDEX

This index shows more than 2,000 brands—including names of periodicals, television programs, popular movies, and other "brand-equivalent" names. Each brand name is followed by one or more numerals; these are entry numbers; they are arranged sequentially, with the first mention of the brand shown first.

Brands Index

Brands Index

APPENDIX I

SIC COVERAGE

This appendix lists the Standard Industrial Classification codes (SICs) included in *Market Share Reporter*. Page numbers are shown following each SIC category; the page shown indicates the first occurrence of an SIC. *NEC* stands for not elsewhere classified.

Agricultural Production - Crops

0110 Cash grains, p. 7
0111 Wheat, p. 7
0112 Rice, p. 8
0115 Corn, p. 8
0116 Soybeans, p. 8
0119 Cash grains, nec, p. 8
0131 Cotton, p. 10
0132 Tobacco, p. 10
0133 Sugarcane and sugar beets, p. 11
0134 Irish potatoes, p. 11
0161 Vegetables and melons, p. 11
0171 Berry crops, p. 12
0173 Tree nuts, p. 12
0174 Citrus fruits, p. 13
0175 Deciduous tree fruits, p. 13
0181 Ornamental nursery products, p. 14
0182 Food crops grown under cover, p. 17
0191 General farms, primarily crop, p. 17

Agricultural Production - Livestock

0213 Hogs, p. 18
0214 Sheep and goats, p. 18
0250 Poultry and eggs, p. 18
0251 Broiler, fryer, and roaster chickens, p. 19
0252 Chicken eggs, p. 19
0253 Turkeys and turkey eggs, p. 19
0272 Horses and other equines, p. 20
0279 Animal specialties, nec, p. 20

Agricultural Services

0752 Animal specialty services, p. 21

Forestry

0811 Timber tracts, p. 22

Fishing, Hunting, and Trapping

0910 Commercial fishing, p. 23
0971 Hunting, trapping, game propagation, p. 23

Metal Mining

1000 Metal mining, p. 25
1041 Gold ores, p. 25
1044 Silver ores, p. 26
1061 Ferroalloy ores, except vanadium, p. 26
1094 Uranium-radium-vanadium ores, p. 26

Coal Mining

1220 Bituminous coal and lignite mining, p. 27

Oil and Gas Extraction

1311 Crude petroleum and natural gas, p. 28
1321 Natural gas liquids, p. 28
1381 Drilling oil and gas wells, p. 29

Nonmetallic Minerals, Except Fuels

1420 Crushed and broken stone, p. 31
1422 Crushed and broken limestone, p. 31
1429 Crushed and broken stone, nec, p. 31
1450 Clay, ceramic, & refractory minerals, p. 32
1474 Potash, soda, and borate minerals, p. 32

General Building Contractors

1521 Single-family housing construction, p. 33

Heavy Construction, Except Building

1600 Heavy construction, ex. building, p. 38
1611 Highway and street construction, p. 38
1623 Water, sewer, and utility lines, p. 38

Paper and Allied Products

Printing and Publishing

Chemicals and Allied Products

Petroleum and Coal Products

Rubber and Misc. Plastics Products

Leather and Leather Products

Stone, Clay, and Glass Products

Primary Metal Industries

Fabricated Metal Products

Appendix: SIC Nomenclature

Appendix: SIC Nomenclature

SIC TO NAICS CONVERSION GUIDE

AGRICULTURE, FORESTRY, & FISHING

0111 Wheat
NAICS 11114　Wheat Farming
0112 Rice
NAICS 11116　Rice Farming
0115 Corn
NAICS 11115　Corn Farming
0116 Soybeans
NAICS 11111　Soybean Farming
0119 Cash Grains, nec
NAICS 11113　Dry Pea & Bean Farming
NAICS 11112　Oilseed Farming
NAICS 11115　Corn Farming
NAICS 111191 Oilseed & Grain Combination Farming
NAICS 111199 All Other Grain Farming
0131 Cotton
NAICS 11192　Cotton Farming
0132 Tobacco
NAICS 11191　Tobacco Farming
0133 Sugarcane & Sugar Beets
NAICS 111991 Sugar Beet Farming
NAICS 11193　Sugarcane Farming
0134 Irish Potatoes
NAICS 111211 Potato Farming
0139 Field Crops, Except Cash Grains, nec
NAICS 11194　Hay Farming
NAICS 111992 Peanut Farming
NAICS 111219 Other Vegetable & Melon Farming
NAICS 111998 All Other Miscellaneous Crop Farming
0161 Vegetables & Melons
NAICS 111219 Other Vegetable & Melon Farming
0171 Berry Crops
NAICS 111333 Strawberry Farming
NAICS 111334 Berry Farming
0172 Grapes
NAICS 111332 Grape Vineyards
0173 Tree Nuts
NAICS 111335 Tree Nut Farming
0174 Citrus Fruits
NAICS 11131　Orange Groves
NAICS 11132　Citrus Groves
0175 Deciduous Tree Fruits
NAICS 111331 Apple Orchards
NAICS 111339 Other Noncitrus Fruit Farming
0179 Fruits & Tree Nuts, nec
NAICS 111336 Fruit & Tree Nut Combination Farming
NAICS 111339 Other Noncitrus Fruit Farming
0181 Ornamental Floriculture & Nursery Products
NAICS 111422 Floriculture Production
NAICS 111421 Nursery & Tree Production
0182 Food Crops Grown under Cover
NAICS 111411 Mushroom Production
NAICS 111419 Other Food Crops Grown under Cover
0191 General Farms, Primarily Crop
NAICS 111998 All Other Miscellaneous Crop Farming
0211 Beef Cattle Feedlots
NAICS 112112 Cattle Feedlots
0212 Beef Cattle, Except Feedlots
NAICS 112111 Beef Cattle Ranching & Farming

0213 Hogs
NAICS 11221　Hog & Pig Farming
0214 Sheep & Goats
NAICS 11241　Sheep Farming
NAICS 11242　Goat Farming
0219 General Livestock, Except Dairy & Poultry
NAICS 11299　All Other Animal Production
0241 Dairy Farms
NAICS 112111 Beef Cattle Ranching & Farming
NAICS 11212　Dairy Cattle & Milk Production
0251 Broiler, Fryers, & Roaster Chickens
NAICS 11232　Broilers & Other Meat-type Chicken
　　　　　　　Production
0252 Chicken Eggs
NAICS 11231　Chicken Egg Production
0253 Turkey & Turkey Eggs
NAICS 11233　Turkey Production
0254 Poultry Hatcheries
NAICS 11234　Poultry Hatcheries
0259 Poultry & Eggs, nec
NAICS 11239　Other Poultry Production
0271 Fur-bearing Animals & Rabbits
NAICS 11293　Fur-bearing Animal & Rabbit Production
0272 Horses & Other Equines
NAICS 11292　Horse & Other Equine Production
0273 Animal Aquaculture
NAICS 112511 Finfish Farming & Fish Hatcheries
NAICS 112512 Shellfish Farming
NAICS 112519 Other Animal Aquaculture
0279 Animal Specialities, nec
NAICS 11291　Apiculture
NAICS 11299　All Other Animal Production
0291 General Farms, Primarily Livestock & Animal Specialties
NAICS 11299　All Other Animal Production
0711 Soil Preparation Services
NAICS 115112 Soil Preparation, Planting & Cultivating
0721 Crop Planting, Cultivating & Protecting
NAICS 48122　Nonscheduled Speciality Air Transportation
NAICS 115112 Soil Preparation, Planting & Cultivating
0722 Crop Harvesting, Primarily by Machine
NAICS 115113 Crop Harvesting, Primarily by Machine
0723 Crop Preparation Services for Market, Except Cotton Ginning
NAICS 115114 Postharvest Crop Activities
0724 Cotton Ginning
NAICS 115111 Cotton Ginning
0741 Veterinary Service for Livestock
NAICS 54194　Veterinary Services
0742 Veterinary Services for Animal Specialties
NAICS 54194　Veterinary Services
0751 Livestock Services, Except Veterinary
NAICS 311611 Animal Slaughtering
NAICS 11521　Support Activities for Animal Production
0752 Animal Specialty Services, Except Veterinary
NAICS 11521　Support Activities for Animal Production
NAICS 81291　Pet Care Services
0761 Farm Labor Contractors & Crew Leaders
NAICS 115115 Farm Labor Contractors & Crew Leaders
0762 Farm Management Services
NAICS 115116 Farm Management Services
0781 Landscape Counseling & Planning
NAICS 54169　Other Scientific & Technical Consulting
　　　　　　　Services
NAICS 54132　Landscape Architectural Services

0782 Lawn & Garden Services
NAICS 56173   Landscaping Services
0783 Ornamental Shrub & Tree Services
NAICS 56173   Landscaping Services
0811 Timber Tracts
NAICS 111421 Nursery & Tree Production
NAICS 11311   Timber Tract Operations
0831 Forest Nurseries & Gathering of Forest Products
NAICS 111998 All Other Miscellaneous Crop
NAICS 11321   Forest Nurseries & Gathering of Forest
Products
0851 Forestry Services
NAICS 11531   Support Activities for Forestry
0912 Finfish
NAICS 114111 Finfish Fishing
0913 Shellfish
NAICS 114112 Shellfish Fishing
0919 Miscellaneous Marine Products
NAICS 114119 Other Marine Fishing
NAICS 111998 All Other Miscellaneous Crop Farming
0921 Fish Hatcheries & Preserves
NAICS 112511 Finfish Farming & Fish Hatcheries
NAICS 112512 Shellfish Farming
0971 Hunting, Trapping, & Game Propagation
NAICS 11421   Hunting & Trapping

MINING INDUSTRIES

1011 Iron Ores
NAICS 21221   Iron Ore Mining
1021 Copper Ores
NAICS 212234 Copper Ore & Nickel Ore Mining
1031 Lead & Zinc Ores
NAICS 212231 Lead Ore & Zinc Ore Mining
1041 Gold Ores
NAICS 212221 Gold Ore Mining
1044 Silver Ores
NAICS 212222 Silver Ore Mining
1061 Ferroalloy Ores, Except Vanadium
NAICS 212234 Copper Ore & Nickel Ore Mining
NAICS 212299 Other Metal Ore Mining
1081 Metal Mining Services
NAICS 213115 Support Activities for Metal Mining
NAICS 54136   Geophysical Surveying & Mapping Services
1094 Uranium-radium-vanadium Ores
NAICS 212291 Uranium-radium-vanadium Ore Mining
1099 Miscellaneous Metal Ores, nec
NAICS 212299 Other Metal Ore Mining
1221 Bituminous Coal & Lignite Surface Mining
NAICS 212111 Bituminous Coal & Lignite Surface Mining
1222 Bituminous Coal Underground Mining
NAICS 212112 Bituminous Coal Underground Mining
1231 Anthracite Mining
NAICS 212113 Anthracite Mining
1241 Coal Mining Services
NAICS 213114 Support Activities for Coal Mining
1311 Crude Petroleum & Natural Gas
NAICS 211111 Crude Petroleum & Natural Gas Extraction
1321 Natural Gas Liquids
NAICS 211112 Natural Gas Liquid Extraction
1381 Drilling Oil & Gas Wells
NAICS 213111 Drilling Oil & Gas Wells

1382 Oil & Gas Field Exploration Services
NAICS 48122   Nonscheduled Speciality Air Transportation
NAICS 54136   Geophysical Surveying & Mapping Services
NAICS 213112 Support Activities for Oil & Gas Field
Operations
1389 Oil & Gas Field Services, nec
NAICS 213113 Other Oil & Gas Field Support Activities
1411 Dimension Stone
NAICS 212311 Dimension Stone Mining & Quarry
1422 Crushed & Broken Limestone
NAICS 212312 Crushed & Broken Limestone Mining &
Quarrying
1423 Crushed & Broken Granite
NAICS 212313 Crushed & Broken Granite Mining &
Quarrying
1429 Crushed & Broken Stone, nec
NAICS 212319 Other Crushed & Broken Stone Mining &
Quarrying
1442 Construction Sand & Gravel
NAICS 212321 Construction Sand & Gravel Mining
1446 Industrial Sand
NAICS 212322 Industrial Sand Mining
1455 Kaolin & Ball Clay
NAICS 212324 Kaolin & Ball Clay Mining
1459 Clay, Ceramic, & Refractory Minerals, nec
NAICS 212325 Clay & Ceramic & Refractory Minerals Mining
1474 Potash, Soda, & Borate Minerals
NAICS 212391 Potash, Soda, & Borate Mineral Mining
1475 Phosphate Rock
NAICS 212392 Phosphate Rock Mining
1479 Chemical & Fertilizer Mineral Mining, nec
NAICS 212393 Other Chemical & Fertilizer Mineral Mining
1481 Nonmetallic Minerals Services Except Fuels
NAICS 213116 Support Activities for Non-metallic Minerals
NAICS 54136   Geophysical Surveying & Mapping Services
1499 Miscellaneous Nonmetallic Minerals, Except Fuels
NAICS 212319 Other Crushed & Broken Stone Mining or
Quarrying
NAICS 212399 All Other Non-metallic Mineral Mining

CONSTRUCTION INDUSTRIES

1521 General Contractors-single-family Houses
NAICS 23321   Single Family Housing Construction
**1522 General Contractors-residential Buildings, Other than
Single-family**
NAICS 23332   Commercial & Institutional Building
Construction
NAICS 23322   Multifamily Housing Construction
1531 Operative Builders
NAICS 23321   Single Family Housing Construction
NAICS 23322   Multifamily Housing Construction
NAICS 23331   Manufacturing & Industrial Building
Construction
NAICS 23332   Commercial & Institutional Building
Construction
1541 General Contractors-industrial Buildings & Warehouses
NAICS 23332   Commercial & Institutional Building
Construction
NAICS 23331   Manufacturing & Industrial Building
Construction

1542 General Contractors-nonresidential Buildings, Other than Industrial Buildings & Warehouses
NAICS 23332   Commercial & Institutional Building Construction

1611 Highway & Street Construction, Except Elevated Highways
NAICS 23411   Highway & Street Construction

1622 Bridge, Tunnel, & Elevated Highway Construction
NAICS 23412   Bridge & Tunnel Construction

1623 Water, Sewer, Pipeline, & Communications & Power Line Construction
NAICS 23491   Water, Sewer & Pipeline Construction
NAICS 23492   Power & Communication Transmission Line Construction

1629 Heavy Construction, nec
NAICS 23493   Industrial Nonbuilding Structure Construction
NAICS 23499   All Other Heavy Construction

1711 Plumbing, Heating, & Air-conditioning
NAICS 23511   Plumbing, Heating & Air-conditioning Contractors

1721 Painting & Paper Hanging
NAICS 23521   Painting & Wall Covering Contractors

1731 Electrical Work
NAICS 561621   Security Systems Services
NAICS 23531   Electrical Contractors

1741 Masonry, Stone Setting & Other Stone Work
NAICS 23541   Masonry & Stone Contractors

1742 Plastering, Drywall, Acoustical & Insulation Work
NAICS 23542   Drywall, Plastering, Acoustical & Insulation Contractors

1743 Terrazzo, Tile, Marble, & Mosaic Work
NAICS 23542   Drywall, Plastering, Acoustical & Insulation Contractors
NAICS 23543   Tile, Marble, Terrazzo & Mosaic Contractors

1751 Carpentry Work
NAICS 23551   Carpentry Contractors

1752 Floor Laying & Other Floor Work, nec
NAICS 23552   Floor Laying & Other Floor Contractors

1761 Roofing, Siding, & Sheet Metal Work
NAICS 23561   Roofing, Siding, & Sheet Metal Contractors

1771 Concrete Work
NAICS 23542   Drywall, Plastering, Acoustical & Insulation Contractors
NAICS 23571   Concrete Contractors

1781 Water Well Drilling
NAICS 23581   Water Well Drilling Contractors

1791 Structural Steel Erection
NAICS 23591   Structural Steel Erection Contractors

1793 Glass & Glazing Work
NAICS 23592   Glass & Glazing Contractors

1794 Excavation Work
NAICS 23593   Excavation Contractors

1795 Wrecking & Demolition Work
NAICS 23594   Wrecking & Demolition Contractors

1796 Installation or Erection of Building Equipment, nec
NAICS 23595   Building Equipment & Other Machinery Installation Contractors

1799 Special Trade Contractors, nec
NAICS 23521   Painting & Wall Covering Contractors
NAICS 23592   Glass & Glazing Contractors
NAICS 56291   Remediation Services
NAICS 23599   All Other Special Trade Contractors

FOOD & KINDRED PRODUCTS

2011 Meat Packing Plants
NAICS 311611   Animal Slaughtering

2013 Sausages & Other Prepared Meats
NAICS 311612   Meat Processed from Carcasses

2015 Poultry Slaughtering & Processing
NAICS 311615   Poultry Processing
NAICS 311999   All Other Miscellaneous Food Manufacturing

2021 Creamery Butter
NAICS 311512   Creamery Butter Manufacturing

2022 Natural, Processed, & Imitation Cheese
NAICS 311513   Cheese Manufacturing

2023 Dry, Condensed, & Evaporated Dairy Products
NAICS 311514   Dry, Condensed, & Evaporated Milk Manufacturing

2024 Ice Cream & Frozen Desserts
NAICS 31152   Ice Cream & Frozen Dessert Manufacturing

2026 Fluid Milk
NAICS 311511   Fluid Milk Manufacturing

2032 Canned Specialties
NAICS 311422   Specialty Canning
NAICS 311999   All Other Miscellaneous Food Manufacturing

2033 Canned Fruits, Vegetables, Preserves, Jams, & Jellies
NAICS 311421   Fruit & Vegetable Canning

2034 Dried & Dehydrated Fruits, Vegetables, & Soup Mixes
NAICS 311423   Dried & Dehydrated Food Manufacturing
NAICS 311211   Flour Milling

2035 Pickled Fruits & Vegetables, Vegetables Sauces & Seasonings, & Salad Dressings
NAICS 311421   Fruit & Vegetable Canning
NAICS 311941   Mayonnaise, Dressing, & Other Prepared Sauce Manufacturing

2037 Frozen Fruits, Fruit Juices, & Vegetables
NAICS 311411   Frozen Fruit, Juice, & Vegetable Processing

2038 Frozen Specialties, nec
NAICS 311412   Frozen Specialty Food Manufacturing

2041 Flour & Other Grain Mill Products
NAICS 311211   Flour Milling

2043 Cereal Breakfast Foods
NAICS 31192   Coffee & Tea Manufacturing
NAICS 31123   Breakfast Cereal Manufacturing

2044 Rice Milling
NAICS 311212   Rice Milling

2045 Prepared Flour Mixes & Doughs
NAICS 311822   Flour Mixes & Dough Manufacturing from Purchased Flour

2046 Wet Corn Milling
NAICS 311221   Wet Corn Milling

2047 Dog & Cat Food
NAICS 311111   Dog & Cat Food Manufacturing

2048 Prepared Feed & Feed Ingredients for Animals & Fowls, Except Dogs & Cats
NAICS 311611   Animal Slaughtering
NAICS 311119   Other Animal Food Manufacturing

2051 Bread & Other Bakery Products, Except Cookies & Crackers
NAICS 311812   Commercial Bakeries

2052 Cookies & Crackers
NAICS 311821   Cookie & Cracker Manufacturing
NAICS 311919   Other Snack Food Manufacturing
NAICS 311812   Commercial Bakeries

2053 Frozen Bakery Products, Except Bread
NAICS 311813 Frozen Bakery Product Manufacturing
2061 Cane Sugar, Except Refining
NAICS 311311 Sugarcane Mills
2062 Cane Sugar Refining
NAICS 311312 Cane Sugar Refining
2063 Beet Sugar
NAICS 311313 Beet Sugar Manufacturing
2064 Candy & Other Confectionery Products
NAICS 31133   Confectionery Manufacturing from Purchased
Chocolate
NAICS 31134   Non-chocolate Confectionery Manufacturing
2066 Chocolate & Cocoa Products
NAICS 31132   Chocolate & Confectionery Manufacturing from
Cacao Beans
2067 Chewing Gum
NAICS 31134   Non-chocolate Confectionery Manufacturing
2068 Salted & Roasted Nuts & Seeds
NAICS 311911 Roasted Nuts & Peanut Butter Manufacturing
2074 Cottonseed Oil Mills
NAICS 311223 Other Oilseed Processing
NAICS 311225 Fats & Oils Refining & Blending
2075 Soybean Oil Mills
NAICS 311222 Soybean Processing
NAICS 311225 Fats & Oils Refining & Blending
2076 Vegetable Oil Mills, Except Corn, Cottonseed, & Soybeans
NAICS 311223 Other Oilseed Processing
NAICS 311225 Fats & Oils Refining & Blending
2077 Animal & Marine Fats & Oils
NAICS 311613 Rendering & Meat By-product Processing
NAICS 311711 Seafood Canning
NAICS 311712 Fresh & Frozen Seafood Processing
NAICS 311225 Edible Fats & Oils Manufacturing
**2079 Shortening, Table Oils, Margarine, & Other Edible Fats &
Oils, nec**
NAICS 311225 Edible Fats & Oils Manufacturing
NAICS 311222 Soybean Processing
NAICS 311223 Other Oilseed Processing
2082 Malt Beverages
NAICS 31212   Breweries
2083 Malt
NAICS 311213 Malt Manufacturing
2084 Wines, Brandy, & Brandy Spirits
NAICS 31213   Wineries
2085 Distilled & Blended Liquors
NAICS 31214   Distilleries
2086 Bottled & Canned Soft Drinks & Carbonated Waters
NAICS 312111 Soft Drink Manufacturing
NAICS 312112 Bottled Water Manufacturing
2087 Flavoring Extracts & Flavoring Syrups nec
NAICS 31193   Flavoring Syrup & Concentrate Manufacturing
NAICS 311942 Spice & Extract Manufacturing
NAICS 311999 All Other Miscellaneous Food Manufacturing
2091 Canned & Cured Fish & Seafood
NAICS 311711 Seafood Canning
2092 Prepared Fresh or Frozen Fish & Seafoods
NAICS 311712 Fresh & Frozen Seafood Processing
2095 Roasted Coffee
NAICS 31192   Coffee & Tea Manufacturing
NAICS 311942 Spice & Extract Manufacturing
2096 Potato Chips, Corn Chips, & Similar Snacks
NAICS 311919 Other Snack Food Manufacturing

2097 Manufactured Ice
NAICS 312113 Ice Manufacturing
2098 Macaroni, Spaghetti, Vermicelli, & Noodles
NAICS 311823 Pasta Manufacturing
2099 Food Preparations, nec
NAICS 311423 Dried & Dehydrated Food Manufacturing
NAICS 111998 All Other Miscellaneous Crop Farming
NAICS 31134   Non-chocolate Confectionery Manufacturing
NAICS 311911 Roasted Nuts & Peanut Butter Manufacturing
NAICS 311991 Perishable Prepared Food Manufacturing
NAICS 31183   Tortilla Manufacturing
NAICS 31192   Coffee & Tea Manufacturing
NAICS 311941 Mayonnaise, Dressing, & Other Prepared Sauce
Manufacturing
NAICS 311942 Spice & Extract Manufacturing
NAICS 311999 All Other Miscellaneous Food Manufacturing

TOBACCO PRODUCTS

2111 Cigarettes
NAICS 312221 Cigarette Manufacturing
2121 Cigars
NAICS 312229 Other Tobacco Product Manufacturing
2131 Chewing & Smoking Tobacco & Snuff
NAICS 312229 Other Tobacco Product Manufacturing
2141 Tobacco Stemming & Redrying
NAICS 312229 Other Tobacco Product Manufacturing
NAICS 31221   Tobacco Stemming & Redrying

TEXTILE MILL PRODUCTS

2211 Broadwoven Fabric Mills, Cotton
NAICS 31321   Broadwoven Fabric Mills
2221 Broadwoven Fabric Mills, Manmade Fiber & Silk
NAICS 31321   Broadwoven Fabric Mills
2231 Broadwoven Fabric Mills, Wool
NAICS 31321   Broadwoven Fabric Mills
NAICS 313311 Broadwoven Fabric Finishing Mills
NAICS 313312 Textile & Fabric Finishing Mills
**2241 Narrow Fabric & Other Smallware Mills: Cotton, Wool,
Silk, & Manmade Fiber**
NAICS 313221 Narrow Fabric Mills
2251 Women's Full-length & Knee-length Hosiery, Except Socks
NAICS 315111 Sheer Hosiery Mills
2252 Hosiery, nec
NAICS 315111 Sheer Hosiery Mills
NAICS 315119 Other Hosiery & Sock Mills
2253 Knit Outerwear Mills
NAICS 315191 Outerwear Knitting Mills
2254 Knit Underwear & Nightwear Mills
NAICS 315192 Underwear & Nightwear Knitting Mills
2257 Weft Knit Fabric Mills
NAICS 313241 Weft Knit Fabric Mills
NAICS 313312 Textile & Fabric Finishing Mills
2258 Lace & Warp Knit Fabric Mills
NAICS 313249 Other Knit Fabric & Lace Mills
NAICS 313312 Textile & Fabric Finishing Mills
2259 Knitting Mills, nec
NAICS 315191 Outerwear Knitting Mills
NAICS 315192 Underwear & Nightwear Knitting Mills
NAICS 313241 Weft Knit Fabric Mills
NAICS 313249 Other Knit Fabric & Lace Mills

2261 Finishers of Broadwoven Fabrics of Cotton
NAICS 313311 Broadwoven Fabric Finishing Mills
2262 Finishers of Broadwoven Fabrics of Manmade Fiber & Silk
NAICS 313311 Broadwoven Fabric Finishing Mills
2269 Finishers of Textiles, nec
NAICS 313311 Broadwoven Fabric Finishing Mills
NAICS 313312 Textile & Fabric Finishing Mills
2273 Carpets & Rugs
NAICS 31411 Carpet & Rug Mills
2281 Yarn Spinning Mills
NAICS 313111 Yarn Spinning Mills
2282 Yarn Texturizing, Throwing, Twisting, & Winding Mills
NAICS 313112 Yarn Texturing, Throwing & Twisting Mills
NAICS 313312 Textile & Fabric Finishing Mills
2284 Thread Mills
NAICS 313113 Thread Mills
NAICS 313312 Textile & Fabric Finishing Mills
2295 Coated Fabrics, Not Rubberized
NAICS 31332 Fabric Coating Mills
2296 Tire Cord & Fabrics
NAICS 314992 Tire Cord & Tire Fabric Mills
2297 Nonwoven Fabrics
NAICS 31323 Nonwoven Fabric Mills
2298 Cordage & Twine
NAICS 314991 Rope, Cordage & Twine Mills
2299 Textile Goods, nec
NAICS 31321 Broadwoven Fabric Mills
NAICS 31323 Nonwoven Fabric Mills
NAICS 313312 Textile & Fabric Finishing Mills
NAICS 313221 Narrow Fabric Mills
NAICS 313113 Thread Mills
NAICS 313111 Yarn Spinning Mills
NAICS 314999 All Other Miscellaneous Textile Product Mills

APPAREL & OTHER FINISHED PRODUCTS MADE FROM FABRICS & SIMILAR MATERIALS

2311 Men's & Boys' Suits, Coats & Overcoats
NAICS 315211 Men's & Boys' Cut & Sew Apparel Contractors
NAICS 315222 Men's & Boys' Cut & Sew Suit, Coat, & Overcoat Manufacturing
2321 Men's & Boys' Shirts, Except Work Shirts
NAICS 315211 Men's & Boys' Cut & Sew Apparel Contractors
NAICS 315223 Men's & Boys' Cut & Sew Shirt, Manufacturing
2322 Men's & Boys' Underwear & Nightwear
NAICS 315211 Men's & Boys' Cut & Sew Apparel Contractors
NAICS 315221 Men's & Boys' Cut & Sew Underwear & Nightwear Manufacturing
2323 Men's & Boys' Neckwear
NAICS 315993 Men's & Boys' Neckwear Manufacturing
2325 Men's & Boys' Trousers & Slacks
NAICS 315211 Men's & Boys' Cut & Sew Apparel Contractors
NAICS 315224 Men's & Boys' Cut & Sew Trouser, Slack, & Jean Manufacturing
2326 Men's & Boys' Work Clothing
NAICS 315211 Men's & Boys' Cut & Sew Apparel Contractors
NAICS 315225 Men's & Boys' Cut & Sew Work Clothing Manufacturing
2329 Men's & Boys' Clothing, nec
NAICS 315211 Men's & Boys' Cut & Sew Apparel Contractors

NAICS 315228 Men's & Boys' Cut & Sew Other Outerwear Manufacturing
NAICS 315299 All Other Cut & Sew Apparel Manufacturing
2331 Women's, Misses', & Juniors' Blouses & Shirts
NAICS 315212 Women's & Girls' Cut & Sew Apparel Contractors
NAICS 315232 Women's & Girls' Cut & Sew Blouse & Shirt Manufacturing
2335 Women's, Misses' & Junior's Dresses
NAICS 315212 Women's & Girls' Cut & Sew Apparel Contractors
NAICS 315233 Women's & Girls' Cut & Sew Dress Manufacturing
2337 Women's, Misses' & Juniors' Suits, Skirts & Coats
NAICS 315212 Women's & Girls' Cut & Sew Apparel Contractors
NAICS 315234 Women's & Girls' Cut & Sew Suit, Coat, Tailored Jacket, & Skirt Manufacturing
2339 Women's, Misses' & Juniors' Outerwear, nec
NAICS 315999 Other Apparel Accessories & Other Apparel Manufacturing
NAICS 315212 Women's & Girls' Cut & Sew Apparel Contractors
NAICS 315299 All Other Cut & Sew Apparel Manufacturing
NAICS 315238 Women's & Girls' Cut & Sew Other Outerwear Manufacturing
2341 Women's, Misses, Children's, & Infants' Underwear & Nightwear
NAICS 315212 Women's & Girls' Cut & Sew Apparel Contractors
NAICS 315211 Men's & Boys' Cut & Sew Apparel Contractors
NAICS 315231 Women's & Girls' Cut & Sew Lingerie, Loungewear, & Nightwear Manufacturing
NAICS 315221 Men's & Boys' Cut & Sew Underwear & Nightwear Manufacturing
NAICS 315291 Infants' Cut & Sew Apparel Manufacturing
2342 Brassieres, Girdles, & Allied Garments
NAICS 315212 Women's & Girls' Cut & Sew Apparel Contractors
NAICS 315231 Women's & Girls' Cut & Sew Lingerie, Loungewear, & Nightwear Manufacturing
2353 Hats, Caps, & Millinery
NAICS 315991 Hat, Cap, & Millinery Manufacturing
2361 Girls', Children's & Infants' Dresses, Blouses & Shirts
NAICS 315291 Infants' Cut & Sew Apparel Manufacturing
NAICS 315223 Men's & Boys' Cut & Sew Shirt, Manufacturing
NAICS 315211 Men's & Boys' Cut & Sew Apparel Contractors
NAICS 315232 Women's & Girls' Cut & Sew Blouse & Shirt Manufacturing
NAICS 315233 Women's & Girls' Cut & Sew Dress Manufacturing
NAICS 315212 Women's & Girls' Cut & Sew Apparel Contractors
2369 Girls', Children's & Infants' Outerwear, nec
NAICS 315291 Infants' Cut & Sew Apparel Manufacturing
NAICS 315222 Men's & Boys' Cut & Sew Suit, Coat, & Overcoat Manufacturing
NAICS 315224 Men's & Boys' Cut & Sew Trouser, Slack, & Jean Manufacturing
NAICS 315228 Men's & Boys' Cut & Sew Other Outerwear Manufacturing
NAICS 315221 Men's & Boys' Cut & Sew Underwear & Nightwear Manufacturing
NAICS 315211 Men's & Boys' Cut & Sew Apparel Contractors

NAICS 315234 Women's & Girls' Cut & Sew Suit, Coat, Tailored Jacket, & Skirt Manufacturing

NAICS 315238 Women's & Girls' Cut & Sew Other Outerwear Manufacturing

NAICS 315231 Women's & Girls' Cut & Sew Lingerie, Loungewear, & Nightwear Manufacturing

NAICS 315212 Women's & Girls' Cut & Sew Apparel Contractors

2371 Fur Goods

NAICS 315292 Fur & Leather Apparel Manufacturing

2381 Dress & Work Gloves, Except Knit & All-leather

NAICS 315992 Glove & Mitten Manufacturing

2384 Robes & Dressing Gowns

NAICS 315231 Women's & Girls' Cut & Sew Lingerie, Loungewear, & Nightwear Manufacturing

NAICS 315221 Men's & Boys' Cut & Sew Underwear & Nightwear Manufacturing

NAICS 315211 Men's & Boys' Cut & Sew Apparel Contractors

NAICS 315212 Women's & Girls' Cut & Sew Apparel Contractors

2385 Waterproof Outerwear

NAICS 315222 Men's & Boys' Cut & Sew Suit, Coat, & Overcoat Manufacturing

NAICS 315234 Women's & Girls' Cut & Sew Suit, Coat, Tailored Jacket, & Skirt Manufacturing

NAICS 315228 Men's & Boys' Cut & Sew Other Outerwear Manufacturing

NAICS 315238 Women's & Girls' Cut & Sew Other Outerwear Manufacturing

NAICS 315291 Infants' Cut & Sew Apparel Manufacturing

NAICS 315999 Other Apparel Accessories & Other Apparel Manufacturing

NAICS 315211 Men's & Boys' Cut & Sew Apparel Contractors

NAICS 315212 Women's & Girls' Cut & Sew Apparel Contractors

2386 Leather & Sheep-lined Clothing

NAICS 315292 Fur & Leather Apparel Manufacturing

2387 Apparel Belts

NAICS 315999 Other Apparel Accessories & Other Apparel Manufacturing

2389 Apparel & Accessories, nec

NAICS 315999 Other Apparel Accessories & Other Apparel Manufacturing

NAICS 315299 All Other Cut & Sew Apparel Manufacturing

NAICS 315231 Women's & Girls' Cut & Sew Lingerie, Loungewear, & Nightwear Manufacturing

NAICS 315212 Women's & Girls' Cut & Sew Apparel Contractors

NAICS 315211 Mens' & Boys' Cut & Sew Apparel Contractors

2391 Curtains & Draperies

NAICS 314121 Curtain & Drapery Mills

2392 Housefurnishings, Except Curtains & Draperies

NAICS 314911 Textile Bag Mills

NAICS 339994 Broom, Brush & Mop Manufacturing

NAICS 314129 Other Household Textile Product Mills

2393 Textile Bags

NAICS 314911 Textile Bag Mills

2394 Canvas & Related Products

NAICS 314912 Canvas & Related Product Mills

2395 Pleating, Decorative & Novelty Stitching, & Tucking for the Trade

NAICS 314999 All Other Miscellaneous Textile Product Mills

NAICS 315211 Mens' & Boys' Cut & Sew Apparel Contractors

NAICS 315212 Women's & Girls' Cut & Sew Apparel Contractors

2396 Automotive Trimmings, Apparel Findings, & Related Products

NAICS 33636 Motor Vehicle Fabric Accessories & Seat Manufacturing

NAICS 315999 Other Apparel Accessories, & Other Apparel Manufacturing

NAICS 323113 Commercial Screen Printing

NAICS 314999 All Other Miscellaneous Textile Product Mills

2397 Schiffli Machine Embroideries

NAICS 313222 Schiffli Machine Embroidery

2399 Fabricated Textile Products, nec

NAICS 33636 Motor Vehicle Fabric Accessories & Seat Manufacturing

NAICS 315999 Other Apparel Accessories & Other Apparel Manufacturing

NAICS 314999 All Other Miscellaneous Textile Product Mills

LUMBER & WOOD PRODUCTS, EXCEPT FURNITURE

2411 Logging

NAICS 11331 Logging

2421 Sawmills & Planing Mills, General

NAICS 321913 Softwood Cut Stock, Resawing Lumber, & Planing

NAICS 321113 Sawmills

NAICS 321914 Other Millwork

NAICS 321999 All Other Miscellaneous Wood Product Manufacturing

2426 Hardwood Dimension & Flooring Mills

NAICS 321914 Other Millwork

NAICS 321999 All Other Miscellaneous Wood Product Manufacturing

NAICS 337139 Other Wood Furniture Manufacturing

NAICS 321912 Hardwood Dimension Mills

2429 Special Product Sawmills, nec

NAICS 321113 Sawmills

NAICS 321913 Softwood Cut Stock, Resawing Lumber, & Planing

NAICS 321999 All Other Miscellaneous Wood Product Manufacturing

2431 Millwork

NAICS 321911 Wood Window & Door Manufacturing

NAICS 321914 Other Millwork

2434 Wood Kitchen Cabinets

NAICS 337131 Wood Kitchen Cabinet & Counter Top Manufacturing

2435 Hardwood Veneer & Plywood

NAICS 321211 Hardwood Veneer & Plywood Manufacturing

2436 Softwood Veneer & Plywood

NAICS 321212 Softwood Veneer & Plywood Manufacturing

2439 Structural Wood Members, nec

NAICS 321913 Softwood Cut Stock, Resawing Lumber, & Planing

NAICS 321214 Truss Manufacturing

NAICS 321213 Engineered Wood Member Manufacturing

2441 Nailed & Lock Corner Wood Boxes & Shook

NAICS 32192 Wood Container & Pallet Manufacturing

2448 Wood Pallets & Skids

NAICS 32192 Wood Container & Pallet Manufacturing

2449 Wood Containers, nec
NAICS 32192   Wood Container & Pallet Manufacturing
2451 Mobile Homes
NAICS 321991 Manufactured Home Manufacturing
2452 Prefabricated Wood Buildings & Components
NAICS 321992 Prefabricated Wood Building Manufacturing
2491 Wood Preserving
NAICS 321114 Wood Preservation
2493 Reconstituted Wood Products
NAICS 321219 Reconstituted Wood Product Manufacturing
2499 Wood Products, nec
NAICS 339999 All Other Miscellaneous Manufacturing
NAICS 337139 Other Wood Furniture Manufacturing
NAICS 337148 Other Nonwood Furniture Manufacturing
NAICS 32192   Wood Container & Pallet Manufacturing
NAICS 321999 All Other Miscellaneous Wood Product
Manufacturing

FURNITURE & FIXTURES

2511 Wood Household Furniture, Except Upholstered
NAICS 337122 Wood Household Furniture Manufacturing
2512 Wood Household Furniture, Upholstered
NAICS 337121 Upholstered Household Furniture
Manufacturing
2514 Metal Household Furniture
NAICS 337124 Metal Household Furniture Manufacturing
2515 Mattresses, Foundations, & Convertible Beds
NAICS 33791   Mattress Manufacturing
NAICS 337132 Upholstered Wood Household Furniture
Manufacturing
2517 Wood Television, Radio, Phonograph & Sewing Machine Cabinets
NAICS 337139 Other Wood Furniture Manufacturing
2519 Household Furniture, nec
NAICS 337143 Household Furniture (except Wood & Metal)
Manufacturing
2521 Wood Office Furniture
NAICS 337134 Wood Office Furniture Manufacturing
2522 Office Furniture, Except Wood
NAICS 337141 Nonwood Office Furniture Manufacturing
2531 Public Building & Related Furniture
NAICS 33636   Motor Vehicle Fabric Accessories & Seat
Manufacturing
NAICS 337139 Other Wood Furniture Manufacturing
NAICS 337148 Other Nonwood Furniture Manufacturing
NAICS 339942 Lead Pencil & Art Good Manufacturing
2541 Wood Office & Store Fixtures, Partitions, Shelving, & Lockers
NAICS 337131 Wood Kitchen Cabinet & Counter Top
Manufacturing
NAICS 337135 Custom Architectural Woodwork, Millwork, &
Fixtures
NAICS 337139 Other Wood Furniture Manufacturing
2542 Office & Store Fixtures, Partitions Shelving, & Lockers, Except Wood
NAICS 337145 Nonwood Showcase, Partition, Shelving, &
Locker Manufacturing
2591 Drapery Hardware & Window Blinds & Shades
NAICS 33792   Blind & Shade Manufacturing
2599 Furniture & Fixtures, nec
NAICS 339113 Surgical Appliance & Supplies Manufacturing
NAICS 337139 Other Wood Furniture Manufacturing

NAICS 337148 Other Nonwood Furniture Manufacturing

PAPER & ALLIED PRODUCTS

2611 Pulp Mills
NAICS 32211   Pulp Mills
NAICS 322121 Paper Mills
NAICS 32213   Paperboard Mills
2621 Paper Mills
NAICS 322121 Paper Mills
NAICS 322122 Newsprint Mills
2631 Paperboard Mills
NAICS 32213   Paperboard Mills
2652 Setup Paperboard Boxes
NAICS 322213 Setup Paperboard Box Manufacturing
2653 Corrugated & Solid Fiber Boxes
NAICS 322211 Corrugated & Solid Fiber Box Manufacturing
2655 Fiber Cans, Tubes, Drums, & Similar Products
NAICS 322214 Fiber Can, Tube, Drum, & Similar Products
Manufacturing
2656 Sanitary Food Containers, Except Folding
NAICS 322215 Non-folding Sanitary Food Container
Manufacturing
2657 Folding Paperboard Boxes, Including Sanitary
NAICS 322212 Folding Paperboard Box Manufacturing
2671 Packaging Paper & Plastics Film, Coated & Laminated
NAICS 322221 Coated & Laminated Packaging Paper &
Plastics Film Manufacturing
NAICS 326112 Unsupported Plastics Packaging Film & Sheet
Manufacturing
2672 Coated & Laminated Paper, nec
NAICS 322222 Coated & Laminated Paper Manufacturing
2673 Plastics, Foil, & Coated Paper Bags
NAICS 322223 Plastics, Foil, & Coated Paper Bag
Manufacturing
NAICS 326111 Unsupported Plastics Bag Manufacturing
2674 Uncoated Paper & Multiwall Bags
NAICS 322224 Uncoated Paper & Multiwall Bag
Manufacturing
2675 Die-cut Paper & Paperboard & Cardboard
NAICS 322231 Die-cut Paper & Paperboard Office Supplies
Manufacturing
NAICS 322292 Surface-coated Paperboard Manufacturing
NAICS 322298 All Other Converted Paper Product
Manufacturing
2676 Sanitary Paper Products
NAICS 322291 Sanitary Paper Product Manufacturing
2677 Envelopes
NAICS 322232 Envelope Manufacturing
2678 Stationery, Tablets, & Related Products
NAICS 322233 Stationery, Tablet, & Related Product
Manufacturing
2679 Converted Paper & Paperboard Products, nec
NAICS 322215 Non-folding Sanitary Food Container
Manufacturing
NAICS 322222 Coated & Laminated Paper Manufacturing
NAICS 322231 Die-cut Paper & Paperboard Office Supplies
Manufacturing
NAICS 322298 All Other Converted Paper Product
Manufacturing

PRINTING, PUBLISHING, & ALLIED INDUSTRIES

2711 Newspapers: Publishing, or Publishing & Printing
NAICS 51111 Newspaper Publishers
2721 Periodicals: Publishing, or Publishing & Printing
NAICS 51112 Periodical Publishers
2731 Books: Publishing, or Publishing & Printing
NAICS 51223 Music Publishers
NAICS 51113 Book Publishers
2732 Book Printing
NAICS 323117 Book Printing
2741 Miscellaneous Publishing
NAICS 51114 Database & Directory Publishers
NAICS 51223 Music Publishers
NAICS 511199 All Other Publishers
2752 Commercial Printing, Lithographic
NAICS 323114 Quick Printing
NAICS 323110 Commercial Lithographic Printing
2754 Commercial Printing, Gravure
NAICS 323111 Commercial Gravure Printing
2759 Commercial Printing, nec
NAICS 323113 Commercial Screen Printing
NAICS 323112 Commercial Flexographic Printing
NAICS 323114 Quick Printing
NAICS 323115 Digital Printing
NAICS 323119 Other Commercial Printing
2761 Manifold Business Forms
NAICS 323116 Manifold Business Form Printing
2771 Greeting Cards
NAICS 323110 Commercial Lithographic Printing
NAICS 323111 Commercial Gravure Printing
NAICS 323112 Commercial Flexographic Printing
NAICS 323113 Commercial Screen Printing
NAICS 323119 Other Commercial Printing
NAICS 511191 Greeting Card Publishers
2782 Blankbooks, Loose-leaf Binders & Devices
NAICS 323110 Commercial Lithographic Printing
NAICS 323111 Commercial Gravure Printing
NAICS 323112 Commercial Flexographic Printing
NAICS 323113 Commercial Screen Printing
NAICS 323119 Other Commercial Printing
NAICS 323118 Blankbook, Loose-leaf Binder & Device
Manufacturing
2789 Bookbinding & Related Work
NAICS 323121 Tradebinding & Related Work
2791 Typesetting
NAICS 323122 Prepress Services
2796 Platemaking & Related Services
NAICS 323122 Prepress Services

CHEMICALS & ALLIED PRODUCTS

2812 Alkalies & Chlorine
NAICS 325181 Alkalies & Chlorine Manufacturing
2813 Industrial Gases
NAICS 32512   Industrial Gas Manufacturing
2816 Inorganic Pigments
NAICS 325131 Inorganic Dye & Pigment Manufacturing
NAICS 325182 Carbon Black Manufacturing
2819 Industrial Inorganic Chemicals, nec
NAICS 325998 All Other Miscellaneous Chemical Product
Manufacturing

NAICS 331311 Alumina Refining
NAICS 325131 Inorganic Dye & Pigment Manufacturing
NAICS 325188 All Other Basic Inorganic Chemical
Manufacturing
2821 Plastics Material Synthetic Resins, & Nonvulcanizable Elastomers
NAICS 325211 Plastics Material & Resin Manufacturing
2822 Synthetic Rubber
NAICS 325212 Synthetic Rubber Manufacturing
2823 Cellulosic Manmade Fibers
NAICS 325221 Cellulosic Manmade Fiber Manufacturing
2824 Manmade Organic Fibers, Except Cellulosic
NAICS 325222 Noncellulosic Organic Fiber Manufacturing
2833 Medicinal Chemicals & Botanical Products
NAICS 325411 Medicinal & Botanical Manufacturing
2834 Pharmaceutical Preparations
NAICS 325412 Pharmaceutical Preparation Manufacturing
2835 In Vitro & in Vivo Diagnostic Substances
NAICS 325412 Pharmaceutical Preparation Manufacturing
NAICS 325413 In-vitro Diagnostic Substance Manufacturing
2836 Biological Products, Except Diagnostic Substances
NAICS 325414 Biological Product Manufacturing
2841 Soaps & Other Detergents, Except Speciality Cleaners
NAICS 325611 Soap & Other Detergent Manufacturing
2842 Speciality Cleaning, Polishing, & Sanitary Preparations
NAICS 325612 Polish & Other Sanitation Good Manufacturing
2843 Surface Active Agents, Finishing Agents, Sulfonated Oils, & Assistants
NAICS 325613 Surface Active Agent Manufacturing
2844 Perfumes, Cosmetics, & Other Toilet Preparations
NAICS 32562   Toilet Preparation Manufacturing
NAICS 325611 Soap & Other Detergent Manufacturing
2851 Paints, Varnishes, Lacquers, Enamels, & Allied Products
NAICS 32551   Paint & Coating Manufacturing
2861 Gum & Wood Chemicals
NAICS 325191 Gum & Wood Chemical Manufacturing
2865 Cyclic Organic Crudes & Intermediates, & Organic Dyes & Pigments
NAICS 32511   Petrochemical Manufacturing
NAICS 325132 Organic Dye & Pigment Manufacturing
NAICS 325192 Cyclic Crude & Intermediate Manufacturing
2869 Industrial Organic Chemicals, nec
NAICS 32511   Petrochemical Manufacturing
NAICS 325188 All Other Inorganic Chemical Manufacturing
NAICS 325193 Ethyl Alcohol Manufacturing
NAICS 32512   Industrial Gas Manufacturing
NAICS 325199 All Other Basic Organic Chemical
Manufacturing
2873 Nitrogenous Fertilizers
NAICS 325311 Nitrogenous Fertilizer Manufacturing
2874 Phosphatic Fertilizers
NAICS 325312 Phosphatic Fertilizer Manufacturing
2875 Fertilizers, Mixing Only
NAICS 325314 Fertilizer Manufacturing
2879 Pesticides & Agricultural Chemicals, nec
NAICS 32532   Pesticide & Other Agricultural Chemical
Manufacturing
2891 Adhesives & Sealants
NAICS 32552   Adhesive & Sealant Manufacturing
2892 Explosives
NAICS 32592   Explosives Manufacturing
2893 Printing Ink
NAICS 32591   Printing Ink Manufacturing

2895 Carbon Black
NAICS 325182 Carbon Black Manufacturing
2899 Chemicals & Chemical Preparations, nec
NAICS 32551　Paint & Coating Manufacturing
NAICS 311942 Spice & Extract Manufacturing
NAICS 325199 All Other Basic Organic Chemical
　　　　　　Manufacturing
NAICS 325998 All Other Miscellaneous Chemical Product
　　　　　　Manufacturing

PETROLEUM REFINING & RELATED INDUSTRIES

2911 Petroleum Refining
NAICS 32411　Petroleum Refineries
2951 Asphalt Paving Mixtures & Blocks
NAICS 324121 Asphalt Paving Mixture & Block Manufacturing
2952 Asphalt Felts & Coatings
NAICS 324122 Asphalt Shingle & Coating Materials
　　　　　　Manufacturing
2992 Lubricating Oils & Greases
NAICS 324191 Petroleum Lubricating Oil & Grease
　　　　　　Manufacturing 2999

RUBBER & MISCELLANEOUS PLASTICS PRODUCTS

3011 Tires & Inner Tubes
NAICS 326211 Tire Manufacturing
3021 Rubber & Plastics Footwear
NAICS 316211 Rubber & Plastics Footwear Manufacturing
3052 Rubber & Plastics Hose & Belting
NAICS 32622　Rubber & Plastics Hoses & Belting
　　　　　　Manufacturing
3053 Gaskets, Packing, & Sealing Devices
NAICS 339991 Gasket, Packing, & Sealing Device
　　　　　　Manufacturing
3061 Molded, Extruded, & Lathe-cut Mechanical Rubber Products
NAICS 326291 Rubber Product Manufacturing for Mechanical
　　　　　　Use
3069 Fabricated Rubber Products, nec
NAICS 31332　Fabric Coating Mills
NAICS 326192 Resilient Floor Covering Manufacturing
NAICS 326299 All Other Rubber Product Manufacturing
3081 Unsupported Plastics Film & Sheet
NAICS 326113 Unsupported Plastics Film & Sheet
　　　　　　Manufacturing
3082 Unsupported Plastics Profile Shapes
NAICS 326121 Unsupported Plastics Profile Shape
　　　　　　Manufacturing
3083 Laminated Plastics Plate, Sheet, & Profile Shapes
NAICS 32613　Laminated Plastics Plate, Sheet, & Shape
　　　　　　Manufacturing
3084 Plastic Pipe
NAICS 326122 Plastic Pipe & Pipe Fitting Manufacturing
3085 Plastics Bottles
NAICS 32616　Plastics Bottle Manufacturing
3086 Plastics Foam Products
NAICS 32615　Urethane & Other Foam Product
　　　　　　Manufacturing
NAICS 32614　Polystyrene Foam Product Manufacturing

3087 Custom Compounding of Purchased Plastics Resins
NAICS 325991 Custom Compounding of Purchased Resin
3088 Plastics Plumbing Fixtures
NAICS 326191 Plastics Plumbing Fixtures Manufacturing
3089 Plastics Products, nec
NAICS 326122 Plastics Pipe & Pipe Fitting Manufacturing
NAICS 326121 Unsupported Plastics Profile Shape
　　　　　　Manufacturing
NAICS 326199 All Other Plastics Product Manufacturing

LEATHER & LEATHER PRODUCTS

3111 Leather Tanning & Finishing
NAICS 31611　Leather & Hide Tanning & Finishing
3131 Boot & Shoe Cut Stock & Findings
NAICS 321999 All Other Miscellaneous Wood Product
　　　　　　Manufacturing
NAICS 339993 Fastener, Button, Needle, & Pin Manufacturing
NAICS 316999 All Other Leather Good Manufacturing
3142 House Slippers
NAICS 316212 House Slipper Manufacturing
3143 Men's Footwear, Except Athletic
NAICS 316213 Men's Footwear Manufacturing
3144 Women's Footwear, Except Athletic
NAICS 316214 Women's Footwear Manufacturing
3149 Footwear, Except Rubber, nec
NAICS 316219 Other Footwear Manufacturing
3151 Leather Gloves & Mittens
NAICS 315992 Glove & Mitten Manufacturing
3161 Luggage
NAICS 316991 Luggage Manufacturing
3171 Women's Handbags & Purses
NAICS 316992 Women's Handbag & Purse Manufacturing
3172 Personal Leather Goods, Except Women's Handbags & Purses
NAICS 316993 Personal Leather Good Manufacturing
3199 Leather Goods, nec
NAICS 316999 All Other Leather Good Manufacturing

STONE, CLAY, GLASS, & CONCRETE PRODUCTS

3211 Flat Glass
NAICS 327211 Flat Glass Manufacturing
3221 Glass Containers
NAICS 327213 Glass Container Manufacturing
3229 Pressed & Blown Glass & Glassware, nec
NAICS 327212 Other Pressed & Blown Glass & Glassware
　　　　　　Manufacturing
3231 Glass Products, Made of Purchased Glass
NAICS 327215 Glass Product Manufacturing Made of
　　　　　　Purchased Glass
3241 Cement, Hydraulic
NAICS 32731　Hydraulic Cement Manufacturing
3251 Brick & Structural Clay Tile
NAICS 327121 Brick & Structural Clay Tile Manufacturing
3253 Ceramic Wall & Floor Tile
NAICS 327122 Ceramic Wall & Floor Tile Manufacturing
3255 Clay Refractories
NAICS 327124 Clay Refractory Manufacturing

3259 Structural Clay Products, nec
NAICS 327123 Other Structural Clay Product Manufacturing

3261 Vitreous China Plumbing Fixtures & China & Earthenware Fittings & Bathroom Accessories
NAICS 327111 Vitreous China Plumbing Fixture & China & Earthenware Fittings & Bathroom Accessories Manufacturing

3262 Vitreous China Table & Kitchen Articles
NAICS 327112 Vitreous China, Fine Earthenware & Other Pottery Product Manufacturing

3263 Fine Earthenware Table & Kitchen Articles
NAICS 327112 Vitreous China, Fine Earthenware & Other Pottery Product Manufacturing

3264 Porcelain Electrical Supplies
NAICS 327113 Porcelain Electrical Supply Manufacturing

3269 Pottery Products, nec
NAICS 327112 Vitreous China, Fine Earthenware, & Other Pottery Product Manufacturing

3271 Concrete Block & Brick
NAICS 327331 Concrete Block & Brick Manufacturing

3272 Concrete Products, Except Block & Brick
NAICS 327999 All Other Miscellaneous Nonmetallic Mineral Product Manufacturing
NAICS 327332 Concrete Pipe Manufacturing
NAICS 32739 Other Concrete Product Manufacturing

3273 Ready-mixed Concrete
NAICS 32732 Ready-mix Concrete Manufacturing

3274 Lime
NAICS 32741 Lime Manufacturing

3275 Gypsum Products
NAICS 32742 Gypsum & Gypsum Product Manufacturing

3281 Cut Stone & Stone Products
NAICS 327991 Cut Stone & Stone Product Manufacturing

3291 Abrasive Products
NAICS 332999 All Other Miscellaneous Fabricated Metal Product Manufacturing
NAICS 32791 Abrasive Product Manufacturing

3292 Asbestos Products
NAICS 33634 Motor Vehicle Brake System Manufacturing
NAICS 327999 All Other Miscellaneous Nonmetallic Mineral Product Manufacturing

3295 Minerals & Earths, Ground or Otherwise Treated
NAICS 327992 Ground or Treated Mineral & Earth Manufacturing

3296 Mineral Wool
NAICS 327993 Mineral Wool Manufacturing

3297 Nonclay Refractories
NAICS 327125 Nonclay Refractory Manufacturing

3299 Nonmetallic Mineral Products, nec
NAICS 32742 Gypsum & Gypsum Product Manufacturing
NAICS 327999 All Other Miscellaneous Nonmetallic Mineral Product Manufacturing

PRIMARY METALS INDUSTRIES

3312 Steel Works, Blast Furnaces , & Rolling Mills
NAICS 324199 All Other Petroleum & Coal Products Manufacturing
NAICS 331111 Iron & Steel Mills

3313 Electrometallurgical Products, Except Steel
NAICS 331112 Electrometallurgical Ferroalloy Product Manufacturing

NAICS 331492 Secondary Smelting, Refining, & Alloying of Nonferrous Metals

3315 Steel Wiredrawing & Steel Nails & Spikes
NAICS 331222 Steel Wire Drawing
NAICS 332618 Other Fabricated Wire Product Manufacturing

3316 Cold-rolled Steel Sheet, Strip, & Bars
NAICS 331221 Cold-rolled Steel Shape Manufacturing

3317 Steel Pipe & Tubes
NAICS 33121 Iron & Steel Pipes & Tubes Manufacturing from Purchased Steel

3321 Gray & Ductile Iron Foundries
NAICS 331511 Iron Foundries

3322 Malleable Iron Foundries
NAICS 331511 Iron Foundries

3324 Steel Investment Foundries
NAICS 331512 Steel Investment Foundries

3325 Steel Foundries, nec
NAICS 331513 Steel Foundries

3331 Primary Smelting & Refining of Copper
NAICS 331411 Primary Smelting & Refining of Copper

3334 Primary Production of Aluminum
NAICS 331312 Primary Aluminum Production

3339 Primary Smelting & Refining of Nonferrous Metals, Except Copper & Aluminum
NAICS 331419 Primary Smelting & Refining of Nonferrous Metals

3341 Secondary Smelting & Refining of Nonferrous Metals
NAICS 331314 Secondary Smelting & Alloying of Aluminum
NAICS 331423 Secondary Smelting, Refining, & Alloying of Copper
NAICS 331492 Secondary Smelting, Refining, & Alloying of Nonferrous Metals

3351 Rolling, Drawing, & Extruding of Copper
NAICS 331421 Copper Rolling, Drawing, & Extruding

3353 Aluminum Sheet, Plate, & Foil
NAICS 331315 Aluminum Sheet, Plate, & Foil Manufacturing

3354 Aluminum Extruded Products
NAICS 331316 Aluminum Extruded Product Manufacturing

3355 Aluminum Rolling & Drawing, nec
NAICS 331319 Other Aluminum Rolling & Drawing,

3356 Rolling, Drawing, & Extruding of Nonferrous Metals, Except Copper & Aluminum
NAICS 331491 Nonferrous Metal Rolling. Drawing, & Extruding

3357 Drawing & Insulating of Nonferrous Wire
NAICS 331319 Other Aluminum Rolling & Drawing
NAICS 331422 Copper Wire Drawing
NAICS 331491 Nonferrous Metal Rolling, Drawing, & Extruding
NAICS 335921 Fiber Optic Cable Manufacturing
NAICS 335929 Other Communication & Energy Wire Manufacturing

3363 Aluminum Die-castings
NAICS 331521 Aluminum Die-castings

3364 Nonferrous Die-castings, Except Aluminum
NAICS 331522 Nonferrous Die-castings

3365 Aluminum Foundries
NAICS 331524 Aluminum Foundries

3366 Copper Foundries
NAICS 331525 Copper Foundries

3369 Nonferrous Foundries, Except Aluminum & Copper
NAICS 331528 Other Nonferrous Foundries

3398 Metal Heat Treating
NAICS 332811 Metal Heat Treating
3399 Primary Metal Products, nec
NAICS 331111 Iron & Steel Mills
NAICS 331314 Secondary Smelting & Alloying of Aluminum
NAICS 331423 Secondary Smelting, Refining & Alloying of Copper
NAICS 331492 Secondary Smelting, Refining, & Alloying of Nonferrous Metals
NAICS 332618 Other Fabricated Wire Product Manufacturing
NAICS 332813 Electroplating, Plating, Polishing, Anodizing, & Coloring

FABRICATED METAL PRODUCTS, EXCEPT MACHINERY & TRANSPORTATION EQUIPMENT

3411 Metal Cans
NAICS 332431 Metal Can Manufacturing
3412 Metal Shipping Barrels, Drums, Kegs & Pails
NAICS 332439 Other Metal Container Manufacturing
3421 Cutlery
NAICS 332211 Cutlery & Flatware Manufacturing
3423 Hand & Edge Tools, Except Machine Tools & Handsaws
NAICS 332212 Hand & Edge Tool Manufacturing
3425 Saw Blades & Handsaws
NAICS 332213 Saw Blade & Handsaw Manufacturing
3429 Hardware, nec
NAICS 332439 Other Metal Container Manufacturing
NAICS 332919 Other Metal Valve & Pipe Fitting Manufacturing
NAICS 33251 Hardware Manufacturing
3431 Enameled Iron & Metal Sanitary Ware
NAICS 332998 Enameled Iron & Metal Sanitary Ware Manufacturing
3432 Plumbing Fixture Fittings & Trim
NAICS 332913 Plumbing Fixture Fitting & Trim Manufacturing
NAICS 332999 All Other Miscellaneous Fabricated Metal Product Manufacturing
3433 Heating Equipment, Except Electric & Warm Air Furnaces
NAICS 333414 Heating Equipment Manufacturing
3441 Fabricated Structural Metal
NAICS 332312 Fabricated Structural Metal Manufacturing
3442 Metal Doors, Sash, Frames, Molding, & Trim Manufacturing
NAICS 332321 Metal Window & Door Manufacturing
3443 Fabricated Plate Work
NAICS 332313 Plate Work Manufacturing
NAICS 33241 Power Boiler & Heat Exchanger Manufacturing
NAICS 33242 Metal Tank Manufacturing
NAICS 333415 Air-conditioning & Warm Air Heating Equipment & Commercial & Industrial Refrigeration Equipment Manufacturing
3444 Sheet Metal Work
NAICS 332322 Sheet Metal Work Manufacturing
NAICS 332439 Other Metal Container Manufacturing
3446 Architectural & Ornamental Metal Work
NAICS 332323 Ornamental & Architectural Metal Work Manufacturing
3448 Prefabricated Metal Buildings & Components
NAICS 332311 Prefabricated Metal Building & Component Manufacturing

3449 Miscellaneous Structural Metal Work
NAICS 332114 Custom Roll Forming
NAICS 332312 Fabricated Structural Metal Manufacturing
NAICS 332321 Metal Window & Door Manufacturing
NAICS 332323 Ornamental & Architectural Metal Work Manufacturing
3451 Screw Machine Products
NAICS 332721 Precision Turned Product Manufacturing
3452 Bolts, Nuts, Screws, Rivets, & Washers
NAICS 332722 Bolt, Nut, Screw, Rivet, & Washer Manufacturing
3462 Iron & Steel Forgings
NAICS 332111 Iron & Steel Forging
3463 Nonferrous Forgings
NAICS 332112 Nonferrous Forging
3465 Automotive Stamping
NAICS 33637 Motor Vehicle Metal Stamping
3466 Crowns & Closures
NAICS 332115 Crown & Closure Manufacturing
3469 Metal Stamping, nec
NAICS 339911 Jewelry Manufacturing
NAICS 332116 Metal Stamping
NAICS 332214 Kitchen Utensil, Pot & Pan Manufacturing
3471 Electroplating, Plating, Polishing, Anodizing, & Coloring
NAICS 332813 Electroplating, Plating, Polishing, Anodizing, & Coloring
3479 Coating, Engraving, & Allied Services, nec
NAICS 339914 Costume Jewelry & Novelty Manufacturing
NAICS 339911 Jewelry Manufacturing
NAICS 339912 Silverware & Plated Ware Manufacturing
NAICS 332812 Metal Coating, Engraving, & Allied Services to Manufacturers
3482 Small Arms Ammunition
NAICS 332992 Small Arms Ammunition Manufacturing
3483 Ammunition, Except for Small Arms
NAICS 332993 Ammunition Manufacturing
3484 Small Arms
NAICS 332994 Small Arms Manufacturing
3489 Ordnance & Accessories, nec
NAICS 332995 Other Ordnance & Accessories Manufacturing 3491
3492 Fluid Power Valves & Hose Fittings
NAICS 332912 Fluid Power Valve & Hose Fitting Manufacturing
3493 Steel Springs, Except Wire
NAICS 332611 Steel Spring Manufacturing
3494 Valves & Pipe Fittings, nec
NAICS 332919 Other Metal Valve & Pipe Fitting Manufacturing
NAICS 332999 All Other Miscellaneous Fabricated Metal Product Manufacturing
3495 Wire Springs
NAICS 332612 Wire Spring Manufacturing
NAICS 334518 Watch, Clock, & Part Manufacturing
3496 Miscellaneous Fabricated Wire Products
NAICS 332618 Other Fabricated Wire Product Manufacturing
3497 Metal Foil & Leaf
NAICS 322225 Laminated Aluminum Foil Manufacturing for Flexible Packaging Uses
NAICS 332999 All Other Miscellaneous Fabricated Metal Product Manufacturing
3498 Fabricated Pipe & Pipe Fittings
NAICS 332996 Fabricated Pipe & Pipe Fitting Manufacturing

3499 Fabricated Metal Products, nec
NAICS 337148 Other Nonwood Furniture Manufacturing
NAICS 332117 Powder Metallurgy Part Manufacturing
NAICS 332439 Other Metal Container Manufacturing
NAICS 33251 Hardware Manufacturing
NAICS 332919 Other Metal Valve & Pipe Fitting
Manufacturing
NAICS 339914 Costume Jewelry & Novelty Manufacturing
NAICS 332999 All Other Miscellaneous Fabricated Metal
Product Manufacturing

INDUSTRIAL & COMMERCIAL MACHINERY & COMPUTER EQUIPMENT

3511 Steam, Gas, & Hydraulic Turbines, & Turbine Generator Set Units
NAICS 333611 Turbine & Turbine Generator Set Unit
Manufacturing
3519 Internal Combustion Engines, nec
NAICS 336399 All Other Motor Vehicle Parts Manufacturing
NAICS 333618 Other Engine Equipment Manufacturing
3523 Farm Machinery & Equipment
NAICS 333111 Farm Machinery & Equipment Manufacturing
NAICS 332323 Ornamental & Architectural Metal Work
Manufacturing
NAICS 332212 Hand & Edge Tool Manufacturing
NAICS 333922 Conveyor & Conveying Equipment
Manufacturing
3524 Lawn & Garden Tractors & Home Lawn & Garden Equipment
NAICS 333112 Lawn & Garden Tractor & Home Lawn &
Garden Equipment Manufacturing
NAICS 332212 Hand & Edge Tool Manufacturing
3531 Construction Machinery & Equipment
NAICS 33651 Railroad Rolling Stock Manufacturing
NAICS 333923 Overhead Traveling Crane, Hoist, & Monorail
System Manufacturing
NAICS 33312 Construction Machinery Manufacturing
3532 Mining Machinery & Equipment, Except Oil & Gas Field Machinery & Equipment
NAICS 333131 Mining Machinery & Equipment Manufacturing
3533 Oil & Gas Field Machinery & Equipment
NAICS 333132 Oil & Gas Field Machinery & Equipment
Manufacturing
3534 Elevators & Moving Stairways
NAICS 333921 Elevator & Moving Stairway Manufacturing
3535 Conveyors & Conveying Equipment
NAICS 333922 Conveyor & Conveying Equipment
Manufacturing
3536 Overhead Traveling Cranes, Hoists & Monorail Systems
NAICS 333923 Overhead Traveling Crane, Hoist & Monorail
System Manufacturing
3537 Industrial Trucks, Tractors, Trailers, & Stackers
NAICS 333924 Industrial Truck, Tractor, Trailer, & Stacker
Machinery Manufacturing
NAICS 332999 All Other Miscellaneous Fabricated Metal
Product Manufacturing
NAICS 332439 Other Metal Container Manufacturing
3541 Machine Tools, Metal Cutting Type
NAICS 333512 Machine Tool Manufacturing
3542 Machine Tools, Metal Forming Type
NAICS 333513 Machine Tool Manufacturing

3543 Industrial Patterns
NAICS 332997 Industrial Pattern Manufacturing
3544 Special Dies & Tools, Die Sets, Jigs & Fixtures, & Industrial Molds
NAICS 333514 Special Die & Tool, Die Set, Jig, & Fixture
Manufacturing
NAICS 333511 Industrial Mold Manufacturing
3545 Cutting Tools, Machine Tool Accessories, & Machinists' Precision Measuring Devices
NAICS 333515 Cutting Tool & Machine Tool Accessory
Manufacturing
NAICS 332212 Hand & Edge Tool Manufacturing
3546 Power-driven Handtools
NAICS 333991 Power-driven Hand Tool Manufacturing
3547 Rolling Mill Machinery & Equipment
NAICS 333516 Rolling Mill Machinery & Equipment
Manufacturing
3548 Electric & Gas Welding & Soldering Equipment
NAICS 333992 Welding & Soldering Equipment Manufacturing
NAICS 335311 Power, Distribution, & Specialty Transformer
Manufacturing
3549 Metalworking Machinery, nec
NAICS 333518 Other Metalworking Machinery Manufacturing
3552
3553 Woodworking Machinery
NAICS 33321 Sawmill & Woodworking Machinery
Manufacturing
3554 Paper Industries Machinery
NAICS 333291 Paper Industry Machinery Manufacturing
3555 Printing Trades Machinery & Equipment
NAICS 333293 Printing Machinery & Equipment
Manufacturing
3556 Food Products Machinery
NAICS 333294 Food Product Machinery Manufacturing
3559 Special Industry Machinery, nec
NAICS 33322 Rubber & Plastics Industry Machinery
Manufacturing
NAICS 333319 Other Commercial & Service Industry
Machinery Manufacturing
NAICS 333295 Semiconductor Manufacturing Machinery
NAICS 333298 All Other Industrial Machinery Manufacturing
3561 Pumps & Pumping Equipment
NAICS 333911 Pump & Pumping Equipment Manufacturing
3562 Ball & Roller Bearings
NAICS 332991 Ball & Roller Bearing Manufacturing
3563 Air & Gas Compressors
NAICS 333912 Air & Gas Compressor Manufacturing
3564 Industrial & Commercial Fans & Blowers & Air Purification Equipment
NAICS 333411 Air Purification Equipment Manufacturing
NAICS 333412 Industrial & Commercial Fan & Blower
Manufacturing
3565 Packaging Machinery
NAICS 333993 Packaging Machinery Manufacturing
3566 Speed Changers, Industrial High-speed Drives, & Gears
NAICS 333612 Speed Changer, Industrial High-speed Drive, &
Gear Manufacturing
3567 Industrial Process Furnaces & Ovens
NAICS 333994 Industrial Process Furnace & Oven
Manufacturing
3568 Mechanical Power Transmission Equipment, nec
NAICS 333613 Mechanical Power Transmission Equipment
Manufacturing

3569 General Industrial Machinery & Equipment, nec
NAICS 333999 All Other General Purpose Machinery
Manufacturing

3571 Electronic Computers
NAICS 334111 Electronic Computer Manufacturing

3572 Computer Storage Devices
NAICS 334112 Computer Storage Device Manufacturing

3575 Computer Terminals
NAICS 334113 Computer Terminal Manufacturing

3577 Computer Peripheral Equipment, nec
NAICS 334119 Other Computer Peripheral Equipment
Manufacturing

3578 Calculating & Accounting Machines, Except Electronic Computers
NAICS 334119 Other Computer Peripheral Equipment
Manufacturing
NAICS 333313 Office Machinery Manufacturing

3579 Office Machines, nec
NAICS 339942 Lead Pencil & Art Good Manufacturing
NAICS 334518 Watch, Clock, & Part Manufacturing
NAICS 333313 Office Machinery Manufacturing

3581 Automatic Vending Machines
NAICS 333311 Automatic Vending Machine Manufacturing

3582 Commercial Laundry, Drycleaning, & Pressing Machines
NAICS 333312 Commercial Laundry, Drycleaning, & Pressing
Machine Manufacturing

3585 Air-conditioning & Warm Air Heating Equipment & Commercial & Industrial Refrigeration Equipment
NAICS 336391 Motor Vehicle Air Conditioning Manufacturing
NAICS 333415 Air Conditioning & Warm Air Heating
Equipment & Commercial & Industrial
Refrigeration Equipment Manufacturing

3586 Measuring & Dispensing Pumps
NAICS 333913 Measuring & Dispensing Pump Manufacturing

3589 Service Industry Machinery, nec
NAICS 333319 Other Commercial and Service Industry
Machinery Manufacturing

3592 Carburetors, Pistons, Piston Rings & Valves
NAICS 336311 Carburetor, Piston, Piston Ring & Valve
Manufacturing

3593 Fluid Power Cylinders & Actuators
NAICS 333995 Fluid Power Cylinder & Actuator
Manufacturing

3594 Fluid Power Pumps & Motors
NAICS 333996 Fluid Power Pump & Motor Manufacturing

3596 Scales & Balances, Except Laboratory
NAICS 333997 Scale & Balance Manufacturing

3599 Industrial & Commercial Machinery & Equipment, nec
NAICS 336399 All Other Motor Vehicle Part Manufacturing
NAICS 332999 All Other Miscellaneous Fabricated Metal
Product Manufacturing
NAICS 333319 Other Commercial & Service Industry
Machinery Manufacturing
NAICS 33271 Machine Shops
NAICS 333999 All Other General Purpose Machinery
Manufacturing

ELECTRONIC & OTHER ELECTRICAL EQUIPMENT & COMPONENTS, EXCEPT COMPUTER EQUIPMENT

3612 Power, Distribution, & Specialty Transformers
NAICS 335311 Power, Distribution, & Specialty Transformer
Manufacturing

3613 Switchgear & Switchboard Apparatus
NAICS 335313 Switchgear & Switchboard Apparatus
Manufacturing

3621 Motors & Generators
NAICS 335312 Motor & Generator Manufacturing

3624 Carbon & Graphite Products
NAICS 335991 Carbon & Graphite Product Manufacturing

3625 Relays & Industrial Controls
NAICS 335314 Relay & Industrial Control Manufacturing

3629 Electrical Industrial Apparatus, nec
NAICS 335999 All Other Miscellaneous Electrical Equipment
& Component Manufacturing

3631 Household Cooking Equipment
NAICS 335221 Household Cooking Appliance Manufacturing

3632 Household Refrigerators & Home & Farm Freezers
NAICS 335222 Household Refrigerator & Home Freezer
Manufacturing

3633 Household Laundry Equipment
NAICS 335224 Household Laundry Equipment Manufacturing

3634 Electric Housewares & Fans
NAICS 335211 Electric Housewares & Fan Manufacturing

3635 Household Vacuum Cleaners
NAICS 335212 Household Vacuum Cleaner Manufacturing

3639 Household Appliances, nec
NAICS 335212 Household Vacuum Cleaner Manufacturing
NAICS 333298 All Other Industrial Machinery Manufacturing
NAICS 335228 Other Household Appliance Manufacturing

3641 Electric Lamp Bulbs & Tubes
NAICS 33511 Electric Lamp Bulb & Part Manufacturing

3643 Current-carrying Wiring Devices
NAICS 335931 Current-carrying Wiring Device Manufacturing

3644 Noncurrent-carrying Wiring Devices
NAICS 335932 Noncurrent-carrying Wiring Device
Manufacturing

3645 Residential Electric Lighting Fixtures
NAICS 335121 Residential Electric Lighting Fixture
Manufacturing

3646 Commercial, Industrial, & Institutional Electric Lighting Fixtures
NAICS 335122 Commercial, Industrial, & Institutional Electric
Lighting Fixture Manufacturing

3647 Vehicular Lighting Equipment
NAICS 336321 Vehicular Lighting Equipment Manufacturing

3648 Lighting Equipment, nec
NAICS 335129 Other Lighting Equipment Manufacturing

3651 Household Audio & Video Equipment
NAICS 33431 Audio & Video Equipment Manufacturing 3652
NAICS 51222 Integrated Record Production/distribution

3661 Telephone & Telegraph Apparatus
NAICS 33421 Telephone Apparatus Manufacturing
NAICS 334416 Electronic Coil, Transformer, & Other Inductor
Manufacturing
NAICS 334418 Printed Circuit/electronics Assembly
Manufacturing

3663 Radio & Television Broadcasting & Communication Equipment
NAICS 33422   Radio & Television Broadcasting & Wireless Communications Equipment Manufacturing

3669 Communications Equipment, nec
NAICS 33429   Other Communication Equipment Manufacturing

3671 Electron Tubes
NAICS 334411 Electron Tube Manufacturing

3672 Printed Circuit Boards
NAICS 334412 Printed Circuit Board Manufacturing

3674 Semiconductors & Related Devices
NAICS 334413 Semiconductor & Related Device Manufacturing

3675 Electronic Capacitors
NAICS 334414 Electronic Capacitor Manufacturing

3676 Electronic Resistors
NAICS 334415 Electronic Resistor Manufacturing

3677 Electronic Coils, Transformers, & Other Inductors
NAICS 334416 Electronic Coil, Transformer, & Other Inductor Manufacturing

3678 Electronic ConNECtors
NAICS 334417 Electronic ConNECtor Manufacturing

3679 Electronic Components, nec
NAICS 33422   Radio & Television Broadcasting & Wireless Communications Equipment Manufacturing
NAICS 334418 Printed Circuit/electronics Assembly Manufacturing
NAICS 336322 Other Motor Vehicle Electrical & Electronic Equipment Manufacturing
NAICS 334419 Other Electronic Component Manufacturing

3691 Storage Batteries
NAICS 335911 Storage Battery Manufacturing

3692 Primary Batteries, Dry & Wet
NAICS 335912 Dry & Wet Primary Battery Manufacturing

3694 Electrical Equipment for Internal Combustion Engines
NAICS 336322 Other Motor Vehicle Electrical & Electronic Equipment Manufacturing

3695 Magnetic & Optical Recording Media
NAICS 334613 Magnetic & Optical Recording Media Manufacturing

3699 Electrical Machinery, Equipment, & Supplies, nec
NAICS 333319 Other Commercial & Service Industry Machinery Manufacturing
NAICS 333618 Other Engine Equipment Manufacturing
NAICS 334119 Other Computer Peripheral Equipment Manufacturing Classify According to Function
NAICS 335129 Other Lighting Equipment Manufacturing
NAICS 335999 All Other Miscellaneous Electrical Equipment & Component Manufacturing

TRANSPORTATION EQUIPMENT

3711 Motor Vehicles & Passenger Car Bodies
NAICS 336111 Automobile Manufacturing
NAICS 336112 Light Truck & Utility Vehicle Manufacturing
NAICS 33612   Heavy Duty Truck Manufacturing
NAICS 336211 Motor Vehicle Body Manufacturing
NAICS 336992 Military Armored Vehicle, Tank, & Tank Component Manufacturing

3713 Truck & Bus Bodies
NAICS 336211 Motor Vehicle Body Manufacturing

3714 Motor Vehicle Parts & Accessories
NAICS 336211 Motor Vehicle Body Manufacturing
NAICS 336312 Gasoline Engine & Engine Parts Manufacturing
NAICS 336322 Other Motor Vehicle Electrical & Electronic Equipment Manufacturing
NAICS 33633   Motor Vehicle Steering & Suspension Components Manufacturing
NAICS 33634   Motor Vehicle Brake System Manufacturing
NAICS 33635   Motor Vehicle Transmission & Power Train Parts Manufacturing
NAICS 336399 All Other Motor Vehicle Parts Manufacturing

3715 Truck Trailers
NAICS 336212 Truck Trailer Manufacturing

3716 Motor Homes
NAICS 336213 Motor Home Manufacturing

3721 Aircraft
NAICS 336411 Aircraft Manufacturing

3724 Aircraft Engines & Engine Parts
NAICS 336412 Aircraft Engine & Engine Parts Manufacturing
3728
NAICS 336413 Other Aircraft Part & Auxiliary Equipment Manufacturing

3731 Ship Building & Repairing
NAICS 336611 Ship Building & Repairing

3732 Boat Building & Repairing
NAICS 81149   Other Personal & Household Goods Repair & Maintenance
NAICS 336612 Boat Building

3743 Railroad Equipment
NAICS 333911 Pump & Pumping Equipment Manufacturing
NAICS 33651   Railroad Rolling Stock Manufacturing

3751 Motorcycles, Bicycles, & Parts
NAICS 336991 Motorcycle, Bicycle, & Parts Manufacturing

3761 Guided Missiles & Space Vehicles
NAICS 336414 Guided Missile & Space Vehicle Manufacturing
3764

3769 Guided Missile Space Vehicle Parts & Auxiliary Equipment, nec
NAICS 336419 Other Guided Missile & Space Vehicle Parts & Auxiliary Equipment Manufacturing

3792 Travel Trailers & Campers
NAICS 336214 Travel Trailer & Camper Manufacturing

3795 Tanks & Tank Components
NAICS 336992 Military Armored Vehicle, Tank, & Tank Component Manufacturing

3799 Transportation Equipment, nec
NAICS 336214 Travel Trailer & Camper Manufacturing
NAICS 332212 Hand & Edge Tool Manufacturing
NAICS 336999 All Other Transportation Equipment Manufacturing

MEASURING, ANALYZING, & CONTROLLING INSTRUMENTS

3812 Search, Detection, Navigation, Guidance, Aeronautical, & Nautical Systems & Instruments
NAICS 334511 Search, Detection, Navigation, Guidance, Aeronautical, & Nautical System & Instrument Manufacturing

3821 Laboratory Apparatus & Furniture
NAICS 339111 Laboratory Apparatus & Furniture Manufacturing

3822 Automatic Controls for Regulating Residential & Commercial Environments & Appliances
NAICS 334512 Automatic Environmental Control Manufacturing for Regulating Residential, Commercial, & Appliance Use

3823 Industrial Instruments for Measurement, Display, & Control of Process Variables & Related Products
NAICS 334513 Instruments & Related Product Manufacturing for Measuring Displaying, & Controlling Industrial Process Variables

3824 Totalizing Fluid Meters & Counting Devices
NAICS 334514 Totalizing Fluid Meter & Counting Device Manufacturing

3825 Instruments for Measuring & Testing of Electricity & Electrical Signals
NAICS 334416 Electronic Coil, Transformer, & Other Inductor Manufacturing
NAICS 334515 Instrument Manufacturing for Measuring & Testing Electricity & Electrical Signals

3826 Laboratory Analytical Instruments
NAICS 334516 Analytical Laboratory Instrument Manufacturing

3827 Optical Instruments & Lenses
NAICS 333314 Optical Instrument & Lens Manufacturing

3829 Measuring & Controlling Devices, nec
NAICS 339112 Surgical & Medical Instrument Manufacturing
NAICS 334519 Other Measuring & Controlling Device Manufacturing

3841 Surgical & Medical Instruments & Apparatus
NAICS 339112 Surgical & Medical Instrument Manufacturing

3842 Orthopedic, Prosthetic, & Surgical Appliances & Supplies
NAICS 339113 Surgical Appliance & Supplies Manufacturing
NAICS 334510 Electromedical & Electrotherapeutic Apparatus Manufacturing

3843 Dental Equipment & Supplies
NAICS 339114 Dental Equipment & Supplies Manufacturing

3844 X-ray Apparatus & Tubes & Related Irradiation Apparatus
NAICS 334517 Irradiation Apparatus Manufacturing

3845 Electromedical & Electrotherapeutic Apparatus
NAICS 334517 Irradiation Apparatus Manufacturing
NAICS 334510 Electromedical & Electrotherapeutic Apparatus Manufacturing

3851 Ophthalmic Goods
NAICS 339115 Ophthalmic Goods Manufacturing

3861 Photographic Equipment & Supplies
NAICS 333315 Photographic & Photocopying Equipment Manufacturing
NAICS 325992 Photographic Film, Paper, Plate & Chemical Manufacturing

3873 Watches, Clocks, Clockwork Operated Devices & Parts
NAICS 334518 Watch, Clock, & Part Manufacturing

MISCELLANEOUS MANUFACTURING INDUSTRIES

3911 Jewelry, Precious Metal
NAICS 339911 Jewelry Manufacturing

3914 Silverware, Plated Ware, & Stainless Steel Ware
NAICS 332211 Cutlery & Flatware Manufacturing
NAICS 339912 Silverware & Plated Ware Manufacturing

3915 Jewelers' Findings & Materials, & Lapidary Work
NAICS 339913 Jewelers' Material & Lapidary Work Manufacturing

3931 Musical Instruments
NAICS 339992 Musical Instrument Manufacturing

3942 Dolls & Stuffed Toys
NAICS 339931 Doll & Stuffed Toy Manufacturing

3944 Games, Toys, & Children's Vehicles, Except Dolls & Bicycles
NAICS 336991 Motorcycle, Bicycle & Parts Manufacturing
NAICS 339932 Game, Toy, & Children's Vehicle Manufacturing

3949 Sporting & Athletic Goods, nec
NAICS 33992 Sporting & Athletic Good Manufacturing

3951 Pens, Mechanical Pencils & Parts
NAICS 339941 Pen & Mechanical Pencil Manufacturing

3952 Lead Pencils, Crayons, & Artist's Materials
NAICS 337139 Other Wood Furniture Manufacturing
NAICS 337139 Other Wood Furniture Manufacturing
NAICS 325998 All Other Miscellaneous Chemical Manufacturing
NAICS 339942 Lead Pencil & Art Good Manufacturing

3953 Marking Devices
NAICS 339943 Marking Device Manufacturing

3955 Carbon Paper & Inked Ribbons
NAICS 339944 Carbon Paper & Inked Ribbon Manufacturing

3961 Costume Jewelry & Costume Novelties, Except Precious Metals
NAICS 339914 Costume Jewelry & Novelty Manufacturing

3965 Fasteners, Buttons, Needles, & Pins
NAICS 339993 Fastener, Button, Needle & Pin Manufacturing

3991 Brooms & Brushes
NAICS 339994 Broom, Brush & Mop Manufacturing

3993 Signs & Advertising Specialties
NAICS 33995 Sign Manufacturing

3995 Burial Caskets
NAICS 339995 Burial Casket Manufacturing

3996 Linoleum, Asphalted-felt-base, & Other Hard Surface Floor Coverings, nec
NAICS 326192 Resilient Floor Covering Manufacturing

3999 Manufacturing Industries, nec
NAICS 337148 Other Nonwood Furniture Manufacturing
NAICS 321999 All Other Miscellaneous Wood Product Manufacturing
NAICS 31611 Leather & Hide Tanning & Finishing
NAICS 335121 Residential Electric Lighting Fixture Manufacturing
NAICS 325998 All Other Miscellaneous Chemical Product Manufacturing
NAICS 332999 All Other Miscellaneous Fabricated Metal Product Manufacturing
NAICS 326199 All Other Plastics Product Manufacturing
NAICS 323112 Commercial Flexographic Printing
NAICS 323111 Commercial Gravure Printing
NAICS 323110 Commercial Lithographic Printing
NAICS 323113 Commercial Screen Printing
NAICS 323119 Other Commercial Printing
NAICS 332212 Hand & Edge Tool Manufacturing
NAICS 339999 All Other Miscellaneous Manufacturing

TRANSPORTATION, COMMUNICATIONS, ELECTRIC, GAS, & SANITARY SERVICES

4011 Railroads, Line-haul Operating
NAICS 482111 Line-haul Railroads
4013 Railroad Switching & Terminal Establishments
NAICS 482112 Short Line Railroads
NAICS 48821 Support Activities for Rail Transportation
4111 Local & Suburban Transit
NAICS 485111 Mixed Mode Transit Systems
NAICS 485112 Commuter Rail Systems
NAICS 485113 Bus & Motor Vehicle Transit Systems
NAICS 485119 Other Urban Transit Systems
NAICS 485999 All Other Transit & Ground Passenger
              Transportation
4119 Local Passenger Transportation, nec
NAICS 62191 Ambulance Service
NAICS 48541 School & Employee Bus Transportation
NAICS 48711 Scenic & Sightseeing Transportation , Land
NAICS 485991 Special Needs Transportation
NAICS 485999 All Other Transit & Ground Passenger
              Transportation
NAICS 48532 Limousine Service
4121 Taxicabs
NAICS 48531 Taxi Service
4131 Intercity & Rural Bus Transportation
NAICS 48521 Interurban & Rural Bus Transportation
4141 Local Bus Charter Service
NAICS 48551 Charter Bus Industry
4142 Bus Charter Service, Except Local
NAICS 48551 Charter Bus Industry
4151 School Buses
NAICS 48541 School & Employee Bus Transportation
4173 Terminal & Service Facilities for Motor Vehicle Passenger Transportation
NAICS 48849 Other Support Activities for Road
              Transportation
4212 Local Trucking Without Storage
NAICS 562111 Solid Waste Collection
NAICS 562112 Hazardous Waste Collection
NAICS 562119 Other Waste Collection
NAICS 48411 General Freight Trucking, Local
NAICS 48421 Used Household & Office Goods Moving
NAICS 48422 Specialized Freight Trucking, Local
4213 Trucking, Except Local
NAICS 484121 General Freight Trucking, Long-distance,
              Truckload
NAICS 484122 General Freight Trucking, Long-distance, less
              than Truckload
NAICS 48421 Used Household & Office Goods Moving
NAICS 48423 Specialized Freight Trucking, Long-distance
4214 Local Trucking with Storage
NAICS 48411 General Freight Trucking, Local
NAICS 48421 Used Household & Office Goods Moving
NAICS 48422 Specialized Freight Trucking, Local
4215 Couriers Services Except by Air
NAICS 49211 Couriers
NAICS 49221 Local Messengers & Local Delivery
4221 Farm Product Warehousing & Storage
NAICS 49313 Farm Product Storage Facilities
4222 Refrigerated Warehousing & Storage
NAICS 49312 Refrigerated Storage Facilities

4225 General Warehousing & Storage
NAICS 49311 General Warehousing & Storage Facilities
NAICS 53113 Lessors of Miniwarehouses & Self Storage
              Units
4226 Special Warehousing & Storage, nec
NAICS 49312 Refrigerated Warehousing & Storage Facilities
NAICS 49311 General Warehousing & Storage Facilities
NAICS 49319 Other Warehousing & Storage Facilities
4231 Terminal & Joint Terminal Maintenance Facilities for Motor Freight Transportation
NAICS 48849 Other Support Activities for Road
              Transportation
4311 United States Postal Service
NAICS 49111 Postal Service
4412 Deep Sea Foreign Transportation of Freight
NAICS 483111 Deep Sea Freight Transportation
4424 Deep Sea Domestic Transportation of Freight
NAICS 483113 Coastal & Great Lakes Freight Transportation
4432 Freight Transportation on the Great Lakes - St. Lawrence Seaway
NAICS 483113 Coastal & Great Lakes Freight Transportation
4449 Water Transportation of Freight, nec
NAICS 483211 Inland Water Freight Transportation
4481 Deep Sea Transportation of Passengers, Except by Ferry
NAICS 483112 Deep Sea Passenger Transportation
NAICS 483114 Coastal & Great Lakes Passenger
              Transportation
4482 Ferries
NAICS 483114 Coastal & Great Lakes Passenger
              Transportation
NAICS 483212 Inland Water Passenger Transportation
4489 Water Transportation of Passengers, nec
NAICS 483212 Inland Water Passenger Transportation
NAICS 48721 Scenic & Sightseeing Transportation, Water
4491 Marine Cargo Handling
NAICS 48831 Port & Harbor Operations
NAICS 48832 Marine Cargo Handling
4492 Towing & Tugboat Services
NAICS 483113 Coastal & Great Lakes Freight Transportation
NAICS 483211 Inland Water Freight Transportation
NAICS 48833 Navigational Services to Shipping
4493 Marinas
NAICS 71393 Marinas
4499 Water Transportation Services, nec
NAICS 532411 Commercial Air, Rail, & Water Transportation
              Equipment Rental & Leasing
NAICS 48831 Port & Harbor Operations
NAICS 48833 Navigational Services to Shipping
NAICS 48839 Other Support Activities for Water
              Transportation
4512 Air Transportation, Scheduled
NAICS 481111 Scheduled Passenger Air Transportation
NAICS 481112 Scheduled Freight Air Transportation
4513 Air Courier Services
NAICS 49211 Couriers
4522 Air Transportation, Nonscheduled
NAICS 62191 Ambulance Services
NAICS 481212 Nonscheduled Chartered Freight Air
              Transportation
NAICS 481211 Nonscheduled Chartered Passenger Air
              Transportation
NAICS 48122 Nonscheduled Speciality Air Transportation
NAICS 48799 Scenic & Sightseeing Transportation , Other

4581 Airports, Flying Fields, & Airport Terminal Services
NAICS 488111 Air Traffic Control
NAICS 488112 Airport Operations, Except Air Traffic Control
NAICS 56172 Janitorial Services
NAICS 48819 Other Support Activities for Air Transportation

4612 Crude Petroleum Pipelines
NAICS 48611 Pipeline Transportation of Crude Oil

4613 Refined Petroleum Pipelines
NAICS 48691 Pipeline Transportation of Refined Petroleum Products

4619 Pipelines, nec
NAICS 48699 All Other Pipeline Transportation

4724 Travel Agencies
NAICS 56151 Travel Agencies

4725 Tour Operators
NAICS 56152 Tour Operators

4729 Arrangement of Passenger Transportation, nec
NAICS 488999 All Other Support Activities for Transportation
NAICS 561599 All Other Travel Arrangement & Reservation Services

4731 Arrangement of Transportation of Freight & Cargo
NAICS 541618 Other Management Consulting Services
NAICS 48851 Freight Transportation Arrangement

4741 Rental of Railroad Cars
NAICS 532411 Commercial Air, Rail, & Water Transportation Equipment Rental & Leasing
NAICS 48821 Support Activities for Rail Transportation

4783 Packing & Crating
NAICS 488991 Packing & Crating

4785 Fixed Facilities & Inspection & Weighing Services for Motor Vehicle Transportation
NAICS 48839 Other Support Activities for Water Transportation
NAICS 48849 Other Support Activities for Road Transportation

4789 Transportation Services, nec
NAICS 488999 All Other Support Activities for Transportation
NAICS 48711 Scenic & Sightseeing Transportation, Land
NAICS 48821 Support Activities for Rail Transportation

4812 Radiotelephone Communications
NAICS 513321 Paging
NAICS 513322 Cellular & Other Wireless Telecommunications
NAICS 51333 Telecommunications Resellers

4813 Telephone Communications, Except Radiotelephone
NAICS 51331 Wired Telecommunications Carriers
NAICS 51333 Telecommunications Resellers

4822 Telegraph & Other Message Communications
NAICS 51331 Wired Telecommunications Carriers

4832 Radio Broadcasting Stations
NAICS 513111 Radio Networks
NAICS 513112 Radio Stations

4833 Television Broadcasting Stations
NAICS 51312 Television Broadcasting

4841 Cable & Other Pay Television Services
NAICS 51321 Cable Networks
NAICS 51322 Cable & Other Program Distribution

4899 Communications Services, nec
NAICS 513322 Cellular & Other Wireless Telecommunications
NAICS 51334 Satellite Telecommunications
NAICS 51339 Other Telecommunications

4911 Electric Services
NAICS 221111 Hydroelectric Power Generation
NAICS 221112 Fossil Fuel Electric Power Generation
NAICS 221113 Nuclear Electric Power Generation

NAICS 221119 Other Electric Power Generation
NAICS 221121 Electric Bulk Power Transmission & Control
NAICS 221122 Electric Power Distribution

4922 Natural Gas Transmission
NAICS 48621 Pipeline Transportation of Natural Gas

4923 Natural Gas Transmission & Distribution
NAICS 22121 Natural Gas Distribution
NAICS 48621 Pipeline Transportation of Natural Gas

4924 Natural Gas Distribution
NAICS 22121 Natural Gas Distribution

4925 Mixed, Manufactured, or Liquefied Petroleum Gas Production And/or Distribution
NAICS 22121 Natural Gas Distribution

4931 Electric & Other Services Combined
NAICS 221111 Hydroelectric Power Generation
NAICS 221112 Fossil Fuel Electric Power Generation
NAICS 221113 Nuclear Electric Power Generation
NAICS 221119 Other Electric Power Generation
NAICS 221121 Electric Bulk Power Transmission & Control
NAICS 221122 Electric Power Distribution
NAICS 22121 Natural Gas Distribution

4932 Gas & Other Services Combined
NAICS 22121 Natural Gas Distribution

4939 Combination Utilities, nec
NAICS 221111 Hydroelectric Power Generation
NAICS 221112 Fossil Fuel Electric Power Generation
NAICS 221113 Nuclear Electric Power Generation
NAICS 221119 Other Electric Power Generation
NAICS 221121 Electric Bulk Power Transmission & Control
NAICS 221122 Electric Power Distribution
NAICS 22121 Natural Gas Distribution

4941 Water Supply
NAICS 22131 Water Supply & Irrigation Systems

4952 Sewerage Systems
NAICS 22132 Sewage Treatment Facilities

4953 Refuse Systems
NAICS 562111 Solid Waste Collection
NAICS 562112 Hazardous Waste Collection
NAICS 56292 Materials Recovery Facilities
NAICS 562119 Other Waste Collection
NAICS 562211 Hazardous Waste Treatment & Disposal
NAICS 562212 Solid Waste Landfills
NAICS 562213 Solid Waste Combustors & Incinerators
NAICS 562219 Other Nonhazardous Waste Treatment & Disposal

4959 Sanitary Services, nec
NAICS 488112 Airport Operations, Except Air Traffic Control
NAICS 56291 Remediation Services
NAICS 56171 Exterminating & Pest Control Services
NAICS 562998 All Other Miscellaneous Waste Management Services

4961 Steam & Air-conditioning Supply
NAICS 22133 Steam & Air-conditioning Supply

4971 Irrigation Systems
NAICS 22131 Water Supply & Irrigation Systems

WHOLESALE TRADE

5012 Automobiles & Other Motor Vehicles
NAICS 42111 Automobile & Other Motor Vehicle Wholesalers

5013 Motor Vehicle Supplies & New Parts
NAICS 44131   Automotive Parts & Accessories Stores - Retail
NAICS 42112   Motor Vehicle Supplies & New Part Wholesalers

5014 Tires & Tubes
NAICS 44132   Tire Dealers - Retail
NAICS 42113   Tire & Tube Wholesalers

5015 Motor Vehicle Parts, Used
NAICS 42114   Motor Vehicle Part Wholesalers

5021 Furniture
NAICS 44211   Furniture Stores
NAICS 42121   Furniture Wholesalers

5023 Home Furnishings
NAICS 44221   Floor Covering Stores
NAICS 42122   Home Furnishing Wholesalers

5031 Lumber, Plywood, Millwork, & Wood Panels
NAICS 44419   Other Building Material Dealers
NAICS 42131   Lumber, Plywood, Millwork, & Wood Panel Wholesalers

5032 Brick, Stone & Related Construction Materials
NAICS 44419   Other Building Material Dealers
NAICS 42132   Brick, Stone & Related Construction Material Wholesalers

5033 Roofing, Siding, & Insulation Materials
NAICS 42133   Roofing, Siding, & Insulation Material Wholesalers

5039 Construction Materials, nec
NAICS 44419   Other Building Material Dealers
NAICS 42139   Other Construction Material Wholesalers

5043 Photographic Equipment & Supplies
NAICS 42141   Photographic Equipment & Supplies Wholesalers

5044 Office Equipment
NAICS 42142   Office Equipment Wholesalers

5045 Computers & Computer Peripheral Equipment & Software
NAICS 42143   Computer & Computer Peripheral Equipment & Software Wholesalers
NAICS 44312   Computer & Software Stores - Retail

5046 Commercial Equipment, nec
NAICS 42144   Other Commercial Equipment Wholesalers

5047 Medical, Dental, & Hospital Equipment & Supplies
NAICS 42145   Medical, Dental & Hospital Equipment & Supplies Wholesalers
NAICS 446199 All Other Health & Personal Care Stores - Retail

5048 Ophthalmic Goods
NAICS 42146   Ophthalmic Goods Wholesalers

5049 Professional Equipment & Supplies, nec
NAICS 42149   Other Professional Equipment & Supplies Wholesalers
NAICS 45321   Office Supplies & Stationery Stores - Retail

5051 Metals Service Centers & Offices
NAICS 42151   Metals Service Centers & Offices

5052 Coal & Other Minerals & Ores
NAICS 42152   Coal & Other Mineral & Ore Wholesalers

5063 Electrical Apparatus & Equipment Wiring Supplies, & Construction Materials
NAICS 44419   Other Building Material Dealers
NAICS 42161   Electrical Apparatus & Equipment, Wiring Supplies & Construction Material Wholesalers

5064 Electrical Appliances, Television & Radio Sets
NAICS 42162   Electrical Appliance, Television & Radio Set Wholesalers

5065 Electronic Parts & Equipment, Not Elsewhere Classified
NAICS 42169   Other Electronic Parts & Equipment Wholesalers

5072 Hardware
NAICS 42171   Hardware Wholesalers

5074 Plumbing & Heating Equipment & Supplies
NAICS 44419   Other Building Material Dealers
NAICS 42172   Plumbing & Heating Equipment & Supplies Wholesalers

5075 Warm Air Heating & Air-conditioning Equipment & Supplies
NAICS 42173   Warm Air Heating & Air-conditioning Equipment & Supplies Wholesalers

5078 Refrigeration Equipment & Supplies
NAICS 42174   Refrigeration Equipment & Supplies Wholesalers

5082 Construction & Mining Machinery & Equipment
NAICS 42181   Construction & Mining Machinery & Equipment Wholesalers

5083 Farm & Garden Machinery & Equipment
NAICS 42182   Farm & Garden Machinery & Equipment Wholesalers
NAICS 44421   Outdoor Power Equipment Stores - Retail

5084 Industrial Machinery & Equipment
NAICS 42183   Industrial Machinery & Equipment Wholesalers

5085 Industrial Supplies
NAICS 42183   Industrial Machinery & Equipment Wholesalers
NAICS 42184   Industrial Supplies Wholesalers
NAICS 81131   Commercial & Industrial Machinery & Equipment Repair & Maintenence

5087 Service Establishment Equipment & Supplies
NAICS 42185   Service Establishment Equipment & Supplies Wholesalers
NAICS 44612   Cosmetics, Beauty Supplies, & Perfume Stores

5088 Transportation Equipment & Supplies, Except Motor Vehicles
NAICS 42186   Transportation Equipment & Supplies Wholesalers

5091 Sporting & Recreational Goods & Supplies
NAICS 42191   Sporting & Recreational Goods & Supplies Wholesalers

5092 Toys & Hobby Goods & Supplies
NAICS 42192   Toy & Hobby Goods & Supplies Wholesalers

5093 Scrap & Waste Materials
NAICS 42193   Recyclable Material Wholesalers

5094 Jewelry, Watches, Precious Stones, & Precious Metals
NAICS 42194   Jewelry, Watch , Precious Stone, & Precious Metal Wholesalers

5099 Durable Goods, nec
NAICS 42199   Other Miscellaneous Durable Goods Wholesalers

5111 Printing & Writing Paper
NAICS 42211   Printing & Writing Paper Wholesalers

5112 Stationery & Office Supplies
NAICS 45321   Office Supplies & Stationery Stores
NAICS 42212   Stationery & Office Supplies Wholesalers

5113 Industrial & Personal Service Paper
NAICS 42213   Industrial & Personal Service Paper Wholesalers

5122 Drugs, Drug Proprietaries, & Druggists' Sundries
NAICS 42221   Drugs, Drug Proprietaries, & Druggists' Sundries Wholesalers

5131 Piece Goods, Notions, & Other Dry Goods
NAICS 313311 Broadwoven Fabric Finishing Mills
NAICS 313312 Textile & Fabric Finishing Mills
NAICS 42231 Piece Goods, Notions, & Other Dry Goods
           Wholesalers
5136 Men's & Boys' Clothing & Furnishings
NAICS 42232 Men's & Boys' Clothing & Furnishings
           Wholesalers
5137 Women's Children's & Infants' Clothing & Accessories
NAICS 42233 Women's, Children's, & Infants' Clothing &
           Accessories Wholesalers
5139 Footwear
NAICS 42234 Footwear Wholesalers
5141 Groceries, General Line
NAICS 42241 General Line Grocery Wholesalers
5142 Packaged Frozen Foods
NAICS 42242 Packaged Frozen Food Wholesalers
5143 Dairy Products, Except Dried or Canned
NAICS 42243 Dairy Products Wholesalers
5144 Poultry & Poultry Products
NAICS 42244 Poultry & Poultry Product Wholesalers
5145 Confectionery
NAICS 42245 Confectionery Wholesalers
5146 Fish & Seafoods
NAICS 42246 Fish & Seafood Wholesalers
5147 Meats & Meat Products
NAICS 311612 Meat Processed from Carcasses
NAICS 42247 Meat & Meat Product Wholesalers
5148 Fresh Fruits & Vegetables
NAICS 42248 Fresh Fruit & Vegetable Wholesalers
5149 Groceries & Related Products, nec
NAICS 42249 Other Grocery & Related Product Wholesalers
5153 Grain & Field Beans
NAICS 42251 Grain & Field Bean Wholesalers
5154 Livestock
NAICS 42252 Livestock Wholesalers
5159 Farm-product Raw Materials, nec
NAICS 42259 Other Farm Product Raw Material Wholesalers
5162 Plastics Materials & Basic Forms & Shapes
NAICS 42261 Plastics Materials & Basic Forms & Shapes
           Wholesalers
5169 Chemicals & Allied Products, nec
NAICS 42269 Other Chemical & Allied Products Wholesalers
5171 Petroleum Bulk Stations & Terminals
NAICS 454311 Heating Oil Dealers
NAICS 454312 Liquefied Petroleum Gas Dealers
NAICS 42271 Petroleum Bulk Stations & Terminals
**5172 Petroleum & Petroleum Products Wholesalers, Except Bulk
     Stations & Terminals**
NAICS 42272 Petroleum & Petroleum Products Wholesalers
5181 Beer & Ale
NAICS 42281 Beer & Ale Wholesalers
5182 Wine & Distilled Alcoholic Beverages
NAICS 42282 Wine & Distilled Alcoholic Beverage
           Wholesalers
5191 Farm Supplies
NAICS 44422 Nursery & Garden Centers - Retail
NAICS 42291 Farm Supplies Wholesalers
5192 Books, Periodicals, & Newspapers
NAICS 42292 Book, Periodical & Newspaper Wholesalers
5193 Flowers, Nursery Stock, & Florists' Supplies
NAICS 42293 Flower, Nursery Stock & Florists' Supplies
           Wholesalers
NAICS 44422 Nursery & Garden Centers - Retail

5194 Tobacco & Tobacco Products
NAICS 42294 Tobacco & Tobacco Product Wholesalers
5198 Paint, Varnishes, & Supplies
NAICS 42295 Paint, Varnish & Supplies Wholesalers
NAICS 44412 Paint & Wallpaper Stores
5199 Nondurable Goods, nec
NAICS 54189 Other Services Related to Advertising
NAICS 42299 Other Miscellaneous Nondurable Goods
           Wholesalers

RETAIL TRADE

5211 Lumber & Other Building Materials Dealers
NAICS 44411 Home Centers
NAICS 42131 Lumber, Plywood, Millwork & Wood Panel
           Wholesalers
NAICS 44419 Other Building Material Dealers
5231 Paint, Glass, & Wallpaper Stores
NAICS 42295 Paint, Varnish & Supplies Wholesalers
NAICS 44419 Other Building Material Dealers
NAICS 44412 Paint & Wallpaper Stores
5251 Hardware Stores
NAICS 44413 Hardware Stores
5261 Retail Nurseries, Lawn & Garden Supply Stores
NAICS 44422 Nursery & Garden Centers
NAICS 453998 All Other Miscellaneous Store Retailers
NAICS 44421 Outdoor Power Equipment Stores
5271 Mobile Home Dealers
NAICS 45393 Manufactured Home Dealers
5311 Department Stores
NAICS 45211 Department Stores
5331 Variety Stores
NAICS 45299 All Other General Merchandise Stores
5399 Miscellaneous General Merchandise Stores
NAICS 45291 Warehouse Clubs & Superstores
NAICS 45299 All Other General Merchandise Stores
5411 Grocery Stores
NAICS 44711 Gasoline Stations with Convenience Stores
NAICS 44511 Supermarkets & Other Grocery Stores
NAICS 45291 Warehouse Clubs & Superstores
NAICS 44512 Convenience Stores
5421 Meat & Fish Markets, Including Freezer Provisioners
NAICS 45439 Other Direct Selling Establishments
NAICS 44521 Meat Markets
NAICS 44522 Fish & Seafood Markets
5431 Fruit & Vegetable Markets
NAICS 44523 Fruit & Vegetable Markets
5441 Candy, Nut, & Confectionery Stores
NAICS 445292 Confectionary & Nut Stores
5451 Dairy Products Stores
NAICS 445299 All Other Specialty Food Stores
5461 Retail Bakeries
NAICS 722213 Snack & Nonalcoholic Beverage Bars
NAICS 311811 Retail Bakeries
NAICS 445291 Baked Goods Stores
5499 Miscellaneous Food Stores
NAICS 44521 Meat Markets
NAICS 722211 Limited-service Restaurants
NAICS 446191 Food Supplement Stores
NAICS 445299 All Other Specialty Food Stores
5511 Motor Vehicle Dealers
NAICS 44111 New Car Dealers

5521 Motor Vehicle Dealers
NAICS 44112 Used Car Dealers
5531 Auto & Home Supply Stores
NAICS 44132 Tire Dealers
NAICS 44131 Automotive Parts & Accessories Stores
5541 Gasoline Service Stations
NAICS 44711 Gasoline Stations with Convenience Store
NAICS 44719 Other Gasoline Stations
5551 Boat Dealers
NAICS 441222 Boat Dealers
5561 Recreational Vehicle Dealers
NAICS 44121 Recreational Vehicle Dealers
5571 Motorcycle Dealers
NAICS 441221 Motorcycle Dealers
5599 Automotive Dealers, nec
NAICS 441229 All Other Motor Vehicle Dealers
5611 Men's & Boys' Clothing & Accessory Stores
NAICS 44811 Men's Clothing Stores
NAICS 44815 Clothing Accessories Stores
5621 Women's Clothing Stores
NAICS 44812 Women's Clothing Stores
5632 Women's Accessory & Specialty Stores
NAICS 44819 Other Clothing Stores
NAICS 44815 Clothing Accessories Stores
5641 Children's & Infants' Wear Stores
NAICS 44813 Children's & Infants' Clothing Stores
5651 Family Clothing Stores
NAICS 44814 Family Clothing Stores
5661 Shoe Stores
NAICS 44821 Shoe Stores
5699 Miscellaneous Apparel & Accessory Stores
NAICS 315 Included in Apparel Manufacturing Subsector Based on Type of Garment Produced
NAICS 44819 Other Clothing Stores
NAICS 44815 Clothing Accessories Stores
5712 Furniture Stores
NAICS 337133 Wood Household Furniture, Except Upholstered, Manufacturing
NAICS 337131 Wood Kitchen Cabinet & Counter Top Manufacturing
NAICS 337132 Upholstered Household Furniture Manufacturing
NAICS 44211 Furniture Stores
5713 Floor Covering Stores
NAICS 44221 Floor Covering Stores
5714 Drapery, Curtain, & Upholstery Stores
NAICS 442291 Window Treatment Stores
NAICS 45113 Sewing, Needlework & Piece Goods Stores
NAICS 314121 Curtain & Drapery Mills
5719 Miscellaneous Homefurnishings Stores
NAICS 442291 Window Treatment Stores
NAICS 442299 All Other Home Furnishings Stores
5722 Household Appliance Stores
NAICS 443111 Household Appliance Stores
5731 Radio, Television, & Consumer Electronics Stores
NAICS 443112 Radio, Television, & Other Electronics Stores
NAICS 44131 Automotive Parts & Accessories Stores
5734 Computer & Computer Software Stores
NAICS 44312 Computer & Software Stores
5735 Record & Prerecorded Tape Stores
NAICS 45122 Prerecorded Tape, Compact Disc & Record Stores

5736 Musical Instrument Stores
NAICS 45114 Musical Instrument & Supplies Stores
5812 Eating & Drinking Places
NAICS 72211 Full-service Restaurants
NAICS 722211 Limited-service Restaurants
NAICS 722212 Cafeterias
NAICS 722213 Snack & Nonalcoholic Beverage Bars
NAICS 72231 Foodservice Contractors
NAICS 72232 Caterers
NAICS 71111 Theater Companies & Dinner Theaters
5813 Drinking Places
NAICS 72241 Drinking Places
5912 Drug Stores & Proprietary Stores
NAICS 44611 Pharmacies & Drug Stores
5921 Liquor Stores
NAICS 44531 Beer, Wine & Liquor Stores
5932 Used Merchandise Stores
NAICS 522298 All Other Non-depository Credit Intermediation
NAICS 45331 Used Merchandise Stores
5941 Sporting Goods Stores & Bicycle Shops
NAICS 45111 Sporting Goods Stores
5942 Book Stores
NAICS 451211 Book Stores
5943 Stationery Stores
NAICS 45321 Office Supplies & Stationery Stores
5944 Jewelry Stores
NAICS 44831 Jewelry Stores
5945 Hobby, Toy, & Game Shops
NAICS 45112 Hobby, Toy, & Game Stores
5946 Camera & Photographic Supply Stores
NAICS 44313 Camera & Photographic Supplies Stores
5947 Gift, Novelty, & Souvenir Shops
NAICS 45322 Gift, Novelty & Souvenir Stores
5948 Luggage & Leather Goods Stores
NAICS 44832 Luggage & Leather Goods Stores
5949 Sewing, Needlework, & Piece Goods Stores
NAICS 45113 Sewing, Needlework & Piece Goods Stores
5961 Catalog & Mail-order Houses
NAICS 45411 Electronic Shopping & Mail-order Houses
5962 Automatic Merchandising Machine Operator
NAICS 45421 Vending Machine Operators
5963 Direct Selling Establishments
NAICS 72233 Mobile Caterers
NAICS 45439 Other Direct Selling Establishments
5983 Fuel Oil Dealers
NAICS 454311 Heating Oil Dealers
5984 Liquefied Petroleum Gas Dealers
NAICS 454312 Liquefied Petroleum Gas Dealers
5989 Fuel Dealers, nec
NAICS 454319 Other Fuel Dealers
5992 Florists
NAICS 45311 Florists
5993 Tobacco Stores & Stands
NAICS 453991 Tobacco Stores
5994 News Dealers & Newsstands
NAICS 451212 News Dealers & Newsstands
5995 Optical Goods Stores
NAICS 339117 Eyeglass & Contact Lens Manufacturing
NAICS 44613 Optical Goods Stores
5999 Miscellaneous Retail Stores, nec
NAICS 44612 Cosmetics, Beauty Supplies & Perfume Stores
NAICS 446199 All Other Health & Personal Care Stores
NAICS 45391 Pet & Pet Supplies Stores

NAICS 45392   Art Dealers
NAICS 443111 Household Appliance Stores
NAICS 443112 Radio, Television & Other Electronics Stores
NAICS 44831   Jewelry Stores
NAICS 453999 All Other Miscellaneous Store Retailers

FINANCE, INSURANCE, & REAL ESTATE

6011 Federal Reserve Banks
NAICS 52111   Monetary Authorities-central Banks
6019 Central Reserve Depository Institutions, nec
NAICS 52232   Financial Transactions Processing, Reserve, &
              Clearing House Activities
6021 National Commercial Banks
NAICS 52211   Commercial Banking
NAICS 52221   Credit Card Issuing
NAICS 523991 Trust, Fiduciary & Custody Activities
6022 State Commercial Banks
NAICS 52211   Commercial Banking
NAICS 52221   Credit Card Issuing
NAICS 52219   Other Depository Intermediation
NAICS 523991 Trust, Fiduciary & Custody Activities
6029 Commercial Banks, nec
NAICS 52211   Commercial Banking
6035 Savings Institutions, Federally Chartered
NAICS 52212   Savings Institutions
6036 Savings Institutions, Not Federally Chartered
NAICS 52212   Savings Institutions
6061 Credit Unions, Federally Chartered
NAICS 52213   Credit Unions
6062 Credit Unions, Not Federally Chartered
NAICS 52213   Credit Unions
6081 Branches & Agencies of Foreign Banks
NAICS 522293 International Trade Financing
NAICS 52211   Commercial Banking
NAICS 522298 All Other Non-depository Credit
              Intermediation
6082 Foreign Trade & International Banking Institutions
NAICS 522293 International Trade Financing
6091 Nondeposit Trust Facilities
NAICS 523991 Trust, Fiduciary, & Custody Activities
6099 Functions Related to Deposit Banking, nec
NAICS 52232   Financial Transactions Processing, Reserve, &
              Clearing House Activities
NAICS 52313   Commodity Contracts Dealing
NAICS 523991 Trust, Fiduciary, & Custody Activities
NAICS 523999 Miscellaneous Financial Investment Activities
NAICS 52239   Other Activities Related to Credit
              Intermediation
6111 Federal & Federally Sponsored Credit Agencies
NAICS 522293 International Trade Financing
NAICS 522294 Secondary Market Financing
NAICS 522298 All Other Non-depository Credit
              Intermediation
6141 Personal Credit Institutions
NAICS 52221   Credit Card Issuing
NAICS 52222   Sales Financing
NAICS 522291 Consumer Lending
**6153 Short-term Business Credit Institutions, Except
     Agricultural**
NAICS 52222   Sales Financing
NAICS 52232   Financial Transactions Processing, Reserve, &
              Clearing House Activities

NAICS 522298 All Other Non-depository Credit
              Intermediation
6159 Miscellaneous Business Credit Institutions
NAICS 52222   Sales Financing
NAICS 532   Included in Rental & Leasing Services
              Subsector by Type of Equipment & Method of
              Operation
NAICS 522293 International Trade Financing
NAICS 522298 All Other Non-depository Credit
              Intermediation
6162 Mortgage Bankers & Loan Correspondents
NAICS 522292 Real Estate Credit
NAICS 52239   Other Activities Related to Credit
              Intermediation
6163 Loan Brokers
NAICS 52231   Mortgage & Other Loan Brokers
6211 Security Brokers, Dealers, & Flotation Companies
NAICS 52311   Investment Banking & Securities Dealing
NAICS 52312   Securities Brokerage
NAICS 52391   Miscellaneous Intermediation
NAICS 523999 Miscellaneous Financial Investment Activities
6221 Commodity Contracts Brokers & Dealers
NAICS 52313   Commodity Contracts Dealing
NAICS 52314   Commodity Brokerage
6231 Security & Commodity Exchanges
NAICS 52321   Securities & Commodity Exchanges
6282 Investment Advice
NAICS 52392   Portfolio Management
NAICS 52393   Investment Advice
**6289 Services Allied with the Exchange of Securities or
     Commodities, nec**
NAICS 523991 Trust, Fiduciary, & Custody Activities
NAICS 523999 Miscellaneous Financial Investment Activities
6311 Life Insurance
NAICS 524113 Direct Life Insurance Carriers
NAICS 52413   Reinsurance Carriers
6321 Accident & Health Insurance
NAICS 524114 Direct Health & Medical Insurance Carriers
NAICS 52519   Other Insurance Funds
NAICS 52413   Reinsurance Carriers
6324 Hospital & Medical Service Plans
NAICS 524114 Direct Health & Medical Insurance Carriers
NAICS 52519   Other Insurance Funds
NAICS 52413   Reinsurance Carriers
6331 Fire, Marine, & Casualty Insurance
NAICS 524126 Direct Property & Casualty Insurance Carriers
NAICS 52519   Other Insurance Funds
NAICS 52413   Reinsurance Carriers
6351 Surety Insurance
NAICS 524126 Direct Property & Casualty Insurance Carriers
NAICS 52413   Reinsurance Carriers
6361 Title Insurance
NAICS 524127 Direct Title Insurance Carriers
NAICS 52413   Reinsurance Carriers
6371 Pension, Health, & Welfare Funds
NAICS 52392   Portfolio Management
NAICS 524292 Third Party Administration for Insurance &
              Pension Funds
NAICS 52511   Pension Funds
NAICS 52512   Health & Welfare Funds
6399 Insurance Carriers, nec
NAICS 524128 Other Direct Insurance Carriers

6411 Insurance Agents, Brokers, & Service
NAICS 52421   Insurance Agencies & Brokerages
NAICS 524291 Claims Adjusters
NAICS 524292 Third Party Administrators for Insurance & Pension Funds
NAICS 524298 All Other Insurance Related Activities

6512 Operators of Nonresidential Buildings
NAICS 71131   Promoters of Performing Arts, Sports & Similar Events with Facilities
NAICS 53112   Lessors of Nonresidential Buildings

6513 Operators of Apartment Buildings
NAICS 53111   Lessors of Residential Buildings & Dwellings

6514 Operators of Dwellings Other than Apartment Buildings
NAICS 53111   Lessors of Residential Buildings & Dwellings

6515 Operators of Residential Mobile Home Sites
NAICS 53119   Lessors of Other Real Estate Property

6517 Lessors of Railroad Property
NAICS 53119   Lessors of Other Real Estate Property

6519 Lessors of Real Property, nec
NAICS 53119   Lessors of Other Real Estate Property

6531 Real Estate Agents & Managers
NAICS 53121   Offices of Real Estate Agents & Brokers
NAICS 81399   Other Similar Organizations
NAICS 531311 Residential Property Managers
NAICS 531312 Nonresidential Property Managers
NAICS 53132   Offices of Real Estate Appraisers
NAICS 81222   Cemeteries & Crematories
NAICS 531399 All Other Activities Related to Real Estate

6541 Title Abstract Offices
NAICS 541191 Title Abstract & Settlement Offices

6552 Land Subdividers & Developers, Except Cemeteries
NAICS 23311   Land Subdivision & Land Development

6553 Cemetery Subdividers & Developers
NAICS 81222   Cemeteries & Crematories

6712 Offices of Bank Holding Companies
NAICS 551111 Offices of Bank Holding Companies

6719 Offices of Holding Companies, nec
NAICS 551112 Offices of Other Holding Companies

6722 Management Investment Offices, Open-end
NAICS 52591   Open-end Investment Funds

6726 Unit Investment Trusts, Face-amount Certificate Offices, & Closed-end Management Investment Offices
NAICS 52599   Other Financial Vehicles

6732 Education, Religious, & Charitable Trusts
NAICS 813211 Grantmaking Foundations

6733 Trusts, Except Educational, Religious, & Charitable
NAICS 52392   Portfolio Management
NAICS 523991 Trust, Fiduciary, & Custody Services
NAICS 52519   Other Insurance Funds
NAICS 52592   Trusts, Estates, & Agency Accounts

6792 Oil Royalty Traders
NAICS 523999 Miscellaneous Financial Investment Activities
NAICS 53311   Owners & Lessors of Other Non-financial Assets

6794 Patent Owners & Lessors
NAICS 53311   Owners & Lessors of Other Non-financial Assets

6798 Real Estate Investment Trusts
NAICS 52593   Real Estate Investment Trusts

6799 Investors, nec
NAICS 52391   Miscellaneous Intermediation
NAICS 52392   Portfolio Management
NAICS 52313   Commodity Contracts Dealing
NAICS 523999 Miscellaneous Financial Investment Activities

SERVICE INDUSTRIES

7011 Hotels & Motels
NAICS 72111   Hotels & Motels
NAICS 72112   Casino Hotels
NAICS 721191 Bed & Breakfast Inns
NAICS 721199 All Other Traveler Accommodation

7021 Rooming & Boarding Houses
NAICS 72131   Rooming & Boarding Houses

7032 Sporting & Recreational Camps
NAICS 721214 Recreational & Vacation Camps

7033 Recreational Vehicle Parks & Campsites
NAICS 721211 Rv & Campgrounds

7041 Organization Hotels & Lodging Houses, on Membership Basis
NAICS 72111   Hotels & Motels
NAICS 72131   Rooming & Boarding Houses

7211 Power Laundries, Family & Commercial
NAICS 812321 Laundries, Family & Commercial

7212 Garment Pressing, & Agents for Laundries
NAICS 812391 Garment Pressing & Agents for Laundries

7213 Linen Supply
NAICS 812331 Linen Supply

7215 Coin-operated Laundry & Drycleaning
NAICS 81231   Coin-operated Laundries & Drycleaners

7216 Drycleaning Plants, Except Rug Cleaning
NAICS 812322 Drycleaning Plants

7217 Carpet & Upholstery Cleaning
NAICS 56174   Carpet & Upholstery Cleaning Services

7218 Industrial Launderers
NAICS 812332 Industrial Launderers

7219 Laundry & Garment Services, nec
NAICS 812331 Linen Supply
NAICS 81149   Other Personal & Household Goods Repair & Maintenance
NAICS 812399 All Other Laundry Services

7221 Photographic Studios, Portrait
NAICS 541921 Photographic Studios, Portrait

7231 Beauty Shops
NAICS 812112 Beauty Salons
NAICS 812113 Nail Salons
NAICS 611511 Cosmetology & Barber Schools

7241 Barber Shops
NAICS 812111 Barber Shops
NAICS 611511 Cosmetology & Barber Schools

7251 Shoe Repair Shops & Shoeshine Parlors
NAICS 81143   Footwear & Leather Goods Repair

7261 Funeral Services & Crematories
NAICS 81221   Funeral Homes
NAICS 81222   Cemeteries & Crematories

7291 Tax Return Preparation Services
NAICS 541213 Tax Preparation Services

7299 Miscellaneous Personal Services, nec
NAICS 62441   Child Day Care Services
NAICS 812191 Diet & Weight Reducing Centers
NAICS 53222   Formal Wear & Costume Rental
NAICS 812199 Other Personal Care Services
NAICS 81299   All Other Personal Services

7311 Advertising Agencies
NAICS 54181   Advertising Agencies

7312 Outdoor Advertising Services
NAICS 54185   Display Advertising

7313 Radio, Television, & Publishers' Advertising Representatives
NAICS 54184 Media Representatives
7319 Advertising, nec
NAICS 481219 Other Nonscheduled Air Transportation
NAICS 54183 Media Buying Agencies
NAICS 54185 Display Advertising
NAICS 54187 Advertising Material Distribution Services
NAICS 54189 Other Services Related to Advertising
7322 Adjustment & Collection Services
NAICS 56144 Collection Agencies
NAICS 561491 Repossession Services
7323 Credit Reporting Services
NAICS 56145 Credit Bureaus
7331 Direct Mail Advertising Services
NAICS 54186 Direct Mail Advertising
7334 Photocopying & Duplicating Services
NAICS 561431 Photocopying & Duplicating Services
7335 Commercial Photography
NAICS 48122 Nonscheduled Speciality Air Transportation
NAICS 541922 Commercial Photography
7336 Commercial Art & Graphic Design
NAICS 54143 Commercial Art & Graphic Design Services
7338 Secretarial & Court Reporting Services
NAICS 56141 Document Preparation Services
NAICS 561492 Court Reporting & Stenotype Services
7342 Disinfecting & Pest Control Services
NAICS 56172 Janitorial Services
NAICS 56171 Exterminating & Pest Control Services
7349 Building Cleaning & Maintenance Services, nec
NAICS 56172 Janitorial Services
7352 Medical Equipment Rental & Leasing
NAICS 532291 Home Health Equipment Rental
NAICS 53249 Other Commercial & Industrial Machinery & Equipment Rental & Leasing
7353 Heavy Construction Equipment Rental & Leasing
NAICS 23499 All Other Heavy Construction
NAICS 532412 Construction, Mining & Forestry Machinery & Equipment Rental & Leasing
7359 Equipment Rental & Leasing, nec
NAICS 53221 Consumer Electronics & Appliances Rental
NAICS 53231 General Rental Centers
NAICS 532299 All Other Consumer Goods Rental
NAICS 532412 Construction, Mining & Forestry Machinery & Equipment Rental & Leasing
NAICS 532411 Commercial Air, Rail, & Water Transportation Equipment Rental & Leasing
NAICS 562991 Septic Tank & Related Services
NAICS 53242 Office Machinery & Equipment Rental & Leasing
NAICS 53249 Other Commercial & Industrial Machinery & Equipment Rental & Leasing
7361 Employment Agencies
NAICS 541612 Human Resources & Executive Search Consulting Services
NAICS 56131 Employment Placement Agencies
7363 Help Supply Services
NAICS 56132 Temporary Help Services
NAICS 56133 Employee Leasing Services
7371 Computer Programming Services
NAICS 541511 Custom Computer Programming Services
7372 Prepackaged Software
NAICS 51121 Software Publishers
NAICS 334611 Software Reproducing

7373 Computer Integrated Systems Design
NAICS 541512 Computer Systems Design Services
7374 Computer Processing & Data Preparation & Processing Services
NAICS 51421 Data Processing Services
7375 Information Retrieval Services
NAICS 514191 On-line Information Services
7376 Computer Facilities Management Services
NAICS 541513 Computer Facilities Management Services
7377 Computer Rental & Leasing
NAICS 53242 Office Machinery & Equipment Rental & Leasing
7378 Computer Maintenance & Repair
NAICS 44312 Computer & Software Stores
NAICS 811212 Computer & Office Machine Repair & Maintenance
7379 Computer Related Services, nec
NAICS 541512 Computer Systems Design Services
NAICS 541519 Other Computer Related Services
7381 Detective, Guard, & Armored Car Services
NAICS 561611 Investigation Services
NAICS 561612 Security Guards & Patrol Services
NAICS 561613 Armored Car Services
7382 Security Systems Services
NAICS 561621 Security Systems Services
7383 News Syndicates
NAICS 51411 New Syndicates
7384 Photofinishing Laboratories
NAICS 812921 Photo Finishing Laboratories
NAICS 812922 One-hour Photo Finishing
7389 Business Services, nec
NAICS 51224 Sound Recording Studios
NAICS 51229 Other Sound Recording Industries
NAICS 541199 All Other Legal Services
NAICS 81299 All Other Personal Services
NAICS 54137 Surveying & Mapping Services
NAICS 54141 Interior Design Services
NAICS 54142 Industrial Design Services
NAICS 54134 Drafting Services
NAICS 54149 Other Specialized Design Services
NAICS 54189 Other Services Related to Advertising
NAICS 54193 Translation & Interpretation Services
NAICS 54135 Building Inspection Services
NAICS 54199 All Other Professional, Scientific & Technical Services
NAICS 71141 Agents & Managers for Artists, Athletes, Entertainers & Other Public Figures
NAICS 561422 Telemarketing Bureaus
NAICS 561432 Private Mail Centers
NAICS 561439 Other Business Service Centers
NAICS 561491 Repossession Services
NAICS 56191 Packaging & Labeling Services
NAICS 56179 Other Services to Buildings & Dwellings
NAICS 561599 All Other Travel Arrangement & Reservation Services
NAICS 56192 Convention & Trade Show Organizers
NAICS 561591 Convention & Visitors Bureaus
NAICS 52232 Financial Transactions, Processing, Reserve & Clearing House Activities
NAICS 561499 All Other Business Support Services
NAICS 56199 All Other Support Services
7513 Truck Rental & Leasing, Without Drivers
NAICS 53212 Truck, Utility Trailer & Rv Rental & Leasing

Appendix: SIC/NAICS Conversion

7514 Passenger Car Rental
  NAICS 532111 Passenger Cars Rental
7515 Passenger Car Leasing
  NAICS 532112 Passenger Cars Leasing
7519 Utility Trailer & Recreational Vehicle Rental
  NAICS 53212 Truck, Utility Trailer & Rv Rental & Leasing
7521 Automobile Parking
  NAICS 81293 Parking Lots & Garages
7532 Top, Body, & Upholstery Repair Shops & Paint Shops
  NAICS 811121 Automotive Body, Paint, & Upholstery Repair
        & Maintenance
7533 Automotive Exhaust System Repair Shops
  NAICS 811112 Automotive Exhaust System Repair
7534 Tire Retreading & Repair Shops
  NAICS 326212 Tire Retreading
  NAICS 811198 All Other Automotive Repair & Maintenance
7536 Automotive Glass Replacement Shops
  NAICS 811122 Automotive Glass Replacement Shops
7537 Automotive Transmission Repair Shops
  NAICS 811113 Automotive Transmission Repair
7538 General Automotive Repair Shops
  NAICS 811111 General Automotive Repair
7539 Automotive Repair Shops, nec
  NAICS 811118 Other Automotive Mechanical & Electrical
        Repair & Maintenance
7542 Carwashes
  NAICS 811192 Car Washes
7549 Automotive Services, Except Repair & Carwashes
  NAICS 811191 Automotive Oil Change & Lubrication Shops
  NAICS 48841 Motor Vehicle Towing
  NAICS 811198 All Other Automotive Repair & Maintenance
7622 Radio & Television Repair Shops
  NAICS 811211 Consumer Electronics Repair & Maintenance
  NAICS 443112 Radio, Television & Other Electronics Stores
7623 Refrigeration & Air-conditioning Services & Repair Shops
  NAICS 443111 Household Appliance Stores
  NAICS 81131 Commercial & Industrial Machinery &
        Equipment Repair & Maintenance
  NAICS 811412 Appliance Repair & Maintenance
7629 Electrical & Electronic Repair Shops, nec
  NAICS 443111 Household Appliance Stores
  NAICS 811212 Computer & Office Machine Repair &
        Maintenance
  NAICS 811213 Communication Equipment Repair &
        Maintenance
  NAICS 811219 Other Electronic & Precision Equipment
        Repair & Maintenance
  NAICS 811412 Appliance Repair & Maintenance
  NAICS 811211 Consumer Electronics Repair & Maintenance
7631 Watch, Clock, & Jewelry Repair
  NAICS 81149 Other Personal & Household Goods Repair &
        Maintenance
7641 Reupholster & Furniture Repair
  NAICS 81142 Reupholstery & Furniture Repair
7692 Welding Repair
  NAICS 81149 Other Personal & Household Goods Repair &
        Maintenance
7694 Armature Rewinding Shops
  NAICS 81131 Commercial & Industrial Machinery &
        Equipment Repair & Maintenance
  NAICS 335312 Motor & Generator Manufacturing
7699 Repair Shops & Related Services, nec
  NAICS 561622 Locksmiths
  NAICS 562991 Septic Tank & Related Services

NAICS 56179 Other Services to Buildings & Dwellings
NAICS 48839 Other Supporting Activities for Water
        Transportation
NAICS 45111 Sporting Goods Stores
NAICS 81131 Commercial & Industrial Machinery &
        Equipment Repair & Maintenance
NAICS 11521 Support Activities for Animal Production
NAICS 811212 Computer & Office Machine Repair &
        Maintenance
NAICS 811219 Other Electronic & Precision Equipment
        Repair & Maintenance
NAICS 811411 Home & Garden Equipment Repair &
        Maintenance
NAICS 811412 Appliance Repair & Maintenance
NAICS 81143 Footwear & Leather Goods Repair
NAICS 81149 Other Personal & Household Goods Repair &
        Maintenance
7812 Motion Picture & Video Tape Production
  NAICS 51211 Motion Picture & Video Production
7819 Services Allied to Motion Picture Production
  NAICS 512191 Teleproduction & Other Post-production
        Services
  NAICS 56131 Employment Placement Agencies
  NAICS 53222 Formal Wear & Costumes Rental
  NAICS 53249 Other Commercial & Industrial Machinery &
        Equipment Rental & Leasing
  NAICS 541214 Payroll Services
  NAICS 71151 Independent Artists, Writers, & Performers
  NAICS 334612 Prerecorded Compact Disc , Tape, & Record
        Manufacturing
  NAICS 512199 Other Motion Picture & Video Industries
7822 Motion Picture & Video Tape Distribution
  NAICS 42199 Other Miscellaneous Durable Goods
        Wholesalers
  NAICS 51212 Motion Picture & Video Distribution
7829 Services Allied to Motion Picture Distribution
  NAICS 512199 Other Motion Picture & Video Industries
  NAICS 51212 Motion Picture & Video Distribution
7832 Motion Picture Theaters, Except Drive-ins.
  NAICS 512131 Motion Picture Theaters, Except Drive-in
7833 Drive-in Motion Picture Theaters
  NAICS 512132 Drive-in Motion Picture Theaters
7841 Video Tape Rental
  NAICS 53223 Video Tapes & Disc Rental
7911 Dance Studios, Schools, & Halls
  NAICS 71399 All Other Amusement & Recreation Industries
  NAICS 61161 Fine Arts Schools
7922 Theatrical Producers & Miscellaneous Theatrical Services
  NAICS 56131 Employment Placement Agencies
  NAICS 71111 Theater Companies & Dinner Theaters
  NAICS 71141 Agents & Managers for Artists, Athletes,
        Entertainers & Other Public Figures
  NAICS 71112 Dance Companies
  NAICS 71131 Promoters of Performing Arts, Sports, &
        Similar Events with Facilities
  NAICS 71132 Promoters of Performing Arts, Sports, &
        Similar Events Without Facilities
  NAICS 51229 Other Sound Recording Industries
  NAICS 53249 Other Commercial & Industrial Machinery &
        Equipment Rental & Leasing
7929 Bands, Orchestras, Actors, & Other Entertainers & Entertainment Groups
  NAICS 71113 Musical Groups & Artists
  NAICS 71151 Independent Artists, Writers, & Performers

NAICS 71119　Other Performing Arts Companies

7933 Bowling Centers
NAICS 71395　Bowling Centers

7941 Professional Sports Clubs & Promoters
NAICS 711211 Sports Teams & Clubs
NAICS 71141　Agents & Managers for Artists, Athletes, Entertainers , & Other Public Figures
NAICS 71132　Promoters of Arts, Sports & Similar Events Without Facilities
NAICS 71131　Promoters of Arts, Sports, & Similar Events with Facilities
NAICS 711219 Other Spectator Sports

7948 Racing, Including Track Operations
NAICS 711212 Race Tracks
NAICS 711219 Other Spectator Sports

7991 Physical Fitness Facilities
NAICS 71394　Fitness & Recreational Sports Centers

7992 Public Golf Courses
NAICS 71391　Golf Courses & Country Clubs

7993 Coin Operated Amusement Devices
NAICS 71312　Amusement Arcades
NAICS 71329　Other Gambling Industries
NAICS 71399　All Other Amusement & Recreation Industries

7996 Amusement Parks
NAICS 71311　Amusement & Theme Parks

7997 Membership Sports & Recreation Clubs
NAICS 48122　Nonscheduled Speciality Air Transportation
NAICS 71391　Golf Courses & Country Clubs
NAICS 71394　Fitness & Recreational Sports Centers
NAICS 71399　All Other Amusement & Recreation Industries

7999 Amusement & Recreation Services, nec
NAICS 561599 All Other Travel Arrangement & Reservation Services
NAICS 48799　Scenic & Sightseeing Transportation, Other
NAICS 71119　Other Performing Arts Companies
NAICS 711219 Other Spectator Sports
NAICS 71392　Skiing Facilities
NAICS 71394　Fitness & Recreational Sports Centers
NAICS 71321　Casinos
NAICS 71329　Other Gambling Industries
NAICS 71219　Nature Parks & Other Similar Institutions
NAICS 61162　Sports & Recreation Instruction
NAICS 532292 Recreational Goods Rental
NAICS 48711　Scenic & Sightseeing Transportation, Land
NAICS 48721　Scenic & Sightseeing Transportation, Water
NAICS 71399　All Other Amusement & Recreation Industries

8011 Offices & Clinics of Doctors of Medicine
NAICS 621493 Freestanding Ambulatory Surgical & Emergency Centers
NAICS 621491 Hmo Medical Centers
NAICS 621112 Offices of Physicians, Mental Health Specialists
NAICS 621111 Offices of Physicians

8021 Offices & Clinics of Dentists
NAICS 62121　Offices of Dentists

8031 Offices & Clinics of Doctors of Osteopathy
NAICS 621111 Offices of Physicians
NAICS 621112 Offices of Physicians, Mental Health Specialists

8041 Offices & Clinics of Chiropractors
NAICS 62131　Offices of Chiropractors

8042 Offices & Clinics of Optometrists
NAICS 62132　Offices of Optometrists

8043 Offices & Clinics of Podiatrists
NAICS 621391 Offices of Podiatrists

8049 Offices & Clinics of Health Practitioners, nec
NAICS 62133　Offices of Mental Health Practitioners
NAICS 62134　Offices of Physical, Occupational, & Speech Therapists & Audiologists
NAICS 621399 Offices of All Other Miscellaneous Health Practitioners

8051 Skilled Nursing Care Facilities
NAICS 623311 Continuing Care Retirement Communities
NAICS 62311　Nursing Care Facilities

8052 Intermediate Care Facilities
NAICS 623311 Continuing Care Retirement Communities
NAICS 62321　Residential Mental Retardation Facilities
NAICS 62311　Nursing Care Facilities

8059 Nursing & Personal Care Facilities, nec
NAICS 623311 Continuing Care Retirement Communities
NAICS 62311　Nursing Care Facilities

8062 General Medical & Surgical Hospitals
NAICS 62211　General Medical & Surgical Hospitals

8063 Psychiatric Hospitals
NAICS 62221　Psychiatric & Substance Abuse Hospitals

8069 Specialty Hospitals, Except Psychiatric
NAICS 62211　General Medical & Surgical Hospitals
NAICS 62221　Psychiatric & Substance Abuse Hospitals
NAICS 62231　Specialty Hospitals

8071 Medical Laboratories
NAICS 621512 Diagnostic Imaging Centers
NAICS 621511 Medical Laboratories

8072 Dental Laboratories
NAICS 339116 Dental Laboratories

8082 Home Health Care Services
NAICS 62161　Home Health Care Services

8092 Kidney Dialysis Centers
NAICS 621492 Kidney Dialysis Centers

8093 Specialty Outpatient Facilities, nec
NAICS 62141　Family Planning Centers
NAICS 62142　Outpatient Mental Health & Substance Abuse Centers
NAICS 621498 All Other Outpatient Care Facilities

8099 Health & Allied Services, nec
NAICS 621991 Blood & Organ Banks
NAICS 54143　Graphic Design Services
NAICS 541922 Commercial Photography
NAICS 62141　Family Planning Centers
NAICS 621999 All Other Miscellaneous Ambulatory Health Care Services

8111 Legal Services
NAICS 54111　Offices of Lawyers

8211 Elementary & Secondary Schools
NAICS 61111　Elementary & Secondary Schools

8221 Colleges, Universities, & Professional Schools
NAICS 61131　Colleges, Universities & Professional Schools

8222 Junior Colleges & Technical Institutes
NAICS 61121　Junior Colleges

8231 Libraries
NAICS 51412　Libraries & Archives

8243 Data Processing Schools
NAICS 611519 Other Technical & Trade Schools
NAICS 61142　Computer Training

8244 Business & Secretarial Schools
NAICS 61141　Business & Secretarial Schools

8249 Vocational Schools, nec
NAICS 611513 Apprenticeship Training
NAICS 611512 Flight Training
NAICS 611519 Other Technical & Trade Schools

8299 Schools & Educational Services, nec
NAICS 48122 Nonscheduled speciality Air Transportation
NAICS 611512 Flight Training
NAICS 611692 Automobile Driving Schools
NAICS 61171 Educational Support Services
NAICS 611691 Exam Preparation & Tutoring
NAICS 61161 Fine Arts Schools
NAICS 61163 Language Schools
NAICS 61143 Professional & Management Development
      Training Schools
NAICS 611699 All Other Miscellaneous Schools & Instruction

8322 Individual & Family Social Services
NAICS 62411 Child & Youth Services
NAICS 62421 Community Food Services
NAICS 624229 Other Community Housing Services
NAICS 62423 Emergency & Other Relief Services
NAICS 62412 Services for the Elderly & Persons with
      Disabilities
NAICS 624221 Temporary Shelters
NAICS 92215 Parole Offices & Probation Offices
NAICS 62419 Other Individual & Family Services

8331 Job Training & Vocational Rehabilitation Services
NAICS 62431 Vocational Rehabilitation Services

8351 Child Day Care Services
NAICS 62441 Child Day Care Services

8361 Residential Care
NAICS 623312 Homes for the Elderly
NAICS 62322 Residential Mental Health & Substance Abuse
      Facilities
NAICS 62399 Other Residential Care Facilities

8399 Social Services, nec
NAICS 813212 Voluntary Health Organizations
NAICS 813219 Other Grantmaking & Giving Services
NAICS 813311 Human Rights Organizations
NAICS 813312 Environment, Conservation & Wildlife
      Organizations
NAICS 813319 Other Social Advocacy Organizations

8412 Museums & Art Galleries
NAICS 71211 Museums
NAICS 71212 Historical Sites

8422 Arboreta & Botanical or Zoological Gardens
NAICS 71213 Zoos & Botanical Gardens
NAICS 71219 Nature Parks & Other Similar Institutions

8611 Business Associations
NAICS 81391 Business Associations

8621 Professional Membership Organizations
NAICS 81392 Professional Organizations

8631 Labor Unions & Similar Labor Organizations
NAICS 81393 Labor Unions & Similar Labor Organizations

8641 Civic, Social, & Fraternal Associations
NAICS 81341 Civic & Social Organizations
NAICS 81399 Other Similar Organizations
NAICS 92115 American Indian & Alaska Native Tribal
      Governments
NAICS 62411 Child & Youth Services

8651 Political Organizations
NAICS 81394 Political Organizations

8661 Religious Organizations
NAICS 81311 Religious Organizations

8699 Membership Organizations, nec
NAICS 81341 Civic & Social Organizations
NAICS 81391 Business Associations
NAICS 813312 Environment, Conservation, & Wildlife
      Organizations

NAICS 561599 All Other Travel Arrangement & Reservation
      Services
NAICS 81399 Other Similar Organizations

8711 Engineering Services
NAICS 54133 Engineering Services

8712 Architectural Services
NAICS 54131 Architectural Services

8713 Surveying Services
NAICS 48122 Nonscheduled Air Speciality Transportation
NAICS 54136 Geophysical Surveying & Mapping Services
NAICS 54137 Surveying & Mapping Services

8721 Accounting, Auditing, & Bookkeeping Services
NAICS 541211 Offices of Certified Public Accountants
NAICS 541214 Payroll Services
NAICS 541219 Other Accounting Services

8731 Commercial Physical & Biological Research
NAICS 54171 Research & Development in the Physical
      Sciences & Engineering Sciences
NAICS 54172 Research & Development in the Life Sciences

**8732 Commercial Economic, Sociological, & Educational
   Research**
NAICS 54173 Research & Development in the Social Sciences
      & Humanities
NAICS 54191 Marketing Research & Public Opinion Polling

8733 Noncommercial Research Organizations
NAICS 54171 Research & Development in the Physical
      Sciences & Engineering Sciences
NAICS 54172 Research & Development in the Life Sciences
NAICS 54173 Research & Development in the Social Sciences
      & Humanities

8734 Testing Laboratories
NAICS 54194 Veterinary Services
NAICS 54138 Testing Laboratories

8741 Management Services
NAICS 56111 Office Administrative Services
NAICS 23   Included in Construction Sector by Type of
      Construction

8742 Management Consulting Services
NAICS 541611 Administrative Management & General
      Management Consulting Services
NAICS 541612 Human Resources & Executive Search Services
NAICS 541613 Marketing Consulting Services
NAICS 541614 Process, Physical, Distribution & Logistics
      Consulting Services

8743 Public Relations Services
NAICS 54182 Public Relations Agencies

8744 Facilities Support Management Services
NAICS 56121 Facilities Support Services

8748 Business Consulting Services, nec
NAICS 61171 Educational Support Services
NAICS 541618 Other Management Consulting Services
NAICS 54169 Other Scientific & Technical Consulting
      Services

8811 Private Households
NAICS 81411 Private Households

8999 Services, nec
NAICS 71151 Independent Artists, Writers, & Performers
NAICS 51221 Record Production
NAICS 54169 Other Scientific & Technical Consulting
      Services
NAICS 51223 Music Publishers
NAICS 541612 Human Resources & Executive Search
      Consulting Services
NAICS 514199 All Other Information Services

NAICS 54162   Environmental Consulting Services

PUBLIC ADMINISTRATION

9111 Executive Offices
NAICS 92111   Executive Offices
9121 Legislative Bodies
NAICS 92112   Legislative Bodies
9131 Executive & Legislative Offices, Combined
NAICS 92114   Executive & Legislative Offices, Combined
9199 General Government, nec
NAICS 92119   All Other General Government
9211 Courts
NAICS 92211   Courts
9221 Police Protection
NAICS 92212   Police Protection
9222 Legal Counsel & Prosecution
NAICS 92213   Legal Counsel & Prosecution
9223 Correctional Institutions
NAICS 92214   Correctional Institutions
9224 Fire Protection
NAICS 92216   Fire Protection
9229 Public Order & Safety, nec
NAICS 92219   All Other Justice, Public Order, & Safety
9311 Public Finance, Taxation, & Monetary Policy
NAICS 92113   Public Finance
9411 Administration of Educational Programs
NAICS 92311   Administration of Education Programs
9431 Administration of Public Health Programs
NAICS 92312   Administration of Public Health Programs
9441 Administration of Social, Human Resource & Income Maintenance Programs
NAICS 92313   Administration of Social, Human Resource & Income Maintenance Programs
9451 Administration of Veteran's Affairs, Except Health Insurance
NAICS 92314   Administration of Veteran's Affairs
9511 Air & Water Resource & Solid Waste Management
NAICS 92411   Air & Water Resource & Solid Waste Management
9512 Land, Mineral, Wildlife, & Forest Conservation
NAICS 92412   Land, Mineral, Wildlife, & Forest Conservation
9531 Administration of Housing Programs
NAICS 92511   Administration of Housing Programs
9532 Administration of Urban Planning & Community & Rural Development
NAICS 92512   Administration of Urban Planning & Community & Rural Development
9611 Administration of General Economic Programs
NAICS 92611   Administration of General Economic Programs
9621 Regulations & Administration of Transportation Programs
NAICS 488111 Air Traffic Control
NAICS 92612   Regulation & Administration of Transportation Programs
9631 Regulation & Administration of Communications, Electric, Gas, & Other Utilities
NAICS 92613   Regulation & Administration of Communications, Electric, Gas, & Other Utilities
9641 Regulation of Agricultural Marketing & Commodity
NAICS 92614   Regulation of Agricultural Marketing & Commodity

9651 Regulation, Licensing, & Inspection of Miscellaneous Commercial Sectors
NAICS 92615   Regulation, Licensing, & Inspection of Miscellaneous Commercial Sectors
9661 Space Research & Technology
NAICS 92711   Space Research & Technology
9711 National Security
NAICS 92811   National Security
9721 International Affairs
NAICS 92812   International Affairs
9999 Nonclassifiable Establishments
NAICS 99999   Unclassified Establishments

NAICS TO SIC CONVERSION GUIDE

AGRICULTURE, FORESTRY, FISHING, & HUNTING

11111   Soybean Farming
SIC 0116 Soybeans
11112   Oilseed Farming
SIC 0119 Cash Grains, nec
11113   Dry Pea & Bean Farming
SIC 0119 Cash Grains, nec
11114   Wheat Farming
SIC 0111 Wheat
11115   Corn Farming
SIC 0115 Corn
SIC 0119 Cash Grains, nec
11116   Rice Farming
SIC 0112 Rice
111191 Oilseed & Grain Combination Farming
SIC 0119 Cash Grains, nec
111199 All Other Grain Farming
SIC 0119 Cash Grains, nec
111211 Potato Farming
SIC 0134 Irish Potatoes
111219 Other Vegetable & Melon Farming
SIC 0161 Vegetables & Melons
SIC 0139 Field Crops Except Cash Grains
11131   Orange Groves
SIC 0174 Citrus Fruits
11132   Citrus Groves
SIC 0174 Citrus Fruits
111331 Apple Orchards
SIC 0175 Deciduous Tree Fruits
111332 Grape Vineyards
SIC 0172 Grapes
111333 Strawberry Farming
SIC 0171 Berry Crops
111334 Berry Farming
SIC 0171 Berry Crops
111335 Tree Nut Farming
SIC 0173 Tree Nuts
111336 Fruit & Tree Nut Combination Farming
SIC 0179 Fruits & Tree Nuts, nec
111339 Other Noncitrus Fruit Farming
SIC 0175 Deciduous Tree Fruits
SIC 0179 Fruit & Tree Nuts, nec
111411 Mushroom Production
SIC 0182 Food Crops Grown Under Cover
111419 Other Food Crops Grown Under Cover
SIC 0182 Food Crops Grown Under Cover
111421 Nursery & Tree Production
SIC 0181 Ornamental Floriculture & Nursery Products
SIC 0811 Timber Tracts
111422 Floriculture Production
SIC 0181 Ornamental Floriculture & Nursery Products
11191   Tobacco Farming
SIC 0132 Tobacco
11192   Cotton Farming
SIC 0131 Cotton
11193   Sugarcane Farming
SIC 0133 Sugarcane & Sugar Beets

11194   Hay Farming
SIC 0139 Field Crops, Except Cash Grains, nec
111991 Sugar Beet Farming
SIC 0133 Sugarcane & Sugar Beets
111992 Peanut Farming
SIC 0139 Field Crops, Except Cash Grains, nec
111998 All Other Miscellaneous Crop Farming
SIC 0139 Field Crops, Except Cash Grains, nec
SIC 0191 General Farms, Primarily Crop
SIC 0831 Forest Products
SIC 0919 Miscellaneous Marine Products
SIC 2099 Food Preparations, nec
112111 Beef Cattle Ranching & Farming
SIC 0212 Beef Cattle, Except Feedlots
SIC 0241 Dairy Farms
112112 Cattle Feedlots
SIC 0211 Beef Cattle Feedlots
11212   Dairy Cattle & Milk Production
SIC 0241 Dairy Farms
11213   Dual Purpose Cattle Ranching & Farming
No SIC equivalent
11221   Hog & Pig Farming
SIC 0213 Hogs
11231   Chicken Egg Production
SIC 0252 Chicken Eggs
11232   Broilers & Other Meat Type Chicken Production
SIC 0251 Broiler, Fryers, & Roaster Chickens
11233   Turkey Production
SIC 0253 Turkey & Turkey Eggs
11234   Poultry Hatcheries
SIC 0254 Poultry Hatcheries
11239   Other Poultry Production
SIC 0259 Poultry & Eggs, nec
11241   Sheep Farming
SIC 0214 Sheep & Goats
11242   Goat Farming
SIC 0214 Sheep & Goats
112511 Finfish Farming & Fish Hatcheries
SIC 0273 Animal Aquaculture
SIC 0921 Fish Hatcheries & Preserves
112512 Shellfish Farming
SIC 0273 Animal Aquaculture
SIC 0921 Fish Hatcheries & Preserves
112519 Other Animal Aquaculture
SIC 0273 Animal Aquaculture
11291   Apiculture
SIC 0279 Animal Specialties, nec
11292   Horse & Other Equine Production
SIC 0272 Horses & Other Equines
11293   Fur-Bearing Animal & Rabbit Production
SIC 0271 Fur-Bearing Animals & Rabbits
11299   All Other Animal Production
SIC 0219 General Livestock, Except Dairy & Poultry
SIC 0279 Animal Specialties, nec
SIC 0291 General Farms, Primarily Livestock & Animal
          Specialties;
11311   Timber Tract Operations
SIC 0811 Timber Tracts
11321   Forest Nurseries & Gathering of Forest Products
SIC 0831 Forest Nurseries & Gathering of Forest Products
11331   Logging
SIC 2411 Logging

114111 Finfish Fishing
 SIC 0912 Finfish
114112 Shellfish Fishing
 SIC 0913 Shellfish
114119 Other Marine Fishing
 SIC 0919 Miscellaneous Marine Products
11421 Hunting & Trapping
 SIC 0971 Hunting & Trapping, & Game Propagation;
115111 Cotton Ginning
 SIC 0724 Cotton Ginning
115112 Soil Preparation, Planting, & Cultivating
 SIC 0711 Soil Preparation Services
 SIC 0721 Crop Planting, Cultivating, & Protecting
115113 Crop Harvesting, Primarily by Machine
 SIC 0722 Crop Harvesting, Primarily by Machine
115114 Other Postharvest Crop Activities
 SIC 0723 Crop Preparation Services For Market, Except Cotton
    Ginning
115115 Farm Labor Contractors & Crew Leaders
 SIC 0761 Farm Labor Contractors & Crew Leaders
115116 Farm Management Services
 SIC 0762 Farm Management Services
11521 Support Activities for Animal Production
 SIC 0751 Livestock Services, Except Veterinary
 SIC 0752 Animal Specialty Services, Except Veterinary
 SIC 7699 Repair Services, nec
11531 Support Activities for Forestry
 SIC 0851 Forestry Services

MINING

211111 Crude Petroleum & Natural Gas Extraction
 SIC 1311 Crude Petroleum & Natural Gas
211112 Natural Gas Liquid Extraction
 SIC 1321 Natural Gas Liquids
212111 Bituminous Coal & Lignite Surface Mining
 SIC 1221 Bituminous Coal & Lignite Surface Mining
212112 Bituminous Coal Underground Mining
 SIC 1222 Bituminous Coal Underground Mining
212113 Anthracite Mining
 SIC 1231 Anthracite Mining
21221 Iron Ore Mining
 SIC 1011 Iron Ores
212221 Gold Ore Mining
 SIC 1041 Gold Ores
212222 Silver Ore Mining
 SIC 1044 Silver Ores
212231 Lead Ore & Zinc Ore Mining
 SIC 1031 Lead & Zinc Ores
212234 Copper Ore & Nickel Ore Mining
 SIC 1021 Copper Ores
212291 Uranium-Radium-Vanadium Ore Mining
 SIC 1094 Uranium-Radium-Vanadium Ores
212299 All Other Metal Ore Mining
 SIC 1061 Ferroalloy Ores, Except Vanadium
 SIC 1099 Miscellaneous Metal Ores, nec
212311 Dimension Stone Mining & Quarrying
 SIC 1411 Dimension Stone
212312 Crushed & Broken Limestone Mining & Quarrying
 SIC 1422 Crushed & Broken Limestone
212313 Crushed & Broken Granite Mining & Quarrying
 SIC 1423 Crushed & Broken Granite

212319 Other Crushed & Broken Stone Mining & Quarrying
 SIC 1429 Crushed & Broken Stone, nec
 SIC 1499 Miscellaneous Nonmetallic Minerals, Except Fuels
212321 Construction Sand & Gravel Mining
 SIC 1442 Construction Sand & Gravel
212322 Industrial Sand Mining
 SIC 1446 Industrial Sand
212324 Kaolin & Ball Clay Mining
 SIC 1455 Kaolin & Ball Clay
212325 Clay & Ceramic & Refractory Minerals Mining
 SIC 1459 Clay, Ceramic, & Refractory Minerals, nec
212391 Potash, Soda, & Borate Mineral Mining
 SIC 1474 Potash, Soda, & Borate Minerals
212392 Phosphate Rock Mining
 SIC 1475 Phosphate Rock
212393 Other Chemical & Fertilizer Mineral Mining
 SIC 1479 Chemical & Fertilizer Mineral Mining, nec
212399 All Other Nonmetallic Mineral Mining
 SIC 1499 Miscellaneous Nonmetallic Minerals, Except Fuels
213111 Drilling Oil & Gas Wells
 SIC 1381 Drilling Oil & Gas Wells
213112 Support Activities for Oil & Gas Operations
 SIC 1382 Oil & Gas Field Exploration Services
 SIC 1389 Oil & Gas Field Services, nec
213113 Other Gas & Field Support Activities
 SIC 1389 Oil & Gas Field Services, nec
213114 Support Activities for Coal Mining
 SIC 1241 Coal Mining Services
213115 Support Activities for Metal Mining
 SIC 1081 Metal Mining Services
**213116 Support Activities for Nonmetallic Minerals, Except
    Fuels**
 SIC 1481 Nonmetallic Minerals Services, Except Fuels

UTILITIES

221111 Hydroelectric Power Generation
 SIC 4911 Electric Services
 SIC 4931 Electric & Other Services Combined
 SIC 4939 Combination Utilities, nec
221112 Fossil Fuel Electric Power Generation
 SIC 4911 Electric Services
 SIC 4931 Electric & Other Services Combined
 SIC 4939 Combination Utilities, nec
221113 Nuclear Electric Power Generation
 SIC 4911 Electric Services
 SIC 4931 Electric & Other Services Combined
 SIC 4939 Combination Utilities, nec
221119 Other Electric Power Generation
 SIC 4911 Electric Services
 SIC 4931 Electric & Other Services Combined
 SIC 4939 Combination Utilities, nec
221121 Electric Bulk Power Transmission & Control
 SIC 4911 Electric Services
 SIC 4931 Electric & Other Services Combined
 SIC 4939 Combination Utilities, NEC
221122 Electric Power Distribution
 SIC 4911 Electric Services
 SIC 4931 Electric & Other Services Combined
 SIC 4939 Combination Utilities, nec
22121 Natural Gas Distribution
 SIC 4923 Natural Gas Transmission & Distribution
 SIC 4924 Natural Gas Distribution

SIC 4925 Mixed, Manufactured, or Liquefied Petroleum Gas Production and/or Distribution
SIC 4931 Electronic & Other Services Combined
SIC 4932 Gas & Other Services Combined
SIC 4939 Combination Utilities, nec
22131 Water Supply & Irrigation Systems
SIC 4941 Water Supply
SIC 4971 Irrigation Systems
22132 Sewage Treatment Facilities
SIC 4952 Sewerage Systems
22133 Steam & Air-Conditioning Supply
SIC 4961 Steam & Air-Conditioning Supply

CONSTRUCTION

23311 Land Subdivision & Land Development
SIC 6552 Land Subdividers & Developers, Except Cemeteries
23321 Single Family Housing Construction
SIC 1521 General contractors-Single-Family Houses
SIC 1531 Operative Builders
23322 Multifamily Housing Construction
SIC 1522 General Contractors-Residential Building, Other Than Single-Family
SIC 1531 Operative Builders
23331 Manufacturing & Industrial Building Construction
SIC 1531 Operative Builders
SIC 1541 General Contractors-Industrial Buildings & Warehouses
23332 Commercial & Institutional Building Construction
SIC 1522 General Contractors-Residential Building Other than Single-Family
SIC 1531 Operative Builders
SIC 1541 General Contractors-Industrial Buildings & Warehouses
SIC 1542 General Contractor-Nonresidential Buildings, Other than Industrial Buildings & Warehouses
23411 Highway & Street Construction
SIC 1611 Highway & Street Construction, Except Elevated Highways
23412 Bridge & Tunnel Construction
SIC 1622 Bridge, Tunnel, & Elevated Highway Construction
2349 Other Heavy Construction
23491 Water, Sewer, & Pipeline Construction
SIC 1623 Water, Sewer, Pipeline, & Communications & Power Line Construction
23492 Power & Communication Transmission Line Construction
SIC 1623 Water, Sewer, Pipelines, & Communications & Power Line Construction
23493 Industrial Nonbuilding Structure Construction
SIC 1629 Heavy Construction, nec
23499 All Other Heavy Construction
SIC 1629 Heavy Construction, nec
SIC 7353 Construction Equipment Rental & Leasing
23511 Plumbing, Heating & Air-Conditioning Contractors
SIC 1711 Plumbing, Heating & Air-Conditioning
23521 Painting & Wall Covering Contractors
SIC 1721 Painting & Paper Hanging
SIC 1799 Special Trade Contractors, nec
23531 Electrical Contractors
SIC 1731 Electrical Work

23541 Masonry & Stone Contractors
SIC 1741 Masonry, Stone Setting & Other Stone Work
23542 Drywall, Plastering, Acoustical & Insulation Contractors
SIC 1742 Plastering, Drywall, Acoustical, & Insulation Work
SIC 1743 Terrazzo, Tile, Marble & Mosaic work
SIC 1771 Concrete Work
23543 Tile, Marble, Terrazzo & Mosaic Contractors
SIC 1743 Terrazzo, Tile, Marble, & Mosaic Work
23551 Carpentry Contractors
SIC 1751 Carpentry Work
23552 Floor Laying & Other Floor Contractors
SIC 1752 Floor Laying & Other Floor Work, nec
23561 Roofing, Siding & Sheet Metal Contractors
SIC 1761 Roofing, Siding, & Sheet Metal Work
23571 Concrete Contractors
SIC 1771 Concrete Work
23581 Water Well Drilling Contractors
SIC 1781 Water Well Drilling
23591 Structural Steel Erection Contractors
SIC 1791 Structural Steel Erection
23592 Glass & Glazing Contractors
SIC 1793 Glass & Glazing Work
SIC 1799 Specialty Trade Contractors, nec
23593 Excavation Contractors
SIC 1794 Excavation Work
23594 Wrecking & Demolition Contractors
SIC 1795 Wrecking & Demolition Work
23595 Building Equipment & Other Machinery Installation Contractors
SIC 1796 Installation of Erection of Building Equipment, nec
23599 All Other Special Trade Contractors
SIC 1799 Special Trade Contractors, nec

FOOD MANUFACTURING

311111 Dog & Cat Food Manufacturing
SIC 2047 Dog & Cat Food
311119 Other Animal Food Manufacturing
SIC 2048 Prepared Feeds & Feed Ingredients for Animals & Fowls, Except Dogs & Cats
311211 Flour Milling
SIC 2034 Dehydrated Fruits, Vegetables & Soup Mixes
SIC 2041 Flour & Other Grain Mill Products
311212 Rice Milling
SIC 2044 Rice Milling
311213 Malt Manufacturing
SIC 2083 Malt
311221 Wet Corn Milling
SIC 2046 Wet Corn Milling
311222 Soybean Processing
SIC 2075 Soybean Oil Mills
SIC 2079 Shortening, Table Oils, Margarine, & Other Edible Fats & Oils, nec
311223 Other Oilseed Processing
SIC 2074 Cottonseed Oil Mills
SIC 2079 Shortening, Table Oils, Margarine & Other Edible Fats & Oils, nec
SIC 2076 Vegetable Oil Mills, Except Corn, Cottonseed, & Soybean
311225 Edible Fats & Oils Manufacturing
SIC 2077 Animal & Marine Fats & Oil, nec
SIC 2074 Cottonseed Oil Mills
SIC 2075 Soybean Oil Mills

SIC 2076 Vegetable Oil Mills, Except Corn, Cottonseed, &
Soybean
SIC 2079 Shortening, Table Oils, Margarine, & Other Edible
Fats & Oils, nec
31123   Breakfast Cereal Manufacturing
SIC 2043 Cereal Breakfast Foods
311311 Sugarcane Mills
SIC 2061 Cane Sugar, Except Refining
311312 Cane Sugar Refining
SIC 2062 Cane Sugar Refining
311313 Beet Sugar Manufacturing
SIC 2063 Beet Sugar
**31132   Chocolate & Confectionery Manufacturing from Cacao
Beans**
SIC 2066 Chocolate & Cocoa Products
31133   Confectionery Manufacturing from Purchased Chocolate
SIC 2064 Candy & Other Confectionery Products
31134   Non-Chocolate Confectionery Manufacturing
SIC 2064 Candy & Other Confectionery Products
SIC 2067 Chewing Gum
SIC 2099 Food Preparations, nec
311411 Frozen Fruit, Juice & Vegetable Processing
SIC 2037 Frozen Fruits, Fruit Juices, & Vegetables
311412 Frozen Specialty Food Manufacturing
SIC 2038 Frozen Specialties, NEC
311421 Fruit & Vegetable Canning
SIC 2033 Canned Fruits, Vegetables, Preserves, Jams, & Jellies
SIC 2035 Pickled Fruits & Vegetables, Vegetable Sauces, &
Seasonings & Salad Dressings
311422 Specialty Canning
SIC 2032 Canned Specialties
311423 Dried & Dehydrated Food Manufacturing
SIC 2034 Dried & Dehydrated Fruits, Vegetables & Soup
Mixes
SIC 2099 Food Preparation, nec
311511 Fluid Milk Manufacturing
SIC 2026 Fluid Milk
311512 Creamery Butter Manufacturing
SIC 2021 Creamery Butter
311513 Cheese Manufacturing
SIC 2022 Natural, Processed, & Imitation Cheese
311514 Dry, Condensed, & Evaporated Milk Manufacturing
SIC 2023 Dry, Condensed & Evaporated Dairy Products
31152   Ice Cream & Frozen Dessert Manufacturing
SIC 2024 Ice Cream & Frozen Desserts
311611 Animal Slaughtering
SIC 0751 Livestock Services, Except Veterinary
SIC 2011 Meat Packing Plants
SIC 2048 Prepared Feeds & Feed Ingredients for Animals &
Fowls, Except Dogs & Cats
311612 Meat Processed from Carcasses
SIC 2013 Sausages & Other Prepared Meats
SIC 5147 Meat & Meat Products
311613 Rendering & Meat By-product Processing
SIC 2077 Animal & Marine Fats & Oils
311615 Poultry Processing
SIC 2015 Poultry Slaughtering & Processing
311711 Seafood Canning
SIC 2077 Animal & Marine Fats & Oils
SIC 2091 Canned & Cured Fish & Seafood
311712 Fresh & Frozen Seafood Processing
SIC 2077 Animal & Marine Fats & Oils
SIC 2092 Prepared Fresh or Frozen Fish & Seafood

311811 Retail Bakeries
SIC 5461 Retail Bakeries
311812 Commercial Bakeries
SIC 2051 Bread & Other Bakery Products, Except Cookies &
Crackers
SIC 2052 Cookies & Crackers
311813 Frozen Bakery Product Manufacturing
SIC 2053 Frozen Bakery Products, Except Bread
311821 Cookie & Cracker Manufacturing
SIC 2052 Cookies & Crackers
**311822 Flour Mixes & Dough Manufacturing from Purchased
Flour**
SIC 2045 Prepared Flour Mixes & Doughs
311823 Pasta Manufacturing
SIC 2098 Macaroni, Spaghetti, Vermicelli & Noodles
31183   Tortilla Manufacturing
SIC 2099 Food Preparations, nec
311911 Roasted Nuts & Peanut Butter Manufacturing
SIC 2068 Salted & Roasted Nuts & Seeds
SIC 2099 Food Preparations, nec
311919 Other Snack Food Manufacturing
SIC 2052 Cookies & Crackers
SIC 2096 Potato Chips, Corn Chips, & Similar Snacks
31192   Coffee & Tea Manufacturing
SIC 2043 Cereal Breakfast Foods
SIC 2095 Roasted Coffee
SIC 2099 Food Preparations, nec
31193   Flavoring Syrup & Concentrate Manufacturing
SIC 2087 Flavoring Extracts & Flavoring Syrups
**311941 Mayonnaise, Dressing & Other Prepared Sauce
Manufacturing**
SIC 2035 Pickled Fruits & Vegetables, Vegetable Seasonings, &
Sauces & Salad Dressings
SIC 2099 Food Preparations, nec
311942 Spice & Extract Manufacturing
SIC 2087 Flavoring Extracts & Flavoring Syrups
SIC 2095 Roasted Coffee
SIC 2099 Food Preparations, nec
SIC 2899 Chemical Preparations, nec
311991 Perishable Prepared Food Manufacturing
SIC 2099 Food Preparations, nec
311999 All Other Miscellaneous Food Manufacturing
SIC 2015 Poultry Slaughtering & Processing
SIC 2032 Canned Specialties
SIC 2087 Flavoring Extracts & Flavoring Syrups
SIC 2099 Food Preparations, nec

BEVERAGE & TOBACCO PRODUCT MANUFACTURING

312111 Soft Drink Manufacturing
SIC 2086 Bottled & Canned Soft Drinks & Carbonated Water
312112 Bottled Water Manufacturing
SIC 2086 Bottled & Canned Soft Drinks & Carbonated Water
312113 Ice Manufacturing
SIC 2097 Manufactured Ice
31212   Breweries
SIC 2082 Malt Beverages
31213   Wineries
SIC 2084 Wines, Brandy, & Brandy Spirits
31214   Distilleries
SIC 2085 Distilled & Blended Liquors

31221 Tobacco Stemming & Redrying
SIC 2141 Tobacco Stemming & Redrying
312221 Cigarette Manufacturing
SIC 2111 Cigarettes
312229 Other Tobacco Product Manufacturing
SIC 2121 Cigars
SIC 2131 Chewing & Smoking Tobacco & Snuff
SIC 2141 Tobacco Stemming & Redrying

TEXTILE MILLS

313111 Yarn Spinning Mills
SIC 2281 Yarn Spinning Mills
SIC 2299 Textile Goods, nec
313112 Yarn Texturing, Throwing & Twisting Mills
SIC 2282 Yarn Texturing, Throwing, Winding Mills
313113 Thread Mills
SIC 2284 Thread Mills
SIC 2299 Textile Goods, NEC
31321 Broadwoven Fabric Mills
SIC 2211 Broadwoven Fabric Mills, Cotton
SIC 2221 Broadwoven Fabric Mills, Manmade Fiber & Silk
SIC 2231 Broadwoven Fabric Mills, Wool
SIC 2299 Textile Goods, nec
313221 Narrow Fabric Mills
SIC 2241 Narrow Fabric & Other Smallware Mills: Cotton,
Wool, Silk & Manmade Fiber
SIC 2299 Textile Goods, nec
313222 Schiffli Machine Embroidery
SIC 2397 Schiffli Machine Embroideries
31323 Nonwoven Fabric Mills
SIC 2297 Nonwoven Fabrics
SIC 2299 Textile Goods, nec
313241 Weft Knit Fabric Mills
SIC 2257 Weft Knit Fabric Mills
SIC 2259 Knitting Mills nec
313249 Other Knit Fabric & Lace Mills
SIC 2258 Lace & Warp Knit Fabric Mills
SIC 2259 Knitting Mills nec
313311 Broadwoven Fabric Finishing Mills
SIC 2231 Broadwoven Fabric Mills, Wool
SIC 2261 Finishers of Broadwoven Fabrics of Cotton
SIC 2262 Finishers of Broadwoven Fabrics of Manmade Fiber
& Silk
SIC 2269 Finishers of Textiles, nec
SIC 5131 Piece Goods & Notions
313312 Textile & Fabric Finishing Mills
SIC 2231 Broadwoven Fabric Mills, Wool
SIC 2257 Weft Knit Fabric Mills
SIC 2258 Lace & Warp Knit Fabric Mills
SIC 2269 Finishers of Textiles, nec
SIC 2282 Yarn Texturizing, Throwing, Twisting, & Winding
Mills
SIC 2284 Thread Mills
SIC 2299 Textile Goods, nec
SIC 5131 Piece Goods & Notions
31332 Fabric Coating Mills
SIC 2295 Coated Fabrics, Not Rubberized
SIC 3069 Fabricated Rubber Products, nec

TEXTILE PRODUCT MILLS

31411 Carpet & Rug Mills
SIC 2273 Carpets & Rugs
314121 Curtain & Drapery Mills
SIC 2391 Curtains & Draperies
SIC 5714 Drapery, Curtain, & Upholstery Stores
314129 Other Household Textile Product Mills
SIC 2392 Housefurnishings, Except Curtains & Draperies
314911 Textile Bag Mills
SIC 2392 Housefurnishings, Except Curtains & Draperies
SIC 2393 Textile Bags
314912 Canvas & Related Product Mills
SIC 2394 Canvas & Related Products
314991 Rope, Cordage & Twine Mills
SIC 2298 Cordage & Twine
314992 Tire Cord & Tire Fabric Mills
SIC 2296 Tire Cord & Fabrics
314999 All Other Miscellaneous Textile Product Mills
SIC 2299 Textile Goods, nec
SIC 2395 Pleating, Decorative & Novelty Stitching, & Tucking
for the Trade
SIC 2396 Automotive Trimmings, Apparel Findings, & Related
Products
SIC 2399 Fabricated Textile Products, nec

APPAREL MANUFACTURING

315111 Sheer Hosiery Mills
SIC 2251 Women's Full-Length & Knee-Length Hosiery,
Except socks
SIC 2252 Hosiery, nec
315119 Other Hosiery & Sock Mills
SIC 2252 Hosiery, nec
315191 Outerwear Knitting Mills
SIC 2253 Knit Outerwear Mills
SIC 2259 Knitting Mills, nec
315192 Underwear & Nightwear Knitting Mills
SIC 2254 Knit Underwear & Nightwear Mills
SIC 2259 Knitting Mills, nec
315211 Men's & Boys' Cut & Sew Apparel Contractors
SIC 2311 Men's & Boys' Suits, Coats, & Overcoats
SIC 2321 Men's & Boys' Shirts, Except Work Shirts
SIC 2322 Men's & Boys' Underwear & Nightwear
SIC 2325 Men's & Boys' Trousers & Slacks
SIC 2326 Men's & Boys' Work Clothing
SIC 2329 Men's & Boys' Clothing, nec
SIC 2341 Women's, Misses', Children's, & Infants' Underwear
& Nightwear
SIC 2361 Girls', Children's, & Infants' Dresses, Blouses &
Shirts
SIC 2369 Girls', Children's, & Infants' Outerwear, nec
SIC 2384 Robes & Dressing Gowns
SIC 2385 Waterproof Outerwear
SIC 2389 Apparel & Accessories, nec
SIC 2395 Pleating, Decorative & Novelty Stitching, & Tucking
for the Trade
315212 Women's & Girls' Cut & Sew Apparel Contractors
SIC 2331 Women's, Misses', & Juniors' Blouses & Shirts
SIC 2335 Women's, Misses' & Juniors' Dresses
SIC 2337 Women's, Misses', & Juniors' Suits, Skirts, & Coats
SIC 2339 Women's, Misses', & Juniors' Outerwear, nec

SIC 2341 Women's, Misses', Children's, & Infants' Underwear & Nightwear
SIC 2342 Brassieres, Girdles, & Allied Garments
SIC 2361 Girls', Children's, & Infants' Dresses, Blouses, & Shirts
SIC 2369 Girls', Children's, & Infants' Outerwear, nec
SIC 2384 Robes & Dressing Gowns
SIC 2385 Waterproof Outerwear
SIC 2389 Apparel & Accessories, nec
SIC 2395 Pleating, Decorative & Novelty Stitching, & Tucking for the Trade
315221 Men's & Boys' Cut & Sew Underwear & Nightwear Manufacturing
SIC 2322 Men's & Boys' Underwear & Nightwear
SIC 2341 Women's, Misses', Children's, & Infants' Underwear & Nightwear
SIC 2369 Girls', Children's, & Infants' Outerwear, nec
SIC 2384 Robes & Dressing Gowns
315222 Men's & Boys' Cut & Sew Suit, Coat & Overcoat Manufacturing
SIC 2311 Men's & Boys' Suits, Coats, & Overcoats
SIC 2369 Girls', Children's, & Infants' Outerwear, nec
SIC 2385 Waterproof Outerwear
315223 Men's & Boys' Cut & Sew Shirt Manufacturing
SIC 2321 Men's & Boys' Shirts, Except Work Shirts
SIC 2361 Girls', Children's, & Infants' Dresses, Blouses, & Shirts
315224 Men's & Boys' Cut & Sew Trouser, Slack & Jean Manufacturing
SIC 2325 Men's & Boys' Trousers & Slacks
SIC 2369 Girls', Children's, & Infants' Outerwear, NEC
315225 Men's & Boys' Cut & Sew Work Clothing Manufacturing
SIC 2326 Men's & Boys' Work Clothing
315228 Men's & Boys' Cut & Sew Other Outerwear Manufacturing
SIC 2329 Men's & Boys' Clothing, nec
SIC 2369 Girls', Children's, & Infants' Outerwear, nec
SIC 2385 Waterproof Outerwear
315231 Women's & Girls' Cut & Sew Lingerie, Loungewear & Nightwear Manufacturing
SIC 2341 Women's, Misses', Children's, & Infants' Underwear & Nightwear
SIC 2342 Brassieres, Girdles, & Allied Garments
SIC 2369 Girls', Children's, & Infants' Outerwear, nec
SIC 2384 Robes & Dressing Gowns
SIC 2389 Apparel & Accessories, NEC
315232 Women's & Girls' Cut & Sew Blouse & Shirt Manufacturing
SIC 2331 Women's, Misses', & Juniors' Blouses & Shirts
SIC 2361 Girls', Children's, & Infants' Dresses, Blouses & Shirts
315233 Women's & Girls' Cut & Sew Dress Manufacturing
SIC 2335 Women's, Misses', & Juniors' Dresses
SIC 2361 Girls', Children's, & Infants' Dresses, Blouses & Shirts
315234 Women's & Girls' Cut & Sew Suit, Coat, Tailored Jacket & Skirt Manufacturing
SIC 2337 Women's, Misses', & Juniors' Suits, Skirts, & Coats
SIC 2369 Girls', Children's, & Infants' Outerwear, nec
SIC 2385 Waterproof Outerwear
315238 Women's & Girls' Cut & Sew Other Outerwear Manufacturing
SIC 2339 Women's, Misses', & Juniors' Outerwear, nec
SIC 2369 Girls', Children's, & Infants' Outerwear, nec

SIC 2385 Waterproof Outerwear
315291 Infants' Cut & Sew Apparel Manufacturing
SIC 2341 Women's, Misses', Children's, & Infants' Underwear & Nightwear
SIC 2361 Girls', Children's, & Infants' Dresses, Blouses, & Shirts
SIC 2369 Girls', Children's, & Infants' Outerwear, nec
SIC 2385 Waterproof Outerwear
315292 Fur & Leather Apparel Manufacturing
SIC 2371 Fur Goods
SIC 2386 Leather & Sheep-lined Clothing
315299 All Other Cut & Sew Apparel Manufacturing
SIC 2329 Men's & Boys' Outerwear, nec
SIC 2339 Women's, Misses', & Juniors' Outerwear, nec
SIC 2389 Apparel & Accessories, nec
315991 Hat, Cap & Millinery Manufacturing
SIC 2353 Hats, Caps, & Millinery
315992 Glove & Mitten Manufacturing
SIC 2381 Dress & Work Gloves, Except Knit & All-Leather
SIC 3151 Leather Gloves & Mittens
315993 Men's & Boys' Neckwear Manufacturing
SIC 2323 Men's & Boys' Neckwear
315999 Other Apparel Accessories & Other Apparel Manufacturing
SIC 2339 Women's, Misses', & Juniors' Outerwear, nec
SIC 2385 Waterproof Outerwear
SIC 2387 Apparel Belts
SIC 2389 Apparel & Accessories, nec
SIC 2396 Automotive Trimmings, Apparel Findings, & Related Products
SIC 2399 Fabricated Textile Products, nec

LEATHER & ALLIED PRODUCT MANUFACTURING

31611 Leather & Hide Tanning & Finishing
SIC 3111 Leather Tanning & Finishing
SIC 3999 Manufacturing Industries, nec
316211 Rubber & Plastics Footwear Manufacturing
SIC 3021 Rubber & Plastics Footwear
316212 House Slipper Manufacturing
SIC 3142 House Slippers
316213 Men's Footwear Manufacturing
SIC 3143 Men's Footwear, Except Athletic
316214 Women's Footwear Manufacturing
SIC 3144 Women's Footwear, Except Athletic
316219 Other Footwear Manufacturing
SIC 3149 Footwear Except Rubber, NEC
316991 Luggage Manufacturing
SIC 3161 Luggage
316992 Women's Handbag & Purse Manufacturing
SIC 3171 Women's Handbags & Purses
316993 Personal Leather Good Manufacturing
SIC 3172 Personal Leather Goods, Except Women's Handbags & Purses
316999 All Other Leather Good Manufacturing
SIC 3131 Boot & Shoe Cut Stock & Findings
SIC 3199 Leather Goods, nec

WOOD PRODUCT MANUFACTURING

321113 Sawmills
SIC 2421 Sawmills & Planing Mills, General
SIC 2429 Special Product Sawmills, nec

321114 Wood Preservation
SIC 2491 Wood Preserving

321211 Hardwood Veneer & Plywood Manufacturing
SIC 2435 Hardwood Veneer & Plywood

321212 Softwood Veneer & Plywood Manufacturing
SIC 2436 Softwood Veneer & Plywood

321213 Engineered Wood Member Manufacturing
SIC 2439 Structural Wood Members, nec

321214 Truss Manufacturing
SIC 2439 Structural Wood Members, nec

321219 Reconstituted Wood Product Manufacturing
SIC 2493 Reconstituted Wood Products

321911 Wood Window & Door Manufacturing
SIC 2431 Millwork

321912 Hardwood Dimension Mills
SIC 2426 Hardwood Dimension & Flooring Mills

321913 Softwood Cut Stock, Resawing Lumber, & Planing
SIC 2421 Sawmills & Planing Mills, General
SIC 2429 Special Product Sawmills, nec
SIC 2439 Structural Wood Members, nec

321914 Other Millwork
SIC 2421 Sawmills & Planing Mills, General
SIC 2426 Hardwood Dimension & Flooring Mills
SIC 2431 Millwork

32192 Wood Container & Pallet Manufacturing
SIC 2441 Nailed & Lock Corner Wood Boxes & Shook
SIC 2448 Wood Pallets & Skids
SIC 2449 Wood Containers, NEC
SIC 2499 Wood Products, nec

321991 Manufactured Home Manufacturing
SIC 2451 Mobile Homes

321992 Prefabricated Wood Building Manufacturing
SIC 2452 Prefabricated Wood Buildings & Components

321999 All Other Miscellaneous Wood Product Manufacturing
SIC 2426 Hardwood Dimension & Flooring Mills
SIC 2499 Wood Products, nec
SIC 3131 Boot & Shoe Cut Stock & Findings
SIC 3999 Manufacturing Industries, nec
SIC 2421 Sawmills & Planing Mills, General
SIC 2429 Special Product Sawmills, nec

PAPER MANUFACTURING

32211 Pulp Mills
SIC 2611 Pulp Mills

322121 Paper Mills
SIC 2611 Pulp Mills
SIC 2621 Paper Mills

322122 Newsprint Mills
SIC 2621 Paper Mills

32213 Paperboard Mills
SIC 2611 Pulp Mills
SIC 2631 Paperboard Mills

322211 Corrugated & Solid Fiber Box Manufacturing
SIC 2653 Corrugated & Solid Fiber Boxes

322212 Folding Paperboard Box Manufacturing
SIC 2657 Folding Paperboard Boxes, Including Sanitary

322213 Setup Paperboard Box Manufacturing
SIC 2652 Setup Paperboard Boxes

322214 Fiber Can, Tube, Drum, & Similar Products Manufacturing
SIC 2655 Fiber Cans, Tubes, Drums, & Similar Products

322215 Non-Folding Sanitary Food Container Manufacturing
SIC 2656 Sanitary Food Containers, Except Folding
SIC 2679 Converted Paper & Paperboard Products, NEC

322221 Coated & Laminated Packaging Paper & Plastics Film Manufacturing
SIC 2671 Packaging Paper & Plastics Film, Coated & Laminated

322222 Coated & Laminated Paper Manufacturing
SIC 2672 Coated & Laminated Paper, nec
SIC 2679 Converted Paper & Paperboard Products, nec

322223 Plastics, Foil, & Coated Paper Bag Manufacturing
SIC 2673 Plastics, Foil, & Coated Paper Bags

322224 Uncoated Paper & Multiwall Bag Manufacturing
SIC 2674 Uncoated Paper & Multiwall Bags

322225 Laminated Aluminum Foil Manufacturing for Flexible Packaging Uses
SIC 3497 Metal Foil & Leaf

322231 Die-Cut Paper & Paperboard Office Supplies Manufacturing
SIC 2675 Die-Cut Paper & Paperboard & Cardboard
SIC 2679 Converted Paper & Paperboard Products, nec

322232 Envelope Manufacturing
SIC 2677 Envelopes

322233 Stationery, Tablet, & Related Product Manufacturing
SIC 2678 Stationery, Tablets, & Related Products

322291 Sanitary Paper Product Manufacturing
SIC 2676 Sanitary Paper Products

322292 Surface-Coated Paperboard Manufacturing
SIC 2675 Die-Cut Paper & Paperboard & Cardboard

322298 All Other Converted Paper Product Manufacturing
SIC 2675 Die-Cut Paper & Paperboard & Cardboard
SIC 2679 Converted Paper & Paperboard Products, NEC

PRINTING & RELATED SUPPORT ACTIVITIES

323110 Commercial Lithographic Printing
SIC 2752 Commercial Printing, Lithographic
SIC 2771 Greeting Cards
SIC 2782 Blankbooks, Loose-leaf Binders & Devices
SIC 3999 Manufacturing Industries, nec

323111 Commercial Gravure Printing
SIC 2754 Commercial Printing, Gravure
SIC 2771 Greeting Cards
SIC 2782 Blankbooks, Loose-leaf Binders & Devices
SIC 3999 Manufacturing Industries, nec

323112 Commercial Flexographic Printing
SIC 2759 Commercial Printing, NEC
SIC 2771 Greeting Cards
SIC 2782 Blankbooks, Loose-leaf Binders & Devices
SIC 3999 Manufacturing Industries, nec

323113 Commercial Screen Printing
SIC 2396 Automotive Trimmings, Apparel Findings, & Related Products
SIC 2759 Commercial Printing, nec
SIC 2771 Greeting Cards
SIC 2782 Blankbooks, Loose-leaf Binders & Devices
SIC 3999 Manufacturing Industries, nec

323114 Quick Printing
SIC 2752 Commercial Printing, Lithographic
SIC 2759 Commercial Printing, nec
323115 Digital Printing
SIC 2759 Commercial Printing, nec
323116 Manifold Business Form Printing
SIC 2761 Manifold Business Forms
323117 Book Printing
SIC 2732 Book Printing
323118 Blankbook, Loose-leaf Binder & Device Manufacturing
SIC 2782 Blankbooks, Loose-leaf Binders & Devices
323119 Other Commercial Printing
SIC 2759 Commercial Printing, nec
SIC 2771 Greeting Cards
SIC 2782 Blankbooks, Loose-leaf Binders & Devices
SIC 3999 Manufacturing Industries, nec
323121 Tradebinding & Related Work
SIC 2789 Bookbinding & Related Work
323122 Prepress Services
SIC 2791 Typesetting
SIC 2796 Platemaking & Related Services

PETROLEUM & COAL PRODUCTS MANUFACTURING

32411 Petroleum Refineries
SIC 2911 Petroleum Refining
324121 Asphalt Paving Mixture & Block Manufacturing
SIC 2951 Asphalt Paving Mixtures & Blocks
324122 Asphalt Shingle & Coating Materials Manufacturing
SIC 2952 Asphalt Felts & Coatings
324191 Petroleum Lubricating Oil & Grease Manufacturing
SIC 2992 Lubricating Oils & Greases
324199 All Other Petroleum & Coal Products Manufacturing
SIC 2999 Products of Petroleum & Coal, nec
SIC 3312 Blast Furnaces & Steel Mills

CHEMICAL MANUFACTURING

32511 Petrochemical Manufacturing
SIC 2865 Cyclic Organic Crudes & Intermediates, & Organic
         Dyes & Pigments
SIC 2869 Industrial Organic Chemicals, nec
32512 Industrial Gas Manufacturing
SIC 2813 Industrial Gases
SIC 2869 Industrial Organic Chemicals, nec
325131 Inorganic Dye & Pigment Manufacturing
SIC 2816 Inorganic Pigments
SIC 2819 Industrial Inorganic Chemicals, nec
325132 Organic Dye & Pigment Manufacturing
SIC 2865 Cyclic Organic Crudes & Intermediates, & Organic
         Dyes & Pigments
325181 Alkalies & Chlorine Manufacturing
SIC 2812 Alkalies & Chlorine
325182 Carbon Black Manufacturing
SIC 2816 Inorganic pigments
SIC 2895 Carbon Black
325188 All Other Basic Inorganic Chemical Manufacturing
SIC 2819 Industrial Inorganic Chemicals, nec
SIC 2869 Industrial Organic Chemicals, nec

325191 Gum & Wood Chemical Manufacturing
SIC 2861 Gum & Wood Chemicals
325192 Cyclic Crude & Intermediate Manufacturing
SIC 2865 Cyclic Organic Crudes & Intermediates & Organic
         Dyes & Pigments
325193 Ethyl Alcohol Manufacturing
SIC 2869 Industrial Organic Chemicals
325199 All Other Basic Organic Chemical Manufacturing
SIC 2869 Industrial Organic Chemicals, nec
SIC 2899 Chemical & Chemical Preparations, nec
325211 Plastics Material & Resin Manufacturing
SIC 2821 Plastics Materials, Synthetic & Resins, &
         Nonvulcanizable Elastomers
325212 Synthetic Rubber Manufacturing
SIC 2822 Synthetic Rubber
325221 Cellulosic Manmade Fiber Manufacturing
SIC 2823 Cellulosic Manmade Fibers
325222 Noncellulosic Organic Fiber Manufacturing
SIC 2824 Manmade Organic Fibers, Except Cellulosic
325311 Nitrogenous Fertilizer Manufacturing
SIC 2873 Nitrogenous Fertilizers
325312 Phosphatic Fertilizer Manufacturing
SIC 2874 Phosphatic Fertilizers
325314 Fertilizer Manufacturing
SIC 2875 Fertilizers, Mixing Only
32532 Pesticide & Other Agricultural Chemical Manufacturing
SIC 2879 Pesticides & Agricultural Chemicals, nec
325411 Medicinal & Botanical Manufacturing
SIC 2833 Medicinal Chemicals & Botanical Products
325412 Pharmaceutical Preparation Manufacturing
SIC 2834 Pharmaceutical Preparations
SIC 2835 In-Vitro & In-Vivo Diagnostic Substances
325413 In-Vitro Diagnostic Substance Manufacturing
SIC 2835 In-Vitro & In-Vivo Diagnostic Substances
325414 Biological Product Manufacturing
SIC 2836 Biological Products, Except Diagnostic Substance
32551 Paint & Coating Manufacturing
SIC 2851 Paints, Varnishes, Lacquers, Enamels & Allied
         Products
SIC 2899 Chemicals & Chemical Preparations, nec
32552 Adhesive & Sealant Manufacturing
SIC 2891 Adhesives & Sealants
325611 Soap & Other Detergent Manufacturing
SIC 2841 Soaps & Other Detergents, Except Specialty Cleaners
SIC 2844 Toilet Preparations
325612 Polish & Other Sanitation Good Manufacturing
SIC 2842 Specialty Cleaning, Polishing, & Sanitary Preparations
325613 Surface Active Agent Manufacturing
SIC 2843 Surface Active Agents, Finishing Agents, Sulfonated
         Oils, & Assistants
32562 Toilet Preparation Manufacturing
SIC 2844 Perfumes, Cosmetics, & Other Toilet Preparations
32591 Printing Ink Manufacturing
SIC 2893 Printing Ink
32592 Explosives Manufacturing
SIC 2892 Explosives
325991 Custom Compounding of Purchased Resin
SIC 3087 Custom Compounding of Purchased Plastics Resin
**325992 Photographic Film, Paper, Plate & Chemical
         Manufacturing**
SIC 3861 Photographic Equipment & Supplies

325998 All Other Miscellaneous Chemical Product Manufacturing
SIC 2819 Industrial Inorganic Chemicals, nec
SIC 2899 Chemicals & Chemical Preparations, nec
SIC 3952 Lead Pencils & Art Goods
SIC 3999 Manufacturing Industries, nec

PLASTICS & RUBBER PRODUCTS MANUFACTURING

326111 Unsupported Plastics Bag Manufacturing
SIC 2673 Plastics, Foil, & Coated Paper Bags

326112 Unsupported Plastics Packaging Film & Sheet Manufacturing
SIC 2671 Packaging Paper & Plastics Film, Coated, & Laminated

326113 Unsupported Plastics Film & Sheet Manufacturing
SIC 3081 Unsupported Plastics Film & Sheets

326121 Unsupported Plastics Profile Shape Manufacturing
SIC 3082 Unsupported Plastics Profile Shapes
SIC 3089 Plastics Product, nec

326122 Plastics Pipe & Pipe Fitting Manufacturing
SIC 3084 Plastics Pipe
SIC 3089 Plastics Products, nec

32613 Laminated Plastics Plate, Sheet & Shape Manufacturing
SIC 3083 Laminated Plastics Plate, Sheet & Profile Shapes

32614 Polystyrene Foam Product Manufacturing
SIC 3086 Plastics Foam Products

32615 Urethane & Other Foam Product Manufacturing
SIC 3086 Plastics Foam Products

32616 Plastics Bottle Manufacturing
SIC 3085 Plastics Bottles

326191 Plastics Plumbing Fixture Manufacturing
SIC 3088 Plastics Plumbing Fixtures

326192 Resilient Floor Covering Manufacturing
SIC 3069 Fabricated Rubber Products, nec
SIC 3996 Linoleum, Asphalted-Felt-Base, & Other Hard Surface Floor Coverings, nec

326199 All Other Plastics Product Manufacturing
SIC 3089 Plastics Products, nec
SIC 3999 Manufacturing Industries, nec

326211 Tire Manufacturing
SIC 3011 Tires & Inner Tubes

326212 Tire Retreading
SIC 7534 Tire Retreading & Repair Shops

32622 Rubber & Plastics Hoses & Belting Manufacturing
SIC 3052 Rubber & Plastics Hose & Belting

326291 Rubber Product Manufacturing for Mechanical Use
SIC 3061 Molded, Extruded, & Lathe-Cut Mechanical Rubber Goods

326299 All Other Rubber Product Manufacturing
SIC 3069 Fabricated Rubber Products, nec

NONMETALLIC MINERAL PRODUCT MANUFACTURING

327111 Vitreous China Plumbing Fixture & China & Earthenware Fittings & Bathroom Accessories Manufacturing
SIC 3261 Vitreous China Plumbing Fixtures & China & Earthenware Fittings & Bathroom Accessories

327112 Vitreous China, Fine Earthenware & Other Pottery Product Manufacturing
SIC 3262 Vitreous China Table & Kitchen Articles
SIC 3263 Fine Earthenware Table & Kitchen Articles
SIC 3269 Pottery Products, nec

327113 Porcelain Electrical Supply Manufacturing
SIC 3264 Porcelain Electrical Supplies

327121 Brick & Structural Clay Tile Manufacturing
SIC 3251 Brick & Structural Clay Tile

327122 Ceramic Wall & Floor Tile Manufacturing
SIC 3253 Ceramic Wall & Floor Tile

327123 Other Structural Clay Product Manufacturing
SIC 3259 Structural Clay Products, nec

327124 Clay Refractory Manufacturing
SIC 3255 Clay Refractories

327125 Nonclay Refractory Manufacturing
SIC 3297 Nonclay Refractories

327211 Flat Glass Manufacturing
SIC 3211 Flat Glass

327212 Other Pressed & Blown Glass & Glassware Manufacturing
SIC 3229 Pressed & Blown Glass & Glassware, nec

327213 Glass Container Manufacturing
SIC 3221 Glass Containers

327215 Glass Product Manufacturing Made of Purchased Glass
SIC 3231 Glass Products Made of Purchased Glass

32731 Hydraulic Cement Manufacturing
SIC 3241 Cement, Hydraulic

32732 Ready-Mix Concrete Manufacturing
SIC 3273 Ready-Mixed Concrete

327331 Concrete Block & Brick Manufacturing
SIC 3271 Concrete Block & Brick

327332 Concrete Pipe Manufacturing
SIC 3272 Concrete Products, Except Block & Brick

32739 Other Concrete Product Manufacturing
SIC 3272 Concrete Products, Except Block & Brick

32741 Lime Manufacturing
SIC 3274 Lime

32742 Gypsum & Gypsum Product Manufacturing
SIC 3275 Gypsum Products
SIC 3299 Nonmetallic Mineral Products, nec

32791 Abrasive Product Manufacturing
SIC 3291 Abrasive Products

327991 Cut Stone & Stone Product Manufacturing
SIC 3281 Cut Stone & Stone Products

327992 Ground or Treated Mineral & Earth Manufacturing
SIC 3295 Minerals & Earths, Ground or Otherwise Treated

327993 Mineral Wool Manufacturing
SIC 3296 Mineral Wool

327999 All Other Miscellaneous Nonmetallic Mineral Product Manufacturing
SIC 3272 Concrete Products, Except Block & Brick
SIC 3292 Asbestos Products
SIC 3299 Nonmetallic Mineral Products, nec

PRIMARY METAL MANUFACTURING

331111 Iron & Steel Mills
SIC 3312 Steel Works, Blast Furnaces , & Rolling Mills
SIC 3399 Primary Metal Products, nec

331112 Electrometallurgical Ferroalloy Product Manufacturing
SIC 3313 Electrometallurgical Products, Except Steel

33121 Iron & Steel Pipes & Tubes Manufacturing from Purchased Steel
SIC 3317 Steel Pipe & Tubes

331221 Cold-Rolled Steel Shape Manufacturing
SIC 3316 Cold-Rolled Steel Sheet, Strip & Bars

331222 Steel Wire Drawing
SIC 3315 Steel Wiredrawing & Steel Nails & Spikes

331311 Alumina Refining
SIC 2819 Industrial Inorganic Chemicals, nec

331312 Primary Aluminum Production
SIC 3334 Primary Production of Aluminum

331314 Secondary Smelting & Alloying of Aluminum
SIC 3341 Secondary Smelting & Refining of Nonferrous Metals
SIC 3399 Primary Metal Products, nec

331315 Aluminum Sheet, Plate & Foil Manufacturing
SIC 3353 Aluminum Sheet, Plate, & Foil

331316 Aluminum Extruded Product Manufacturing
SIC 3354 Aluminum Extruded Products

331319 Other Aluminum Rolling & Drawing
SIC 3355 Aluminum Rolling & Drawing, nec
SIC 3357 Drawing & Insulating of Nonferrous Wire

331411 Primary Smelting & Refining of Copper
SIC 3331 Primary Smelting & Refining of Copper

331419 Primary Smelting & Refining of Nonferrous Metal
SIC 3339 Primary Smelting & Refining of Nonferrous Metals, Except Copper & Aluminum

331421 Copper Rolling, Drawing & Extruding
SIC 3351 Rolling, Drawing, & Extruding of Copper

331422 Copper Wire Drawing
SIC 3357 Drawing & Insulating of Nonferrous Wire

331423 Secondary Smelting, Refining, & Alloying of Copper
SIC 3341 Secondary Smelting & Refining of Nonferrous Metals
SIC 3399 Primary Metal Products, nec

331491 Nonferrous Metal Rolling, Drawing & Extruding
SIC 3356 Rolling, Drawing & Extruding of Nonferrous Metals, Except Copper & Aluminum
SIC 3357 Drawing & Insulating of Nonferrous Wire

331492 Secondary Smelting, Refining, & Alloying of Nonferrous Metal
SIC 3313 Electrometallurgical Products, Except Steel
SIC 3341 Secondary Smelting & Reining of Nonferrous Metals
SIC 3399 Primary Metal Products, nec

331511 Iron Foundries
SIC 3321 Gray & Ductile Iron Foundries
SIC 3322 Malleable Iron Foundries

331512 Steel Investment Foundries
SIC 3324 Steel Investment Foundries

331513 Steel Foundries,
SIC 3325 Steel Foundries, nec

331521 Aluminum Die-Castings
SIC 3363 Aluminum Die-Castings

331522 Nonferrous Die-Castings
SIC 3364 Nonferrous Die-Castings, Except Aluminum

331524 Aluminum Foundries
SIC 3365 Aluminum Foundries

331525 Copper Foundries
SIC 3366 Copper Foundries

331528 Other Nonferrous Foundries
SIC 3369 Nonferrous Foundries, Except Aluminum & Copper

FABRICATED METAL PRODUCT MANUFACTURING

332111 Iron & Steel Forging
SIC 3462 Iron & Steel Forgings

332112 Nonferrous Forging
SIC 3463 Nonferrous Forgings

332114 Custom Roll Forming
SIC 3449 Miscellaneous Structural Metal Work

332115 Crown & Closure Manufacturing
SIC 3466 Crowns & Closures

332116 Metal Stamping
SIC 3469 Metal Stampings, nec

332117 Powder Metallurgy Part Manufacturing
SIC 3499 Fabricated Metal Products, nec

332211 Cutlery & Flatware Manufacturing
SIC 3421 Cutlery
SIC 3914 Silverware, Plated Ware, & Stainless Steel Ware

332212 Hand & Edge Tool Manufacturing
SIC 3423 Hand & Edge Tools, Except Machine Tools & Handsaws
SIC 3523 Farm Machinery & Equipment
SIC 3524 Lawn & Garden Tractors & Home Lawn & Garden Equipment
SIC 3545 Cutting Tools, Machine Tools Accessories, & Machinist Precision Measuring Devices
SIC 3799 Transportation Equipment, nec
SIC 3999 Manufacturing Industries, nec

332213 Saw Blade & Handsaw Manufacturing
SIC 3425 Saw Blades & Handsaws

332214 Kitchen Utensil, Pot & Pan Manufacturing
SIC 3469 Metal Stampings, nec

332311 Prefabricated Metal Building & Component Manufacturing
SIC 3448 Prefabricated Metal Buildings & Components

332312 Fabricated Structural Metal Manufacturing
SIC 3441 Fabricated Structural Metal
SIC 3449 Miscellaneous Structural Metal Work

332313 Plate Work Manufacturing
SIC 3443 Fabricated Plate Work

332321 Metal Window & Door Manufacturing
SIC 3442 Metal Doors, Sash, Frames, Molding & Trim
SIC 3449 Miscellaneous Structural Metal Work

332322 Sheet Metal Work Manufacturing
SIC 3444 Sheet Metal Work

332323 Ornamental & Architectural Metal Work Manufacturing
SIC 3446 Architectural & Ornamental Metal Work
SIC 3449 Miscellaneous Structural Metal Work
SIC 3523 Farm Machinery & Equipment

33241   Power Boiler & Heat Exchanger Manufacturing
SIC 3443 Fabricated Plate Work

33242   Metal Tank Manufacturing
SIC 3443 Fabricated Plate Work

332431 Metal Can Manufacturing
SIC 3411 Metal Cans

332439 Other Metal Container Manufacturing
SIC 3412 Metal Shipping Barrels, Drums, Kegs, & Pails
SIC 3429 Hardware, nec
SIC 3444 Sheet Metal Work
SIC 3499 Fabricated Metal Products, nec
SIC 3537 Industrial Trucks, Tractors, Trailers, & Stackers

33251   Hardware Manufacturing
SIC 3429 Hardware, nec
SIC 3499 Fabricated Metal Products, nec

332611 Steel Spring Manufacturing
SIC 3493 Steel Springs, Except Wire
332612 Wire Spring Manufacturing
SIC 3495 Wire Springs
332618 Other Fabricated Wire Product Manufacturing
SIC 3315 Steel Wiredrawing & Steel Nails & Spikes
SIC 3399 Primary Metal Products, nec
SIC 3496 Miscellaneous Fabricated Wire Products
33271 Machine Shops
SIC 3599 Industrial & Commercial Machinery & Equipment, nec
332721 Precision Turned Product Manufacturing
SIC 3451 Screw Machine Products
332722 Bolt, Nut, Screw, Rivet & Washer Manufacturing
SIC 3452 Bolts, Nuts, Screws, Rivets, & Washers
332811 Metal Heat Treating
SIC 3398 Metal Heat Treating
332812 Metal Coating, Engraving , & Allied Services to Manufacturers
SIC 3479 Coating, Engraving, & Allied Services, nec
332813 Electroplating, Plating, Polishing, Anodizing & Coloring
SIC 3399 Primary Metal Products, nec
SIC 3471 Electroplating, Plating, Polishing, Anodizing, & Coloring
332911 Industrial Valve Manufacturing
SIC 3491 Industrial Valves
332912 Fluid Power Valve & Hose Fitting Manufacturing
SIC 3492 Fluid Power Valves & Hose Fittings
SIC 3728 Aircraft Parts & Auxiliary Equipment, nec
332913 Plumbing Fixture Fitting & Trim Manufacturing
SIC 3432 Plumbing Fixture Fittings & Trim
332919 Other Metal Valve & Pipe Fitting Manufacturing
SIC 3429 Hardware, nec
SIC 3494 Valves & Pipe Fittings, nec
SIC 3499 Fabricated Metal Products, nec
332991 Ball & Roller Bearing Manufacturing
SIC 3562 Ball & Roller Bearings
332992 Small Arms Ammunition Manufacturing
SIC 3482 Small Arms Ammunition
332993 Ammunition Manufacturing
SIC 3483 Ammunition, Except for Small Arms
332994 Small Arms Manufacturing
SIC 3484 Small Arms
332995 Other Ordnance & Accessories Manufacturing
SIC 3489 Ordnance & Accessories, nec
332996 Fabricated Pipe & Pipe Fitting Manufacturing
SIC 3498 Fabricated Pipe & Pipe Fittings
332997 Industrial Pattern Manufacturing
SIC 3543 Industrial Patterns
332998 Enameled Iron & Metal Sanitary Ware Manufacturing
SIC 3431 Enameled Iron & Metal Sanitary Ware
332999 All Other Miscellaneous Fabricated Metal Product Manufacturing
SIC 3291 Abrasive Products
SIC 3432 Plumbing Fixture Fittings & Trim
SIC 3494 Valves & Pipe Fittings, nec
SIC 3497 Metal Foil & Leaf
SIC 3499 Fabricated Metal Products, NEC
SIC 3537 Industrial Trucks, Tractors, Trailers, & Stackers
SIC 3599 Industrial & Commercial Machinery & Equipment, nec
SIC 3999 Manufacturing Industries, nec

MACHINERY MANUFACTURING

333111 Farm Machinery & Equipment Manufacturing
SIC 3523 Farm Machinery & Equipment
333112 Lawn & Garden Tractor & Home Lawn & Garden Equipment Manufacturing
SIC 3524 Lawn & Garden Tractors & Home Lawn & Garden Equipment
33312 Construction Machinery Manufacturing
SIC 3531 Construction Machinery & Equipment
333131 Mining Machinery & Equipment Manufacturing
SIC 3532 Mining Machinery & Equipment, Except Oil & Gas Field Machinery & Equipment
333132 Oil & Gas Field Machinery & Equipment Manufacturing
SIC 3533 Oil & Gas Field Machinery & Equipment
33321 Sawmill & Woodworking Machinery Manufacturing
SIC 3553 Woodworking Machinery
33322 Rubber & Plastics Industry Machinery Manufacturing
SIC 3559 Special Industry Machinery, nec
333291 Paper Industry Machinery Manufacturing
SIC 3554 Paper Industries Machinery
333292 Textile Machinery Manufacturing
SIC 3552 Textile Machinery
333293 Printing Machinery & Equipment Manufacturing
SIC 3555 Printing Trades Machinery & Equipment
333294 Food Product Machinery Manufacturing
SIC 3556 Food Products Machinery
333295 Semiconductor Machinery Manufacturing
SIC 3559 Special Industry Machinery, nec
333298 All Other Industrial Machinery Manufacturing
SIC 3559 Special Industry Machinery, nec
SIC 3639 Household Appliances, nec
333311 Automatic Vending Machine Manufacturing
SIC 3581 Automatic Vending Machines
333312 Commercial Laundry, Drycleaning & Pressing Machine Manufacturing
SIC 3582 Commercial Laundry, Drycleaning & Pressing Machines
333313 Office Machinery Manufacturing
SIC 3578 Calculating & Accounting Machinery, Except Electronic Computers
SIC 3579 Office Machines, nec
333314 Optical Instrument & Lens Manufacturing
SIC 3827 Optical Instruments & Lenses
333315 Photographic & Photocopying Equipment Manufacturing
SIC 3861 Photographic Equipment & Supplies
333319 Other Commercial & Service Industry Machinery Manufacturing
SIC 3559 Special Industry Machinery, nec
SIC 3589 Service Industry Machinery, nec
SIC 3599 Industrial & Commercial Machinery & Equipment, nec
SIC 3699 Electrical Machinery, Equipment & Supplies, nec
333411 Air Purification Equipment Manufacturing
SIC 3564 Industrial & Commercial Fans & Blowers & Air Purification Equipment
333412 Industrial & Commercial Fan & Blower Manufacturing
SIC 3564 Industrial & Commercial Fans & Blowers & Air Purification Equipment
333414 Heating Equipment Manufacturing
SIC 3433 Heating Equipment, Except Electric & Warm Air Furnaces

SIC 3634 Electric Housewares & Fans

333415 Air-Conditioning & Warm Air Heating Equipment & Commercial & Industrial Refrigeration Equipment Manufacturing

SIC 3443 Fabricated Plate Work

SIC 3585 Air-Conditioning & Warm Air Heating Equipment & Commercial & Industrial Refrigeration Equipment

333511 Industrial Mold Manufacturing

SIC 3544 Special Dies & Tools, Die Sets, Jigs & Fixtures, & Industrial Molds

333512 Machine Tool Manufacturing

SIC 3541 Machine Tools, Metal Cutting Type

333513 Machine Tool Manufacturing

SIC 3542 Machine Tools, Metal Forming Type

333514 Special Die & Tool, Die Set, Jig & Fixture Manufacturing

SIC 3544 Special Dies & Tools, Die Sets, Jigs & Fixtures, & Industrial Molds

333515 Cutting Tool & Machine Tool Accessory Manufacturing

SIC 3545 Cutting Tools, Machine Tool Accessories, & Machinists' Precision Measuring Devices

333516 Rolling Mill Machinery & Equipment Manufacturing

SIC 3547 Rolling Mill Machinery & Equipment

333518 Other Metalworking Machinery Manufacturing

SIC 3549 Metalworking Machinery, nec

333611 Turbine & Turbine Generator Set Unit Manufacturing

SIC 3511 Steam, Gas, & Hydraulic Turbines, & Turbine Generator Set Units

333612 Speed Changer, Industrial High-Speed Drive & Gear Manufacturing

SIC 3566 Speed Changers, Industrial High-Speed Drives, & Gears

333613 Mechanical Power Transmission Equipment Manufacturing

SIC 3568 Mechanical Power Transmission Equipment, nec

333618 Other Engine Equipment Manufacturing

SIC 3519 Internal Combustion Engines, nec

SIC 3699 Electrical Machinery, Equipment & Supplies, nec

333911 Pump & Pumping Equipment Manufacturing

SIC 3561 Pumps & Pumping Equipment

SIC 3743 Railroad Equipment

333912 Air & Gas Compressor Manufacturing

SIC 3563 Air & Gas Compressors

333913 Measuring & Dispensing Pump Manufacturing

SIC 3586 Measuring & Dispensing Pumps

333921 Elevator & Moving Stairway Manufacturing

SIC 3534 Elevators & Moving Stairways

333922 Conveyor & Conveying Equipment Manufacturing

SIC 3523 Farm Machinery & Equipment

SIC 3535 Conveyors & Conveying Equipment

333923 Overhead Traveling Crane, Hoist & Monorail System Manufacturing

SIC 3536 Overhead Traveling Cranes, Hoists, & Monorail Systems

SIC 3531 Construction Machinery & Equipment

333924 Industrial Truck, Tractor, Trailer & Stacker Machinery Manufacturing

SIC 3537 Industrial Trucks, Tractors, Trailers, & Stackers

333991 Power-Driven Hand Tool Manufacturing

SIC 3546 Power-Driven Handtools

333992 Welding & Soldering Equipment Manufacturing

SIC 3548 Electric & Gas Welding & Soldering Equipment

333993 Packaging Machinery Manufacturing

SIC 3565 Packaging Machinery

333994 Industrial Process Furnace & Oven Manufacturing

SIC 3567 Industrial Process Furnaces & Ovens

333995 Fluid Power Cylinder & Actuator Manufacturing

SIC 3593 Fluid Power Cylinders & Actuators

333996 Fluid Power Pump & Motor Manufacturing

SIC 3594 Fluid Power Pumps & Motors

333997 Scale & Balance Manufacturing

SIC 3596 Scales & Balances, Except Laboratory

333999 All Other General Purpose Machinery Manufacturing

SIC 3599 Industrial & Commercial Machinery & Equipment, nec

SIC 3569 General Industrial Machinery & Equipment, nec

COMPUTER & ELECTRONIC PRODUCT MANUFACTURING

334111 Electronic Computer Manufacturing

SIC 3571 Electronic Computers

334112 Computer Storage Device Manufacturing

SIC 3572 Computer Storage Devices

334113 Computer Terminal Manufacturing

SIC 3575 Computer Terminals

334119 Other Computer Peripheral Equipment Manufacturing

SIC 3577 Computer Peripheral Equipment, nec

SIC 3578 Calculating & Accounting Machines, Except Electronic Computers

SIC 3699 Electrical Machinery, Equipment & Supplies, nec

33421 Telephone Apparatus Manufacturing

SIC 3661 Telephone & Telegraph Apparatus

33422 Radio & Television Broadcasting & Wireless Communications Equipment Manufacturing

SIC 3663 Radio & Television Broadcasting & Communication Equipment

SIC 3679 Electronic Components, nec

33429 Other Communications Equipment Manufacturing

SIC 3669 Communications Equipment, nec

33431 Audio & Video Equipment Manufacturing

SIC 3651 Household Audio & Video Equipment

334411 Electron Tube Manufacturing

SIC 3671 Electron Tubes

334412 Printed Circuit Board Manufacturing

SIC 3672 Printed Circuit Boards

334413 Semiconductor & Related Device Manufacturing

SIC 3674 Semiconductors & Related Devices

334414 Electronic Capacitor Manufacturing

SIC 3675 Electronic Capacitors

334415 Electronic Resistor Manufacturing

SIC 3676 Electronic Resistors

334416 Electronic Coil, Transformer, & Other Inductor Manufacturing

SIC 3661 Telephone & Telegraph Apparatus

SIC 3677 Electronic Coils, Transformers, & Other Inductors

SIC 3825 Instruments for Measuring & Testing of Electricity & Electrical Signals

334417 Electronic Connector Manufacturing

SIC 3678 Electronic Connectors

334418 Printed Circuit/Electronics Assembly Manufacturing

SIC 3679 Electronic Components, nec

SIC 3661 Telephone & Telegraph Apparatus

334419 Other Electronic Component Manufacturing
SIC 3679 Electronic Components, nec
334510 Electromedical & Electrotherapeutic Apparatus Manufacturing
SIC 3842 Orthopedic, Prosthetic & Surgical Appliances & Supplies
SIC 3845 Electromedical & Electrotherapeutic Apparatus
334511 Search, Detection, Navigation, Guidance, Aeronautical, & Nautical System & Instrument Manufacturing
SIC 3812 Search, Detection, Navigation, Guidance, Aeronautical, & Nautical Systems & Instruments
334512 Automatic Environmental Control Manufacturing for Residential, Commercial & Appliance Use
SIC 3822 Automatic Controls for Regulating Residential & Commercial Environments & Appliances
334513 Instruments & Related Products Manufacturing for Measuring, Displaying, & Controlling Industrial Process Variables
SIC 3823 Industrial Instruments for Measurement, Display, & Control of Process Variables; & Related Products
334514 Totalizing Fluid Meter & Counting Device Manufacturing
SIC 3824 Totalizing Fluid Meters & Counting Devices
334515 Instrument Manufacturing for Measuring & Testing Electricity & Electrical Signals
SIC 3825 Instruments for Measuring & Testing of Electricity & Electrical Signals
334516 Analytical Laboratory Instrument Manufacturing
SIC 3826 Laboratory Analytical Instruments
334517 Irradiation Apparatus Manufacturing
SIC 3844 X-Ray Apparatus & Tubes & Related Irradiation Apparatus
SIC 3845 Electromedical & Electrotherapeutic Apparatus
334518 Watch, Clock, & Part Manufacturing
SIC 3495 Wire Springs
SIC 3579 Office Machines, nec
SIC 3873 Watches, Clocks, Clockwork Operated Devices, & Parts
334519 Other Measuring & Controlling Device Manufacturing
SIC 3829 Measuring & Controlling Devices, nec
334611 Software Reproducing
SIC 7372 Prepackaged Software
334612 Prerecorded Compact Disc , Tape, & Record Reproducing
SIC 3652 Phonograph Records & Prerecorded Audio Tapes & Disks
SIC 7819 Services Allied to Motion Picture Production
334613 Magnetic & Optical Recording Media Manufacturing
SIC 3695 Magnetic & Optical Recording Media

ELECTRICAL EQUIPMENT, APPLIANCE, & COMPONENT MANUFACTURING

33511 Electric Lamp Bulb & Part Manufacturing
SIC 3641 Electric Lamp Bulbs & Tubes
335121 Residential Electric Lighting Fixture Manufacturing
SIC 3645 Residential Electric Lighting Fixtures
SIC 3999 Manufacturing Industries, nec
335122 Commercial, Industrial & Institutional Electric Lighting Fixture Manufacturing
SIC 3646 Commercial, Industrial, & Institutional Electric Lighting Fixtures

335129 Other Lighting Equipment Manufacturing
SIC 3648 Lighting Equipment, nec
SIC 3699 Electrical Machinery, Equipment, & Supplies, nec
335211 Electric Housewares & Fan Manufacturing
SIC 3634 Electric Housewares & Fans
335212 Household Vacuum Cleaner Manufacturing
SIC 3635 Household Vacuum Cleaners
SIC 3639 Household Appliances, nec
335221 Household Cooking Appliance Manufacturing
SIC 3631 Household Cooking Equipment
335222 Household Refrigerator & Home Freezer Manufacturing
SIC 3632 Household Refrigerators & Home & Farm Freezers
335224 Household Laundry Equipment Manufacturing
SIC 3633 Household Laundry Equipment
335228 Other Household Appliance Manufacturing
SIC 3639 Household Appliances, nec
335311 Power, Distribution & Specialty Transformer Manufacturing
SIC 3548 Electric & Gas Welding & Soldering Equipment
SIC 3612 Power, Distribution, & Speciality Transformers
335312 Motor & Generator Manufacturing
SIC 3621 Motors & Generators
SIC 7694 Armature Rewinding Shops
335313 Switchgear & Switchboard Apparatus Manufacturing
SIC 3613 Switchgear & Switchboard Apparatus
335314 Relay & Industrial Control Manufacturing
SIC 3625 Relays & Industrial Controls
335911 Storage Battery Manufacturing
SIC 3691 Storage Batteries
335912 Dry & Wet Primary Battery Manufacturing
SIC 3692 Primary Batteries, Dry & Wet
335921 Fiber-Optic Cable Manufacturing
SIC 3357 Drawing & Insulating of Nonferrous Wire
335929 Other Communication & Energy Wire Manufacturing
SIC 3357 Drawing & Insulating of Nonferrous Wire
335931 Current-Carrying Wiring Device Manufacturing
SIC 3643 Current-Carrying Wiring Devices
335932 Noncurrent-Carrying Wiring Device Manufacturing
SIC 3644 Noncurrent-Carrying Wiring Devices
335991 Carbon & Graphite Product Manufacturing
SIC 3624 Carbon & Graphite Products
335999 All Other Miscellaneous Electrical Equipment & Component Manufacturing
SIC 3629 Electrical Industrial Apparatus, nec
SIC 3699 Electrical Machinery, Equipment, & Supplies, nec

TRANSPORTATION EQUIPMENT MANUFACTURING

336111 Automobile Manufacturing
SIC 3711 Motor Vehicles & Passenger Car Bodies
336112 Light Truck & Utility Vehicle Manufacturing
SIC 3711 Motor Vehicles & Passenger Car Bodies
33612 Heavy Duty Truck Manufacturing
SIC 3711 Motor Vehicles & Passenger Car Bodies
336211 Motor Vehicle Body Manufacturing
SIC 3711 Motor Vehicles & Passenger Car Bodies
SIC 3713 Truck & Bus Bodies
SIC 3714 Motor Vehicle Parts & Accessories
336212 Truck Trailer Manufacturing
SIC 3715 Truck Trailers

336213 Motor Home Manufacturing
SIC 3716 Motor Homes

336214 Travel Trailer & Camper Manufacturing
SIC 3792 Travel Trailers & Campers
SIC 3799 Transportation Equipment, nec

336311 Carburetor, Piston, Piston Ring & Valve Manufacturing
SIC 3592 Carburetors, Pistons, Piston Rings, & Valves

336312 Gasoline Engine & Engine Parts Manufacturing
SIC 3714 Motor Vehicle Parts & Accessories

336321 Vehicular Lighting Equipment Manufacturing
SIC 3647 Vehicular Lighting Equipment

336322 Other Motor Vehicle Electrical & Electronic Equipment Manufacturing
SIC 3679 Electronic Components, nec
SIC 3694 Electrical Equipment for Internal Combustion Engines
SIC 3714 Motor Vehicle Parts & Accessories

33633 Motor Vehicle Steering & Suspension Components Manufacturing
SIC 3714 Motor Vehicle Parts & Accessories

33634 Motor Vehicle Brake System Manufacturing
SIC 3292 Asbestos Products
SIC 3714 Motor Vehicle Parts & Accessories

33635 Motor Vehicle Transmission & Power Train Parts Manufacturing
SIC 3714 Motor Vehicle Parts & Accessories

33636 Motor Vehicle Fabric Accessories & Seat Manufacturing
SIC 2396 Automotive Trimmings, Apparel Findings, & Related Products
SIC 2399 Fabricated Textile Products, nec
SIC 2531 Public Building & Related Furniture

33637 Motor Vehicle Metal Stamping
SIC 3465 Automotive Stampings

336391 Motor Vehicle Air-Conditioning Manufacturing
SIC 3585 Air-Conditioning & Warm Air Heating Equipment & Commercial & Industrial Refrigeration Equipment

336399 All Other Motor Vehicle Parts Manufacturing
SIC 3519 Internal Combustion Engines, nec
SIC 3599 Industrial & Commercial Machinery & Equipment, NEC
SIC 3714 Motor Vehicle Parts & Accessories

336411 Aircraft Manufacturing
SIC 3721 Aircraft

336412 Aircraft Engine & Engine Parts Manufacturing
SIC 3724 Aircraft Engines & Engine Parts

336413 Other Aircraft Part & Auxiliary Equipment Manufacturing
SIC 3728 Aircraft Parts & Auxiliary Equipment, nec

336414 Guided Missile & Space Vehicle Manufacturing
SIC 3761 Guided Missiles & Space Vehicles

336415 Guided Missile & Space Vehicle Propulsion Unit & Propulsion Unit Parts Manufacturing
SIC 3764 Guided Missile & Space Vehicle Propulsion Units & Propulsion Unit Parts

336419 Other Guided Missile & Space Vehicle Parts & Auxiliary Equipment Manufacturing
SIC 3769 Guided Missile & Space Vehicle Parts & Auxiliary Equipment

33651 Railroad Rolling Stock Manufacturing
SIC 3531 Construction Machinery & Equipment
SIC 3743 Railroad Equipment

336611 Ship Building & Repairing
SIC 3731 Ship Building & Repairing

336612 Boat Building
SIC 3732 Boat Building & Repairing

336991 Motorcycle, Bicycle, & Parts Manufacturing
SIC 3944 Games, Toys, & Children's Vehicles, Except Dolls & Bicycles
SIC 3751 Motorcycles, Bicycles & Parts

336992 Military Armored Vehicle, Tank & Tank Component Manufacturing
SIC 3711 Motor Vehicles & Passenger Car Bodies
SIC 3795 Tanks & Tank Components

336999 All Other Transportation Equipment Manufacturing
SIC 3799 Transportation Equipment, nec

FURNITURE & RELATED PRODUCT MANUFACTURING

337121 Upholstered Household Furniture Manufacturing
SIC 2512 Wood Household Furniture, Upholstered
SIC 2515 Mattress, Foundations, & Convertible Beds
SIC 5712 Furniture

337122 Nonupholstered Wood Household Furniture Manufacturing
SIC 2511 Wood Household Furniture, Except Upholstered
SIC 5712 Furniture Stores

337124 Metal Household Furniture Manufacturing
SIC 2514 Metal Household Furniture

337125 Household Furniture Manufacturing
SIC 2519 Household Furniture, NEC

337127 Institutional Furniture Manufacturing
SIC 2531 Public Building & Related Furniture
SIC 2599 Furniture & Fixtures, nec
SIC 3952 Lead Pencils, Crayons, & Artist's Materials
SIC 3999 Manufacturing Industries, nec

337129 Wood Television, Radio, & Sewing Machine Cabinet Manufacturing
SIC 2517 Wood Television, Radio, Phonograph, & Sewing Machine Cabinets

337131 Wood Kitchen & Counter Top Manufacturing
SIC 2434 Wood Kitchen Cabinets
SIC 2541 Wood Office & Store Fixtures, Partitions, Shelving, & Lockers
SIC 5712 Furniture Stores

337132 Upholstered Wood Household Furniture Manufacturing
SIC 2515 Mattresses, Foundations, & Convertible Beds
SIC 5712 Furniture Stores

337133 Wood Household Furniture
SIC 5712 Furniture Stores

337134 Wood Office Furniture Manufacturing
SIC 2521 Wood Office Furniture

337135 Custom Architectural Woodwork, Millwork, & Fixtures
SIC 2541 Wood Office & Store Fixtures, Partitions, Shelving, and Lockers

337139 Other Wood Furniture Manufacturing
SIC 2426 Hardwood Dimension & Flooring Mills
SIC 2499 Wood Products, nec
SIC 2517 Wood Television, Radio, Phonograph, & Sewing Machine Cabinets
SIC 2531 Public Building & Related Furniture
SIC 2541 Wood Office & Store Fixtures, Partitions., Shelving, & Lockers
SIC 2599 Furniture & Fixtures, nec
SIC 3952 Lead Pencils, Crayons, & Artist's Materials

337141 Nonwood Office Furniture Manufacturing
SIC 2522 Office Furniture, Except Wood
337143 Household Furniture Manufacturing
SIC 2519 Household Furniture, NEC
337145 Nonwood Showcase, Partition, Shelving, & Locker Manufacturing
SIC 2542 Office & Store Fixtures, Partitions, Shelving, & Lockers, Except Wood
337148 Other Nonwood Furniture Manufacturing
SIC 2499 Wood Products, NEC
SIC 2531 Public Building & Related Furniture
SIC 2599 Furniture & Fixtures, nec
SIC 3499 Fabricated Metal Products, nec
SIC 3952 Lead Pencils, Crayons, & Artist's Materials
SIC 3999 Manufacturing Industries, nec
337212 Custom Architectural Woodwork & Millwork Manufacturing
SIC 2541 Wood Office & Store Fixtures, Partitions, Shelving, & Lockers
337214 Nonwood Office Furniture Manufacturing
SIC 2522 Office Furniture, Except Wood
337215 Showcase, Partition, Shelving, & Locker Manufacturing
SIC 2542 Office & Store Fixtures, Partitions, Shelving & Lockers, Except Wood
SIC 2541 Wood Office & Store Fixtures, Partitions, Shelving, & Lockers
SIC 2426 Hardwood Dimension & Flooring Mills
SIC 3499 Fabricated Metal Products, nec
33791 Mattress Manufacturing
SIC 2515 Mattresses, Foundations & Convertible Beds
33792 Blind & Shade Manufacturing
SIC 2591 Drapery Hardware & Window Blinds & Shades

MISCELLANEOUS MANUFACTURING

339111 Laboratory Apparatus & Furniture Manufacturing
SIC 3829 Measuring & Controlling Devices, nec
339112 Surgical & Medical Instrument Manufacturing
SIC 3841 Surgical & Medical Instruments & Apparatus
SIC 3829 Measuring & Controlling Devices, nec
339113 Surgical Appliance & Supplies Manufacturing
SIC 2599 Furniture & Fixtures, nec
SIC 3842 Orthopedic, Prosthetic, & Surgical Appliances & Supplies
339114 Dental Equipment & Supplies Manufacturing
SIC 3843 Dental Equipment & Supplies
339115 Ophthalmic Goods Manufacturing
SIC 3851 Opthalmic Goods
SIC 5995 Optical Goods Stores
339116 Dental Laboratories
SIC 8072 Dental Laboratories 339117 Eyeglass & Contact Lens Manufacturing
SIC 5995 Optical Goods Stores
339911 Jewelry Manufacturing
SIC 3469 Metal Stamping, nec
SIC 3479 Coating, Engraving, & Allied Services, nec
SIC 3911 Jewelry, Precious Metal
339912 Silverware & Plated Ware Manufacturing
SIC 3479 Coating, Engraving, & Allied Services, nec
SIC 3914 Silverware, Plated Ware, & Stainless Steel Ware
339913 Jewelers' Material & Lapidary Work Manufacturing
SIC 3915 Jewelers' Findings & Materials, & Lapidary Work

339914 Costume Jewelry & Novelty Manufacturing
SIC 3479 Coating, Engraving, & Allied Services, nec
SIC 3499 Fabricated Metal Products, nec
SIC 3961 Costume Jewelry & Costume Novelties, Except Precious Metal
33992 Sporting & Athletic Goods Manufacturing
SIC 3949 Sporting & Athletic Goods, nec
339931 Doll & Stuffed Toy Manufacturing
SIC 3942 Dolls & Stuffed Toys
339932 Game, Toy, & Children's Vehicle Manufacturing
SIC 3944 Games, Toys, & Children's Vehicles, Except Dolls & Bicycles
339941 Pen & Mechanical Pencil Manufacturing
SIC 3951 Pens, Mechanical Pencils, & Parts
339942 Lead Pencil & Art Good Manufacturing
SIC 2531 Public Buildings & Related Furniture
SIC 3579 Office Machines, nec
SIC 3952 Lead Pencils, Crayons, & Artists' Materials
339943 Marking Device Manufacturing
SIC 3953 Marking Devices
339944 Carbon Paper & Inked Ribbon Manufacturing
SIC 3955 Carbon Paper & Inked Ribbons
33995 Sign Manufacturing
SIC 3993 Signs & Advertising Specialties
339991 Gasket, Packing, & Sealing Device Manufacturing
SIC 3053 Gaskets, Packing, & Sealing Devices
339992 Musical Instrument Manufacturing
SIC 3931 Musical Instruments
339993 Fastener, Button, Needle & Pin Manufacturing
SIC 3965 Fasteners, Buttons, Needles, & Pins
SIC 3131 Boat & Shoe Cut Stock & Findings
339994 Broom, Brush & Mop Manufacturing
SIC 3991 Brooms & Brushes
SIC 2392 Housefurnishings, Except Curtains & Draperies
339995 Burial Casket Manufacturing
SIC 3995 Burial Caskets
339999 All Other Miscellaneous Manufacturing
SIC 2499 Wood Products, NEC
SIC 3999 Manufacturing Industries, nec

WHOLESALE TRADE

42111 Automobile & Other Motor Vehicle Wholesalers
SIC 5012 Automobiles & Other Motor Vehicles
42112 Motor Vehicle Supplies & New Part Wholesalers
SIC 5013 Motor Vehicle Supplies & New Parts
42113 Tire & Tube Wholesalers
SIC 5014 Tires & Tubes
42114 Motor Vehicle Part Wholesalers
SIC 5015 Motor Vehicle Parts, Used
42121 Furniture Wholesalers
SIC 5021 Furniture
42122 Home Furnishing Wholesalers
SIC 5023 Homefurnishings
42131 Lumber, Plywood, Millwork & Wood Panel Wholesalers
SIC 5031 Lumber, Plywood, Millwork, & Wood Panels
SIC 5211 Lumber & Other Building Materials Dealers - Retail
42132 Brick, Stone & Related Construction Material Wholesalers
SIC 5032 Brick, Stone, & Related Construction Materials
42133 Roofing, Siding & Insulation Material Wholesalers
SIC 5033 Roofing, Siding, & Insulation Materials

42139 Other Construction Material Wholesalers
SIC 5039 Construction Materials, nec

42141 Photographic Equipment & Supplies Wholesalers
SIC 5043 Photographic Equipment & Supplies

42142 Office Equipment Wholesalers
SIC 5044 Office Equipment

42143 Computer & Computer Peripheral Equipment & Software Wholesalers
SIC 5045 Computers & Computer Peripherals Equipment & Software

42144 Other Commercial Equipment Wholesalers
SIC 5046 Commercial Equipment, nec

42145 Medical, Dental & Hospital Equipment & Supplies Wholesalers
SIC 5047 Medical, Dental & Hospital Equipment & Supplies

42146 Ophthalmic Goods Wholesalers
SIC 5048 Ophthalmic Goods

42149 Other Professional Equipment & Supplies Wholesalers
SIC 5049 Professional Equipment & Supplies, nec

42151 Metal Service Centers & Offices
SIC 5051 Metals Service Centers & Offices

42152 Coal & Other Mineral & Ore Wholesalers
SIC 5052 Coal & Other Mineral & Ores

42161 Electrical Apparatus & Equipment, Wiring Supplies & Construction Material Wholesalers
SIC 5063 Electrical Apparatus & Equipment, Wiring Supplies & Construction Materials

42162 Electrical Appliance, Television & Radio Set Wholesalers
SIC 5064 Electrical Appliances, Television & Radio Sets

42169 Other Electronic Parts & Equipment Wholesalers
SIC 5065 Electronic Parts & Equipment, nec

42171 Hardware Wholesalers
SIC 5072 Hardware

42172 Plumbing & Heating Equipment & Supplies Wholesalers
SIC 5074 Plumbing & Heating Equipment & Supplies

42173 Warm Air Heating & Air-Conditioning Equipment & Supplies Wholesalers
SIC 5075 Warm Air Heating & Air-Conditioning Equipment & Supplies

42174 Refrigeration Equipment & Supplies Wholesalers
SIC 5078 Refrigeration Equipment & Supplies

42181 Construction & Mining Machinery & Equipment Wholesalers
SIC 5082 Construction & Mining Machinery & Equipment

42182 Farm & Garden Machinery & Equipment Wholesalers
SIC 5083 Farm & Garden Machinery & Equipment

42183 Industrial Machinery & Equipment Wholesalers
SIC 5084 Industrial Machinery & Equipment
SIC 5085 Industrial Supplies

42184 Industrial Supplies Wholesalers
SIC 5085 Industrial Supplies

42185 Service Establishment Equipment & Supplies Wholesalers
SIC 5087 Service Establishment Equipment & Supplies Wholesalers

42186 Transportation Equipment & Supplies Wholesalers
SIC 5088 Transportation Equipment and Supplies, Except Motor Vehicles

42191 Sporting & Recreational Goods & Supplies Wholesalers
SIC 5091 Sporting & Recreational Goods & Supplies

42192 Toy & Hobby Goods & Supplies Wholesalers
SIC 5092 Toys & Hobby Goods & Supplies

42193 Recyclable Material Wholesalers
SIC 5093 Scrap & Waste Materials

42194 Jewelry, Watch, Precious Stone & Precious Metal Wholesalers
SIC 5094 Jewelry, Watches, Precious Stones, & Precious Metals

42199 Other Miscellaneous Durable Goods Wholesalers
SIC 5099 Durable Goods, nec
SIC 7822 Motion Picture & Video Tape Distribution

42211 Printing & Writing Paper Wholesalers
SIC 5111 Printing & Writing Paper

42212 Stationary & Office Supplies Wholesalers
SIC 5112 Stationery & Office Supplies

42213 Industrial & Personal Service Paper Wholesalers
SIC 5113 Industrial & Personal Service Paper

42221 Drug, Drug Proprietaries & Druggists' Sundries Wholesalers
SIC 5122 Drugs, Drug Proprietaries, & Druggists' Sundries

42231 Piece Goods, Notions & Other Dry Goods Wholesalers
SIC 5131 Piece Goods, Notions, & Other Dry Goods

42232 Men's & Boys' Clothing & Furnishings Wholesalers
SIC 5136 Men's & Boys' Clothing & Furnishings

42233 Women's, Children's, & Infants' & Accessories Wholesalers
SIC 5137 Women's, Children's, & Infants' Clothing & Accessories

42234 Footwear Wholesalers
SIC 5139 Footwear

42241 General Line Grocery Wholesalers
SIC 5141 Groceries, General Line

42242 Packaged Frozen Food Wholesalers
SIC 5142 Packaged Frozen Foods

42243 Dairy Product Wholesalers
SIC 5143 Dairy Products, Except Dried or Canned

42244 Poultry & Poultry Product Wholesalers
SIC 5144 Poultry & Poultry Products

42245 Confectionery Wholesalers
SIC 5145 Confectionery

42246 Fish & Seafood Wholesalers
SIC 5146 Fish & Seafoods

42247 Meat & Meat Product Wholesalers
SIC 5147 Meats & Meat Products

42248 Fresh Fruit & Vegetable Wholesalers
SIC 5148 Fresh Fruits & Vegetables

42249 Other Grocery & Related Products Wholesalers
SIC 5149 Groceries & Related Products, nec

42251 Grain & Field Bean Wholesalers
SIC 5153 Grain & Field Beans

42252 Livestock Wholesalers
SIC 5154 Livestock

42259 Other Farm Product Raw Material Wholesalers
SIC 5159 Farm-Product Raw Materials, nec

42261 Plastics Materials & Basic Forms & Shapes Wholesalers
SIC 5162 Plastics Materials & Basic Forms & Shapes

42269 Other Chemical & Allied Products Wholesalers
SIC 5169 Chemicals & Allied Products, nec

42271 Petroleum Bulk Stations & Terminals
SIC 5171 Petroleum Bulk Stations & Terminals

42272 Petroleum & Petroleum Products Wholesalers
SIC 5172 Petroleum & Petroleum Products Wholesalers, Except Bulk Stations & Terminals

42281 Beer & Ale Wholesalers
SIC 5181 Beer & Ale

42282 Wine & Distilled Alcoholic Beverage Wholesalers
SIC 5182 Wine & Distilled Alcoholic Beverages
42291 Farm Supplies Wholesalers
SIC 5191 Farm Supplies
42292 Book, Periodical & Newspaper Wholesalers
SIC 5192 Books, Periodicals, & Newspapers
42293 Flower, Nursery Stock & Florists' Supplies Wholesalers
SIC 5193 Flowers, Nursery Stock, & Florists' Supplies
42294 Tobacco & Tobacco Product Wholesalers
SIC 5194 Tobacco & Tobacco Products
42295 Paint, Varnish & Supplies Wholesalers
SIC 5198 Paints, Varnishes, & Supplies
SIC 5231 Paint, Glass & Wallpaper Stores
42299 Other Miscellaneous Nondurable Goods Wholesalers
SIC 5199 Nondurable Goods, nec

RETAIL TRADE

44111 New Car Dealers
SIC 5511 Motor Vehicle Dealers, New and Used
44112 Used Car Dealers
SIC 5521 Motor Vehicle Dealers, Used Only
44121 Recreational Vehicle Dealers
SIC 5561 Recreational Vehicle Dealers
441221 Motorcycle Dealers
SIC 5571 Motorcycle Dealers
441222 Boat Dealers
SIC 5551 Boat Dealers
441229 All Other Motor Vehicle Dealers
SIC 5599 Automotive Dealers, NEC
44131 Automotive Parts & Accessories Stores
SIC 5013 Motor Vehicle Supplies & New Parts
SIC 5731 Radio, Television, & Consumer Electronics Stores
SIC 5531 Auto & Home Supply Stores
44132 Tire Dealers
SIC 5014 Tires & Tubes
SIC 5531 Auto & Home Supply Stores
44211 Furniture Stores
SIC 5021 Furniture
SIC 5712 Furniture Stores
44221 Floor Covering Stores
SIC 5023 Homefurnishings
SIC 5713 Floor Coverings Stores
442291 Window Treatment Stores
SIC 5714 Drapery, Curtain, & Upholstery Stores
SIC 5719 Miscellaneous Homefurnishings Stores
442299 All Other Home Furnishings Stores
SIC 5719 Miscellaneous Homefurnishings Stores
443111 Household Appliance Stores
SIC 5722 Household Appliance Stores
SIC 5999 Miscellaneous Retail Stores, nec
SIC 7623 Refrigeration & Air-Conditioning Service & Repair Shops
SIC 7629 Electrical & Electronic Repair Shops, nec
443112 Radio, Television & Other Electronics Stores
SIC 5731 Radio, Television, & Consumer Electronics Stores
SIC 5999 Miscellaneous Retail Stores, nec
SIC 7622 Radio & Television Repair Shops
44312 Computer & Software Stores
SIC 5045 Computers & Computer Peripheral Equipment & Software
SIC 7378 Computer Maintenance & Repair '
SIC 5734 Computer & Computer Software Stores

44313 Camera & Photographic Supplies Stores
SIC 5946 Camera & Photographic Supply Stores
44411 Home Centers
SIC 5211 Lumber & Other Building Materials Dealers
44412 Paint & Wallpaper Stores
SIC 5198 Paints, Varnishes, & Supplies
SIC 5231 Paint, Glass, & Wallpaper Stores
44413 Hardware Stores
SIC 5251 Hardware Stores
44419 Other Building Material Dealers
SIC 5031 Lumber, Plywood, Millwork, & Wood Panels
SIC 5032 Brick, Stone, & Related Construction Materials
SIC 5039 Construction Materials, nec
SIC 5063 Electrical Apparatus & Equipment, Wiring Supplies, & Construction Materials
SIC 5074 Plumbing & Heating Equipment & Supplies
SIC 5211 Lumber & Other Building Materials Dealers
SIC 5231 Paint, Glass, & Wallpaper Stores
44421 Outdoor Power Equipment Stores
SIC 5083 Farm & Garden Machinery & Equipment
SIC 5261 Retail Nurseries, Lawn & Garden Supply Stores
44422 Nursery & Garden Centers
SIC 5191 Farm Supplies
SIC 5193 Flowers, Nursery Stock, & Florists' Supplies
SIC 5261 Retail Nurseries, Lawn & Garden Supply Stores
44511 Supermarkets & Other Grocery Stores
SIC 5411 Grocery Stores
44512 Convenience Stores
SIC 5411 Grocery Stores
44521 Meat Markets
SIC 5421 Meat & Fish Markets, Including Freezer Provisioners
SIC 5499 Miscellaneous Food Stores
44522 Fish & Seafood Markets
SIC 5421 Meat & Fish Markets, Including Freezer Provisioners
44523 Fruit & Vegetable Markets
SIC 5431 Fruit & Vegetable Markets
445291 Baked Goods Stores
SIC 5461 Retail Bakeries
445292 Confectionery & Nut Stores
SIC 5441 Candy, Nut & Confectionery Stores
445299 All Other Specialty Food Stores
SIC 5499 Miscellaneous Food Stores
SIC 5451 Dairy Products Stores
44531 Beer, Wine & Liquor Stores
SIC 5921 Liquor Stores
44611 Pharmacies & Drug Stores
SIC 5912 Drug Stores & Proprietary Stores
44612 Cosmetics, Beauty Supplies & Perfume Stores
SIC 5087 Service Establishment Equipment & Supplies
SIC 5999 Miscellaneous Retail Stores, nec
44613 Optical Goods Stores
SIC 5995 Optical Goods Stores
446191 Food Supplement Stores
SIC 5499 Miscellaneous Food Stores
446199 All Other Health & Personal Care Stores
SIC 5047 Medical, Dental, & Hospital Equipment & Supplies
SIC 5999 Miscellaneous Retail Stores, nec
44711 Gasoline Stations with Convenience Stores
SIC 5541 Gasoline Service Station
SIC 5411 Grocery Stores
44719 Other Gasoline Stations
SIC 5541 Gasoline Service Station

44811 Men's Clothing Stores
SIC 5611 Men's & Boys' Clothing & Accessory Stores
44812 Women's Clothing Stores
SIC 5621 Women's Clothing Stores
44813 Children's & Infants' Clothing Stores
SIC 5641 Children's & Infants' Wear Stores
44814 Family Clothing Stores
SIC 5651 Family Clothing Stores
44815 Clothing Accessories Stores
SIC 5611 Men's & Boys' Clothing & Accessory Stores
SIC 5632 Women's Accessory & Specialty Stores
SIC 5699 Miscellaneous Apparel & Accessory Stores
44819 Other Clothing Stores
SIC 5699 Miscellaneous Apparel & Accessory Stores
SIC 5632 Women's Accessory & Specialty Stores
44821 Shoe Stores
SIC 5661 Shoe Stores
44831 Jewelry Stores
SIC 5999 Miscellaneous Retailer, nec
SIC 5944 Jewelry Stores
44832 Luggage & Leather Goods Stores
SIC 5948 Luggage & Leather Goods Stores
45111 Sporting Goods Stores
SIC 7699 Repair Shops & Related Services, NEC
SIC 5941 Sporting Goods Stores & Bicycle Shops
45112 Hobby, Toy & Game Stores
SIC 5945 Hobby, Toy, & Game Stores
45113 Sewing, Needlework & Piece Goods Stores
SIC 5714 Drapery, Curtain, & Upholstery Stores
SIC 5949 Sewing, Needlework, & Piece Goods Stores
45114 Musical Instrument & Supplies Stores
SIC 5736 Musical Instruments Stores
451211 Book Stores
SIC 5942 Book Stores
451212 News Dealers & Newsstands
SIC 5994 News Dealers & Newsstands
45122 Prerecorded Tape, Compact Disc & Record Stores
SIC 5735 Record & Prerecorded Tape Stores
45211 Department Stores
SIC 5311 Department Stores
45291 Warehouse Clubs & Superstores
SIC 5399 Miscellaneous General Merchandise Stores
SIC 5411 Grocery Stores
45299 All Other General Merchandise Stores
SIC 5399 Miscellaneous General Merchandise Stores
SIC 5331 Variety Stores
45311 Florists
SIC 5992 Florists
45321 Office Supplies & Stationery Stores
SIC 5049 Professional Equipment & Supplies, nec
SIC 5112 Stationery & Office Supplies
SIC 5943 Stationery Stores
45322 Gift, Novelty & Souvenir Stores
SIC 5947 Gift, Novelty, & Souvenir Shops
45331 Used Merchandise Stores
SIC 5932 Used Merchandise Stores
45391 Pet & Pet Supplies Stores
SIC 5999 Miscellaneous Retail Stores, NEC
45392 Art Dealers
SIC 5999 Miscellaneous Retail Stores, nec
45393 Manufactured Home Dealers
SIC 5271 Mobile Home Dealers

453991 Tobacco Stores
SIC 5993 Tobacco Stores & Stands
453999 All Other Miscellaneous Store Retailers
SIC 5999 Miscellaneous Retail Stores, nec
SIC 5261 Retail Nurseries, Lawn & Garden Supply Stores
45411 Electronic Shopping & Mail-Order Houses
SIC 5961 Catalog & Mail-Order Houses
45421 Vending Machine Operators
SIC 5962 Automatic Merchandise Machine Operators
454311 Heating Oil Dealers
SIC 5171 Petroleum Bulk Stations & Terminals
SIC 5983 Fuel Oil Dealers
454312 Liquefied Petroleum Gas Dealers
SIC 5171 Petroleum Bulk Stations & Terminals
SIC 5984 Liquefied Petroleum Gas Dealers
454319 Other Fuel Dealers
SIC 5989 Fuel Dealers, nec
45439 Other Direct Selling Establishments
SIC 5421 Meat & Fish Markets, Including Freezer Provisioners
SIC 5963 Direct Selling Establishments

TRANSPORTATION & WAREHOUSING

481111 Scheduled Passenger Air Transportation
SIC 4512 Air Transportation, Scheduled
481112 Scheduled Freight Air Transportation
SIC 4512 Air Transportation, Scheduled
481211 Nonscheduled Chartered Passenger Air Transportation
SIC 4522 Air Transportation, Nonscheduled
481212 Nonscheduled Chartered Freight Air Transportation
SIC 4522 Air Transportation, Nonscheduled
481219 Other Nonscheduled Air Transportation
SIC 7319 Advertising, nec
48122 Nonscheduled Speciality Air Transportation
SIC 0721 Crop Planting, Cultivating, & Protecting
SIC 1382 Oil & Gas Field Exploration Services
SIC 4522 Air Transportation, Nonscheduled
SIC 7335 Commercial Photography
SIC 7997 Membership Sports & Recreation Clubs
SIC 8299 Schools & Educational Services, nec
SIC 8713 Surveying Services
482111 Line-Haul Railroads
SIC 4011 Railroads, Line-Haul Operating
482112 Short Line Railroads
SIC 4013 Railroad Switching & Terminal Establishments
483111 Deep Sea Freight Transportation
SIC 4412 Deep Sea Foreign Transportation of Freight
483112 Deep Sea Passenger Transportation
SIC 4481 Deep Sea Transportation of Passengers, Except by Ferry
483113 Coastal & Great Lakes Freight Transportation
SIC 4424 Deep Sea Domestic Transportation of Freight
SIC 4432 Freight Transportation on the Great Lakes - St. Lawrence Seaway
SIC 4492 Towing & Tugboat Services
483114 Coastal & Great Lakes Passenger Transportation
SIC 4481 Deep Sea Transportation of Passengers, Except by Ferry
SIC 4482 Ferries
483211 Inland Water Freight Transportation
SIC 4449 Water Transportation of Freight, nec
SIC 4492 Towing & Tugboat Services

483212 Inland Water Passenger Transportation
SIC 4482 Ferries
SIC 4489 Water Transportation of Passengers, nec

48411 General Freight Trucking, Local
SIC 4212 Local Trucking without Storage
SIC 4214 Local Trucking with Storage

484121 General Freight Trucking, Long-Distance, Truckload
SIC 4213 Trucking, Except Local

484122 General Freight Trucking, Long-Distance, Less Than Truckload
SIC 4213 Trucking, Except Local

48421 Used Household & Office Goods Moving
SIC 4212 Local Trucking Without Storage
SIC 4213 Trucking, Except Local
SIC 4214 Local Trucking With Storage

48422 Specialized Freight Trucking, Local
SIC 4212 Local Trucking without Storage
SIC 4214 Local Trucking with Storage

48423 Specialized Freight Trucking, Long-Distance
SIC 4213 Trucking, Except Local

485111 Mixed Mode Transit Systems
SIC 4111 Local & Suburban Transit

485112 Commuter Rail Systems
SIC 4111 Local & Suburban Transit

485113 Bus & Motor Vehicle Transit Systems
SIC 4111 Local & Suburban Transit

485119 Other Urban Transit Systems
SIC 4111 Local & Suburban Transit

48521 Interurban & Rural Bus Transportation
SIC 4131 Intercity & Rural Bus Transportation

48531 Taxi Service
SIC 4121 Taxicabs

48532 Limousine Service
SIC 4119 Local Passenger Transportation, nec

48541 School & Employee Bus Transportation
SIC 4151 School Buses
SIC 4119 Local Passenger Transportation, nec

48551 Charter Bus Industry
SIC 4141 Local Charter Bus Service
SIC 4142 Bus Charter Services, Except Local

485991 Special Needs Transportation
SIC 4119 Local Passenger Transportation, nec

485999 All Other Transit & Ground Passenger Transportation
SIC 4111 Local & Suburban Transit
SIC 4119 Local Passenger Transportation, nec

48611 Pipeline Transportation of Crude Oil
SIC 4612 Crude Petroleum Pipelines

48621 Pipeline Transportation of Natural Gas
SIC 4922 Natural Gas Transmission
SIC 4923 Natural Gas Transmission & Distribution

48691 Pipeline Transportation of Refined Petroleum Products
SIC 4613 Refined Petroleum Pipelines

48699 All Other Pipeline Transportation
SIC 4619 Pipelines, nec

48711 Scenic & Sightseeing Transportation, Land
SIC 4119 Local Passenger Transportation, nec
SIC 4789 Transportation Services, nec
SIC 7999 Amusement & Recreation Services, nec

48721 Scenic & Sightseeing Transportation, Water
SIC 4489 Water Transportation of Passengers, nec
SIC 7999 Amusement & Recreation Services, nec

48799 Scenic & Sightseeing Transportation, Other
SIC 4522 Air Transportation, Nonscheduled
SIC 7999 Amusement & Recreation Services, nec

488111 Air Traffic Control
SIC 4581 Airports, Flying Fields, & Airport Terminal Services
SIC 9621 Regulation & Administration of Transportation Programs

488112 Airport Operations, except Air Traffic Control
SIC 4581 Airports, Flying Fields, & Airport Terminal Services
SIC 4959 Sanitary Services, nec

488119 Other Airport Operations
SIC 4581 Airports, Flying Fields, & Airport Terminal Services
SIC 4959 Sanitary Services, nec

48819 Other Support Activities for Air Transportation
SIC 4581 Airports, Flying Fields, & Airport Terminal Services

48821 Support Activities for Rail Transportation
SIC 4013 Railroad Switching & Terminal Establishments
SIC 4741 Rental of Railroad Cars
SIC 4789 Transportation Services, nec

48831 Port & Harbor Operations
SIC 4491 Marine Cargo Handling
SIC 4499 Water Transportation Services, nec

48832 Marine Cargo Handling
SIC 4491 Marine Cargo Handling

48833 Navigational Services to Shipping
SIC 4492 Towing & Tugboat Services
SIC 4499 Water Transportation Services, nec

48839 Other Support Activities for Water Transportation
SIC 4499 Water Transportation Services, nec
SIC 4785 Fixed Facilities & Inspection & Weighing Services for Motor Vehicle Transportation
SIC 7699 Repair Shops & Related Services, nec

48841 Motor Vehicle Towing
SIC 7549 Automotive Services, Except Repair & Carwashes

48849 Other Support Activities for Road Transportation
SIC 4173 Terminal & Service Facilities for Motor Vehicle Passenger Transportation
SIC 4231 Terminal & Joint Terminal Maintenance Facilities for Motor Freight Transportation
SIC 4785 Fixed Facilities & Inspection & Weighing Services for Motor Vehicle Transportation

48851 Freight Transportation Arrangement
SIC 4731 Arrangement of Transportation of Freight & Cargo

488991 Packing & Crating
SIC 4783 Packing & Crating

488999 All Other Support Activities for Transportation
SIC 4729 Arrangement of Passenger Transportation, nec
SIC 4789 Transportation Services, nec

49111 Postal Service
SIC 4311 United States Postal Service

49211 Couriers
SIC 4215 Courier Services, Except by Air
SIC 4513 Air Courier Services

49221 Local Messengers & Local Delivery
SIC 4215 Courier Services, Except by Air

49311 General Warehousing & Storage Facilities
SIC 4225 General Warehousing & Storage
SIC 4226 Special Warehousing & Storage, nec

49312 Refrigerated Storage Facilities
SIC 4222 Refrigerated Warehousing & Storage
SIC 4226 Special Warehousing & Storage, nec

49313 Farm Product Storage Facilities
SIC 4221 Farm Product Warehousing & Storage

49319 Other Warehousing & Storage Facilities
SIC 4226 Special Warehousing & Storage, nec

INFORMATION

51111 Newspaper Publishers
SIC 2711 Newspapers: Publishing or Publishing & Printing
51112 Periodical Publishers
SIC 2721 Periodicals: Publishing or Publishing & Printing
51113 Book Publishers
SIC 2731 Books: Publishing or Publishing & Printing
51114 Database & Directory Publishers
SIC 2741 Miscellaneous Publishing
511191 Greeting Card Publishers
SIC 2771 Greeting Cards
511199 All Other Publishers
SIC 2741 Miscellaneous Publishing
51121 Software Publishers
SIC 7372 Prepackaged Software
51211 Motion Picture & Video Production
SIC 7812 Motion Picture & Video Tape Production
51212 Motion Picture & Video Distribution
SIC 7822 Motion Picture & Video Tape Distribution
SIC 7829 Services Allied to Motion Picture Distribution
512131 Motion Picture Theaters, Except Drive-Ins.
SIC 7832 Motion Picture Theaters, Except Drive-In
512132 Drive-In Motion Picture Theaters
SIC 7833 Drive-In Motion Picture Theaters
512191 Teleproduction & Other Post-Production Services
SIC 7819 Services Allied to Motion Picture Production
512199 Other Motion Picture & Video Industries
SIC 7819 Services Allied to Motion Picture Production
SIC 7829 Services Allied to Motion Picture Distribution
51221 Record Production
SIC 8999 Services, nec
51222 Integrated Record Production/Distribution
SIC 3652 Phonograph Records & Prerecorded Audio Tapes & Disks
51223 Music Publishers
SIC 2731 Books: Publishing or Publishing & Printing
SIC 2741 Miscellaneous Publishing
SIC 8999 Services, nec
51224 Sound Recording Studios
SIC 7389 Business Services, nec
51229 Other Sound Recording Industries
SIC 7389 Business Services, nec
SIC 7922 Theatrical Producers & Miscellaneous Theatrical Services
513111 Radio Networks
SIC 4832 Radio Broadcasting Stations
513112 Radio Stations
SIC 4832 Radio Broadcasting Stations
51312 Television Broadcasting
SIC 4833 Television Broadcasting Stations
51321 Cable Networks
SIC 4841 Cable & Other Pay Television Services
51322 Cable & Other Program Distribution
SIC 4841 Cable & Other Pay Television Services
51331 Wired Telecommunications Carriers
SIC 4813 Telephone Communications, Except Radiotelephone
SIC 4822 Telegraph & Other Message Communications
513321 Paging
SIC 4812 Radiotelephone Communications
513322 Cellular & Other Wireless Telecommunications
SIC 4812 Radiotelephone Communications
SIC 4899 Communications Services, nec

51333 Telecommunications Resellers
SIC 4812 Radio Communications
SIC 4813 Telephone Communications, Except Radiotelephone
51334 Satellite Telecommunications
SIC 4899 Communications Services, NEC
51339 Other Telecommunications
SIC 4899 Communications Services, NEC
51411 News Syndicates
SIC 7383 News Syndicates
51412 Libraries & Archives
SIC 8231 Libraries
514191 On-Line Information Services
SIC 7375 Information Retrieval Services
514199 All Other Information Services
SIC 8999 Services, nec
51421 Data Processing Services
SIC 7374 Computer Processing & Data Preparation & Processing Services

FINANCE & INSURANCE

52111 Monetary Authorities - Central Bank
SIC 6011 Federal Reserve Banks
52211 Commercial Banking
SIC 6021 National Commercial Banks
SIC 6022 State Commercial Banks
SIC 6029 Commercial Banks, nec
SIC 6081 Branches & Agencies of Foreign Banks
52212 Savings Institutions
SIC 6035 Savings Institutions, Federally Chartered
SIC 6036 Savings Institutions, Not Federally Chartered
52213 Credit Unions
SIC 6061 Credit Unions, Federally Chartered
SIC 6062 Credit Unions, Not Federally Chartered
52219 Other Depository Credit Intermediation
SIC 6022 State Commercial Banks
52221 Credit Card Issuing
SIC 6021 National Commercial Banks
SIC 6022 State Commercial Banks
SIC 6141 Personal Credit Institutions
52222 Sales Financing
SIC 6141 Personal Credit Institutions
SIC 6153 Short-Term Business Credit Institutions, Except Agricultural .
SIC 6159 Miscellaneous Business Credit Institutions
522291 Consumer Lending
SIC 6141 Personal Credit Institutions
522292 Real Estate Credit
SIC 6162 Mortgage Bankers & Loan Correspondents
522293 International Trade Financing
SIC 6081 Branches & Agencies of Foreign Banks
SIC 6082 Foreign Trade & International Banking Institutions
SIC 6111 Federal & Federally-Sponsored Credit Agencies
SIC 6159 Miscellaneous Business Credit Institutions
522294 Secondary Market Financing
SIC 6111 Federal & Federally Sponsored Credit Agencies
522298 All Other Nondepository Credit Intermediation
SIC 5932 Used Merchandise Stores
SIC 6081 Branches & Agencies of Foreign Banks
SIC 6111 Federal & Federally-Sponsored Credit Agencies
SIC 6153 Short-Term Business Credit Institutions, Except Agricultural
SIC 6159 Miscellaneous Business Credit Institutions

52231 Mortgage & Other Loan Brokers
SIC 6163 Loan Brokers
52232 Financial Transactions Processing, Reserve, & Clearing House Activities
SIC 6019 Central Reserve Depository Institutions, nec
SIC 6099 Functions Related to Depository Banking, nec
SIC 6153 Short-Term Business Credit Institutions, Except Agricultural
SIC 7389 Business Services, nec
52239 Other Activities Related to Credit Intermediation
SIC 6099 Functions Related to Depository Banking, nec
SIC 6162 Mortgage Bankers & Loan Correspondents
52311 Investment Banking & Securities Dealing
SIC 6211 Security Brokers, Dealers, & Flotation Companies
52312 Securities Brokerage
SIC 6211 Security Brokers, Dealers, & Flotation Companies
52313 Commodity Contracts Dealing
SIC 6099 Functions Related to depository Banking, nec
SIC 6799 Investors, nec
SIC 6221 Commodity Contracts Brokers & Dealers
52314 Commodity Brokerage
SIC 6221 Commodity Contracts Brokers & Dealers
52321 Securities & Commodity Exchanges
SIC 6231 Security & Commodity Exchanges
52391 Miscellaneous Intermediation
SIC 6211 Securities Brokers, Dealers & Flotation Companies
SIC 6799 Investors, nec
52392 Portfolio Management
SIC 6282 Investment Advice
SIC 6371 Pension, Health, & Welfare Funds
SIC 6733 Trust, Except Educational, Religious, & Charitable
SIC 6799 Investors, nec
52393 Investment Advice
SIC 6282 Investment Advice
523991 Trust, Fiduciary & Custody Activities
SIC 6021 National Commercial Banks
SIC 6022 State Commercial Banks
SIC 6091 Nondepository Trust Facilities
SIC 6099 Functions Related to Depository Banking, nec
SIC 6289 Services Allied With the Exchange of Securities or Commodities, nec
SIC 6733 Trusts, Except Educational, Religious, & Charitable
523999 Miscellaneous Financial Investment Activities
SIC 6099 Functions Related to Depository Banking, nec
SIC 6211 Security Brokers, Dealers, & Flotation Companies
SIC 6289 Services Allied With the Exchange of Securities or Commodities, nec
SIC 6799 Investors, nec
SIC 6792 Oil Royalty Traders
524113 Direct Life Insurance Carriers
SIC 6311 Life Insurance
524114 Direct Health & Medical Insurance Carriers
SIC 6324 Hospital & Medical Service Plans
SIC 6321 Accident & Health Insurance
524126 Direct Property & Casualty Insurance Carriers
SIC 6331 Fire, Marine, & Casualty Insurance
SIC 6351 Surety Insurance
524127 Direct Title Insurance Carriers
SIC 6361 Title Insurance
524128 Other Direct Insurance Carriers
SIC 6399 Insurance Carriers, nec
52413 Reinsurance Carriers
SIC 6311 Life Insurance
SIC 6321 Accident & Health Insurance

SIC 6324 Hospital & Medical Service Plans
SIC 6331 Fire, Marine, & Casualty Insurance
SIC 6351 Surety Insurance
SIC 6361 Title Insurance
52421 Insurance Agencies & Brokerages
SIC 6411 Insurance Agents, Brokers & Service
524291 Claims Adjusters
SIC 6411 Insurance Agents, Brokers & Service
524292 Third Party Administration for Insurance & Pension Funds
SIC 6371 Pension, Health, & Welfare Funds
SIC 6411 Insurance Agents, Brokers & Service
524298 All Other Insurance Related Activities
SIC 6411 Insurance Agents, Brokers & Service
52511 Pension Funds
SIC 6371 Pension, Health, & Welfare Funds
52512 Health & Welfare Funds
SIC 6371 Pension, Health, & Welfare Funds
52519 Other Insurance Funds
SIC 6321 Accident & Health Insurance
SIC 6324 Hospital & Medical Service Plans
SIC 6331 Fire, Marine, & Casualty Insurance
SIC 6733 Trusts, Except Educational, Religious, & Charitable
52591 Open-End Investment Funds
SIC 6722 Management Investment Offices, Open-End
52592 Trusts, Estates, & Agency Accounts
SIC 6733 Trusts, Except Educational, Religious, & Charitable
52593 Real Estate Investment Trusts
SIC 6798 Real Estate Investment Trusts
52599 Other Financial Vehicles
SIC 6726 Unit Investment Trusts, Face-Amount Certificate Offices, & Closed-End Management Investment Offices

REAL ESTATE & RENTAL & LEASING

53111 Lessors of Residential Buildings & Dwellings
SIC 6513 Operators of Apartment Buildings
SIC 6514 Operators of Dwellings Other Than Apartment Buildings
53112 Lessors of Nonresidential Buildings
SIC 6512 Operators of Nonresidential Buildings
53113 Lessors of Miniwarehouses & Self Storage Units
SIC 4225 General Warehousing & Storage
53119 Lessors of Other Real Estate Property
SIC 6515 Operators of Residential Mobile Home Sites
SIC 6517 Lessors of Railroad Property
SIC 6519 Lessors of Real Property, nec
53121 Offices of Real Estate Agents & Brokers
SIC 6531 Real Estate Agents Managers
531311 Residential Property Managers
SIC 6531 Real Estate Agents & Managers
531312 Nonresidential Property Managers
SIC 6531 Real Estate Agents & Managers
53132 Offices of Real Estate Appraisers
SIC 6531 Real Estate Agents & Managers
531399 All Other Activities Related to Real Estate
SIC 6531 Real Estate Agents & Managers
532111 Passenger Car Rental
SIC 7514 Passenger Car Rental
532112 Passenger Car Leasing
SIC 7515 Passenger Car Leasing

53212 Truck, Utility Trailer, & RV Rental & Leasing
SIC 7513 Truck Rental & Leasing Without Drivers
SIC 7519 Utility Trailers & Recreational Vehicle Rental

53221 Consumer Electronics & Appliances Rental
SIC 7359 Equipment Rental & Leasing, nec

53222 Formal Wear & Costume Rental
SIC 7299 Miscellaneous Personal Services, nec
SIC 7819 Services Allied to Motion Picture Production

53223 Video Tape & Disc Rental
SIC 7841 Video Tape Rental

532291 Home Health Equipment Rental
SIC 7352 Medical Equipment Rental & Leasing

532292 Recreational Goods Rental
SIC 7999 Amusement & Recreation Services, nec

532299 All Other Consumer Goods Rental
SIC 7359 Equipment Rental & Leasing, nec

53231 General Rental Centers
SIC 7359 Equipment Rental & Leasing, nec

532411 Commercial Air, Rail, & Water Transportation Equipment Rental & Leasing
SIC 4499 Water Transportation Services, nec
SIC 4741 Rental of Railroad Cars
SIC 7359 Equipment Rental & Leasing, nec

532412 Construction, Mining & Forestry Machinery & Equipment Rental & Leasing
SIC 7353 Heavy Construction Equipment Rental & Leasing
SIC 7359 Equipment Rental & Leasing, nec

53242 Office Machinery & Equipment Rental & Leasing
SIC 7359 Equipment Rental & Leasing
SIC 7377 Computer Rental & Leasing

53249 Other Commercial & Industrial Machinery & Equipment Rental & Leasing
SIC 7352 Medical Equipment Rental & Leasing
SIC 7359 Equipment Rental & Leasing, nec
SIC 7819 Services Allied to Motion Picture Production
SIC 7922 Theatrical Producers & Miscellaneous Theatrical Services

53311 Owners & Lessors of Other Nonfinancial Assets
SIC 6792 Oil Royalty Traders
SIC 6794 Patent Owners & Lessors

PROFESSIONAL, SCIENTIFIC, & TECHNICAL SERVICES

54111 Offices of Lawyers
SIC 8111 Legal Services

541191 Title Abstract & Settlement Offices
SIC 6541 Title Abstract Offices

541199 All Other Legal Services
SIC 7389 Business Services, nec

541211 Offices of Certified Public Accountants
SIC 8721 Accounting, Auditing, & Bookkeeping Services

541213 Tax Preparation Services
SIC 7291 Tax Return Preparation Services

541214 Payroll Services
SIC 7819 Services Allied to Motion Picture Production
SIC 8721 Accounting, Auditing, & Bookkeeping Services

541219 Other Accounting Services
SIC 8721 Accounting, Auditing, & Bookkeeping Services

54131 Architectural Services
SIC 8712 Architectural Services

54132 Landscape Architectural Services
SIC 0781 Landscape Counseling & Planning

54133 Engineering Services
SIC 8711 Engineering Services

54134 Drafting Services
SIC 7389 Business Services, nec

54135 Building Inspection Services
SIC 7389 Business Services, nec

54136 Geophysical Surveying & Mapping Services
SIC 8713 Surveying Services
SIC 1081 Metal Mining Services
SIC 1382 Oil & Gas Field Exploration Services
SIC 1481 Nonmetallic Minerals Services, Except Fuels

54137 Surveying & Mapping Services
SIC 7389 Business Services, nec
SIC 8713 Surveying Services

54138 Testing Laboratories
SIC 8734 Testing Laboratories

54141 Interior Design Services
SIC 7389 Business Services, nec

54142 Industrial Design Services
SIC 7389 Business Services, nec

54143 Commercial Art & Graphic Design Services
SIC 7336 Commercial Art & Graphic Design
SIC 8099 Health & Allied Services, nec

54149 Other Specialized Design Services
SIC 7389 Business Services, nec

541511 Custom Computer Programming Services
SIC 7371 Computer Programming Services

541512 Computer Systems Design Services
SIC 7373 Computer Integrated Systems Design
SIC 7379 Computer Related Services, nec

541513 Computer Facilities Management Services
SIC 7376 Computer Facilities Management Services

541519 Other Computer Related Services
SIC 7379 Computer Related Services, nec

541611 Administrative Management & General Management Consulting Services
SIC 8742 Management Consulting Services

541612 Human Resources & Executive Search Consulting Services
SIC 8742 Management Consulting Services
SIC 7361 Employment Agencies
SIC 8999 Services, nec

541613 Marketing Consulting Services
SIC 8742 Management Consulting Services

541614 Process, Physical, Distribution & Logistics Consulting Services
SIC 8742 Management Consulting Services

541618 Other Management Consulting Services
SIC 4731 Arrangement of Transportation of Freight & Cargo
SIC 8748 Business Consulting Services, nec

54162 Environmental Consulting Services
SIC 8999 Services, nec

54169 Other Scientific & Technical Consulting Services
SIC 0781 Landscape Counseling & Planning
SIC 8748 Business Consulting Services, nec
SIC 8999 Services, nec

54171 Research & Development in the Physical Sciences & Engineering Sciences
SIC 8731 Commercial Physical & Biological Research
SIC 8733 Noncommercial Research Organizations

54172 Research & Development in the Life Sciences
SIC 8731 Commercial Physical & Biological Research
SIC 8733 Noncommercial Research Organizations
54173 Research & Development in the Social Sciences & Humanities
SIC 8732 Commercial Economic, Sociological, & Educational Research
SIC 8733 Noncommercial Research Organizations
54181 Advertising Agencies
SIC 7311 Advertising Agencies
54182 Public Relations Agencies
SIC 8743 Public Relations Services
54183 Media Buying Agencies
SIC 7319 Advertising, nec
54184 Media Representatives
SIC 7313 Radio, Television, & Publishers' Advertising Representatives
54185 Display Advertising
SIC 7312 Outdoor Advertising Services
SIC 7319 Advertising, nec
54186 Direct Mail Advertising
SIC 7331 Direct Mail Advertising Services
54187 Advertising Material Distribution Services
SIC 7319 Advertising, NEC
54189 Other Services Related to Advertising
SIC 7319 Advertising, nec
SIC 5199 Nondurable Goods, nec
SIC 7389 Business Services, nec
54191 Marketing Research & Public Opinion Polling
SIC 8732 Commercial Economic, Sociological, & Educational Research
541921 Photography Studios, Portrait
SIC 7221 Photographic Studios, Portrait
541922 Commercial Photography
SIC 7335 Commercial Photography
SIC 8099 Health & Allied Services, nec
54193 Translation & Interpretation Services
SIC 7389 Business Services, NEC
54194 Veterinary Services
SIC 0741 Veterinary Services for Livestock
SIC 0742 Veterinary Services for Animal Specialties
SIC 8734 Testing Laboratories
54199 All Other Professional, Scientific & Technical Services
SIC 7389 Business Services

MANAGEMENT OF COMPANIES & ENTERPRISES

551111 Offices of Bank Holding Companies
SIC 6712 Offices of Bank Holding Companies
551112 Offices of Other Holding Companies
SIC 6719 Offices of Holding Companies, nec
551114 Corporate, Subsidiary, & Regional Managing Offices
No SIC equivalent

ADMINISTRATIVE & SUPPORT, WASTE MANAGEMENT & REMEDIATION SERVICES

56111 Office Administrative Services
SIC 8741 Management Services

56121 Facilities Support Services
SIC 8744 Facilities Support Management Services
56131 Employment Placement Agencies
SIC 7361 Employment Agencies
SIC 7819 Services Allied to Motion Pictures Production
SIC 7922 Theatrical Producers & Miscellaneous Theatrical Services
56132 Temporary Help Services
SIC 7363 Help Supply Services
56133 Employee Leasing Services
SIC 7363 Help Supply Services
56141 Document Preparation Services
SIC 7338 Secretarial & Court Reporting
561421 Telephone Answering Services
SIC 7389 Business Services, nec
561422 Telemarketing Bureaus
SIC 7389 Business Services, nec
561431 Photocopying & Duplicating Services
SIC 7334 Photocopying & Duplicating Services
561432 Private Mail Centers
SIC 7389 Business Services, nec
561439 Other Business Service Centers
SIC 7334 Photocopying & Duplicating Services
SIC 7389 Business Services, nec
56144 Collection Agencies
SIC 7322 Adjustment & Collection Services
56145 Credit Bureaus
SIC 7323 Credit Reporting Services
561491 Repossession Services
SIC 7322 Adjustment & Collection
SIC 7389 Business Services, nec
561492 Court Reporting & Stenotype Services
SIC 7338 Secretarial & Court Reporting
561499 All Other Business Support Services
SIC 7389 Business Services, NEC
56151 Travel Agencies
SIC 4724 Travel Agencies
56152 Tour Operators
SIC 4725 Tour Operators
561591 Convention & Visitors Bureaus
SIC 7389 Business Services, nec
561599 All Other Travel Arrangement & Reservation Services
SIC 4729 Arrangement of Passenger Transportation, nec
SIC 7389 Business Services, nec
SIC 7999 Amusement & Recreation Services, nec
SIC 8699 Membership Organizations, nec
561611 Investigation Services
SIC 7381 Detective, Guard, & Armored Car Services
561612 Security Guards & Patrol Services
SIC 7381 Detective, Guard, & Armored Car Services
561613 Armored Car Services
SIC 7381 Detective, Guard, & Armored Car Services
561621 Security Systems Services
SIC 7382 Security Systems Services
SIC 1731 Electrical Work
561622 Locksmiths
SIC 7699 Repair Shops & Related Services, nec
56171 Exterminating & Pest Control Services
SIC 4959 Sanitary Services, NEC
SIC 7342 Disinfecting & Pest Control Services
56172 Janitorial Services
SIC 7342 Disinfecting & Pest Control Services
SIC 7349 Building Cleaning & Maintenance Services, nec
SIC 4581 Airports, Flying Fields, & Airport Terminal Services

56173 Landscaping Services
SIC 0782 Lawn & Garden Services
SIC 0783 Ornamental Shrub & Tree Services

56174 Carpet & Upholstery Cleaning Services
SIC 7217 Carpet & Upholstery Cleaning

56179 Other Services to Buildings & Dwellings
SIC 7389 Business Services, nec
SIC 7699 Repair Shops & Related Services, nec

56191 Packaging & Labeling Services
SIC 7389 Business Services, nec

56192 Convention & Trade Show Organizers
SIC 7389 Business Services, NEC

56199 All Other Support Services
SIC 7389 Business Services, nec

562111 Solid Waste Collection
SIC 4212 Local Trucking Without Storage
SIC 4953 Refuse Systems

562112 Hazardous Waste Collection
SIC 4212 Local Trucking Without Storage
SIC 4953 Refuse Systems

562119 Other Waste Collection
SIC 4212 Local Trucking Without Storage
SIC 4953 Refuse Systems

562211 Hazardous Waste Treatment & Disposal
SIC 4953 Refuse Systems

562212 Solid Waste Landfill
SIC 4953 Refuse Systems

562213 Solid Waste Combustors & Incinerators
SIC 4953 Refuse Systems

562219 Other Nonhazardous Waste Treatment & Disposal
SIC 4953 Refuse Systems

56291 Remediation Services
SIC 1799 Special Trade Contractors, nec
SIC 4959 Sanitary Services, nec

56292 Materials Recovery Facilities
SIC 4953 Refuse Systems

562991 Septic Tank & Related Services
SIC 7359 Equipment Rental & Leasing, nec
SIC 7699 Repair Shops & Related Services, nec

562998 All Other Miscellaneous Waste Management Services
SIC 4959 Sanitary Services, nec

EDUCATIONAL SERVICES

61111 Elementary & Secondary Schools
SIC 8211 Elementary & Secondary Schools

61121 Junior Colleges
SIC 8222 Junior Colleges & Technical Institutes

61131 Colleges, Universities & Professional Schools
SIC 8221 Colleges, Universities, & Professional Schools

61141 Business & Secretarial Schools
SIC 8244 Business & Secretarial Schools

61142 Computer Training
SIC 8243 Data Processing Schools

61143 Professional & Management Development Training Schools
SIC 8299 Schools & Educational Services, nec

611511 Cosmetology & Barber Schools
SIC 7231 Beauty Shops
SIC 7241 Barber Shops

611512 Flight Training
SIC 8249 Vocational Schools, nec
SIC 8299 Schools & Educational Services, nec

611513 Apprenticeship Training
SIC 8249 Vocational Schools, nec

611519 Other Technical & Trade Schools
SIC 8249 Vocational Schools, NEC
SIC 8243 Data Processing Schools

61161 Fine Arts Schools
SIC 8299 Schools & Educational Services, nec
SIC 7911 Dance Studios, Schools, & Halls

61162 Sports & Recreation Instruction
SIC 7999 Amusement & Recreation Services, nec

61163 Language Schools
SIC 8299 Schools & Educational Services, nec

611691 Exam Preparation & Tutoring
SIC 8299 Schools & Educational Services, nec

611692 Automobile Driving Schools
SIC 8299 Schools & Educational Services, nec

611699 All Other Miscellaneous Schools & Instruction
SIC 8299 Schools & Educational Services, nec

61171 Educational Support Services
SIC 8299 Schools & Educational Services nec
SIC 8748 Business Consulting Services, nec

HEALTH CARE & SOCIAL ASSISTANCE

621111 Offices of Physicians
SIC 8011 Offices & Clinics of Doctors of Medicine
SIC 8031 Offices & Clinics of Doctors of Osteopathy

621112 Offices of Physicians, Mental Health Specialists
SIC 8011 Offices & Clinics of Doctors of Medicine
SIC 8031 Offices & Clinics of Doctors of Osteopathy

62121 Offices of Dentists
SIC 8021 Offices & Clinics of Dentists

62131 Offices of Chiropractors
SIC 8041 Offices & Clinics of Chiropractors

62132 Offices of Optometrists
SIC 8042 Offices & Clinics of Optometrists

62133 Offices of Mental Health Practitioners
SIC 8049 Offices & Clinics of Health Practitioners, nec

62134 Offices of Physical, Occupational & Speech Therapists & Audiologists
SIC 8049 Offices & Clinics of Health Practitioners, nec

621391 Offices of Podiatrists
SIC 8043 Offices & Clinics of Podiatrists

621399 Offices of All Other Miscellaneous Health Practitioners
SIC 8049 Offices & Clinics of Health Practitioners, nec

62141 Family Planning Centers
SIC 8093 Speciality Outpatient Facilities, NEC
SIC 8099 Health & Allied Services, nec

62142 Outpatient Mental Health & Substance Abuse Centers
SIC 8093 Specialty Outpatient Facilities, nec

621491 HMO Medical Centers
SIC 8011 Offices & Clinics of Doctors of Medicine

621492 Kidney Dialysis Centers
SIC 8092 Kidney Dialysis Centers

621493 Freestanding Ambulatory Surgical & Emergency Centers
SIC 8011 Offices & Clinics of Doctors of Medicine

621498 All Other Outpatient Care Centers
SIC 8093 Specialty Outpatient Facilities, nec

621511 Medical Laboratories
SIC 8071 Medical Laboratories

621512 Diagnostic Imaging Centers
SIC 8071 Medical Laboratories

62161 Home Health Care Services
SIC 8082 Home Health Care Services
62191 Ambulance Services
SIC 4119 Local Passenger Transportation, nec
SIC 4522 Air Transportation, Nonscheduled
621991 Blood & Organ Banks
SIC 8099 Health & Allied Services, nec
621999 All Other Miscellaneous Ambulatory Health Care Services
SIC 8099 Health & Allied Services, nec
62211 General Medical & Surgical Hospitals
SIC 8062 General Medical & Surgical Hospitals
SIC 8069 Specialty Hospitals, Except Psychiatric
62221 Psychiatric & Substance Abuse Hospitals
SIC 8063 Psychiatric Hospitals
SIC 8069 Specialty Hospitals, Except Psychiatric
62231 Specialty Hospitals
SIC 8069 Specialty Hospitals, Except Psychiatric
62311 Nursing Care Facilities
SIC 8051 Skilled Nursing Care Facilities
SIC 8052 Intermediate Care Facilities
SIC 8059 Nursing & Personal Care Facilities, nec
62321 Residential Mental Retardation Facilities
SIC 8052 Intermediate Care Facilities
62322 Residential Mental Health & Substance Abuse Facilities
SIC 8361 Residential Care
623311 Continuing Care Retirement Communities
SIC 8051 Skilled Nursing Care Facilities
SIC 8052 Intermediate Care Facilities
SIC 8059 Nursing & Personal Care Facilities, nec
623312 Homes for the Elderly
SIC 8361 Residential Care
62399 Other Residential Care Facilities
SIC 8361 Residential Care
62411 Child & Youth Services
SIC 8322 Individual & Family Social Services
SIC 8641 Civic, Social, & Fraternal Organizations
62412 Services for the Elderly & Persons with Disabilities
SIC 8322 Individual & Family Social Services
62419 Other Individual & Family Services
SIC 8322 Individual & Family Social Services
62421 Community Food Services
SIC 8322 Individual & Family Social Services
624221 Temporary Shelters
SIC 8322 Individual & Family Social Services
624229 Other Community Housing Services
SIC 8322 Individual & Family Social Services
62423 Emergency & Other Relief Services
SIC 8322 Individual & Family Social Services
62431 Vocational Rehabilitation Services
SIC 8331 Job Training & Vocational Rehabilitation Services
62441 Child Day Care Services
SIC 8351 Child Day Care Services
SIC 7299 Miscellaneous Personal Services, nec

ARTS, ENTERTAINMENT, & RECREATION

71111 Theater Companies & Dinner Theaters
SIC 5812 Eating Places
SIC 7922 Theatrical Producers & Miscellaneous Theatrical Services

71112 Dance Companies
SIC 7922 Theatrical Producers & Miscellaneous Theatrical Services
71113 Musical Groups & Artists
SIC 7929 Bands, Orchestras, Actors, & Entertainment Groups
71119 Other Performing Arts Companies
SIC 7929 Bands, Orchestras, Actors, & Entertainment Groups
SIC 7999 Amusement & Recreation Services, nec
711211 Sports Teams & Clubs
SIC 7941 Professional Sports Clubs & Promoters
711212 Race Tracks
SIC 7948 Racing, Including Track Operations
711219 Other Spectator Sports
SIC 7941 Professional Sports Clubs & Promoters
SIC 7948 Racing, Including Track Operations
SIC 7999 Amusement & Recreation Services, nec
71131 Promoters of Performing Arts, Sports & Similar Events with Facilities
SIC 6512 Operators of Nonresidential Buildings
SIC 7922 Theatrical Procedures & Miscellaneous Theatrical Services
SIC 7941 Professional Sports Clubs & Promoters
71132 Promoters of Performing Arts, Sports & Similar Events without Facilities
SIC 7922 Theatrical Producers & Miscellaneous Theatrical Services
SIC 7941 Professional Sports Clubs & Promoters
71141 Agents & Managers for Artists, Athletes, Entertainers & Other Public Figures
SIC 7389 Business Services, nec
SIC 7922 Theatrical Producers & Miscellaneous Theatrical Services
SIC 7941 Professional Sports Clubs & Promoters
71151 Independent Artists, Writers, & Performers
SIC 7819 Services Allied to Motion Picture Production
SIC 7929 Bands, Orchestras, Actors, & Other Entertainers & Entertainment Services
SIC 8999 Services, nec
71211 Museums
SIC 8412 Museums & Art Galleries
71212 Historical Sites
SIC 8412 Museums & Art Galleries
71213 Zoos & Botanical Gardens
SIC 8422 Arboreta & Botanical & Zoological Gardens
71219 Nature Parks & Other Similar Institutions
SIC 7999 Amusement & Recreation Services, nec
SIC 8422 Arboreta & Botanical & Zoological Gardens
71311 Amusement & Theme Parks
SIC 7996 Amusement Parks
71312 Amusement Arcades
SIC 7993 Coin-Operated Amusement Devices
71321 Casinos
SIC 7999 Amusement & Recreation Services, nec
71329 Other Gambling Industries
SIC 7993 Coin-Operated Amusement Devices
SIC 7999 Amusement & Recreation Services, nec
71391 Golf Courses & Country Clubs
SIC 7992 Public Golf Courses
SIC 7997 Membership Sports & Recreation Clubs
71392 Skiing Facilities
SIC 7999 Amusement & Recreation Services, nec
71393 Marinas
SIC 4493 Marinas

71394 Fitness & Recreational Sports Centers
SIC 7991 Physical Fitness Facilities
SIC 7997 Membership Sports & Recreation Clubs
SIC 7999 Amusement & Recreation Services, nec
71395 Bowling Centers
SIC 7933 Bowling Centers
71399 All Other Amusement & Recreation Industries
SIC 7911 Dance Studios, Schools, & Halls
SIC 7993 Amusement & Recreation Services, nec
SIC 7997 Membership Sports & Recreation Clubs
SIC 7999 Amusement & Recreation Services, nec

ACCOMMODATION & FOODSERVICES

72111 Hotels & Motels
SIC 7011 Hotels & Motels
SIC 7041 Organization Hotels & Lodging Houses, on
Membership Basis
72112 Casino Hotels
SIC 7011 Hotels & Motels
721191 Bed & Breakfast Inns
SIC 7011 Hotels & Motels
721199 All Other Traveler Accommodation
SIC 7011 Hotels & Motels
721211 RV Parks & Campgrounds
SIC 7033 Recreational Vehicle Parks & Campgrounds
721214 Recreational & Vacation Camps
SIC 7032 Sporting & Recreational Camps
72131 Rooming & Boarding Houses
SIC 7021 Rooming & Boarding Houses
SIC 7041 Organization Hotels & Lodging Houses, on
Membership Basis
72211 Full-Service Restaurants
SIC 5812 Eating Places
722211 Limited-Service Restaurants
SIC 5812 Eating Places
SIC 5499 Miscellaneous Food Stores
722212 Cafeterias
SIC 5812 Eating Places
722213 Snack & Nonalcoholic Beverage Bars
SIC 5812 Eating Places
SIC 5461 Retail Bakeries
72231 Foodservice Contractors
SIC 5812 Eating Places
72232 Caterers
SIC 5812 Eating Places
72233 Mobile Caterers
SIC 5963 Direct Selling Establishments
72241 Drinking Places
SIC 5813 Drinking Places

OTHER SERVICES

811111 General Automotive Repair
SIC 7538 General Automotive Repair Shops
811112 Automotive Exhaust System Repair
SIC 7533 Automotive Exhaust System Repair Shops
811113 Automotive Transmission Repair
SIC 7537 Automotive Transmission Repair Shops

811118 Other Automotive Mechanical & Electrical Repair &
Maintenance
SIC 7539 Automotive Repair Shops, nec
811121 Automotive Body, Paint & Upholstery Repair &
Maintenance
SIC 7532 Top, Body, & Upholstery Repair Shops & Paint
Shops
811122 Automotive Glass Replacement Shops
SIC 7536 Automotive Glass Replacement Shops
811191 Automotive Oil Change & Lubrication Shops
SIC 7549 Automotive Services, Except Repair & Carwashes
811192 Car Washes
SIC 7542 Carwashes
811198 All Other Automotive Repair & Maintenance
SIC 7534 Tire Retreading & Repair Shops
SIC 7549 Automotive Services, Except Repair & Carwashes
811211 Consumer Electronics Repair & Maintenance
SIC 7622 Radio & Television Repair Shops
SIC 7629 Electrical & Electronic Repair Shops, nec
811212 Computer & Office Machine Repair & Maintenance
SIC 7378 Computer Maintenance & Repair
SIC 7629 Electrical & Electronic Repair Shops, nec
SIC 7699 Repair Shops & Related Services, nec
811213 Communication Equipment Repair & Maintenance
SIC 7622 Radio & Television Repair Shops
SIC 7629 Electrical & Electronic Repair Shops, nec
811219 Other Electronic & Precision Equipment Repair &
Maintenance
SIC 7629 Electrical & Electronic Repair Shops, nec
SIC 7699 Repair Shops & Related Services, NEC
81131 Commercial & Industrial Machinery & Equipment
Repair & Maintenance
SIC 7699 Repair Shops & Related Services, nec
SIC 7623 Refrigerator & Air-Conditioning Service & Repair
Shops
SIC 7694 Armature Rewinding Shops
811411 Home & Garden Equipment Repair & Maintenance
SIC 7699 Repair Shops & Related Services, nec
811412 Appliance Repair & Maintenance
SIC 7623 Refrigeration & Air-Conditioning Service & Repair
Shops
SIC 7629 Electrical & Electronic Repair Shops, NEC
SIC 7699 Repairs Shops & Related Services, nec
81142 Reupholstery & Furniture Repair
SIC 7641 Reupholstery & Furniture Repair
81143 Footwear & Leather Goods Repair
SIC 7251 Shoe Repair & Shoeshine Parlors
SIC 7699 Repair Shops & Related Services
81149   Other Personal & Household Goods Repair &
Maintenance
SIC 3732 Boat Building & Repairing
SIC 7219 Laundry & Garment Services, nec
SIC 7631 Watch, Clock, & Jewelry Repair
SIC 7692 Welding Repair
SIC 7699 Repair Shops & Related Services, nec
812111 Barber Shops
SIC 7241 Barber Shops
812112 Beauty Salons
SIC 7231 Beauty Shops
812113 Nail Salons
SIC 7231 Beauty Shops
812191 Diet & Weight Reducing Centers
SIC 7299 Miscellaneous Personal Services, nec

812199 Other Personal Care Services
SIC 7299 Miscellaneous Personal Services, nec,
81221 Funeral Homes
SIC 7261 Funeral Services & Crematories
81222 Cemeteries & Crematories
SIC 6531 Real Estate Agents & Managers
SIC 6553 Cemetery Subdividers & Developers
SIC 7261 Funeral Services & Crematories
81231 Coin-Operated Laundries & Drycleaners
SIC 7215 Coin-Operated Laundry & Drycleaning
812321 Laundries, Family & Commercial
SIC 7211 Power Laundries, Family & Commercial
812322 Drycleaning Plants
SIC 7216 Drycleaning Plants, Except Rug Cleaning
812331 Linen Supply
SIC 7213 Linen Supply
SIC 7219 Laundry & Garment Services, nec,
812332 Industrial Launderers
SIC 7218 Industrial Launderers
812391 Garment Pressing, & Agents for Laundries
SIC 7212 Garment Pressing & Agents for Laundries
812399 All Other Laundry Services
SIC 7219 Laundry & Garment Services, NEC
81291 Pet Care Services
SIC 0752 Animal Speciality Services, Except Veterinary
812921 Photo Finishing Laboratories
SIC 7384 Photofinishing Laboratories
812922 One-Hour Photo Finishing
SIC 7384 Photofinishing Laboratories
81293 Parking Lots & Garages
SIC 7521 Automobile Parking
81299 All Other Personal Services
SIC 7299 Miscellaneous Personal Services, nec
SIC 7389 Miscellaneous Business Services
81311 Religious Organizations
SIC 8661 Religious Organizations
813211 Grantmaking Foundations
SIC 6732 Educational, Religious, & Charitable Trust
813212 Voluntary Health Organizations
SIC 8399 Social Services, nec
813219 Other Grantmaking & Giving Services
SIC 8399 Social Services, NEC
813311 Human Rights Organizations
SIC 8399 Social Services, nec
813312 Environment, Conservation & Wildlife Organizations
SIC 8399 Social Services, nec
SIC 8699 Membership Organizations, nec
813319 Other Social Advocacy Organizations
SIC 8399 Social Services, NEC
81341 Civic & Social Organizations
SIC 8641 Civic, Social, & Fraternal Organizations
SIC 8699 Membership Organizations, nec
81391 Business Associations
SIC 8611 Business Associations
SIC 8699 Membership Organizations, nec
81392 Professional Organizations
SIC 8621 Professional Membership Organizations
81393 Labor Unions & Similar Labor Organizations
SIC 8631 Labor Unions & Similar Labor Organizations
81394 Political Organizations
SIC 8651 Political Organizations
81399 Other Similar Organizations
SIC 6531 Real Estate Agents & Managers
SIC 8641 Civic, Social, & Fraternal Organizations

SIC 8699 Membership Organizations, nec
81411 Private Households
SIC 8811 Private Households

PUBLIC ADMINISTRATION

92111 Executive Offices
SIC 9111 Executive Offices
92112 Legislative Bodies
SIC 9121 Legislative Bodies
92113 Public Finance
SIC 9311 Public Finance, Taxation, & Monetary Policy
92114 Executive & Legislative Offices, Combined
SIC 9131 Executive & Legislative Offices, Combined
92115 American Indian & Alaska Native Tribal Governments
SIC 8641 Civic, Social, & Fraternal Organizations
92119 All Other General Government
SIC 9199 General Government, nec
92211 Courts
SIC 9211 Courts
92212 Police Protection
SIC 9221 Police Protection
92213 Legal Counsel & Prosecution
SIC 9222 Legal Counsel & Prosecution
92214 Correctional Institutions
SIC 9223 Correctional Institutions
92215 Parole Offices & Probation Offices
SIC 8322 Individual & Family Social Services
92216 Fire Protection
SIC 9224 Fire Protection
92219 All Other Justice, Public Order, & Safety
SIC 9229 Public Order & Safety, nec
92311 Administration of Education Programs
SIC 9411 Administration of Educational Programs
92312 Administration of Public Health Programs
SIC 9431 Administration of Public Health Programs
92313 Administration of Social, Human Resource & Income Maintenance Programs
SIC 9441 Administration of Social, Human Resource & Income Maintenance Programs
92314 Administration of Veteran's Affairs
SIC 9451 Administration of Veteran's Affairs, Except Health Insurance
92411 Air & Water Resource & Solid Waste Management
SIC 9511 Air & Water Resource & Solid Waste Management
92412 Land, Mineral, Wildlife, & Forest Conservation
SIC 9512 Land, Mineral, Wildlife, & Forest Conservation
92511 Administration of Housing Programs
SIC 9531 Administration of Housing Programs
92512 Administration of Urban Planning & Community & Rural Development
SIC 9532 Administration of Urban Planning & Community & Rural Development
92611 Administration of General Economic Programs
SIC 9611 Administration of General Economic Programs
92612 Regulation & Administration of Transportation Programs
SIC 9621 Regulations & Administration of Transportation Programs
92613 Regulation & Administration of Communications, Electric, Gas, & Other Utilities
SIC 9631 Regulation & Administration of Communications, Electric, Gas, & Other Utilities

92614 Regulation of Agricultural Marketing & Commodities
SIC 9641 Regulation of Agricultural Marketing & Commodities
**92615 Regulation, Licensing, & Inspection of Miscellaneous
Commercial Sectors**
SIC 9651 Regulation, Licensing, & Inspection of Miscellaneous
Commercial Sectors
92711 Space Research & Technology
SIC 9661 Space Research & Technology
92811 National Security
SIC 9711 National Security
92812 International Affairs
SIC 9721 International Affairs
99999 Unclassified Establishments
SIC 9999 Nonclassifiable Establishments

APPENDIX III

ANNOTATED SOURCE LIST

The following listing provides the names, publishers, addresses, telephone and fax numbers (if available), and frequency of publications for the primary sources used in *Market Share Reporter*.

Adhesives Age, Communication Channels Inc., 6255 Barfield Rd, Atlanta, GA 30328, *Telephone:* (256-9800, *Fax:* (404) 256-3116, *Published:* monthly.

Adhesives & Sealants Industry, Communication Channels Inc., 6255 Barfield Rd., Atlanta, GA 30328, *Telephone:* (404) 256-9800, *Fax:* (404) 256-3116, *Published:* monthly.

Advanced Coatings & Surface Technology, Freedonia Group, 767 Beta Drive, Cleveland, OH 44143, *Telephone:* (440) 684-9611.

Advertising Age, Crain Communications, Inc., 220 E. 42nd St., New York, NY 10017, *Telephone:* (212) 210-0725, *Fax:* (212) 210-0111, *Published:* weekly.

Adweek, BPI Communications, Merchandise Mart, Suite 396, Chicago, IL 60654, *Telephone:* (800) 722-6658, *Fax:* (312) 464-8540, *Published:* weekly.

Aftermarket Business, Advanstar Communications, Inc., 7500 Old Oak Blvd., Cleveland, OH 44130-3343, *Published:* monthly.

Ag Lender, 11701 Boorman Drive, St. Louis, MO 63146, *Telephone:* (800) 535-2342.

AgExporter, U.S. Government Printing Office, Superintendent of Documents, Washington D.C. 20402, *Telephone:* (202) 783-3238, *Fax:* (202) 275-0019.

Air Cargo World, Journal of Commerce Inc., 1230 National Press Building, Washington D.C. 20045, *Telephone:* (202) 783-1148, *Published:* monthly.

Air Conditioning, Heating and Refrigeration News, Business News Publishing Co., P.O. Box 2600, Troy, MI 48007, *Telephone:* (313) 362-3700, *Fax:* (313) 362-0317.

Air Transport World, 600 Summer St., P.O. Box 1361, Stamfort, CT 06904, Telephone: (203) 348-7531.

Albuquerque Journal, Albuquerque Publishing Co., 7777 Jefferson NE, Albuquerque, NM 87109, *Telephone:* (505) 823-3393.

Albuquerque Tribune, Albuquerque Publishing Co., 7777 Jefferson NE, Albuquerque, NM 87109, *Telephone:* (505) 823-3393.

American Banker, American Banker Inc., 1 State St, New York, NY 10023, *Telephone:* (212) 408-1480, *Fax:* (212) 943-2984, *Published:* Mon. - Fri.

American Business Review, University of New Haven, 300 Orange Avenue, West Haven CT 06516.

American Ceramic Society Bulletin, American Ceramic Society, 735 Ceramic Place, Westerville, OH 43081-8720, *Published:* monthly, *Price:* $50 per year for nonmembers and libraries.

American Demographics, Media Central, 470 Park Avenue South, 8th Floor, New York, NY 10016, *Telephone:* (800) 529-7502, *Published:* monthly, Price: $89 a year; $99 Canada.

American Lawyer, 600 3rd Avenue, New York 10016, *Telephone:* (212) 973-2800, *Fax:* (212) 972-6258, *Published:* monthly, with combined issues, *Price:* $135, $265, home; $525 office.

American Nurseryman, American Nurseryman Publishing Co., 77 W. Washington St., Ste. 2100, Chicago, IL 60602-2801, *Telephone:* (312) 782-5505, *Fax:* (312) 782-3232.

American Printer, Maclean Hunter Publishing Co., 29 N. Wacker Dr., Chicago, IL 60606. *Published:* monthly.

American School & University, North American Publishing Co., 401 N. Broad St., Philadelphia, PA 19106, *Telephone:* (215) 238-4200, *Fax:* (215) 238-4227, *Published:* monthly.

Amusement Business, BPI Communications Inc., Box 24970, Nashville, TN 37202, *Telephone:* (615)321-4250, *Fax:* (615) 327-1575. *Published:* weekly.

Appliance, Dana Chase Publications Inc., 1110 Jorie Blvd., CS 9019, Ste. 203, Hinsdale, IL 60521, *Telephone:* (708) 990 - 3484, *Fax:* (708) 990 - 0078, *Published:* monthly, *Price:* $60.

Appliance Manufacturer, Business News Publishing Co., 755 W. Big Beaver Rd., Ste. 1000, Troy, MI 48084-4900, *Telephone:* (313) 362-3700, *Fax:* (313) 244-6439, *Published:* monthly.

Arizona Republic, Phoenix Newspaper Inc., P.O. Box 1950, Phoenix, AZ 85001, *Telephone:* (602) 271-8000, *Fax:* (602) 271-8500, *Published:* daily.

Arkansas Business, 201 E. Markham, P.O. Box 3686, Little Rock, AR 72203, *Telephone:* (501)372-1443 Fax: (501) 375-3623, *Published:* weekly, *Price:* $38 per year.

Atlanta Journal-Constitution, 72 Marietta St., NW Atlanta, GA 30303, *Telephone:* (404) 526 - 5151, *Published:* daily.

Austin American-Statesman, P.O. Box 670, Austin, TX 78767, *Telephone:* (512) 445-3745, *Fax:* (512) 445-3800.

Auto Rental News, Quist Publishing, 210 Madison Ave., number 1108, New York, NY 10016-3802, Published: monthly, but not in August.

Automatic Merchandiser, Johnson Hill Press Inc., 1233 Janesville Ave., Fort Atkinson, WI 53538, *Telephone:* (414) 563-6388, *Fax:* (414) 563-1699, *Published:* monthly.

Automotive News, Crain Communications Inc., 380 Woodbridge, Detroit, MI 48207, *Telephone:* (313) 446-6000, *Fax:* (313) 446-0347.

AVG, Meister Publishing Co., 37733 Euclid Ave., Willoughby, OH 44094-5992, *Telephone:* (216) 942-2000, *Fax:* (216) 942-0662, *Published:* monthly.

Aviation Week & Space Technology, McGraw Hill Inc., 1221 Avenue of the Americas, New York, NY 10020, *Telephone:* (212) 512-2294, *Fax:* (212) 869-7799, *Published:* weekly.

Baking & Snack, Sosland Publishing Co., 4800 Main St., Ste 100, Kansas City, MO 64112, *Telephone:* (816) 756-1000.

Bank Systems & Technology, Miller Freeman Inc., 1515 Broadway, New York, NY 10036, *Telephone:* (212) 869-1300.

Banking Strategies, Bank Administration Institute, One North Franklin, Chicago, IL 60606, *Telephone:* (312) 553-4600, Price: $59.

Battery & EV Technology, BCC Inc., 25 Van Zant, Norwalk, C 06855-1781.

Behavioral Health Business News, Manisses Communications Group, 208 Governor Street, Providence, RI 02906.

Best's Review, A.M. Best Co. Inc., Ambest Rd., Oldwick, NJ 08858, *Telephone:* (908) 439-2200, *Fax:* (908) 439-3363, *Published:* monthly.

Beverage Aisle, Advanstar Communications, Inc., 7500 Old Oak Blvd., Cleveland OH 44130.

Beverage Dynamics, Jobson Publishing Corp., 100 Avenues of the Americas, 9th Floor, New York, NY 10013, *Telephone:* (212) 274-7000, *Fax:* (212) 431-0500.

Beverage Industry, Advanstar Communications, Inc., 7500 Old Oak Blvd., Cleveland OH 44130, *Telephone:* (216) 243-8100, *Fax:* (216) 891-2651, *Published:* monthly, *Price:* $40 per year.

Beverage World, Keller International Publishing Corp., 150 Great Neck Rd., Great Neck, NY 11021, *Telephone:* (516) 829-9210, *Fax:* (516) 829-5414, *Published:* monthly.

Bicycle Retailer & Industry News, 502 W. Cordova Rd., Santa Fe, NM 87501, *Telephone:* (505) 988-5099, *Fax:* (505) 988-7224, *Published:* monthly.

Billboard, BPI Communications, 1515 Broadway, 14th FL, New York, NY 10036, *Telephone*: (212) 764-7300, *Fax:* (212) 536-5358.

Biomedical Market Newsletter, 3237 Idaho Place, Costa Mesa, CA 92626-2207, *Telephone:* (714) 434-9500, *Fax:* (714) 434-9755.

The Blade, 541 Superior St., Toledo, OH 43660, *Telephone:* (419) 724-6000.

Bobbin, Bobbin Blenheim Media Corp., 1110 Shop Rd, Columbia, SC 29202.

The Boston Globe, 135 Morrisey Boulevard, P.O. Box 2378, Boston, MA 02107-2378, *Telephone:* (617) 929-2000.

Boston Herald, 1 Herald Sq., Boston, MA 02106-2096, *Telephone:* (617) 426-3000, *Fax:* (617) 426-1869.

Brandweek, Adweek L.P., 1515 Broadway, New York, NY 10036, *Telephone:* (212) 536-5336. *Published:* weekly, except no issue in the last week of Dec.

Broadcasting & Cable, Cahners Publishing Co., 1705 DeSales Street, N.W., Washington, DC 20036, *Telephone:* (800) 554-5729 or (202) 659-2340, *Fax:* (202) 331-1732.

BSB, Capital Cities/ABC/Chilton, Chilton Way, Radnor, PA 19089, *Telephone:* (215) 964-4000, *Fax:* (215) 964-4981.

BtoB, Crain Communications Inc., 220 E 42nd St., New York, NY 10017, *Telephone:* (202) 210-0725, *Fax:* (212) 210-0111, *Published:* weekly.

Buffalo Business First, 472 Delaware St., Buffalo, NY 14202.

Builder, Hanley-Wood Inc., 655 15th St. N.W., Ste. 475, Washington, D.C. 20005, *Telephone:* (202) 737-0717, *Fax:* (202) 737-2439, *Published:* monthly.

Building Design & Construction, Cahners Publishing Co., 1350 E. Touhy Ave., Des Plaines, IL 60018, *Telephone:* (708) 635-8800, *Fax:* (708) 299-8622, *Published:* monthly.

Burlington Free Press, 191 College Street, Burlington VT 05402-0010, *Telephone:* (802) 863-3441, *Fax:* (802) 862-5622.

Business 2.0, 5 Thomas Mellon Circle, Suite 305, San Francisco, CA 94134.

Business Forms, Labels & Systems, North American Publishing Co., 401 N Broad Street, Philadelphia, PA 19108, *Telephone:* (215) 238-5300, *Fax:* (215) 238-5457, *Published:* 2x/mo, *Price:* $24.

Business Mexico, American Chamber of Commerce, A.C., Lucerna 78, Col. Juarez, DEL. Cuahtemoc, Mexico City, Mexico, *Telephone:* 705-0995, *Published:* monthly.

Business Record, 100 4th Street, Des Moines IA 50309, Telephone: (515) 288-3336, Fax: (515) 288-0309, Published: weekly.

Business Review (Albany, NY), P.O. Box 15081, Albany, NY 12212-5081, *Telephone:* (518) 437-9855, *Fax:* (518) 437-0764, *Published:* weekly, *Price:* $45.

Business Travel News, CMP Publications, 600 Community Drive, Manhasset, NY 11030, *Telephone:* (516) 365-4600, *Fax:* (516) 562-5474.

BusinessWeek, McGraw-Hill Inc., 1221 Avenue of the Americas, New York, NY 10020. *Published:* weekly, *Price:* U.S.: $46.95 per year; Canada: $69 CDN per year.

Buyouts, 195 Broadway, New York, NY.

C&EN, American Chemical Society, Dept. L-0011, Columbus, OH 43210, *Telephone:* (800) 333-9511 or (614) 447-3776. *Published:* weekly, except last week in December, *Price:* U.S.: $100 per year, $198 for 2 years; elsewhere: $148 per year, $274 for 2 years.

Cabling Installation & Maintenance, PennWell, 98 Spit Brook Rd., Nashua, NH 03062, *Telephone:* (603) 891-0123.

Calgary Herald, 215 16th St SE, Calgary, AB T2P OW8, *Telephone:* (403) 235-7100.

Canadian Business, CB Media Limited, 70 Esplanade, Second Floor, Toronto MSE IR2 Canada, *Telephone:* (416) 364-4266, *Fax:* (416) 364-2783. *Published:*

monthly, *Price:* Canada: $24 per year, $60 for 3 years; Elsewhere: $40 per year, $100 for 3 years.

Canadian Machinery and Metalworking, Maclean Hunter, 777 Bay St., Toronto, ON Canada, *Telephone:* (416) 596-5772, *Fax:* (416) 593-3162, *Published:* monthly.

Canadian Mining Journal, Southern Business Communications, 1450 Don Mills Rd., Don Mills, ON Canada M3B 2X7, *Telephone:* (416) 445-6641.

Canadian Packaging, Maclean Hunter, 777 Bay St., Toronto, ON Canada, *Telephone:* (416) 596-5772, *Fax*: (416) 593-3162, *Published:* monthly.

Canadian Underwriter, Southern Business Communications, 1450 Don Mills Rd, Don Mills Ontario, Canada M3B 2X7.

Candy Business, Advanstar Communications Inc., 7500 Old Oak Blvd, Cleveland, OH 44130, *Telephone:* (216) 891-2612, *Fax:* (216) 891-2651, *Published:* monthly.

Candy Industry, Advanstar Communications Inc., 7500 Old Oak Blvd, Cleveland, OH 44130, *Telephone:* (216) 891-2612, *Fax:* (216) 891-2651, *Published:* monthly.

Cardline, One State Street Plaza, 27th fl, New York, NY 10004, *Telephone*: (800) 221-1809.

Cards International, Faulkner & Grey, 11 Penn Plaza, New York, NY 10001.

Catalog Age, Cowles Business Media, 911 Hope St., Six River Bend Center, P.O. Box 4949, Stanford, CT 06907-0949, *Telephone:* (203) 358-9900, *Published:* monthly.

Census of State and Law Enforcement, U.S. Government Printing Office, Superintendent of Documents, Washington D.C. 20402, *Telephone:* (202) 783-3238, *Fax:* (202) 275-0019.

Ceramic Bulletin, American Ceramic Society, 735 Ceramic Place, Westerville, OH 43081-8720, *Published:* monthly, *Price:* $50.

Ceramic Industry, Business News Publishing Co., 5900 Harper Road, Suite 109, Solon, OH 44139, *Telephone:* (216) 498-9214, *Fax:* (216) 498-9121. *Published:* monthly, *Price:* U.S.: $53 per year; Mexico: $63; Canada: $66.71 (includes postage & GST).

Chain Drug Review, Racher Press, 220 5th Ave, New York, NY 10001, *Telephone:* (212) 213-6000, *Fax:* (212) 725-3961.

Chain Leader, Attn: Reader Services, 1350 E. Touhy Ave, PO Box 5080, Des Plaines, IL 60017-5080.

Charlotte Business Journal, 120 W Morehead St., Suite 200, Charlotte, NC 28202.

Charlotte Observer, Knight-Ridder, 1 Herald Drive, Miami, FL 33132, *Telephone:* (305) 376-3800, *Published:* daily.

Chemical Market Reporter, Schnell Publishing Co., Inc., 80 Broad St., New York, NY 1004-2203, *Telephone:* (212) 248-4177, *Fax:* (212) 248-4903, *Published:* weekly.

Chemical Week, Chemical Week Associates, P.O. Box 7721, Riverton, NJ 08077-7721, *Telephone:* (609) 786-0401, *Published:* weekly, except four combination issues (total of 49 issues), *Price:* U.S.: $99 per year; Canada: $129 per year. Single copies $8 in U.S. and $10 elsewhere.

Child Care Information Exchange, Exchange Press Inc., P.O. 2890, Redmond, WA 98073, *Telephone:* (800) 221-2864, *Published:* bimonthly, *Price:* $35 per year.

Children's Business, Fairchild Publications, 7 W 34th St., New York, NY 10001, *Telephone:* (212) 630-4520, *Fax:* (212) 630-4511.

The Christian Science Monitor, Christian Science Publishing Society, One Norway St., Boston, MA 02115, *Telephone:* (800) 456-2220, *Published:* daily, except weekends and holidays.

The Cincinnati Post, E.W. Scripps Co., 125 E Court St., Cincinnati, OH 45202, *Telephone:* (513) 352-2000, *Fax:* (513) 621-3962.

CircuiTree, BNP, 755 West Big Beaver, Ste 100, Troy, MI 48084, *Telephone:* (248)362-3700.

Coatings World, 70 Hilltop Road, Ramsey, NJ 07466.

ColoradoBiz, Wiesner Publishing, 7009 S. Potomoac Street, Suite 200, Centennial, CO 80112, *Telephone:* (303) 397-7600.

Comic Buyer's Guide, Krause Publications Inc., 700 E State St., Iola, WI 54990-0001, *Telephone:* (715) 445-2214, *Fax:* (715) 445-4087, *Published:* weekly, *Price:* $38.95 a year.

Commercial Carrier Journal, Capital Cities/ABC/Chilton Co., Chilton Way, Radnor, PA 19089, *Telephone:* (215) 964 4000, *Fax:* (215) 964-4981.

Community Banker, 5704 71st Street, Lubbock, TX 79424.

Computer Reseller News, CMP Media, One Jericho Plaza, Jericho, NY 11753, *Published:* weekly, *Price:* $199, Canada $224.

Computing Canada, Plesman Publications Ltd., 2005 Sheppard Ave. E., 4th Fl., Willowsdale, ON, Canada M2J 5B1, *Telephone:* (416) 497-9562, *Fax:* (416) 497-9427. *Published:* biweekly.

Concrete Construction, The Aberdeen Group, 426 S. Weestgate, Addison, IL 60101-9929, *Telephone:* (708) 543-0870, *Fax:* (708) 543-3112, *Published:* monthly.

Concrete Products, Maclean Hunter Publishing, 29 N Wacker Drive, Chicago, IL 60606, *Telephone:* (312) 726-2802, *Fax:* (312) 726-2574.

Confectioner, American Publishing Corp., 17400 Dallas Pkway, Number 121, Dallas, TX 752-7305, *Telephone:* (214) 250-3630, *Fax:* (214) 250-3733.

Construction Equipment, Cahners PublishingCo., 1350 E. Touhy Ave., Des Plaines, IL 60018, *Telephone:* (708) 635-8800, *Fax:* (708) 390-2690.

Consumer Electronics, CEA, 2500 Wilson Blvd., Arlington, VA 22201-3834.

Control Engineering, Cahners PublishingCo., 1350 E. Touhy Ave., Des Plaines, IL 60018, *Telephone:* (708) 635-8800, *Fax:* (708) 390-2690.

Convenience Store News, BMT Publications Inc., 7 Penn Plaza, New York, NY 10001-3900, *Telephone:* (212) 594-4120, *Fax:* (212) 714-0514, *Published:* 16x/yr.

Cosmetic Surgery Times, 7500 Old Oak Blvd, Cleveland, OH 44130, *Telephone:* (800) 225-4569.

Cosmetics International, 307 Linen Hall, 162/ 168 Regent Street, London, W1R 5TB, United Kingdom, *Telephone:* (020) 7434-1530, *Fax:* (020) 7437-0915.

Cosmetics Magazine, Rogers Media, One Mount Pleasant Road, 7th fl, Toronto, Ontario, Canada.

Courier Journal, 525 W Broadway P.O. Box 740031, Louisville KY 40201-7431, *Telephone:* (502) 582-4011.

Crain's Chicago Business, Crain Communications Inc., 740 N. Rush St., Chicago, IL 60611, *Telephone:* (312) 649-5411.

Crain's Detroit Business, Crain Communications Inc., 1400 Woodbridge, Detroit, MI 48207-3187, *Telephone:* (313) 446-6000. *Published:* weekly, except semiweekly the fourth week in May.

Crain's New York Business, Crain Communications, Inc., 220 E. 42nd St., New York, NY 10017, *Telephone:* (212) 210-0100, *Fax:* (212) 210-0799. *Published:* weekly.

Credit Card Management, Faulkner & Gray Inc., 11 Penn Plaza, 17th FL, New York, NY 10001, *Telephone:* (212) 766-7800, *Fax:* (212) 766-0142.

Crop Production, U.S. Government Printing Office, Superintendent of Documents, Washington D.C. 20402, *Telephone:* (202) 783-3238, *Fax:* (202) 275-0019.

Daily Business Review, 330 Clematis Street, Via Jardin, Suite 114, West Palm Beach, FL 33401, *Telephone:* (561) 820-2060, *Fax:* (561) 820-2077.

Daily Herald, P.O. Box 280, Arlinton Heights, IL 60193, *Telephone:* (847) 427-4300.

Daily News Record, Cahners Publishing Co., 275 Washington St., Newton, MA 02158, *Telephone:* (617) 558-4243, *Fax:* (617) 558-4759, *Published:* 2x/mo.

Dairy Field, Stagnito Communications Inc., 155 Pfingsten Road, Suite 205, Deerfield, IL 60015, *Telephone:* (847) 205-5660, *Fax:* (847) 205-5680.

Dairy Foods, Gorman Publishing Co., 8750 W. Bryn Mawr Ave., Chicago, IL 60062, *Telephone:* (312) 693-3200. *Published:* monthly, except semimonthly in Aug.

Datamonitor Industry Market Research, Datamonitor USA, 1 Park Avenue, 14th Floor, New York, NY 10016-5802.

Dayton Daily News, P.O. Box 1287, Dayton, OH 45401-1287.

Dealernews, Advanstar Communications Inc., 1700 E Dyer Rd., Ste. 250, Santa Ana, CA 92705, *Telephone:* (714) 252-5300, *Fax:* (714) 261-9790, *Published:* monthly.

Dealerscope, North American Publishing Co., 401 N Broad St, Philadelphia, PA 19108.

The Denver Post, 1560 Broadway, Denver, CO 80202, Telephone: (303) 820-1201, *Published*: daily.

Des Moines Register, 715 Locust St., Des Moines, IA 50309, Telephone: (800) 247-5346, Published: daily.

Detroit Free Press, Knight-Ridder, Inc., 1 Herald Plaza, Miami, FL 33132, *Telephone:* (305) 376-3800, *Published:* daily.

Detroit News, Detroit News Inc., 615 Lafayette, Detroit, MI 48226, *Telephone:* (313) 222-2300, *Published:* daily.

Diesel Progress, Diesel & Gas Turbine Publications, 20855 Watertown Road, Suite 220, Waukesha, WI 53186.

Do-It-Yourself-Retailing, National Retail Hardware Assn., 5822 W. 74th St., Indianapolis, IN 46278-1756, *Telephone:* (317) 297-1190, *Fax:* (317) 328-4354, *Published:* monthly, *Price: $8; $2 single issue.*

Drug Store News, Lehbhar-Friedman Inc., 425 Park Ave, New York, NY 10022, *Telephone:* (212) 756-5000, *Fax:* (212) 838-9487, *Published:* 2x/mo.

Drug Topics, Medical Economics Publishing, 5 Paragon Drive, Montvale, NJ 0764 1742, *Telephone:* (201) 358-7200, *Fax:* (201) 573-1045.

DSN Retailing Today, Lebharr-Friedmann Inc., 425 Park Ave., New York, NY 10022, *Telephone:* (212) 756-5100, *Fax:* (212) 756-5125.

Duty-Free News International, Euromoney, Nestor House, Playhouse Yard, London EC4V 5EX, United Kingdom.

Ear, Nose & Throat Journal, Medquest Communications, 3800 Lakeside Avenue, Suite 201, Cleveland, OH 44114, *Telephone:* (216) 391-9100, *Published:* monthly.

EBN, Cahners Publishing Co., 275 Washington, Newton, MA 02158-1630, *Telephone:* (617) 964-3030, *Fax:* (617) 558-4470.

The Economist, The Economist Bldg, 111 W. 57th St., New York, NY 10019, *Telephone:* (212) 541-5730,

Fax: (212) 541-9378, *Published:* weekly, *Cost:* $110; $3.50 per single issue.

Econtent, Online Inc., 213 Danbury Rd., Wilton, CT 06897-4007, *Telephone:* (203) 761-1466, *Fax:* (203) 761-1444.

Edmonton Journal, 5325 Allard Way, Edmonton, Alberta, Canada, T6h 5B8, *Telephone:* (780) 436-1250, *Fax:* (780) 438-8448.

Educational Marketer, Simba Information, PO Box 4234, 11 River Bend Drive South, Stamford, CT 06907-0234.

Egg Industry, Watt Publishing Co., 122 S. Wesley Ave., Mount Morris, IL 61054-1497, *Telephone:* (815) 734-4171, *Fax:* (815) 734-4201, *Published:* bi-monthly.

El Paso Times, 300 N. Campbell St., El Paso, TX 7999.

Electric Light & Power, 1421 S Sheridan Road, Tulsa, OK 74112, *Telephone:* (918) 832-9249, *Fax:* (918) 831-9875, *Published:* monthly.

Electric Vehicle Online Today, EIN Publishing, 119 South Fairfax, Alexandria, Virgina 22314.

Electronic Business, Cahners Publishing Co., 275 Washington, Newton, MA 02158-1630, *Telephone:* (617) 964-3030, *Fax:* (617) 558-4470.

Electronic Education Report, Simba Information, PO Box 4234, 11 River Bend Drive South, Stamford, CT 06907-0234.

Electronic Engineering Times, CMP Publications, 600 Community Drive, Manhasset, NY 11030, *Telephone:* (516) 562-5000, *Fax:* (516) 562-5995.

Electronic News, Electronic News Publishing Corp., 488 Madison Ave., New York, NY 10022, *Telephone:* (212) 909-5924, *Published:* weekly, except last week of Dec.

Employee Benefit News, Enterprise Communications, 1483 Chain Bridge Rd., Ste 202, McLean, VA 22101-4599, *Telephone:* (703) 448-0322, *Fax:* (703) 827-0720, *Published*: monthly, *Price:* $56; $62 in Canada and Mexico.

ENR , McGraw-Hill Inc., Fulfillment Manager, ENR, P.O. Box 518, Highstown, NJ 08520, *Telephone:* (609) 426-7070 or (212) 512-3549, *Fax:* (212) 512-3150, *Published:* weekly, *Price:* U.S.: $89 per year; Canada: $75 per year. Single copies $5 in U.S.

Entertainment Marketing Letter, EMP Communications, 160 mercer St, New York, NY 10012, *Telephone:* (212) 941-0099, *Fax:* (212) 941-1622.

Entertainment Weekly, Time-Warner Inc., 1675 Broadway, New York, NY 10019, *Published:* weekly.

European Cosmetics Market, Wilmington Publishing, 6-14 Underwood St., London N1 7JQ, U.K.

E Week, 10 Presidents Landing, Medford, MA 02155, *Telephone:* (781) 393-3700.

Fairfield County Business Journal, Westfair Communications, 22 Saw Mill River Rd., Hawthorne, NY 10532, *Telephone:* (914) 347-5200, *Fax:* (914) 347-5576, *Published:* weekly, *Price:* $36.

Family Practice News, International Medical News Group, 770 Lexington Ave., New York, NY 10021, *Telephone:* (212) 888-3232, *Fax:* (212) 421-0106, *Published:* 2x/mo. *Price:* $96.

Farms and Land in Farms, U.S. Government Printing Office, Superintendent of Documents, Washington D.C. 20402, *Telephone:* (202) 783-3238, *Fax:* (202) 275-0019.

Feedstuffs, Miller Publishing Co., 12400 Whitewater Dr., Ste. 1600, Minnetonka, MN 55343, *Telephone:* (612) 931-0211.

Finance and Commerce, 615 S. 7th St, Minneapolis MN 55415.

Financial Times, FT Publications Inc., 14 East 60th Street, New York, NY 21002, *Telephone:* (212) 752-4500, *Fax:* (212) 319-0704, *Published:* daily, except for Sundays and holidays, *Price:* $425.

Floor Focus, 28 Old Stone Hill, Pound Ridge, NY 10576, *Telephone:* (914) 764-0556, *Fax:* (914) 764-0560.

Floriculture, U.S. Government Printing Office, Superintendent of Documents, Washington D.C. 20402, *Telephone:* (202) 783-3238, *Fax:* (202) 275-0019.

Florida Bar News, 651 E. Jefferson, Tallahassee, FL 32399-2300, *Telephone:* (850) 561-5600.

Florida Times-Union, Morris Communications, P.O. Box 936, Augusta, GA 30913-0936, *Telephone:* (706) 724-0851.

Florida Today, Cape Publications, P.O. Box 41900, Melbourne, FL 32941, *Telephone:* (407) 242-3500, *Fax:* (407) 242-6618, *Published:* daily, *Price:* $143 local, $208 out of area.

Florida Trend, Trend Magazines, PO Box 611, Saint Petersburg, FL 33731.

Food in Canada, Rogers Media Inc., 777 Bay Street, 6th Floor, Toronto, Ontario, Canada M5W 1A7, *Published:* monthly.

Food Institute Report, Food Insitute, Elwood Park, New Jersey.

Food Management, Penton Publishing, 1100 Superior, Cleveland, OH 44114, *Telephone:* (216) 696-7000, *Fax:* (216) 696-0836, *Published:* monthly.

Footwear News, Fairchild Publications, 7 W. 34th Street, New York, NY 10001, *Telephone:* (212) 630-4000, *Published:* weekly.

Forbes, Forbes, Inc., P.O. Box 10048, Des Moines, IA 50340-0048, *Telephone:* (800) 888-9896, *Published:* 27 issues per year, *Price:* U.S.: $54 per year; Canada: $95 per year (includes GST).

Forging, Penton Industries, Penton Media Building, 1300 E 9th St, Cleveland, OH 44114, *Telephone:* (216) 931-9141, *Fax:* (216) 931-9678.

Formulary, 7500 Old Oak Blvd, Cleveland, OH 44310, *Telephone:* (800) 225-4569.

Fortune, Time Inc., Time & Life Building, Rockefeller Center, New York, NY 10020-1393, *Published:* twice monthly, except two issues combined into a single issue at year-end, *Price:* U.S.: $57 per year; Canada: $65 per year.

Free Inquiry, Council for Secular Humanism, P.O. Box 664, Amherst, NY 14226-0664, *Telephone:* (800) 458-1366, *Fax:* (716) 636-1733.

Frozen Food Age, Maclean Hunter, 4 Stamford Four, Stamford, CT 06901-1201, *Telephone:* (203) 325-3500, *Published:* weekly.

Frozen Fruit Digest, 271 Madison Ave, New York, NY 10016.

Fuel Oil News, Hunter Publishing, 950 Lee St., Des Plaines, IL 60016, *Telephone:* (708) 296-0770, *Fax:* (708) 296-8821, *Published:* monthly.

Furniture Today, Cahners Publishing Co., 200 S. Main St., P.O. Box 2754, High Point, NC 27261, *Telephone:* (919) 889-0113, *Published:* weekly.

Games Analyst, Informa Media Group, Mortimer House, 37-41 Mortimer Street, London W1T 3JH, Untied Kingdom.

Gas Processors Report, Chemical Week Associates, 110 William St., New York, NY 10038, *Telephone:* (212) 621-4900, *Fax:* (212) 621-4949, *Published:* weekly, *Price:* $797 a year.

Gifts & Decorative Accessories, Geyer-McAllister Publications, 51 Madison Ave., New York, NY 10010, *Telephone:* (212) 689-4411, *Fax:* (212) 683-7929.

Global Cosmetic Industry, Advanstar Communications, 270 Madison Ave., New York, NY 10016.

Globe and Mail, 444 Front St. W., Toronto, ON, Canada M5V 2S9, *Telephone:* (416) 585-5000, *Fax:* (416) 585-5085, *Published:* Mon.-Sat. (Morn.).

Golf World, 5520 Park Ave, Trumbull, CT 06611.

Golf World Business, 5520 Park Ave., Trumbull, CT 06611.

Government Executive, National Journal Inc., 1730 M. NW, Ste 1100, Washington D.C. 20036, *Telephone:* (202) 862-0600.

Graphic Arts Monthly, Cahners Publishing Company, 44 Cook St., Denver, CO 80206-5800, *Telephone:* (800) 637-6089.

Greater Baton Rouge Business Report, Louisiana Business, P.O. Box 1949, Baton Rouge, LA 70821, *Telephone:* (504) 928-1700, *Fax:* (504) 923-3448, *Published:* biweekly, *Price:* $24; free to qualified subscribers.

Grocery Headquarters, Delta Communications Inc., 455 N. Cityfront Plaza Drive, Chicago, IL 60611, *Telephone:* (312) 222-2000, *Fax:* (312) 222-2026, *Published:* monthly.

Hawaii Business, Hawaii Business Publishing, 825 Keeamoku St., P.O. Box 913, Honolulu, HI 96808, *Telephone:* (808) 946-3978, *Fax:* (808) 947-8498, *Price:* $18.

Health Products Business, Cygnus Publishing, P.O. Box 803, Ft. Atkinson, WI 53538-0803.

Healthcare Purchasing News, 7650 So. Tamiami Trail Suite Suite 10, Sarasota, FL 34231, *Telephone:* (941) 927-9345, *Fax:* (941) 927-9588.

The Hearing Journal, The Laux Company Inc., 63 Great Rd., Maynard, MA 01754-2025, *Telephone:* (508) 897-5552, *Fax:* (508) 897-6824, *Published:* monthly.

HFN, 7 E. 12th St., New York, NY 10003. *Published:* weekly.

Hogs and Pigs, U.S. Government Printing Office, Superintendent of Documents, Washington D.C. 20402, *Telephone:* (202) 783-3238, *Fax:* (202) 275-0019.

Hollywood Reporter, 5055 Wilshire Blvd, 6th Fl, Los Angeles, CA 90036, *Telephone:* (213) 525-2000, *Fax:* (213) 525-2377, *Published:* weekdays.

Home Accents Today, 1350 E. Touhy Ave, PO Box 5080, Des Plaines, IL 60017-5080.

Home Care, 2104 Harvell Circle, Bellevue NE 68005, *Telephone:* (866) 505-7173, *Fax:* (402) 293-0741.

Home Channel News, Lebhar-Friedman Inc., 425 Park Avenue, New York, NY 10022, *Telephone:* (212) 756-5228, *Published:* 22x/yr.

Home Textiles Today, Cahners Publishing Co., 249 W 17th St., New York, NY 10011, *Telephone:* (212) 337-6900.

Hospital Materials Management, Aspen Publishers, 200 Orchard Ridge Dr., Ste. 200, Gaithersburg, MD 20878, Telephone: (301) 417-7500, Fax: (301) 417-7550.

Hotel & Motel Management, Advanstar Communications, Inc., 7500 Old Oak Blvd., Cleveland, OH 44130, *Telephone:* (216) 826-2839.

Household and Personal Products Industry, Rodman Publishing, 17 S. Franklin Turnpike, Box 555, Ramsey, NJ 07446, *Telephone:* (201) 825-2552, *Fax:* (201) 825-0553, *Published:* monthly.

Houston Chronicle, 801 Texas Ave., Houston, TX 77002, *Telephone*: (713) 220-7171, *Fax:* (713) 220-6677.

ICS Cleaning Specialist, 22801 Ventura Blvd, #115, Woodland Hills, CA 91364, *Telephone* (818) 224-8035, *Fax:* (818) 224-8042.

Implement & Tractor, Farm Press Publications, P.O. Bopx 1420, Clarksdale, MS 38614, *Telephone:* (601)

624-8503, *Fax:* (601) 627-1977, *Published:* monthly, *Price:* $15.

Indianapolis Business Journal, IBJ Corp., 431 N Pennsylvania St., Indianapolis, IN 46204, *Telephone:* (317) 634-6200, Fax: (317) 263-5060, *Published:* weekly, *Price:* $54.

The Indianapolis Star, Indianapolis Newspapers Inc., 307 N. Pennsylvania St., Indianapolis, IN 46204, *Telephone:* (317) 633-1157, *Fax:* (317) 633-1174.

Industrial Distribution, Cahners Publishing Company, 275 Washington Street, Newton, MA 02158, *Telephone:* (617) 964-3030, *Published:* monthly.

Industrial Paint & Powder, 1050 IL Route Suite 200, Bensenville, IL 60106, *Published:* monthly.

Infoworld, Infoworld Publishing Co., 155 Bovet Rd., Ste. 800, San Mateo, CA 94402, *Telephone:* (415) 572-7341, *Published:* weekly.

Ink World, 70 Hilltop Road, Ramsey NJ 07446.

Institutional Investor, 488 Madison Ave., New York, NY 10022, *Telephone:* (212) 303-3300, *Fax:* (212) 303-3171, *Published:* monthly.

Interavia, Swissair Centre, 31 Route de l'Aeroport, P.O. Box 437, 1215 Geneva 15 Switzerland, Switzerland, *Telephone:* (902) 788-2788, *Published:* monthly, *Price:* $128.

Investment News, 711 Third Avenue, Third floor, New York, NY 10017, *Telephone:* (212) 210-0759, *Fax:* (212) 210-0117.

Investor's Business Daily, P.O. Box 661750, Los Angeles, CA 90066-8950, *Published:* daily, except weekends and holidays, *Price:* $128 per year.

JCK's High-Volume Retailer, Capital Cities/ABC/Chilton, Chilton Way, Radnor, PA 19089, *Telephone:* (215) 964-4000, *Fax:* (215) 964-4947.

JofC Week, Journal of Commerce Inc., Two World Trade Center, 27th Floor, New York, NY 10048, *Telephone:* (800) 331-1341, *Fax:* (973) 848-7259.

Journal News, 228 Court St, Hamilton OH 45011.

Journal of Commerce, Journal of Commerce Inc., Two World Trade Center, 27th Floor, New York, NY 10048, *Telephone:* (800) 331-1341, *Fax:* (973) 848-7259.

Kingston Whig-Standard, Osprey Media, P.O. Box 2300, 6 Cataraqui St., Kingston, Ontario, Canada K7L 4Z7, *Telephone:* (613) 544-5000.

Kitchen & Bath Business, Miller Freeman, 1515 Broadway, New York, NY 10036, *Telephone:* (212) 869-1300, *Fax:* (212) 302-6273.

Label & Narrow Web, 70 HilltopRoad, Ramsey, NJ 07446,*Telephone:* (201) 825-2552, *Fax:* (201) 825-0553.

Laser Focus World, PennWell Publishing Co., 1 Technology Park Drive, Westford, MA 01886, *Telephone:* (508) 692-0700, *Fax:* (508) 692-9415.

Latin America Telecom, IGI Group, 320 Washington, Suite 302, Boston, MA 02135, *Telephone:* (800) 323-1088, *Fax:* (617) 782-5735.

Latin Trade, Freedom Communications Inc., 200 South Bicauyne Blvd., Suite 1150, Miami, FL 33131, *Published:* monthly.

Lightwave, PennWell Publishing Co., 1 Technology Park Drive, Westford, MA 01886, *Telephone:* (508) 692-0700, *Fax:* (508) 692-8391.

Limousine & Chauffered Transportation, 21061 S Western Ave, Torrance, CA 90501, *Telephone:* (310) 533-2400.

LLA, Laurentian Media Inc., 501 Oakdale Rd., Downsview, ON, Canada M3N 1W7, *Telephone*: (416) 746-7360, *Fax:* (416) 746-1421.

Lodging Hospitality, Penton Publishing, 1100 Superior Ave., Cleveland, OH 44114, *Telephone:* (216) 696-7000, *Fax:* (216) 696-7658.

Logging & Sawmilling Journal, P.O. Box 86670, 211 East 1st Street, North Vancouver BC, V7L 4L2, *Telephone:* (604) 990-9970, *Fax:* (604) 990-9971.

Long Island Business News, 2150 Smithtown Ave., Ronkonkoma, New York 11779.

Los Angeles Business Journal, Los Angeles, CA 92005-0001, *Telephone:* (800) 404-5225.

Los Angeles Times, The Times Mirror Company, Times Mirror Square, Los Angeles, CA 90053, *Telephone:* (800) LA TIMES.

LP/GAS, Advanstar Communications, 131 West First Street, Duluth, MN 55802-2065, *Published:* monthly, *Price:* $40.

Lubricants World, Chemical Week Associates, 110 William Street, New York, NY 10138, *Telephone:* (212) 621-4900, *Fax:* (212) 621-4949.

Macleans, 7th Floor, 777 Bay Street, Toronto, ON M5W 1A7, *Published:* weekly.

Managed Healthcare Executive, 7500 Old Oak Blvd, Cleveland, OH 44130.

Munuged Medicare & Medicaid, AIS, 1100 17th St., NW Ste 300, Washington D.C., 20036.

The Manufacturing Confectioner, The Manufacturing Confectioner Publishing Company, 175 Rock Rd., Glen Rock, NJ 07452, *Telephone:* (201) 652-2655, *Fax:* (201) 652-3419, *Published:* 12 times per year, *Price:* $25 per year, single copies $10 each, except $25 for April and July issues.

Marketing Magazine, Maclean Hunter Canadian Publishing, P.O. Box 4541, Buffalo, NY 14240-4541, *Telephone:* (800) 567-0444, *Fax:* (416) 946-1679, *Price:* Canada: $59.50 per year, $98.50 for 2 years, $125 for 3 years; U.S.: $90 per year.

Material Handling Product News, Gordon Publications, 301 Gibraltar Drive, P.O. Box 650, Morris Plains, NJ 07950-0650, *Telephone:* (201) 292-5100, *Fax:* (201) 539-3476.

Meat Retailer, Stagnito Communications Inc., 155 Pfingsten Road, Suite 205, Deerfield, IL 60015, *Telephone:* (847) 205-5660, *Fax:* (847) 205-5680.

Med Ad News, Engel Communications, 820 Bear Taven Rd., Ste 302, West Trenton, NJ 08628, *Telephone:* (609) 530-0044, *Fax:* (609) 530-0207.

Mediaweek, Adweek, LP, PO Box 1976, Danbury, CT 06813-1976, *Telephone:* (800) 722-6658, *Published:* weekly.

Medical Marketing & Media, CPS Communications, 7200 West Camino Real, Ste. 215, Boca Raton, FL 33433, *Telephone:* (407) 368-9301, *Fax:* (407) 368-7870, *Published:* monthly, *Price:* $75 per year.

Meetings & Conventions, Reed Travel Group, 500 Plaza Drive, Secaucus, NJ 07096, *Telephone:* (201) 902-1700, *Fax:* (201) 319-1796.

Mergers & Acquisitions Journal, One State Street Palza, 27th fl, New York, NY 10004, *Telephone:* (212) 803-8200.

Mergers & Acquisitions Report, One State Street Palza, 27th fl, New York, NY 10004, *Telephone:* (212) 803-8200.

Metal Center News, 2000 Clearwater Dr., Pak brook, IL 60523.

Metalworkers Insiders Report, P.O. Box 107, Larchmont, New York, 10538, *Telephone:* (914) 834-2300.

Metro Magazine, Bobit Publishing, 2512 Artesia Blvd, Redondo Beach, CA 90278, *Telephone:* (310) 376-8788, *Fax:* (310) 376-9043, *Published:* 7x/yr., *Price:* $12.

Michigan Retailer, Michigan Retailers Association, 221 North Pine Street, Lansing, MI 48933, *Published:* 10x/yr. *Price:* $20.

Milling & Baking News, Sosland Publishing Co., 4800 Main St., Ste. 100, Kansas City, MO 64112, *Telephone:* (816) 756-1000, *Fax:* (816) 756-0494.

Milwaukee Journal-Sentinel, Journal/Sentinel Inc., P.O. Box 371, 53201, *Telephone:* (414) 224-2000, *Published:* Mon-Sat.

MMR, Racher Press, 220 5th Ave., New York, NY 1001, *Telephone:* (212) 213-6000, *Fax:* (212) 213-6101, *Published:* biweekly.

Modern Casting, American Foundrymen's Society, 505 State St., Des Plaines, IL 60016-8399, *Telephone:* (708) 824-0181.

Modern Materials Handling, Cahners Publishing, 271 Washington St, Newton, MA 02158, *Telephone:* (617) 964-3030, *Fax:* (617) 558-4402.

Modern Plastics, McGraw-Hill, P.O. Box 481, Highstwon, NJ 08520, *Telephone:* (800) 525-5003, *Published:* monthly.

Modern Tire Dealer, Bill Communications Inc., PO Box 3599, Akron, OH 44309-3599, *Telephone:* (216) 867-4401, *Fax:* (216) 867-0019, *Published:* 14x/yr.

Montgomery Advertiser, 425 Molton St., Montgomery AL 36101, *Telephone:* (334) 262-1611.

The Morning Call, 101 N. 6th St., Allentown, PA 18105, *Telephone:* (215) 820-6646, *Published:* daily.

Mortgage Banking, Mortgage Bankers Assn of America, 1125 15th St. NW, Washington D.C. 20005, *Telephone:* (202) 861-6500, *Fax:* (202) 872-0186, *Published:* monthly.

Mortgage Servicing News, Thomas Financial Mortgage Publications.

Mortgage Technology, One Station Place, Stamford, CT 06902, *Telephone:* (203) 969-8700, *Fax:* (203) 977-8354.

Motor Trend, Peterson Publishing, 8490 Sunset Blvd, Los Angeles, CA 90069, *Telephone:* (213) 854-2222.

Music & Copyright, Informa, Mortimer House, 37-41 Mortimer Street, London W1T 3JH, Untied Kingdom.

Music Trades, P.O. Box 432, 80 West St., Englewood, NJ 07631, *Telephone:* (201) 871-1965, *Fax:* (201) 871-0455, *Published:* monthly.

National Defense, 2111 Wilson Boulevard, Suite 400, Arlington VA 2201-3061, *Telephone:* (703) 522-1820, *Fax:* (703) 522-1885.

National Floor Trends, 22801 Ventura Blvd, #115, Woodland Hills, CA 91364, *Telephone:* (818) 224-8035, *Fax:* (818) 224-8042.

National Jeweler, Miller Freeman, 1515 Broadway, New York, NY 10036, *Telephone:* (212) 626-2380, *Fax:* (212) 944-7164, *Published*: 2x/mo.

National Mortgage News, National Thrift News Inc., 212 W. 35th St., 13th FL, New York, NY 10001, *Telephone:* (212) 563-4008, *Fax:* (212) 564-8879, *Published:* 39x/yr.

National Petroleum News, Hunter Publishing, 950 Lee St., Des Plaines, IL 60016, *Telephone:* (708) 296-0770, *Fax:* (708) 296-8821, *Published*: monthly.

National Post, 300 1450 Don Mills Road, Don Mills, Ontario Canada, *Telephone:* (416) 383-2300, *Fax*: (416) 442-2209.

National Provisioner, 15 W. Huron St., Chicago, IL 60610, *Telephone:* (312) 944-3380, *Fax:* (312) 944-3709.

National Real Estate Investor, Communications Channels, 6255 Barfield, Atlanta, GA 30328, *Telephone:* (404) 256-9800, *Published: monthly.*

National Underwriter, The National Underwriter Co., 505 Gest St., Cincinnati, OH 45203, *Telephone:* (800) 543-0874, *Fax:* (800) 874-1916, *Published:* weekly, except last week in December, *Price:* U.S.: $77 per year, $130 for 2 years; Canada: $112 per year, $130 for 2 years.

Nation's Restaurant News, Lebhar-Friedman, Inc., Subscription Dept., P.O. Box 31179, Tampa, FL 33631-3179, *Telephone:* (800) 447-7133. *Published:* weekly on Mondays, except the first Monday in July and the last Monday in December, *Price:* $34.50 per year and $55 for 2 years for professionals in the field; $89 per year for those allied to field.

Natural Foods Merchandiser, 1401 Pearl Street, Boulder, CO 80302, Telephone: (303) 939-8440, Fax: (303) 939-9886.

Natural Gas Week, Energy Intelligence, 5 East 37th Street, 5th Floor, New York, NY 10016.

Network World, Network World, 161 Worcester Rd, Framingham, MA 01701-9172, *Telephone:* (508) 875-6400, *Published:* weekly.

New Mexico Business Weekly, 116 Central Ave., SW Suite 202, Albuquerque, NM 87102, *Telephone:* (505) 768-7008.

The New York Times, New York Times Co., 229 W. 43rd St., New York, NY 10036, *Telephone:* (212) 556-1234. *Published:* daily.

News Journal, P.O. Box 15505, Wilmington, DE 19850, Telephone: (800) 235-9100.

Newsweek, Newsweek Inc., 444 Madison Ave., New York, NY 10022, *Telephone:* (212) 350-4000, Published: weekly.

Nikkei Weekly, 1-9-5 Otemachi, Chiyoda-ku, Tokyo, 100-66 Japan.

Non-Profit Times, 120 Littleton Road, Sutie 120, Parsippany, NJ 07054-1803, *Telephone:* (973) 394-1800, *Fax:* (973) 394-2888, *Published:* 24x/yr.

Nonwovens Industry, Rodman Publishing, 17 S. Franklin Turnpike, P.O. Box 555, Ramsey, NJ 07446, *Telephone:* (201) 825-2552, *Fax:* (201) 825-0553, *Published:* monthly, *Price:* $48, or free to qualified subscribers.

Nursery Retailer, Brantwood Publications, 3023 Eastland Blvd, Ste. 103, Clearwater, FL 34621-4106, *Telephone:* (813) 796-3877, *Fax:* (813) 791-4126, *Published:* 6x/yr.

Nutraceuticals World, 70 Hilltop Road, Ramsey, NJ 07446, *Telephone:* (201) 825-2552, *Fax:* (201) 825-0553.

Oil & Gas Journal, PennWell Publishing CO., PO Box 2002, Tulsa, OK 74101, *Telephone:* (800) 633-1656, *Published:* weekly.

Oilweek, June Warren Publishing, 9915-56 Avenue NW, Edmonton Alberta Canada T6E 5L7

Orange County Register, 625 N Grand Ave, P.O. Box 11626, Santa Ana, CA 92711, *Telephone:* (714) 835-1234, *Fax:* (714) 542-5037.

Ottawa Citizen, P.O. Box 5020, 1101 Baxter Rd, Ottawa, ON K2C 3M4.

Paint & Coatings Industry, 755 W Big Bewaver Rd, Ste. 1000, Troy, MI 48083, *Published:* monthly.

Paperboard Packaging, Advanstar Communications Inc., 131 West First Street, Duluth, MN 55802, *Telephone:* (218) 723-9477, *Fax:* (218) 723-9437, *Published:* monthly, *Price:* U.S.: $39 per year, $58 for 2 years; Canada: $59 per year, $88 for 2 years.

Pest Control, Advanstar Communications, 7500 Old Oak Blvd, Cleveland, OH 44130.

Pet Product News, Fancy Publications, P.O. Box 6050, Mission Viejo, CA 9260, *Telephone:* (213) 385-2222, *Published:* monthly.

Pipeline & Gas Journal, Oildom Publishing Company of Texas Inc., 3314 Mercer St., Houston, TX 77027, *Telephone:* (713) 622-0676, *Fax:* (713) 623-4768, *Published:* monthly.

Pit & Quarry, Edgell Communications, 7500 Old Oak Blvd, Cleveland, OH 44130, *Telephone:* (216) 243-8100, *Fax:* (216) 891-2726, *Published:* monthly.

Pittsburgh Business Times, MCP Inc., 2313 E Carson St., Pittsburgh, PA 15203, *Telephone:* (412) 481-6397, *Fax:* (412) 481-9956, *Published:* weekly.

Pittsburgh Post-Gazette, 34 Blvd of the Allies, Pittsburgh, PA 1522, *Telephone:* (800) 228-6397.

Plastics News, Crain Communications, 965 E. Jefferson, Detroit, MI 48207-3185, *Published:* weekly.

Plastics Technology, 29 W 34th St, 8th Fl, New York, NY 10001, *Telephone:* (646) 827-4848, *Fax:* (513) 527-8801.

Playthings, Geyer-McAllister Publications, Inc., 51 Madison Ave., New York, NY 10010, *Telephone:* (212) 689-4411, *Fax:* (212) 683-7929, *Published:* monthly, except semimonthly in May.

Plumbing & Mechanical, Horton Publishing, 1350 E Touhy Ave, 100 E, Rosemont, IL 60018, *Published:* monthly.

Polymers Paint Colour Journal, DMG Media, *Telephone:* (44) 1737 855079.

Pool & Spa Marketing, Hubbard Marketing & Publishing, 46 Crockford Blvd, Scarborough, ON, Canada M1R 3C3, *Telephone:* (416) 752-2500, *Fax:* (416) 752-2748, *Published:* monthly, *Price:* $20.

Pool & Spa News, Leisure Publications, 3923 W 6th St., Los Angeles, CA 90020, *Telephone:* (213) 385-3926, *Fax:* (213) 383-1152, *Published:* 2x/mo.

PR Week, PR Publications Ltd., 220 Fifth Ave., New York, NY 10001, *Telephone:* (212) 532-9200, *Fax:* (212) 532-9200, *Published:* 49x/yr.

Practical Accountant, Faulkner & Gray, Inc., 11 Penn Plaza, 17th Floor, New York, NY 10001, *Telephone:* (800) 535-8403 or (212) 967-7060, *Published:* monthly, *Price:* U.S.: $60 per year; Elsewhere: $79 per year.

Prepared Foods, Cahners Publishing Company, 44 Cook St., Denver, CO 80217-3377, *Telephone:* (303) 388-4511, *Published:* monthly.

Printing Impressions, North American Publishing Co., 401 N Broad St., Philadelphia, PA 19108, *Telephone:* (215) 238-5300, *Fax:* (215) 238-5457.

Private Label Buyer, Stagnito Communications Inc., 155 Pfingsten Road, Suite 205, Deerfield, IL 60015, *Telephone:* (847) 205-5660, *Fax:* (847) 205-5680.

Professional Builder, Cahners Publishing, 1350 E Touhy Ave, Des Plaines, IL 60018, *Telephone:* (708) 635-8800, *Fax:* (708) 635-9950.

Professional Candy Buyer, Adams Business Media, 2101 S. Arlington Heights Rd., Arlington Heights, IL 60005-4142.

Professional Carwashing & Detailing Online, National Trade Publications, 13 Century Hill, Latham NY 12110, *Telephone:* (518) 783-1281, *Fax:* (518) 783-1386.

Progressive Grocer, 263 Tresser Blvd., Stamford, CT 06901, *Telephone:* (203) 325-3500, *Published:* monthly, *Price:* U.S.: $75 per year; Canada: $86 per year; single copies $9 each.

Promo, 2104 Harvell Circle, Bellvue, NE 68005.

Property Week, Ludgate House, 245 Blackfriars Rd, London SE1 9UY, UK.

Publishers Weekly, Cahners Publishing Company, ESP Computer Services, 19110 Van Ness Ave., Torrance, CA 90501-1170, *Telephone:* (800) 278-2991, *Published:* weekly, *Price:* U.S.: $129 per year; Canada: $177 per year (includes GST).

Pulp & Paper, Miller Freeman Inc., P.O. Box 1065, Skokie, IL 60076-8065, *Telephone:* (800) 682-8297, *Published:* monthly, *Price:* free to those in pulp, paper, and board manufacturing and paper converting firms; Others in U.S.: $100 per year.

Purchasing, Cahners Publishing Company, 44 Cook St., Denver, CO 80217-3377, *Telephone:* (303) 388-4511. *Published:* semimonthly, except monthly in January, February, July, August, December, and one extra issue in March and September, *Price:* U.S.: $84.95 per year; Canada: $133.95 per year; Mexico: $124.95 per year.

Quick Frozen Foods International, EW Williams Publishing Co., 2125 Center Ave., Ste. 305, Fort Lee, NJ 07024, *Telephone:* (201) 592-7007, *Fax:* (201) 592-7171, *Published:* monthly.

R&D Magazine, Cahners Publishing Company, 275 Washington St, Newton, MA 02158, Telephone: (708) 635-8800, Fax: (708) 390-2618, Published: monthly.

Railway Age, Simmons-Boardman Publishing, 345 Hudson St., New York, NY 10014, *Telephone:* (212) 620-7200, *Fax:* (212) 633-1165, *Published:* monthly.

RCR, RCR Publications, 777 East Speer Blvd., Denver, CO 80203.

Real Estate Alert, 5 Marine View Plaza, Ste. 301, Hoboken, NJ 07030-5795, *Telephone:* (201) 659-1700, *Fax:* (201) 659-4141.

Realtor, 430 N Michigan Ave, Chicago, IL 60611-4087.

The Record, 150 River St., Hackensack, NJ 07601.

Refrigerated & Frozen Foods, Stagnito Communications, 1935 Sherman Rd., Northbrook, IL 60062, *Telephone:* (847) 205-5660, *Fax:* (847) 205-5680, *Published:* monthly.

Refrigerated Transporter, Tunnell Publications, P.O. Box 66010, Houston, TX 77266, *Telephone:* (713) 528-8124, *Fax:* (713) 523-8384.

Reinsurance, Lafferty Group, 82 Bishops Bridge Road, London W2 6BB UK, *Telephone:* (44) 0 20 7563 5786.

Research Alert, EPM Communications, 160 Mercer Street, 3rd Floor, New York, NY 10012.

Research Studies, Freedonia Group, 767 Beta Drive, Cleveland, OH 44143, *Telephone:* (440) 684-9600.

Restaurant Business, Penton Publishing, 1100 Superior Ave., Cleveland, OH 44114, *Telephone:* (216) 696-7000.

Restaurant Hospitality, Penton Media, 1300 E 9th St, Cleveland, OH 44114.

Restaurants & Institutions, Cahners Publishing Co., 1350 Touhy Ave., Cahners Plaza, Des Plaines, IL 60017-5080, *Telephone:* (312) 635-8800.

Retail Merchandiser, Schwartz Publications, 233 Park Ave, New York, NY 1003, *Telephone:* (212) 979-4860.

Roanoke Times, 201 W Campbell, P.O. Box 2491, Roanoke VA 24010, *Telephone:* (800) 346-1234.

Rochester Democrat, Gannett Co., 1 Gannett Dr, White Plains, NY 10604-3498.

Rockford Register Star, 99 E. State St., Rockford, IL 61104.

Rocky Mountain News, 400 West Colfax, Denver, CO 80204.

Rolling Stone, Staight Arrow Publishers, 1290 Avenue of the Americas, New York NY 10104, *Telephone:* (212) 484-1616, *Fax:* (212) 767-8209.

Rubber & Plastics News, Crain Communications, 1725 Merriman Road, Ste. 300, Akron, OH 44313, *Telephone:* (330) 836-9180, *Fax:* (33) 836-1005, *Published:* weekly.

Rubber World, P.O. Box 5451, 1867 W. Market St., Akron, OH 44313-6901, *Telephone:* (330) 864-2122, *Fax:* (330) 864-5298.

RV Business, P.O. Box 17126, North Hollywood, CA 91615-9925, *Published:* monthly.

St. Louis Post Dispatch, 400 South 4th Street, Ste 1200, St. Louis, MO 63102, *Published:* daily.

San Diego Business Journal, 4909 Murphy Canyon, number 200, San Diego, CA 92123, *Telephone:* (619) 277-6359, *Fax:* (619) 571-3628.

San Francisco Chronicle, Chroncile Publishing Co., 901 Mission St., San Francisco, CA 94103-2988, *Telephone:* (415) 777-1111, *Fax:* (415) 512-8196.

San Jose Mercury News, Knight-Ridder Inc., 1 Herald Plaza, Miami, Fl 33132, *Published:* daily.

Sarasota Herald-Tribune, 801 S. Tamiami Trail, Sarasota, FL 34236, *Telephone:* (813) 953-7755, *Fax:* (813) 957-5235.

Satellite News, 800 Siesta Way, Sonoma, CA 95476, *Telephone:* (707) 939-9306, *Fax:* (707) 939-9235.

School Bus Fleet, Bobit Publishing, 2512 Artesia Blvd, Redondo Beach, CA 90278, *Telephone:* (310) 376-8788, *Fax:* (310) 376-9043.

School Foodservice & Nutrition, ASFSA, 700 South Washington, Suite 300, Alexandria, VA 22314, *Telephone:* (703) 739-3900, *Fax:* (703) 739-3915.

Screen Digest, EMAP Media, 33-39 Bowling Green Lane, London EC1R ODA, *Telephone:* 44 (0)171 396-8000, *Published:* weekly.

SDM, Cahners Publishing Co., 1350 E. Touhy Ave., Des Plaines, IL 60018, *Telephone:* (708) 635-8800, *Fax:* (708) 299-8622.

Seafood Business, Journal Publications, P.O. Box 98, Rockland, ME 04841, *Telephone:* (207) 594-6222, *Fax:* (207) 594-8978, *Published:* 6x/yr.

Seattle Times, P.O. Box 70, Seattle WA 98111, *Published:* daily.

Securities Industry News, One State Street, 27th Floor, New York, NY 10004, *Telephone:* (888) 280-4820, *Fax:* (301) 545-4836.

Sensor Business Digest, 1 Phoenix Mill Lane, Peterborough, NH 03458, *Telephone:* (603) 924-5400.

Sheep & Goats, U.S. Government Printing Office, Superintendent of Documents, Washington D.C. 20402, *Telephone:* (202) 783-3238, *Fax:* (202) 275-0010.

Shooting Industry, Publishers Development Corp., 591 Camino de la Reina, Ste. 200, San Diego, CA 92108, *Telephone:* (619) 297-8520, *Fax:* (619) 297-5353, *Published:* monthly, *Price:* $25.

Shopping Center World, Communications Channels, Inc., 6255 Barfield Rd., Altanta, GA 30328, *Telephone:* (404) 256-9800.

Snack Food & Wholesale Bakery, Stagnito Publishing Co., 1935 Shermer Rd., Ste. 100, Northbrook, IL 60062-5354, *Telephone:* (708) 205-5660, *Fax:* (708) 205-5680, *Published:* monthly, *Price:* free to qualified subscribers; $45 per year to all others.

Soap & Cosmetics, 455 Broad Hollow Road, Melville, NY 11747-4722, *Published:* monthly.

Spectroscopy, 859 Willamette, Eugene OR 97401, *Telephone:* (541) 343-1200.

Sporting Goods Business, Gralla Publications, Inc., 1515 Broadway, New York, NY 10036, *Telephone:* (212) 869-1300.

Star-Ledger, 1 Star-Ledger Plaza, Newark, NJ 07102, Telephone: (973) 392-4141.

Star Tribune, 425 Portland Ave., Minneapolis, MN 55488, *Telephone:* (612) 673-4000.

StateWays, Adams BeverageGroup, 17 High Street, Norwalk, CT 06851, *Telephone:* (203) 855-8499, *Fax:* (203) 855-9446.

Stores, NRF Enterprises Inc., 100 West 31st St., New York, NY 10001, *Published:* monthly, *Price:* U.S./Canada: $49 per year, $80 for 2 years, $120 for 3 years.

Supermarket News, Fairchild Publications, 7 W. 34th St., New York, NY 10001, *Telephone:* (212) 630-4750, *Fax:* (212) 630-4760.

Supply House Times, Horton Publishing, 1350 Touhy Ave. Ste. 100E, Rosemont, IL 60018-3358.

Tape-Disc Business, PBI Media, 1201 Seven Locks Road, Suite 300, Potomac, MD 20854, *Telephone:* (301) 354-2000.

Technology Access Report, 80 South Early Street, Alexandria, VA 22304-633, *Telephone:* (800) 733-1556.

Telecom Manager's Voice Report, CCMI, 1130 Rockville Pike, Suite 1100, Rockville MD 20852, Telephone: (888) 275-2264.

Telephony, Intersec Publishing Corp., 9800 Metcalf, Overland Park, KS 66282-2960, *Published:* monthly.

Time, Time, Inc., Time & Life Bldg., Rockefeller Center, New York, NY 10020-1393, *Telephone:* (800) 843-8463, *Published:* weekly.

Tire Business, Crain Communcations, Inc., 1725 Merriman Rd., Ste. 300, Akron, OH 44313-5251, *Telephone:* (216) 836-9180, *Fax:* (216) 836-1005.

Tradeshow Week, 5700 Wilshire Blvd, Ste 120, Los Angeles, CA 90036, *Telephone:* (323) 965-2437, *Fax:* (323) 965-2407.

Trailer Body Business, Tunnell Publications, P.O. Box 66010, Houston, TX 77266.

Training & Development, American Society for Training and Development Inc., 1640 King Street, P.O.

Box 1443, Alexandria, VA 22313-2043, *Telephone:* (703) 683-8100, *Published:* monthly.

Transplant News, Transplant Communications, 401 W Fallbrook, Suite 114, Fresno, CA 93711, *Telephone:* (800) 689-4262, *Fax:* (559) 435-8099.

Transport Technology Today, 2615 Three Oaks Blvd, 1B, Cary, IL 60013, *Telephone:* (847) 359-6100.

Transportation & Distribution, Penton Publishing, 1100 Superior Ave., Cleveland, OH 44114-2543, *Telephone:* (216) 696-7000, *Fax:* (216) 696-4135, *Published:* monthly, *Price:* $45.

Transportation Builder, ARTA Building, 1010 Massachusetts Ave, NW Washington D.C. 20001-5402.

Turkeys Raised, U.S. Government Printing Office, Superintendent of Documents, Washington D.C. 20402, *Telephone*: (202) 783-3238, *Fax:* (202) 275-0010.

TWICE, Cahners Publishing, 249 W 17th St, New York, NY 10010, *Telephone:* (212) 645-0067, *Price:* $35.

Underground Construction, Oldom Publishing, P.O. Box 219368, Houston, TX 77218-9368, *Telephone:* (281) 558-6930, *Fax:* (281) 558-7029.

U.S. News & World Report, 2400 N. St. NW, Washington, D.C. 20037, *Telephone:* (202) 955-2000, *Published:* weekly.

Urban Land, 1025 Thomas Jefferson Street, NW, Suite 500 West, Washington D.C. 20007, *Telephone*: (800) 321-5011.

USA TODAY, Gannett Co., Inc., 1000 Wilson Blvd., Arlington, VA 22229, *Telephone:* (703) 276-3400. *Published:* Mon.-Fri.

Utility Business, Intertec Publishing, 707 Westchester, White Plains, NY.

Vancouver Province, 1-200 Granville Street, Vancouver, BC Canada V6C 3N3, *Telephone:* (604) 605-2222.

Vancouver Sun, 1-200 Granville Street, Vancouver, BC Canada V6C 3N3, *Telephone:* (604) 605-2111.

VAR Business, CMP Media Inc., 1 Jericho Plaza A, Jericho NY 11753, *Telephone:* (516) 733-6700, *Published:* weekly.

Variety, 475 Park Ave., South, New York, NY 10016, *Telephone:* (212) 779-1100, *Fax:* (212) 779-0026. *Published:* weekly.

Video Business, Capital Cities/ABC/Chilton CO., Chilton Way, Radnor, PA 19089, *Telephone:* (215) 964-4000, *Fax:* (215) 964-4285, *Published:* weekly.

Video Store, Advanstar Communications Inc., 1700 E. Dyer Rd., Ste 250, Santa Ana, CA 92705, *Telephone:* (714) 252-5300.

Wall Street Journal, Dow Jones & Co. Inc., 200 Liberty St., New York, NY 10281, *Telephone:* (212) 416-2000. *Published:* Mon.-Fri.

WARD's Dealer Business, Ward's Communications, 28 W. Adams, Detroit, MI 48226, *Telephone:* (313) 962-4456. *Published:* monthly.

Warehousing Management, 275 Washington Street, Newton, MA 02458, *Telephone:* (617) 964-3030, *Fax:* (617) 558-4327.

The Washington Post, The Washington Post, 1150 15th St., N.W., Washington, DC 20071, *Published:* daily.

Washington Technology, Tech News Inc., 1953 Gallows Road, Ste. 130, Vienna, VA 22182.

Washington Times, News World Communications, 3600 New York Ave, NE Washington D.C. 20002, *Telephone:* (202) 636-3028, *Fax:* (202) 526-9348.

Waste News, 1725 Merriman Road, Akron, OH 44313.

Waste Treatment Technology Times, BCC 25 Van Zant, Norwalk CT 06855, *Telephone:* (203) 853-4266.

WattPoultryUSA, WATT Publishing, 122 S. Wesley Ave., Mt. Morris, IL 61054, *Telephone:* (815) 734-4171, *Fax:* (815) 734-4201.

Wearable Business, Intertec Publishing, 707 Westchester, White Plains, NY, *Published:* monthly.

Wichita Business Journal, American City Business Journal, 110 St. Main Street, Ste. 200, Wichita, KS 67202, *Published:* weekly.

Windows & Door, NGA, 8200 Greensboro, Ste 302, McLean VA, *Telephone:* (703) 442-4890, *Fax:* (703) 442-0630.

Wines & Vines, Hiaring Co., 1800 Lincoln Ave., San Rafael, CA 94901-1298, *Telephone:* (415) 453-9700, *Fax:* (415) 453-2517, *Published:* monthly, *Price:* $32 per year without directory; $77.50 per year including directory.

Wireless Satellite, IGI Group, 320 Washington Street, Suite 302, Boston, MA 02135, *Telephone:* (800) 323-1088, *Fax:* (617) 782-5735.

Wood & Wood Products, Vance Publishing Corp., 400 Knightsbridge Pkway., Lincolnshire, IL 60069, *Telephone:* (708) 634-4347, *Fax:* (708) 634-4379, Published: monthly, except semimonthly in March.

Wood Markets, Suite 501 Granville Street, Vancouver BC Canada V6C 1X8, *Telephone:* (604) 801-5998, *Fax:* (604) 801-5997.

Workboat, Diversified Business Comm., 121 Free Street, P.O. Box 7437, Portland ME 04112-7437.

World Oil, Gulf Publishing, 3301 Allen Pkway, PO Box 2608, Houston, TX 77242, *Telephone:* (713) 529-4301, *Fax:* (713) 520-4433.

World Tobacco, World Media, ITdQueensway Hosue 2, Queensway Redhill Survey RH1 1QSUK, Telephone (44) 0 1737 855294.

World Trade, 23211 South Point Dr, Suite 101, Laguna Hills, CA 92653, *Telephone:* (949) 830-1340, *Fax:* (949) 830-1328.

WWD, Fairchild Publications, 7 E. 12th St., New York, NY 10003, *Telephone:* (212) 741-4000, *Fax:* (212) 337-3225. *Published:* weekly.

Youth Markets Alert, EPM Communications, 160 Mercer Street, 3rd Floor, New York, NY 10012.